Revolutionizing the Healthcare Sector with AI

Babita Singla
Chitkara Business School, Chitkara University, Punjab, India

Kumar Shalender
Chitkara Business School, Chitkara University, Punjab, India

Katja Stamer
DHBW Stuttgart Campus Horb, Germany

A volume in the Advances in Medical Technologies and Clinical Practice (AMTCP) Book Series

Published in the United States of America by
IGI Global
Medical Information Science Reference (an imprint of IGI Global)
701 E. Chocolate Avenue
Hershey PA, USA 17033
Tel: 717-533-8845
Fax: 717-533-8661
E-mail: cust@igi-global.com
Web site: http://www.igi-global.com

Copyright © 2024 by IGI Global. All rights reserved. No part of this publication may be reproduced, stored or distributed in any form or by any means, electronic or mechanical, including photocopying, without written permission from the publisher.
Product or company names used in this set are for identification purposes only. Inclusion of the names of the products or companies does not indicate a claim of ownership by IGI Global of the trademark or registered trademark.

Library of Congress Cataloging-in-Publication Data

CIP Pending

Revolutionizing the Healthcare Sector with AI
Babita Singla, Kumar Shalender, Katja Stamer
2024 Medical Information Science Reference

ISBN: 979-8-3693-3731-8
eISBN: 979-8-3693-3732-5

British Cataloguing in Publication Data
A Cataloguing in Publication record for this book is available from the British Library.

All work contributed to this book is new, previously-unpublished material.
The views expressed in this book are those of the authors, but not necessarily of the publisher.

For electronic access to this publication, please contact: eresources@igi-global.com.

Advances in Medical Technologies and Clinical Practice (AMTCP) Book Series

Srikanta Patnaik
SOA University, India
Priti Das
S.C.B. Medical College, India

ISSN:2327-9354
EISSN:2327-9370

MISSION

Medical technological innovation continues to provide avenues of research for faster and safer diagnosis and treatments for patients. Practitioners must stay up to date with these latest advancements to provide the best care for nursing and clinical practices.

The **Advances in Medical Technologies and Clinical Practice (AMTCP) Book Series** brings together the most recent research on the latest technology used in areas of nursing informatics, clinical technology, biomedicine, diagnostic technologies, and more. Researchers, students, and practitioners in this field will benefit from this fundamental coverage on the use of technology in clinical practices.

Coverage

- Biometrics
- Clinical High-Performance Computing
- Clinical Studies
- Diagnostic Technologies
- Neural Engineering
- Patient-Centered Care

IGI Global is currently accepting manuscripts for publication within this series. To submit a proposal for a volume in this series, please contact our Acquisition Editors at Acquisitions@igi-global.com or visit: http://www.igi-global.com/publish/.

The (ISSN) is published by IGI Global, 701 E. Chocolate Avenue, Hershey, PA 17033-1240, USA, www.igi-global.com. This series is composed of titles available for purchase individually; each title is edited to be contextually exclusive from any other title within the series. For pricing and ordering information please visit http://www.igi-global.com/book-series/advances-medical-technologies-clinical-practice/73682. Postmaster: Send all address changes to above address. Copyright © IGI Global. All rights, including translation in other languages reserved by the publisher. No part of this series may be reproduced or used in any form or by any means – graphics, electronic, or mechanical, including photocopying, recording, taping, or information and retrieval systems – without written permission from the publisher, except for non commercial, educational use, including classroom teaching purposes. The views expressed in this series are those of the authors, but not necessarily of IGI Global.

Titles in this Series

For a list of additional titles in this series, please visit: www.igi-global.com/book-series

Revolutionizing Healthcare Treatment With Sensor Technology
Sima Das (Bengal College of Engineering and Technology, India) Parijat Bhowmick (Indian Institute of Technology, Guwahati, India) and Dr. Kitmo (National Advanced School of Engineering of Maroua, University of Maroua, Cameroon)
Medical Information Science Reference • copyright 2024 • 371pp • H/C (ISBN: 9798369327623) • US $495.00 (our price)

Clinical and Comparative Research on Maternal Health
P. Paramasivan (Dhaanish Ahmed College of Engineering, India) S. Suman Rajest (Dhaanish Ahmed College of Engineering, India) Karthikeyan Chinnusamy (Veritas, USA) R. Regin (SRM Institute of Science and Technology, India) and Ferdin Joe John Joseph (Thai-Nichi Institute of Technology, Thailand)
Medical Information Science Reference • copyright 2024 • 259pp • H/C (ISBN: 9798369359419) • US $415.00 (our price)

Advancements in Clinical Medicine
P. Paramasivan (Dhaanish Ahmed College of Engineering, India) S. Suman Rajest (Dhaanish Ahmed College of Engineering, India) Karthikeyan Chinnusamy (Veritas, USA) R. Regin (SRM Institute of Science and Technology, India) and Ferdin Joe John Joseph (Thai-Nichi Institute of Technology, Thailand)
Medical Information Science Reference • copyright 2024 • 426pp • H/C (ISBN: 9798369359464) • US $495.00 (our price)

Advances in Computational Intelligence for the Healthcare Industry 4.0
Imdad Ali Shah (School of Computing Science, Taylor's University, Malaysia) and Quratulain Sial (Aga Khan University Hospital, Karachi, Pakistan)
Engineering Science Reference • copyright 2024 • 371pp • H/C (ISBN: 9798369323335) • US $425.00 (our price)

701 East Chocolate Avenue, Hershey, PA 17033, USA
Tel: 717-533-8845 x100 • Fax: 717-533-8661
E-Mail: cust@igi-global.com • www.igi-global.com

Table of Contents

Preface ix

Chapter 1
Artificial Intelligence in Healthcare 1
    Aruna Sharma, Chitkara University, India

Chapter 2
Evolution of Generative AI in Healthcare 26
    Nikita Thakur, Chitkara University, India

Chapter 3
Revolutionizing Healthcare: The Transformative Impact of Artificial
Intelligence 54
    Manoj Govindaraj, VelTech Rangarajan Dr. Sagunthala R&D Institute
        of Science and Technology, India
    D. Anitha Kumari, Vels Institute of Science, Technology, and Advanced
        Studies, India
    Parvez Khan, Atria University, India
    Ravishankar Krishnan, VelTech Rangarajan Dr. Sagunthala R&D
        Institute of Science and Technology, India
    Chandramowleeswaran Gnanasekaran, VelTech Rangarajan Dr.
        Sagunthala R&D Institute of Science and Technology, India
    Jenifer Lawrence, Woldia University, Ethiopia

Chapter 4
Generative AI in Healthcare: Opportunities, Challenges, and Future
Perspectives 79
    D. Helen, SRM Institute of Science and Technology, India
    N. V. Suresh, ASET College of Science and Technology, Chennai, India

Chapter 5
Navigating the Promise and Perils of Generative AI in Healthcare 91
    Shenson Joseph, Texas Tech University, USA
    Qurat Ul-Ain, University of Agriculture, Faisalabad, Pakistan
    Sidra Nosheen, University of Agriculture, Faisalabad, Pakistan
    Munir Ahmad, Survey of Pakistan, Pakistan
    Rida Fatima, Comsats University, Islamabad, Pakistan

Chapter 6
Exploring Augmented Reality, Virtual Reality, and Machine Learning for
Delivering Better Value in the Healthcare Sector 111
    Zeenal Punamiya, Chitkara School of Health Sciences, Chitkara
        University, Punjab, India
    Navita Gupta, Chitkara School of Health Sciences, Chitkara University,
        Punjab, India
    Sagar Anil Patil, D.Y. Patil University, Navi Mumbai, India

Chapter 7
AI Strategies for Delivering Better Value in the Healthcare Sector 131
    Partap Singh, Lovely Professional University, India
    Partap Singh, Lovely Professional University, India

Chapter 8
Redefining Healthcare: Artificial Intelligence's Revolutionary Effect............... 157
    Simanpreet Kaur, Department of Commerce, Chandigarh School of
        Business, Jhanjeri, India
    Anjali, Department of Commerce, Chandigarh School of Business,
        Jhanjeri, India

Chapter 9
Innovations in Healthcare: Exploring the Dualities of Generative AI............... 178
    A. Karthiayani, Symbiosis International University (Deemed), India

Chapter 10
Mapping the AI Landscape in Healthcare Quality: A Bibliometrics Analysis.. 207
    S. Baranidharan, Christ University, India
    Raja Narayanan, Dayananda Sagar University, India

Chapter 11
Technology Adoption Roadmap for Delivering Superior Services in the
Healthcare Industry 229
    Nripendra Singh, Pennsylvania Western University, USA
    Kumar Shalender, Chitkara Business School, Chitkara University,
        Punjab, India
    Babita Singla, Chitkara Business School, Chitkara University, Punjab,
        India
    Sandhir Sharma, Chitkara Business School, Chitkara University,
        Punjab, India

Chapter 12
Navigating the Crossroads: Stakeholder Perspectives in Healthcare Innovation238
    Ravishankar Krishnan, Vel Tech Rangarajan Dr.Sagunthala R&D
        Institute of Science and Technology, India
    Saravana Mahesan S., Vel Tech Rangarajan Dr.Sagunthala R&D
        Institute of Science and Technology, India
    G. Manoj, Vel Tech Rangarajan Dr.Sagunthala R&D Institute of Science
        and Technology, India
    Kannan G., St. Peter's Institute of Higher Education and Research, India
    Perumal Elantheraiyan, Vel Tech Rangarajan Dr.Sagunthala R&D
        Institute of Science and Technology, India
    Logasakthi Kandasamy, RV University, India

Chapter 13
Operational Efficiency and Cost Reduction: The Role of AI in Healthcare
Administration 262
    N. V. Suresh, ASET College of Science and Technology, India
    Ananth Selvakumar, ASET College of Science and Technology, India
    Gajalaksmi Sridhar, ASET College of Science and Technology, India
    S. Catherine, SRM Institute of Science and Technology, India

Chapter 14
Mathematical Modelling in the Analysis of Viral Diseases and
Communicable Diseases 273
    Saravanan D., The ICFAI Foundation for Higher Education (IFHE),
        India
    Vaithyasubramanian Subramanian, Dwaraka Doss Goverdhan Doss
        Vaishnav College, India
    Delhi Babu R., Department of Mathematics, Sathyabama Institute of
        Science and Technology, India
    Sundararajan R., Department of Mathematics, PSNA College of
        Engineering and Technology, India
    Kirubhashankar C. K., Department of Mathematics, Sathyabama
        Institute of Science and Technology, India
    Vengata Krishnan K., Department of Mathematics and Computer
        Science, Sri Sathya Sai Institute of Higher Learning, India

Chapter 15
Promises and Perils of Generative AI in the Healthcare Sector 293
    Pratibha Garg, Amity University, India

Chapter 16
FutureCare: AI Robots Revolutionizing Health and Healing 311
    Jaspreet Kaur, Chandigarh University, India

Chapter 17
Generative AI Revolution: Shaping the Future of Healthcare Innovation 341
    Manikandan Arunachalam, Department of Electronics and
        Communication Engineering, Amrita Vishwa Vidyapeetham, India
    Chitransh Chiranjeev, Department of Electronics and Communication
        Engineering, Amrita School of Engineering, India
    Barshan Mondal, Department of Electronics and Communication
        Engineering, Amrita School of Engineering, India
    Sanjay T., JP Morgan, USA

Chapter 18
Generative Intelligence: Sculpting Tomorrow's Healthcare Solutions 365
    Jaspreet Kaur, Chandigarh University, India

Compilation of References 393

About the Contributors 444

Index 449

Preface

Artificial Intelligence (AI) is leading the way in this revolutionary technological revolution that has come about with the advent of the 21st century. In particular, artificial intelligence (AI) technologies are revolutionizing the healthcare industry by redefining our understanding, diagnosis, and treatment of medical diseases. It is a privilege for us as the editors of this extensive volume, *Revolutionizing the Healthcare Sector With AI*, to offer an assortment of cutting-edge studies and perspectives that shed light on the complex ways in which AI is influencing the healthcare industry.

Experts in the field collaborated to write this book, which aims to explore the depth and breadth of AI applications in healthcare. Every chapter explores a different facet of AI, offering a comprehensive examination of the state of the art, new trends, and potential paths forward. Our objective is to provide a comprehensive overview of how AI is improving patient care, changing the face of healthcare, and solving challenging medical issues.

Chapter Overview:
1. Artificial Intelligence in Healthcare: A broad overview of AI's applications in healthcare, highlighting key technologies, innovations, and their transformative potential.
2. Evolution of Generative AI in Healthcare: An examination of how generative AI technologies have evolved and affected healthcare, highlighting how they could completely transform diagnosis and treatment.
3. Revolutionizing Healthcare: The Transformative Impact of Artificial Intelligence: A comprehensive examination of the transformative impact of AI on healthcare, highlighting key advancements and future directions.
4. Generative AI in Healthcare: Opportunities, Challenges, and Future Perspectives: A thorough investigation into the possible effects and opportunities that generative AI may bring to the healthcare industry, with an emphasis on emerging trends.
5. Navigating the Promise and Perils of Generative AI in Healthcare: An analysis of the promises and perils associated with generative AI in healthcare, offering a balanced perspective on its potential and risks.

Preface

6. Exploring Augmented Reality, Virtual Reality, and Machine Learning for Delivering Better Value in the Healthcare Sector: A thorough examination of the ways in which healthcare delivery and patient engagement are improved through the use of AR, VR, and machine learning.
7. AI Strategies for Delivering Better Value in the Healthcare Sector: An investigation of the strategic application of AI with the goal of boosting patient outcomes and operational efficiency in healthcare value delivery.
8. Redefining Healthcare: Artificial Intelligence's Revolutionary Effect: A broad look at how AI is redefining healthcare, driving revolutionary changes across the industry.
9. Innovations in Healthcare: Exploring the Dualities of Generative AI: An exploration of the dualities and paradoxes inherent in generative AI, and their implications for healthcare innovation.
10. Mapping the AI Landscape in Healthcare Quality: A Bibliometrics Analysis: A bibliometric analysis mapping the AI landscape in healthcare quality, identifying key trends, research areas, and future directions.
11. Technology Adoption Roadmap for Delivering superior Services in Healthcare Industry: This chapter specifically focuses on the utility of technology adoption for stakeholders in the healthcare ecosystem so that maximum advantage could be given to the underserved population.
12. Navigating the Crossroads: Stakeholder Perspectives in Healthcare Innovation: An exploration of stakeholder perspectives on healthcare innovation, highlighting the roles and viewpoints of various actors in the ecosystem.
13. Operational Efficiency and Cost Reduction: The Role of AI in Healthcare Administration: Examination of how AI is enhancing operational efficiency and reducing costs in healthcare administration.
14. Mathematical Modelling in the Analysis of Viral Diseases and Communicable Diseases: This chapter provides a wide range of factors that play a role in mathematical models of epidemiology and public health policy
15. Promises and Perils of Generative AI in Healthcare Sector: This chapter provides a critical view of the promises and perils associated with generative AI in the healthcare sector.
16. Future Care: AI Robots Revolutionizing Health and Healing: An outlook on how AI-powered robots will change patient care and healthcare delivery in the future.
17. Generative AI Revolution: Shaping the Future of Healthcare Innovation: This chapter examines how generative AI is driving innovation in healthcare, shaping new paradigms in medical research and practice.
18. Generative Intelligence: Sculpting Tomorrow's Healthcare Solutions: Insight into how generative intelligence is being harnessed to create advanced healthcare solutions that address complex medical needs.

This volume serves as a crucial resource for healthcare professionals, researchers, policymakers, and anyone interested in the intersection of AI and healthcare. We hope this book will inspire further research, innovation, and ethical considerations in the ongoing journey to revolutionize healthcare with artificial intelligence.

Babita Singla
Chitkara Business School, Chitkara University, Punjab, India

Kumar Shalender
Chitkara Business School, Chitkara University, Punjab, India

Katja Stamer
DHBW Stuttgart Campus Horb, Germany

Introduction

Babita Singla
Chitkara University, India

Kumar Shalender
Chitkara University, India

The role of artificial intelligence (AI) in enhancing the services in the Healthcare sector is becoming prominent. There are many use cases of AI in the healthcare sector today and to further catalyse AI adoption, this edited title *Revolutionizing the Healthcare Sector With AI* is likely to play a very important role. The book has been edited is edited by Dr. Babita Singla, Dr. Kumar Shalender, and Dr. Katja Stamer.

The edited book title is a wonderful compilation of AI applications in the healthcare sector with a specific focus on developing theoretical frameworks, conceptual models, and practical recommendations for the stakeholders in the industry. It is likely to guide the participating entities in the Healthcare ecosystem on how to conceptualize, develop, and implement the technology in both daily routine care procedures and specialized diseases. The book is equally focused on the development and implementation of AI technologies in the healthcare sector so that it can deliver holistic benefits to the industry players.

While accepting the contributions from various authors, we specifically focused on covering all important aspects of AI integration in the Healthcare sector. The book contains chapters on the ethical issues related to AI, the moral implications of the use of technology, and how to create awareness among stakeholders for better utilising AI in the industry. The guidelines offered by the book can also play an important role in enhancing the functional effectiveness as well as operational efficiency of Healthcare procedures by integrating technology in different forms and manners.

Another distinctive point of the book title is the contributions of the various authors specifically delving into detail about the specialised applications related to the theme of AI in the Healthcare sector. Authors have contributed to a diversified range of topics related to AI applications in the Health Care industry. The title contains the chapters on how application of the AI can help in cardiovascular diseases and cervical cancer treatment.

The book also deals with issues such as obstetrics and how the use of AI tools and technology can prove instrumental in the entire process. Also, against the backdrop of rising incidents of Cyber-attacks, we have accepted the contributions from authors related to the cyber security challenges related to the implementation of AI in the healthcare sector.

In sum, this book title will help all stakeholders in the technology and healthcare ecosystem to utilise AI effectively and efficiently. The book also offers recommendations to administrators, regulators, and policymakers so that an open and constructive policy framework can be made to encourage the adoption of AI in the healthcare sector.

We are very thankful to all contributors for taking the time out and offering valuable contributions to make this book possible. We humbly acknowledge the fact that without their support and contribution, this book wouldn't have been possible. It is only through their contribution we can present this edited title and make this revolution happen today.

Chapter 1
Artificial Intelligence in Healthcare

Aruna Sharma
Chitkara University, India

ABSTRACT

Artificial intelligence (AI) has experienced fast enlargement in current years. The term AI refers to the intelligence exhibited by machines, contrasting with that of humans or other living organisms. Utilizing AI expertise in healthcare has led to significant advancements in disease diagnosis, organization, and prediction; benefit both patients and healthcare professional. This book chapter aims to delve into the conceptual framework of confidence in AI concerning health, grounded not only in expert opinion but also in rigorous conceptual research and solid empirical evidence. It specifically focuses on clinical decision-manufacture, patient data investigation and diagnostics, analytical medication, physical condition services organization, and clinical making decisions, providing enhanced analysis and conduct decision help in healthcare settings.

1. INTRODUCTION

The term artificial intelligence (AI) in computer science deals with the development of intelligent computer systems. This intelligent system is akin in relation to behavioral intelligence in humans. Artificial intelligence (AI) can be used to create computers that are capable of reasoning similarly to humans. Robotics, specialist system, automated speech recognition software, translation programs, the creation of normal speech statement, audio analyzers, simulators, and theorems for addressing issues are a few of its uses (Hamet. P, and Tremblay, J. 2017). While AI is clearly important, the phrase itself lacks a well agreed definition. In general, the term refers

DOI: 10.4018/979-8-3693-3731-8.ch001

to computer techniques that simulate cognitive processes associated with human capacity, including thinking, learning and adapting, perceiving with the senses, and interaction. In the last ten years, Artificial intelligence(AI) has a large contact on human survival and is used in many different fields, such engineering, communications, manufacturing, and healthcare. (Massalha, S. et al. 2018). The primary forces behind AI are enormous gains in processing power and even larger improvements in data production. Many high-tech businesses have achieved near-human or even superior performance on tasks by integrating enhanced algorithms that enable deep neural network training: These include speech recognition, picture processing, chess playing, and self-driving cars. It is predictable that artificial intelligence(AI) will bring about the next significant change in the field of healthcare (Becker. A.2019).AI-based healthcare systems enhance disease detection, prognosis, and therapy; benefit both patients and healthcare practitioners. AI in healthcare has the possible to help doctors, patients, and healthcare provider in four habits: through controlling or avoiding difficulties; by actively assisting with patient attention throughout diagnosis and/or course of action; by figuring out the illness's pathology and the most effective line of action; and by Assessing the probability of success of treatment and looking at the disease start previous to start treatment (Labovitz, D. et al.2017).Among the most exciting the application of AI in healthcare has the potential to enhance the precision of analysis and therapy. In contrast to the majority of occupations, medical experts may diagnose symptoms more swiftly with its assistance. Artificial intelligence (AI) can imitate the prediction capacity of human being physician and get better diagnosis precision by rapidly analyzing patients' electronic health information both vertically and horizontally. AI can also improve the quality of life of a patient, help with the comprehension of complex symptoms, and promote treatment plan adherence. For instance, an AI system helped stroke patients who were taking anticoagulants to take their medications more consistently (Islam, M.et al.2021). By examining bibliometrics on papers related to AI in healthcare, Researchers are able to have a deeper comprehension of the evolution of AI investigate in this field as well as the future paths of trends and modifications. The quickly growing corpus of AI research in healthcare makes it easier to apply AI intervention to enhance the health of both patients and caregivers, which opens up opportunities for practitioners and policymakers to seize (Guo, Y. et al.2020).

2. SCOPE

Here, the phrase "explainable AI" refers, in a broad sense to a clarifying agent that reveals the fundamental rationale for its own or a new agent decisions. Nonetheless, it's critical to keep in mind that "more AI" is not the solution to explainable AI. The problem lies at the intersection of human-agent interaction. Human-agent interaction (HAI) is the point where artificial intelligence, social science, and human-computer interface (HCI) converge (Fig. 1) (Kwon, M.et al.2018).

Figure 1. Scope of 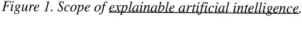explainable artificial intelligence.

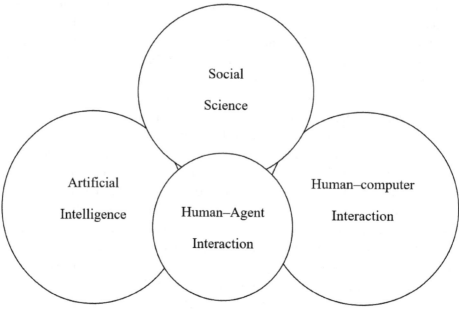

3. TYPES OF AI OF RELEVANCE OF HEALTHCARE

Though the particular tasks and processes that each of these technologies supports varies greatly, most of the technologies that make up artificial intelligence are immediately applicable to the healthcare industry. A few exacting Artificial Intelligence (AI)-based technologies that are very pertinent to the healthcare industries are enumerated hereunder (Jeong, H. and Shi, L. 2018).

3.1 Machine Learning

This area of artificial intelligence analyzes relationships, recent data, and historical data using an algorithm (Lee, S. et al.2018). This study can be used to forecast the best course of treatment for specific patients. It is furthermore necessary for streamlining and improving healthcare administration and procedures. Data annotators are an essential part of machine learning. It uses MRI and CT images to more accurately identify tumor cells (Vial, A. et al. 2018).

3.2 Natural Processing Language(NLP):

It is the method by which a machine reads andunderstandpassage or words. NLP can facilitate in the investigation of patient health check data and offer suggestions to raise the standard of methods used and improve patient outcomes (Choi, B.et al. 2018). AI frequently uses natural language processing, or NLP, to analyze and categorize medical records. The system functions as intended after it grasps what the user is attempting to communicate (Bou Assi, E,et al. 2018).

3.3 Expert Systems Based on Rules:

For the past few, they have been extensively utilized in the healthcare sector for decades. "Clinical decision support and their use is still widespread nowadays. These days, a lot of electronic health record suppliers bundle a position of policies utilizing their systems. Knowledge engineers and human experts are needed for expert systems to produce a collection of guidelines in a particular knowledge domain (Davenport, T., and Kalakota, R. 2019).They are simple to understand and, for the most part, work well. However, when there are many rules—usually more than a little thousand—and when those rules begin to conflict with one another, they be inclined to fall apart (Sakai, K., and Yamada, K. 2019).

3.4 Physical Robots:

Physical robotics is becoming more and more widespread in the medicalProfession as a form of AI. Robots for delivering medical supplies were initially developed by scientists. However, there are now more sophisticated robots available (Martens, F. M. J., et al. 2010). These robots can operate in tandem with people and are quickly trained to do certain jobs. They possess greater intelligence because Artificial Intelligence is built into the operating system (brain).. Surgical robots are another kind of robot that have been present in operating rooms since 2000. Opportunities in this field of artificial intelligence are still being sought after (Vial, A., 2018).

3.5 Robotic Process Automation:

The development of this AI technology has primarily focused on administrative goals. Robotic process automation (RPA) is less expensive than other artificial intelligence techniques. Despite the name, this procedure is really performed by a certain kind of computer software rather than by robots (Davenport, T. H. 2021). In the healthcare sector, RPA is used to record in the early hours authorizations, charge, and keep informed patient medical information. It can be used to extract data when paired with other technologies, including photo recognition (Dahmani, K.,et al. 2016).

4. INFORMATION PROCESSING AND ALGORITHM IMPLEMENTATION

There are four basic categories into which artificial intelligence is used within biomedicine. In order to address healthcare-related issues, the first three categories covered in this section are made to effectively process vast amounts of records and give users with fastentrance to information. These applications pertain to basic research activities, methods for natural language processing, and living help for the aged and disabled. We'll examine the final class of AI applications, which deals with illness prediction and diagnosis.

4.1 AI for Living Assistance

Applications of artificial intelligence (AI) coupled with intelligent robotic systems are creating new opportunities to enhance the standard of living for the aged and crippled living in assisted living. A summary of smart tools and features for the home for those who are losing their autonomy (PLA) was just released (Rabhi, Y., et al. 2018). Wireless sensor networks, AI, and data mining provide the foundation of the intelligent solution models. NNs can be qualified to recognize definitefigure-processing techniques to translate human face emotions into commands. Moreover, facial appearancestudy-base human-machine interfacefacilitateuser to with impairments to drive mobility devices and automated vehicles for aid that lack the need for a direction control or physical sensors (Hudec, M., and Smutny, Z. 2017). Blind people can coexist industries like electronics and informatics with the aid of RUDO, a "ambient intelligent system" (Tumpa, S. N., et al. 2017). This intelligent assistant has numerous tasks that can be utilized by blind individuals with a single user interface. During critical periods of becoming pregnant, an AI-powered "smart assistant" can offer dietary guidance and other essential recommendations to expectant mothers. with the use of "cloud-based communication media between all people concerned" and its own intelligence, it may offer recommendations at "an advanced level."(Wu, Q., et al. 2015).Senior fall hazards and related problems can be decreased with a fall detection system based on radar Doppler time-frequency signatures and a sparse Bayesian classifier (García-Vázquez, J. P., et al 2010). Actually, systems for "smart communication architecture" or ambient assisted living(AAL) have been residential to permit artificial intelligence(AI) to interpret in order gathered starting diverse technologies or communication channels to determine the frequency of events in the network environment and the assistance needs of senior citizens (Lloret, J., et al. 2015). Smart homes with "ambient intelligence" can help older people age in place by offering activity awareness and subsequent activity support. This allows people to age in place, or in the house. For instance, older persons with typical pharmaceutical tasks may benefit from the SALSA intelligent agent, which performs activity-aware screening for activity limits and safety awareness. Machine learning may identify potentially risky behavior in motion and gait analysis and start safety procedures (Abacha, A. B., and Zweigenbaum, P. 2015).

4.2 AI in the Analysis of Biological Data

Notable developments in natural language processing for applications in the biological sciences. Retrieving accurate and timely answer to consumerquestion from a file of papers and datasets is the aim of biological question answering, or BioQA. Therefore, it makes sense to assume that algorithms for natural language processing will search for answers that are instructive (Sarrouti, M., and El Alaoui, S. O. 2017). It is necessary to first categorize the biological questions in order to get pertinent information from the responses. Nearly 90% of biomedical inquiries can be accurately categorized by machine learning into four main categories. A biomedical document retrieval system with intelligence can then be used to efficiently extract the sections of the records that are most likely to contain the answers to the biomedical inquiries. An innovative technique for handling among primary categories of BioQA can effectively extract information from binary responses: the generator for yes-or-no answers, which is based on word sentiment analysis (Sarrouti, M., and El Alaoui, S. O. 2017). Clinical information merging, comparison, and conflict resolution are three crucial tasks that can take precedence when dealing with biomedical data that has been gathered over an extended period of time from many sources. These have historically been human-performed, labor-intensive, time-consuming, and unsatisfying tasks. AI has demonstrated the ability to execute these tasks with results that are just as precise as those generated by a qualified assessor, increasing both productivity and accuracy. Furthermore, medical narrative data needs to be naturally language processed in order to relieve individuals of the laborious task of maintaining logic and structures while following chronological occurrences. (ML) can handle high-complexity clinical data (like text and other related biological data types) and apply the learned knowledge to a range of applications. It can also be used to integrate logic reasoning into the dataset (Handelman, G. S., et al. 2018).

4.3 AI in Biomedical Research

Beyond its potential use as a virtual doctor for illness diagnosis, treatment, and prognosis, artificial intelligence is also a powerful tool for biomedical research. Artificial intelligence could accelerate the global screening and indexing of scholarly papers related to biological research and innovation projects. Tumor-suppressor processes, the extraction of information on protein–protein interactions, the creation of genetic associations for the human genome to help translate genomic findings into medical procedures, and other issues are among the most recent study areas in this direction (Kanevsky, J., et al. 2016). Furthermore, by applying a semantic graph-based AI technique, biomedical researchers can effectively complete the difficult work of summarizing the literature on a particular topic of interest. Furthermore, biomedical researchers can benefit from artificial intelligence (AI) when the amount of study papers grows too large for them to handle by using it to help search and prioritize relevant literature. This makes it possible for scientists to develop and evaluate concise scientific ideas, which are crucial for biomedical research. For instance, scholars might use AI to create and evaluate hypotheses by ranking and screening figures of interest in the growing body of literature (Bou Assi, E., et al. 2018).

Research in the field of biomedicine can examine the "consciousness" that some intelligent medical equipment are exhibiting. Computational modeling assistants, or CMAs, are intelligent agents that assist biomedical researchers in creating "executable" simulation models from conceptual models. A comprehensive overview of the contacts and process flow between human researchers. A variety of techniques, databases, and information are offered to the CMA. Biological models are used to express the researcher's hypothesis and are fed into the CMA. The researchers' hypotheses are translated into concrete simulation models by the CMA's intelligence, which allows it to integrate all of this data and these models. Following a study and selection of the top models by the researcher, the CMA creates simulation codes for the models that were chosen. Thus, the CMA facilitates a markedly expedited research process and increased production. Furthermore, certain intelligent robots may serve as guides for scientific study in fields including plastic surgery, oral surgery, and biomedical imaging. A discussion on the relationship between biomedical engineering and human and machine consciousness has been held in order to better comprehend the implications of this progress(Tran, B. X., et al. 2019).

5. ROLE OF AI IN DISEASES PREDICTION

Nowadays, Artificial Intelligence is utilized in many different medical care applications. It's been applied specifically to signal and picture processing, in addition to function modification prediction, including the prevention of strokes, bladder control, and epileptic seizures. Two typical case studies are presented below: the prediction of bladder volume and the prediction of epileptic seizures (Mendez, A., et al. 2013).

5.1. Bladder Volume Prediction

The patient's medical condition becomes complicated whenever the bladder's storage and urine functions are involved are compromised due to aging, neurological illnesses, or spinal cord damage. These days, implantable brain stimulators can help patients who are drug-refractory regain some of their bladder function. In order to improve the safety and effectiveness of neuroprostheses via conditional neurostimulation, a bladder sensor that recognizes stored urine is needed (Manyika, J., et al. 2017). This mechanism administers electrical stimulation only when necessary. Typically, data is transmitted and the implant is powered by a wireless link suited between the two halves. The interior component operates several functions, including keeping tracks of neutral signals, processing sensory information signals on-chip (to varying degrees, depending on application), neurostimulation of allocated nerves via communication with the external unit, logical control of implanted unit operations, and functional electrical stimulation (FES) approaches. The external unit receives the recorded signal from the internal unit, uses it to execute more intricate algorithms, and returns the appropriate neurostimulation commands when more signal processing is required to carry out more intricate algorithms that require additional computing capabilities and are not suitable for implantation due to their size, power consumption, temperature rise, electromagnetic emission, and other factors. The implant-user and implant-computer interfaces are combined in the external base station for more flexibility (Assi, E. B., et al.2017).

5.2 Epilepsy Seizure Forecast:

One of the most severe neurological disorders is epilepsy, a neurodegenerative illness distinguished by frequent, unexpected, and spontaneous seizures. Although long-term medication-based therapy is the primary line of treatment for most patients, over one-third of them are refractory. Nonetheless, because of the extremely poor success rates and anxiety associated with consequences, the use of epilepsy surgery is still quite uncommon. If successful, researching the possibility of seizure prediction could result in the development of innovative interventional methods

(Howbert, J. J., et al.2014). Even though the first seizure-forecasting studies date back to the 1970s, there have been significant obstacles to a sufficient assessment of seizure prediction performances, including the small number of seizure events, the scarcity of intracranial electroencephalography (iEEG) recordings, and the limited scope of interictal epochs. Remarkably, iEEG signals obtained from canines that are naturally epileptic and have been implanted with the NeuroVista ambulatory monitoring device are available via the ieeg.org web portal (Gagliano, L.,et al. 2018). The seizure onset zone, however, was not made known or accessible. With the use of the previously mentioned canine data, our team looked into the feasibility of predicting seizures. The electrodes inside the epileptic network were then quantitatively identified using a directed transfer function (DTF). To determine which characteristics are most indicative of the preictal stage, a genetic algorithm was utilized. A novel fitness function that is impervious to skewed data distributions was put forth by us. An average sensitivity of 84.82% at a time-in-warning of 10% was obtained on the held-out dataset, indicating an improvement over previous seizure prediction performances (W Shi, T., et al. 2017)

5.3 Disease Diagnostics and Prediction

The greatest pressing requirement for artificial intelligence in biomedicine is in the diagnosis of disease. Numerous fascinating discoveries have been made in this subject. Medical professionals may now identify a wide range of ailments more rapidly and precisely thanks to artificial intelligence. One of the primary diagnostic categories is the use of biosensors or biochips for in vitro diagnostics. To evaluate gene expression, for example, machine learning (ML) can be applied. ML is an essential diagnostic tool that involves using microarray data to classify and find anomalies. One new usage is the classification of cancer microarray data for cancer diagnosis. (Vashistha, R., et al. 2018). Integrated artificial intelligence (AI) in biosensors and related point-of-care testing (POCT) devices can help detect cardiovascular diseases early (Foster, K. R., et al. 2014). AI can help with cancer patient diagnosis and prognosis, especially colon cancer patients. Researchers have also pointed out important limitations of machine learning in biological diagnostics and suggested ways to mitigate these limitations (Hamada, M., et al. 2018) a result, AI for prognostics and diagnostics continues to show great promise. Medical imaging, which uses two dimensions, and signal processing, which uses one dimension, are two other crucial classes of illness diagnosis. These techniques have been applied to the diagnosis, treatment, and prognosis of illness. AI has been applied to one-dimensional signal processing (Stacey, W. C. 2018). for biomedical signal feature extraction, including electrocardiography (ECG) (Krishnan, S., and Athavale, Y. 2018). electromyography (EMG), and electroencephalography (EEG)

(Rai, H. M., and Chatterjee, K. 2018). One important application of EEG is seizure prediction in epilepsy. To lessen seizures' detrimental consequences on patients, seizure prediction is essential. Lately, (AI) has come to be recognized as one of the essentials components of a reliable and accurate prediction system. Predictions are now achievable thanks to deep learning (Kiral-Kornek, I., et al. 2018), additionally; a mobile system can incorporate the prediction platform. Additionally, biological image processing-based diagnoses are greatly impacted by AI (Elkin, P. L., et al.2018). To enhance image quality and analytical effectiveness, artificial intelligence has been applied to image segmentation, multidimensional imaging, and thermal imaging. AI can also be utilized in portable ultrasound devices, making ultrasonography a useful diagnosis tool for a variety of illnesses in impoverished countries, even for those without medical training (Safdar, S., et al. 2018).

In addition to the applications outlined above, artificial intelligence (AI) can benefit traditional decision support systems (DSSs) by improving the accuracy of diagnoses and simplifying the handling of illnesses to reduce staff workloads. For example, the diagnosis and treatment of tropical and cardiovascular diseases, as well as the integrated care of cancer, and the ease of diagnostic decision-making have all benefited from the application of artificial intelligence (AI). These applications demonstrate that AI has the potential to be a useful tool for controlling and even forecasting patient ailments and diseases at the time of diagnosis(Díaz, Ó., et al. 2019).

6. APPLICATION OF AI IN HEALTHCARE

Here are a few of the application of artificial intelligence in medicine application employed in the medical field:

6.1 AI for Drug Discovery:

Pharmaceutical businesses have benefited from the use of AItechnology in healthcare by expediting the drug discovery process. However, it automates the process of identifying targets. In addition, AI in healthcare 2021 helps in drug repurposing through the analysis of off-target chemicals. As a result, AI drug discovery speeds up and reduces repetitive work in the healthcare and AI industries (Lv, J., et a.l 2021).There exist several therapies developed by leading biopharmaceutical companies. Pfizer is assisting in the development of immuno-oncology medications by making use of IBM Watson, a machine learning-based system. (Chan, H. S., et al. 2019).Sanofi has chosen to use Exscientia's artificial intelligence (AI) platform to find drugs for metabolic diseases, while Roche subsidiary Genentech is relying on a system from GNS Healthcare in Cambridge, Massachusetts to assist with its search for cancer treatments. Almost all of the major biopharmaceutical companies have similar internal initiatives or alliances. AI and ML could usher in a new era of more effective, economical, and expeditious medication discovery, if proponents of these approaches are correct. The majority of specialists believe that these tools will grow more and more significant in the future, however some are skeptical. For scientists, this change offers both opportunities and challenges, particularly when the techniques are coupled with automation (Angus, D. C. 2020).

6.2 AI in Clinical Trials:

In a research project, individuals get recently made drugs to evaluateTheir efficacy. It's been really expensive money and time to complete this. But the success rate is really low. Thus, clinical trial automation has proven to be beneficial for AI and the medical field. Artificial intelligence and healthcare also assist in eliminating time-consuming data monitoring procedures. AI-assisted clinical studies also produce astonishingly accurate outcomes and manage enormous data collections. The subsequent items are a few of the most popular AI applications for clinical trials in healthcare:

6.3 Intelligent Clinical Trials:

The most dependable technique for confirming the effectiveness and safety of novel medications are still obtained through traditional "linear and sequential" clinical studies. Developed mainly for the assessment of pharmaceuticals for the mass market, the long-standing, well-tried protocol consisting of discrete and well-defined stages of randomised controlled trials (RCTs) has mostly not altered in the last few decades. Artificial intelligence has the potential to shorten the duration of clinical trial cycles, increase productivity, and enhance clinical development outcomes. This paper, which examines AI's effects on the biopharma value chain, is the third in the series (Mayorga-Ruiz, I.,et al. 2019).The large volumes of scientific and research data that biopharma businesses can today access from a number of sources are cited to as "real-world data" (RWD). However, they frequently lack the skills and resources needed to exploit this data effectively. Through the use of advanced analytics and predictive AI models to uncover RWD, researchers may find important patients and investigators, learn more about diseases, and develop innovative clinical study designs [83].Clinical trial data can be cleaned, compiled, coded, preserved, and retained with the use of AI algorithms and a productive digital infrastructure. Additionally, improved electronic data capture (EDC) could reduce the impact of human error in data collection and enable smooth system integration (Luengo-Oroz, M.,et al. 2020).

6.4 Collaboration on Clinical Trials and Sharing of Models:

Scientists from all disciplines are collaborating in an incredible endeavor to support the COVID-19 reaction. For leveraging AI tools to have a worldwide impact, scalable data, model, and code sharing strategies, application localization, and cross-border cooperation are all required (Lip, S., et al. 2020).

6.5 Applications of AI Require Data.

At the international, national, and local levels, there are now a number of COVID-19-focused data-sharing programs in progress that target the three application sizes. Genomic sequences, genetic studies, structures of protein, patient clinical data, health check imaging, event information, and epidemiological data, movement data, comments on social media, news items, and scholarly papers are a few of the materials. The risk of innovations being limited to certain projects and communities gives rise to the problem of hyper-fragmentation in data-sharing activities. New applications could be developed and distributed more quickly if Scalable methods for sharing code, models, and data were available. Currently, international, open, complete, comparable and validated exchange of data activities will be helpful in establishing connections and promoting collaboration between varied community and geography(Pumplun, L., et al. 2021).Through worldwide multi-stakeholder AI cooperation, open science can accelerate the distribution of information and the development of national health systems' capabilities (Sucharitha, G., and Chary, D. V. 2021). For instance, the Epidemic Intelligence from Open Sources (EIOS) network makes use of open source data to facilitate the early identification, confirmation, and evaluation of risks and hazards to public health (Harrer, S.,et al. 2019). Governments, international organization, and research institutes make up the network of practice for health care intelligence. They work together to evaluate and exchange information about outbreak events in real time, adhering to the idea that cooperation is preferable to competition in early detection. Epidemiologists believe that international standards and database interoperability could help promote coordinated response and decision-making at the international, national, and local levels. It will be necessary to include public health interventions, health system resource capacity, environmental factors, and COVID-19's social effects in order to comprehend the epidemiologic characteristics and risk profiles of different demographic groups as the pandemic spreads (Harrer, S.,et al. 2019). Few initiatives exist today that trade trained artificial intelligence (AI) models for any of the above uses, aside from data sharing. Among the challenges are those posed by particular computational, design, and infrastructure requirements; a lack of documentation; problems with verification and interpretability; and legal considerations pertaining to intellectual property and secrecy. Exchange of approved and pre-trained AI models could facilitate faster situational adaptation. Algorithms with broad potential include those that are used to diagnose diseases from images, calculate patient outcomes, clean false information based on patterns that spread through social media, and extract informationgraph from bigdatabase of educationalpublication (Ting, D. S., et al. 2018).

6.6 Patient Care:

AI has an influence on patient results in the medical field. Medical AI companies develop aorganization that supports the tolerant in every way. Clinical intelligence also providesinsight to patients to help them enhance their standard of living by analyzing their medical data. The following are some notable examples of systems for clinical intelligence that enhance patient care.

6.7 Maternal Care:

The following is one potential strategy for identifying high-risk moms, reducing the fatality rate, and preventing postpartum problems: Analyzing electronic health records and artificial intelligence (AI) to predict if expecting moms are much more likely to experience complications during delivery.using digital technologies to increase patient access to high-acuity (more frequent, more advanced care) during pregnancy. When giving birth in low-acuity clinics, high-risk obstetric patients are more likely to experience severe maternal morbidity as compared to giving birth in higher-acuity clinics with stronger resources and clinical experience (Shi, D., et al. 2019).

6.8 Healthcare Robotics:

Some medical robots provide patients with additional assistance beyond professionals. on behalf ofcase, Robots that exoskeletons can aid disabled People stroll once again and regain their independence (Cruciger, O.,et al. 2016). Another example of technology in use is a smart prosthesis. It is possible to wrap these bionic limbs with bionic skin and connect them to the user's muscles.The sensors that these bionic limbs attach to make them more accurate and responsive than natural body parts.Rehabilitation and surgery can be aided by robots.For instance, The Hybrid Assistive Limb (HAL) exoskeleton from Cyberdyne uses sensors affixed to the skin to detect electrical signals in the patient's body and moves at the join accordingly (Hummel, P., and Braun, M. 2020). This technology aids in patients' rehabilitation from ailments such spinal cord injuries and strokes that result in abnormalities of the lower limbs (Hummel, P., and Braun, M. 2020).

6.9 Genetics AI Data-Driven Medicine:

The modern healthcare user has become more involved in their personal health care, including genome sequencing to customizing our health position based on in sequence from our health and movementmonitor. Putting all of this hugeinformation together and combining it will allow us to anticipate our health and medical state more precisely. Individualized medical therapies potentially are enabled by data-driven medicine, which may also improve the precision of and speed of genetic illness identification (Singh, M., and Nath, G. 2022).

6.10 AI-powered Stethoscope:

The ability to obtain readings even in loud environments is a major benefit, which is not possible with standard stethoscopes and enables more precise diagnosis. Since the digital gadget does not require expertise to use, Records are available for anyone to obtain and telemeter to the physician (Ji, S.,et al. 2020). This also lowers their chance of contracting COVID-19 and makes it easier to provide patients who are chronically sick and live in distant areas with better healthcare.Due to advances in (AI) andML, computers are now able to discern patterns and anomalies in disease from enormous volumes of clinical data. The same concept applies here since blood that circulates around a blood clot in the blood vessels is not the same as blood that flows through normal arteries (Lubarsky, B. 2010).

7. ARTIFICIAL INTELLIGENCE'S DRAWBACKS AND POSSIBLE SOLUTIONS IN THE HEALTHCARE SECTOR

7.1 Data Collection Concern:

The initial issue is the difficulty in obtaining significantinformation.LargeDL and ML models require datasets to correctly categorize or forecast a broad spectrum of employment. The most important progress in machine learning's capacity to produce increasingly complex and correct algorithms has come from industries allowing for simple access to big datasets. The healthcare industry has a difficult-problemamong regard to in sequenceconvenience (Lubarsky, B. 2010).. Given that patient reportare usually regarded as confidential, institutions are hesitant to exchange health data by nature. An additional problem is that once an algorithm is employed for the first time, data may not always be readily available. Ideally, machine learning based system would continually get better with supplementary data provided to their guidanceplace. The business may be resistant internally, making this complicated to implement. As said, the successful use of artificial intelligence and information technology in the healthcare sector calls for a change in perspective from treating patients as unique individuals to enhancing healthcare. Certain It's possible for contemporary algorithms to function on a unimodal or smaller scale in contrast to multimodal instruction, and the growing use of make unclearcompute servers may help to alleviate the opposite problem of store these ever increasing datasets (Khan, B.,et al. 2023).

7.2 Algorithms Developments Concerns:

Potentially skewed results could arise due to biases in the methods used to acquire the data that guided the model's design. Poor prediction results, for instance, could result from minorities being underrepresented because of racial biases in the dataset's creation. Creating training sets with multiple ethnic backgrounds is single of numerous methods to combat this bias. Still, some AI models can handle bias on their own; one such model is the stereotype neural network, which currently exists and lessens the impact of such confusing characteristics. If these tactics are effective in eradicating bias in the actual world, only time will tell (Fernandes, M.,et al. 2020). As AI technology advances, it offers a new issue later thaninformationcompilation. As soon as the algorithm finds insignificant relationships stuck between patient characteristics and outcome, over fitting takes place. It occurs when there are an excessive number of factors affecting the result, leading to inaccurate forecasts by the algorithm. Because of this, even if the algorithm works well when used with the training dataset, it could produce inaccurate results when used with subsequent occurrences. Data leaks are another source of concern the method's ability to predict occurrences outside of the training dataset are diminished if the algorithm achieves extremely high predicted accuracy because aIt's possible that a covariate in the dataset misreferred to the result. However, in order to solve this issue, a fresh dataset is necessary in order to verify the findings (Gama, F.,et al.2022)(Lee, S. I.,et al.2018).

7.3 Moral Issues:

The topic of artificial intelligence has raised ethical debates since its Conception. The Accountability is the primary issue, not privacy or data safety issue that were previously discussed. Because of the dire repercussions of bad decisions, specially in the health check industry, the present scheme mandates that someone be made to answer for their actions. Artificial intelligence (AI) is perceived as a "black box" by some academics due to the difficulty in deciphering algorithmic reasoning. Lower-stakes applications, such non-medical ones that focus on efficiency or operational improvement, may be less vulnerable to the "black-box" issue when it comes to algorithms. Despite this, When considering applications of AI that try to improve medical outcome—especially in the event of errors—the accountability concern becomes more important. It is therefore difficult to determine who is to fault in the occurrence of an organization breakdown. It could be challenging to hold the physician responsible because they had no involvement in the development or supervision of the algorithm. on the other hand, it can also appear that the developer is to blame, which is unrelated to the therapeutic setting. In China and Hong Kong, it is illegal for artificial intelligence to be used to determine morality in the healthcare sector (Díaz, Ó.,et al.2019).

7.4 Social Concerns:

People have consistently been concerned the application of artificial Intelligence (AI)in the healthcare sector may eventually replace them in their jobs. Some people are opposed toward and mistrustful of AI-based projects because they think they will be replaced. However, a large portion of this perspective is based on an incorrect understanding of artificial intelligence as a whole. AI just means that jobs will need to be changed, not that they will become obsolete (Cruciger, O., et al. 2016). This is even before factoring in How long will it take for artificial intelligence to advance to the point where it can successfully replace medical professionals. Because medical process are human-centered and fundamentally unpredictable, they can never be as exact or well-organized as algorithms. Although reasonable, mistrust about AI is clearly detrimental and keeps the technology from gaining widespread use. However, ignorance could lead to exaggerated expectations about the capabilities and outcomes of artificial intelligence. The people may lose hope if they think AI is capable of more than it presently does. There needs to be a greater public discussion about AI in healthcare to dispel these beliefs held by doctors and patients (Alami, H., et al. 2021).

7.5 Clinical Implementation Concerns:

The major difficulty to the winning application of AI based medications is the lack of empirical data supporting the treatments' effectiveness in intendedscientifictrial. Since mainly study on Artificial Intelligences (AI) use has been conducted in a mutual setting, We're not sure much about how technology ultimately has an impact on patient outcomes. For the most part, AI research in healthcare has been carried out in non-medical settings. This raises the possibility that extrapolating study results may prove demanding. The gold standard in the field of medicine, randomized controlled trials, but it can't demonstrate how AI enhances medical care. Businesses are disinclined to undertake artificial intelligence (AI)-based solutions because of a require of pertinent information and inconsistent research feature. (Denti, L., and Hemlin, S. 2012).if everyone agreed that artificial intelligence was being used. It may have been used more successfully if it had been integrated into medical processes. The availability of information systems is a prerequisite for load reduction efficacy. Artificial Intelligence (AI)-powered behavior shouldn't make it more difficult for doctors to look through or analyze electronic medical records. The cost of the equipment incorporates both time and money needed to instruct health care providers on how to operate the skill correctly. There are currently few documented examples of effectively integrating AI into clinical treatment, and the majority of these situations are still in the experimental phase (Hagendorff, T. 2020)

7.6 Biased and Discriminatory Algorithms:

Along with social andcultural issues, "bias" is a problem in the technology realm as well. Bad design or inaccurate or unbalanced data sent into algorithms can result in technology artifacts and biased software. Therefore, AI only widens the income gap by perpetuating the age, gender, and racial inequality that already exists in our society. It's highly likely that You are aware of Amazon's contentious hiring experiment from a few years ago. Artificial intelligence (AI) was employed in the applicant search tool to grade candidates on a five-star rating system, akin to how Amazon customers review things (Schönberger, D. 2019). After ten years of data collecting, computer models that Amazon used to screen job applications were biased against candidates whose resumes featured the word "women" and toward male prospects (Tantin, A., et al.2020).

REFERENCES

Abacha, A. B., & Zweigenbaum, P. (2015). MEANS: A medical question-answering system combining NLP techniques and semantic Web technologies. *Information Processing & Management*, 51(5), 570–594. 10.1016/j.ipm.2015.04.006

Alami, H., Lehoux, P., Denis, J. L., Motulsky, A., Petitgand, C., Savoldelli, M., Rouquet, R., Gagnon, M.-P., Roy, D., & Fortin, J. P. (2021). Organizational readiness for artificial intelligence in health care: Insights for decision-making and practice. *Journal of Health Organization and Management*, 35(1), 106–114. 10.1108/JHOM-03-2020-0074

Angus, D. C. (2020). Randomized clinical trials of artificial intelligence. *Journal of the American Medical Association*, 323(11), 1043–1045. 10.1001/jama.2020.1039

Assi, E. B., Nguyen, D. K., Rihana, S., & Sawan, M. (2017). Towards accurate prediction of epileptic seizures: A review. *Biomedical Signal Processing and Control*, 34, 144–157. 10.1016/j.bspc.2017.02.001

Becker, A. (2019). Artificial intelligence in medicine: What is it doing for us today? *Health Policy and Technology*, 8(2), 198–205. 10.1016/j.hlpt.2019.03.004

Bou Assi, E., Gagliano, L., Rihana, S., Nguyen, D. K., & Sawan, M. (2018). Bispectrum features and multilayer perceptron classifier to enhance seizure prediction. *Scientific Reports*, 8(1), 15491. 10.1038/s41598-018-33969-9

Chan, H. S., Shan, H., Dahoun, T., Vogel, H., & Yuan, S. (2019). Advancing drug discovery via artificial intelligence. *Trends in Pharmacological Sciences*, 40(8), 592–604. 10.1016/j.tips.2019.06.004

Choi, B. K., Dayaram, T., Parikh, N., Wilkins, A. D., Nagarajan, M., Novikov, I. B., Bachman, B. J., Jung, S. Y., Haas, P. J., Labrie, J. L., Pickering, C. R., Adikesavan, A. K., Regenbogen, S., Kato, L., Lelescu, A., Buchovecky, C. M., Zhang, H., Bao, S. H., Boyer, S., & Lichtarge, O. (2018). Literature-based automated discovery of tumor suppressor p53 phosphorylation and inhibition by NEK2. *Proceedings of the National Academy of Sciences of the United States of America*, 115(42), 10666–10671. 10.1073/pnas.1806643115

Cruciger, O., Schildhauer, T. A., Meindl, R. C., Tegenthoff, M., Schwenkreis, P., Citak, M., & Aach, M. (2016). Impact of locomotion training with a neurologic controlled hybrid assistive limb (HAL) exoskeleton on neuropathic pain and health related quality of life (HRQoL) in chronic SCI: A case study. *Disability and Rehabilitation. Assistive Technology*, 11(6), 529–534.

Cruciger, O., Schildhauer, T. A., Meindl, R. C., Tegenthoff, M., Schwenkreis, P., Citak, M., & Aach, M. (2016). Impact of locomotion training with a neurologic controlled hybrid assistive limb (HAL) exoskeleton on neuropathic pain and health related quality of life (HRQoL) in chronic SCI: A case study. *Disability and Rehabilitation. Assistive Technology*, 11(6), 529–534.

Dahmani, K., Tahiri, A., Habert, O., & Elmeftouhi, Y. (2016, April). An intelligent model of home support for people with loss of autonomy: A novel approach. In *2016 International Conference on Control, Decision and Information Technologies (CoDIT)* (pp. 182-185). IEEE. 10.1109/CoDIT.2016.7593557

Davenport, T., & Kalakota, R. (2019). The potential for artificial intelligence in healthcare. *Future Healthcare Journal*, 6(2), 94–98. 10.7861/futurehosp.6-2-94

Davenport, T. H. (2021). Artificial Intelligence in Healthcare: Promise and Reality. *Healthcare Informatics: Strategies for the Digital Era*, 227.

Denti, L., & Hemlin, S. (2012). Leadership and innovation in organizations: A systematic review of factors that mediate or moderate the relationship. *International Journal of Innovation Management*, 16(03), 1240007. 10.1142/S1363919612400075

Díaz, Ó., Dalton, J. A., & Giraldo, J. (2019). Artificial intelligence: A novel approach for drug discovery. *Trends in Pharmacological Sciences*, 40(8), 550–551. 10.1016/j.tips.2019.06.005

Díaz, Ó., Dalton, J. A., & Giraldo, J. (2019). Artificial intelligence: A novel approach for drug discovery. *Trends in Pharmacological Sciences*, 40(8), 550–551. 10.1016/j.tips.2019.06.005

Elkin, P. L., Schlegel, D. R., Anderson, M., Komm, J., Ficheur, G., & Bisson, L. (2018). Artificial intelligence: Bayesian versus heuristic method for diagnostic decision support. *Applied Clinical Informatics*, 9(02), 432–439. 10.1055/s-0038-1656547

Fernandes, M., Vieira, S. M., Leite, F., Palos, C., Finkelstein, S., & Sousa, J. M. (2020). Clinical decision support systems for triage in the emergency department using intelligent systems: A review. *Artificial Intelligence in Medicine*, 102, 101762. 10.1016/j.artmed.2019.101762

Foster, K. R., Koprowski, R., & Skufca, J. D. (2014). Machine learning, medical diagnosis, and biomedical engineering research-commentary. *Biomedical Engineering Online*, 13(1), 1–9. 10.1186/1475-925X-13-94

Gagliano, L., Assi, E. B., Nguyen, D. K., Rihana, S., & Sawan, M. (2018). Bilateral preictal signature of phase-amplitude coupling in canine epilepsy. *Epilepsy Research*, 139, 123–128. 10.1016/j.eplepsyres.2017.11.009

Gama, F., Tyskbo, D., Nygren, J., Barlow, J., Reed, J., & Svedberg, P. (2022). Implementation frameworks for artificial intelligence translation into health care practice: Scoping review. *Journal of Medical Internet Research*, 24(1), e32215. 10.2196/32215

García-Vázquez, J. P., Rodríguez, M. D., Tentori, M., Saldaña-Jimenez, D., Andrade, Á. G., & Espinoza, A. N. (2010). An Agent-based Architecture for Developing Activity-Aware Systems for Assisting Elderly. *Journal of Universal Computer Science*, 16(12), 1500–1520.

Guo, Y., Hao, Z., Zhao, S., Gong, J., & Yang, F. (2020). Artificial intelligence in health care: Bibliometric analysis. *Journal of Medical Internet Research*, 22(7), e18228. 10.2196/18228

Hagendorff, T. (2020). The ethics of AI ethics: An evaluation of guidelines. *Minds and Machines*, 30(1), 99–120. 10.1007/s11023-020-09517-8

Hamada, M., Zaidan, B. B., & Zaidan, A. A. (2018). A systematic review for human EEG brain signals based emotion classification, feature extraction, brain condition, group comparison. *Journal of Medical Systems*, 42(9), 1–25. 10.1007/s10916-018-1020-8

Hamet, P., & Tremblay, J. (2017). Artificial intelligence in medicine. *Metabolism: Clinical and Experimental*, 69, S36–S40. 10.1016/j.metabol.2017.01.011

Handelman, G. S., Kok, H. K., Chandra, R. V., Razavi, A. H., Lee, M. J., & Asadi, H. (2018). eDoctor: Machine learning and the future of medicine. *Journal of Internal Medicine*, 284(6), 603–619. 10.1111/joim.12822

Harrer, S., Shah, P., Antony, B., & Hu, J. (2019). Artificial intelligence for clinical trial design. *Trends in Pharmacological Sciences*, 40(8), 577–591. 10.1016/j.tips.2019.05.005

Howbert, J. J., Patterson, E. E., Stead, S. M., Brinkmann, B., Vasoli, V., Crepeau, D., Vite, C. H., Sturges, B., Ruedebusch, V., Mavoori, J., Leyde, K., Sheffield, W. D., Litt, B., & Worrell, G. A. (2014). Forecasting seizures in dogs with naturally occurring epilepsy. *PLoS One*, 9(1), e81920. 10.1371/journal.pone.0081920

Hudec, M., & Smutny, Z. (2017). RUDO: A home ambient intelligence system for blind people. *Sensors (Basel)*, 17(8), 1926. 10.3390/s17081926

Hummel, P., & Braun, M. (2020). Just data? Solidarity and justice in data-driven medicine. *Life Sciences, Society and Policy*, 16(1), 1–18. 10.1186/s40504-020-00101-7

Islam, M. M., Poly, T. N., Alsinglawi, B., Lin, L. F., Chien, S. C., Liu, J. C., & Jian, W. S. (2021, April). Application of artificial intelligence in COVID-19 pandemic: Bibliometric analysis. []). MDPI.]. *Health Care*, 9(4), 441.

Jeong, H., & Shi, L. (2018). Memristor devices for neural networks. *Journal of Physics. D, Applied Physics*, 52(2), 023003. 10.1088/1361-6463/aae223

Ji, S., Gu, Q., Weng, H., Liu, Q., Zhou, P., Chen, J., . . . Wang, T. (2020, April). De-Health: all your online health information are belong to us. In *2020 IEEE 36th International Conference on Data Engineering (ICDE)* (pp. 1609-1620). IEEE. 10.1109/ICDE48307.2020.00143

Kanevsky, J., Corban, J., Gaster, R., Kanevsky, A., Lin, S., & Gilardino, M. (2016). Big data and machine learning in plastic surgery: A new frontier in surgical innovation. *Plastic and Reconstructive Surgery*, 137(5), 890e–897e. 10.1097/PRS.0000000000002088

Khan, B., Fatima, H., Qureshi, A., Kumar, S., Hanan, A., Hussain, J., & Abdullah, S. (2023). Drawbacks of artificial intelligence and their potential solutions in the healthcare sector. *Biomedical Materials & Devices*, 1(2), 1–8. 10.1007/s44174-023-00063-2

Kiral-Kornek, I., Roy, S., Nurse, E., Mashford, B., Karoly, P., Carroll, T., Payne, D., Saha, S., Baldassano, S., O'Brien, T., Grayden, D., Cook, M., Freestone, D., & Harrer, S. (2018). Epileptic seizure prediction using big data and deep learning: Toward a mobile system. *EBioMedicine*, 27, 103–111. 10.1016/j.ebiom.2017.11.032

Krishnan, S., & Athavale, Y. (2018). Trends in biomedical signal feature extraction. *Biomedical Signal Processing and Control*, 43, 41–63. 10.1016/j.bspc.2018.02.008

Kwon, M. W., Baek, M. H., Hwang, S., Park, K., Jang, T., Kim, T., Lee, J., Cho, S., & Park, B. G. (2018). Integrate-and-fire neuron circuit using positive feedback field effect transistor for low power operation. *Journal of Applied Physics*, 124(15), 152107. 10.1063/1.5031929

Labovitz, D. L., Shafner, L., Reyes Gil, M., Virmani, D., & Hanina, A. (2017). Using artificial intelligence to reduce the risk of nonadherence in patients on anticoagulation therapy. *Stroke*, 48(5), 1416–1419. 10.1161/STROKEAHA.116.016281

Lee, S. I., Celik, S., Logsdon, B. A., Lundberg, S. M., Martins, T. J., Oehler, V. G., Estey, E. H., Miller, C. P., Chien, S., Dai, J., Saxena, A., Blau, C. A., & Becker, P. S. (2018). A machine learning approach to integrate big data for precision medicine in acute myeloid leukemia. *Nature Communications*, 9(1), 42. 10.1038/s41467-017-02465-5

Lee, S. I., Celik, S., Logsdon, B. A., Lundberg, S. M., Martins, T. J., Oehler, V. G., Estey, E. H., Miller, C. P., Chien, S., Dai, J., Saxena, A., Blau, C. A., & Becker, P. S. (2018). A machine learning approach to integrate big data for precision medicine in acute myeloid leukemia. *Nature Communications*, 9(1), 42. 10.1038/s41467-017-02465-5

Lip, S., Visweswaran, S., & Padmanabhan, S. (2020). Transforming Clinical Trials with Artificial Intelligence. In *Artificial Intelligence* (pp. 297–306). Productivity Press. 10.4324/9780429317415-17

Lloret, J., Canovas, A., Sendra, S., & Parra, L. (2015). A smart communication architecture for ambient assisted living. *IEEE Communications Magazine*, 53(1), 26–33. 10.1109/MCOM.2015.7010512

Lubarsky, B. (2010). Re-identification of "anonymized data". *Georgetown Law Technology Review. Available online:*https://www. georgetownlawtechreview.org/re-identification-of-anonymized-data/GLTR-04-2017*(accessed on 10 September 2021).*

Luengo-Oroz, M., Hoffmann Pham, K., Bullock, J., Kirkpatrick, R., Luccioni, A., Rubel, S., Wachholz, C., Chakchouk, M., Biggs, P., Nguyen, T., Purnat, T., & Mariano, B. (2020). Artificial intelligence cooperation to support the global response to COVID-19. *Nature Machine Intelligence*, 2(6), 295–297. 10.1038/s42256-020-0184-3

Lv, J., Dong, B., Lei, H., Shi, G., Wang, H., Zhu, F., Wen, C., Zhang, Q., Fu, L., Gu, X., Yuan, J., Guan, Y., Xia, Y., Zhao, L., & Chen, H. (2021). Artificial intelligence-assisted auscultation in detecting congenital heart disease. *European Heart Journal. Digital Health*, 2(1), 119–124. 10.1093/ehjdh/ztaa017

Manyika, J., Chui, M., Miremadi, M., Bughin, J., George, K., Willmott, P., & Dewhurst, M. (2017). A future that works: AI, automation, employment, and productivity. *McKinsey Global Institute Research. Tech. Rep*, 60, 1–135.

Martens, F. M. J., Van Kuppevelt, H. J. M., Beekman, J. A. C., Rijkhoff, N. J. M., & Heesakkers, J. P. F. A. (2010). Limited value of bladder sensation as a trigger for conditional neurostimulation in spinal cord injury patients. *Neurourology and Urodynamics*, 29(3), 395–400. 10.1002/nau.20770

Massalha, S., Clarkin, O., Thornhill, R., Wells, G., & Chow, B. J. (2018). Decision support tools, systems, and artificial intelligence in cardiac imaging. *The Canadian Journal of Cardiology*, 34(7), 827–838. 10.1016/j.cjca.2018.04.032

Mayorga-Ruiz, I., Jiménez-Pastor, A., Fos-Guarinos, B., López-González, R., García-Castro, F., & Alberich-Bayarri, Á. (2019). The role of AI in clinical trials. *Artificial Intelligence in Medical Imaging: Opportunities, applications and risks*, 231-243.

Mendez, A., Belghith, A., & Sawan, M. (2013). A DSP for sensing the bladder volume through afferent neural pathways. *IEEE Transactions on Biomedical Circuits and Systems*, 8(4), 552–564. 10.1109/TBCAS.2013.2282087

Pumplun, L., Fecho, M., Wahl, N., Peters, F., & Buxmann, P. (2021). Adoption of machine learning systems for medical diagnostics in clinics: Qualitative interview study. *Journal of Medical Internet Research*, 23(10), e29301. 10.2196/29301

Rabhi, Y., Mrabet, M., & Fnaiech, F. (2018). A facial expression controlled wheelchair for people with disabilities. *Computer Methods and Programs in Biomedicine*, 165, 89–105. 10.1016/j.cmpb.2018.08.013

Rai, H. M., & Chatterjee, K. (2018). A unique feature extraction using MRDWT for automatic classification of abnormal heartbeat from ECG big data with multilayered probabilistic neural network classifier. *Applied Soft Computing*, 72, 596–608. 10.1016/j.asoc.2018.04.005

Safdar, S., Zafar, S., Zafar, N., & Khan, N. F. (2018). Machine learning based decision support systems (DSS) for heart disease diagnosis: A review. *Artificial Intelligence Review*, 50(4), 597–623. 10.1007/s10462-017-9552-8

Sakai, K., & Yamada, K. (2019). Machine learning studies on major brain diseases: 5-year trends of 2014–2018. *Japanese Journal of Radiology*, 37(1), 34–72. 10.1007/s11604-018-0794-4

Sarrouti, M., & El Alaoui, S. O. (2017). A machine learning-based method for question type classification in biomedical question answering. *Methods of Information in Medicine*, 56(03), 209–216. 10.3414/ME16-01-0116

Sarrouti, M., & El Alaoui, S. O. (2017). A yes/no answer generator based on sentiment-word scores in biomedical question answering. [IJHISI]. *International Journal of Healthcare Information Systems and Informatics*, 12(3), 62–74. 10.4018/IJHISI.2017070104

Schönberger, D. (2019). Artificial intelligence in healthcare: A critical analysis of the legal and ethical implications. *International Journal of Law and Information Technology*, 27(2), 171–203. 10.1093/ijlit/eaz004

Shi, D., Zhang, W., Zhang, W., & Ding, X. (2019). A review on lower limb rehabilitation exoskeleton robots. *Chinese Journal of Mechanical Engineering*, 32(1), 1–11. 10.1186/s10033-019-0389-8

Shi, W., Kah, W. S., Mohamad, M. S., Moorthy, K., Deris, S., Sjaugi, M. F., Omatu, S., Corchado, J. M., & Kasim, S. (2017). A review of gene selection tools in classifying cancer microarray data. *Current Bioinformatics*, 12(3), 202–212. 10.2174/1574893610666151026215104

Singh, M., & Nath, G. (2022). Artificial intelligence and anesthesia: A narrative review. *Saudi Journal of Anaesthesia*, 16(1), 86. 10.4103/sja.sja_669_21

Stacey, W. C. (2018). Seizure prediction is possible–now let's make it practical. *EBioMedicine*, 27, 3–4. 10.1016/j.ebiom.2018.01.006

Sucharitha, G., & Chary, D. V. (2021). Predicting the effect of Covid-19 by using Artificial Intelligence: A case study. *Materials today. Proceedings*.

Tantin, A., Assi, E. B., van Asselt, E., Hached, S., & Sawan, M. (2020). Predicting urinary bladder voiding by means of a linear discriminant analysis: Validation in rats. *Biomedical Signal Processing and Control*, 55, 101667. 10.1016/j.bspc.2019.101667

Ting, D. S., Liu, Y., Burlina, P., Xu, X., Bressler, N. M., & Wong, T. Y. (2018). AI for medical imaging goes deep. *Nature Medicine*, 24(5), 539–540. 10.1038/s41591-018-0029-3

Tran, B. X., Vu, G. T., Ha, G. H., Vuong, Q. H., Ho, M. T., Vuong, T. T., La, V.-P., Ho, M.-T., Nghiem, K.-C., Nguyen, H., Latkin, C., Tam, W., Cheung, N.-M., Nguyen, H.-K., Ho, C., & Ho, R. C. (2019). Global evolution of research in artificial intelligence in health and medicine: A bibliometric study. *Journal of Clinical Medicine*, 8(3), 360. 10.3390/jcm8030360

Tumpa, S. N., Islam, A. B., & Ankon, M. T. M. (2017, September). Smart care: An intelligent assistant for pregnant mothers. In *2017 4th International Conference on Advances in Electrical Engineering (ICAEE)* (pp. 754-759). IEEE.

Vashistha, R., Dangi, A. K., Kumar, A., Chhabra, D., & Shukla, P. (2018). Futuristic biosensors for cardiac health care: an artificial intelligence approach. *3 Biotech*, 8, 1-11.

Vial, A., Stirling, D., Field, M., Ros, M., Ritz, C., Carolan, M., Holloway, L., & Miller, A. A. (2018). The role of deep learning and radiomic feature extraction in cancer-specific predictive modelling: A review. *Translational Cancer Research*, 7(3), 803–816. 10.21037/tcr.2018.05.02

Wu, Q., Zhang, Y. D., Tao, W., & Amin, M. G. (2015). Radar-based fall detection based on Doppler time–frequency signatures for assisted living. *IET Radar, Sonar & Navigation*, 9(2), 164–172. 10.1049/iet-rsn.2014.0250

Chapter 2
Evolution of Generative AI in Healthcare

Nikita Thakur
Chitkara University, India

ABSTRACT

AI in healthcare is not a coincidental development; rather, it is a revolutionary force that has the potential to completely alter patient experiences and medical practices. Artificial intelligence (AI) methods, and processes of natural language, especially machine learning, are progressively effective in the health profession and education. Generative AI is one of the common types of artificial intelligence that should be used for making and creating new data, such as text, images, and music. This technology could transform completely healthcare by contributing to new approaches to improve the care of the patient, develop new treatments, and diagnose diseases. Nowadays, Generative AI plays a significant part in healthcare to improve mental health, New drug discovery, personalized medicine, Improved diagnosis, More efficient surgery, and enhanced rehabilitation. Potential hazards, however, include the use of biases or inaccurate statistics for algorithms to train them, relying too heavily on generative AI lacking supervision of humans, concealment issues with patients, besides the moral ramifications of applying AI to decision-making for medical. Oversight and careful regulation are required to assurance that the generative AI's promises in neuro-interventional surgeries are appreciated while minimizing its potential perils. AI has had a huge impact on healthcare, changing the sector in a variety of ways. In the end, it has saved lives by lowering expenses and raising the standard of care. We accept that true artificial intelligence (AI) will have a big impact on healthcare services in the future. Machine learning is the prime technology forward precision medicine, which is commonly perceived as a much-needed advancement in healthcare. We trust AI will eventually become accomplished in providing that diagnosis and treatment recommendations, even still early creativities in that area

DOI: 10.4018/979-8-3693-3731-8.ch002

Copyright © 2024, IGI Global. Copying or distributing in print or electronic forms without written permission of IGI Global is prohibited.

have demonstrated stimulating.

INTRODUCTION

There is a rebellion captivating in the healthcare division right now. An increasing shortage of medical specialists and rising overall healthcare costs are the root causes of this revolution. Consequently, the healthcare sector is seeking to introduce novel information technology-driven approaches and procedures that have the potential to reduce expenses and address these increasing challenges. Worldwide healthcare systems provoke massive encounters, such as an aging population, high expenditures, waste, and limited access. Healthcare systems are stressed by pandemics such as the coronavirus (COVID-19), which can lead to several issues including inadequate or imprecise diagnostic testing, overworked specialists, and a lack of information (Greenberg et al., 2020) (Pavli et al., 2021).

More importantly, a health crisis such as COVID-19 or the emergence of HIV in the 1980s highlights the momentousness of the complications with our healthcare systems. We can reimagine and actualize care and back office health systems as healthcare crises degenerate current problems, such as incapable access to healthcare, a deficiency of on-demand healthcare services, excessive responsibilities, and a lack of price transparency (Maphumulo

& Bhengu, 2019). Innovations in knowledge are being comprised progressively. The irresistible capacity of data that wants to be managed averts surgeons from waiting up to time on modern therapeutic progressions, which mains to burnout among healthcare professionals.

Revolutions in technology are being embraced gradually. The overwhelming volume of data that needs to be processed prevents doctors from staying up to date on the newest medical advancements, which leads to burnout among healthcare specialists (Maphumulo & Bhengu, 2019).

- **Generative AI in healthcare**

A well-liked division of artificial intelligence (AI) so-called machine learning varieties uses huge data sets to invent patterns in the communications between different factors. These approaches can lead researchers and resources in the most creative tracks, harvest novel schemes, and expose previously anonymous connections. Frequent manufacturing, counting finance, mechanical driving, smart homes, etc., can benefit from the application of machine learning. Frequent Machine learning is utilized in medicine to generate automated clinical decision provision systems. Expertise applications can now impersonate human thought processes by using generative AI to interpret information and learn from alterations in predictable consequences (Dwivedi et al.,2023) (Nishant et al., 2020). Generative AI has human-like services which are essential for the transformation of how they are individually engaged with technology. Human-AI collaborative conversation systems, for example, could be used in customer service (Wet et al., 2022), Social robots may have an impression on normative conformance (Qin et al., 2022) While chatbots powered by artificial intelligence (AI) could be used in classrooms to give students instantaneous, interactive support and better suit their requirements (Chen et al., 2022) (Nishant et al., 2020).

This Generative AI-enabled technology is shifting the paradigm toward healthcare which is very beneficial for the healthcare industries (Chem et al., 2023). More exactly, healthcare providers can enhance market accomplishment by applying responsible AI (Kumar et al., 2023), whereas AI is very supportive and enables a connection with the management systems to enhance their innovative services and use of this AI is a very supportive system to automatically diagnose mental disorders orders, (Tutun et al., 2023) and to enhance medical diagnostic determinations (Jussupow et al., 2021). Even with all its potential advantages, Generative AI still has to suffer from many challenges which would be the failure of its operations. More precisely, generative AI algorithms would cause adverse health outcomes and incorrect treatment because of their automated preserved prejudices and adverse health outcomes (e.g., ignoring gender distinctions). This would be the main detriment of patients and healthcare providers towards generative AI. Human beings have lost their knowledge because of AI (Fugener et al., 2021). Users may likewise dispute about implementation or refuse the use of generative AI owing to apprehensions about privacy protection and whether AI would ultimately replace humans (Chiu et al., 2021). Novel technologies are anxious about users' attitudes toward generative AI like AI designers, managers, and scholars regulating the implementation of AI (chi et al., 2023) (Gursoy et al., 2019). The aforementioned studies have recommended that perceived cognitive and AI capabilities of operations, observations of AI's efficiency, apparent negative effects of AI, and users' reactions may be vital factors in encouraging a good attitude towards AI (Chiu et al., 2021) (Gursoy et al., 2019). These all demonstrate the need for additional study on the deployment of generative AI. Nonetheless, it's possible that the TAM and UTAUT technology adoption models—among others—are ill-suited to describe people's inclination to embrace generative AI. These all determine the need for supplementary education on the arrangement of generative AI. Nevertheless, it's conceivable that the TAM and UTAUT technology adoption representations—amongst others—are ill-suited to a pronounced common predisposition to squeeze generative AI. Non-intelligent and Traditional use technologies are used initially for exploring (Gursoy et al., 2019). One of the greatest significant influences in the acceptance of AI in healthcare should be customers' trust, which is obstructed by AI-specific features together with personalization, loss of privacy, and anthropomorphism (Liu et al., 2022). As a consequence, future studies on generative AI in healthcare have to think about including the exceptional features of generative AI in their research model (Ooi et al., 2023).

- **Routine Information Gathering**

Concluded clear communication with patients, hesitation resolve, and data summarization for healthcare consultants, generative AI can improve the effectiveness of data get-togethers and commentary. Through inquiring beset questions in a conversational style, an AI system can support medical authorities gather patient medical histories. AI's measurements to access health information exchanges (HIEs) and bring together medical records of patients, examine them, and generate appropriate investigations constructed on the patient role in medical antiquity is alternative profit. AI can, for illustration, authorize whether patients are after their prescribed routines or stopped taking cross-referencing the patient's medication list to recognize any conflicting prescriptions in light of new prescriptions through their existing health complications. This technique helps to accumulate a further complete medical history for the separate, which the doctors utilize to treat them more effectively. By organizing a more systematic medical history for the patient, the process helps the medics give them better care (Yaraghi et al., 2024).

- **Diagnosis**

AI has established the ability to recover diagnostic procedures, predominantly for conditions for which a substantial amount of data is accessible. However, there are immobile difficulties in making accurate analyses and dropping biases, specifically for unusual diseases with tiny data representations. This deficiency of data types it extra problematic for AI to detect rare diseases, and as a consequence, AI might not be occupied well because of the slight knowledge model. AI systems must have access to comprehensive datasets, even in common conditions where data are profuse, to enhance their performance and prevent the appearance of a balkanized AI scene in which health systems are higher through admittance to large amounts of proprietary data outpace their smaller counterparts. This is approximately what will be discussed below. AI systems must have access to comprehensive datasets, even in common conditions where data are abundant, to increase their performance and avoid the emergence of a balkanized AI landscape in which higher health systems with access to enormous quantities of exclusive statistics outstrip their slighter corresponding item. This is something that will be discussed below.

Only publicly available data is used for training the generative AI systems that are currently available, such as ChatGPT. Depend exclusively on basic AI models for therapeutic analysis would be untimely without enchanting into justification the amusing medical olden times gathered after considerable challenges to medical records for digitization. Thus, AI on large medical datasets and healthcare specialists should use caution when applying generative AI for analysis. Healthcare professionals must reduce any dangers even after their AI systems have been trained on substantial and adequate medical datasets. They should generate specialized methods in which AI supports doctors diagnose complications rather than enchanting their place—in other words, where AI serves as a beneficial implement rather than a replacement (Yaraghi et al., 2024).

- **Surgeons and AI collaborations**

AI takes the possibility to variety the health care system more streamlined and efficient by repurposing the purposes moderately rather than replacing them. Does this suggest that medical doctors who use AI take the place of those who don't? This entitlement that AI will replace doctors has increased a proportion of traction later (Haupt & Marks, 2023). The declaration is precise. AI-assisted therapeutic verdicts consume the possibility to be more precise than individuals made without it, as they diminish patient risk and develop efficiency, quality, and service (Miller & Browm, 2018). But then "collaboration" stays a feasible income of allowing the "use" of AI. Construction on the ideas of human-AI collaboration and human-in-the-loop, an agenda used for attaching AI's probable can be formulated (Wu et al., 2022) (Cai et al., 2019). To exploit outcomes, the approach of the Human-in-the-Loop (HITL) strains a supportive association between humanoid knowledge and AI. AI delivers insights to complete collaborative managerial, and individuals use their information to variety the eventual decision. This diminishes biases or imprecisions by producing organization and quality control to validate AI predictions.

As a consequence of communal learning, the enterprise cares for enduring expansion and advancement. This improves acceptance and trust uniform supplementary. To confirm accountability, transparency, and explainability in AI verdicts, ethical moralities are crucial. More adaptable thanks to AI for the feedback of humans which makes it accomplish handling complex illustrations that energy beyond training data. HITL valor be used in the healthcare business since therapeutic authorities with the required drill could exert AI to monitor, authorize, and through the procedure, interpret AI outputs, and suggest responses to improve AI's accuracy and capabilities. Recent research emphasized AI's collaborative nature and surgeons by representing how it might expand the accuracy of problem-solving and clinical decisions when corresponding through conversant human evaluation (Cai et al., 2019). In instruction to stun the inconsistencies, this collaboration can further support a value suggestion that is regularly unnoticed. In situations by inadequate possessions, such rural areas or emerging regions, AI has a advanced worth to activate as an added tool or technique of knowledge augmentation, to adjacent knowledge gaps and recover patient education, diagnosis, and communication although reducing language barriers (Wahi et al., 2018). Nevertheless, as an alternative to presence entirely reliant on separate decisions completed in healthcare settings, these association with AI and choice provision tools are completely available through the approval of administrations (Sezgin et al., 2023).

- **AI algorithms in medicine.**

Relatively few AI tools consume employed in medical practice, even though AI systems have constantly established their efficiency in a huge variety of historic medical surveys (Wiens et al., 2019). Critics point out that in real medical conditions, AI systems would not be as useful in preparation as surveying statistics would display; their capacity be besides slow otherwise composite, or their dealings per individual strength prime to unsuspected complications (Kanagasingam et al., 2018) (Beede et al., 2020) (Kiani et al., 2020). Retrospective in silico datasets as well go over a severe filtering and cleaning procedure, which can reduce their representativeness of authentic medical practice. This gap between theory and practice can be occupied through prospective studies and randomized controlled trials (RCTs), which more carefully demonstrate that AI models can be used in authentic healthcare settings and have assessable, valuable possessions. RCTs have lately remained used to estimate the worth of AI in health care. An all-inclusive depiction of AI's encouragement on medical systems is provided by the numerous other metrics that have been employed in addition to accuracy to assess the knowledge's helpfulness (Lin et al., 2019) (Gong et al., 2020) (Wang et al., 2020) (Hollon et al., 2020) (Philips et al., 2019). In a single RCT, for illustration, the length of time patients persisted within the target glucose range was evaluated to assess the effectiveness of an AI system for managing insulin quantities. The average duration of hypotension episodes was tracked in an education appraising an intensive care system for intraoperative hypotension; then the turnaround time reduction of an arrangement that selected belongings of intracranial hemorrhage for humanoid appraisal was used to evaluate its efficiency (Nimri et al., 2020) (Winberge et al., 2020). Upcoming guidelines were identical to STARD-AI and current procedures like AI-specific extensions to CONSORT and SPIRIT guidelines could support regulating medical AI reportage, counting clinical trial protocols and results, simplifying the community's facility to segment discoveries, and systematically scrutinizing the utility of medicinal AI (Wismuller & Geerts, 2020) (Liu et al., 2020). Some AI arrangements have innovative beginning challenging to deployment in recent years, in advance administrative support and circumnavigating regulatory complications. By permitting subsidies for the practice of two specific AI systems for therapeutic picture identification, the Centre designed for Medicaid Services and Medicare, which authorizes public assurance compensation expenses, has aided in the acceptance of AI in scientific situations (Rivera et al., 2020). Moreover, a 2020 education revealed that the US

Food and Drug Administration (FDA) is appreciating AI possessions at a faster rate, with machine learning (ML) existing single sort of AI (Panjamapirom et al., 20222). These expansions are frequently in the form of FDA clearances, which are less rigorous than whole approvals but cover the method for the submission of AI/ML systems in authentic clinical conditions. It is critical to communicate that the evidence used for these regulatory clearances regularly contains single-institution, retrospective data that is considered proprietary and is mostly unpublished. It is remarkable to indicate that the evidence applied for these supervisory authorizations frequently comprises retrospective, single-institution statistics that are observed as proprietary, and unreported.

- **Types of AI of relevance in Health care**

As a substitute of existence a single piece of knowledge, artificial intelligence is a cluster of them. Though the accurate professions and progressions that this knowledge assists vary significantly, the common of them have immediate consequences for healthcare manufacturing. The subsequent lists and designates limited detailed AI skills that are identically substantial to the health care business.

Machine Learning

Machine learning is an arithmetic technique that turns representations into statistics and consents representations to "learn" over data-driven prototypical exercises. One of the maximum predominant categories of AI is machine learning; according to a 2018 Deloitte survey of 1,100 US executives whose administrations were previously discovered AI, 63% of the companies surveyed were via machine learning. There are abundant dissimilarities in this broad approach, which is the source of many AI organizations (Loucks et al., 2018). Meticulousness medication, which envisages which dealing routines are probable to remain operative for a persistent constructed on the variability of persistent features and the treatment environment, is the most general usage of conventional machine learning in the healthcare industry. Supervised learning is the procedure of consuming a training dataset for which the termination adjustable (such as the onset of disease) is known. This is essential for the massive mainstream of machine education and accuracy medication submissions (Lee et al., 2018). Neural systems remain a additional cultured category of machine learning. Technologically advanced in the 1960s, these systems have remained extensively used in healthcare investigations for numerous years, predominantly in submissions including categories, such as expecting the probability that a persistent will bond with a detailed infection. Its tactics are difficulties given outputs, inputs, and adjustable weightiness, or "features," that connect inputs and outputs. While there has been some evaluation of the way neurons interpret indications, the similarity to the operation of intelligence is not identical (Sordo et al., 2002).

Neural network models and deep learning through numerous coatings of appearances or variable quantities that expect consequences remain the maximum cultured categories of machine learning. Today's graphics have faster processing cold and unit schemes might expose thousands of hidden features in such models. Deep learning is regularly rummaged in the therapeutic field to classify conceivably malicious tumours in radiological imageries (Fakoor et al., 2013). Deep learning is being used more and more in radio mics to recognize clinically significant structures in imaging data that are imperceptible to the human eye (Vial et al., 2018). The most common submissions for radiomics and deep education are in image analysis associated with oncology. Once collected, these automated methods for image investigation—recognized as computer-aided detection, or CAD—appear to suggest improved indicative accurateness than the previous group. Deep learning remains a form of natural language processing (NLP), which is enlightened beneath, and is also being utilized more and more for speech recognition. A human observer would regularly discover little meaning in individual features of a deep education model, in distinction to prior techniques of statistical analysis. Subsequently, the description of the model's marks may be tremendously stimulating or conceivably incredible.

- **Rule-Based Expert System**

In the 1980s, practiced organizations that trusted groups of "if-then" instructions conquered AI knowledge and remained extensively working in both individuals and succeeding epochs for commercial determinations. They have remained extensively used in the healthcare business for "clinical decision support" determinations aimed at the preceding scarce decades, besides their use is motionless and extensive currently. A set of strategies is presently provided by numerous electronic health record (EHR) providers sideways with their systems (Vial et al., 2018). To generate a conventional of rules in a convinced knowledge domain, knowledge engineers and human specialists are needed. They remain modest to grasp besides functioning effectively awake to a degree. But they tend to collapse when there are a lot of rules—characteristically further than a limited thousand—and when individual rules flinch to contradict one another. Additionally, the situation might be stimulating and time-consuming to adjust the rules if the acquaintance province changes. Healthcare field, novel approaches constructed on statistics algorithms, and machine learning are steadily swapping them (Davenport et al., 2019).

- **Physical Robots**

Near about 200,000 robots are installed in maximum industries every year globally, physical robots are by now well known. In surroundings like warehouses and factories, they convey ready-determined responsibilities together with lifting, welding, assembling belongings, or everchanging carrying health to hospitals. In the previous few years, robots have learned to work smarter than humans and are calmer to train by managing them through a desired program. Moreover, once further AI structures are involved in their "brainpower"—essentially, their functioning organizations—they have developed further cultured. It seems convincing that physical robots' motivation ultimately incorporates the identical improvements in trendy intellect that we've perceived in other pitches of artificial intelligence (Davenport et al., 2019). Surgical robots, which remained initially authorized in the United States in 2000, give doctors "superpowers" by attracting their visualization, allowing them to make precise, fewer offensive openings, seams injuries, and other errands. Then human specialists remain to a variety of significant decisions. Prostate, Gynecological, and head and neck operations are among the communal clinical dealings accomplished with robotic support (Hussain et al., 2014).

- **Robotic Process automatic**

This technology, managerially structured digital responsibilities involving statistics organizations remain accomplished as if via a humanoid employer observing a conventional of strategies and scripts. These are less expensive, humbler to sequence, and behave compared to other forms of AI. Robots aren't essentially tangled in robotic process automation (RPA); as a substitute, computer plans successively on servers located. Toward occupation of a semi-intelligent user of the schemes, depends on workflow, business rules, and "presentation layer" construction with the evidence systems. They are hired in the medicinal arena for tedious responsibilities like prior endorsement, billing, and patient record information. It can be used in combination with further technologies, such as image acknowledgment, to excerpt statistics from conveyed snapshots and arrive at transactional systems (Hussain et al., 2014).

Though these technologies have remained conversed as dispersed objects, nearby in an upward tendency of their grouping besides combination; for example, image appreciation is presence combined through RPA, and automata are getting "brains" power-driven by AI. It's conceivable that these knowledges will be associated with such an amount in the upcoming that complex explanations develop further real or faithful.

- **Diagnosis and Treatment**

AI has been mainly intensive on treatment and disease diagnosis since at least the 1970s when Stanford developed MYCIN to recognize bloodborne bacterial infections. Despite the presentation's promise the exactly categorizing and treating infections, these and other early rule-based systems were not combined interested in clinical practice. They were poorly integrated with medical record systems and scientific developments, and they did not suggestively beat human diagnosticians (Bush, 2018). Recently the media has agreed to IBM's Watson a portion of attention owed to its importance on precision medicine, precisely the recognition and treatment of cancer. Watson types practice of individually natural linguistic processing and machine learning techniques. However, once customers maximized how thought-provoking it was to train Watson to delicacy exact types of oncology and participate Watson into care systems and events, their preliminary enthusiasm for this high-tech use diminished. Watson is a gathering of "cognitive services," such as language and speech, machine and vision learning-based or data-analysis software, which stays accessible through application programming interfaces (APIs). Though mainstream spectators believe that Watson APIs are precisely conceivable, giving malignance appears like an extremely supercilious area. Competition from free "open source" agendas accessible by approximately contractors, similar to Google's TensorFlow, has also offended Watson and other proprietary programs (Buchanan & Shortlife et al., 1984) (Ross & Swetlitz, 2017). Difficulties with AI implementation wave numerous healthcare organizations. Rule-based systems that are combined hooked on EHR systems are normally utilized, smoothly at the NHS, then they are not as accurate as additional algorithmic schemes that are constructed on machine learning. These rule-based clinical decision support systems are stimulating to maintain as therapeutically empathic developments, nevertheless, they are commonly unable to handle the explosion of data and material based on genomic, proteomic, metabolic, and other "omic-based" approaches to care (Davenport, 2018).

Nevertheless, it is mainly understood in IT businesses and investigative labs rather than clinical practice, that this situation is preliminary for transformation. Here is rarely a week that permits a research lab not to privilege to consume a scheme used for smearing big data or AI to diagnose and treatment of a disease with as great correctness as or even more than human consultants (Care, 2014). Although approximately of these findings utilize extra categories of depictions, such as for the scanning of retinal or genomic-based precision medicine, various of these discoveries are based on radiological image investigation (Lona, 2018). These varieties of detections, which originated on statistically-based machine learning models, are fetching in a new period of indication- and probability-based medication, which is mainly received then offerings frequent complications for patient-clinician dealings and medicinal integrities (Schmidt et al., 2018) (Aronson & Rehm, 2015). The same difficulties are present and thoroughly functioned on by impresarios and tech corporations. For illustration, Google is employed with health distribution systems to advance immense statistics estimate representations that aware doctors to high-risk infections like heart failure and sepsis. AI-derived image interpretation algorithms are existence established by Google, Enlitic, and numerous other firms. Jvion delivers a "clinical success machine" that inventions the patient role greatest likely to profit since rehabilitation and those who are most at risk. Respectively these possibly will help doctors of medicine make conclusions around which analysis and progression of dealing to commend for the affected role in patient (Rysavy., 2013). "Population health" machine learning representations are also used by payers and healthcare workers to forecast populaces by the risk of precise sicknesses or coincidences, as well as to get ahead of readmissions to hospitals. These models are probable to be moderately predictive, but infrequently they are undersupplied in significant evidence that could expand the predictive power, such as the socioeconomic situation of the patient (Rysavy., 2013) (Rajkomar et al., 2018) (Shimabukuro et al., 2017) (NaitAicha et al., 2017). However, mixing AI-based diagnosis and treatment recommendations into clinical workflows and EHR systems can rarely be tough, irrespective of whether they are algorithmic or rules-based in nature. More prospective than not, these integration complications have prohibited AI from being present extensively. Furthermore, a portion of AI-based therapeutic analytical and treatment tools offered by tech companies are either stand-alone solutions or focus on a single area of health care. Even though they are immobile in the early stages, some EHR workers have in progress to integrate retiring AI competencies (beyond rule-based clinical decision support) into their products. Providers will have to wait for EHR vendors to mature more AI capabilities, or take on huge integration projects themselves (Low et al., 2015).

- **Use of AI algorithms in medicine.**

Relatively few AI tools are applied in medical practice, even though AI organizations have been dependably established to be efficacious in an extensive series of surveying therapeutic educations. Critics point out that in real medical circumstances, AI systems would non be as advantageous in practice as retrospective data would display; their strength is too slow or composite, or their collaboration by person capacity main to surprising complications (Wiens et al., 2019) (Kmagasingan et al., 2018) (Beede et al., 2020) (Kiani et al., 2020). Retrospective in silico datasets too go over a difficult filtering and cleaning procedure, which can decrease their representativeness of concrete medical practice. This gap between theory and practice can be occupied by prospective investigations and randomized controlled trials (RCTs), which more systematically demonstrate that AI models can be used in definite healthcare settings and have assessable, advantageous things. RCTs have freshly been used to assess the worth of AI in healthcare. An inclusive image of AI's effect on medical systems is provided in the frequent other metrics that have been working in addition to accuracy to estimate the knowledge's practicality (Lin et al., 2019) (Gong et al., 2020) (Wang et al., 2020)

(Hollon et al., 2020) (Phillips et al., 2019). For occurrence, the dimension of patients spent within the mark glucose assortment was measured in an RCT assessing an AI scheme for dealing insulin prescriptions; the average duration of hypotension episodes was tracked in a study evaluating a monitoring system for intraoperative hypotension; then the turnaround time reduction of a system that flagged cases of intracranial hemorrhage for human review was used to measure its efficiency. Upcoming guidelines similar to STARD-AI and recent guidelines comparable AI-specific extensions to SPIRIT and CONSORT guidelines could help standardize medical AI reporting, including clinical trial protocols and results, smoothing the community's capability to share findings and carefully survey the utility of medical AI (Nimri et al., 2020) (Winberge et al., 2020) (Wismuller et al., 2020) (Liu et al., 2020) (Rivera et al., 2020). Convinced AI schemes have advanced from testing to deployment in recent years, acquiring administrative support, and obstacles of legal navigating. By authorizing funding for the use of two particular AI systems for medical picture identification, the Centre for Medicare and Medicaid Services, which authorizes communal assurance compensation expenditures, has assisted in the implementation of AI in medical situations. Moreover, in 2020 studies exposed that the US Food and Drug Administration (FDA) is approving AI properties at a fast-tracked rate, through machine learning (ML) existence single category of AI (Panjamapirom, A.et al., 2022) (Benjamens, S.,et al.,2020).

- **Interpretation of medical Images By Deep Learning**

Deep learning, in which networks excerpt direct patterns from whole statistics, has shown impressive consequences in picture classification in recent years. As an effect, medical AI research has burst into fields like pathology, radiology, ophthalmology, and gastroenterology specialisms that significantly trust the clarification of depictions. AI organizations have meaningfully improved the correctness of radiological occupations, such as cardiac function estimation, lung cancer screening, and mammography interpretation. This will not only discover diagnosis but also be used for treatment and risk assessment. AI system is the one, for example, that stayed qualified to expect the three-year risk of lung cancer created on clinical information and computed tomography (CT) readings from radiologists. The development of follow-up CT scans for cancer patients power then be completed using these predictions, enhancing the present screening protocols. Artificial Intellect is getting closer to being employed and consuming actual inspiration in radiology cheers to the justification of these schemes on an increasing number of prospective evaluations frequent and clinical sites (Wu, N.,et al., 20219)(McKinney, S. M., et al., 2020)(Ghorbani, A., et al., 2020)(Ghorbani, A., et al., 2020)(Ardila, D., et al., 2019)(Huynh, E., et al., 2020). Therefore whole-slide imaging, and artificial intelligence (AI) in pathology have made momentous advancements in the analysis of cancer and the provision of new disease insights. Slides' areas of interest have been successfully recognized by consuming models, which might advance the analysis progression. Even beyond the opportunity of expert pathologist reviews, deep neural networks can be trained to recognize structural variants or powerful mutations, as well as to regulate the primary tumor origin. Furthermore, associated with outmoded marking and histologic subtyping, AI was established to make supplementary precise persistence predictions for the variability of tumor types (Huang, P.,et al., 2019)(Kather, J. N.,et al., 2019)(Jackson, H. W.,et al., 2020)(Campanella, G.,et al., 2019)(Fu, Y.,et al., 2020). These investigations have exposed how AI can recover the accuracy, efficiency, and usefulness of pathology interpretations.

Furthermore, profound education has better-quality gastroenterology, particularly colonoscopy, a critical procedure for the primary detection of colorectal cancer. With accuracy on par with skilled endoscopists, profound education has been useful to mechanically regulate whether colonic irrigation lesions are carcinomatous. Additionally, AI systems have been developed to assist endoscopists because, during the inspection, tumors and further probable disease pointers are regularly missed. This knowledge has been established to grow endoscopists' measurements to recognize irregularities, which might intensify sensitivity and grow the investigative dependability of colonoscopy(Zhou, D., et al., 2020)(Zhao S,et al., 2019)(Freedman, D.,et al., 2019).

In the field of ophthalmology, deep learning models have realized widespread submission, important to momentous progressions in deployment. In accumulation to measurement model performance, previous studies have observed just how these models disturb popular communications with health systems. For illustration, a study of rummage-sale interviews and human observation to look at just how an AI system meant for screening eye diseases pretentious patient understanding and therapeutic systems. Supplementary investigations probing the financial belongings of AI in the ophthalmology field have exposed that, in certain situations, such as the analysis of diabetic retinopathy, fully or semi-automated AI screening might consequence in charge savings (Milea, D., et al., 2020) (Wolf, R. M.,et al., 2020) (Xie, Y.,et al., 2020).

- **Robotic-Assisted Surgical Systems (RASS) and Computer Assisted Surgery (CAS)**

Subsequently 1985, the RASS was utilized in the variability of medical specialisms, such as general surgery, orthopaedical surgery, urology, gastrointestinal surgery, spine surgery, gynecology, thoracic surgery, and heart surgery. Based on the degree of autonomous activity, RASS has been divided into three types: shared control surgery, telesurgical, and supervisory controlled surgery (Kwoh, Y. S.,et al., 1988). In conservative surgery, surgeons are partial to working on what their eyes can see, and open surgery is the only means to opinion a patient. A minute incision can be used to implant instruments and cameras that a surgeon can use with RASS to do operations with extreme precision. The goal of the least invasive technique is to decrease postoperative complications and expedite patient recovery. Furthermore,

RASS can minimize the physical strain on medical employees. With RASS, it is also conceivable to pucker all applicable evidence, together with videotapes of the procedure, as well as the movements and cutting and sewing actions that receipt residence while the operation is present and completed. This data might then be used for added analysis, refining, and rationalization of the medical process. Internationally, there are RASS manufacturer's contributions to robotic medical provisions. In this education, we describe DaVinci, a RASS developed by Intuitive Surgical Inc. that is now one of the most prevalent. As of September 2019, DaVinci had 5406 installed bases (Väänänen, A.,et al., 2021). A further approach for assisted surgical systems is called CAS. Although robot-assisted surgery (RASS) essences on the physical surgery robot, its control and applications, and its applications, computer-aided surgery (CAS) technology usages computer technology to design surgeries and improves surgeon guidance during surgeries. Techniques recognized as computer-aided surgery (CAS) can be rummage-sale to moreover directly participate in surgery or provision the navigation or positioning of surgical paraphernalia (Aboushelib, M. N.,et al., 2008). Preoperatively, intraoperatively, and for decorative surgical efficiency and efficacy following surgery, CAS has a variety of uses in the surgical workplace. Preoperative planning, surgical navigation, diagnostics, image analysis and processing, and the expansion of a virtual image from the patient are amongst the main fundamentals of CAS. A significant contributor to the development of RASS has been CAS. An added approach for assisted surgical systems is termed CAS. Although robot-assisted surgery (RASS) essences on the physical surgery robot, its control and applications, and its applications, computer-aided surgery (CAS) technology practices computer technology to design surgeries and improves surgeon guidance during surgeries. Techniques used in CAS can either aggressively participate in surgery or benefit from instrument navigation or placement. A diversity of applications designed for preoperative and intraoperative care, as well as for attractive surgical efficiency and efficacy postnatal surgery, are available in CAS. The group of virtual images from the patient, analysis, image processing and analysis, preoperative planning, surgical simulations, and surgical navigation are among the primary elements of CAS. The development of RASS has been significantly influenced by CAS (Kenngott, H. G.,et al., 2015). According to Canadian research which is conducted in 2011 to measure the clinical 95 effectiveness of robotic surgery technology originated that when compared to open or laparoscopic surgery, robotic surgery (RASS) in hysterectomy, prostatectomy, nephrectomy, and cardiac surgery produced frequent assistance with clinical outcomes, counting quicker hospice stays, subordinate transfusion and blood loss rate, and fewer complications. Laparoscopic prostatectomy is one of the RASS measures with straight recovery times; open prostatectomy and open hysterectomy have longer recovery times. The review also assessed the economic evidence for hysterectomy, nephrectomy, heart surgery, and prostatectomy. In contrast to laparoscopic and open surgery, cost study exposed that tumbling hospital breaks after robotic radical prostatectomy also occasioned lesser hospitalization expenditures. On the other hand, the outlay of buying and preserving surgical robots will type it so that around 75% of dealings linking robot assistance will be more costly. However, a higher RASS consumption rate can save costs. In 2017, a systematic investigation was directed to measure the compensations for the patient role, costs, and surgeon conditions linked to the use of RASS in gynecological oncology. The learning exploratory the cost and efficacy of robotic hepatectomy discovered that the RASS group qualified a 20% longer operational time, a 35% shorter length of stay, 10% higher perioperative expenses, and 36% lower postoperative costs once compared to the group experiencing steady open surgery. General expenditures for RASS were 22% fewer in the study than for open surgery. The patient groups suffering open surgery and RASS knowledgeable equivalent complications (Kenngott, H. G.,et al., 2015).

Virtual Nurse Assistants (VNAs) for Healthcare

As a result of present digitalization, virtual assistants—which are already present and used in other business segments—remain used by healthcare organizations and contributors to healthcare processes. Hospitals can reduce the number of unpredicted hospital visits and the workload of medicinal operations by applying virtual nurse assistants. These apps aimed at virtual subordinates consume the ability to express, listen, and propose propositions and advice. Studies on the use of embodied conversational agents (ECAs) in healthcare over the previous 20 centuries have revealed that using chatbots or conversational agents suggestively recovers persistent consequences. The greatest of these ECAs have qualified user input, which is utilized in prevalent survey categories like utterance or multichoice. Fresh progressions in artificial intelligence (AI) technology, machine learning (ML), together with natural language processing (NLP), and neural networks (NN), have permitted the growth of virtual agents and virtual assistants that can fake humanoid language by using casual systems (Laranjo, L.,et al., 2018)(Radziwill, N. M. and Benton, M. C. 2017). The maximum conclusions for condition coverage, accuracy of suggested conditions, and urgency recommendation performance remained confirmed with 200 vignettes of depiction of real-world conditions and compared to five general practitioners (GPs) in another study that inspected frequent symptom assessment applications. With condition recommendation coverage of 99% and top-3 conditions suggestion 70.50% (GPs average 82.10%), as well as 97% accuracy for safe urgency advice (GPs average, 97%), service ADA accomplished the best results (Chambers, D.,et al., 2019).

Sensely is another VNA platform. Its avatar, a digital nurse, employments machine learning methods. It makes use of the patient's medical history information and keeps track of the patient's standing. The VNA can also plan follow-up treatments, agenda appointments, and fill in the time between doctor visits. In 2019, 72 patients with determined heart failure participated in a clinical site platform trial. Results displayed that, in judgment to the traditional care technique, the platform was able to decrease readmission rates by 75% and patient monitoring expenditures by 66% (Sensely. 2019).

Medication Management and medication error reduction (MMMER)

In accumulation to tumbling healthcare prices meaningfully, efficient MMMER services can decrease preventable injuries and mortalities. In the United States, the predictable annual costs of drug-related death and morbidity as a result of suboptimal medication therapy were $528 billion. This amounts to 16% of the total 2016 US healthcare expenditure. Errors with prescription medications result in significant morbidity, mortality, and needless medicinal expenditures. According to a National Audit Commission report, preparation faults and misuse explanation for 7000 deaths in the United States each year, underlining the essential requirement of the enchanting preventive act (Watanabe, J. H.,et al., 2018) (Williams, D. J. 2007).

Improving medical safety: A system for recognizing medication errors was established by MedAware. Researchers originate that this machine learning (ML) approach was therapeutically effective in identifying 75% of possible medication errors or problems, with 18.80% of the valid warnings being categorised as having medium clinical value and 56.20% as having high clinical value (Schiff, G. D.,et al., 2017).

REFERENCES

Aboushelib, M. N., de Jager, N., Kleverlaan, C. J., Feilzer, A. J., Blatz, M. B., Oppes, S., & Holst, S. (2008). Hip reconstruction. *Quintessence International*, 39, 23–32.

Ardila, D., Kiraly, A. P., Bharadwaj, S., Choi, B., Reicher, J. J., Peng, L., Tse, D., Etemadi, M., Ye, W., Corrado, G., Naidich, D. P., & Shetty, S. (2019). End-to-end lung cancer screening with three-dimensional deep learning on low-dose chest computed tomography. *Nature Medicine*, 25(6), 954–961. 10.1038/s41591-019-0447-x

Aronson, S. J., & Rehm, H. L. (2015). Building the foundation for genomics in precision medicine. *Nature*, 526(7573), 336–342. 10.1038/nature15816

Beede, E., Baylor, E., Hersch, F., Iurchenko, A., Wilcox, L., Ruamviboonsuk, P., & Vardoulakis, L. M. (2020, April). A human-centered evaluation of a deep learning system deployed in clinics for the detection of diabetic retinopathy. In *Proceedings of the 2020 CHI conference on human factors in computing systems* (pp. 1-12). 10.1145/3313831.3376718

Beede, E., Baylor, E., Hersch, F., Iurchenko, A., Wilcox, L., Ruamviboonsuk, P., & Vardoulakis, L. M. (2020, April). A human-centered evaluation of a deep learning system deployed in clinics for the detection of diabetic retinopathy. In *Proceedings of the 2020 CHI conference on human factors in computing systems* (pp. 1-12). 10.1145/3313831.3376718

Benjamens, S., Dhunnoo, P., & Meskó, B. (2020). The state of artificial intelligence-based FDA-approved medical devices and algorithms: An online database. *NPJ Digital Medicine*, 3(1), 118. 10.1038/s41746-020-00324-0

Buchanan, B. G., & Shortliffe, E. H. (1984). *Rule based expert systems: the mycin experiments of the stanford heuristic programming project (the Addison-Wesley series in artificial intelligence)*. Addison-Wesley Longman Publishing Co., Inc.

Bush, J. (2018). How AI is taking the scut work out of health care. *Harvard Business Review*, •••, 5.

Cai, C. J., Winter, S., Steiner, D., Wilcox, L., & Terry, M. (2019). " Hello AI": uncovering the onboarding needs of medical practitioners for human-AI collaborative decision-making. *Proceedings of the ACM on Human-computer Interaction*, 3(CSCW), 1-24. 10.1145/3359206

Campanella, G., Hanna, M. G., Geneslaw, L., Miraflor, A., Werneck Krauss Silva, V., Busam, K. J., Brogi, E., Reuter, V. E., Klimstra, D. S., & Fuchs, T. J. (2019). Clinical-grade computational pathology using weakly supervised deep learning on whole slide images. *Nature Medicine*, 25(8), 1301–1309. 10.1038/s41591-019-0508-1

Care, N. R. (2012). *Measuring Shared Decision Making–A Review of Research Evidence: A Report for the Shared Decision Making Programme in Partnership with Capita Group Plc*. National Health Service, Department of Health.

Carr-Brown, J., & Berlucchi, M. (2016). *Pre-primary care: an untapped global health opportunity*. Your.

Chambers, D., Cantrell, A. J., Johnson, M., Preston, L., Baxter, S. K., Booth, A., & Turner, J. (2019). Digital and online symptom checkers and health assessment/triage services for urgent health problems: Systematic review. *BMJ Open*, 9(8), e027743. 10.1136/bmjopen-2018-027743

Chen, X., Xie, H., Li, Z., Cheng, G., Leng, M., & Wang, F. L. (2023). Information fusion and artificial intelligence for smart healthcare: A bibliometric study. *Information Processing & Management*, 60(1), 103113. 10.1016/j.ipm.2022.103113

Chen, Y., Jensen, S., Albert, L. J., Gupta, S., & Lee, T. (2023). Artificial intelligence (AI) student assistants in the classroom: Designing chatbots to support student success. *Information Systems Frontiers*, 25(1), 161–182. 10.1007/s10796-022-10291-4

Chi, O. H., Chi, C. G., Gursoy, D., & Nunkoo, R. (2023). Customers' acceptance of artificially intelligent service robots: The influence of trust and culture. *International Journal of Information Management*, 70, 102623. 10.1016/j.ijinfomgt.2023.102623

Chiu, Y. T., Zhu, Y. Q., & Corbett, J. (2021, October 1). In the hearts and minds of employees: A model of pre-adoptive appraisal toward artificial intelligence in organizations. *International Journal of Information Management*, 60, 102379. 10.1016/j.ijinfomgt.2021.102379

Davenport, T., & Kalakota, R. (2019). The potential for artificial intelligence in healthcare. *Future Healthcare Journal*, 6(2), 94–98. 10.7861/futurehosp.6-2-94

Davenport, T. H. (2018). *The AI advantage: How to put the artificial intelligence revolution to work*. mit Press..

Davenport, T. H., & Glaser, J. (2002). Just-in-time delivery comes to knowledge management. *Harvard Business Review*, 80(7), 107–111.

Dwivedi, Y. K., Kshetri, N., Hughes, L., Slade, E. L., Jeyaraj, A., Kar, A. K., Baabdullah, A. M., Koohang, A., Raghavan, V., Ahuja, M., Albanna, H., Albashrawi, M. A., Al-Busaidi, A. S., Balakrishnan, J., Barlette, Y., Basu, S., Bose, I., Brooks, L., Buhalis, D., & Wright, R. (2023). "So what if ChatGPT wrote it?" Multidisciplinary perspectives on opportunities, challenges and implications of generative conversational AI for research, practice and policy. *International Journal of Information Management*, 71, 102642. 10.1016/j.ijinfomgt.2023.102642

Fakoor, R., Ladhak, F., Nazi, A., & Huber, M. (2013, June). Using deep learning to enhance cancer diagnosis and classification. In *Proceedings of the international conference on machine learning* (Vol. 28, pp. 3937-3949). New York, NY, USA: ACM.

Freedman, D., Blau, Y., Katzir, L., Aides, A., Shimshoni, I., Veikherman, D., Golany, T., Gordon, A., Corrado, G., Matias, Y., & Rivlin, E. (2020). Detecting deficient coverage in colonoscopies. *IEEE Transactions on Medical Imaging*, 39(11), 3451–3462. 10.1109/TMI.2020.2994221

Fu, Y., Jung, A. W., Torne, R. V., Gonzalez, S., Vöhringer, H., Shmatko, A., Yates, L. R., Jimenez-Linan, M., Moore, L., & Gerstung, M. (2020). Pan-cancer computational histopathology reveals mutations, tumor composition and prognosis. *Nature Cancer*, 1(8), 800–810. 10.1038/s43018-020-0085-8

Fügener, A., Grahl, J., Gupta, A., & Ketter, W. (2021). Will humans-in-the-loop become borgs? Merits and pitfalls of working with AI. [MISQ]. *Management Information Systems Quarterly*, 45(3), 1527–1556. 10.25300/MISQ/2021/16553

Ghorbani, A., Ouyang, D., Abid, A., He, B., Chen, J. H., Harrington, R. A., Liang, D. H., Ashley, E. A., & Zou, J. Y. (2020). Deep learning interpretation of echocardiograms. *NPJ Digital Medicine*, 3(1), 10. 10.1038/s41746-019-0216-8

Ghorbani, A., Ouyang, D., Abid, A., He, B., Chen, J. H., Harrington, R. A., Liang, D. H., Ashley, E. A., & Zou, J. Y. (2020). Deep learning interpretation of echocardiograms. *NPJ Digital Medicine*, 3(1), 10. 10.1038/s41746-019-0216-8

Gong, D., Wu, L., Zhang, J., Mu, G., Shen, L., Liu, J., Wang, Z., Zhou, W., An, P., Huang, X., Jiang, X., Li, Y., Wan, X., Hu, S., Chen, Y., Hu, X., Xu, Y., Zhu, X., Li, S., & Yu, H. (2020). Detection of colorectal adenomas with a real-time computer-aided system (ENDOANGEL): A randomised controlled study. *The Lancet. Gastroenterology & Hepatology*, 5(4), 352–361. 10.1016/S2468-1253(19)30413-3

Gong, D., Wu, L., Zhang, J., Mu, G., Shen, L., Liu, J., Wang, Z., Zhou, W., An, P., Huang, X., Jiang, X., Li, Y., Wan, X., Hu, S., Chen, Y., Hu, X., Xu, Y., Zhu, X., Li, S., & Yu, H. (2020). Detection of colorectal adenomas with a real-time computer-aided system (ENDOANGEL): A randomised controlled study. *The Lancet. Gastroenterology & Hepatology*, 5(4), 352–361. 10.1016/S2468-1253(19)30413-3

Greenberg, N., Docherty, M., Gnanapragasam, S., & Wessely, S. (2020). Managing mental health challenges faced by healthcare workers during covid-19 pandemic. *bmj, 368*.

Gursoy, D., Chi, O. H., Lu, L., & Nunkoo, R. (2019). Consumers acceptance of artificially intelligent (AI) device use in service delivery. *International Journal of Information Management*, 49, 157–169. 10.1016/j.ijinfomgt.2019.03.008

Gursoy, D., Chi, O. H., Lu, L., & Nunkoo, R. (2019). Consumers acceptance of artificially intelligent (AI) device use in service delivery. *International Journal of Information Management*, 49, 157–169. 10.1016/j.ijinfomgt.2019.03.008

Haupt, C. E., & Marks, M. (2023). AI-generated medical advice—GPT and beyond. *Journal of the American Medical Association*, 329(16), 1349–1350. 10.1001/jama.2023.5321

Hollon, T. C., Pandian, B., Adapa, A. R., Urias, E., Save, A. V., Khalsa, S. S. S., Eichberg, D. G., D'Amico, R. S., Farooq, Z. U., Lewis, S., Petridis, P. D., Marie, T., Shah, A. H., Garton, H. J. L., Maher, C. O., Heth, J. A., McKean, E. L., Sullivan, S. E., Hervey-Jumper, S. L., & Orringer, D. A. (2020). Near real-time intraoperative brain tumor diagnosis using stimulated Raman histology and deep neural networks. *Nature Medicine*, 26(1), 52–58. 10.1038/s41591-019-0715-9

Hollon, T. C., Pandian, B., Adapa, A. R., Urias, E., Save, A. V., Khalsa, S. S. S., Eichberg, D. G., D'Amico, R. S., Farooq, Z. U., Lewis, S., Petridis, P. D., Marie, T., Shah, A. H., Garton, H. J. L., Maher, C. O., Heth, J. A., McKean, E. L., Sullivan, S. E., Hervey-Jumper, S. L., & Orringer, D. A. (2020). Near real-time intraoperative brain tumor diagnosis using stimulated Raman histology and deep neural networks. *Nature Medicine*, 26(1), 52–58. 10.1038/s41591-019-0715-9

Huang, P., Lin, C. T., Li, Y., Tammemagi, M. C., Brock, M. V., Atkar-Khattra, S., Xu, Y., Hu, P., Mayo, J. R., Schmidt, H., Gingras, M., Pasian, S., Stewart, L., Tsai, S., Seely, J. M., Manos, D., Burrowes, P., Bhatia, R., Tsao, M.-S., & Lam, S. (2019). Prediction of lung cancer risk at follow-up screening with low-dose CT: A training and validation study of a deep learning method. *The Lancet. Digital Health*, 1(7), e353–e362. 10.1016/S2589-7500(19)30159-1

Hussain, A., Malik, A., Halim, M. U., & Ali, A. M. (2014). The use of robotics in surgery: A review. *International Journal of Clinical Practice*, 68(11), 1376–1382. 10.1111/ijcp.12492

Huynh, E., Hosny, A., Guthier, C., Bitterman, D. S., Petit, S. F., Haas-Kogan, D. A., Kann, B., Aerts, H. J. W. L., & Mak, R. H. (2020). Artificial intelligence in radiation oncology. *Nature Reviews. Clinical Oncology*, 17(12), 771–781. 10.1038/s41571-020-0417-8

Jackson, H. W., Fischer, J. R., Zanotelli, V. R., Ali, H. R., Mechera, R., Soysal, S. D., Moch, H., Muenst, S., Varga, Z., Weber, W. P., & Bodenmiller, B. (2020). The single-cell pathology landscape of breast cancer. *Nature*, 578(7796), 615–620. 10.1038/s41586-019-1876-x

Jussupow, E., Spohrer, K., Heinzl, A., & Gawlitza, J. (2021). Augmenting medical diagnosis decisions? An investigation into physicians' decision-making process with artificial intelligence. *Information Systems Research*, 32(3), 713–735. 10.1287/isre.2020.0980

Kanagasingam, Y., Xiao, D., Vignarajan, J., Preetham, A., Tay-Kearney, M. L., & Mehrotra, A. (2018). Evaluation of artificial intelligence–based grading of diabetic retinopathy in primary care. *JAMA Network Open*, 1(5), e182665–e182665. 10.1001/jamanetworkopen.2018.2665

Kanagasingam, Y., Xiao, D., Vignarajan, J., Preetham, A., Tay-Kearney, M. L., & Mehrotra, A. (2018). Evaluation of artificial intelligence–based grading of diabetic retinopathy in primary care. *JAMA Network Open*, 1(5), e182665–e182665. 10.1001/jamanetworkopen.2018.2665

Kather, J. N., Pearson, A. T., Halama, N., Jäger, D., Krause, J., Loosen, S. H., Marx, A., Boor, P., Tacke, F., Neumann, U. P., Grabsch, H. I., Yoshikawa, T., Brenner, H., Chang-Claude, J., Hoffmeister, M., Trautwein, C., & Luedde, T. (2019). Deep learning can predict microsatellite instability directly from histology in gastrointestinal cancer. *Nature Medicine*, 25(7), 1054–1056. 10.1038/s41591-019-0462-y

Kenngott, H. G., Wagner, M., Nickel, F., Wekerle, A. L., Preukschas, A., Apitz, M., Schulte, T., Rempel, R., Mietkowski, P., Wagner, F., Termer, A., & Müller-Stich, B. P. (2015). Computer-assisted abdominal surgery: New technologies. *Langenbeck's Archives of Surgery*, 400(3), 273–281. 10.1007/s00423-015-1289-8

Kiani, A., Uyumazturk, B., Rajpurkar, P., Wang, A., Gao, R., Jones, E., Yu, Y., Langlotz, C. P., Ball, R. L., Montine, T. J., Martin, B. A., Berry, G. J., Ozawa, M. G., Hazard, F. K., Brown, R. A., Chen, S. B., Wood, M., Allard, L. S., Ylagan, L., & Shen, J. (2020). Impact of a deep learning assistant on the histopathologic classification of liver cancer. *NPJ Digital Medicine*, 3(1), 23. 10.1038/s41746-020-0232-8

Kiani, A., Uyumazturk, B., Rajpurkar, P., Wang, A., Gao, R., Jones, E., Yu, Y., Langlotz, C. P., Ball, R. L., Montine, T. J., Martin, B. A., Berry, G. J., Ozawa, M. G., Hazard, F. K., Brown, R. A., Chen, S. B., Wood, M., Allard, L. S., Ylagan, L., & Shen, J. (2020). Impact of a deep learning assistant on the histopathologic classification of liver cancer. *NPJ Digital Medicine*, 3(1), 23. 10.1038/s41746-020-0232-8

Kumar, P., Dwivedi, Y. K., & Anand, A. (2023). Responsible artificial intelligence (AI) for value formation and market performance in healthcare: The mediating role of patient's cognitive engagement. *Information Systems Frontiers*, 25(6), 2197–2220. 10.1007/s10796-021-10136-6

Kumar, P., Sharma, S. K., & Dutot, V. (2023). Artificial intelligence (AI)-enabled CRM capability in healthcare: The impact on service innovation. *International Journal of Information Management*, 69, 102598. 10.1016/j.ijinfomgt.2022.102598

Kwoh, Y. S., Hou, J., Jonckheere, E. A., & Hayati, S. (1988). A robot with improved absolute positioning accuracy for CT guided stereotactic brain surgery. *IEEE Transactions on Biomedical Engineering*, 35(2), 153–160. 10.1109/10.1354

Laranjo, L., Dunn, A. G., Tong, H. L., Kocaballi, A. B., Chen, J., Bashir, R., Surian, D., Gallego, B., Magrabi, F., Lau, A. Y. S., & Coiera, E. (2018). Conversational agents in healthcare: A systematic review. *Journal of the American Medical Informatics Association : JAMIA*, 25(9), 1248–1258. 10.1093/jamia/ocy072

Lee, S. I., Celik, S., Logsdon, B. A., Lundberg, S. M., Martins, T. J., Oehler, V. G., Estey, E. H., Miller, C. P., Chien, S., Dai, J., Saxena, A., Blau, C. A., & Becker, P. S. (2018). A machine learning approach to integrate big data for precision medicine in acute myeloid leukemia. *Nature Communications*, 9(1), 42. 10.1038/s41467-017-02465-5

Lin, H., Li, R., Liu, Z., Chen, J., Yang, Y., Chen, H., Lin, Z., Lai, W., Long, E., Wu, X., Lin, D., Zhu, Y., Chen, C., Wu, D., Yu, T., Cao, Q., Li, X., Li, J., Li, W., & Liu, Y. (2019). Diagnostic efficacy and therapeutic decision-making capacity of an artificial intelligence platform for childhood cataracts in eye clinics: A multicentre randomized controlled trial. *EClinicalMedicine*, 9, 52–59. 10.1016/j.eclinm.2019.03.001

Lin, H., Li, R., Liu, Z., Chen, J., Yang, Y., Chen, H., Lin, Z., Lai, W., Long, E., Wu, X., Lin, D., Zhu, Y., Chen, C., Wu, D., Yu, T., Cao, Q., Li, X., Li, J., Li, W., & Liu, Y. (2019). Diagnostic efficacy and therapeutic decision-making capacity of an artificial intelligence platform for childhood cataracts in eye clinics: A multicentre randomized controlled trial. *EClinicalMedicine*, 9, 52–59. 10.1016/j.eclinm.2019.03.001

Liu, K., & Tao, D. (2022). The roles of trust, personalization, loss of privacy, and anthropomorphism in public acceptance of smart healthcare services. *Computers in Human Behavior*, 127, 107026. 10.1016/j.chb.2021.107026

Liu, X., Rivera, S. C., Moher, D., Calvert, M. J., Denniston, A. K., Ashrafian, H., & Yau, C. (2020). Reporting guidelines for clinical trial reports for interventions involving artificial intelligence: The CONSORT-AI extension. *The Lancet. Digital Health*, 2(10), e537–e548. 10.1016/S2589-7500(20)30218-1

Liu, X., Rivera, S. C., Moher, D., Calvert, M. J., Denniston, A. K., Ashrafian, H., & Yau, C. (2020). Reporting guidelines for clinical trial reports for interventions involving artificial intelligence: The CONSORT-AI extension. *The Lancet. Digital Health*, 2(10), e537–e548. 10.1016/S2589-7500(20)30218-1

Loria, K. (2018). Putting the AI in radiology. *Radiology Today*, 19(1), 10.

Loucks, J., Davenport, T., & Schatsky, D. (2018). State of AI in the Enterprise. *Deloitte Insights Report.*.

Low, L. L., Lee, K. H., Hock Ong, M. E., Wang, S., Tan, S. Y., Thumboo, J., & Liu, N. (2015). Predicting 30-day readmissions: Performance of the LACE index compared with a regression model among general medicine patients in Singapore. *BioMed Research International*, 2015, 2015. 10.1155/2015/169870

Maphumulo, W. T., & Bhengu, B. R. (2019). Challenges of quality improvement in the healthcare of South Africa post-apartheid: A critical review. *Curationis*, 42(1), 1–9. 10.4102/curationis.v42i1.1901

McKinney, S. M., Sieniek, M., Godbole, V., Godwin, J., Antropova, N., Ashrafian, H., Back, T., Chesus, M., Corrado, G. S., Darzi, A., Etemadi, M., Garcia-Vicente, F., Gilbert, F. J., Halling-Brown, M., Hassabis, D., Jansen, S., Karthikesalingam, A., Kelly, C. J., King, D., & Shetty, S. (2020). International evaluation of an AI system for breast cancer screening. *Nature*, 577(7788), 89–94. 10.1038/s41586-019-1799-6

Milea, D., Najjar, R. P., Jiang, Z., Ting, D., Vasseneix, C., Xu, X., Aghsaei Fard, M., Fonseca, P., Vanikieti, K., Lagrèze, W. A., La Morgia, C., Cheung, C. Y., Hamann, S., Chiquet, C., Sanda, N., Yang, H., Mejico, L. J., Rougier, M.-B., Kho, R., & Biousse, V. (2020). Artificial intelligence to detect papilledema from ocular fundus photographs. *The New England Journal of Medicine*, 382(18), 1687–1695. 10.1056/NEJMoa1917130

Miller, D. D., & Brown, E. W. (2018). Artificial intelligence in medical practice: The question to the answer? *The American Journal of Medicine*, 131(2), 129–133. 10.1016/j.amjmed.2017.10.035

Nait Aicha, A., Englebienne, G., Van Schooten, K. S., Pijnappels, M., & Kröse, B. (2018). Deep learning to predict falls in older adults based on daily-life trunk accelerometry. *Sensors (Basel)*, 18(5), 1654. 10.3390/s18051654

Nimri, R., Battelino, T., Laffel, L. M., Slover, R. H., Schatz, D., Weinzimer, S. A., & Phillip, M. (2020). Insulin dose optimization using an automated artificial intelligence-based decision support system in youths with type 1 diabetes. *Nature Medicine*, 26(9), 1380–1384. 10.1038/s41591-020-1045-7

Nimri, R., Battelino, T., Laffel, L. M., Slover, R. H., Schatz, D., Weinzimer, S. A., & Phillip, M. (2020). Insulin dose optimization using an automated artificial intelligence-based decision support system in youths with type 1 diabetes. *Nature Medicine*, 26(9), 1380–1384. 10.1038/s41591-020-1045-7

Nishant, R., Kennedy, M., & Corbett, J. (2020). Artificial intelligence for sustainability: Challenges, opportunities, and a research agenda. *International Journal of Information Management*, 53, 102104. 10.1016/j.ijinfomgt.2020.102104

Ooi, K. B., Tan, G. W. H., Al-Emran, M., Al-Sharafi, M. A., Capatina, A., Chakraborty, A., . . . Hoffman, Y. (2022). Promoting Interoperability and Quality Payment Programs: The Evolving Paths of Meaningful Use. In *Health Informatics* (pp. 165-190). Productivity Press.

Panjamapirom, A. T., Levinthal, N., & Hoffman, Y. (2022). Promoting Interoperability and Quality Payment Programs: The Evolving Paths of Meaningful Use. In *Health Informatics* (pp. 165-190). Productivity Press.

Pavli, A., Theodoridou, M., & Maltezou, H. C. (2021). Post-COVID syndrome: Incidence, clinical spectrum, and challenges for primary healthcare professionals. *Archives of Medical Research*, 52(6), 575–581. 10.1016/j.arcmed.2021.03.010

Phillips, M., Marsden, H., Jaffe, W., Matin, R. N., Wali, G. N., Greenhalgh, J., McGrath, E., James, R., Ladoyanni, E., Bewley, A., Argenziano, G., & Palamaras, I. (2019). Assessment of accuracy of an artificial intelligence algorithm to detect melanoma in images of skin lesions. *JAMA Network Open*, 2(10), e1913436–e1913436. 10.1001/jamanetworkopen.2019.13436

Phillips, M., Marsden, H., Jaffe, W., Matin, R. N., Wali, G. N., Greenhalgh, J., McGrath, E., James, R., Ladoyanni, E., Bewley, A., Argenziano, G., & Palamaras, I. (2019). Assessment of accuracy of an artificial intelligence algorithm to detect melanoma in images of skin lesions. *JAMA Network Open*, 2(10), e1913436–e1913436. 10.1001/jamanetworkopen.2019.13436

Qin, X., Chen, C., Yam, K. C., Cao, L., Li, W., Guan, J., Zhao, P., Dong, X., & Lin, Y. (2022). Adults still can't resist: A social robot can induce normative conformity. *Computers in Human Behavior*, 127, 107041. 10.1016/j.chb.2021.107041

Radziwill, N. M., & Benton, M. C. (2017). Evaluating quality of chatbots and intelligent conversational agents. *arXiv preprint arXiv:1704.04579*.

Rajkomar, A., Oren, E., Chen, K., Dai, A. M., Hajaj, N., Hardt, M., Liu, P. J., Liu, X., Marcus, J., Sun, M., Sundberg, P., Yee, H., Zhang, K., Zhang, Y., Flores, G., Duggan, G. E., Irvine, J., Le, Q., Litsch, K., & Dean, J. (2018). Scalable and accurate deep learning with electronic health records. *NPJ Digital Medicine*, 1(1), 18. 10.1038/s41746-018-0029-1

Rivera, S. C., Liu, X., Chan, A. W., Denniston, A. K., Calvert, M. J., Ashrafian, H., & Yau, C. (2020). Guidelines for clinical trial protocols for interventions involving artificial intelligence: The SPIRIT-AI extension. *The Lancet. Digital Health*, 2(10), e549–e560. 10.1016/S2589-7500(20)30219-3

Rivera, S. C., Liu, X., Chan, A. W., Denniston, A. K., Calvert, M. J., Ashrafian, H., & Yau, C. (2020). Guidelines for clinical trial protocols for interventions involving artificial intelligence: The SPIRIT-AI extension. *The Lancet. Digital Health*, 2(10), e549–e560. 10.1016/S2589-7500(20)30219-3

Ross, C., & Swetlitz, I. (2017). IBM pitched its Watson supercomputer as a revolution in cancer care. It's nowhere close. *Stat*.

Rysavy, M. (2013). Evidence-based medicine: A science of uncertainty and an art of probability. *AMA Journal of Ethics*, 15(1), 4–8. 10.1001/virtualmentor.2013.15.1.fred1-1301

Schaffter, T., Buist, D. S., Lee, C. I., Nikulin, Y., Ribli, D., Guan, Y., Lotter, W., Jie, Z., Du, H., Wang, S., Feng, J., Feng, M., Kim, H.-E., Albiol, F., Albiol, A., Morrell, S., Wojna, Z., Ahsen, M. E., Asif, U., & Jung, H. (2020). Evaluation of combined artificial intelligence and radiologist assessment to interpret screening mammograms. *JAMA Network Open*, 3(3), e200265–e200265. 10.1001/jamanetworkopen.2020.0265

Schiff, G. D., Volk, L. A., Volodarskaya, M., Williams, D. H., Walsh, L., Myers, S. G., Bates, D. W., & Rozenblum, R. (2017). Screening for medication errors using an outlier detection system. *Journal of the American Medical Informatics Association : JAMIA*, 24(2), 281–287. 10.1093/jamia/ocw171

Schmidt-Erfurth, U., Bogunovic, H., Sadeghipour, A., Schlegl, T., Langs, G., Gerendas, B. S., Osborne, A., & Waldstein, S. M. (2018). Machine learning to analyze the prognostic value of current imaging biomarkers in neovascular age-related macular degeneration. *Ophthalmology Retina*, 2(1), 24–30. 10.1016/j.oret.2017.03.015

Sensely. (2019). An integrated payer/provider wanted to intervene in a timelier manner with its Chronic Heart Failure (CHF) patients.

Sezgin, E. (2023). Artificial intelligence in healthcare: Complementing, not replacing, doctors and healthcare providers. *Digital Health*, 9, 20552076231186520. 10.1177/20552076231186520

Shimabukuro, D. W., Barton, C. W., Feldman, M. D., Mataraso, S. J., & Das, R. (2017). Effect of a machine learning-based severe sepsis prediction algorithm on patient survival and hospital length of stay: A randomised clinical trial. *BMJ Open Respiratory Research*, 4(1), e000234. 10.1136/bmjresp-2017-000234

Sordo, M. (2002). Introduction to neural networks in healthcare. *Open clinical: Knowledge management for medical care*.

Tutun, S., Johnson, M. E., Ahmed, A., Albizri, A., Irgil, S., Yesilkaya, I., Ucar, E. N., Sengun, T., & Harfouche, A. (2023). An AI-based decision support system for predicting mental health disorders. *Information Systems Frontiers*, 25(3), 1261–1276. 10.1007/s10796-022-10282-5

Väänänen, A., Haataja, K., Vehviläinen-Julkunen, K., & Toivanen, P. (2021). AI in healthcare: A narrative review. *F1000 Research*, 10, 6. 10.12688/f1000research.26997.2

Vial, A., Stirling, D., Field, M., Ros, M., Ritz, C., Carolan, M., Holloway, L., & Miller, A. A. (2018). The role of deep learning and radiomic feature extraction in cancer-specific predictive modelling: A review. *Translational Cancer Research*, 7(3), 803–816. 10.21037/tcr.2018.05.02

Wahl, B., Cossy-Gantner, A., Germann, S., & Schwalbe, N. R. (2018). Artificial intelligence (AI) and global health: How can AI contribute to health in resource-poor settings? *BMJ Global Health*, 3(4), e000798. 10.1136/bmjgh-2018-000798

Wang, P., Liu, X., Berzin, T. M., Brown, J. R. G., Liu, P., Zhou, C., & Zhou, G. (2020). Effect of a deep-learning computer-aided detection system on adenoma detection during colonoscopy (CADe-DB trial): A double-blind randomised study. *The Lancet. Gastroenterology & Hepatology*, 5(4), 343–351. 10.1016/S2468-1253(19)30411-X

Wang, P., Liu, X., Berzin, T. M., Brown, J. R. G., Liu, P., Zhou, C., & Zhou, G. (2020). Effect of a deep-learning computer-aided detection system on adenoma detection during colonoscopy (CADe-DB trial): A double-blind randomised study. *The Lancet. Gastroenterology & Hepatology*, 5(4), 343–351. 10.1016/S2468-1253(19)30411-X

Watanabe, J. H., McInnis, T., & Hirsch, J. D. (2018). Cost of prescription drug–related morbidity and mortality. *The Annals of Pharmacotherapy*, 52(9), 829–837. 10.1177/1060028018765159

Wei, Y., Lu, W., Cheng, Q., Jiang, T., & Liu, S. (2022). How humans obtain information from AI: Categorizing user messages in human-AI collaborative conversations. *Information Processing & Management*, 59(2), 102838. 10.1016/j.ipm.2021.102838

Wiens, J., Saria, S., Sendak, M., Ghassemi, M., Liu, V. X., Doshi-Velez, F., Jung, K., Heller, K., Kale, D., Saeed, M., Ossorio, P. N., Thadaney-Israni, S., & Goldenberg, A. (2019). Do no harm: A roadmap for responsible machine learning for health care. *Nature Medicine*, 25(9), 1337–1340. 10.1038/s41591-019-0548-6

Wiens, J., Saria, S., Sendak, M., Ghassemi, M., Liu, V. X., Doshi-Velez, F., Jung, K., Heller, K., Kale, D., Saeed, M., Ossorio, P. N., Thadaney-Israni, S., & Goldenberg, A. (2019). Do no harm: A roadmap for responsible machine learning for health care. *Nature Medicine*, 25(9), 1337–1340. 10.1038/s41591-019-0548-6

Wijnberge, M., Geerts, B. F., Hol, L., Lemmers, N., Mulder, M. P., Berge, P., Schenk, J., Terwindt, L. E., Hollmann, M. W., Vlaar, A. P., & Veelo, D. P. (2020). Effect of a machine learning–derived early warning system for intraoperative hypotension vs standard care on depth and duration of intraoperative hypotension during elective noncardiac surgery: The HYPE randomized clinical trial. *Journal of the American Medical Association*, 323(11), 1052–1060. 10.1001/jama.2020.0592

Wijnberge, M., Geerts, B. F., Hol, L., Lemmers, N., Mulder, M. P., Berge, P., Schenk, J., Terwindt, L. E., Hollmann, M. W., Vlaar, A. P., & Veelo, D. P. (2020). Effect of a machine learning–derived early warning system for intraoperative hypotension vs standard care on depth and duration of intraoperative hypotension during elective noncardiac surgery: The HYPE randomized clinical trial. *Journal of the American Medical Association*, 323(11), 1052–1060. 10.1001/jama.2020.0592

Williams, D. J. (2007). Medication errors. *Journal-Royal College of Physicians of Edinburgh*, 37(4), 343.

Wismüller, A., & Stockmaster, L. (2020, February). A prospective randomized clinical trial for measuring radiology study reporting time on Artificial Intelligence-based detection of intracranial hemorrhage in emergent care head CT. In *Medical Imaging 2020: Biomedical Applications in Molecular, Structural, and Functional Imaging* (Vol. 11317, pp. 144-150). SPIE. 10.1117/12.2552400

Wismüller, A., & Stockmaster, L. (2020, February). A prospective randomized clinical trial for measuring radiology study reporting time on Artificial Intelligence-based detection of intracranial hemorrhage in emergent care head CT. In *Medical Imaging 2020: Biomedical Applications in Molecular, Structural, and Functional Imaging* (Vol. 11317, pp. 144-150). SPIE. 10.1117/12.2552400

Wolf, R. M., Channa, R., Abramoff, M. D., & Lehmann, H. P. (2020). Cost-effectiveness of autonomous point-of-care diabetic retinopathy screening for pediatric patients with diabetes. *JAMA Ophthalmology*, 138(10), 1063–1069. 10.1001/jamaophthalmol.2020.3190

Wong, L. W. (2023). The potential of generative artificial intelligence across disciplines: Perspectives and future directions. *Journal of Computer Information Systems*, ●●●, 1–32.

Wu, N., Phang, J., Park, J., Shen, Y., Huang, Z., Zorin, M., Jastrzebski, S., Fevry, T., Katsnelson, J., Kim, E., Wolfson, S., Parikh, U., Gaddam, S., Lin, L. L. Y., Ho, K., Weinstein, J. D., Reig, B., Gao, Y., Toth, H., & Geras, K. J. (2019). Deep neural networks improve radiologists' performance in breast cancer screening. *IEEE Transactions on Medical Imaging*, 39(4), 1184–1194. 10.1109/TMI.2019.2945514

Wu, X., Xiao, L., Sun, Y., Zhang, J., Ma, T., & He, L. (2022). A survey of human-in-the-loop for machine learning. *Future Generation Computer Systems*, 135, 364–381. 10.1016/j.future.2022.05.014

Xie, Y., Nguyen, Q. D., Hamzah, H., Lim, G., Bellemo, V., Gunasekeran, D. V., Yip, M. Y. T., Qi Lee, X., Hsu, W., Li Lee, M., Tan, C. S., Tym Wong, H., Lamoureux, E. L., Tan, G. S. W., Wong, T. Y., Finkelstein, E. A., & Ting, D. S. (2020). Artificial intelligence for teleophthalmology-based diabetic retinopathy screening in a national programme: An economic analysis modelling study. *The Lancet. Digital Health*, 2(5), e240–e249. 10.1016/S2589-7500(20)30060-1

Yaraghi, N. (2024). *Generative AI in health care: Opportunities, challenges, and policy*. Health Affairs Forefront.

Zhao, S., Wang, S., Pan, P., Xia, T., Chang, X., Yang, X., Guo, L., Meng, Q., Yang, F., Qian, W., Xu, Z., Wang, Y., Wang, Z., Gu, L., Wang, R., Jia, F., Yao, J., Li, Z., & Bai, Y. (2019, May 1). Magnitude, risk factors, and factors associated with adenoma miss rate of tandem colonoscopy: A systematic review and meta-analysis. *Gastroenterology*, 156(6), 1661–1674. 10.1053/j.gastro.2019.01.260

Zhou, D., Tian, F., Tian, X., Sun, L., Huang, X., Zhao, F., Zhou, N., Chen, Z., Zhang, Q., Yang, M., Yang, Y., Guo, X., Li, Z., Liu, J., Wang, J., Wang, J., Wang, B., Zhang, G., Sun, B., & Li, X. (2020). Diagnostic evaluation of a deep learning model for optical diagnosis of colorectal cancer. *Nature Communications*, 11(1), 2961. 10.1038/s41467-020-16777-6

Chapter 3
Revolutionizing Healthcare:
The Transformative Impact of Artificial Intelligence

Manoj Govindaraj
https://orcid.org/0000-0003-2830-7875
VelTech Rangarajan Dr. Sagunthala R&D Institute of Science and Technology, India

D. Anitha Kumari
Vels Institute of Science, Technology, and Advanced Studies, India

Parvez Khan
Atria University, India

Ravishankar Krishnan
VelTech Rangarajan Dr. Sagunthala R&D Institute of Science and Technology, India

Chandramowleeswaran Gnanasekaran
VelTech Rangarajan Dr. Sagunthala R&D Institute of Science and Technology, India

Jenifer Lawrence
https://orcid.org/0000-0002-4115-1521
Woldia University, Ethiopia

ABSTRACT

Artificial Intelligence (AI) is currently revolutionizing different aspects of the healthcare industry, making it a transformative force in the modern healthcare setting. This book chapter thoroughly analyses the significant influence of artificial intelligence (AI) on healthcare systems, carefully examining important applications and their consequences. A comprehensive investigation is carried out on the incorporation of diagnostic algorithms, predictive analytics, and personalized medicine, revealing their capacity to redefine the established level of medical treatment. The chapter specifically examines the impact of machine learning and deep learning techniques

DOI: 10.4018/979-8-3693-3731-8.ch003

Copyright © 2024, IGI Global. Copying or distributing in print or electronic forms without written permission of IGI Global is prohibited.

on medical imaging, highlighting their ability to improve diagnostic accuracy and efficiency. Moreover, the study explores AI-powered predictive models that not only transform preventive care but also enhance disease management and patient outcomes. The chapter examines the ethical implications of using AI in healthcare, while also discussing the importance of responsible and transparent methods.

INTRODUCTION

The field of artificial intelligence has undergone significant advancements since the creation of the initial AI program in 1951 by Christopher Strachey. During that period, artificial intelligence was in its early stages of development and predominantly focused on academic research. John McCarthy convened the Dartmouth Conference in 1956, during which he introduced the phrase "Artificial Intelligence." This event signalled the commencement of the contemporary era of artificial intelligence. During the 1960s and 1970s, the field of AI research primarily concentrated on the development of rule-based systems and expert systems. Nevertheless, this method was constrained by the requirement for more computational resources and data.

The impact of artificial intelligence (AI) is already profound and will continue to grow in industries including healthcare, finance, and transportation. Intelligent tutoring systems have been developed using artificial intelligence (AI) within the academic domain. These systems are computer programs that possess the ability to adjust and cater to the specific requirements of each individual student. These programs have enhanced student academic performance in several disciplines, such as mathematics and science. AI has been employed in research to evaluate vast datasets and discern intricate patterns that would pose challenges for human detection. Consequently, this has resulted in significant advancements in domains such as genomics and drug development. AI is reshaping traditional paradigms and ushering in a new era of innovation in the healthcare sector.

This chapter delves into the profound implications of AI in healthcare, aiming to provide a comprehensive analysis of its transformative impact. By examining key applications, challenges, and future possibilities, this chapter seeks to elucidate the multifaceted role of AI in revolutionizing healthcare systems worldwide.

Background of the Study

The healthcare landscape is undergoing a rapid transformation driven by advancements in AI technologies. Traditional methods of diagnosis, treatment, and patient care are being augmented and, in some cases, supplanted by AI-driven solutions.

This transformation is fuelled by the unprecedented growth in healthcare data, coupled with the increasing computational power and sophistication of AI algorithms.

The possible advantages of AI in healthcare, notwithstanding these obstacles, are incontestable. By leveraging AI technologies, healthcare systems have the opportunity to streamline processes, optimize resource utilization, and ultimately improve patient outcomes. This chapter aims to explore these opportunities and challenges comprehensively, offering insights into how AI can be harnessed to revolutionize healthcare delivery in the years to come. AI technologies, such as machine learning, natural language processing, and robotics, are being increasingly integrated into various healthcare applications, ranging from diagnostics and treatment planning to patient care and administrative tasks. One of the key areas where AI is making a significant impact is in diagnostics. AI-powered imaging technologies, such as deep learning algorithms, are enabling more accurate and faster interpretation of medical images, leading to early detection of diseases such as cancer. These technologies can analyze vast amounts of imaging data, helping radiologists make more informed decisions (Shen et al., 2017). Another area where AI is revolutionizing healthcare is in personalized medicine. By analyzing genetic, clinical, and lifestyle data, AI algorithms can identify patterns and predict individual patient responses to treatments. This approach allows for more targeted and effective treatment plans, minimizing side effects and improving patient outcomes (Obermeyer et al., 2016). AI is also transforming the way healthcare is delivered. Virtual health assistants and chatbots powered by AI are providing patients with access to personalized medical information and advice, reducing the burden on healthcare providers and improving patient satisfaction (Laranjo et al., 2018). Additionally, AI-powered robots are being used in hospitals for tasks such as patient monitoring, medication delivery, and disinfection, freeing up healthcare staff to focus on more complex care tasks (Huang et al., 2021). AI is having a substantial influence on personalised treatment options, particularly in the field of oncology. AI systems can utilise genetic information and tumour characteristics to find distinct biomarkers and genetic mutations that could potentially impact therapy responses. This allows healthcare providers to choose specific treatments that are more likely to be successful and reduce the risk of negative side effects. Furthermore, AI can aid in forecasting the probability of illness relapse, directing surveillance tactics, and enhancing long-term therapy techniques. (Potter, K., Blessing, E., & Mohamed, S. 2024)

Artificial intelligence is also transforming the approaches to treating chronic diseases. Through the examination of clinical data, lifestyle factors, and patient-reported results, artificial intelligence (AI) algorithms can detect patterns and create customised treatment strategies for medical ailments like diabetes, cardiovascular diseases, and autoimmune disorders. These customised approaches can enhance the effectiveness of drug regimes, dietary suggestions, and lifestyle adjustments, leading to improved disease control and better patient results.

However, despite the numerous benefits AI offers, there are also challenges and ethical considerations. Issues such as data privacy, bias in AI algorithms, and the impact on the healthcare workforce need to be carefully addressed to ensure that AI is deployed responsibly and ethically (Char et al., 2018).

AI in Healthcare: Changing India's Healthcare Landscape

In India, AI in healthcare is growing fast and could be worth a lot of money in a few years. AI helps make personalized treatment plans, allows doctors to see patients from far away, and even finds new medicines faster.

Entering the third decade of the 21st century, the influence of AI in the Indian healthcare sector is undeniable. India is currently experiencing a notable increase in the implementation of artificial intelligence (AI) in healthcare, encompassing several aspects such as diagnosis, treatment, and beyond. Recent figures indicate that the Indian healthcare AI industry is projected to reach USD 1.6 billion by 2025, exhibiting a compound annual growth rate (CAGR) of 40.5% from 2020 to 2025.

Within the domain of healthcare, scholars have intensively investigated the capacity of Artificial Intelligence (AI) to revolutionize the sector. The report titled "Deep Learning for Healthcare: Review, Opportunities, and Challenges" authored by Arjun Panwar, R. Balachandar, and M. Akila, provides insights into the profound potential of artificial intelligence (AI) in the field of healthcare. This research highlights the significant improvement in diagnostic accuracy that can be achieved by analyzing medical pictures, such as X-rays and MRIs, using deep learning techniques, namely convolutional neural networks (CNNs) and recurrent neural networks (RNNs).

AI-driven predictive analytics play a crucial role in identifying individuals with a high susceptibility to diseases such as diabetes, cardiovascular ailments, and cancer. Sophisticated algorithms examine extensive datasets, considering genetic, lifestyle, and clinical data, in order to offer tailored treatment strategies. This method not only enhances patient outcomes but also diminishes the economic burden of therapy.

Telemedicine has become an essential component of healthcare in India, particularly in light of the COVID-19 pandemic. AI-powered telehealth solutions provide immediate consultations, enabling patients to remotely communicate with doctors from the convenience of their residences. Remote monitoring devices, in conjunction with AI algorithms, monitor patients' vital signs and offer timely alerts regarding any health concerns.

Artificial intelligence is significantly diminishing the duration and expenses related to the process of medication discovery. Machine learning models evaluate the molecular structures and provide predictions about prospective medication candidates. India has the potential to greatly benefit from AI-driven drug research and development, thanks to its thriving pharmaceutical industry. Statistics indicate that artificial intelligence (AI) is enabling pharmaceutical businesses to achieve savings of up to 60% in drug discovery expenses.

Research papers on AI in healthcare provide significant insights into the potential benefits and difficulties associated with this technology. Researchers stress the importance of responsible use of AI, considering privacy, ethics, and regulatory factors, while utilizing AI's capacity to enhance healthcare results. Ongoing research is crucial in developing the responsible integration of AI into the healthcare environment as it continues to expand.

RESEARCH QUESTION

How does the integration of Artificial Intelligence (AI) revolutionize healthcare systems, particularly in terms of diagnostic accuracy, treatment outcomes, and patient care?

Objective

This chapter aims to comprehensively analyse the transformative impact of Artificial Intelligence (AI) on healthcare systems, focusing on its ability to enhance diagnostic accuracy, treatment outcomes, and patient care. Specific objectives include:
1. Investigating the incorporation of AI-powered diagnostic algorithms, predictive analytics, and personalized medicine in healthcare.
2. Exploring the application of AI-driven predictive models in preventive care, disease management, and enhancing patient outcomes.
3. Analyzing the ethical implications of AI integration in healthcare and the importance of responsible and transparent methods.
4. Discussing challenges related to data security and interoperability in the adoption of AI in healthcare.

METHODOLOGY

To achieve the objectives outlined above, the chapter will conduct a comprehensive review of existing literature, scholarly articles, and relevant research studies on the integration of AI in healthcare to understand current trends, challenges, and opportunities. Analyzing real-world case studies and examples of AI implementation in healthcare settings to illustrate the practical implications and outcomes.

INCORPORATION OF AI-POWERED DIAGNOSTIC ALGORITHMS, PREDICTIVE ANALYTICS, AND PERSONALIZED MEDICINE IN HEALTHCARE.

Improvements in predictive analytics, tailored medication, and diagnostic accuracy have resulted from the use of artificial intelligence (AI) in healthcare. An outline of current research on healthcare integration of AI-powered diagnostic algorithms, predictive analytics, and personalised medicine is the goal of this literature review.

AI-driven algorithms for diagnosis: Various medical imaging tasks, including abnormality detection and illness diagnosis, have been impressively handled by AI-powered diagnostic algorithms. An example of a study that showcases the potential of deep learning algorithms to enhance early detection and treatment is Ardila et al. (2019), which found that an algorithm could detect lung cancer on low-dose chest CT images just as well as radiologists. Another study that looked at an AI system for breast cancer screening by McKinney et al. (2020) came to the same conclusion: it was very sensitive and specific, which could make it useful as a mammography diagnostic assistance.

Clinical decision support systems now include AI algorithms to aid doctors in diagnosis and therapy planning, in addition to medical imaging. Clinical decision-making and patient care could be enhanced by the deep learning model that Rajkomar et al. (2018) created utilizing EHRs to forecast patient outcomes.

Predictive Analytics: Predictive analytics, powered by AI and machine learning techniques, has emerged as a valuable tool for forecasting disease trends and identifying high-risk populations. Obermeyer and Emanuel (2016) discuss the use of predictive analytics in identifying patients at high risk of adverse events, enabling proactive interventions to prevent complications and improve outcomes. Additionally, predictive analytics plays a crucial role in population health management by identifying individuals at risk of chronic diseases and enabling targeted interventions to reduce morbidity and mortality.

Personalized Medicine: The goal of precision medicine, another name for personalized medicine, is to modify a patient's course of therapy according to their specific traits, including their genes and way of life. AI technologies play a crucial role in personalized medicine by analyzing large datasets of clinical and genomic data to identify optimal treatment strategies and predict treatment responses (Ashley 2016). For example, pharmacogenomic algorithms analyse genetic variations to predict drug responses and guide medication selection, improving therapeutic outcomes and reducing adverse effects.

Examining Elaborate Medical Data: Artificial intelligence systems have extraordinary proficiency in managing extensive quantities of data, a prevalent attribute of medical datasets. They possess the ability to rapidly analyse this data in order to discern trends, abnormalities, or patterns that would need a significant amount of time or be unattainable for humans to perceive.

Enhancing Diagnostic Precision: Artificial intelligence algorithms have the capability to assist clinicians in achieving more precise disease diagnoses. AI-driven systems in radiology have the capability to identify anomalies in imaging scans with a notable level of accuracy, resulting in prompt and more precise diagnosis.

Improving Treatment Planning: Artificial intelligence aids in developing individualized treatment plans by taking into account several elements such as a patient's genetic data, lifestyle, medical history, and present health state. Consequently, this leads to therapies that are precisely customized to suit the unique needs of each patient, thereby potentially enhancing the final results.

Enhancing Efficiency in Healthcare Services: In addition to its clinical uses, AI also assists in streamlining administrative processes, including scheduling, billing, and patient record management. This contributes to an overall improvement in the efficiency of healthcare services.

The role of artificial intelligence (AI) in healthcare is revolutionary, providing unparalleled tools for analyzing intricate data and improving diagnostic and treatment procedures. This breakthrough enhances the capacities of healthcare practitioners and holds the potential for a future when personalized and efficient healthcare is more readily available.

Moreover, AI-driven precision oncology platforms leverage genomic profiling and machine learning techniques to match cancer patients with targeted therapies based on their tumour molecular profiles, improving treatment efficacy and patient outcomes (8).

Overall, the incorporation of AI-powered diagnostic algorithms, predictive analytics, and personalized medicine in healthcare holds promise for improving diagnostic accuracy, predicting disease outcomes, and tailoring treatments to individual patient needs. However, challenges such as data privacy, algorithm bias, and regulatory compliance must be addressed to realize the full potential of AI in healthcare.

AI-DRIVEN PREDICTIVE MODELS IN PREVENTIVE CARE, DISEASE MANAGEMENT, AND ENHANCING PATIENT OUTCOMES

AI-driven predictive models hold immense promise in revolutionizing healthcare delivery by leveraging vast amounts of data to predict disease onset, progression, and patient response to treatments. This literature review aims to explore the current state of AI-driven predictive models in preventive care, disease management, and their impact on patient outcomes.

Predictive Models in Preventive Care: Preventive care plays a crucial role in reducing the burden of disease and improving population health. AI-driven predictive models are increasingly being utilized to identify individuals at high risk of developing various health conditions, enabling proactive interventions to prevent disease onset. For instance, studies by Li et al. (2019) demonstrated the effectiveness of AI algorithms in predicting cardiovascular events by analyzing electronic health records and incorporating multiple data sources such as genetic information and lifestyle factors. Similarly, the research conducted by Wang et al. (2020) showcased the utility of machine learning algorithms in identifying individuals at risk of developing type 2 diabetes based on demographic, clinical, and behavioural data.

Disease Management: Effective disease management is essential for improving patient outcomes and reducing healthcare costs. AI-driven predictive models offer valuable insights into disease progression, treatment response, and personalized care strategies. For example, a study by Topol (2019) highlighted the potential of AI-based predictive analytics in oncology for optimizing treatment regimens and predicting patient outcomes based on genomic profiling and tumour characteristics. Furthermore, research by Johnson et al. (2021) demonstrated the efficacy of AI-powered predictive models in managing chronic conditions such as asthma and COPD by forecasting exacerbations and facilitating timely interventions.

Enhancing Patient Outcomes: The integration of AI-driven predictive models into clinical practice has the potential to significantly enhance patient outcomes by enabling personalized and proactive care delivery. By analyzing vast datasets and identifying patterns, AI algorithms can assist healthcare providers in making more informed decisions tailored to individual patient needs. For instance, a study by Rajkumar et al. (2018) showed that AI models could accurately predict patient outcomes such as mortality, readmission, and length of hospital stay, thereby facilitating early interventions and improving overall care quality. Additionally, research by Chen et al. (2021) demonstrated the utility of AI-driven predictive models in optimizing medication adherence and reducing adverse drug events, leading to improved patient safety and outcomes.

In preventive care, AI-driven predictive models are being used to identify individuals at high risk of developing various health conditions, allowing healthcare providers to intervene early and prevent disease progression. For example, a study by Choi et al. (2016) used machine learning algorithms to predict the onset of diabetes in patients with prediabetes, enabling early interventions such as lifestyle modifications and medication therapy to prevent the development of diabetes. Similarly, AI models have been employed to predict cardiovascular events and other chronic diseases, enabling healthcare providers to implement targeted preventive measures (Li et al., 2019).

In disease management, AI-driven predictive models are helping healthcare providers optimize treatment strategies and improve patient outcomes. For instance, in oncology, AI algorithms analyze genomic data to predict individual patient responses to treatments, enabling oncologists to personalize treatment regimens and improve therapeutic outcomes (Topol, 2019). Additionally, AI models are being used to predict disease progression and identify optimal treatment pathways, enhancing clinical decision-making and patient care (Johnson et al., 2021).

Furthermore, AI-driven predictive models are enhancing patient outcomes by enabling personalized and proactive care delivery. These models analyse vast datasets to identify patterns and predict patient outcomes, helping healthcare providers make more informed decisions tailored to individual patient needs. For example, a study by Rajkumar et al. (2018) showed that AI models could accurately predict patient outcomes such as mortality, readmission, and length of hospital stay, enabling early interventions and improving overall care quality. Additionally, AI models are being used to optimize medication adherence and reduce adverse drug events, leading to improved patient safety and outcomes (Chen et al., 2021).

To address the variables related to the transformative impact of artificial intelligence (AI) in healthcare, several powerful tools can be employed. One significant scope is the application of AI in medical imaging, which enhances the accuracy and speed of diagnosis. AI-powered tools like convolutional neural networks (CNNs) have shown remarkable performance in image analysis, aiding in early detection of diseases such as cancer (Litjens et al., 2017). Additionally, natural language processing (NLP) is a powerful tool that can extract valuable information from unstructured clinical notes and literature, facilitating clinical decision-making and research (Miotto et al., 2017). AI can also revolutionize personalized medicine by analyzing vast amounts of genomic data to predict individual responses to treatments (Topol, 2019). These tools demonstrate the potential of AI to transform healthcare delivery and outcomes.

AI-driven predictive models hold immense potential in transforming preventive care, disease management, and patient outcomes. By leveraging advanced algorithms and vast datasets, these models enable proactive interventions, personalized treatment strategies, and improved clinical decision-making. Moving forward, continued research and collaboration between healthcare professionals, data scientists, and policymakers are essential to harnessing the power of AI in optimizing preventive care, disease management, and patient outcomes.

ETHICAL IMPLICATIONS OF AI INTEGRATION IN HEALTHCARE: IMPORTANCE OF RESPONSIBLE AND TRANSPARENT METHODS

The use of AI in healthcare has the ability to completely transform the way patients are diagnosed, treated, and cared for. While AI holds great potential, it also brings with it important ethical concerns that must be thoroughly addressed. This study explores the ethical implications of AI integration in healthcare, focusing on the importance of responsible and transparent methods in addressing these concerns.

Ethical Implications of AI Integration:

Patient Privacy and Data Security: AI algorithms in healthcare often rely on large datasets containing sensitive patient information. Ensuring patient privacy and data security is paramount to maintain trust and confidentiality. Studies by Mittelstadt et al. (2016) and Abouelmehdi et al. (2018) highlight the need for robust data encryption, anonymization techniques, and adherence to privacy regulations to protect patient data from unauthorized access or misuse.

Algorithmic Bias and Fairness: AI algorithms can be susceptible to bias, which may result in unfair treatment or disparities in healthcare delivery. Responsible AI development involves identifying and mitigating bias through rigorous testing and validation. Research by Obermeyer et al. (2019) and Buolamwini and Gebru (2018) emphasizes the importance of transparent reporting of algorithmic performance across demographic groups to ensure fairness and equity in healthcare decision-making.

Clinical Decision Support and Autonomy: AI-powered clinical decision support systems have the potential to improve diagnostic accuracy and treatment outcomes. However, concerns arise regarding the autonomy of healthcare providers and overreliance on algorithmic recommendations. Studies by Char et al. (2020) and Cabitza et al. (2017) underscore the need for transparent communication between AI systems and healthcare professionals to ensure that AI algorithms complement rather than replace clinical judgment.

Accountability and Liability: Defining accountability and liability for algorithmic errors or adverse outcomes presents challenges in AI-driven healthcare. Responsible AI integration requires clear delineation of responsibilities between developers, healthcare providers, and regulatory agencies. Research by Mittelstadt et al. (2016) and Cohen and Adar (2019) stress the importance of transparent documentation of AI algorithms and mechanisms for accountability in case of errors or adverse events.

Informed Consent and Patient Empowerment: Informed consent is essential for ethical healthcare practice, yet AI-driven interventions may complicate this process. Transparent communication with patients about the use of AI technologies in their care is crucial for promoting informed consent and shared decision-making. Studies by Caine and Hanania (2018) and Kerasidou and Kingori (2018) advocate for empowering patients with knowledge and agency regarding AI-driven healthcare interventions.

Case Study Examples

Ethical implications of AI integration in healthcare highlight the importance of responsible and transparent methods in addressing concerns related to patient privacy, fairness, autonomy, accountability, and informed consent. By prioritizing ethical considerations in AI development and implementation, healthcare stakeholders can harness the benefits of AI technologies while upholding ethical principles and preserving trust in the healthcare system.

Patient Privacy and Data Security:

Case Study: In 2015, UCLA Health System suffered a cyberattack compromising the personal and medical information of approximately 4.5 million individuals. The breach, attributed to hackers exploiting a vulnerability in the hospital's network, exposed sensitive data including names, Social Security numbers, medical conditions, and treatment histories. This incident underscored the importance of robust data security measures in healthcare to protect patient information. The breach raised significant ethical concerns regarding patient privacy and data security. Healthcare organizations are entrusted with sensitive patient information, and breaches can lead to identity theft, financial fraud, and other serious consequences for patients. It highlighted the need for responsible data handling practices and the implementation of stringent security measures to safeguard patient data. Sengupta, S., & Eason, K. (2017).

Algorithmic Bias and Fairness:

Case Study: In 2018, a study published in science revealed racial bias in a widely used algorithm used to determine the level of care for patients with complex health needs. The algorithm, which aimed to predict which patients would benefit most from extra care, was found to prioritize white patients over black patients who were equally sick. This bias resulted in black patients receiving fewer services despite having similar healthcare needs. The case highlighted the ethical implications of algorithmic bias in healthcare. AI algorithms are increasingly used to support clinical decision-making, but if these algorithms are biased, they can perpetuate and exacerbate existing healthcare disparities. It underscored the importance of fairness

CHALLENGES OF DATA SECURITY AND INTEROPERABILITY IN THE ADOPTION OF AI IN HEALTHCARE

The adoption of AI in healthcare is hindered by several challenges, particularly in the realms of data security and interoperability. This literature review explores existing research on the challenges related to data security and interoperability in the adoption of AI in healthcare.

Data Security Challenges:

Sensitive Nature of Healthcare Data: There are stringent privacy requirements in place to protect healthcare data, which includes genomic information, medical pictures, and patient records. Protecting patient privacy and preserving faith in healthcare systems depend on keeping this data secure and private. Strong data encryption, access controls, and audit trails are crucial for protecting patient data from misuse or unauthorized access, according to studies by Kuo et al. (2018) and Abouelmehdi et al. (2018).

Cybersecurity Threats: Healthcare organizations are increasingly vulnerable to cyberattacks, including ransomware, phishing, and data breaches. AI-driven healthcare systems present lucrative targets for cybercriminals due to the valuable patient information they contain. Research by Kierkegaard (2019) and Brown (2019) underscores the need for proactive cybersecurity measures, such as network segmentation, intrusion detection systems, and employee training, to mitigate the risk of data breaches and ensure the integrity of AI-driven healthcare systems.

Interoperability Challenges:

Fragmented IT Systems: Healthcare IT infrastructure is often fragmented, with disparate systems and databases that use different standards, formats, and protocols for data exchange. This lack of interoperability makes it challenging to integrate AI algorithms seamlessly into existing workflows and share insights across healthcare settings. Studies by Adler-Milstein et al. (2017) and Evans et al. (2020) emphasize the need for standardized data formats, application programming interfaces (APIs), and interoperability frameworks to facilitate the seamless exchange of data between disparate systems.

Data Silos and Vendor Lock-In: Healthcare organizations may encounter difficulties in accessing and sharing data due to proprietary formats and vendor-specific interfaces. This creates data silos that impede interoperability and hinder the adoption of AI technologies. Research by Raghupathi and Raghupathi (2018) and Adler-Milstein et al. (2020) suggests that addressing vendor lock-in requires collaboration between healthcare stakeholders, policymakers, and technology vendors to promote open standards and interoperable solutions.

The problem of data security and interoperability is one of the primary challenges to the broad use of AI in healthcare. Protecting the confidentiality of patient information is critical for retaining faith in healthcare systems powered by artificial intelligence. However, healthcare organizations often face challenges in securely storing, transmitting, and accessing large volumes of diverse data from disparate sources. Furthermore, interoperability issues arise due to the fragmented nature of healthcare IT systems, which may use different standards, formats, and protocols for data exchange. This lack of interoperability makes it difficult to integrate AI algorithms seamlessly into existing workflows and share insights across healthcare settings. Addressing these challenges requires collaboration between healthcare stakeholders, policymakers, and technology providers to develop robust data security frameworks, standardized data formats, and interoperability protocols. Additionally, implementing encryption techniques, access controls, and audit trails can help safeguard patient data while facilitating secure data sharing for AI-driven insights. Ultimately, overcoming the challenges related to data security and interoperability is essential to unlock the full potential of AI in healthcare and improve patient outcomes.

TRANSFORMATIVE IMPACT OF ARTIFICIAL INTELLIGENCE

One of the most revolutionary technologies of our time, artificial intelligence (AI) is changing the way many industries and parts of society work. Here are some key areas where AI is making a significant difference:

Automation and Efficiency: AI makes it possible to automate mundane jobs, which helps organizations save money, work faster, and simplify their processes. The manufacturing, logistics, and customer service sectors are prime examples of this.

Data Analysis and Insights: AI algorithms can process large volumes of data at high speeds, extracting valuable insights and patterns that humans might overlook. This capability is revolutionizing fields like finance, healthcare, and marketing, where data-driven decision-making is critical.

Personalization and Recommendation Systems: AI-powered recommendation engines analyse user preferences and behaviour to deliver personalized recommendations, driving engagement and sales in sectors such as e-commerce, streaming services, and content platforms.

Healthcare Advancements: Medical imaging analysis, medication development, individualized treatment programs, and disease prevention predictive analytics are just a few of the ways artificial intelligence is changing healthcare. These advancements have the potential to improve patient health outcomes while decreasing healthcare costs generally.

Autonomous Vehicles and Transportation: Autonomous vehicle development is being propelled by AI, which is reshaping logistics and transportation. Transportation networks may be optimized, congestion might be reduced, and safety could be enhanced by self-driving cars, trucks, drones, and delivery robots.

Natural Language Processing and Communication: Machines can now comprehend, analyse, and even create their own language with the help of natural language processing (NLP) technology powered by artificial intelligence. Improvements in language translation, sentiment analysis, chatbots, virtual assistants, and accessibility have resulted from these improvements.

Environmental Sustainability: AI is being used to address environmental challenges through applications like predictive modelling for climate change, optimization of energy consumption, and monitoring of wildlife and ecosystems. These efforts contribute to sustainability and conservation efforts.

Cybersecurity and Fraud Detection: AI enhances cybersecurity by detecting and mitigating threats in real-time, identifying patterns of suspicious behaviour, and preventing fraud across digital platforms and financial transactions.

Education and Training: AI-driven learning platforms cater to each student's unique requirements, tailor lessons to their specific progress, and offer specific comments and assistance. Virtual tutors, adaptive learning platforms, and educational games are transforming the way people learn and acquire new skills.

Ethical and Societal Implications: As AI becomes more integrated into daily life, it raises important ethical and societal questions regarding privacy, bias, job displacement, and algorithmic accountability. Addressing these challenges is crucial to ensuring that AI technologies benefit society as a whole.

The transformative impact of AI is far-reaching and multifaceted, touching virtually every aspect of our lives and reshaping industries, economies, and societies around the world. As AI continues to evolve, it will be essential to harness its potential responsibly and ethically to maximize its benefits while mitigating risks.

Artificial Intelligence (AI) stands at the forefront of technological innovation, wielding transformative power across industries and societal spheres. Its impact is profound, touching every aspect of human existence, from the way we work and communicate to how we navigate healthcare and transportation. Through automation, AI streamlines operations, driving efficiency and cost reduction in sectors ranging from manufacturing to customer service. Moreover, its prowess in data analysis unlocks valuable insights from vast datasets, revolutionizing decision-making in finance, healthcare, and marketing. AI's ability to personalize experiences through recommendation systems and natural language processing not only enhances user engagement but also fosters greater accessibility and communication. In healthcare, AI facilitates groundbreaking advancements in medical imaging, drug discovery, and personalized treatment plans, promising improved patient outcomes and cost savings. Beyond these practical applications, AI fuels innovation in autonomous vehicles, environmental sustainability efforts, cybersecurity, and education, reshaping industries and addressing global challenges. However, this transformative power also raises ethical and societal concerns, necessitating thoughtful consideration of issues like privacy, bias, and job displacement. As AI continues to evolve, its transformative impact underscores the need for responsible development and governance to ensure its benefits are equitably distributed and its risks mitigated.

BENEFITS FOR IMPLEMENTATION OF AI IN HEALTHCARE

A. Diagnosis with AI: Timely and accurate diagnosis is one of the biggest challenges in healthcare. Systems driven by AI have proven to be quite effective in assisting doctors with the diagnosis of various illnesses. These systems evaluate massive volumes of genetic data, medical images, and patient records using cutting-edge machine learning algorithms and deep learning techniques. This data can be processed and analyzed by AI algorithms to improve the diagnostic process by identifying patterns, detecting anomalies, and providing valuable insights. Some examples of AI diagnostic technologies that have found successful use are computer-aided detection (CAD) and computer-aided diagnosis (CADx) systems. Radiologists, for example, can use AI algorithms to sift through X-ray, CT, and MRI pictures to find anomalies and aid in their diagnoses. A similar trend has emerged in the medical profession, where AI algorithms are helping pathologists analyse tissue samples and detect malignant cells. Integrating AI into the diagnostic process requires a number of steps. The most important thing is to gather a lot of medical data and keep it in a safe and convenient way. By including more datasets, the trained models are further tested and improved. Integrating the AI models into clinical workflows improves diagnosis accuracy and patient outcomes by giving healthcare practitioners quick insights and help.

B. Treatment with AI: After establishing a diagnosis, AI can be highly advantageous in guiding treatment decisions. AI-powered clinical decision support systems (CDSS) analyze patient data, therapy options, and relevant scientific literature to provide healthcare practitioners with evidence-based recommendations. These technologies can facilitate the improvement of treatment regimens, aid in the selection of appropriate medications and dosages, and predict any adverse effects or drug interactions. Moreover, with the utilization of customized medical methodologies, AI has the potential to enhance the results of treatments. AI systems can utilize patient-specific data, like genetic profiles and electronic health records, to identify patterns and predict patient responses to different treatments. This enables medical practitioners to tailor medicines to individual patients, thereby improving efficacy and minimizing adverse effects. In order to be utilized in therapy, it is imperative to connect AI algorithms with electronic health record (EHR) systems and other clinical datasets. To train the AI models, a diverse range of information such as patient profiles, treatment outcomes, and medical literature is required. The training process can incorporate many approaches such as supervised learning, reinforcement learning, and others. To ensure safety, address ethical considerations, and comply with regulations, the utilization of AI in therapy requires a close collaboration among AI experts, healthcare professionals, and regulatory bodies.

C. Prediction with AI: AI has found significant application in healthcare, particularly in the field of prediction. AI systems can examine extensive datasets to identify patterns and trends that aid in predicting patient outcomes and the evolution of illnesses. AI can provide valuable information on prognosis, risk assessment, and therapy response through the use of machine learning algorithms. Artificial intelligence-driven predictive analytics can aid in identifying people with a higher propensity to develop specific illnesses or conditions. AI systems can analyse genetic information, electronic health data, and lifestyle characteristics to identify individuals who have a higher likelihood of acquiring diabetes or cardiovascular disease. These prognostications enable the implementation of timely preventive measures and interventions, thereby improving patient outcomes and reducing healthcare costs. The application of AI in prediction involves the utilization of clinical data, lifestyle data, environmental data, and other diverse data sources. The healthcare industry is experiencing a swift and significant change due to the advancements in artificial intelligence, particularly in the areas of diagnosis, treatment, and prediction. Artificial intelligence (AI) systems aid medical professionals in accurately diagnosing patients, guiding treatment decisions, and predicting patient outcomes. Incorporating AI models into clinical workflows necessitates adherence to appropriate protocols for training, involving the acquisition and analysis of vast quantities of medical data. While AI has great promise for enhancing healthcare, there remain challenges to address, such as ensuring data security and privacy, resolving ethical dilemmas, and fostering collaboration between AI researchers and healthcare professionals. Nevertheless, the latest advancements in AI technology exhibit significant potential for improving patient care, reducing expenses, and achieving superior healthcare outcomes.

DISCUSSION

The chapter comprehensively analyses the transformative impact of Artificial Intelligence (AI) on healthcare systems, focusing on its ability to enhance diagnostic accuracy, treatment outcomes, and patient care. It investigates the incorporation of AI-powered diagnostic algorithms, predictive analytics, and personalized medicine in healthcare, exploring how these technologies are revolutionizing the field. Moreover, it discusses the ethical implications of AI integration in healthcare and emphasizes the importance of responsible and transparent methods to address concerns related to patient privacy, fairness, autonomy, accountability, and informed consent. Furthermore, the chapter highlights challenges related to data security and interoperability in the adoption of AI in healthcare, underscoring the need for robust data security frameworks, standardized data formats, and interoperability protocols to realize the full potential of AI in improving patient outcomes. To achieve these objectives, the chapter conducts a comprehensive review of existing literature, scholarly articles, and relevant research studies, analyzing real-world case studies and examples of AI implementation in healthcare settings to illustrate practical implications and outcomes. It concludes by emphasizing the transformative impact of AI across various sectors and aspects of society, while also recognizing the importance of responsible development and governance to maximize benefits and mitigate risks.

The use of AI has the potential to greatly improve the precision and efficiency of medical diagnostics. The technology is able to discover anomalies and trends in patient data that could be indicative of diseases by using machine learning techniques. Artificial intelligence systems can examine X-rays, CT scans, and MRI pictures to spot possible anomalies. Training deep learning models on massive datasets allows for the early identification of cancer and other diseases by seeing small patterns in medical pictures. Treatment strategies can be optimized for specific patients using AI approaches. Algorithms powered by artificial intelligence can analyse a patient's medical history, genetic data, and therapy response data to provide individualized treatment recommendations. Machine learning models can help healthcare providers make educated decisions by predicting the effectiveness and possible negative effects of different treatment regimens.

a comprehensive overview of the transformative impact of artificial intelligence (AI) in healthcare, emphasizing its potential to improve diagnostic accuracy, treatment outcomes, and patient care. However, there is a potential overemphasis on the positive aspects of AI integration, while underemphasizing the challenges and ethical implications associated with its adoption.

In terms of potential solutions, the chapter suggests prioritizing the integration of AI technologies in medical imaging and predictive models for preventive care. Standardized protocols for data security and interoperability are recommended to ensure a seamless and secure exchange of patient information. Additionally, collaboration between healthcare organizations and policymakers is encouraged to develop ethical guidelines for the responsible use of AI in clinical settings.

While these recommendations are valuable, they may oversimplify the complexities involved in integrating AI in healthcare. The chapter could benefit from a more nuanced discussion of the challenges, such as data privacy, algorithm bias, and the impact on the healthcare workforce, and how these challenges can be addressed in a responsible and transparent manner. Furthermore, the chapter could explore the role of stakeholders, including patients, healthcare providers, and technology developers, in shaping the future of AI in healthcare and ensuring its ethical implementation.

Main Findings:

Incorporation of AI in Healthcare: The incorporation of AI-powered diagnostic algorithms, predictive analytics, and personalized medicine in healthcare has led to significant advancements in diagnostic accuracy, predictive modeling, and tailored treatment plans. AI algorithms have demonstrated remarkable capabilities in medical imaging tasks, clinical decision support, and population health management. They have the potential to improve early detection, optimize treatment regimens, and enhance patient outcomes.

AI-driven Predictive Models: AI-driven predictive models have transformative potential in preventive care, disease management, and enhancing patient outcomes. These models enable proactive interventions, personalized treatment strategies, and improved clinical decision making. By leveraging vast datasets and advanced algorithms, AI predicts disease trends, identifies high-risk populations, and forecasts treatment responses, leading to improved population health and reduced healthcare costs.

Ethical Implications: The integration of AI in healthcare raises ethical considerations related to patient privacy, algorithmic bias, clinical autonomy, accountability, and informed consent. Responsible and transparent methods are crucial to address these concerns and uphold ethical principles in AI development and implementation. Measures such as robust data encryption, fair algorithmic design, transparent reporting, and patient empowerment are essential to ensure ethical AI integration in healthcare.

Challenges of Data Security and Interoperability: Challenges related to data security and interoperability hinder the widespread adoption of AI in healthcare. Healthcare data is highly sensitive, and ensuring its security and confidentiality is paramount to maintain patient trust. Interoperability issues arise due to fragmented IT systems and disparate data formats, impeding the seamless exchange of information and integration of AI algorithms. Collaboration between stakeholders and policymakers is necessary to develop standardized data formats, interoperability frameworks, and robust data security measures.

Suggestions:

Investment in AI Research and Development: Continued investment in AI research and development is essential to drive innovation and overcome challenges in healthcare. Funding initiatives should prioritize the development of AI algorithms, predictive models, and ethical guidelines to ensure responsible AI integration and maximize its potential benefits in healthcare.

Development of Ethical Frameworks: Healthcare organizations should develop ethical frameworks and guidelines to govern the responsible use of AI in healthcare. These frameworks should address ethical considerations such as patient privacy, algorithmic bias, clinical autonomy, and accountability, fostering transparency, fairness, and trust in AI-driven healthcare systems.

Collaboration and Knowledge Sharing: Collaboration between healthcare professionals, data scientists, policymakers, and technology vendors is crucial to address challenges related to data security, interoperability, and ethical concerns. Knowledge sharing and interdisciplinary collaboration can facilitate the development of standardized protocols, best practices, and innovative solutions for AI integration in healthcare.

Regulatory Oversight and Compliance: Regulatory agencies should establish clear guidelines and standards for the ethical use of AI in healthcare, ensuring compliance with privacy regulations, fair algorithmic design, and transparent reporting practices. Regulatory oversight is essential to safeguard patient rights, mitigate risks, and promote responsible AI integration in healthcare.

Education and Training: Healthcare professionals should receive education and training on AI technologies, ethical considerations, and best practices for integrating AI into clinical workflows. Training programs should emphasize the importance of patient privacy, algorithmic transparency, and informed consent, empowering healthcare professionals to navigate ethical challenges and leverage AI effectively in patient care.

IMPLICATION OF THE STUDY

The study, titled "Revolutionizing Healthcare: The Transformative Impact of Artificial Intelligence," presents a comprehensive analysis of how AI is reshaping healthcare systems. By focusing on its capacity to enhance diagnostic accuracy, treatment outcomes, and patient care, the study highlights AI's pivotal role in revolutionizing clinical practice. Through the incorporation of AI-powered diagnostic algorithms, predictive analytics, and personalized medicine, healthcare providers can harness the power of AI to optimize patient care and improve outcomes. Furthermore, the study delves into the ethical implications of AI integration in healthcare, emphasizing the importance of responsible and transparent methods to address concerns surrounding patient privacy, fairness, autonomy, accountability, and informed consent. By acknowledging and navigating these ethical considerations, healthcare organizations can build trust and ensure the ethical deployment of AI technologies. Additionally, the study identifies challenges related to data security and interoperability, underlining the necessity for robust data security frameworks, standardized data formats, and interoperability protocols. By addressing these challenges, healthcare systems can fully leverage the potential of AI to enhance patient outcomes while safeguarding data integrity and privacy. Overall, the study underscores the transformative impact of AI on healthcare delivery and emphasizes the need for continued research, collaboration, and regulatory oversight to ensure ethical and effective AI integration in healthcare.

Managerial Implication

Strategic planning is crucial, requiring organizations to integrate AI into their strategic processes to fully realize its potential (Wickramasinghe et al., 2021). This involves identifying areas where AI can enhance operational efficiency, improve patient outcomes, and drive innovation. Effective resource allocation is also essential, with managers needing to invest in AI technologies, train staff, and redesign workflows to accommodate AI-driven processes (Jiang et al., 2017). Developing and implementing ethical guidelines for AI use is paramount, ensuring patient privacy and data security, mitigating algorithmic bias, and promoting transparency and accountability (Char et al., 2018). Collaboration among healthcare professionals, data scientists, and technology experts is key to developing and implementing AI solutions effectively (Obermeyer et al., 2019). Change management is critical to managing the transition to AI-driven healthcare, addressing resistance to change, providing adequate training and support, and monitoring the impact on organizational culture (Cabitza et al., 2017). A culture of continuous improvement should be adopted to optimize the use of AI in healthcare, regularly evaluating AI applications and adapting strategies based on feedback and lessons learned (Topol, 2019). Ultimately, AI should be used to enhance patient-centric care, aligning with patient needs and preferences to improve outcomes and experiences (Laranjo et al., 2018). By considering these implications, healthcare organizations can effectively leverage AI to drive positive change in healthcare delivery.

Implications for Researchers:

The study provides researchers with valuable insights into the transformative impact of Artificial Intelligence (AI) on healthcare systems. It highlights areas for further investigation, such as the development of AI-powered diagnostic algorithms, predictive analytics, and personalized medicine. Researchers can explore the effectiveness of AI technologies in improving diagnostic accuracy, treatment outcomes, and patient care through empirical studies and clinical trials. Moreover, the study underscores the importance of addressing ethical considerations and challenges related to data security and interoperability in AI integration in healthcare. Researchers can contribute to the field by developing ethical frameworks, protocols, and best practices for the responsible deployment of AI technologies in healthcare settings. Additionally, the study encourages interdisciplinary collaboration between researchers from various fields, including computer science, healthcare, ethics, and policy, to advance knowledge and innovation in AI-driven healthcare.

Implications for Society:

The study has significant implications for society, as it highlights the potential of AI to revolutionize healthcare delivery and improve patient outcomes. By leveraging AI-powered diagnostic algorithms, predictive analytics, and personalized medicine, healthcare systems can enhance the quality, efficiency, and accessibility of care. This has far-reaching implications for public health, as AI technologies can facilitate early detection, prevention, and management of diseases, ultimately reducing healthcare costs and improving population health. Moreover, the study emphasizes the importance of addressing ethical concerns and ensuring transparency, fairness, and accountability in AI integration in healthcare. By promoting responsible AI deployment and fostering trust and confidence in AI-driven healthcare systems, society can reap the benefits of AI while mitigating potential risks and challenges.

Implications for Academicians:

Academicians can draw upon the findings of the study to enrich teaching, research, and academic discourse in various disciplines. The study provides a comprehensive overview of the transformative impact of AI on healthcare systems, offering academicians valuable insights into current trends, challenges, and opportunities in the field. Academicians can integrate discussions on AI ethics, data security, and interoperability into curricula and academic programs to educate students and professionals about the ethical and social implications of AI integration in healthcare. Furthermore, the study encourages academicians to engage in interdisciplinary research collaborations and knowledge exchange initiatives to advance understanding and innovation in AI-driven healthcare. By fostering a culture of responsible AI development and governance, academicians can contribute to the ethical and sustainable deployment of AI technologies in healthcare and society at large.

CONCLUSION

The integration of artificial intelligence (AI) in healthcare holds immense promise for revolutionizing diagnostic accuracy, treatment outcomes, and patient care. Through AI-powered diagnostic algorithms, predictive analytics, and personalized medicine, significant advancements have been made in various areas of healthcare, including medical imaging analysis, disease management, and preventive care. However, alongside these transformative benefits come important ethical considerations, such as patient privacy, algorithmic bias, clinical autonomy, accountability, and informed consent. Addressing these concerns requires responsible and transparent methods in AI development and implementation. Furthermore, challenges related to data security and interoperability must be overcome through collaboration between stakeholders, investment in research and development, development of ethical frameworks, regulatory oversight, education, and training. By navigating these challenges effectively, healthcare systems can harness the full potential of AI to improve patient outcomes while upholding ethical principles and maintaining trust in the healthcare system.

REFERENCES

Abouelmehdi, K., Beni-Hessane, A., & Khaloufi, H. (2018). Big healthcare data: Preserving security and privacy. *Journal of Big Data*, 5(1), 1–34. 10.1186/s40537-017-0110-7

Adler-Milstein, J., Holmgren, A. J., Kralovec, P., Worzala, C., & Searcy, T. (2017). Electronic health record adoption in US hospitals: Progress continues, but challenges persist. *Health Affairs*, 36(8), 1567–1574. 10.1377/hlthaff.2017.0446

Adler-Milstein, J., Lin, S. C., & Jha, A. K. (2020). The number of health information exchange efforts is declining, leaving the viability of broad clinical data exchange uncertain. *Health Affairs*, 39(1), 63–71. 10.1377/hlthaff.2019.00539

Amisha, M., Malik, P., Pathania, M., & Rathaur, V. K. (2019). Overview of artificial intelligence in medicine. *Journal of Family Medicine and Primary Care*, 8(7), 2328–2331. 10.4103/jfmpc.jfmpc_440_19

Ashley, E. A. (2016). Towards precision medicine. *Nature Reviews. Genetics*, 17(9), 507–522. 10.1038/nrg.2016.86

Buolamwini, J., & Gebru, T. (2018). Gender shades: Intersectional accuracy disparities in commercial gender classification. Proceedings of Machine Learning Research, 81, 1-15. http://proceedings.mlr.press/v81/buolamwini18a.html

Cabitza, F., Rasoini, R., & Gensini, G. F. (2017). Unintended consequences of machine learning in medicine. *Journal of the American Medical Association*, 318(6), 517–518. 10.1001/jama.2017.7797

Caine, K., & Hanania, R. (2018). Patients want granular privacy control over health information in electronic medical records. *Journal of the American Medical Informatics Association : JAMIA*, 25(8), 967–969. 10.1093/jamia/ocy026

Char, D. S., Shah, N. H., & Magnus, D.Implementing Machine Learning in Health Care Workgroup. (2020). Implementing machine learning in health care—Addressing ethical challenges. *The New England Journal of Medicine*, 378(11), 981–983. 10.1056/NEJMp1714229

Chen, J. H., & Asch, S. M.Machine Learning in Medicine Workgroup. (2021). Machine learning and prediction in medicine: Beyond the peak of inflated expectations. *The New England Journal of Medicine*, 384(23), 2077–2082. 10.1056/NEJMsb2029340

Cohen, D., & Adar, E. (2019). How do you know? Building and measuring trust in AI. arXiv preprint arXiv:1912.08968. https://arxiv.org/abs/1912.08968

Evans, R. S.Electronic Health Record Information, Utah Sentinel Surveillance Network and Intermountain Healthcare Clinical Genetics Institute. (2020). Electronic health records: Then, now, and in the future. *Yearbook of Medical Informatics*, 29(1), 242–249. 10.1055/s-0040-1713158

Huang, C., Xu, L., Shi, Y., & Zhang, L. (2021). A comprehensive review of artificial intelligence in the diagnosis and treatment of breast cancer. *Journal of Cancer Research and Clinical Oncology*, 147(1), 7–24.

Jiang, F., Jiang, Y., Zhi, H., Dong, Y., Li, H., Ma, S., Wang, Y., Dong, Q., Shen, H., & Wang, Y. (2017). Artificial intelligence in healthcare: Past, present and future. *Stroke and Vascular Neurology*, 2(4), 230–243. 10.1136/svn-2017-000101

Johnson, A. E., Pollard, T. J., & Mark, R. G. (2021). Reproducibility in critical care: A mortality prediction case study. *Journal of the American Medical Informatics Association : JAMIA*, 28(2), 333–343. 10.1093/jamia/ocaa208

Kerasidou, A., & Kingori, P. (2018). Ethical, social, and cultural issues in the use of personalized genomic medicine in Africa. *Personalized Medicine*, 15(5), 385–397. 10.2217/pme-2018-0021

Kierkegaard, P. (2019). The state of ransomware in healthcare organizations: 2019. *Cybersecurity*, 2(1), 1–8. 10.1186/s42400-019-0021-8

Kuo, A. M., Borycki, E. M., & Kushniruk, A. W. (2018). Cybersecurity in healthcare: A narrative review of trends, threats and ways forward. *The HIM Journal*, 47(2), 63–75. 10.1177/1833358317703175

Laranjo, L., Dunn, A. G., Tong, H. L., Kocaballi, A. B., Chen, J., Bashir, R., & Bates, D. W. (2018). Conversational agents in healthcare: A systematic review. *Journal of the American Medical Informatics Association : JAMIA*, 25(9), 1248–1258. 10.1093/jamia/ocy072

Li, Y., Lu, J., Hu, Y., & Chang, C. (2019). Predicting acute cardiovascular events with a large-scale, densely connected deep learning network. *Nature Medicine*, 25(12), 1869–1873. 10.1038/s41591-019-0613-7

McKinney, S. M., Sieniek, M., Godbole, V., Godwin, J., Antropova, N., Ashrafian, H., Back, T., Chesus, M., Corrado, G. S., Darzi, A., Etemadi, M., Garcia-Vicente, F., Gilbert, F. J., Halling-Brown, M., Hassabis, D., Jansen, S., Karthikesalingam, A., Kelly, C. J., King, D., & Shetty, S. (2020). International evaluation of an AI system for breast cancer screening. *Nature*, 577(7788), 89–94. 10.1038/s41586-019-1799-6

Mittelstadt, B. D., Allo, P., Taddeo, M., Wachter, S., & Floridi, L. (2016). The ethics of algorithms: Mapping the debate. *Big Data & Society*, 3(2), 1–21. 10.1177/2053951716679679

Obermeyer, Z., & Emanuel, E. J. (2016). Predicting the future—Big data, machine learning, and clinical medicine. *The New England Journal of Medicine*, 375(13), 1216–1219. 10.1056/NEJMp1606181

Obermeyer, Z., Powers, B., Vogeli, C., & Mullainathan, S. (2019). Dissecting racial bias in an algorithm used to manage the health of populations. *Science*, 366(6464), 447–453. 10.1126/science.aax2342

Patel, V. L., Shortliffe, E. H., Stefanelli, M., Szolovits, P., Berthold, M. R., Bellazzi, R., & Geissbuhler, A. (2018). The coming of age of artificial intelligence in medicine. *Artificial Intelligence in Medicine*, 46(1), 5–17. 10.1016/j.artmed.2008.07.017

. Potter, K., Blessing, E., & Mohamed, S. (2024). Revolutionizing Healthcare: The Transformative Impact of Artificial Intelligence.

Raghupathi, W., & Raghupathi, V. (2018). Big data analytics in healthcare: Promise and potential. *Health Information Science and Systems*, 6(1), 1–10. 10.1007/s13755-018-0061-6

Rajkomar, A., Oren, E., Chen, K., Dai, A. M., Hajaj, N., Hardt, M., & Dean, J. (2018). Scalable and accurate deep learning with electronic health records. *NPJ Digital Medicine*, 1(1), 1–10. 10.1038/s41746-018-0029-1

Sengupta, S., & Eason, K. (2017). Understanding data security and privacy in the era of digital government transformation: A study of India. *Information Systems Frontiers*, 19(2), 245–259.

Topol, E. J. (2019). High-performance medicine: The convergence of human and artificial intelligence. *Nature Medicine*, 25(1), 44–56. 10.1038/s41591-018-0300-7

Wang, F., Casalino, L. P., & Khullar, D. (2018). Deep learning in medicine—Promise, progress, and challenges. *JAMA Internal Medicine*, 178(6), 737–738.

Wang, Y., Tan, J., & Deng, J. (2020). A study on type 2 diabetes mellitus prediction models using different machine learning techniques. *Health Care*, 8(2), 128. 10.3390/healthcare8020128

Wickramasinghe, N., Bali, R. K., & Lehaney, B. (2021). Artificial Intelligence in Healthcare: Strategic Planning and Implementation. In Preethika, B. R., & Devika, S. (Eds.), *Artificial Intelligence in Healthcare: Theory and Application* (pp. 113–130). Springer.

Chapter 4

Generative AI in Healthcare:
Opportunities, Challenges, and Future Perspectives

D. Helen
SRM Institute of Science and Technology, India

N. V. Suresh
 https://orcid.org/0000-0002-0393-6037
ASET College of Science and Technology, Chennai, India

ABSTRACT

In recent years, the rapid development of AI technology Generative AI, has restructured the healthcare industry. Generative AI is a collection of algorithms that uses a large volume of medical data to generate new data in various formats, including medical images, data augmentation, and medicine development. A variety of techniques are employed in Generative AI in the healthcare industry, which includes Generative Adversarial Networks (GANs), Variational Autoencoders (VAEs), AutoRegressive Models, Flow-Based Models, and Probabilistic Graphical Models. Generative AI can applied in various domains in the healthcare sector including drug discovery, medical imaging enhancement, data augmentation, anomaly detection, simulation and training, and predictive modelling. The integration of Generative AI faces some challenges, such as addressing ethical and legal issues related to the use of Artificial Intelligence (AI) in healthcare and synthetic data in clinical decision-making, and ensuring the reliability and interpretability of AI-generated outputs.

DOI: 10.4018/979-8-3693-3731-8.ch004

INTRODUCTION

In healthcare industry Generative AI, comes with new opportunity for treatment, diagnostics, and innovation. The Generative AI can create synthetic data that resembles real data which are used in various healthcare domains, including as pharmaceutical discovery, population health management, precision medicine, genomics, medical imaging, and healthcare analytics (Choi et al., 2017). By analysing pre-defined datasets, Generative AI models like Variational Autoencoders (VAEs) and Generative Adversarial Networks (GANs) are applied in the healthcare sector to produce new patient records, medical pictures, and other healthcare-related data. Additionally, it may be applied to improve machine learning model training datasets. While generative AI has great potential for innovative healthcare, there are still issues with data security, bias reduction, and regulatory compliance. Notwithstanding these challenges, it has the power to totally revolutionise healthcare by opening up new application areas, improving diagnosis accuracy, and encouraging medical research. Generative AI holds the potential to completely change various aspects of healthcare by enhancing research, diagnosis, treatment, and operational effectiveness while resolving issues with scarce data, privacy, and resource availability. By improving diagnosis, treatment, research, and operational efficiency, generative AI has the potential to revolutionize a number of healthcare domains. It can also address challenges including scarce data, privacy concerns, and resource constraints.

TECHNIQUES USED FOR GENERATIVE AI IN HEATHCARE

Generative Adversarial Networks (GANs)

Generative Adversarial Networks (GANs) have attracted considerable attention and usage in the healthcare sector because of its capacity to provide authentic data, improve medical imaging, and expedite drug discovery.

Here is an overview of the applications of GANs in several healthcare fields:

1) **Medical Image Generation and Enhancement**: Generative Adversarial Networks (GANs) are able to generate new medical images that resemble the real images. These newly generated images are useful in the scenario where getting real data is difficult or restricted due to privacy concerns. To train machine learning models, for example, GANs have been used to create simulated images of organs while maintaining patient privacy. Additionally, Generative Adversarial Networks (GANs) can improve the resolution and general quality

of medical images, which can improve diagnosis accuracy and make treatment planning easier.

2) **Data Augmentation and Imputation**: Generative Adversarial Networks (GANs) can produce synthetic samples that accurately represents the underlying data distribution and also improves the quality of existing medical datasets. The improved data can be used to improve machine learning model training, especially when there isn't much labelled data available. GANs can improve dataset integrity and increase the accuracy of prediction models.

3) **Generating medical data for training deep learning models:** Generative AI can generate medical images such as Magnetic Resonance Imaging (MRI) Scans, Electrocardiograms (ECGS), and Histopathological Images (Arora & Arora, 2022). The synthetic data generated by Generative Adversarial Networks (GANs) can be a useful supplement to real datasets, especially when getting labelled data is expensive or scarce. Generative Adversarial Networks (GANs) may be employed to train models in a variety of domains, including medical imaging, time-series data, and patient records, with the aim of detecting anomalies or outliers. By grasping the usual data distribution, GANs may identify anomalies like as tumours in medical images or odd patterns in physiological signals. This functionality can help medical professionals identify and treat ailments in a timely manner.

4) **Personalised Medicine and Treatment Planning:** Generative Adversarial Networks (GANs) may provide personalized medical simulations or treatment plans that are tailored to the distinct features of individual patients. GANs have the potential to anticipate therapeutic outcomes, simulate the progression of illnesses, and improve treatment strategies for precision medicine approaches by leveraging patient-specific data, such as genetic information, medical history, and imaging scans.

Variational Autoencoders (VAE)

VAEs are a useful tool in the healthcare industry because they can efficiently conduct latent space representations, generate new datasets, and learn data distributions (Jadon & Kumar, 2023). VAEs are applied in various domain of healthcare contexts:

1. **Medical Image Reconstruction and Enhancement:** VAEs can enhance the quality and dependability of medical image data by reconstructing high-resolution medical images from low-resolution images. This mechanism can be helpful in a various situations where precise diagnosis and treatment plans depend on the quality of the picture, such as MRIs, CT scans, and ultrasound imaging (Jadon & Kumar, 2023).

2. **Data Imputation and Completion:** VAEs may deal with time-series data, medical pictures, and missing or incomplete data in Electronic Health Records (EHRs). By learning the distribution of the data and producing potential values for missing data, VAE facilitates efficient analysis that helps forecast patient outcomes.
3. **Representation learning and feature extraction:** VAEs are able to learn intricate medical data, including genetic information, clinical factors, and patient demographics. These representations help with downstream tasks like classification, clustering, and anomaly detection by capturing the structure and connections within the dataset.
4. **Molecular Design and Drug development:** VAEs may be used in drug development to create novel molecular structures with desirable properties, such as drug potency, bioavailability, etc. By storing chemical compounds into a continuous latent space, VAEs make it easier to explore and optimise chemical space. This expedites the search for new treatments and potential medications.
5. **Predictive Modelling and Risk Stratification**: By identifying the most important characteristics associated with a range of medical problems, VAEs may perform predictive models for prognosis, illness diagnosis, and risk stratification. By encoding patient data into a latent space representation, VAEs help with the construction of personalised risk scores and prediction algorithms, which are useful for early illness diagnosis.
6. **Personalised Medicine and Treatment Planning**: By identifying each patient's unique features from a variety of healthcare data sources, VAEs may create a personalised treatment plan. Clinical, genomic, and imaging data may be combined by VAEs to provide personalised therapy recommendations, enhance therapeutic interventions, and support precision medicine strategies that are especially tailored to address the particular requirements of patients (Zhang & Boulos, 2023).

Recurrent Neural Networks (RNNs)

RNNs are widely used in healthcare sector due to their proficiency at modelling sequential data and capturing temporal relationships.

The following list includes many uses of recurrent neural networks (RNNs) in the medical field:

1. **Time-series prediction:** Recurrent Neural Networks (RNNs) are used in time series analysis to forecast and assess patient health data over a given period of time. It can analyze blood pressure and heart rate, glucose levels in diabetic individuals, and ECG readings effectively. RNNs can forecast future health

outcomes and assist in the early detection or treatment of illnesses by using historical data to find patterns and trends.

2. **Medical Text Generation:** RNN are used to create Clinical notes, discharge summaries, and diagnostic reports. The generated texts can improve Electronic Health Records (EHRs), expedite the documentation process, and support medical staff in managing patient care (Spector-Bagdady, 2023).

3. **Analyzing Physiological Signals:** RNNs may be used to analyse physiological signals, including Electroencephalography (EEG), Electromyography (EMG), and pulse oximetry. When it comes to diagnosing and scheduling therapy for neurological ailments, sleep disorders, or respiratory difficulties, RNNs can identify patterns that may indicate these symptoms exist.

4. **Clinical Outcome Prediction:** Clinical data, demographics, and medical history are used to predict clinical outcomes, such as patient mortality, hospital readmission, or response to medication, using recurrent neural networks (RNNs). These predictions help medical professionals prioritise treatments, distribute resources efficiently, and improve patient care.

5. **Drug Response Prediction:** Personalised medicine techniques may be implemented by using Recurrent Neural Networks (RNNs) to determine the link between pharmacological treatments and patient responses. RNNs can effectively predict individual medication reactions and the best treatment plans that are tailored to each patient's unique features by using genetic data, gene expression patterns, and clinical considerations.

6. **Healthcare Workflow Optimisation:** Recurrent Neural Networks (RNNs) are employed to augment the efficiency of healthcare workflows, specifically in domains like hospital bed management, resource distribution, and patient scheduling. Recurrent Neural Networks (RNNs) can improve patient flow, reduce wait times, and optimise hospital operations by analysing historical data on patient admissions, discharges, and treatment durations.

7. **Remote Patient Monitoring**: By analysing data from wearable technology, mobile health apps, or telehealth platforms, Recurrent Neural Networks (RNNs) enable remote patient monitoring. Because RNNs continuously monitor physiological signals and activity patterns, they are able to identify early symptoms of deterioration, deliver timely therapies, and provide remote consultations with healthcare specialists.

Transformer Models

Transformer models such as BERT (Bidirectional Encoder Representations from Transformers) and GPT (Generative Pre-trained Transformer) have remarkable abilities in NLP (natural language processing) are more frequently in different areas of the healthcare sector. Here's how transformer models are utilized in healthcare

1. **Clinicial Documentation:** Transformer models are employed to automate clinical documentation procedures by producing accurate medical notes from patient interactions in Electronic Health Records (EHR). They have ability to analyze both structured and unstructured data from Electronic Health Records (EHR) systems, Doctor's notes, lab results, and radiology findings. This assists healthcare practitioners with their documentation duties, resulting in time savings and decreased administrative workload.
2. **Information Extraction from Medical Literature:** The use of Transformer models enables the extraction of relevant information from a wide range of medical literature, including research papers, clinical trials, and medical textbooks. They can recognise fundamental ideas, extract connections between medical entities, and condense textual material, therefore assisting researchers, doctors, and policymakers in acquiring and consolidating pertinent knowledge.
3. **Clinical Decision Support Systems (CDSS):** Clinical Decision Support Systems (CDSS) utilise transformer models to examine patient information, clinical research, and evidence-based guidelines to generate personalised recommendations for diagnosis, therapy, and patient management. They can aid the physicians to understand the complex medical information, recognising possible drug interactions, and forecasting patient outcomes using past data.
4. **Healthcare chatbots and Virtual Assistants**: Transformer models facilitate the development of intelligent virtual assistants and healthcare chatbots. These chatbots and assistants engage with patients and suggest medical guidance, respond to inquiries and provide remote monitoring assistance. They employ Natural Language Processing(NLP) and generation skills to imitate human-like interactions and improve patient engagement and satisfaction.
5. **Clinical Natural Language Processing (NLP):**Transformer model plays a role in creating and enhancing healthcare knowledge graphs and ontologies. Transformer models support various NLP tasks, including Named Entity Recognition (NER), relation extraction, sentiment analysis and entity linking. This helps to extract the clinical data such as diagnoses, symptoms, and treatment plans which enables to perform decision support and computational analysis in healthcare sector.

6. **Healthcare Knowledge Graphs and Ontologies:** Transformer models enhance the development and enhancement of healthcare knowledge graphs and ontologies by extracting semantic links and creating representations of medical ideas, illnesses, therapies, and patient phenotypes. Knowledge graphs enable the integration of data, promote semantic interoperability, and support sophisticated analytics in healthcare systems.

APPLICATIONS OF GENERATIVE AI IN THE HEALTHCARE SECTOR

1. **Personalised Medicine:** Generative AI system use the patient historical data, including genetic information, medical histories, and lifestyle elements, to develop a personalized treatment plans. This system maximizes the effectiveness of the treatment and reduce the negative effects by taking into account the individual features of every patient.
2. **Medical Imaging:** Generative AI approaches, such as generative adversarial networks (GANs), have the ability to improve medical imaging by creating high-resolution images from low-quality inputs or reconstructing images with missing data. This technology enhances the precision of diagnostics and allows healthcare workers to visualise intricate medical situations more efficiently.
3. **Healthcare Simulation:** Generative AI models have the ability to replicate the evolution of diseases, predict patient outcomes, and simulate therapy responses by considering a range of elements including demographic information, medical history, and environmental variables. These simulations aid academics and physicians in examining various scenarios, optimising treatment procedures, and predicting healthcare trends.
4. **Natural Language Processing(NLP):** NLP is a field that involves using advanced AI systems to generate clinical documentation in healthcare. These algorithms may create medical reports, discharge summaries, and treatment plans by analysing both structured and unstructured data sources. This optimises administrative duties, boosts clinical communication, and enhances the overall efficiency of healthcare operations.
5. **Behavioural Modification and Patient Engagement:** AI-driven chatbots and virtual assistants may engage with patients to deliver tailored health advice, track medication compliance, give mental health assistance, and encourage the adoption of good living habits. These treatments promote patient involvement, strengthen adherence to treatment, and ultimately improve health results.

CHALLENGES IN GENERATIVE AI

Generative AI has significant potential in the healthcare sector, but it also encounters certain obstacles that must be resolved for its effective acceptance and implementation:

1. **Data Quality and Quantity:** Generative AI models require huge amounts of high-quality data to acquire significant patterns and provide accurate outputs. Nevertheless, healthcare data frequently exhibits heterogeneity, incompleteness, and noise, which causes difficulties in training robust models. Ensuring data integrity, confidentiality, and protection, availability are major obstacle implementing Generative AI in healthcare sector.
2. **Data Privacy and Security:** The healthcare data needs to be protected securely and privacy regulations should be followed strictly. Generating and using healthcare data should ensure the patient privacy and security.
3. **Data quality and heterogeneity:** The healthcare data typically heterogeneous, noisy, and sparse, so it is very tedious task to train the generative models. Hence the reliability of generated data in healthcare reflects the underlying distribution of real-world healthcare data while taking its unpredictability and quality into consideration.
4. **Clinical Interpretability and Trust:** For usage in clinical settings, generated healthcare data and models need to be trustworthy and understandable. To successfully integrate AI-driven insights into patient care, clinicians need to understand the methods and motivations behind the generation of specific data and forecasts. The generative models can be adopted and accepted by healthcare professionals if the model will essential that they be understood in an interpretable manner.
5. **Fairness and Bias:** Predictions and models derived from healthcare data are frequently skewed because of social inequalities and prejudices. If Generative AI is not rigorously controlled and mitigated, it might reinforce or worsen these prejudices. Preventing unintended effects and guaranteeing equitable healthcare delivery depend on maintaining justice and equity in the creation of healthcare data and m maintaining justice and equity in the creation of healthcare data and models.
6. **Regulatory Compliance:** Applications of Generative AI in healthcare must abide by laws pertaining to data protection, software, and medical devices. Healthcare companies and AI developers have a big problem when attempting to innovate with generative AI technology while navigating the complicated regulatory environment.

7. **Data Scarcity and Imbalance**: These two issues are frequently present in several healthcare areas, such as uncommon illnesses or specialised medical imaging modalities. Such datasets may be too diverse for generative models to fully represent, which would restrict their performance and generalizability. For generative models to be effective in these fields, methods for addressing data imbalance and scarcity must be developed.
8. **Healthcare Validation and Adoption:** Generative AI models takes lot of time and resources to validate the efficiency and safety of for usage in healthcare settings. Adoption by healthcare providers and regulatory approval depend on proving the clinical value, safety, and dependability of produced data and AI-driven insights through thorough validation studies and clinical trials.
9. **Generalization and Transfer Learning:** Generative AI models trained on a specific dataset or domain may not exhibit good generalisation capabilities when applied to different datasets or clinical environments. Transfer learning methods can adapt already trained models for unique healthcare scenarios. However, there are still obstacles to overcome in terms of domain adaptation, data heterogeneity, and model robustness. It is essential to provide techniques for successful transfer learning and domain adaptation in the healthcare field in order to implement generative AI solutions in various clinical applications.
10. **Ethical and Regulatory Considerations:** Ethical and regulatory considerations arise when dealing with Generative AI due to issues around privacy, bias, fairness, and responsibility. Healthcare artificial intelligence (AI) systems must adhere to rules, such as the Health Insurance Portability and Accountability Act (HIPAA), in order to guarantee the privacy and security of patient data. To tackle ethical and regulatory difficulties, it is necessary to establish clear and open governance frameworks, implement strong data governance regulations, and foster multidisciplinary collaboration among healthcare, ethics, and legal professional

OPPORTUNITIES OF GENERATIVE AI IN HEALTHCARE INDUSTRY

Table 1. Opportunities of generative ai in healthcare industry

Opportunity	How Generative AI Contributes	Where it Manifests in Healthcare
Medical Image Generation and Augmentation	Generates synthetic medical images	Pathology, Radiology, medical imaging research

Opportunity	How Generative AI Contributes	Where it Manifests in Healthcare
Drug Discovery and Development	Generates novel molecular structures	drug development, Pharmaceutical research,
Personalized Medicine	Analyzes patient data to generate personalized treatment plans	Oncology, Precision medicine,, chronic disease management
Clinical Decision Support Systems	Generates recommendations for diagnosis and treatment planning	Healthcare analytics, Clinical decision support systems,
Medical Text Generation and Summarization	Automatically generates medical reports and clinical notes	clinical documentation, Electronic health records (EHR),
Healthcare Chatbots and Virtual Assistants	Interacts with patients to provide medical advice and assistance	patient engagement solutions, Telemedicine platforms,
Disease Modeling and Simulation	Simulates disease progression and patient outcomes	public health planning, Epidemiological research,
Data Synthesis and Privacy Preservation	Generates synthetic healthcare data while preserving privacy	data anonymization techniques, Data sharing for research,

CONCLUSION

The field of healthcare might be significantly transformed by Generative AI, which provides a chances to enhance the patient care, expedite procedures, and further medical research. To reach its maximum potential, though, its integration into healthcare systems also brings with it a number of difficulties.

Generative AI presents a number of opportunities, chief among them being the production of artificial data that may supplement scarce datasets, aid in the training of machine learning models, and provide privacy protection. Improved patient outcomes, tailored therapy suggestions, and early illness identification may result from the development of more reliable and accurate prediction models.

Furthermore, realistic medical pictures may be produced using generative AI techniques like GANs and VAEs, which can help with surgical planning, medical education, and diagnostic medical imaging. These developments have the potential to completely transform clinical practice by giving doctors better tools for making decisions and raising the standard of patient care.

Furthermore, via the creation of novel chemical structures, the prediction of drug-target interactions, and the optimisation of drug design procedures, generative models can aid in the discovery and development of new drugs. This has the potential to decrease expenses, quicken the speed of drug discovery, and eventually result in the creation of more potent treatments for a range of illnesses.

But there are also a lot of obstacles that need to be overcome before generative AI is widely used in the healthcare industry. These obstacles include ethical concerns, privacy issues with data, legal restrictions, and the requirement for reliable validation and interpretability of produced outputs. Collaboration amongst stakeholders, including researchers, medical experts, legislators, and regulatory bodies, will be necessary to address these issues.

Looking ahead, generative AI has a bright future in the medical field. We may anticipate further breakthroughs that enhance patient care, advance medical research, and eventually improve global health outcomes as long as technology and this field's research continue to grow. Through the effective management of generative AI's obstacles and utilisation of its potential, we can create a future in healthcare that is more efficient, accessible, and tailored to each individual.

REFERENCES

Arora, A., & Arora, A. (2022). Generative adversarial networks and synthetic patient data: Current challenges and future perspectives. *Future Healthcare Journal*, 9(2), 190–193. 10.7861/fhj.2022-001335928184

Choi, E., Biswal, S., Malin, B., Duke, J., Stewart, W. F., & Sun, J. (2017, November). Generating multi-label discrete patient records using generative adversarial networks. In *Machine learning for healthcare conference* (pp. 286–305). PMLR.

Goodfellow, Pouget-Abadie, Mirza, Xu, Warde-Farley, & Ozair. (2014). *Generative adversarial networks*. Academic Press.

Jadon, A., & Kumar, S. (2023). Leveraging Generative AI Models for Synthetic Data Generation in Healthcare: Balancing Research and Privacy. *2023 International Conference on Smart Applications, Communications and Networking (SmartNets)*, 1-4. 10.1109/SmartNets58706.2023.10215825

Spector-Bagdady, K. (2023). Generative-AI-Generated Challenges for Health Data Research. *The American Journal of Bioethics*, 23(10), 1–5. 10.1080/15265161.2023.225231137831940

Zhang, P., & Boulos, M. (2023). Generative AI in Medicine and Healthcare: Promises, Opportunities and Challenges. *Future Internet*, 15(9), 286. Advance online publication. 10.3390/fi15090286

Chapter 5
Navigating the Promise and Perils of Generative AI in Healthcare

Shenson Joseph
https://orcid.org/0009-0001-5191-5556
Texas Tech University, USA

Qurat Ul-Ain
University of Agriculture, Faisalabad, Pakistan

Sidra Nosheen
University of Agriculture, Faisalabad, Pakistan

Munir Ahmad
https://orcid.org/0000-0003-4836-6151
Survey of Pakistan, Pakistan

Rida Fatima
https://orcid.org/0009-0003-4867-6245
Comsats University, Islamabad, Pakistan

ABSTRACT

Generative AI offers transformative potential in healthcare, enabling advancements from data augmentation to drug discovery. However, its adoption poses ethical, technical, and regulatory hurdles. Issues like bias, data privacy, and ethical use necessitate responsible implementation. Stakeholders must collaborate to navigate these challenges, prioritizing ethical guidelines, robust security measures, and regulatory compliance. Education is crucial to ensure awareness and equip stakeholders to make informed decisions. By fostering trust and accountability, generative AI

DOI: 10.4018/979-8-3693-3731-8.ch005

can revolutionize healthcare responsibly.

INTRODUCTION

In the ever-evolving landscape of healthcare, the integration of artificial intelligence (AI) stands as a pivotal force driving transformative change. The exponential growth of AI technologies has catalyzed a paradigm shift in healthcare delivery, offering unprecedented opportunities to enhance patient outcomes, streamline workflows, and revolutionize clinical decision-making. From accelerating diagnostic processes to facilitating personalized treatment plans, the potential applications of AI in healthcare are vast and multifaceted.

Generative AI, a paradigm that empowers machines to generate new content based on learned patterns from existing data. The integration of generative AI in healthcare emerges as a promising avenue for innovation and advancement. Generative AI technologies have garnered increasing attention for their ability to generate synthetic data, create medical images, and support various facets of medical research. However, as with any disruptive technology, the adoption of generative AI in healthcare necessitates a critical examination of its potential implications, both positive and negative.

Generative AI has the potential to revolutionize medical imaging by creating new, realistic images for better diagnosis and research. It can be used to create more training data for AI models, translate images from one type of scan to another, improve image resolution, and even remove artifacts caused by low radiation doses. However, training these AI models requires a lot of computing power and there are no clear rules yet on how to handle data privacy and who owns the rights to the generated images. Additionally, since medical image analysis can have a big impact on patients' lives, it's essential that these AI-generated images are very accurate (Goyal & Kaushal, 2024). Moreover, generative AI has the potential to revolutionize healthcare by improving diagnosis, treatment, and decision-making through tasks like drug discovery, analyzing medical images, and personalizing medicine. Reddy (2024) argued that careful planning and responsible development are crucial to address ethical concerns, data privacy, and ensure successful integration into healthcare workflows. Frameworks like TAM and NASSS can guide this process, while considering clinician expertise and potential challenges.

Sai et al. (2024) explored the potential of generative artificial intelligence (GAI) in transforming healthcare. The authors argued that GAI can generate new data formats like images and text based on existing information. GAI can be used for simulating diseases to aid in research, analyzing medical images to support diagnosis, personalizing treatment plans, designing prosthetics, and even providing educational materials and chatbots for patient care. The authors also noted that limitations exist in the use of GAI in healthcare such as the need for large amounts of data to train the models, difficulty in understanding how the models work (lack of interpretability), and the necessity for regulatory oversight to ensure safe and ethical use in healthcare. Similarly, Chen & Esmaeilzadeh (2024) noted that while this technology has the potential to improve patient outcomes and accelerate medical discoveries, it also creates opportunities for malicious actors to exploit this data if not properly protected. The authors have explored these challenges throughout the development and implementation of generative AI systems, including data collection, model development, and implementation.

ChatGPT, an example of generative AI, has the potential to be a multifaceted tool in medicine, assisting with tasks like analyzing data to improve diagnoses and treatments, providing quick access to medical information for patients and professionals, and even aiding in medical education. It can also be a boon for evidence-based medicine by analyzing vast datasets and surfacing the most effective treatments (de Souza et al., 2023). The authors endorsed that ChatGPT has limitations, such as the inability to perform physical exams or navigate complex medical situations. Additionally, ethical concerns around bias, misinformation, and data privacy need to be addressed before widespread adoption of generative AI like ChatGPT in healthcare.

Against this backdrop, this chapter seeks to provide a comprehensive overview of the multifaceted landscape surrounding generative AI in healthcare. By fostering a holistic understanding of the opportunities and challenges inherent in the convergence of generative AI and healthcare, this chapter aims to empower stakeholders with the knowledge and insights necessary to navigate this dynamic landscape effectively.

UNDERSTANDING GENERATIVE AI

Generative AI represents a pioneering subset of artificial intelligence (AI) that possesses the remarkable ability to create novel content autonomously. Unlike traditional AI systems that primarily focus on processing and interpreting existing data, generative AI transcends these limitations by actively generating new information that mirrors the underlying patterns and characteristics of the data it has been trained on. At its core, generative AI operates on the principle of learning from examples to produce content that exhibits coherence, realism, and fidelity to the underlying data distribution. This is achieved through the utilization of advanced algorithms and techniques that enable machines to understand and mimic the inherent structure and complexity of the data they encounter.

Generative AI differs from other forms of AI, such as discriminative AI, in terms of its primary objective and mode of operation. While discriminative AI focuses on distinguishing between different classes or categories within a dataset, generative AI is concerned with generating new data points that are indistinguishable from those in the original dataset. This fundamental distinction underscores the unique capabilities and potential applications of generative AI in various domains, including image generation, text synthesis, and data augmentation. Moreover, generative AI has the capacity to generate content that goes beyond mere replication of existing data points. Instead, generative AI algorithms have the ability to produce entirely new instances of data that possess novel combinations of features and characteristics, thereby expanding the scope of possibilities beyond what is present in the training dataset.

Generative AI techniques often involve the utilization of complex neural network architectures, such as generative adversarial networks (GANs) and variational autoencoders (VAEs), which enable machines to learn and mimic the underlying distribution of data in a high-dimensional space. By iteratively refining their representations of the data through training, generative AI models can generate increasingly realistic and diverse content that captures the complexity and variability present in the original dataset.

Generative Adversarial Networks (GANs)

GANs consist of two neural networks – a generator and a discriminator – that engage in a competitive process to generate realistic data. The generator aims to create synthetic data samples that are indistinguishable from real data, while the discriminator aims to distinguish between real and generated data. Through iterative training, GANs learn to generate increasingly realistic content, making them well-suited for tasks such as image generation and data augmentation.

Variational Autoencoders (VAEs)

VAEs are probabilistic models that learn to encode and decode data in a lower-dimensional latent space. They consist of an encoder network that maps input data to a latent space and a decoder network that reconstructs the input data from the latent representation. VAEs enable the generation of diverse and novel data samples by sampling from the learned latent space, making them useful for tasks such as image generation and data synthesis.

Recurrent Neural Networks (RNNs)

RNNs are a class of neural networks designed to handle sequential data by maintaining internal state or memory. They are commonly used in generative AI applications such as natural language processing (NLP) and music composition, where the output depends on the previous inputs and the network's internal state.

Transformer Models

Transformer models, such as the popular GPT (Generative Pre-trained Transformer) series, have revolutionized the field of natural language processing (NLP) and text generation. These models use self-attention mechanisms to capture long-range dependencies in input sequences and generate coherent and contextually relevant text.

POTENTIAL BENEFITS OF GENERATIVE AI IN HEALTHCARE

Generative AI holds immense promise for revolutionizing healthcare across multiple dimensions. Some potential benefits of integrating generative AI into healthcare are depicted in Figure 1 and described below.

Tabular Data Synthesis

Generative AI techniques can generate synthetic data to augment existing healthcare datasets, addressing issues related to data scarcity and imbalance. By creating additional data samples that closely mimic the characteristics of real patient data, generative AI can improve the robustness and generalization of machine learning models trained on limited datasets. For example, Umer & Adnan (2024) noted that generative artificial intelligence techniques, including Variational Autoencoders (VAEs), Generative Adversarial Networks (GANs), and diffusion models, present promising solutions to the challenges encountered in generating diverse and privacy-compliant datasets for training Deep Learning (DL) models in healthcare, particularly in dentistry. They argued that traditional datasets face obstacles such as data privacy regulations, extensive manual annotation requirements, and biases, hampering their scalability and generalizability. However, generative AI techniques offer avenues for producing Synthetic Datasets (SDs) that address these challenges. VAEs employ probabilistic techniques to generate synthetic data, GANs utilize adversarial training to produce realistic images, and diffusion models employ noise addition and removal to create new data. While SDs offer opportunities, but challenges like patient confidentiality, lack of standardized evaluation metrics, biases, and the production of false data necessitate careful mitigation strategies and AI governance for responsible implementation in healthcare.

Similarly, Li et al. (2023) developed a novel Generative Adversarial Network (GAN) model called EHR-M-GAN to generate synthetic but realistic data for AI applications. They tested the model on ICU datasets, the model excels in generating continuous and discrete timeseries data, capturing correlations and temporal dynamics effectively. By utilizing a kernel function and dual-VAE module, EHR-M-GAN surpasses existing benchmarks, showcasing enhanced privacy protection and improved downstream task outcomes. Its ability to model correlations between different types of timeseries data, as demonstrated through metrics like Pearson pairwise correlation, offers promise for data augmentation and classifier performance enhancement. Moreover, Inan et al. (2023) explored the use of deep generative models like the Tabular Variational Autoencoder (TVAE) and Conditional Generative Adversarial Network (CTGAN) to generate synthetic tabular data related to breast tumors for breast cancer classification. The research showed that the TVAE model excels in producing high-quality synthetic data compared to the CTGAN model, and the TabNet architecture proves superior among various machine-learning and deep-learning classifiers. The study emphasized the significance of synthetic data in AI research and the need for interpretable deep-learning models in the medical field, particularly for breast cancer diagnosis and prognosis.

Sharing electronic health records (EHR) data is essential for using Artificial Intelligence (AI) to improve medical research. However, legal and ethical concerns around patient privacy make sharing real EHR data difficult. Yoon et al. (2020) proposed a new method called ADS-GAN to address this challenge. ADS-GAN uses a technique called Generative Adversarial Networks (GANs) to create synthetic data that replicates the statistical properties of real patient data but protects patient identities. ADS-GAN incorporates a quantifiable definition of patient identifiability based on the likelihood of re-identification. The study showed that models trained on synthetic data generated by ADS-GAN perform similarly to models trained on real data, demonstrating the effectiveness of this method.

Medical Image Synthesis

Generative AI algorithms, such as GANs, can generate synthetic medical images with varying pathologies or imaging modalities. This capability is particularly valuable for training and validating medical imaging analysis algorithms, as it allows researchers to create diverse datasets representing different clinical scenarios without the need for extensive manual labeling. This is particularly useful when obtaining large amounts of real medical data is difficult or unethical. GANs work through two neural networks: a generator network that creates new data samples and discriminator network that determines if the samples are real or fake. This process is repeated until the generator network can produce synthetic data indistinguishable from genuine data. While promising in medical image analysis, GANs are still under research to ensure the quality of generated images for clinical applications (Biswas et al., 2023).

In the realm of cardiology, AI also showed promise in medical imaging applications. For example, Olender et al. (2021) introduced introduce a platform utilizing AI to create realistic images based on physiological tissue morphology, offering valuable support for diagnosis and treatment. Additionally, the platform can facilitate the translation between different imaging modalities, incorporate diverse information sources, and reconstruct images with reduced noise. The authors stressed the importance of fostering collaboration between clinical and technical communities to fully harness the capabilities of this technology. Similarly, Xu et al. (2023) used generative adversarial networks to create high-quality, synthetic MRI images of prostate cancer. These images were so realistic that even medical professionals struggled to tell them apart from real ones. This success in creating indistinguishable synthetic images paves the way for future applications in anomaly detection and machine learning for prostate cancer research.

Ali et al. (2022) explored how generative adversarial networks are revolutionizing brain MRI analysis. They noted that GANs can generate synthetic MRI data to improve AI methods, and be directly used for tasks like tumor segmentation and image enhancement. The authors highlighted the potential of GANs in brain MRI analysis, including data generation, segmentation, diagnosis, image reconstruction, and disease progression prediction. They also noted challenges including evaluation metrics, generalizability of AI models, and collaboration between researchers and clinicians.

Personalized Treatment Planning

Generative AI can support the development of personalized treatment plans by analyzing patient data and generating tailored recommendations based on individual health profiles, medical history, and treatment outcomes. By leveraging patient-specific data and predictive modeling techniques, generative AI can assist healthcare providers in optimizing treatment strategies and improving patient outcomes. For example, Goktas et al. (2023) explored the potential of AI chatbots like ChatGPT 4.0 to revolutionize allergy and immunology practice. They asserted that AI chatbots hold promise for improved communication, diagnosis, treatment plans, and documentation in clinics. However, challenges including data privacy, ensuring reliable AI outputs, and ethical considerations need to be addressed. They also reasoned that collaboration between AI developers and medical professionals is key to safely and effectively using AI chatbots to enhance patient care while maintaining ethical standards.

Lawry (2023) asserted that generative AI revolutionizing precision medicine by assisting with tasks like writing medical notes and suggesting treatment plans. It also has the potential to improve drug discovery and development by analyzing patient data to create personalized treatments, all while working collaboratively with doctors. Bečulić et al. (2024) argued that despite promising applications in neurosurgery like personalized treatment plans and education, challenges of reliability, ethics, and bias exist. While ChatGPT showed potential in areas like treatment recommendations and documentation, accuracy limitations require cautious use. Additionally, AI offered potential for personalized medicine and improved communication between doctors and patients, but ethical considerations remain paramount.

Drug Discovery and Development

Generative AI techniques are increasingly being applied in drug discovery and molecular design to accelerate the identification of novel therapeutic compounds. By generating virtual chemical structures and predicting their properties, generative AI models can assist in the design of new drug candidates with optimized efficacy and safety profiles, thereby expediting the drug development process. For example, digital twins of organs, cells, and even entire patients can now be created, allowing researchers to predict how patients might respond to drugs. This could significantly reduce reliance on animal testing and improve the design of clinical trials. Generative AI can can support the development of digital twin, however, challenges regarding interpretability and regulations remain, but generative AI holds immense potential for the future of drug development and clinical trials (Bordukova et al., 2024). Similarly, Wang et al. (2023) explored the potential of ChatGPT to aid in discovering new drugs to treat cocaine addiction. They noted that ChatGPT can analyze massive scientific databases to find relevant information, propose new research avenues, and even help design experiments.

Clinical Text Generation

Generative AI models, such as transformer-based language models, can generate clinical notes, medical reports, and patient summaries based on input data such as electronic health records (EHRs) and medical imaging findings. This capability streamlines documentation processes, reduces administrative burden on healthcare professionals, and improves the accuracy and consistency of clinical documentation. For example, Au Yeung et al. (2023) highlighted the advancements in Large Language Models (LLMs) and their potential applications in healthcare, emphasizing the emergence of specialized models like GatorTron for healthcare-specific tasks. The comparison between ChatGPT and Foresight in forecasting relevant diagnoses based on clinical vignettes sheds light on the performance and nuances of different approaches to generative pretrained transformers. Authors also delved into the capabilities and limitations of these models in handling clinical data and providing accurate predictions.

Patient Education and Engagement

Generative AI-powered chatbots and virtual assistants can provide personalized health education, answer patient queries, and offer support for self-management of chronic conditions. By leveraging natural language processing (NLP) techniques, these virtual agents can deliver tailored information and guidance, empowering patients to make informed decisions about their health and well-being. For example, AI-powered chatbots hold promise for improving kidney transplant care by assisting with decision-making, communication, and efficiency throughout the process. Healthcare professionals could leverage chatbots as clinical decision support tools for real-time access to medical information, while patients could benefit from educational resources and guidance on pre- and post-transplant care, including medication management. Additionally, chatbots have the potential to integrate with existing healthcare systems to improve risk assessment and treatment planning for transplants (Garcia Valencia et al., 2023).

Disease Modeling and Prediction

Generative AI can help in modeling and predicting disease progression, treatment outcomes, and population health trends by analyzing large-scale healthcare data. By identifying patterns and correlations within complex datasets, generative AI models can assist researchers and healthcare providers in forecasting disease trends, allocating resources effectively, and implementing targeted interventions to mitigate health risks. For example, Mardikoraem et al. (2023) outlined the critical role of machine learning (ML) methods, particularly self-supervised and unsupervised techniques, in leveraging large-scale protein sequence data for various protein engineering tasks. Authors asserted that despite the abundance of sequence data, the lack of experimental annotations necessitates the use of ML to extract meaningful features and navigate the protein fitness landscape effectively.

Similarly, James et al. (2023) discussed the challenges in classifying missense variants in the low-density lipoprotein receptor (LDLR) due to its complex structure and function. Authors highlighted the use of deep generative models such as Evolutionary model of Variant Effect (EVE), Evolutionary Scale Modeling (ESM), and AlphaFold 2 (AF2) to predict protein structure and function, particularly in the context of LDLR variants. AF2, ESM, and EVE are evaluated for their effectiveness in predicting variant pathogenicity compared to established methods. According to the analysis, AF2 predicts LDLR structures and estimates variant effects by assessing changes in stability, while ESM and EVE directly estimate the likelihood of variant sequences, though they are challenging to interpret. The study also found that AF2 poorly performs in predicting variant pathogenicity compared to ESM and EVE. While EVE and ESM show comparable performance to established methods like Polyphen-2, SIFT, REVEL, and Primate AI in binary classifications from ClinVar, they exhibit stronger correlations with experimental measures of LDL uptake. Additionally, ESM and EVE demonstrated stronger associations with clinical phenotypes such as serum LDL-C levels and atherosclerotic cardiovascular disease compared to traditional scoring methods.

Figure 1. Potential Benefits of Generative AI in Healthcare

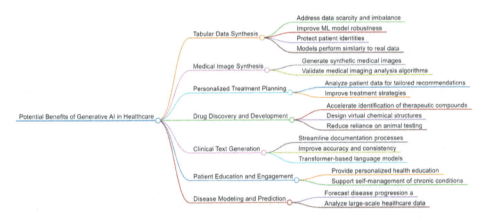

RISKS AND CHALLENGES OF GENERATIVE AI IN HEALTHCARE

While generative AI holds significant promise for advancing healthcare, its adoption also presents several risks and challenges that need to be carefully considered. Some of the key risks and challenges associated with generative AI in healthcare are depicted in Figure 2 and elaborated below.

as and Fairness

AI bias refers to prejudiced results reflecting societal biases in data, algorithms or predictions. Sources of AI bias may include training data, algorithms and cognitive bias from developers (IBM, 2023). The issue of algorithmic bias within the healthcare sector is longstanding. It stems from deep-seated power dynamics entrenched in systems of White supremacy, patriarchy, cisheteronormativity, and colonialism, shaping both the historical trajectory of healthcare and its present-day manifestations (Benjamin, 2019). However, Walker et al. (2023) argued that algorithmic bias serves as a mere symptom of a broader and enduring issue: power disparities concerning the inception, advancement, and application of healthcare technologies.

Generative AI models can inadvertently perpetuate biases present in the training data (Golda et al., 2024), that can lead to unfair or discriminatory outcomes, particularly in healthcare contexts. Biases in healthcare data, such as disparities in disease prevalence across demographic groups, can be amplified by generative AI algorithms, potentially exacerbating existing health inequities. For example, generative AI can misrepresent women and minorities in criminal justice portrayals. These biases could lead to real-world consequences, from unfair treatment based on AI-generated suspect sketches to the perpetuation of stereotypes in advertising and media. Furthermore, the problematic training data used by AI models creates a snowball effect, where biases present in existing data are amplified as AI creates new data (Leonardo & Dina, 2023).

Data Privacy and Security

The rapid growth of AI in healthcare raises privacy concerns, as private companies holding much health data face security risks. Additionally, public-private partnerships on AI may have weak privacy protections, highlighting the need for new regulations to address data security, patient control, and the ability of AI to re-identify anonymized health data. This is further emphasized by data breaches as a major risk and the need for new anonymization methods (Murdoch, 2021). For example, AI is revolutionizing drug discovery by making the process faster and cheaper, while also reducing reliance on animal testing. This approach is already showing promise with several AI-developed compounds reaching clinical trials. However, challenges remain, such as ensuring the accuracy of data used to train AI models and incorporating human expertise in the later stages of drug development (Hasselgren & Oprea, 2024).

The generation and utilization of synthetic patient data by generative AI algorithms raise concerns about data privacy and security. Synthetic data may inadvertently reveal sensitive information about individuals, posing risks to patient confidentiality and privacy. Additionally, there is a risk of unauthorized access or misuse of synthetic data, leading to breaches of patient confidentiality and data security. Chen & Esmaeilzadeh (2024) argued that generative AI has security and privacy risks because it uses a lot of data. It's important to be careful about how this data is collected and used so that patient privacy is protected. Attackers may potentially use generative models to steal sensitive information. Synthetic data could be misused to create deepfakes that violate patient privacy Even de-identified data may be vulnerable to re-identification attacks (Golda et al., 2024).

Ethical Use of AI-generated Content

The ethical implications of using AI-generated content in healthcare, such as synthetic medical images or clinical text, must be carefully considered. Healthcare professionals have a responsibility to ensure the accuracy, reliability, and safety of AI-generated content, as errors or inaccuracies could have serious consequences for patient care and clinical decision-making (Golda et al., 2024).

Regulatory Compliance

The use of generative AI in healthcare may raise regulatory challenges related to compliance with existing regulations and standards, such as the Health Insurance Portability and Accountability Act (HIPAA) in the United States. Ensuring that generative AI applications adhere to regulatory requirements for data privacy, security, and patient consent is essential to mitigate legal and compliance risks. Chen & Esmaeilzadeh (2024) asserted that regulatory issues may include copyright for AI-generated content and lack of human control over AI behavior.

Interpretability and Transparency

Generative AI models are often complex and difficult to interpret, making it challenging to understand how they generate content and why certain decisions are made. Lack of interpretability and transparency can undermine trust in AI-generated outputs and hinder the adoption of generative AI technologies in healthcare settings. Chen & Esmaeilzadeh (2024) asserted that generative AI models can be difficult to understand because of their complex decision making. This can make it hard for doctors to trust the recommendations these models make. There needs to be more research on how to make generative AI models more transparent.

alidation and Reliability

Validating the reliability and accuracy of AI-generated content, such as synthetic medical images or diagnostic predictions, is essential for ensuring patient safety and clinical efficacy. Generative AI models must undergo rigorous testing and validation processes to demonstrate their performance and generalizability across diverse patient populations and clinical scenarios. For example, Chen & Esmaeilzadeh (2024) asserted that generative AI can be used to spread misinformation in healthcare. Malicious actors could manipulate the model to generate fake medical advice or research findings. This could lead to patients making poor decisions about their health

Malicious Use and Adversarial Attacks

Generative AI algorithms are vulnerable to adversarial attacks, where malicious actors manipulate input data to produce unintended or harmful outputs. In healthcare, adversarial attacks on generative AI models could lead to misdiagnosis, treatment errors, or other adverse clinical outcomes, highlighting the importance of robust security measures and safeguards against malicious use. For example, Chen & Esmaeilzadeh (2024) stated that generative AI models in healthcare can be vulnerable to hacking. Attackers could steal sensitive information by hacking into the model or feeding it special prompts. This is a risk for all types of generative AI in healthcare, including medical diagnostics and drug discovery.

Figure 2. Risks and Challenges of Generative AI in Healthcare

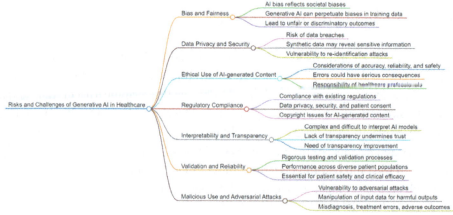

MITIGATING RISKS AND ENSURING RESPONSIBLE IMPLEMENTATION

Mitigating the risks associated with generative AI in healthcare and ensuring its responsible implementation require a multifaceted approach that encompasses ethical, technical, and regulatory considerations. Some to mitigate risks and ensure responsible implementation are elaborated below.

Ethical Guidelines and Frameworks

Develop and adhere to ethical guidelines and frameworks that govern the responsible use of generative AI in healthcare. These guidelines should address issues such as data privacy, fairness, transparency, accountability, and patient consent. Establishing ethical standards promotes trust, transparency, and accountability in the development and deployment of generative AI technologies (Golda et al., 2024).

Bias Detection and Mitigation

Implement measures to detect and mitigate biases in generative AI models to ensure fair and equitable outcomes. Conduct thorough bias assessments during model development and deployment to identify and address potential biases in training data and algorithms. Utilize techniques such as bias auditing, fairness-aware training, and post-processing algorithms to mitigate biases and promote fairness in AI-generated content. There is no one-size-fits-all solution, understanding fairness in context and mitigating bias across data, algorithms, and outputs is crucial. Furthermore, creators must be aware of their own biases and the need for social and legal solutions alongside technical ones (Ntoutsi et al., 2020).

Data Privacy and Security

Implement robust data privacy and security measures to protect patient confidentiality and mitigate the risk of unauthorized access or misuse of healthcare data. Adhere to established data protection regulations, such as HIPAA in the United States or the General Data Protection Regulation (GDPR) in the European Union, and employ encryption, access controls, and anonymization techniques to safeguard sensitive healthcare information. Moreover, Chen & Esmaeilzadeh (2024) argued that Generative Adversarial Networks can be used to improve privacy and security in healthcare. GANs can be used to simulate attack scenarios so researchers can develop better defenses. GANs can also be used to preprocess data before training make it more secure. Further, GANs can also be used to train models that don't reveal sensitive information.

Transparency and Interpretability

Enhance the transparency and interpretability of generative AI models to promote trust and facilitate understanding among healthcare professionals and patients. Provide explanations and visualizations that elucidate how generative AI models generate content and make decisions. Foster open dialogue and collaboration between AI researchers, healthcare professionals, and end-users to ensure that AI-generated outputs are interpretable and actionable.

Validation and Verification

Validate the reliability, accuracy, and safety of AI-generated content through rigorous testing and validation processes. Conduct comprehensive evaluations of generative AI models using diverse datasets and clinical scenarios to assess their performance and generalizability. Establish benchmarks and standards for evaluating generative AI models in healthcare and encourage transparency in reporting results and outcomes. Chen & Esmaeilzadeh (2024) reasoned that healthcare needs careful methods for collecting data to train generative AI. This includes separating clinical and non-clinical data and checking for biases. Data should also be checked for quality and authenticity to prevent attacks.

Regulatory Compliance

Ensure compliance with regulatory requirements and standards governing the use of AI in healthcare, such as HIPAA, GDPR, and regulatory guidelines issued by healthcare regulatory agencies. Work closely with regulatory bodies and policymakers to address regulatory gaps and develop guidelines tailored to the unique challenges and opportunities posed by generative AI in healthcare. There are different regulations for AI in the EU and US. For example, the EU AI Act is a legal framework with mandatory requirements for high-risk AI. Similarly, the US AI Bill of Rights is a non-binding set of principles that organizations can voluntarily adopt (Chen & Esmaeilzadeh, 2024).

Education and Training

Provide education and training programs for healthcare professionals, AI developers, and other stakeholders to increase awareness of the risks and benefits of generative AI in healthcare and promote responsible and ethical use. Equip healthcare professionals with the knowledge and skills necessary to critically evaluate AI-generated content, interpret results, and make informed decisions in clinical practice.

CONCLUSION

Generative AI holds immense potential for revolutionizing healthcare by enabling innovative solutions across various domains. From data augmentation and medical image synthesis to personalized treatment planning and drug discovery, generative AI offers unprecedented opportunities to enhance patient care, streamline workflows, and advance medical research.

However, the adoption of generative AI in healthcare also presents ethical, technical, and regulatory challenges that must be carefully navigated. Risks such as bias and fairness, data privacy and security concerns, and the ethical use of AI-generated content underscore the importance of responsible implementation and ethical practice.

Mitigating these risks requires a concerted effort from stakeholders across the healthcare ecosystem, including healthcare professionals, AI researchers, policymakers, and regulatory agencies. By adhering to ethical guidelines, implementing robust data privacy and security measures, enhancing transparency and interpretability, and ensuring regulatory compliance, stakeholders can foster trust, accountability, and responsible innovation in the deployment of generative AI technologies.

Furthermore, education and training programs are essential to increase awareness of the risks and benefits of generative AI in healthcare and equip stakeholders with the knowledge and skills necessary to make informed decisions and address emerging challenges.

REFERENCES

Ali, H., Biswas, R., Ali, F., Shah, U., Alamgir, A., Mousa, O., & Shah, Z. (2022). The role of generative adversarial networks in brain MRI: a scoping review. In *Insights into Imaging* (Vol. 13, Issue 1). 10.1186/s13244-022-01237-0

Au Yeung, J., Kraljevic, Z., Luintel, A., Balston, A., Idowu, E., Dobson, R. J., & Teo, J. T. (2023). AI chatbots not yet ready for clinical use. *Frontiers in Digital Health*, 5, 1161098. Advance online publication. 10.3389/fdgth.2023.116109837122812

Bečulić, H., Begagić, E., Skomorac, R., Mašović, A., Selimović, E., & Pojskić, M. (2024). ChatGPT's contributions to the evolution of neurosurgical practice and education: A systematic review of benefits, concerns and limitations. *Medicinski Glasnik*, 21(1). Advance online publication. 10.17392/1661-2337950660

Benjamin, R. (2019). *Race after technology: Abolitionist tools for the new Jim code*. John Wiley & Sons.

Biswas, A., Md Abdullah Al, N., Imran, A., Sejuty, A. T., Fairooz, F., Puppala, S., & Talukder, S. (2023). Generative Adversarial Networks for Data Augmentation. In *Data Driven Approaches on Medical Imaging*. 10.1007/978-3-031-47772-0_8

Bordukova, M., Makarov, N., Rodriguez-Esteban, R., Schmich, F., & Menden, M. P. (2024). Generative artificial intelligence empowers digital twins in drug discovery and clinical trials. In *Expert Opinion on Drug Discovery* (Vol. 19, Issue 1). 10.1080/17460441.2023.2273839

Chen, Y., & Esmaeilzadeh, P. (2024). Generative AI in Medical Practice: In-Depth Exploration of Privacy and Security Challenges. In *Journal of Medical Internet Research* (Vol. 26, Issue 1). 10.2196/53008

de Souza, L. L., Fonseca, F. P., Martins, M. D., de Almeida, O. P., Pontes, H. A. R., Coracin, F. L., Lopes, M. A., Khurram, S. A., Santos-Silva, A. R., Hagag, A., & Vargas, P. A. (2023). ChatGPT and medicine: a potential threat to science or a step towards the future? In *Journal of Medical Artificial Intelligence* (Vol. 6). 10.21037/jmai-23-70

Garcia Valencia, O. A., Thongprayoon, C., Jadlowiec, C. C., Mao, S. A., Miao, J., & Cheungpasitporn, W. (2023). Enhancing Kidney Transplant Care through the Integration of Chatbot. In *Healthcare (Switzerland)* (Vol. 11, Issue 18). 10.3390/healthcare11182518

Goktas, P., Karakaya, G., Kalyoncu, A. F., & Damadoglu, E. (2023). Artificial Intelligence Chatbots in Allergy and Immunology Practice: Where Have We Been and Where Are We Going? *The Journal of Allergy and Clinical Immunology. In Practice*, 11(9), 2697–2700. Advance online publication. 10.1016/j.jaip.2023.05.04237301435

Golda, A., Mekonen, K., Pandey, A., Singh, A., Hassija, V., Chamola, V., & Sikdar, B. (2024). Privacy and Security Concerns in Generative AI: A Comprehensive Survey. *IEEE Access : Practical Innovations, Open Solutions*, 12, 48126–48144. 10.1109/ACCESS.2024.3381611

Goyal, S., & Kaushal, L. (2024). Harnessing generative AI: Transformative applications in medical imaging and beyond. *Future Health*, 2, 21–33. Advance online publication. 10.25259/FH_12_2024

Hasselgren, C., & Oprea, T. I. (2024). Artificial Intelligence for Drug Discovery: Are We There Yet? In *Annual Review of Pharmacology and Toxicology* (Vol. 64). 10.1146/annurev-pharmtox-040323-040828

IBM. (2023). *Shedding light on AI bias with real world examples*. https://www.ibm.com/blog/shedding-light-on-ai-bias-with-real-world-examples/

Inan, M. S. K., Hossain, S., & Uddin, M. N. (2023). Data augmentation guided breast cancer diagnosis and prognosis using an integrated deep-generative framework based on breast tumor's morphological information. *Informatics in Medicine Unlocked*, 37, 101171. Advance online publication. 10.1016/j.imu.2023.101171

James, J. K., Norland, K., Johar, A. S., & Kullo, I. J. (2023). Deep generative models of LDLR protein structure to predict variant pathogenicity. *Journal of Lipid Research*, 64(12), 100455. Advance online publication. 10.1016/j.jlr.2023.10045537821076

Lawry, T. (2023). Generative AI and Precision Medicine—The Future Is Not What It Used to Be. *Inside. Precision Medicine*, 10(5), 40–41, 43, 44, 45. Advance online publication. 10.1089/ipm.10.05.08

Leonardo, N., & Dina, B. (2023). *Generative AI Takes Stereotypes and Bias From Bad to Worse*. https://www.bloomberg.com/graphics/2023-generative-ai-bias/

Li, J., Cairns, B. J., Li, J., & Zhu, T. (2023). Generating synthetic mixed-type longitudinal electronic health records for artificial intelligent applications. *NPJ Digital Medicine*, 6(1), 98. Advance online publication. 10.1038/s41746-023-00834-737244963

Mardikoraem, M., Wang, Z., Pascual, N., & Woldring, D. (2023). Generative models for protein sequence modeling: recent advances and future directions. In *Briefings in Bioinformatics* (Vol. 24, Issue 6). 10.1093/bib/bbad358

Murdoch, B. (2021). Privacy and artificial intelligence: Challenges for protecting health information in a new era. *BMC Medical Ethics*, 22(1), 122. Advance online publication. 10.1186/s12910-021-00687-334525993

Ntoutsi, E., Fafalios, P., Gadiraju, U., Iosifidis, V., Nejdl, W., Vidal, M. E., Ruggieri, S., Turini, F., Papadopoulos, S., Krasanakis, E., Kompatsiaris, I., Kinder-Kurlanda, K., Wagner, C., Karimi, F., Fernandez, M., Alani, H., Berendt, B., Kruegel, T., Heinze, C., & Staab, S. (2020). Bias in data-driven artificial intelligence systems—An introductory survey. *Wiley Interdisciplinary Reviews. Data Mining and Knowledge Discovery*, 10(3), e1356. Advance online publication. 10.1002/widm.1356

Olender, M. L., De La Torre Hernández, J. M., Athanasiou, L. S., Nezami, F. R., & Edelman, E. R. (2021). Artificial intelligence to generate medical images: Augmenting the cardiologist's visual clinical workflow. *European Heart Journal. Digital Health*, 2(3), 539–544. Advance online publication. 10.1093/ehjdh/ztab05236713593

Reddy, S. (2024). Generative AI in healthcare: An implementation science informed translational path on application, integration and governance. *Implementation Science : IS*, 19(1), 27. 10.1186/s13012-024-01357-938491544

Sai, S., Gaur, A., Sai, R., Chamola, V., Guizani, M., & Rodrigues, J. J. P. C. (2024). Generative AI for Transformative Healthcare: A Comprehensive Study of Emerging Models, Applications, Case Studies, and Limitations. *IEEE Access : Practical Innovations, Open Solutions*, 12, 31078–31106. Advance online publication. 10.1109/ACCESS.2024.3367715

Umer, F., & Adnan, N. (2024). Generative artificial intelligence: synthetic datasets in dentistry. In *BDJ Open* (Vol. 10, Issue 1). 10.1038/s41405-024-00198-4

Walker, R., Dillard-Wright, J., & Iradukunda, F. (2023). Algorithmic bias in artificial intelligence is a problem—And the root issue is power. *Nursing Outlook*, 71(5), 102023. Advance online publication. 10.1016/j.outlook.2023.10202337579574

Wang, R., Feng, H., & Wei, G. W. (2023). ChatGPT in Drug Discovery: A Case Study on Anticocaine Addiction Drug Development with Chatbots. *Journal of Chemical Information and Modeling*, 63(22), 7189–7209. Advance online publication. 10.1021/acs.jcim.3c0142937956228

Xu, I. R. L., Van Booven, D. J., Goberdhan, S., Breto, A., Porto, J., Alhusseini, M., Algohary, A., Stoyanova, R., Punnen, S., Mahne, A., & Arora, H. (2023). Generative Adversarial Networks Can Create High Quality Artificial Prostate Cancer Magnetic Resonance Images. *Journal of Personalized Medicine*, 13(3), 547. Advance online publication. 10.3390/jpm1303054736983728

Yoon, J., Drumright, L. N., & Van Der Schaar, M. (2020). Anonymization through data synthesis using generative adversarial networks (ADS-GAN). *IEEE Journal of Biomedical and Health Informatics*, 24(8), 2378–2388. Advance online publication. 10.1109/JBHI.2020.298026232167919

Chapter 6
Exploring Augmented Reality, Virtual Reality, and Machine Learning for Delivering Better Value in the Healthcare Sector

Zeenal Punamiya
 https://orcid.org/0000-0002-7829-1165
Chitkara School of Health Sciences, Chitkara University, Punjab, India

Navita Gupta
 https://orcid.org/0000-0002-4163-6406
Chitkara School of Health Sciences, Chitkara University, Punjab, India

Sagar Anil Patil
D.Y. Patil University, Navi Mumbai, India

ABSTRACT

Technological advancements have revolutionized the field of healthcare by offering innovative methods to enhance patient care. With changing demands, it is essential to align them with current advancements. Thus, we explore the strategic utilization of advanced technologies like Artificial Intelligence (AI), Augmented Reality (AR), Virtual Reality (VR), and Machine Learning (ML) to deliver better healthcare. The current challenges are vast and integration of such technologies can help in solving the pain points. Some applications include AR for medical training and surgery, VR for pain relief and patient education, ML for image analysis and predictive analytics, AI for clinical decision support, and process optimization. As we highlight the role

DOI: 10.4018/979-8-3693-3731-8.ch006

Copyright © 2024, IGI Global. Copying or distributing in print or electronic forms without written permission of IGI Global is prohibited.

of technology in healthcare, addressing ethical and regulatory considerations is essential to navigate challenges and guide future implementation directions. Thus, embracing these technologies positively can enhance healthcare value delivery.

INTRODUCTION:

The healthcare industry is facing a multitude of challenges, including rising costs, inefficiencies in care delivery, and disparities in access to quality healthcare services. These challenges are further compounded by an aging population, the increasing prevalence of chronic diseases, and the COVID-19 pandemic. In this context, there is a growing recognition of the need for innovative solutions to improve the efficiency, effectiveness, and affordability of healthcare services. In recent years, various fields have witnessed a rapid boom of technological advancements.

Evolution and History of AI: Christopher Strachey developed the first AI program in 1951. It was at its beginning stage and considered an academic research topic. John McCarthy conducted the Dartmouth Conference in late 1956, where he proposed the term "Artificial Intelligence". Since then, began the era of modern AI (Alowais et al., 2023). During the 1960s and 1970s, AI research highlighted rule-based and expert systems. However, the effectiveness of this method was constrained by the requirement for increased computing resources and data. With advancing years (in the 1980s and 1990s), AI research transitioned to Machine Learning (ML) and Neural Networks. ML and Neural Networks enable machines to learn from existing data and enhance their performance progressively. The developments that happened in this tenure, gave rise to systems such as "IBM Deep Blue". It gained popularity in 1997 when it defeated the great champion, Garry Kasparov. In the 2000s, further research in AI focused on fields such as Computer Vision and Natural Language Processing (NLP). The best examples of AI Virtual assistants are "Siri by Apple" and "Alexa by Amazon". These assistants can understand natural human language and respond to questions (Alowais et al., 2023).

Exploring Augmented Reality, Virtual Reality, and Machine Learning for Delivering

Figure 1. History and Evolution of Artificial Intelligence (Alowais et al., 2023).

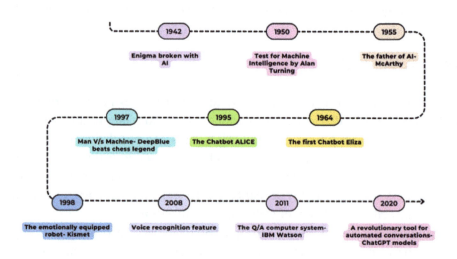

Artificial intelligence is a cumulation of various technologies. The majority of these technologies have a direct and quick connection with the medical field. Physicians first utilized AI to diagnose patients using computer programs in the near 1950s. Since then, there has been a wide interest in and utilization of AI-based applications in various domains of the medical field. This is been caused due to technological advancements in computing programs along with the availability of large data sets for utilization. It has contributed to developing innovative solutions to clinical needs, thereby improving patient care (Topol, 2019). This medical and technological integration is a stepping stone for the overall development of the quality of healthcare delivery in the country. In the ever-changing field of healthcare, it is essential to be updated and synced with the advancements to meet the demands (Wen & Huang, 2022). Focusing on and addressing the above-mentioned issues and demands, AI emerges as a game changer with the ability to tackle the challenges and transform healthcare delivery.

The revolutionizing technology of Artificial Intelligence (AI) is offering innovative solutions to major longstanding problems in the healthcare system covering areas such as diagnosis, treatment, patient care, administration, training, etc (Liu, Tan, & He, 2022). This is possible due to the convergence of AI with other technologies like Augmented Reality (AR), Virtual Reality (VR), Telemedicine, Machine Learning (ML), Deep Learning (DL), Big data informatics, remote monitoring, etc which has eventually helped in driving better value in healthcare delivery (Lau & Staccini, 2019). Thus, we explore the strategic utilization of these advanced technologies with

AI, to provide deeper insights into comprehensive strategies for increasing the value of healthcare in the current, vast pool of challenges in the field. This will not only solve the pain points of the patients but also help in strengthening the workforce.

AI-Enabled Clinical Decision Support System using Machine Learning:

Diseases that are diagnosed early, have a very high chance of getting treated accurately and efficiently. Clinicians are well trained in applying their knowledge and clinical practice together for this but there are chances of errors. Thus, AI technologies come into the picture for early detection and diagnosis, reduction of the workload, streamlining the process, and reducing the burden on healthcare staff. "AI-powered clinical decision support systems (CDSS)" contributes to providing an efficient decision-making process by utilizing patient's data, available resources, knowledge, and expertise. It utilizes machine learning algorithms, natural language processing, and representation to analyze huge collections of patient data, helping healthcare providers provide evidence-based recommendations for the line of diagnosis and treatment (Patel et al., 2009). It segregates the patients based on the characteristics of the patient and disease and helps in suggesting treatment options (Comito ET AL., 2022). A statistical technique of creating models by using data and further training these models to learn and interpret is called as Machine Learning (Wen & Huang, 2022). The commonest form of machine learning used in healthcare is precision medicine. It predicts the range of treatment protocols available and also intimates the probability to success based on multiple attributes and treatment considerations. Various types of machine learning models are used to fulfill different types of requirements in healthcare. A large volume of patient information extracted from electronic health records (EHRs), radiological images, genomic data, and other sources helps in offering curated insights with clear, precise, and quick treatment options (Wright & Sittig, 2008). It also helps in predicting patient outcomes and monitoring the progression of disease. EHR mining is done for prime reasons such as disease identification, disease progression and prediction, electronic phenotype and genotype, treatment options, and adverse drug effects (Comito ET AL., 2022). A few examples of AI-enabled decision support systems are:

Table 1. Examples of AI-enabled Clinical Decision Support System using Machine Learning

Name	Technological basis	Field of Application	Use/ Description
IBM Watson (https://www.ibm.com/watson)	Natural Language Processing, Machine Learning, deep Learning	Oncology	This system helps the oncologist provide curated treatment options to the patients. It utilizes patients' data- signs and symptoms, literature available as input for the system to get solutions as per patients' conditions.
Livongo (https://www.livongo.com/)	Machine Learning and Data Analytics	Remote monitoring	Livongo provides remote patient monitoring for patients with chronic conditions.
Visual Dx (https://www.visualdx.com/)	Machine Learning	Patient Diagnostics	It helps in providing differential diagnosis by utilizing patients' data as input and provides all the possible interventions.
IDx-DR System (https://www.healthvisors.com/en/idx-dr/)	Machine Learning	Diabetes	It is a FDA approved system that provides diagnostic assessment for diabetic retinopathy and macular edema.
StealthStation Surgical Navigation (https://europe.medtronic.com/xd-en/healthcare-professionals/products/neurological/surgical-navigation-systems/stealthstation.html)	Deep Learning and Machine Learning	Surgery	It helps surgeons to navigate precisely and assist them in surgery with precision, efficiency and safety.

The use of AI-powered CDSS can yield substantial improvements in patient safety and healthcare outcomes through enhanced diagnostic precision, optimized treatment strategies, and decreased medical errors thereby helping in better patient outcomes and reducing treatment costs.

AI-enabled Augmented Reality and Virtual Reality in Healthcare

Virtual Reality (VR) and Augmented Reality (AR) are the two booming technologies that are covering almost all the fields. While VR is a technology that has been developing since years ago, AR is quite recent. Both these technologies have the same aim of providing an immersive experience to users where they engage visual and auditory senses in virtual surroundings. The advancement in these technologies has contributed to making the overall experience more realistic, more portable, and more accessible. VR and AR systems can be either head-mounted devices or hand-held devices. VR and AR technologies are mainly used in areas where there is a need to perform a certain task repeatedly and with perfection. A domain with such a requirement is Healthcare. The utilization of AR and VR in Healthcare can be classified as teaching, training, patient education, diagnostics, planning surgeries, and patient education. Healthcare education, training, patient engagement, and rehabilitation have transformed due to newer technologies like AR and VR. In AR technology, digital 3D information is overlaid on the physical world (Dhar et al., 2021). This technology can be used to enhance medical image visualization, surgical planning, and navigation (Barsom, Graafland, & Schijven, 2016). On the other hand, VR technology enables the user to immerse in simulated scenarios, thereby helpful in "virtual surgeries, pain management therapies, and patient rehabilitation" (Jones, Moore, Choo, 2016).

Figure 2. Virtual Continnum (Harashima, 1994)

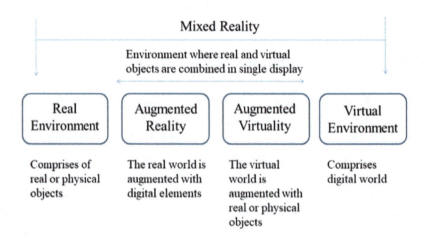

Figure 3. Current Technologies (Https://www.interaction-design.org/literature/article/beyond-ar-vs-vr-what-is-the-difference-between-ar-vs-mr-vs-vr-vs-xr)

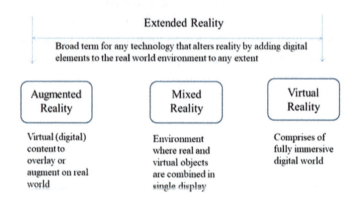

Integration of Artificial Intelligence with AR and VR has helped transform a new era of innovation in healthcare. It is spreading widely in various aspects of the medical field such as treatment, diagnosis, education, training, skill development, and much more. The advantage of having AI integration into these technologies is that it utilizes large patient data, available medical literature, case studies and clinical practice to provide real-time insight and personalized experience to help enhance patient care and the proficiency of the healthcare professional (Chen & Decary, 2020). In the area of treatment, AI-integrated AR and VR systems are helping in surgical planning and navigation. It helps surgeons visualize the difficult and bizarre views of a patient's anatomy and pathology. "Surgical Theatre, a U.S.-based firm", has created artificial intelligence (AI) algorithms that convert conventional medical imaging data into immersive three-dimensional (3D) models, enabling surgeons to see intricate anatomy and precisely plan surgeries. AR is greatly helping in Intraoperative decision-making by overlaying the structures and providing real-time guidance by focusing on critical anatomical landmarks (Barsom, Graafland, & Schijven, 2016). This widely enhances the surgical outcome, thereby reducing the operative time and risk of complications.

AI-enhanced AR and VR platforms have now made it easy to diagnose and interpret medical imaging data more accurately and efficiently. One of the best examples is "EchoPixel". It uses AI algorithms to transform 2D imaging scans into interactive 3D models (McGrath et al., n.d.). This helps the radiologists to hover around the anatomical structures in virtual space, thus helping them to detect abnormalities and raise a concrete diagnosis. Such systems also highlight the most concerning areas and prioritize the cases further, to speed up the diagnosis and treatment process. AI-enabled AR and VR have also revolutionized medical education and clinical training by offering interactive, immersive learning experiences that fill the shortcomings of traditional classrooms. A surgical simulation named "Osso VR", uses AI algorithms to generate a real-like virtual environment that enables students and professionals to practice and develop their skills (McGrath et al., n.d.) (Laver et al., 2017). This helps them in learning complex concepts and procedures in a safe environment, without harming the patient in real life (Dutta et al., 2023). These simulations can be customized as per the proficiency of the learner where it can start from basic and increment the difficulty to achieve mastery (Kumar et al., 2022). Additionally, AI-driven feedback systems offer performance data and tailored advice, enabling users to monitor their development and pinpoint areas in need of improvement. Thus, medical education can now be made more interactive, immersive, engaging, effective and accessible to make better and efficient healthcare professionals to deliver best quality patient care. AI enabled AR and VR is also being helping in skill development in various domains of healthcare. For example, Fundamental Surgery integrates haptic feedback technology in conjunction with AI-driven simulations to mimic the tactile sensations of surgery, giving users the opportunity to hone their motor skills and practice methods in a lifelike virtual environment. Immersion experiences enhance learning and encourage mastery for physicians, whether they are improving complex surgical procedures or gaining diagnostic skills.

A few examples of integration of AI with AR and VR are:

Table 2. Examples of AI-enabled AR and VR in Healthcare

Name	Technological basis	Field of Application	Use/ Description
XRHealth (https://www.xr.health/)	AR and VR	Rehabilitation	It helps in rehabilitation of traumatic brain injury or stroke patients by providing immersive experiences.
MindMotion Go (https://mindmaze.com/mindmotion-go/)	VR	Neurorehabilitation	It provides customized rehabilitation programs based on the condition and severity of the patient.
Psious (https://ameliavirtualcare.com/)	VR	Mental Health Professionals	It is used to treat phobias and anxiety of patients. It can be used for personalized treatments based on the severity of the patients.
Insight Heart (https://apps.apple.com/us/app/insight-heart/id1280845473)	AR	Cardiac anatomy and physiology education	It helps in 360-degree visualization of the heart's anatomy and physiology, thereby helping patients to understand their conditions properly and make informed decisions.

The revolutionization in healthcare is happening in multiple ways due to the integration of AI with AR, VR, and other immersive technologies. It covers wide areas such as diagnostics, treatment, training, skill development etc. These technologies enable healthcare professionals to excel in their practice, improve clinical results, and advance patient care by utilizing AI algorithms to evaluate data and create immersive experiences. The advantages of AR and VR are multiple. It provides time, access, and multiple chances to perform and perfect a certain clinical step/procedure in a safe environment without harming the actual patient and without the constant supervision of a medical professional (Kan Yeung et al., 2021). Thus, the overall training cost is reduced. These technologies can be used for bedridden patients who cannot visit hospitals. The use of AR and VR creates a more interesting and happier environment for the patient. As AI continues to evolve and AR/VR technologies become more sophisticated, the potential for innovation and impact in healthcare is limitless, promising a future where personalized, immersive, and data-driven care is the new standard. The possibilities for innovation and influence in healthcare are endless as AI and AR/VR technology advance, pointing to a time when individualized, immersive, and data-driven treatment will be the norm.

AI-Powered Telemedicine and Remote Monitoring Systems Using Machine Learning and Data Analytics (Shaik et al., 2023)

The scenario that we usually observe for a very long time is that healthcare professionals monitor patients' vitals and status on a regular basis manually. These processes depend on various factors such as the number of patients admitted, amount of clinical workload, working hours and shift of the staff, diagnosis of patients, clinical leadership and guidance. However, this was limited due to scarcity of resources. In order to estimate a patient's vital signs, intrusive equipment requires skin contact with the patient. With noninvasive gadgets that lack contact with patients' bodies and chances for continuous patient monitoring, technological developments in data transmission have reshaped the healthcare sector. The advancements have revolutionized the way that patients' health condition is monitored, making it possible to remotely check on patients in hospitals, patient care facilities, senior living communities, and even in their homes. Remote Patient Monitoring (RPM) is now widely developing in the healthcare field which enables the clinician to provide additional care and support to the patient. Traditionally, it was used to monitor patients in remote rural areas via telehealth and monitor chronic ill patients, and geriatrics using sensor-based devices. But, nowadays, there is a wide usage of RPM in nonintrusive areas of the hospitals like post-operative monitoring, Intensive Care Unit (ICU) pateints etc. RPM is possible due to the Internet of Things (IoT), Telehealth application, sensor-based devices, and wearable devices. By adding noninvasive digital technologies that allow patients to go about their everyday lives, it is conceivable to take these monitoring systems to the next level. Due to AI-powered telemedicine and remote monitoring technologies, it is now possible to provide remote delivery of healthcare services, which allows patients to get access to medical care- anytime, anywhere. Such systems utilize natural language processing (NLP) and chatbots for providing virtual consultations, assessment of symptoms, and management of medicines. With the help of remote monitoring devices, integrated with AI, it is now possible to continuously collect data and analyze them which further helps in early detection of pathologies to provide early interventions. Integration of AI with telemedicine and remote monitoring can help healthcare providers deliver patient-specific care, improve patient treatment plans, and reduce hospital stay costs and further readmissions. By identifying high-risk patients and predicting the course of diseases, machine learning and deep learning algorithms facilitate resource allocation and focused interventions for the best possible healthcare results. A few examples of AI- Powered Telemedicine and Remote Monitoring Systems are as follows:

Table 3. Examples of AI-Powered Telemedicine and Remote Monitoring Systems using Machine Learning and Data Analytics

Name	Technological basis	Field of Application	Use/ Description
Propller Health (https://propellerhealth.com/)	Natural Language Processing, Machine Learning and Data Analytics	Remote monitoring platform for COPD and asthma	It provides a remote monitoring platform for COPD and Asthma patients.
Philips Telehealth Solutions (https://www.philips.co.in/healthcare/e/enterprise-telehealth/hospital-telehealth)	Machine Learning, Data Analytics	Remote monitoring, diagnostics and treatment	It provides telemedicine services like virtual consultations, virtual patient coordination. It helps in predictive analysis for patients who are at risk.
Infermedica (https://infermedica.com/)	Natural Language Processing and Machine Learning	Remote monitoring and telemedicine	This platform analyses the symptoms and data of the patient and suggests treatment options or consultation from clinicians.

AI-driven Big Data Informatics and Predictive Analytics using Machine Learning and Deep Learning

With the technological changes that are constantly occurring, big data is gaining the limelight. Researchers, clinicians, and data scientists are working in collaboration to put continuous and sincere efforts into utilizing the large amount of data that is produced in healthcare. Data is generated from various sources such as electronic health records, medical scans, wearable devices, trials, etc. This data is complex and in a mixed form. To categorize these data- it could be either structured or unstructured. Structured data can be described as systematic data which is extensive and in varied forms. Unstructured data is more complex data (Big Data) that cannot fit in standard data processing format. The traditional tools are incapable of storing, processing, and analyzing the big data due to their huge size and quantity (Batko & Ślęzak, 2022). Thus, a lot of data that is collected remains unutilized which hampers the value of the organization. Big data can be described as a collection of Vs i.e Velocity (the speed at which the data is generated is very fast), Volume (a large volume of data is generated), Variety (different types of data are collected), Variability (inconsistency of data), Veracity (unsure of the authenticity of the data), Visualization (ability to distinguish the data and provide insights), Value (generation of useful information) (Batko & Ślęzak, 2022). Big Data Analytics can be a game-changer to tackle these problems. The synergy of Big Data informatics with AI-driven predictive analytics is helping to improve patient outcomes, customized treatment plans, and informed decision-making by providing hidden and unpredictable chances and complexities from the huge volume of data (Alowais et al., 2023). The data that is collected for big data analytics is gathered and analyzed in a different way to encourage innovation, utilization of resources and give the best patient care (Beam & Kohane, 2018). The data that is collected as structured and unstructured is analyzed by Big data informatics and predictive analytics. It can identify patterns, and relations among the variables and factors, that help in formulating the predictive models and risk categorization for population health management (Matheny et al., 2023). Healthcare practitioners can now get assistance in real-time decision-making due to Clinical decision support systems (CDSS) as it analyze raw data, medical imaging scans, and electronic health records (EHRs) by integrating AI algorithms. Real-time insights are provided to healthcare professionals so that they can make better clinical decisions, and intervention plans, utilization of resources and improve operations of the organization (Dash et al., 2019). Due to Artificial intelligence (AI)-powered predictive analytics, it is now possible to track the population at risk, and the epidemiology of the diseases, generate focused treatment to prevent diseases and promote health (Choi et al., 2016). The use of machine learning (ML) and deep learning techniques helps to improve the accuracy and adaptability of predictive analytics (Nishijima et al., 2016).. The combination of AI-enabled big data informatics and predictive analytics caters to a wide list of advantages for healthcare stakeholders. Early disease identification, curated treatment plans, and advanced patient management lead to improved and better patient outcomes and reduce healthcare costs (Rajkomar et al., 2019). Advancements in speeding the drug development are possible as AI-driven big data informatics helps in chemical library screening, predicting possible drug interactions, and improving compounds for further research (Lavecchia, 2019). Healthcare operations and resource management could be made effective as it is possible to estimate patient demand, streamline workflows, and allocate resources effectively. Due to these, the processes are simplified, resulting in shorter wait times and access to healthcare by more people (Epizitone & Moyan, 2023). The generation of hypotheses and validation of results is now done swiftly due to AI-enabled big data informatics. This helps in medical research and innovation. A few examples of AI-driven Big Data Informatics and Predictive analytics are as follows:

Table 4. AI-driven Big Data Informatics and Predictive Analysis using Machine Learning and Deep Learning

Name	Technological basis	Field of Application	Use/ Description
Sepsis Watch (https://apps.smarthealthit.org/app/sepsis-watch)	Big data informatics, Machine Learning and Deep Learning	Identification of sepsis	This system analyses the clinical notes, and investigations and tracks the patients at risk. It helps in better patient outcomes and reduces deaths due to sepsis.
Zocdoc	Big data informatics and predictive modeling	Appointment scheduling	It helps in scheduling appointments for the patient and also helps clinicians in optimizing income, and access patients to healthcare facilities.

Implementation Strategies

To get the maximum advantage of AI usage, there is a need for better and more systematic implementation of it. A good strategic plan and implementation will help an organization excel and achieve its goals quickly and smoothly. Below are a few major elements that could contribute to successful implementation strategies:

a. Infrastructure: A huge amount of data is generated from various sources in healthcare. To utilize this data properly, it is essential to have a concrete IT infrastructure that is capable of storing such data and further help in analyzing and interpreting the same. Thus, a well-secured and sophisticated system comprising updated software, large storage, and advanced features will help in utilizing the data for AI, ML, and various DL applications. Along with storing, analyzing, and interpreting the data, a good networking infrastructure is vital for organizations to ensure smooth data flow and communication across the various AI system components. A good system will not only secure the data from illegal access but also provide features like encryption, access limits, etc (Yi, Chan, & Petrikat, 2023).

b. Skilled Professionals and timely training: Implementation of AI in healthcare will not be possible without having trained and skilled staff. Good leadership comes into the picture when we talk about the integration of both- the development of

AI systems and implementation in real life. A multi-disciplinary approach of the team members is required. Skilled and qualified members belonging to but not limited to medical, engineering, data scientists, designers, etc will be the bare minimum requirement of the team. Such interdisciplinary teams can bring value from the domain of expertise they hold in conceptualizing, designing, and developing AI-based AAR and VR solutions. The engineers are responsible for putting AI models into practice and integrating them with existing systems. These models are designed by data scientists. Experts from the healthcare field will help in validating the relevancy and effectiveness of the developed AI models and systems. IT specialists are responsible for the effective functioning of AI systems with the integration of IT infrastructure. It would be a waste to have such facilities if the staff who would be using them are not aware and trained about these. With the advances that are constantly taking place in AI, data security, ethical concerns and issues, and using best AI practices, it becomes vital to conduct training and workshops for the staff at frequent intervals. Training could be in the form of workshops, sessions hands-on training, or online courses that would be curated to fulfill the required needs of the healthcare force of the organization (Petersson et al., 2022).

c. Regulatory Compliance: As a large amount of data is collected for integrating with AI, the security and privacy of these data are the prime concern. It is the responsibility of the organizations to follow and abide by the ethical, legal, and high standards of regulations while integrating AI into healthcare. There are several protocols and regulations laid out by every country for data privacy and security. It is the responsibility of the organizations to make sure that they are abiding by those. Regular meetings, audits, system checks, and firewalls should be updated to keep the system in place (Petersson et al., 2022).

d. Engagement of Stakeholders: With the rising need and advancement of AI in healthcare, it is vital to have professionals from various domains come together to implement and execute the complex integration of AI in Healthcare. Collaborations among the inter and intra institute and organizations are important where professionals from medical, engineering law, data scientists, designers, management, policy makers etc can come together and contribute by providing expertise from their own domains. Such collaboration will not only help in streamlining the process but also help in efficient and quick integration and acceptance of AI. Along woht training and educating the staff, it is equally important to educate patients about the newer technology through which they can take get better healthcare and make informed decisions for themselves. Thus, all the stakeholders should be brought together to understand the requirements, concerns, painpoints, and expectations from newer technological integration. Involving patients in this process, helps them feel responsible in the entire process as well as helps in early adoption of the change. Proper and regular communication and feedback loops will ensure that all the stakeholders are informed and involved in the entire process (44).

e. Measurement of Outcome: Any process which is developed, needs to be monitored for efficiency to understand the efficiency, gaps, and scope of development. Thus, key performance (KPIs) should be developed which will help in tracking and assessing the several factors of patient care delivery, including patient outcomes, cost-effectiveness, satisfaction, and efficiency. To increase the acceptance and efficiency of AI. Regular data analysis and feedback mechanisms should be set (Yi et al., 2023; Petersson et al., 2022).

Challenges and Considerations

As AI technology is growing day by day, it is important to tackle challenges that come in the way of implementing AI in healthcare. Below are a few challenges that need to be tackled:

a. Data Availability and Quality: Integrating AI in Machine learning and Deep learning algorithms, needs a large amount of data to interpret, classify, and analyze the data. Inaccessibility to relevant data is one of the major issues. As patients' data is confident, thus patients and organizations are reluctant to share the data for training the AI, and DL models. Another challenge would be the flow of continuous data. ML and DL models work best and are accurate when more and more data is updated in the algorithms. As the data size is large, there may be issues with proper storage of the same. Organizations will have to make arrangements to tackle this situation. To train good quality of AI models and ensure relevant insights, organizations should standardize the quality of data and interoperability (Khan et al., 2023)

b. Security and Privacy: Patient data is extremely sensitive and private, thus governed by strict laws. As health records are sensitive, they are highly probable to get hacked by hackers during security breaches. Healthcare data is extremely sensitive and governed by stringent privacy laws. Due to the severe advancement of AI, there are chances that patients might consider AI systems as human and provide consent. Thus, to protect patients' data, it is the responsibility of the organizations to have strong security and privacy protocols for patients' data (Khan et al., 2023)

c. Algorithm Bias and Interpretability: Due to less amount of data or less developed systems, there could be a chance where AI systems could be non-reliable and biased. There could be negative effects and can hamper the user confidences. Thus, unbiased, transparent and accurate interpretability of the algorithms is essential to encourage the usage of such systems and build confidence among

the healthcare users. There should be explanations of the results generated by AI to gurantee the accountability f the system (Rahman et al., 2023)
d. Clinical Integration and adoption: Technology cannot replace humans but can help in making the work easier and quicker. With this thought, it is essential to encourage clinicians and other healthcare professionals to showcase trust in the newer technology, or else their acceptance of these technologies will be difficult. To encourage and promote the usage and adoption of AI, it is essential to involve stakeholders, provide them with training, and upskill them from time to time will be helpful (Li, Ruijs, & Lu, 2023)
e. Resources and cost constraints: As there is a lot of requirements in setting up and streamlining the entire process, a significant investment must be needed in hiring the right skill set of people, setting up and maintaining the system, technical infrastructures, etc. Organizations can face difficulty in case they have limited resources. Thus, finding the best affordable solution as per the requirement, proper financing sources and allocation of resources efficiently can help in tackling these issues (Li, Ruijs, & Lu, 2023)

Addressing the above challenges actively and adopting best practices can help healthcare organizations harness the full potential of AI in delivering the better value of patient care, thereby improving patient outcomes and the healthcare system as a whole.

CONCLUSION

The synergy of AI with other technologies like AR, VR, ML, DL, Telemedicine, Big data Informatics provides vast opportunities to tackle the challenges of the healthcare system, improve patient outcomes, and optimize the allocation of resources. Through purposeful incorporation of these technologies within clinical processes, educational curricula, and therapeutic strategies, healthcare institutions can harness novel efficiencies, enhance decision-making capabilities, and ultimately provide heightened value to patients, healthcare professionals, and stakeholders alike. Thus, embracing these technologies in a positive and impactful way can contribute to providing better value in healthcare delivery.

REFERENCES

Alowais, S. A., Alghamdi, S. S., Alsuhebany, N., Alqahtani, T., Alshaya, A. I., Almohareb, S. N., Aldairem, A., Alrashed, M., Bin Saleh, K., Badreldin, H. A., Al Yami, M. S., Al Harbi, S., & Albekairy, A. M. (2023). Revolutionizing healthcare: The role of artificial intelligence in clinical practice. *BMC Medical Education*, 23(1), 1–15. 10.1186/s12909-023-04698-z37740191

Barsom, E. Z., Graafland, M., & Schijven, M. P. (2016). Systematic review on the effectiveness of augmented reality applications in medical training. *Surgical Endoscopy*, 30(10), 4174–4183. 10.1007/s00464-016-4800-626905573

Batko, K., & Ślęzak, A. (2022). The use of Big Data Analytics in healthcare. [Internet]. *Journal of Big Data*, 9(1), 3. Advance online publication. 10.1186/s40537-021-00553-435013701

Beam, A. L., & Kohane, I. S. (2018). Big data and machine learning in health care. JAMA -. *Journal of the American Medical Association*, 319(13), 1317–1318. 10.1001/jama.2017.1839129532063

Chen, M., & Decary, M. (2020). Artificial intelligence in healthcare: An essential guide for health leaders. *Healthcare Management Forum*, 33(1), 10–18. 10.1177/0 84047041987312331550922

Choi, E., Bahadori, M. T., Schuetz, A., Stewart, W. F., Sun, J., & Doctor, A. I. (2016, August). Predicting Clinical Events via Recurrent Neural Networks. *JMLR Workshop and Conference Proceedings*, 56, 301–318.28286600

Comito, C., Falcone, D., & Forestiero, A. (2022). AI-Driven Clinical Decision Support: Enhancing Disease Diagnosis Exploiting Patients Similarity. *IEEE Access : Practical Innovations, Open Solutions*, 10, 6878–6888. 10.1109/ACCESS.2022.3142100

Dash, S., Shakyawar, S. K., Sharma, M., & Kaushik, S. (2019). Big data in healthcare: Management, analysis and future prospects. [Internet]. *Journal of Big Data*, 6(1), 54. Advance online publication. 10.1186/s40537-019-0217-0

Dhar, P., Rocks, T., Samarasinghe, R. M., Stephenson, G., & Smith, C. (2021). Augmented reality in medical education: Students' experiences and learning outcomes. [Internet]. *Medical Education Online*, 26(1), 1953953. Advance online publication. 10.1080/10872981.2021.195395334259122

Dutta, R., Mantri, A., Singh, G., & Singh, N. (2023). Measuring the Impact of Augmented Reality in Flipped Learning Mode on Critical Thinking, Learning Motivation, and Knowledge of Engineering Students. *Journal of Science Education and Technology*, 32(6), 1–19. 10.1007/s10956-023-10051-237359120

Epizitone A, Moyane SP, Agbehadji IE. A Systematic Literature Review of Health Information Systems for Healthcare. Healthc. 2023;11(7).

Harashima, H. (1994). Special Issue on Networked Reality. *IEICE Transactions on Information and Systems*, 77(12), 1317.

https://ameliavirtualcare.com/

https://apps.apple.com/us/app/insight-heart/id1280845473

https://apps.smarthealthit.org/app/sepsis-watch

https://europe.medtronic.com/xd-en/healthcare-professionals/products/neurological/surgical-navigation-systems/stealthstation.html

https://infermedica.com/

https://mindmaze.com/mindmotion-go/

https://propellerhealth.com/

https://www.healthvisors.com/en/idx-dr/

https://www.ibm.com/watson

Https://www.interaction-design.org/literature/article/beyond-ar-vs-vr-what-is-the-difference-between-ar-vs-mr-vs-vr-vs-xr. No Title.

https://www.livongo.com/

https://www.philips.co.in/healthcare/e/enterprise-telehealth/hospital-telehealth

https://www.visualdx.com/

https://www.xr.health/.

Jones, T., Moore, T., & Choo, J. (2016). The impact of virtual reality on chronic pain. *PLoS One*, 11(12), 1–10. 10.1371/journal.pone.016752327997539

Kan Yeung, A. W., Tosevska, A., Klager, E., Eibensteiner, F., Laxar, D., & Stoyanov, J.. (2021). Virtual and augmented reality applications in medicine: Analysis of the scientific literature. *Journal of Medical Internet Research*, 23(2).33565986

Kumar, A., Mantri, A., Singh, G., & Kaur, D. (2022). Impact of AR-based collaborative learning approach on knowledge gain of engineering students in embedded system course. *Education and Information Technologies*, 27(5), 1–22. 10.1007/s10639-021-10858-9 khan B, Fatima H, Qureshi A, Kumar S, Hanan A, Hussain J, et al. Drawbacks of Artificial Intelligence and Their Potential Solutions in the Healthcare Sector. Biomed Mater Devices [Internet]. 2023;1(2):731–8. Available from: 10.1007/s44174-023-00063-2

Lavecchia, A. (2019). Deep learning in drug discovery: Opportunities, challenges and future prospects. [Internet]. *Drug Discovery Today*, 24(10), 2017–2032. 10.1016/j.drudis.2019.07.00631377227

Laver, K. E., Lange, B., George, S., Deutsch, J. E., Saposnik, G., & Crotty, M. (2017). Virtual reality for stroke rehabilitation. *Cochrane Database of Systematic Reviews*, 2017(11).29156493

Li, F., Ruijs, N., & Lu, Y. (2023). Ethics & AI: A Systematic Review on Ethical Concerns and Related Strategies for Designing with AI in Healthcare. *AI*, 4(1), 28–53. 10.3390/ai4010003

Liu, C., Tan, Z., & He, M. (2022). Overview of Artificial Intelligence in Medicine. *Artif Intell Med Appl Limitations Futur Dir.*, 41(6), 23–34. 10.1007/978-981-19-1223-8_234874486

Lau, A. Y. S., & Staccini, P. (2019). Artificial Intelligence in Health: New Opportunities, Challenges, and Practical Implications. *Yearbook of Medical Informatics*, 28(1), 174–178. 10.1055/s-0039-167793531419829

Matheny, M., Israni, S. T., Whicher, D., & Ahmed, M. (2023). *Artificial intelligence in health care: The hope, the hype, the promise, the peril.* Artif Intell Heal Care Hope, Hype, Promise, Peril.

McGrath, J. L., Taekman, J. M., Dev, P., Danforth, D. R., Mohan, D., Kman, N., Crichlow, A. B. W., & Bond, W. F. (2018, February). Using Virtual Reality Simulation Environments to Assess Competence for Emergency Medicine Learners. *Academic Emergency Medicine*, 25(2), 186–195. 10.1111/acem.1330828888070

Patel, V. L., Shortliffe, E. H., Stefanelli, M., Szolovits, P., Berthold, M. R., Bellazzi, R., & Abu-Hanna, A. (2009). The coming of age of artificial intelligence in medicine. *Artificial Intelligence in Medicine*, 46(1), 5–17. 10.1016/j.artmed.2008.07.01718790621

Petersson, L., Larsson, I., Nygren, J. M., Nilsen, P., Neher, M., Reed, J. E., Tyskbo, D., & Svedberg, P. (2022). Challenges to implementing artificial intelligence in healthcare: A qualitative interview study with healthcare leaders in Sweden. [Internet]. *BMC Health Services Research*, 22(1), 1–16. 10.1186/s12913-022-08215-835778736

Rahman, A., Hossain, M. S., Muhammad, G., Kundu, D., Debnath, T., Rahman, M., ... Federated learning-based AI approaches in smart healthcare: concepts, taxonomies, challenges and open issues [Internet]. Vol. 26, Cluster Computing. Springer US; 2023. 2271–2311 p. Available from: 10.1007/s10586-022-03658-4

Rajkomar, A., Dean, J., & Kohane, I. (2019). Machine Learning in Medicine. *The New England Journal of Medicine*, 380(14), 1347–1358. 10.1056/NEJM-ra181425930943338

Shaik, T., Tao, X., Higgins, N., Li, L., Gururajan, R., Zhou, X., & Acharya, U. R. (2023). Remote patient monitoring using artificial intelligence: Current state, applications, and challenges. *Wiley Interdisciplinary Reviews. Data Mining and Knowledge Discovery*, 13(2), 1–31. 10.1002/widm.1485

Shickel, B., Tighe, P. J., Bihorac, A., & Rashidi, P. (2017). Deep EHR: A survey of recent advances in deep learning techniques for electronic health record (EHR) analysis. *IEEE Journal of Biomedical and Health Informatics*, 22(5), 1589–1604.

Topol, E. J. (2019). High-performance medicine: The convergence of human and artificial intelligence. [Internet]. *Nature Medicine*, 25(1), 44–56. 10.1038/s41591-018-0300-730617339 Wen, Z., & Huang, H. (2022). The potential for artificial intelligence in healthcare. *Journal of Commercial Biotechnology*, 27(4), 217–224.

Wright, A., & Sittig, D. F. (2008). A four-phase model of the evolution of clinical decision support architectures. *International Journal of Medical Informatics*, 77(10), 641–649. 10.1016/j.ijmedinf.2008.01.00418353713

Yi, C., Chan, T., & Petrikat, D. Journal of Medical and Health Studies Strategic Applications of Artificial Intelligence in Healthcare and Medicine. 2023; Available from: https://creativecommons.org/licenses/by/4.0/

Chapter 7
AI Strategies for Delivering Better Value in the Healthcare Sector

Partap Singh
Lovely Professional University, India

Partap Singh
Lovely Professional University, India

ABSTRACT

Artificial Intelligence (AI) is reforming various industries, and the healthcare sector is no exception. Artificial Intelligence (AI) has emerged as a transformative technology in healthcare, offering promising avenues to enhance patient care, optimize resource utilization, and improve overall value in the healthcare sector. This paper explores the various AI strategies employed in healthcare settings to deliver better value. It examines the application of AI in clinical decision-making, patient engagement, administrative tasks, and healthcare system management. Additionally, it discusses challenges, opportunities, and future directions in leveraging AI for maximizing value in healthcare delivery. The paper settles with recommendations for policymakers, practitioners, and researchers to harness the full potential of AI in healthcare.

INTRODUCTION

The incorporation of Artificial Intelligence (AI) into the healthcare sector symbolizes a transformative paradigm shift, offering unique opportunities to revolutionize diagnosis, patient care, treatment, and administrative processes. AI, categorized by

DOI: 10.4018/979-8-3693-3731-8.ch007

its ability to simulator human cognitive functions such as learning, reasoning, and problem-solving, has emerged as a powerful tool for augmenting the capabilities of healthcare professionals and institutions. This introduction serves as an entry to understanding the multi-layered inferences of AI in healthcare.

The healthcare industry is facing abundant challenges, including rising costs, increasing demand for services, and a growing burden of chronic diseases. These challenges require innovative approaches to healthcare delivery that can improve efficiency, boost patient outcomes, and enhance resource utilization. Against this background, AI has emerged as a disruptive force with the potential to address these encounters by leveraging predictive analytics, machine learning algorithms and data-driven insights, to drive decision-making and improve healthcare delivery.

The amalgamation of AI into the healthcare sector holds huge promise for improving patient care, optimizing healthcare delivery and enhancing clinical decision-making. The Current Landscape of AI in Healthcare is as under:

Overview of AI Technologies in Healthcare

Artificial Intelligence (AI) technologies encompass a diverse array of tools and techniques that have been increasingly integrated into various facets of healthcare. This section provides a comprehensive overview of the AI technologies currently employed in the healthcare sector, including machine learning, natural language processing, computer vision, robotics, and expert systems. Each technology is elucidated with its principles, capabilities, and applications in healthcare settings.

Applications of AI in Medical Diagnosis

AI has demonstrated remarkable potential in medical diagnosis by augmenting the accuracy and efficiency of disease detection across various specialties. This subsection explores the application of AI in medical diagnosis, encompassing fields such as radiology, pathology, dermatology, and ophthalmology. It examines how AI algorithms analyze medical images, laboratory results, and clinical data to assist healthcare professionals in diagnosing diseases with greater precision and speed.

AI-driven Treatment and Therapeutics

Beyond diagnosis, AI plays a pivotal role in guiding treatment decisions and developing innovative therapeutic interventions. This section delves into the applications of AI in treatment planning, drug discovery, personalized medicine, and precision oncology. It elucidates how AI algorithms analyze patient data, genomic information, and biomedical literature to optimize treatment regimens, identify potential drug targets, and tailor therapies to individual patient characteristics.

AI-enabled Patient Care and Monitoring

AI technologies have revolutionized patient care and monitoring by providing real-time insights, predictive analytics, and personalized interventions. This subsection explores how AI is utilized in remote patient monitoring, predictive analytics, virtual health assistants, and wearable devices. It examines how AI algorithms analyze continuous streams of patient data to detect early signs of deterioration, prevent adverse events, and facilitate timely interventions, thereby improving patient outcomes and enhancing healthcare delivery.

Administrative Applications of AI in Healthcare

In addition to clinical applications, AI is increasingly employed to streamline administrative processes, optimize resource allocation, and enhance operational efficiency in healthcare organizations. This section discusses the diverse administrative applications of AI, including revenue cycle management, supply chain optimization, workforce scheduling, and fraud detection. It examines how AI-driven analytics and automation tools enable healthcare providers to minimize administrative burdens, reduce costs, and improve overall organizational performance.

This section provides a comprehensive overview of the current landscape of AI in healthcare, highlighting the diverse applications and transformative potential of AI technologies across clinical, operational, and administrative domains. Through an in-depth exploration of each application area, this research paper aims to elucidate the multifaceted role of AI in revolutionizing healthcare delivery and improving patient outcomes.

LITERATURE REVIEW

Hypotheses Setting

Null Hypothesis (H_0): There is no significant difference in diagnostic care, treatment outcomes, and patient satisfaction between AI-assisted healthcare delivery or traditional approaches.

Alternative Hypothesis (H_1): AI technologies significantly improve diagnostic care, treatment outcomes, and patient satisfaction compared to traditional approaches in healthcare.

Null Hypothesis (H_0):: Addressing key challenges and implementing best AI strategies for the responsible development and deployment of AI in healthcare does not lead to significant improvements in healthcare quality, efficiency, and accessibility or delivery of better values in healthcare.

Alternative Hypothesis (H_2):: Addressing key challenges and implementing best AI strategies for the responsible development and deployment of AI in healthcare leads to significant improvements in healthcare quality, efficiency, accessibility or delivery of better values in healthcare.

Gaurav Jain (2023) mentioned that AI revolutionizes healthcare, balancing quality and cost. Current applications include prediction, NLP, and clinical procedure enhancement. AI improves diagnosis, treatment, and predictive analytics. Chatbots enhance patient experience. Future success relies on AI integration and innovation.

McCarthy (1998) elucidated that artificial intelligence (AI) entails the development of intelligent systems using algorithms to replicate human cognitive processes, such as learning and problem-solving, within the realms of science and engineering.

Andrews (2013) emphasized the significance of experiments in concurrently testing novel concepts, determining efficacy, assimilating insights from both successes and failures, and comprehending underlying principles.

Quinn et al. (2021) underscored the disparity between AI systems and human physicians in terms of reasoning abilities, particularly the absence of the capacity to utilize 'common sense' or clinical intuition inherent in human medical practitioners.

Muehlematter (2020) highlighted the predominant utilization of AI in the automated categorization of medical imagery, with a substantial portion of AI/ML-based medical devices securing approval for radiological applications in both the USA and Europe.

Simonite (2020) documented the approval of Medicare reimbursement for the deployment of the FDA-endorsed AI algorithm 'IDx-DR,' renowned for its high sensitivity and specificity in detecting diabetic retinopathy, by the Centers for Medicare & Medicaid Services.

Gudigar et al. (2021) emphasized the pivotal role of AI in the early detection of COVID-19 using various medical imaging techniques such as X-ray, CT, and ultrasound. Their study showcased the efficacy of handcrafted feature learning (HCFL), deep neural networks (DNN), and hybrid methods in accurately predicting COVID-19 cases.

Khanna et al. (2022) provided an in-depth analysis of AI's contribution to COVID-19 diagnosis, elucidating its utilization in CT scans, X-rays, MRI, and ultrasound. Their research underscored AI's instrumental role in aiding the global battle against the pandemic.

Patel and Tarakji (2021) presented a case study demonstrating the efficacy of wearable digital devices in detecting atrial fibrillation, leading to the precise diagnosis of stroke. This exemplifies the diagnostic support provided by consumer wearable devices, verified by electrophysiologists.

Natarajan et al. (2020) advocated for research addressing sparse tagged data in mental health disorder studies. They noted advancements in wearable devices for online patient monitoring, triggered by the COVID-19 pandemic, facilitating physiological measurements.

Mak et al. (2019) explored AI's potential in predicting drug-target interactions for drug repurposing, thereby advancing clinical trials and mitigating polypharmacology concerns. Their research highlighted AI's role in streamlining drug development processes.

Jadhav (2021) emphasizes the necessity of eXplainable AI (XAI) methods to enhance radiologists' confidence in CT image classification predictions, offering valuable visual insights into the automated workflow.

Hukunda et al. (2023) highlight the effectiveness of apps and online portals for patient-HCP communication, reporting up to a 60% increase in engagement rates. These AI-driven platforms store and manage patient data securely in the cloud, improving health outcomes.

Moon (2023) finds that metaverse physiotherapy (MPT) outperforms conventional methods in treating children with cerebral palsy, reducing perceived COVID-19 risks and enhancing cardiopulmonary and motor function.

Corny et al. (2020) demonstrate the superiority of a hybrid ML-based decision support system in detecting prescribing errors in clinical settings. ML techniques, including NLP and deep learning subsets, are widely utilized in developing AI tools for pharmaceutical services.

Liao (2022) stresses the importance of governance in AI technology implementation in healthcare, ensuring patient safety, clinician confidence, and system accountability. Comprehensive governance frameworks are essential to address challenges across clinical, operational, and leadership domains.

Choudhury and Asan (2022) found clinicians' perceptions of AI in healthcare influenced by factors like risk, trust, workload, and training availability. They suggest integrating AI education into medical and nursing curricula.

Wolf (2020) discovered challenges with deep learning algorithms' explanation abilities, raising legal and trust issues. The opaque nature of AI predictions may undermine public confidence in healthcare systems.

Alami (2021) highlighted the dearth of empirical data validating AI-based drugs' efficacy in clinical settings, hindering their adoption. Institutions hesitate due to insufficient evidence and research quality.

Ackerman (2023) emphasizes AI's vital role in healthcare, optimizing data management, enhancing care coordination, and addressing nurse shortages. Leveraging AI promises transformative value-based care with improved efficiency and patient outcomes.

McKendrick (2023) highlights healthcare's slow adoption of AI, projecting significant cost savings and improved patient care. AI integration offers productivity gains, marking a transformative period in the industry.

Morgan Stanley representatives (2023) foresee AI's transformative impact in healthcare, spanning biopharma, diagnostics, and patient care. While promising enhanced efficiency and revenue, widespread industry adoption remains in its infancy.

Kriwet (2020) explores AI-driven predictive healthcare, leveraging diverse data for disease risk anticipation and proactive preventive measures. This approach aims for improved health outcomes and reduced chronic conditions prevalence by 2030.

Saifi (2013) found that in healthcare, AI offers enhanced diagnosis and treatment precision, facilitating rapid symptom assessment surpassing many experts. Its potential lies in expediting medical processes with increased accuracy.

Kristensen (2019) studied a systematic review on AI-assisted robotic surgery in gynecological oncology reveals comparable safety to traditional methods. However, it notably increases overall costs due to equipment expenditures.

Topo (2019) found that AI algorithms show significant utility in pathology, radiology, and diverse diagnostic domains. Medical futurist Eric Topol's insights underscore AI's pivotal role in advancing medical diagnostics.

Singh (2020) described that AI holds promise in augmenting medical decision-making, potentially supplanting human judgment in certain contexts, offering substantial benefits to healthcare practitioners and patients alike.

Balasubramanian et al. (2023) presented a robust AI framework for UAE healthcare, it highlights transformative potential contingent on regulatory and stakeholder support. Addressing privacy, security, and bias concerns is imperative for sustained impact.

Sivathanu (2021) proposed a comprehensive AI framework for healthcare, it integrates stakeholders, application areas, and technical/managerial aspects. Insights from established frameworks like the TOE model enhance its comprehensiveness.

Mohamadou and Kapen (2020) explored NLP techniques in healthcare, focusing on analyzing, summarizing, clustering, and classifying disease-related information from text and speech data.

Alhasan and Hasaneen (2021) noted that CT scan-based approaches yielded superior results compared to X-rays in healthcare applications, particularly in analyzing blood samples.

Shah (2021) discussed the efficacy of computer vision systems with thermal imaging in public health surveillance, aiding in febrile case screening, face mask detection, social distancing assessment, motion detection, and number plate recognition to enforce COVID-19 regulations.

Carriere (2021) highlighted AI's capability to identify COVID-19 vaccines with enhanced effectiveness and reduced side effects, showcasing its potential in vaccine development and evaluation.

Research Gap

There is a research lacuna in widely examining the continuing socioeconomic consequences of AI amalgamation within healthcare structures. Existing studies chiefly focus on technical facets, overseeing wider societal and economic considerations such as economic impact, workforce dynamics, patient-centered outcomes, and regulatory implications. Exploring these aspects would offer invaluable insights into AI's transformative potential, facilitating the formulation of policies aimed at maximizing benefits while effectively managing associated risks.

Research Objectives:

- To evaluate the impact of AI technologies on healthcare sector;
- To identify Key challenges and opportunities in the adoption of AI in healthcare sector;
- To propose recommendations for maximizing the benefits of AI in healthcare sector.

Research Questions:

- **Objective 1**: To evaluate the impact of AI technologies on healthcare sector,
    - 1.1 Research Question 1: How does the incorporation of artificial intelligence (AI) technologies impact the efficiency and effectiveness of medical diagnosis in healthcare sector?
    - 1.2 Research Question 2: How do AI applications contribute to treatment planning and decision-making processes in healthcare?
    - 1.3 Research Question 3: What role does AI play in patient monitoring and personalized healthcare delivery?

1.4 Research Question 4: How are administrative processes in healthcare transformed by the integration of AI technologies?

- **Objective 2**: To identify Key challenges and opportunities in the adoption of AI in healthcare sector;
  2.1 Research Question 5: What are the primary challenges hindering the widespread adoption of AI technologies in healthcare?
  2.2 Research Question 6: What opportunities exist for leveraging AI to address current limitations and gaps in healthcare delivery?
  2.3 Research Question 7: How do regulatory frameworks impact the development and deployment of AI applications in healthcare
  2.4 Research Question 8: What are the ethical and privacy considerations associated with the use of AI in healthcare, and how can they be addressed?

- **Objective 3:** To propose recommendations for maximizing the benefits of AI in healthcare sector.

  3.1 Research Question 9: What evidence-based recommendations can be proposed for healthcare stakeholders to optimize the integration of AI technologies?
  3.2 Research Question 10: How can policymakers, healthcare providers, technology developers, and patients collaborate to ensure the responsible development and deployment of AI in healthcare?

METHODOLOGY

The methodology employed in this research involves conducting a bibliometric analysis to examine the scholarly literature related to Artificial Intelligence (AI) in the healthcare sector to achieve the objectives of study. This process involves the systematic collection of relevant academic publications from established databases such as PubMed, Scopus, and Web of Science.to capture a comprehensive range of articles focusing on AI applications in healthcare. Further, a case study on Pharm Easy has been conducted to achieve the objectives of study. Moreover, a survey from the website Insiderintelligence.com has been included to understand the impact of Ai on health sector

RESULTS AND DISCUSSION

Survey on the evaluation the impact of AI technologies on healthcare sector

Table 1. Survey on Impact of AI and ML on select healthcare Outcomes in 2022 according to healthcare executive (% of respondents)

Impact	VE	OE	SE	RE	NE
Improving clinical outcomes	23	36	35	7	
Improving operational performance	19	39	36	7	
Improving health system efficiency	13	33	36	9	
Improving Administrative Performance	13	33	36	16	2
Improving Financial Outcome	12	35	39	13	1
Improving Consumer Engagement	13	33	45	8	2

Source: Innowoccer, Healthcare's Data Readiness crisis, conducted by Moring Consult and Insiderintelligence.com

Note: i. VE- Very effective, OE- Often Effective, SE- Sometimes Effective, RE- Rarely Effective NE- Never Effective

ii. Number may not add up to 100% due to rounding

To analyze the impact of AI and ML on select healthcare outcomes as reported by healthcare executives, we can interpret the data provided in Table 1 and Figure 1. This table presents the percentage of respondents who rated the effectiveness of AI and ML in improving various healthcare outcomes, categorized as Very Effective (VE), Often Effective (OE), Sometimes Effective (SE), Rarely Effective (RE), and Never Effective (NE). Let's break down the analysis:

Improving Clinical Outcomes: The data shows that 23% of respondents rated AI and ML as very effective (VE) in improving clinical outcomes, while 36% found it often effective (OE).

Overall, a majority of respondents (23% + 36% = 59%) perceived AI and ML as effective in improving clinical outcomes, indicating a positive impact on patient care and treatment efficacy.

Improving Operational Performance: AI and ML are seen as effective tools for enhancing operational performance in healthcare settings. 19% of respondents rated them as very effective (VE), and 39% found them often effective (OE).

The combined percentage of respondents who rated AI and ML as effective (VE + OE) in improving operational performance is 58%, indicating a significant positive impact on streamlining processes and optimizing resource utilization.

Improving Health System Efficiency: In terms of improving health system efficiency, 13% of respondents rated AI and ML as very effective (VE), while 33% found them often effective (OE).

Despite lower percentages compared to clinical outcomes and operational performance, the combined effectiveness rating (VE + OE = 46%) suggests a considerable impact of AI and ML on enhancing overall healthcare system efficiency.

Improving Administrative Performance: The data indicates that 13% of respondents rated AI and ML as very effective (VE) in improving administrative performance, while 33% found them often effective (OE). However, a noteworthy proportion of respondents (16%) rated them as rarely effective (RE), suggesting potential challenges or limitations in utilizing AI and ML for administrative tasks.

Improving Financial Outcome: In terms of improving financial outcomes, 12% of respondents rated AI and ML as very effective (VE), while 35% found them often effective (OE).

The combined effectiveness rating (VE + OE = 47%) indicates a significant positive impact of AI and ML on financial outcomes, such as revenue optimization and cost containment in healthcare organizations.

Improving Consumer Engagement: AI and ML are perceived as effective tools for improving consumer engagement in healthcare. 13% of respondents rated them as very effective (VE), while 33% found them often effective (OE), and 45% sometimes effective (SE).

With a combined effectiveness rating of 91% (VE + OE + SE), the data highlights the substantial impact of AI and ML on enhancing consumer engagement and patient satisfaction.

Overall Analysis:

The data from healthcare executives indicates a generally positive perception of the effectiveness of AI and ML in various healthcare outcomes. Clinical outcomes, operational performance, and financial outcomes are areas where AI and ML are perceived to have a significant impact, with a majority of respondents rating them as effective or very effective. While AI and ML show promise in improving administrative performance and health system efficiency, there are also challenges highlighted by a proportion of respondents, such as rare effectiveness in administrative tasks. Consumer engagement emerges as a particularly strong area of impact, with the majority of respondents perceiving AI and ML as effective tools for enhancing patient engagement and satisfaction.

AI Strategies for Delivering Better Value in the Healthcare Sector

Figure 1. Survey on Impact of AI and ML on select healthcare Outcomes in 2022 according to healthcare executive.

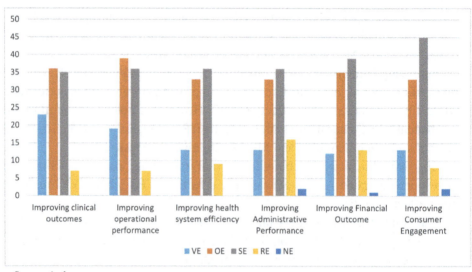

Source: Author

These findings underscore the potential of AI and ML to transform healthcare delivery, but also highlight the need to address challenges and optimize implementation strategies to maximize their effectiveness across different aspects of healthcare operations.

Case Study on Pharm Easy: AI Strategies for Delivering Better Value in the Healthcare Sector

The concept of medicine home delivery has been taken to a new level by the Pharm Easy online medicine delivery app. PharmEasy controls innovative technologies such as machine learning and big data analytics to optimize its medical delivery platform. By flawlessly concerning users with nearby pharmacies and facilitating doorstep delivery of medications, PharmEasy simplifies the process of obtaining essential healthcare products. The platform's data-driven approach enhances efficiency and user experience, ultimately improving access to medications and healthcare services for individuals across the country

One can use the PharmEasy online medicine delivery app to browse through an extensive range of medicines. Each medicine undergoes a 3-step quality check. Whatever be one's medicine requirement, he is sure to locate it in this online pharmacy. One has to do then is to add it to his cart and place the order and get his order delivered quickly. India's beloved online medicine delivery app makes sure that one gets his medicines in record time because team of Farm Easy knows how vital time is in any treatment. Sit back, and their team will have all his medical necessities delivered to one's doorstep.

Online Medicine – One's Online Medical Store in India

Order medicines online at PharmEasy, India's trusted online medicine app. With more than 1 lakh medicines always in stock, one is sure to find what he is looking for, and that too at affordable prices. Besides, extremely stringent sanitization norms are followed at one's favourite online medical store. PharmEasy takes the safety of customers and employees very seriously.

Reasons to Buy Medicine Online from PharmEasy

- 1,200+ cities and 20,000+ Pin codes served
- Express Delivery
- 1 Lakh+ medicines available
- Cash on delivery option available
- Attractive offers
- Cashback option through wallet
- Stringent quality checks
- Garnered the trust of more than 10 million users who have made an online purchase through PharmEasy
- Order Medicines Online

Get 3-Step Quality-checked Medicines

PharmEasy is a one-stop-shop for all someone's healthcare needs. It has 1L+ products to choose from and to buy medicines online at affordable prices from the comforts of one's home in just a few clicks and get him delivered at his doorstep. The entire process of shopping for medicines is hassle-free and convenient. One has to do is search for the products his need on its website or app, add to cart and then proceed with the checkout process. It also offers a scheduled reminder feature to help one stay on track and never miss his important doses.

AI Strategies for Delivering Better Value in the Healthcare Sector

Figure 2. Pharm Easy has great offers, with added discounts and massive e-wallet cashbacks on purchasing medicines:

As of March 31, 2023, PharmEasy's total assets decreased significantly from the previous year, mainly due to a decrease in current assets. However, there was a notable increase in reserves and surplus. Total liabilities decreased, driven by a decline in both non-current and current liabilities compared to the previous year as shown below: -

Table 2. Consolidated Balance sheet of PharmEasy as at March 31, 2023 (Amount in Rs. Million)

Particular	March 31, 2023	March 31, 2022
Assets: Non –current Assets Total Current Assets	57215.53 25348.63	88,961.22 25,022.05
Total Assets	82564.16	113,983.27
Equity and Liabilities: Reserves& Surplus Total Non-current liabilities Total Current Liabilities	14703.77 10265.12 23232.23	60751.91 9472.93 37616.06
Total Equity and Liabilities	82564.16	113,983.27

Analysis of Perception of Customer towards Pharm Easy Platform

1. Rishi Tiwari (April 11, 2023)- "The ordering medicines from PharmEasy is smoot and hassle-free experience. It provides variety of medicines. Their doctor support is always available, if there is need of any help and ordering medicines has become easier."
2. Soanli Khatri (Feb 15, 20230- "The ordering medicines from PharmEasy via WhatsApp or call is much easier and their services are excellent."
3. Vimla Malhotra (Dec 28, 2022)- "The ease of ordering and the availability of all kinds of medicines has made me a repeat customer for long –time. And as a Plus member, I get extra discounts on my orders as well as free delivery."

4. Shakti Menon (November 18, 2022) – "I have been ordering from PharmEasy for my parents for some time now. The convenience of choosing from a wide variety of medicines and getting quick home is helpful. I also get cashback and discounts from time to time. Quite affordable and easy to use overall."
5. Vallabh Thakur (March 23, 2023)- "PharmEasy has been a great help to me as my daughter lives away and I cannot always go out to buy medicines. I find the App very easy to use and their quick home delivery is great. I am happy with their offers too. Surely recommended it."

Interpretation from the Analysis:

Customers perceive PharmEasy as a convenient solution for medicine procurement, praising its smooth ordering process, wide medication selection, and readily available doctor support. Utilizing various channels like WhatsApp or call enhances accessibility. Repeat customers appreciate the ease of ordering, comprehensive medication availability, and benefits of membership like discounts and free delivery. Users, particularly those with limited mobility, value the app's user-friendliness and efficient home delivery, endorsing it as a reliable option for medication needs, especially for remote assistance.

Customers find PharmEasy convenient for ordering medicines with praise for its smooth process, wide selection, doctor support, and various channels for accessibility. Repeat users value membership benefits, user-friendliness, and efficient home delivery, recommending it for medication needs.

PharmEasy's total assets decreased, primarily due to a reduction in current assets. Reserves and surplus increased, while total liabilities decreased, driven by declines in both current and non-current liabilities

A detailed overview of current applications of AI in healthcare

Table 3. Applications of AI in healthcare

Medical Imaging and Diagnostics
Personalized Treatment Plans
Virtual Health Assistants and Telemedicine
Drug Discovery and Development
Predictive Analytics for Hospital Management
Healthcare Administration and Billing
Remote Monitoring and Wearable Devices

Medical Imaging and Diagnostics:

Image Interpretation: AI algorithms analyze medical images (such as X-rays, MRIs, CT scans) to detect anomalies and assist radiologists in diagnosis. For instance, AI can help identify tumors, fractures, or anomalies in organs with high accuracy and speed.

Computer-Aided Detection/Diagnosis (CAD): AI-powered CAD systems assist radiologists by highlighting suspicious areas, leading to more accurate interpretations and early detection of diseases like cancer.

Personalized Treatment Plans:

Predictive Analytics: AI models analyze patient data to predict disease progression, treatment responses, and potential complications. This enables healthcare providers to tailor treatment plans according to individual patient characteristics.

Genomics and Precision Medicine: AI analyzes genomic data to understand genetic predispositions to diseases and develop personalized treatment strategies.

Virtual Health Assistants and Telemedicine:

Chatbots and Virtual Assistants: AI-powered chatbots provide personalized medical advice, schedule appointments, and answer queries, thereby improving patient engagement and accessibility to healthcare services.

Telemedicine Platforms: AI facilitates remote patient monitoring, video consultations, and diagnosis through telemedicine platforms, enhancing healthcare accessibility, especially in rural or underserved areas.

Drug Discovery and Development:

Drug Repurposing: AI algorithms analyze vast datasets to identify existing drugs that could be repurposed for treating new diseases, accelerating the drug development process.

Target Identification and Drug Design: AI assists in identifying disease targets, designing drug molecules, and predicting their efficacy, reducing the time and cost involved in drug discovery.

Predictive Analytics for Hospital Management:

Resource Optimization: AI algorithms forecast patient admission rates, bed occupancy, and staffing requirements, helping hospitals optimize resource allocation and improve operational efficiency.

Early Warning Systems: AI-based predictive models identify patients at risk of deterioration or readmission, enabling proactive interventions and improving patient outcomes.

Healthcare Administration and Billing:

Administrative Automation: AI streamlines administrative tasks such as appointment scheduling, medical coding, and billing, reducing paperwork and administrative burdens on healthcare providers.

Fraud Detection: AI algorithms analyze billing data to detect fraudulent activities and billing errors, ensuring compliance with regulations and reducing healthcare fraud.

Remote Monitoring and Wearable Devices:

IoT Devices and Wearables: AI integrates with wearable devices to monitor patients' vital signs, activity levels, and medication adherence remotely, enabling continuous health monitoring and early intervention for chronic conditions.

These are just a few examples of how AI is transforming various aspects of healthcare delivery, from diagnosis and treatment to administrative tasks and patient management. As AI technology continues to evolve, its impact on healthcare is expected to grow, leading to improved patient outcomes, cost savings, and overall healthcare quality.

Identification of Challenges and Opportunities from literature review

I. Challenges

Security Concerns and Data Privacy: Healthcare data is extremely sensitive and subject to strict privacy guidelines. The incorporation of AI technologies raises concerns about data security, patient confidentiality, and compliance with regulations such as the Health Insurance Portability and Accountability Act. Ensuring robust data privacy protections while leveraging AI for healthcare delivery remains a significant challenge.

i. Data Integration: Healthcare data is often fragmented across multiple systems and formats, making interoperability and data integration challenging. AI applications require access to comprehensive and standardized data from electronic health records (EHRs), medical devices, and other sources to generate meaningful insights. Achieving seamless data interoperability and integration is essential for the effective deployment of AI strategies in healthcare.
ii. Algorithmic Bias and Fairness: AI algorithms are susceptible to bias, resulting in disparities in healthcare delivery and outcomes. Biases may arise from skewed training data, algorithmic design choices, or systemic inequalities in healthcare systems. Algorithmic bias can exacerbate existing disparities in access to care, diagnosis, and treatment, undermining the goal of delivering equitable healthcare services. Mitigating algorithmic bias and promoting fairness in AI-driven healthcare interventions is a pressing challenge.
iii. Ethical Considerations and Regulatory: The rapid evolution of AI technologies outpaces regulatory frameworks and raises ethical questions regarding accountability, bias, and transparency. Regulatory agencies struggle to keep pace with the development and deployment of AI applications in healthcare, leading to uncertainty about legal requirements and ethical standards. Addressing regulatory and ethical challenges is critical to ensuring the responsible use of AI in healthcare and protecting patient interests.
iv. Integration with Clinical Workflows: Integrating AI technologies into clinical workflows presents technical and organizational challenges. Healthcare providers may face resistance to adopting AI tools due to concerns about workflow disruptions, usability issues, and perceived threats to professional autonomy. Effective integration of AI into clinical practice requires user-friendly interfaces, clinician training programs, and interdisciplinary collaboration to ensure seamless adoption and utilization of AI-driven solutions.

II. Opportunities:

i. Enhanced Patient Engagement: AI-powered implements such as virtual assistants, and mobile apps enable proactive communication with patients, providing personalized health information, medication reminders, and lifestyle recommendations. These tools empower patients to take a more active role in their healthcare management, improve medication adherence, and facilitate remote monitoring of chronic conditions. By nurturing patient engagement and self-care, AI contributes to better health outcomes and patient satisfaction.
ii. Superior Clinical Decision-Making: AI technologies have the potential to enhance clinical decision-making by analyzing large volumes of patient data, identifying patterns, and generating actionable insights. AI-powered clinical

decision support systems can assist healthcare providers in diagnosing diseases, predicting treatment outcomes, and personalizing care plans based on individual patient characteristics. By leveraging AI, healthcare organizations can improve diagnostic accuracy, optimize treatment strategies, and ultimately enhance patient outcomes.

iii. Streamlined Administrative Tasks: AI technologies streamline administrative tasks such as appointment scheduling, billing, and medical coding, reducing administrative burden and improving operational efficiency. Natural language processing (NLP) algorithms automate documentation tasks, while robotic process automation (RPA) tools automate repetitive workflows, freeing up healthcare professionals to focus on patient care. By automating administrative processes, AI enhances productivity, reduces costs, and improves the overall efficiency of healthcare operations.

iv. Innovation and Research: AI-driven research and innovation hold promise for advancing medical knowledge, discovering new treatments, and improving healthcare delivery. AI algorithms analyze biomedical data, identify drug targets, and accelerate the drug discovery process. Additionally, AI-enabled precision medicine approaches tailor treatments to individual patient profiles, improving therapeutic efficacy and minimizing adverse effects. By driving research and innovation, AI contributes to scientific progress and the development of cutting-edge healthcare solutions.

v. Population Health Management: AI enables population health management by analyzing large-scale healthcare data to identify at-risk populations, predict disease outbreaks, and implement targeted interventions. Predictive analytics models forecast patient demand, optimize resource allocation, and identify opportunities for preventive care and early intervention. By leveraging AI for population health management, healthcare organizations can improve health outcomes, reduce healthcare costs, and enhance the value of healthcare services at the population level.

In conclusion, while AI strategies offer immense potential to deliver better value in the healthcare sector, addressing challenges such as data privacy, interoperability, bias, and regulatory compliance is essential for realizing the full benefits of AI-driven healthcare innovation. By embracing opportunities to enhance clinical decision-making, patient engagement, administrative efficiency, population health management, and research, healthcare organizations can leverage AI to improve patient outcomes, reduce costs, and advance the quality and accessibility of healthcare services.

Future Directions in AI Research in Healthcare

Looking ahead, several promising avenues for future research in AI and healthcare emerge from the analysis. These include the development of AI-driven decision support systems, real-time monitoring tools, and adaptive interventions that empower healthcare providers and patients to make informed decisions and optimize health outcomes. Furthermore, there is a growing emphasis on human-AI collaboration and co-creation, where AI technologies augment rather than replace human expertise and judgment. This collaborative approach holds the potential to enhance clinical workflows, improve diagnostic accuracy, and personalize patient care while fostering trust and acceptance of AI among healthcare professionals and patients.

Moreover, the integration of AI into population health management, public health surveillance, and disaster response systems presents opportunities to address pressing global health challenges and enhance resilience in the face of emerging infectious diseases, natural disasters, and other health threats. Overall, the future of AI research in healthcare lies in leveraging technological advancements to address complex healthcare challenges, promote health equity, and empower individuals to lead healthier lives. By embracing interdisciplinary collaboration, ethical principles, and patient-centered approaches, AI has the potential to revolutionize healthcare delivery and transform the way we prevent, diagnose, and treat diseases in the 21st century.

Model for Building Effective and Trusted AI-Augmented Healthcare Systems

Ethical Framework and Governance: Establish clear ethical guidelines and governance structures to ensure that AI technologies in healthcare adhere to principles of beneficence, non-maleficence, autonomy, and justice. Develop transparent and accountable processes for data collection, algorithm development, and decision-making to foster trust among patients, clinicians, and other stakeholders.

Data Quality and Privacy Protection: Prioritize data quality assurance measures, including data cleaning, standardization, and validation, to ensure the accuracy, reliability, and integrity of data inputs for AI algorithms. Implement robust privacy protection mechanisms, such as data anonymization, encryption, and access controls, to safeguard patient privacy and comply with regulatory requirements, such as HIPAA and GDPR.

Interoperability and Integration: Promote interoperability standards and open APIs to facilitate seamless integration and interoperability of AI applications with existing healthcare systems, electronic health records (EHRs), and clinical workflows. Foster collaboration and partnerships among healthcare organizations, technology vendors, and research institutions to develop interoperable solutions that enhance care coordination, information exchange, and clinical decision support.

Clinical Validation and Evidence-Based Practice: Conduct rigorous clinical validation studies and real-world evaluations to assess the accuracy, reliability, and clinical utility of AI algorithms across diverse patient populations and clinical settings. Emphasize evidence-based practice and shared decision-making by providing clinicians with transparent information about the strengths, limitations, and uncertainties associated with AI recommendations and predictions.

Clinician Training and User-Centered Design: Provide comprehensive training programs and continuing education opportunities for clinicians, nurses, and other healthcare professionals to enhance their digital literacy, AI fluency, and ability to interpret and act upon AI-generated insights. Adopt a user-centered design approach to develop AI-enabled tools and interfaces that are intuitive, user-friendly, and aligned with clinician workflows, preferences, and needs.

Bias Detection and Mitigation: Implement measures to detect and mitigate biases in AI algorithms and data sources, including algorithmic auditing, bias impact assessments, and fairness-aware machine learning techniques. Promote diversity and inclusivity in AI development teams and datasets to mitigate the risk of algorithmic bias and ensure that AI technologies are equitable and representative of diverse patient populations.

Continuous Monitoring and Feedback Loops: Establish mechanisms for continuous monitoring, evaluation, and feedback to identify performance issues, address user feedback, and iteratively improve the accuracy, safety, and effectiveness of AI algorithms over time. Engage patients, clinicians, and other stakeholders in the co-design and co-development of AI-enabled healthcare solutions to ensure that user needs and preferences are incorporated into the design and optimization process.

Regulatory Compliance and Quality Assurance: Comply with regulatory requirements and industry standards for medical device software, including FDA regulations for AI-based medical devices, CE marking for European markets, and ISO standards for quality management systems.

Implement rigorous quality assurance processes, including software validation, verification, and documentation, to ensure that AI-enabled healthcare systems meet safety, reliability, and performance standards.

Transparency and Explain -ability: Enhance transparency and explain- ability of AI algorithms and decision-making processes by providing clinicians and patients with access to relevant information about the inputs, outputs, and underlying mechanisms of AI models.

Develop tools and techniques for generating interpretable explanations, visualizations, and summaries of AI-generated insights to support clinician understanding, trust, and acceptance of AI recommendations.

Long-Term Sustainability and Scalability: Evaluate the long-term sustainability and scalability of AI-augmented healthcare systems by considering factors such as cost-effectiveness, scalability, interoperability, and alignment with organizational goals and strategic priorities.

Invest in infrastructure, capacity building, and knowledge transfer initiatives to ensure that healthcare organizations have the necessary resources, capabilities, and support systems to deploy, manage, and sustain AI technologies effectively over the long term.

CONCLUSION AND FUTURE IMPLICATIONS

Summary of Findings

Findings from PharmEasy Case Study:
i. PharmEasy utilizes innovative technologies like machine learning and big data analytics for optimized medicine delivery.
ii. Smooth ordering process, wide medication selection, and efficient home delivery enhance user experience.
iii. Repeat users appreciate membership benefits and user-friendliness, recommending PharmEasy for medication needs.

Findings from Survey on AI and ML in Healthcare:
i. AI and ML positively impact healthcare outcomes, especially in clinical and operational domains.
ii. Challenges persist in administrative tasks despite perceived effectiveness.
iii. Financial outcomes benefit, and consumer engagement significantly improves with AI and ML adoption.

Overall Findings:
i. AI significantly improves healthcare outcomes, enhancing diagnosis, treatment, and patient satisfaction.
ii. Challenges in adoption include legal, ethical, and technical concerns, but but promises transformative improvements in quality, efficiency, and accessibility.
iii. AI offers potential in diverse medical domains, including surgery, diagnostics, and public health surveillance.
iv. Applications span diagnostics, treatment prediction, telemedicine, and preventive care.
v. AI frameworks and NLP techniques show promise in enhancing healthcare processes and decision-making.
vi. CT scans and computer vision systems demonstrate superior performance in healthcare applications, particularly during the COVID-19 pandemic.

vii. Future research must address privacy, security, and bias concerns to maximize AI's potential in healthcare delivery.

Implications for Policymakers, Practitioners, and Researchers

The findings underscore implications for policymakers, practitioners, and researchers in healthcare. Policymakers should prioritize regulatory frameworks addressing AI integration, ensuring patient privacy, and mitigating bias. Practitioners can leverage AI tools like PharmEasy for improved medication delivery, emphasizing user-friendly interfaces and efficient service. They must also undergo training to maximize AI benefits while addressing patient concerns. Researchers should focus on interdisciplinary collaboration to address adoption challenges and explore AI's potential in diverse medical domains, including surgery and public health surveillance. Future research must prioritize privacy, security, and bias concerns to ensure ethical AI deployment, fostering trust among stakeholders and optimizing healthcare outcomes.

Recommendations for Future Research

Based on the analysis, future research should prioritize several key areas to advance the integration of AI in healthcare effectively. Firstly, exploring interdisciplinary collaboration is crucial for addressing adoption challenges and maximizing AI's potential across various medical domains. Additionally, researchers should focus on developing robust regulatory frameworks to address privacy, security, and bias concerns, ensuring ethical AI deployment. Investigating the long-term impact of AI on patient outcomes, including diagnosis, treatment efficacy, and satisfaction, is essential. Furthermore, studying the effectiveness of AI-driven interventions, such as PharmEasy, in improving medication delivery and patient engagement can provide valuable insights for practitioners and policymakers. Finally, exploring novel AI techniques, such as explainable AI (XAI), can enhance transparency and trust in AI systems, fostering acceptance among healthcare professionals and patients alike.

Limitation of the Study

While the research provides valuable insights into the impact of AI on healthcare outcomes and the effectiveness of AI-driven interventions like PharmEasy, several limitations should be acknowledged. Firstly, the study relies heavily on survey data, and literature review, which may be subject to biases or limited generalizability. Additionally, the analysis primarily focuses on perceptions and effectiveness ratings from healthcare executives, potentially overlooking perspectives from other stakeholders such as patients or frontline healthcare workers. Moreover, the scope of the study may not encompass all aspects of AI in healthcare, leaving out emerging technologies or applications. Furthermore, the research lacks empirical data on the long-term effects of AI adoption and may not fully capture the complexities of implementing AI strategies in diverse healthcare settings. Future studies could address these limitations by incorporating diverse perspectives, utilizing mixed-methods approaches, and conducting longitudinal evaluations to assess sustained impacts.

Conclusion

Based on the findings and objectives of this research, the evidence overwhelmingly supports rejecting the null hypotheses and accepting the alternative hypotheses. AI technologies have demonstrated significant improvements in diagnostic care, treatment outcomes, patient satisfaction, healthcare quality, efficiency, accessibility, and delivery of better values in healthcare. Through innovative approaches like PharmEasy and AI-driven interventions, healthcare delivery has become more streamlined and patient-centric. Interdisciplinary collaboration, robust regulatory frameworks, and continuous research are vital for maximizing the potential benefits of AI in healthcare while addressing challenges such as privacy, security, and bias concerns. Therefore, this research concludes that AI-assisted healthcare delivery surpasses traditional approaches, offering transformative advancements in healthcare quality and accessibility, aligning with the alternative hypotheses proposed.

REFERENCES

Ackerman, J. (2023, June 28). How AI can add value to value-based care. *Medical Economics*.

Alami, H., Lehoux, P., Denis, J. L., Motulsky, A., Petitgand, C., Savoldelli, M., & Fortin, J. P. (2021). Organizational readiness for artificial intelligence in health care: Insights for decision-making and practice. *Journal of Health Organization and Management*, 35(1), 106–114. 10.1108/JHOM-03-2020-0074

Alhasan, M., & Hasaneen, M. (2021). Digital imaging, technologies and artificial intelligence applications during COVID-19 pandemic. *Computerized Medical Imaging and Graphics*, 91, 101933. 10.1016/j.compmedimag.2021.101933

Bajwa, J., Munir, U., Nori, A., & Williams, B. (2021). Artificial intelligence in healthcare: Transforming the practice of medicine. *Future Healthcare Journal*, 8(2), e188–e194. 10.7861/fhj.2021-0095

Balasubramanian, S., Shukla, V., Islam, N., Upadhyay, A., & Duong, L. (2023). Applying artificial intelligence in healthcare: Lessons from the COVID-19 pandemic. *International Journal of Production Research*, 1–34. 10.1080/00207543.2023.2263102

Carla Kriwet Chief Executive Officer, Connected Care and Health Informatics Here are 3 ways AI will change healthcare by 2030. World Economic forum, Jan 7, 2020

Carriere, J., Shafi, H., Brehon, K., Pohar Manhas, K., Churchill, K., Ho, C., & Tavakoli, M. (2021). Case report: Utilizing AI and NLP to assist with healthcare and rehabilitation during the COVID-19 pandemic. *Frontiers in Artificial Intelligence*, 4, 613637. 10.3389/frai.2021.613637

Choudhury, A., & Asan, O. (2022). Impact of accountability, training, and human factors on the use of artificial intelligence in healthcare: Exploring the perceptions of healthcare practitioners in the US. *Human Factors in Healthcare*, 2, 10002. 10.1016/j.hfh.2022.100021

Corny, J., Rajkumar, A., Martin, O., Dode, X., Lajonchère, J. P., Billuart, O., Bézie, Y., & Buronfosse, A. (2020). A machine learning–based clinical decision support system to identify prescriptions with a high risk of medication error. *Journal of the American Medical Informatics Association : JAMIA*, 27(11), 1688–1694. 10.1093/jamia/ocaa154

Gudigar, A., Raghavendra, U., Nayak, S., Ooi, C. P., Chan, W. Y., Gangavarapu, M. R., Dharmik, C., Samanth, J., Kadri, N. A., Hasikin, K., Barua, P. D., Chakraborty, S., Ciaccio, E. J., & Acharya, U. R. (2021). Role of artificial intelligence in COVID-19 detection. *Sensors (Basel)*, 21(23), 8045. 10.3390/s21238045

Jadhav, S., Deng, G., Zawin, M., & Kaufman, A. E. (2021). COVID-view: Diagnosis of COVID-19 using Chest CT. *IEEE Transactions on Visualization and Computer Graphics*, 28(1), 227–237. 10.1109/TVCG.2021.3114851

Jain, G. (2023) Leveraging AI to redefine value-care proposition. The Times of India, March 29, 2023, 10:38 PM IST Gaurav Jain in Voices, India, TOI

Khanna, V. V., Chadaga, K., Sampathila, N., Prabhu, S., Chadaga, R., & Umakanth, S. (2022). Diagnosing COVID-19 using artificial intelligence: A comprehensive review. *Network Modeling and Analysis in Health Informatics and Bioinformatics*, 11(1), 25. 10.1007/s13721-022-00367-1

Kristensen, S. E., Mosgaard, B. J., Rosendahl, M., Dalsgaard, T., Bjørn, S. F., Frøding, L. P., Kehlet, H., Høgdall, C. K., & Lajer, H. (2017). Robot-assisted surgery in gynecological oncology: Current status and controversies on patient benefits, cost and surgeon conditions–a systematic review. *Acta Obstetricia et Gynecologica Scandinavica*, 96(3), 274–285. 10.1111/aogs.13084

Liao, F., Adelaine, S., Afshar, M., & Patterson, B. W. (2022). Governance of Clinical AI applications to facilitate safe and equitable deployment in a large health system: Key elements and early successes. *Frontiers in Digital Health*, 4, 931439. 10.3389/fdgth.2022.931439

Mak, K. K., & Pichika, M. R. (2019). Artificial intelligence in drug development: Present status and future prospects. *Drug Discovery Today*, 24(3), 773–780. 10.1016/j.drudis.2018.11.014

McKendrick, J. Healthcare May Be the Ultimate Proving Ground for Artificial Intelligence. Forbes, Feb 22, 2023, 12:19pm EST

Mohamadou, Y., Halidou, A., & Kapen, P. T. (2020). A review of mathematical modeling, artificial intelligence and datasets used in the study, prediction and management of COVID-19. *Applied Intelligence*, 50(11), 3913–3925. 10.1007/s10489-020-01770-9

Moon, I., An, Y., Min, S., & Park, C. (2023). Therapeutic Effects of Metaverse Rehabilitation for Cerebral Palsy: A Randomized Controlled Trial. *International Journal of Environmental Research and Public Health*, 20(2), 1578. 10.3390/ijerph20021578

Morgan Stanley representative (2023) "What's NEXT – How AI/ML Could Reshape Healthcare," Morgan Stanley, (June 19, 2023)

Muehlematter, U. J., Daniore, P., & Vokinger, K. N. (2021). Approval of artificial intelligence and machine learning-based medical devices in the USA and Europe (2015–20): A comparative analysis. *The Lancet. Digital Health*, 3(3), e195–e203. 10.1016/S2589-7500(20)30292-2

Natarajan, A., Su, H. W., & Heneghan, C. (2020). Assessment of physiological signs associated with COVID-19 measured using wearable devices. *NPJ Digital Medicine*, 3(1), 156. 10.1038/s41746-020-00363-7

Patel, D., & Tarakji, K. G. (2021). Smartwatch diagnosis of atrial fibrillation in patient with embolic stroke of unknown source: A case report. *Cardiovascular Digital Health Journal*, 2(1), 84–87. 10.1016/j.cvdhj.2021.01.001

Pillai, R., Sivathanu, B., Mariani, M., Rana, N. P., Yang, B., & Dwivedi, Y. K. (2022). Adoption of AI-empowered industrial robots in auto component manufacturing companies. *Production Planning and Control*, 33(16), 1517–1533. 10.1080/09537287.2021.1882689

Quinn, T. P., Senadeera, M., Jacobs, S., Coghlan, S., & Le, V. (2021). Trust and medical AI: The challenges we face and the expertise needed to overcome them. *Journal of the American Medical Informatics Association : JAMIA*, 28(4), 890–894. 10.1093/jamia/ocaa268

Saifi, S., Taylor, A. J., Allen, J., & Hendel, R. (2013). The use of a learning community and online evaluation of utilization for SPECT myocardial perfusion imaging. *JACC: Cardiovascular Imaging*, 6(7), 823–829. 10.1016/j.jcmg.2013.01.012

Shah, H., Shah, S., Tanwar, S., Gupta, R., & Kumar, N. (2021). Fusion of AI techniques to tackle COVID-19 pandemic: Models, incidence rates, and future trends. *Multimedia Systems*, 1–34.

Simonite, T. (2020). The US government will pay doctors to use these AI algorithms. *Wired Magazine, 11*.

Singh, V. I. N. I. T., & Gochhait, S. (2020). The development of artificial intelligence in health and medicine: A bibliometric analysis. *European Journal of Molecular and Clinical Medicine*, 7(6), 2585–2594.

Topol, E. J. (2019). High-performance medicine: The convergence of human and artificial intelligence. *Nature Medicine*, 25(1), 44–56. 10.1038/s41591-018-0300-7

Wolff, J., Pauling, J., Keck, A., & Baumbach, J. (2020). Systematic review of economic impact studies of artificial intelligence in health care. *Journal of Medical Internet Research*, 22(2), e16866. 10.2196/16866

Chapter 8
Redefining Healthcare:
Artificial Intelligence's Revolutionary Effect

Simanpreet Kaur
Department of Commerce, Chandigarh School of Business, Jhanjeri, India

Anjali
Department of Commerce, Chandigarh School of Business, Jhanjeri, India

ABSTRACT

This chapter explores how artificial intelligence (AI) is revolutionising healthcare, with a focus on how AI may improve operational effectiveness, individualised care, and diagnostic accuracy. It examines AI uses in personalised medicine, medical imaging analysis, and predictive analytics, highlighting the profound shifts these technologies bring to the provision of healthcare. Examined are the ethical, privacy, and regulatory issues, emphasising the significance of a responsible and balanced approach to innovation. The chapter also discusses how AI may lessen healthcare inequalities and increase accessibility everywhere. In order to guarantee AI maximises advantages while addressing social problems, it argues for a collaborative approach, recommending continual research, multidisciplinary cooperation, and strong ethical frameworks. Researchers, policymakers, and medical practitioners who are navigating the changing terrain of AI in healthcare.

INTRODUCTION

Healthcare might undergo a revolution thanks to artificial intelligence (AI), which could improve patient outcomes and change the way healthcare is provided. AI-enabled healthcare processes that are more efficient and ethically sound, as well

DOI: 10.4018/979-8-3693-3731-8.ch008

Copyright © 2024, IGI Global. Copying or distributing in print or electronic forms without written permission of IGI Global is prohibited.

as proactive disease prevention, personalised treatment plans, real-time monitoring and intervention, enhanced medical imaging, and real-time monitoring and intervention (Harry, 2023). Personalised treatment plans and increased diagnosis accuracy are made possible by AI algorithms that analyse massive volumes of patient data, including genetic and biomarker data. Moreover, by identifying those who are at risk and facilitating early intervention, AI contributes to proactive illness prevention. In order to improve patient safety and lower hospital readmission rates, wearable technology and AI-powered remote monitoring devices provide real-time monitoring and intervention. Medical imaging is more accurate and efficient thanks to AI algorithms, which facilitates faster diagnosis and treatment. AI also expedites medical operations by automating administrative work and giving patients timely support. But it's also important to handle ethical issues like bias mitigation, data security, and patient privacy. Effective cooperation among healthcare professionals, technologists, politicians, and ethicists is vital in order to optimise the advantages and guarantee a human-centered strategy when incorporating artificial intelligence into healthcare. By using techniques like adaptive learning, predictive analytics, and intelligent tutoring systems, it can improve the efficacy and efficiency of the educational system. AI and machine learning are being used in cybersecurity to address the drawbacks and restrictions of conventional security measures (Pongtambing, et. al. 2023) Additionally, AI is being applied in a number of scientific and technological domains, such as natural language processing, robotics, and image recognition (Ramesh, 2004). AI is divided into two major categories: (i) Narrow AI (Weak AI): AI that has been trained and developed for a particular purpose. Virtual assistants such as Alexa and Siri, image recognition software, and recommendation algorithms employed by online retailers and streaming services are a few examples. (ii) General AI (Strong AI): Capable of understanding, learning, and applying knowledge to a broad range of tasks, this kind of AI demonstrates intelligence akin to that of humans. The goal of achieving general artificial intelligence is still theoretical.

    Deep learning, a subset of machine learning, is a technique that uses neural networks with multiple layers to process complex data. Machine learning is the process of training algorithms on data to generate predictions or decisions. Artificial Intelligence has applications in many different fields, such as customer service, healthcare, finance, transportation, and entertainment. It can increase productivity and accuracy, automate repetitive tasks, enhance human abilities, and open up new avenues for creativity and problem-solving. Aside from job displacement, algorithmic bias, privacy concerns, and the possibility of misuse or unforeseen consequences, artificial intelligence (AI) also brings up ethical, societal, and economic issues. In order to improve humanity's future, it is imperative that we address these issues as AI develops while also maximising its advantages. One of the most promising areas where artificial intelligence (AI) is advancing significantly is the healthcare sector.

Redefining Healthcare

A vast array of career options are available in the rapidly expanding and improving healthcare industry. Tough competition, intricate legal frameworks, and the requirement to remain current with changing healthcare policies make it difficult for students to get employment in the healthcare sector (Banerjee & Basu, 20232023). The use of digital tools and technologies by the healthcare sector, such as Internet of Things (IoT), machine learning, artificial intelligence, and big data analytics, is improving process efficiency and overall quality of care (Ravi et al., 2022).

AI has the potential to change the healthcare sector in a number of ways. It can facilitate effective drug discovery, tailored therapy, and quicker and more accurate diagnosis. By automatically identifying patterns and analysing data, machine learning approaches in healthcare can improve the precision and accuracy of clinicians' work (Kavya et al., 2023). AI has the potential to significantly alter clinical and administrative operations, especially those that involve early diagnosis and detection. Furthermore, medication development, personalised medicine, clinical decision-making, and medical imaging analysis can all benefit from the use of AI (Davenport & Kalakota, 2019). Healthcare issues such as screening and fitness monitoring, testing and diagnosis, and clinical decision-making can be resolved by integrating AI/ML (Wen & Huang, 2022). All things considered, AI has the ability to raise productivity, lower costs, and enhance healthcare outcomes across the board.

Application of Artificial Intelligence in Healthcare

Artificial Intelligence is applicable in the healthcare sector in various forms like: Medical Imaging Analysis: Artificial intelligence (AI) algorithms are able to analyse medical images, including MRIs, CT scans, X-rays, and mammograms, to help radiologists identify abnormalities, diagnose diseases (such as cancer, fractures, and neurological conditions), and rank cases for review. This process results in quicker and more accurate diagnoses:

Predictive Analytics and Early Disease Detection: AI systems examine genetic information, electronic health records (EHRs), and additional patient data to find trends and risk factors linked to specific diseases. Thanks to this, medical professionals can now anticipate and address diseases at an earlier stage of development, which may avert negative health consequences and save medical expenses.

Personalised Treatment Plans: AI examines sizable patient data sets to create customised regimens based on each patient's unique traits, including genetics, medical history, lifestyle choices, and response to therapy. The goal of precision medicine is to maximise therapeutic efficacy while minimising side effects.

Drug Discovery and Development: Artificial Intelligence (AI) finds and predicts potential drug candidates, optimises their properties, and speeds up the process by analysing chemical and biological data. In addition to more effectively meeting unmet medical needs, this can drastically cut the time and expense associated with introducing new drugs to the market.

Chatbots and virtual health assistants powered by AI: These tools offer patients individualised health advice, medication reminders, symptom triage, and appointment scheduling. By answering common questions, these technologies facilitate routine inquiries, increase patient engagement, and improve access to healthcare services.

Remote Monitoring and Telemedicine: AI-enabled remote monitoring devices gather and evaluate patient data in real-time, enabling healthcare providers to keep an eye on patients' health outside of conventional clinical settings. This is known as remote monitoring and telemedicine. AI is used by telemedicine platforms to provide remote consultations, diagnosis, and treatment planning. This improves accessibility and convenience by allowing patients to receive healthcare services from any location.

Healthcare Operations Management: By automating administrative work, effectively allocating hospital resources, and forecasting patient flow and demand, artificial intelligence improves healthcare operations. This increases overall care delivery quality, decreases wait times, and boosts operational efficiency.

Healthcare Billing and Fraud Detection: Artificial intelligence (AI) algorithms examine data from healthcare claims to find irregularities and trends that point to possible fraud. This lowers losses and strengthens the integrity of healthcare systems.

These uses of AI in healthcare show off the technology's potential to revolutionise patient outcomes, increase operational effectiveness, and change the way healthcare is delivered. However, to fully reap the benefits of artificial intelligence in healthcare, issues pertaining to data privacy, security, regulatory compliance, and ethical considerations must be resolved.

Areas of Application of Artificial Intelligence in Healthcare Sector

In many respects, artificial intelligence (AI) is transforming the healthcare sector by providing creative answers to persistent problems. Artificial intelligence (AI) can examine enormous volumes of patient data to find patterns and trends that humans might not notice right away, enabling earlier diagnosis, treatment, and prognosis assessment (Naqvi et al. 2023). Healthcare professionals can easily access and interpret patient data thanks to natural language processing (NLP) systems' ability to extract crucial information from electronic medical records (EMR) (Köse, 2023 & Nabeel, 2023). AI can help with image analysis, resulting in more precise analysis and quick diagnosis of medical images like X-rays and CT scans (Al Kuwaiti et al. 2023). Among the well-known uses of AI in healthcare are:

Redefining Healthcare

1. Medical Imaging: AI systems are able to evaluate medical images, including CT, MRI, and X-rays, to help with the identification and diagnosis of illnesses like cancer, fractures, and neurological disorders. AI can assist radiologists in improving patient outcomes by giving quicker and more accurate interpretations.
2. Drug Development and Discovery: Artificial Intelligence is being utilised to speed up the process of finding new drugs by evaluating enormous volumes of chemical and biological data in order to find promising drug candidates, forecast their effectiveness, and enhance their qualities. This can drastically cut down on the time and expense needed to introduce novel medications to the market.
3. Customised Medicine: Artificial Intelligence allows for the analysis of enormous volumes of patient data, such as genetic data, medical history, lifestyle factors, and treatment results, in order to customise medical interventions for specific patients. Enhancing patient outcomes and reducing side effects, this strategy may result in more focused and efficient treatments.
4. AI-Powered Virtual Health Assistants: Patients can receive customised health advice, symptom evaluation, medication reminders, and appointment scheduling from chatbots and virtual health assistants. In addition to facilitating better patient engagement, these tools also make healthcare services more accessible and less taxing on medical staff.
5. Predictive Analytics: AI systems examine patient data to forecast the possibility of subsequent medical occurrences, such as complications, hospital readmissions, or the advancement of a disease. Healthcare practitioners can take proactive measures to prevent negative outcomes and lower healthcare costs by early identification of patients who are at-risk.
6. Remote Monitoring and Telemedicine: Artificial intelligence (AI)-enabled devices for remote monitoring gather and evaluate patient data instantly, enabling medical professionals to keep an eye on their patients' health outside of conventional clinical settings. By using AI to facilitate remote consultations, diagnosis, and treatment planning, telemedicine platforms improve accessibility and convenience by allowing patients to receive healthcare services from any location.
7. Healthcare Operations Management: AI helps hospitals run more smoothly by predicting patient demand and flow, automating administrative tasks, and effectively managing hospital resources. This increases overall care delivery quality, decreases wait times, and boosts operational efficiency.
8. Mental Health Assistance: AI-powered instruments examine speech, actions, and additional digital indicators to evaluate people's mental well-being, identify early indicators of mental illnesses, and offer tailored interventions and assistance. By filling in the gaps in access to mental health resources, these tools support conventional mental healthcare services.

9. Wearable Health Monitoring Devices: Wearables with artificial intelligence (AI) continuously track physiological variables like blood pressure, heart rate, and activity level to give users real-time health status information. These gadgets support proactive health management and early health issue detection.
10. Medical Research and Knowledge Discovery: Artificial intelligence (AI) algorithms examine a tonne of clinical trial data, research data, and biomedical literature to find patterns, trends, and associations that can guide medical research and hasten scientific discovery.

These uses highlight AI's revolutionary potential in transforming healthcare delivery, enhancing patient outcomes, and promoting innovation and research in medicine.

Importance of Artificial Intelligence in Healthcare Sector

The use of artificial intelligence (AI) in healthcare is growing in significance. It is employed to increase the precision of diagnoses, plan treatments, and make better decisions, all of which eventually improve patient outcomes. (Sezgin, 2023). AI can examine vast volumes of patient data to find patterns and trends that humans might not notice right away, enabling earlier diagnosis and treatment. (Naqvi et al., 2023). Healthcare providers can more easily access and interpret patient data thanks to the use of natural language processing (NLP) systems, which can extract crucial information from electronic medical records (Ali et al. 2023 & Ola, 2023). Healthcare systems benefit greatly from artificial intelligence (AI) in a number of ways, including increased operational efficiency, personalised treatment, and diagnostic precision.

1. Operational Effectiveness: Artificial intelligence (AI) cuts down on manual labour and boosts efficiency in healthcare operations by streamlining administrative duties. AI-powered solutions, for instance, can handle inventory management, billing, and appointment scheduling automatically, freeing up staff members' time to provide patient care.

    "- Reduced wait times, higher patient satisfaction, and better use of healthcare facilities are all possible with predictive analytics driven by AI. It can also forecast patient demand, optimise resource allocation, and improve workflow management.

    - Healthcare companies can reduce downtime and guarantee the availability of vital medical equipment by using AI-driven predictive maintenance to proactively identify equipment failures and maintenance needs.

2. Treatment Customisation: Artificial intelligence (AI) examines enormous volumes of patient data, including genetic data, medical records, and lifestyle variables, to create individualised treatment regimens that meet each patient's

requirements and preferences. Precision medicine is an approach that strives to minimise side effects while optimising treatment efficacy.

Healthcare professionals can make well-informed decisions and deliver individualised care thanks to AI-powered decision support systems, which offer evidence-based recommendations, clinical guidelines, and treatment protocols. Patients are empowered to actively participate in their care and personalised remote healthcare delivery is promoted by AI-enabled remote monitoring devices that continuously track patient health metrics, identify deviations from baseline, and initiate timely interventions.

3. Diagnostic Accuracy: AI improves diagnosis accuracy by examining test results, medical images, and patient symptoms to help medical professionals identify illnesses more precisely and earlier. To increase diagnostic accuracy and lower false-positive rates, artificial intelligence (AI) algorithms, for instance, can identify abnormalities in radiological images, such as MRIs and X-rays. AI systems can now analyse unstructured clinical notes, pathology reports, and electronic health records (EHRs) to extract insightful data and speed up the diagnostic decision-making process. This is made possible by advances in machine learning and natural language processing (NLP). Symptom checkers and medical chatbots are two examples of AI-powered diagnostic tools that reduce diagnostic errors and unnecessary healthcare utilisation by giving patients accurate information, triage services, and advice on where to seek the best medical care.

To put it briefly, artificial intelligence (AI) is critical to enhancing the efficiency of healthcare systems' operations, precision of diagnosis, and personalisation of care. Healthcare organisations may improve patient outcomes, increase efficiency, and provide higher-quality care by utilising AI technologies to optimise resource allocation, provide personalised care, and improve diagnostic capabilities.

Artificial Intelligence in Healthcare: Obstacles and its transformative potential

Although artificial intelligence (AI) has the potential to revolutionise the healthcare sector, there are a number of issues that need to be resolved before it can be successfully integrated and widely used. Transparency, bias, privacy, safety, accountability, justice, and autonomy are some of the ethical issues that AI in healthcare faces (Pasricha, 2023). Events involving threats to data privacy and security, safety issues, bias diagnosis, the potential for hostile entities to commandeer AI, a deficiency in humanistic or interpersonal communication, a concentration of wealth around an AI company, and employment losses have all occurred. (Baihakki et al.

2023). The major obstacles in the path of Artificial intelligence with reference to healthcare industry are:

1. Data Security and Privacy: Sensitive information in the healthcare industry, such as patient records, is subject to stringent privacy laws. For training and validation, AI applications need access to massive amounts of data, which presents issues with data privacy, security lapses, and illegal access. To foster trust and reduce the risks associated with AI in healthcare, it is imperative to guarantee the implementation of strong data protection protocols and adherence to regulatory mandates.
2. Data Quality and Standardisation: Effective integration and analysis of healthcare data is difficult due to its frequent fragmentation, heterogeneity, and storage in multiple formats across multiple systems. The effectiveness and dependability of AI algorithms can be impacted by disparities, incomplete records, and poor data quality.
3. Bias and Fairness: AI systems may carry over biases from the training data, resulting in judgements and predictions that unfairly target particular demographic groups. In order to ensure justice, openness, and equity in the provision of healthcare, biases in AI must be addressed with great care in the selection of data, the design of algorithms, and examination techniques.
4. Ethical and Regulatory Considerations: To preserve professional integrity, safeguard patient rights, and assure safety and efficacy, the healthcare sector is bound by strict ethical and regulatory standards. Respecting ethical principles about patient consent, data confidentiality, and accountability for algorithmic decisions is necessary when integrating AI into healthcare workflows. Regulations such as the Health Insurance Portability and Accountability Act must also be followed.
5. Adoption and Clinical Validation: Before being incorporated into clinical practice, AI technologies must pass a thorough clinical validation process to show their efficacy, dependability, and safety. To gain acceptance from payers, patients, and healthcare providers and promote the widespread adoption of AI solutions, strong evidence must be generated through clinical trials, real-world validation studies, and regulatory approvals.
6. Workforce Readiness and Training: The proficient workforce needed to understand, create, and employ AI technologies is essential for the successful integration of AI in healthcare. For decision-making, patient care, and workflow optimisation, healthcare professionals require training and education on artificial intelligence (AI) principles, tools, and applications.

Notwithstanding these obstacles, AI has enormous potential to revolutionise the healthcare sector. With its revolutionary potential to improve healthcare delivery, diagnosis, and treatment, artificial intelligence (AI) holds great promise. ChatGPT and other AI models can act as co-pilot tools for physicians, completing, summarising, and interpreting reports (Ali et al., 2023). AI technology improves precision diagnosis, allowing for individualised treatment regimens and proactive illness prevention (Harry, 2023). It can help medical professionals analyse medical images remarkably accurately, allowing for the early detection of conditions like cancer (Al Kuwaiti et al., 2023). The transformative potential of Artificial Intelligence is discussed below:

1. Better Diagnosis and Treatment: AI can decipher complicated datasets, such as genetic information, clinical records, and medical images, to help medical professionals predict treatment outcomes, diagnose illnesses earlier, and customise treatment regimens based on unique patient characteristics.
2. Enhanced Patient Outcomes: By enabling prompt interventions, lowering medical errors, and streamlining healthcare delivery pathways, AI-driven interventions like predictive analytics, telemedicine, and remote monitoring can improve patient outcomes.
3. Operational Efficiency and Cost Savings: AI solutions enhance operational efficiency, lessen administrative burden, and save costs for healthcare organisations by streamlining administrative tasks, automating repetitive procedures, and optimising resource allocation.
4. Accelerated Research and Innovation: In order to more effectively address unmet medical needs, artificial intelligence (AI) has the potential to accelerate scientific research and drug development efforts by enabling the analysis of large-scale biomedical data, the identification of novel disease biomarkers, and the discovery of potential drug targets.

Ethical aspects related to artificial intelligence in healthcare

To effectively address the challenges and leverage the revolutionary possibilities of artificial intelligence in healthcare, cooperation between relevant parties is necessary, along with financial and human resource investments, and a dedication to morally sound, accountable, and patient-focused AI implementation approaches. In the years to come, AI has the power to transform healthcare delivery, enhance patient outcomes, and promote medical innovation—all provided these factors are carefully taken into account. But now a days, Artificial intelligence (AI) in healthcare brings up a number of ethical, privacy, and regulatory issues that need to be resolved for responsible and secure implementation. In a number of domains, such as bioinformatics, Industry 5.0, IoT, and aviation, ethical, data privacy, and regulatory issues are major concerns. In order to ensure appropriate privacy measures in the context of IoT, a thorough evaluation of potential benefits and harms, ethical considerations, and GDPR compliance are necessary (Vishi, (2023). In bioinformatics, Orlova et al. (2022) address privacy, informed consent, confidentiality, and other ethical concerns associated with using big databases. They also offer recommendations for medical data safety. The ethical and legal issues related to data privacy in the context of biomedical datasets are covered by Gamze, et al.(2019). It draws attention to the necessity of protecting privacy as well as the difficulties regulators and researchers have in maintaining privacy while encouraging data sharing. The various ethical issues related to Artidficial Intelligence are:

a. The use of AI algorithms can result in unfair or discriminatory outcomes by perpetuating biases found in the training data. This is known as bias and fairness. Transparent algorithmic decision-making, meticulous training data selection, and constant bias monitoring are necessary to ensure fairness in AI.

b. Accountability and Transparency: AI systems frequently function as "black boxes," making it difficult to comprehend how they make decisions. To ensure accountability for AI-driven decisions and to foster trust, it is imperative to set explainability standards, transparency requirements, and accountability mechanisms.

c. Patient autonomy and informed consent: AI-enabled medical interventions may have an effect on patients' right to privacy and autonomy. Transparent communication, informed consent procedures, and opt-out options for patients to refuse AI-driven interventions are all necessary to uphold patient autonomy.

d. Security and Confidentiality: Medical records and imaging are examples of highly sensitive data that must adhere to stringent confidentiality regulations. To stop illegal access, security breaches, and improper use of data, it is crucial to safeguard patient privacy and provide secure healthcare data transmission and storage.

e. Data Ownership and Control: Preserving patient privacy and upholding confidence among patients, healthcare providers, and AI developers requires elucidating data ownership rights and defining precise rules for data sharing, access, and control.

f. De-identification and Anonymization: When using large datasets for training and validation, AI applications frequently need access to them. Before providing patient data to AI developers, it is important to de-identify and anonymize it in order to reduce privacy risks and facilitate innovative research.

Regulations set to curb the issues related to use of artificial intelligence in healthcare

To address the difficulties and dangers involved with using artificial intelligence (AI) in healthcare, regulations are required (McKee & Wouters, 2023). The swift progress in artificial intelligence (AI) has resulted in the creation of intricate large language models (LLMs) that have various uses in healthcare environments. Assuring safety, upholding moral principles, and safeguarding patient privacy should be the major goals of AI legislation in the healthcare industry (Gerke et al., 2020). The FDA and HIPAA are two examples of regulatory entities that have a role in the rules, standards, and best practices that now govern AI in healthcare. It is necessary to address ethical issues such patient confidentiality, data security, algorithmic bias, and decision-making openness. The European Union's proposed AI Act seeks to standardise data security and moral AI in medical research and healthcare services. Healthcare-specific policies that are specifically tailored can guarantee the moral and responsible application of AI technology while promoting creativity. Here are some key rules that are covered:

a. Healthcare Regulation Compliance: AI applications must abide by current regulations, including local privacy laws, medical device regulations, GDPR (General Data Protection Regulation) in the European Union, and HIPAA (Health Insurance Portability and Accountability Act) in the United States. Robust data governance, risk management procedures, and legal knowledge are necessary to ensure regulatory compliance.

b. Rules special to AI: To foster innovation while preserving patient safety, privacy, and ethical standards, AI-specific regulatory frameworks that are adapted to the special features and hazards of AI in healthcare are imperative. To guarantee the security and efficacy of AI-driven medical devices and interventions, regulatory bodies might need to set rules for AI validation, performance assessment, and post-market surveillance.

c. International Cooperation and Standards: Coordinating regulatory standards and encouraging international cooperation can help ensure that artificial intelligence (AI) is developed responsibly and used widely in the healthcare industry. Raising regulatory coherence and promoting cross-border data sharing and innovation can be achieved by standardising terminology, interoperability specifications, and performance metrics for AI technologies.

d. Multidisciplinary cooperation between stakeholders, such as healthcare providers, AI developers, policymakers, ethicists, and patient advocacy organisations, is necessary to address these ethical, data privacy, and regulatory issues. AI has the ability to change healthcare delivery while preserving patient rights and privacy by promoting a culture of responsible innovation and respecting ethical standards.

Future of Artificial Intelligence in Healthcare

AI in healthcare has enormous potential to change the sector in the future. Doctors may use AI models such as ChatGPT as co-pilot tools to help with report completion, summarization, and interpretation (Ali et al., 2023). These models can produce appropriate answers for medical examinations by accessing a large body of medical literature and expertise (Harry, 2023 & Sahu et al., 2023). Improved medical imaging, tailored treatment regimens, real-time monitoring and intervention, and precision diagnosis are all made possible by AI technology. In order to increase diagnostic precision, identify illnesses early, and develop customised treatment plans, they examine patient data (Naveed, 2023). AI also improves patient participation and happiness by streamlining healthcare procedures and automating administrative activities. But there are issues that must be resolved, including prejudice, incomplete or misleading information, data privacy, and ethical issues. Artificial intelligence (AI) in healthcare has enormous potential to change patient care, healthcare delivery, and medical research, among other areas. The following significant events and trends are influencing how AI will be used in healthcare going forward:

Personalized Medicine

Through several significant advancements and trends, artificial intelligence (AI) is allowing personalised medicine, which is revolutionising the healthcare industry. Through dataset analysis and machine learning algorithms, artificial intelligence (AI) is being applied to diagnostics to increase accuracy (Khan, 2023). Utilising patient-specific data and predictive analytics, it also aids in the creation of customised treatment programmes that maximise therapeutic outcomes and reduce adverse effects. By evaluating patient data, including genetics and biomarkers, to develop customised treatment plans, artificial intelligence is revolutionising medicinal techniques (Waden, 2022). By automating processes like appointment scheduling and paperwork, it simplifies medical operations by lowering administrative burdens and mistakes. Chatbots and virtual assistants driven by AI improve patient engagement and satisfaction by promptly addressing issues and classifying symptoms (Mehta, 2023). Through its ability to analyse and understand high-throughput data produced by precision medicine tests, artificial intelligence advances personalised medicine. By analysing complicated data and offering suggestions based on solid evidence, it supports clinical decision-making. Through the analysis of clinical trial results and biological literature, AI also speeds up the process of developing new drugs. These AI trends and advancements are changing healthcare and have the power to both revolutionise the sector and enhance patient outcomes.

Predictive Analytics and Early Disease Detection

Predictive analytics and early illness diagnosis have seen notable trends and advancements in the field of artificial intelligence (AI) in healthcare. Large-scale healthcare data analysis and the identification of complex patterns for illness prediction have been shown to be possible using AI approaches like machine learning and deep learning (Kaur et al., 2020). This makes it possible to diagnose illnesses early and accurately, which improves patient outcomes and lowers healthcare expenditures. AI-powered solutions have the ability to predict patient outcomes and support medical professionals in choosing the best course of action. Furthermore, AI systems are capable of analysing medical pictures, including MRIs and CT scans, improving radiologists' efficiency and precision in spotting abnormalities (Harry, 2023). By identifying people who are at a high risk of acquiring particular disorders, AI in healthcare also makes proactive disease prevention possible. This allows for early intervention and specially designed preventative treatments. All things considered, artificial intelligence (AI) in healthcare is transforming early detection and illness prediction, resulting in better patient care and more efficient healthcare delivery.

Autonomous Healthcare Systems

AI is being applied to healthcare to increase the effectiveness and precision of medical diagnosis, treatment regimens, and decision-making. In order to uncover patterns and trends that may be used for early illness identification and individualised treatment strategies, machine learning algorithms evaluate patient data. Artificial intelligence (AI) further supports natural language processing to extract pertinent data from electronic medical records, making patient data easier to access and analyse (Faye et al., 2023). AI image analysis enables more precise diagnosis of medical pictures such as X-rays and CT scans. AI-driven chatbots and virtual assistants help with routine activities like reminding patients to take their medications and setting up appointments. Systems for predictive analytics predict patient outcomes and assist in making well-informed decisions about therapy (Zhang et al., 2021). Healthcare personnel will be relieved of monotonous chores by autonomous healthcare technologies, such robots, which are being developed to collect vital signs and health data on their own. These technologies can detect patterns in epidemics and employ AI to guarantee accurate readings. The Fourth Industrial Revolution's AI-accelerated digital transformation includes the integration of AI in healthcare, which paves the way for the creation of AI-powered healthcare system models.

Drug Discovery and Development

In healthcare, artificial intelligence (AI) has become a major trend, especially in the area of medication development. AI has the potential to enable personalised treatment, speed up the process of finding novel drug targets, and increase the efficiency of drug discovery procedures. It can find novel drug targets by analysing vast volumes of data, including genetic information, protein structures, and illness pathways. This expedites the drug discovery process and raises the success rate of drug development (Paul et al., 2021). Clinical trials for various drugs have been made possible by AI technologies including multi-property optimisation, generative chemistry, and machine learning. But only with enough ground truth and the right human intervention at later pipeline stages will AI's full promise in drug development be realised (Kohli et al., 2023). AI is also used in the production of pharmaceutical products, enabling the creation of customised drugs and enhancing resource efficiency and economy. All things considered, AI is changing drug research and might completely change the healthcare sector.

Augmented Healthcare Workforce

AI in clinical practice to enhance diagnosis precision, treatment planning, and outcomes for patients is one of the major trends and advancements in AI in healthcare related to the expanded healthcare workforce. Diagnostic imaging and testing, virtual patient care, clinical research and drug development, patient engagement and legal compliance rehabilitation, and administrative services are just a few of the domains in which AI applications have revolutionised healthcare (Sezgin, 2023). Healthcare is integrating augmented intelligence (AuI), which is producing remarkable gains and advantages for all parties involved. Interdisciplinary communication between medical professionals, AuI specialists, engineering professionals, and patients is essential if AuI is to be properly utilised in healthcare (Ilyas, 2022). AI-augmented delivery systems for healthcare may be intentionally designed to gain physician buy-in, acceptance among patients, provider investment, and payer support—all necessary for integrating AI into healthcare workflow (Dai, & Tayur, 2022). Artificial Intelligence (AI) has promise for bettering patient outcomes, cutting expenses, and raising the standard of care provided by healthcare providers.

Ethical and Regulatory Considerations

Regarding ethical and regulatory issues, some of the most significant advancements and trends in AI for healthcare include the rise in international investments in AI-based digital health technologies, such as Japan's Cross-Ministerial Strategic Innovation Promotion Programme (SIP) for a "Innovative AI Hospital System" (Katirai, 2023). The advantages of AI in healthcare are emphasised, including enhanced productivity, accuracy, and efficiency; personalised experiences; and support for decision-making and result prediction (Amedior, 2023). But the quickening pace of AI deployment in healthcare also brings with it difficult moral and legal quandaries, highlighting the necessity for precise healthcare-specific regulations to guarantee the technology is used responsibly and ethically (Khan, 2024). Privacy and security, prejudice and discrimination, explainability and transparency, accountability and responsibility, informed consent, human contact, and empathy are among the ethical ramifications of AI in healthcare. Clear standards for appropriate usage should be established, and the value of interpersonal communication and empathy in patient care should be upheld (Schicktanz et al., 2023). Global use of AI in healthcare can be encouraged by ongoing investigation and advancement of the technology's ethical implications.

Collaborative Innovation Ecosystem

The broad adoption and development of healthcare AI to lessen the workload for medical professionals and provide enhanced medical treatment are some of the key trends and advances in the field in connection to the Collaborative Innovation Ecosystem (Ahmed et al., 2020). Common industry concerns include establishing uniform connection protocols based on next-generation standards and guaranteeing strong security against attacks like ransomware (Wan, 2020). To improve the creation of pertinent frameworks for AI research in healthcare, collaborative relationships between university researchers, medical professionals, and industry specialists in software design and data science are required (Ismail et al., 2022). Problems with the quality of the data utilised and the possibility of insufficient automatic choices impede the application of AI in healthcare. To fully integrate AI into the healthcare ecosystem and achieve its potential, a digital ecosystem strategy might be employed. Using machine learning algorithms to analyse patient data and find patterns for early diagnosis and treatment is one of the major trends and advancements of AI in healthcare (Panwar, 2016). In order to improve patient data access and interpretation, natural language processing algorithms are being utilised to extract critical information from electronic medical records. AI is also being used in image analysis, which will improve the accuracy of medical picture diagnosis (Mukherjee et al., 2023). Healthcare professionals may focus on more sophisticated duties by using AI to automate basic operations. Systems for personalised medicine and predictive analytics are being utilised to anticipate patient outcomes and customise treatment regimens. AI-powered solutions help drug research, screening, diagnosis, and remote care; the COVID-19 pandemic has expedited the use of AI in healthcare (Nallamothu et al., 2023). Data security, privacy violations, and ethical issues are still problems, though. AI in healthcare has a bright future ahead of it, but its deployment will need addressing biases and limitations as well as judicious application.

CONCLUSION

The chapter examines artificial intelligence's (AI) uses, challenges, and revolutionary possibilities in the healthcare sector. With a focus on the interface between technology and patient care, the chapter provides a thorough understanding of how artificial intelligence (AI) is transforming healthcare delivery and upending conventional practices. The importance of artificial intelligence (AI) in enhancing operational efficiency, treatment personalisation, and diagnostic precision in healthcare systems is emphasised in the introduction. It looks at the various applications of AI in medicine, including predictive analytics, medical imaging analysis, and personalised medicine, and offers insights into the big changes these technologies bring about. The possibilities and issues surrounding the application of AI in healthcare are examined in the sections that follow. Examined are ethical, data privacy, and regulatory framework issues with an emphasis on the need to carefully balance innovation and responsible implementation. The chapter also examines how artificial intelligence (AI) can be applied to reduce healthcare disparities and enhance accessibility, emphasising how this technology has the potential to revolutionize the global healthcare system. The chapter ends with a suggestion for an all-encompassing, collaborative approach to maximise the benefits of AI in healthcare. In order to ensure that AI technologies improve patient care while resolving any potential ethical and societal issues, it emphasizes the need for ongoing research, interdisciplinary cooperation, and strong ethical frameworks. Researchers, legislators, and medical professionals will find this chapter to be a very useful resource as they navigate the quickly evolving field of artificial intelligence in healthcare.

REFERENCES

Ahmed, Z., Mohamed, K., Zeeshan, S., & Dong, X. (2020). Artificial intelligence with multi-functional machine learning platform development for better healthcare and precision medicine. *Database (Oxford)*, 2020, baaa010.

Al Kuwaiti, A., Nazer, K., Al-Reedy, A., Al-Shehri, S., Al-Muhanna, A., Subbarayalu, A. V., Al Muhanna, D., & Al-Muhanna, F. A. (2023). A Review of the Role of Artificial Intelligence in Healthcare. *Journal of Personalized Medicine*, 13(6), 951. 10.3390/jpm13060951

Ali, H., Qadir, J., Alam, T., Househ, M., & Shah, Z. (2023). Revolutionizing healthcare with foundation AI models. In *Healthcare Transformation with Informatics and Artificial Intelligence* (pp. 469–470). IOS Press. 10.3233/SHTI230533

Amedior, N. C. (2023). Ethical implications of artificial intelligence in the healthcare sector. *Adv. Multidiscip. Sci. Res. J. Publ*, 36, 1–12.

Baihakki, M. A., & Qutayan, S. M. S. B. (2023). Ethical Issues of Artificial Intelligence (AI) in the Healthcare. Journal of Science. *Technology and Innovation Policy*, 9(1), 32–37. 10.11113/jostip.v9n1.129

Banerjee, R., & Basu, S. (2023). HEALTHCARE INDUSTRY JOBS: OPPORTUNITIES AND CHALLENGES FROM A STUDENT'S PERSPECTIV. *Journal of Social Sciences & Humanities Researches*, 9(7), 1–8. 10.53555/sshr.v9i7.5771

Dai, T., & Tayur, S. (2022). Designing AI-augmented healthcare delivery systems for physician buy-in and patient acceptance. *Production and Operations Management*, 31(12), 4443–4451. 10.1111/poms.13850

Davenport, T., & Kalakota, R. (2019). The potential for artificial intelligence in healthcare. *Future Healthcare Journal*, 6(2), 94–98. 10.7861/futurehosp.6-2-94

Faye, A. S., Sow, O., Diop, M. A., Traore, Y., Ndiaye, J., Gueye, M., & Diop, A. (2023). Autonomous Robot with Artificial Intelligence for Taking Health Constants. *Ozean Journal of Applied Sciences*, 13(7), 963–975. 10.4236/ojapps.2023.137077

Gerke, S., Babic, B., Evgeniou, T., & Cohen, I. G. (2020). The need for a system view to regulate artificial intelligence/machine learning-based software as medical device. *NPJ Digital Medicine*, 3(1), 53. 10.1038/s41746-020-0262-2

Harry, A. (2023). The Future of Medicine: Harnessing the Power of AI for Revolutionizing Healthcare. *International Journal of Multidisciplinary Sciences and Arts*, 2(1), 36–47. 10.47709/ijmdsa.v2i1.2395

Ilyas, M. (2022). Augmented Intelligence for Advancing Healthcare. *Journal of Systemics, Cybernetics and Informatics*, 20(6), 13–19. 10.54808/JSCI.20.06.13

Ismail, A. F. M. F., Sam, M. F. M., Bakar, K. A., Ahamat, A., Adam, S., & Qureshi, M. I. (2022). Artificial Intelligence in Healthcare Business Ecosystem: A Bibliometric Study. International journal of online and biomedical engineering, 18(9), 100-114.

Jha, R. S., Sahoo, P. R., & Mohapatra, S. (2022, November). Healthcare Industry: Embracing Potential of Big Data across Value Chain. In *2022 International Conference on Advancements in Smart, Secure and Intelligent Computing (ASSIC)* (pp. 1-9). IEEE. 10.1109/ASSIC55218.2022.10088406

Katirai, A. (2023). The ethics of advancing artificial intelligence in healthcare: Analyzing ethical considerations for Japan's innovative AI hospital system. *Frontiers in Public Health*, 11, 1142062. 10.3389/fpubh.2023.1142062

Kaur, S., Singla, J., Nkenyereye, L., Jha, S., Prashar, D., Joshi, G. P., El-Sappagh, S., Islam, M. S., & Islam, S. R. (2020). Medical diagnostic systems using artificial intelligence (ai) algorithms: Principles and perspectives. *IEEE Access : Practical Innovations, Open Solutions*, 8, 228049–228069. 10.1109/ACCESS.2020.3042273

Kavya, A., Reddy, G. D., Sree, R. D. S., Jeevitesh, B., Gampala, V., & Thatavarthi, S. (2023, April). Role of Artificial Intelligence (AI) in Healthcare: Covid-19, Cancer and Accident Prevention. In 2023 7th International Conference on Trends in Electronics and Informatics (ICOEI) (pp. 858-864). IEEE.

Khan, A. (2023). Transforming Healthcare through AI: Unleashing the Power of Personalized Medicine. *Int. J. Multidiscip. Sci. Arts*, 2(1), 67–77. 10.47709/ijmdsa.v2i1.2424

Khan, F. (2024). Regulating the Revolution: A Legal Roadmap to Optimizing AI in Healthcare. Minnesota Journal of Law, Science & Technology, Spring.

Kohli, R. K., Santoshi, S., Yadav, S. S., & Chauhan, V. (2023). Applications of AI in Computer-Aided Drug Discovery. In *Applying AI-Based IoT Systems to Simulation-Based Information Retrieval* (pp. 77–89). IGI Global. 10.4018/978-1-6684-5255-4.ch005

Köse, A. (2023). Artificial intelligence in health and applications. In *Integrating digital health strategies for effective administration* (pp. 20–31). IGI Global. 10.4018/978-1-6684-8337-4.ch002

McKee, M., & Wouters, O. J. (2023). The Challenges of Regulating Artificial Intelligence in Healthcare: Comment on" Clinical Decision Support and New Regulatory Frameworks for Medical Devices: Are We Ready for It? A Viewpoint Paper. *International Journal of Health Policy and Management*, 12.

Mehta, V. (2023). Artificial Intelligence in Medicine: Revolutionizing Healthcare for Improved Patient Outcomes. *Journal of Medical Research and Innovation*, 7(2), e000292–e000292. 10.32892/jmri.292

Mukherjee, J., Sharma, R., Dutta, P., & Bhunia, B. (2023). Artificial intelligence in healthcare: A mastery. *Biotechnology & Genetic Engineering Reviews*, 1–50. 10.1080/02648725.2023.2196476

Nabeel, R. (2023). *Artificial intelligence (AI) is intelligence—perceiving, synthesizing, and inferring information—demonstrated by machines, as opposed to intelligence displayed by non-human animals and humans. Example tasks in which this is done include speech recognition, computer vision, translation between (natural) languages, as well as other mappings of inputs. The Oxford English Dictionary of Oxford University Press defines artificial intelligence as (No. sz7mj)*. Center for Open Science.

Nallamothu, P. T., & Cuthrell, K. M. (2023). Artificial Intelligence in Health Sector: Current Status and Future Perspectives. *Asian Journal of Research in Computer Science*, 15(4), 1–14. 10.9734/ajrcos/2023/v15i4325

Naqvi, S. G., Nasir, T., Azam, H., & Zafar, L. (2023). Artificial Intelligence in Healthcare. *Pakistan Journal of Humanities and Social Sciences*, 11(2), 1397–1403. 10.52131/pjhss.2023.1102.0443

Naveed, M. A. (2023). Transforming Healthcare through Artificial Intelligence and Machine Learning. Pakistan Journal of Health Sciences, 01-01.

Ola, A. F. (2023). *Artificial intelligence (AI) is intelligence—perceiving, synthesizing, and inferring information— (No. 37m9k)*. Center for Open Science.

Orlova, N. V., Suvorov, G. N., & Gorbunov, K. S. ETHICS AND LEGAL REGULATION OF USING LARGE DATABASES IN MEDICINE.

Panwar, N., Huang, P., Lee, J., Keane, P. A., Chuan, T. S., Richhariya, A., & Agrawal, R. (2016). Fundus photography in the 21st century—A review of recent technological advances and their implications for worldwide healthcare. *Telemedicine Journal and e-Health*, 22(3), 198–208. 10.1089/tmj.2015.0068

Pasricha, S. (2022). AI Ethics in Smart Healthcare. *IEEE Consumer Electronics Magazine*.

Paul, D., Sanap, G., Shenoy, S., Kalyane, D., Kalia, K., & Tekade, R. K. (2021). Artificial intelligence in drug discovery and development. *Drug Discovery Today*, 26(1), 80–93. 10.1016/j.drudis.2020.10.010

Pongtambing, Y. S., Appa, F. E., Siddik, A. M. A., Sampetoding, E. A., Admawati, H., Purba, A. A., & Manapa, E. S. (2023). Peluang dan Tantangan Kecerdasan Buatan Bagi Generasi Muda. Bakti Sekawan. *Jurnal Pengabdian Masyarakat*, 3(1), 23–28.

Ramesh, A. N., Kambhampati, C., Monson, J. R., & Drew, P. J. (2004). Artificial intelligence in medicine. *Annals of the Royal College of Surgeons of England*, 86(5), 334–338. 10.1308/147870804290

Ravi, P. R., Sarumathi, S., & Ramaswamy, R. (2022). Design principles, modernization and techniques in artificial intelligence for IoT: Advanced technologies, development and challenges. In *Artificial intelligence for internet of things* (pp. 315–333). CRC Press.

Sahu, V. K., Ranjan, A., Paul, M. K., Nagar, S., Devarajan, S., Aich, J., & Basu, S. (2023). AI Techniques and IoT Applications Transforming the Future of Healthcare. In Revolutionizing Healthcare Through Artificial Intelligence and Internet of Things Applications (pp. 210-233). IGI Global. 10.4018/978-1-6684-5422-0.ch014

Schicktanz, S., Welsch, J., Schweda, M., Hein, A., Rieger, J. W., & Kirste, T. (2023). AI-Assisted Ethics? Considerations of AI Simulation for the Ethical Assessment and Design of Assistive Technologies. arXiv preprint arXiv:2305.00566.

Sezgin, E. (2023). Artificial intelligence in healthcare: Complementing, not replacing, doctors and healthcare providers. *Digital Health*, 9, 20552076231186520. 10.1177/20552076231186520

Vishi, K. (2023, June). Privacy and Ethical Considerations of Smart Environments: A Philosophical Approach on Smart Meters. In International Conference on Computational Science and Its Applications (pp. 303-313). Cham: Springer Nature Switzerland. 10.1007/978-3-031-37129-5_25

Waden, J. (2022). Artificial Intelligence and Its Role In The Development Of Personalized Medicine And Drug Control: Artificial Intelligence and Its Role In The Development Of Personalized Medicine And Drug Control. *Wasit Journal of Computer and Mathematics Science*, 1(4), 194–206.

Wan, T. T. (2020). Convergence of artificial intelligence research in healthcare: trends and approaches. Journal of Integrated Design and Process Science, (Preprint), 1-14.

Wen, Z., & Huang, H. (2022). The potential for artificial intelligence in healthcare. *Journal of Commercial Biotechnology*, 27(4).

Zhang, Z., Genc, Y., Wang, D., Ahsen, M. E., & Fan, X. (2021). Effect of ai explanations on human perceptions of patient-facing ai-powered healthcare systems. *Journal of Medical Systems*, 45(6), 64. 10.1007/s10916-021-01743-6

Chapter 9
Innovations in Healthcare:
Exploring the Dualities of Generative AI

A. Karthiayani
Symbiosis International University (Deemed), India

ABSTRACT

This proposed chapter seeks to contribute to the ongoing discourse surrounding the promise and perils of generative AI in healthcare, offering insights and recommendations to guide informed decision-making and policy formulation in this rapidly evolving field. This chapter aims to delve into the revolutionary landscape of healthcare innovations, focusing on the nuanced interplay between promise and perils associated with Generative AI. As healthcare embraces artificial intelligence, the chapter will examine successful implementations, potential benefits, and, equally crucial, the risks and ethical considerations that come with the integration of Generative AI in the healthcare sector.

In recent years, the integration of generative artificial intelligence (AI) technologies into healthcare has marked a pivotal moment in medical history. With the promise of ground-breaking advancements, generative AI stands at the frontier of innovation, ready to revolutionize patient care, medical research, and healthcare delivery. However, this transformative potential does not come without its set of complex ethical, technical, and regulatory challenges. This chapter aims to explore the dynamic landscape of generative AI in healthcare, examining both its immense potential benefits and the inherent risks it brings to the forefront of medical innovation.

Generative AI, characterized by its ability to create novel data sets, images, and medical insights, employs sophisticated models such as deep learning architectures, natural language processing algorithms, generative adversarial networks (GANs),

DOI: 10.4018/979-8-3693-3731-8.ch009

and variational autoencoders (VAEs), (Liu et.al, 2023). These technologies have the power to generate synthetic data, detailed images, comprehensive medical reports, and even novel drug compounds, thereby opening new avenues for patient care and medical research, (Liu et.al, 2023). However, the deployment of these technologies also raises pressing ethical questions, underscores significant technical hurdles, and necessitates careful navigation of regulatory landscapes.

The applications of generative AI in healthcare are vast and varied, promising not only to enhance the quality of patient care but also to accelerate the pace of medical research. From the creation of synthetic patient data that respects privacy concerns to the generation of novel drug compounds that could cure previously untreatable diseases, the innovations brought about by generative AI are nothing short of transformative. Yet, the dualities of such innovations cannot be overlooked. The benefits of generative AI must be carefully weighed against the ethical dilemmas it poses, such as concerns related to data privacy, bias in AI models, and the potential for misuse of synthetic data.

To navigate the complexities of implementing generative AI in healthcare, this chapter will delve into a detailed exploration of these dualities. It will provide a comprehensive overview of the current state of healthcare innovation and discuss the pivotal role of generative AI within this context. Furthermore, it will highlight the importance of exploring these dualities to understand the full spectrum of challenges and opportunities that generative AI presents.

As we embark on this exploration, the following sections will offer an in-depth look at the innovative applications of generative AI in healthcare, the mechanisms behind the technologies driving these innovations, and the ethical, technical, and regulatory considerations that must be addressed. By examining these elements, this introduction sets the stage for a nuanced discussion on the transformative potential of generative AI in healthcare and the critical importance of navigating its inherent dualities for the betterment of patient care and medical research.

THE PROMISE OF GENERATIVE AI IN HEALTHCARE

Generative Artificial Intelligence (AI) is at the cusp of transforming healthcare in unprecedented ways. This technology, through its ability to analyze and synthesize vast amounts of data, is setting the stage for significant enhancements in healthcare delivery, diagnosis, treatment, and drug discovery. This section delves into the transformative potential of generative AI, exploring its capabilities to facilitate early disease detection, enable personalized treatment regimens, enhance patient outcomes, reduce healthcare costs, and democratize access to quality care.

Enhancing Patient Outcomes through Early Detection and Personalized Treatment

One of the most significant impacts of generative AI in healthcare is its potential to improve patient outcomes drastically. By employing advanced algorithms capable of processing and interpreting complex medical data, generative AI technologies can identify subtle patterns and indicators of disease that might elude human detection, (Krishnan, Singh, & Pathania, 2023). This capability is particularly promising in the field of medical imaging, where generative models can enhance the resolution and accuracy of images, facilitating early detection of conditions such as cancer, cardiovascular diseases, and neurological disorders.

Furthermore, generative AI can simulate patient responses to various treatment approaches, enabling healthcare providers to tailor treatments to the individual's genetic makeup, lifestyle, and disease progression. This personalization of care represents a shift from the one-size-fits-all approach to a more nuanced and effective strategy, potentially leading to better treatment outcomes and improved patient satisfaction.

Survey of Potential Benefits and Positive Impacts on Patient Care

The integration of generative AI into healthcare promises a range of benefits that extend beyond individual patient care. By generating synthetic data sets that mimic real patient data, generative AI can aid in training medical professionals, developing more robust diagnostic tools, and conducting research without compromising patient privacy, (Reddy, 2024). This aspect is particularly crucial in areas where patient data is scarce or sensitive, allowing for continued innovation while adhering to ethical standards.

Moreover, generative AI can bridge the gap in healthcare access by providing remote and underserved communities with sophisticated diagnostic and treatment options. Through mobile applications and telehealth services powered by AI, patients in remote areas can receive timely and accurate medical advice, reducing the need for travel and making quality healthcare more accessible to all.

Innovations in Healthcare

Figure 1. Generative AI in patient care (Reddy, 2024)

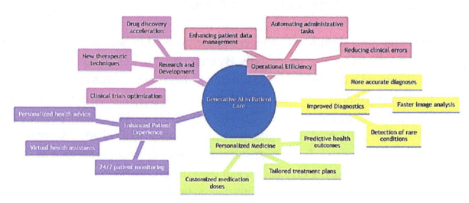

Around the central blue circle labeled "Generative AI in Patient Care," there are branches in purple and green. Each branch points to a specific application or benefit of generative AI.

The purple branches seem to focus on aspects related to research and development and the patient experience:

Drug discovery acceleration, New therapeutic techniques, Research and Development, Clinical trials optimization, Personalized health advice, Virtual health assistants, Enhanced Patient Experience, 24/7 patient monitoring.

The green branches highlight applications related to diagnostics and medicine:

Automating administrative tasks, Reducing clinical errors, More accurate diagnoses, Improved Diagnostics, Faster image analysis, Detection of rare conditions, Predictive health outcomes, Personalized Medicine, Customized medication doses, Tailored treatment plans

Each branch has two different colors, dark at the text and fading to light where it connects to the central concept, likely signifying the various levels of connection to the central idea. The arrangement suggests a comprehensive view of how generative AI integrates into different facets of patient care, highlighting its potential for innovation and improvement in healthcare delivery.

Examination of Efficiency Improvements, Diagnostic Accuracy, and Personalized Treatment Options

The efficiency of healthcare systems stands to gain significantly from the adoption of generative AI. By automating routine tasks, such as data entry and analysis, generative AI can free up medical professionals to focus more on patient care. This increase in efficiency can lead to faster diagnosis, reduced wait times for treatment, and, ultimately, lower healthcare costs.

Diagnostic accuracy is another area where generative AI can make a substantial impact. With its ability to learn from vast datasets, AI can assist in diagnosing diseases with a high degree of precision, reducing the likelihood of human error and the need for invasive diagnostic procedures, (Kumar et al., 2023). For instance, AI algorithms can analyze pathology slides or radiology images to identify disease markers that are not apparent to the human eye.

Lastly, the advent of generative AI paves the way for personalized treatment options that consider the unique characteristics of each patient. By analyzing individual health records, genetic information, and lifestyle factors, AI can help healthcare providers devise treatment plans that are optimized for the best possible outcomes. This approach not only enhances the efficacy of treatments but also minimizes the risk of adverse reactions, paving the way for a new era of personalized medicine.

In summary, the promise of generative AI in healthcare is vast and varied. From revolutionizing early disease detection and enhancing diagnostic accuracy to enabling personalized treatments and improving healthcare accessibility, the potential benefits are profound. As the healthcare industry continues to embrace generative AI, the focus must remain on harnessing this technology to deliver patient-centered care that is efficient, effective, and equitable.

PERILS AND ETHICAL CONSIDERATIONS OF GENERATIVE AI IN HEALTHCARE

The integration of Generative Artificial Intelligence (AI) into healthcare systems heralds a new era of medical innovation, promising to transform patient care, diagnosis, treatment planning, and even personalized medicine. Despite its potential to revolutionize the healthcare industry, the deployment of generative AI is fraught with complex ethical, legal, and social implications. This essay critically examines the perils and ethical considerations of generative AI within the healthcare sector, focusing on patient privacy, data security, algorithmic bias, informed consent, liability issues, and the need for robust regulatory frameworks. It also explores the positive impacts of generative AI through case studies, underscoring the balance between innovation and ethical responsibility.

Potential Risks Associated with Generative AI in Healthcare

The deployment of generative AI in healthcare poses several risks that need to be meticulously addressed. First, patient privacy and data security emerge as primary concerns. The vast amounts of personal health information required to train AI systems heighten the risk of data breaches, potentially compromising patient confidentiality. Second, algorithmic bias poses a significant threat to equitable healthcare delivery. AI systems trained on biased datasets can perpetuate and amplify existing disparities, leading to unequal treatment outcomes. Furthermore, the opaque nature of some AI algorithms can hinder accountability and obscure the decision-making process, making informed consent challenging.

Patient Privacy and Data Security

One of the most pressing concerns with the application of generative AI in healthcare is the risk to patient privacy and data security. AI systems require large datasets for training, including sensitive patient information. The aggregation and processing of this data increase the risk of breaches, which could lead to the exposure of confidential patient information. Such breaches not only violate privacy but also erode trust in healthcare providers and AI systems., (Seh et al., 2020). Ensuring the security of health data against cyber-attacks and unauthorized access is paramount, requiring robust encryption methods and stringent access controls.

Algorithmic Bias and Health Inequities

Algorithmic bias represents another significant risk, with the potential to exacerbate health inequities. AI algorithms can inadvertently perpetuate and amplify existing biases present in the data they are trained on, (Norori et al., 2021). For instance, if a dataset lacks diversity in racial or socioeconomic terms, the AI system might perform less effectively for underrepresented groups, leading to disparities in diagnosis, treatment recommendations, and patient outcomes. Addressing algorithmic bias requires a deliberate effort to use diverse training datasets and implement fairness algorithms that can identify and correct for biases.

Opaque Decision-Making Processes

The "black box" nature of some AI algorithms poses a challenge to transparency and accountability in healthcare decision-making. When clinicians and patients cannot understand how AI systems arrive at their conclusions, it raises concerns about the reliability and trustworthiness of these decisions, (Kiseleva, Kotzinos, &

De Hert, 2022). This opacity can hinder informed consent, where patients have the right to understand the options and potential outcomes of their treatment. Making AI systems more interpretable and explainable is crucial for integrating AI into patient care responsibly.

Erosion of the Patient-Doctor Relationship

The deployment of AI in healthcare also risks altering the fundamental nature of the patient-doctor relationship. The reliance on technology for diagnosis and treatment decisions could diminish the personal interaction and empathy that are core to the therapeutic relationship., (Sauerbrei et al., 2023). Maintaining a balance between leveraging AI for its analytical capabilities and preserving the human aspects of healthcare is essential.

Liability and Accountability in AI-driven Decisions

Finally, the question of liability in the event of errors or adverse outcomes from AI-driven decisions is complex. Determining accountability—whether it lies with the healthcare provider, the AI developers, or elsewhere—is challenging. This uncertainty may hinder the adoption of AI technologies in healthcare settings. Establishing clear legal and ethical guidelines for liability in AI-driven healthcare is crucial for protecting patients and ensuring that the benefits of AI can be realized safely and equitably.

The potential risks associated with generative AI in healthcare are significant and multifaceted, touching on ethical, legal, and social dimensions of healthcare delivery. Mitigating these risks requires a multifaceted approach, including the development of secure data handling practices, measures to ensure the fairness and transparency of AI systems, and policies that preserve the integrity of the patient-doctor relationship, (Naik et al., 2022). As the healthcare industry navigates these challenges, the goal should be to harness the power of AI to improve patient care while safeguarding against the perils that could undermine these advancements.

The integration of Generative Artificial Intelligence (AI) into healthcare holds the promise of transformative benefits but also introduces a range of potential risks that demand careful consideration and management (Zhang & Boulos, 2023). These risks span various dimensions of healthcare delivery, from patient privacy to the integrity of medical decision-making. Understanding these risks is crucial for developing strategies to mitigate them effectively.

Ethical Dilemmas, Privacy Concerns, and Implications for Patient-Doctor Relationships

Generative AI introduces ethical dilemmas centered around the autonomy and dignity of patients. The delegation of certain clinical decisions to AI systems could dilute the humanistic aspects of healthcare, affecting the patient-doctor relationship. Moreover, privacy concerns extend beyond data breaches, encompassing the ethical use of patient data for training AI without explicit consent, (Oniani et al., 2023). This raises questions about autonomy, informed consent, and the right to opt-out of AI-driven care. The impersonal nature of AI interactions could further erode the trust and empathy inherent in patient-doctor relationships, essential for effective healthcare.

The incorporation of Generative AI into healthcare introduces a complex array of ethical dilemmas and privacy concerns that have profound implications for the foundational patient-doctor relationship. These challenges are not only technical but deeply philosophical, touching upon the core values and principles that guide medical practice.

Ethical Dilemmas and the Principle of Autonomy

One of the central ethical dilemmas presented by Generative AI revolves around the principle of patient autonomy. AI's capability to analyze vast datasets and provide treatment recommendations or prognostic predictions raises questions about the extent to which such systems should influence medical decision-making. While AI can augment the decision-making process with insights derived from data beyond a human doctor's capacity to analyze, it also risks overshadowing the patient's or doctor's judgment, potentially leading to choices that may not fully align with the patient's values or preferences, (Abdallah et al., 2023). Ensuring that AI tools serve to support, rather than supplant, informed consent processes is critical.

Privacy Concerns Beyond Data Breaches

Beyond the risk of data breaches, there are nuanced privacy concerns related to the nature of the data Generative AI systems require for optimal functionality. The depth and breadth of personal information—ranging from genetic data to lifestyle information—that can enhance the performance of AI systems pose a dilemma, (Ricciardi, 2023). How much should be shared, and who gets to decide? The aggregation of such sensitive data, even if de-identified, raises the specter of re-identification and misuse. Establishing boundaries for data use, ensuring transparency about how and why data is used, and giving patients control over their information are crucial steps in addressing these concerns.

Implications for the Patient-Doctor Relationship

The patient-doctor relationship is built on trust, communication, and shared decision-making—elements that are challenged by the introduction of AI into healthcare. The potential for AI to act as an intermediary between patient and doctor can dilute the personal interaction that is central to building trust, (Lorenzini et al., 2023). Moreover, the reliance on AI for diagnostic or treatment recommendations could lead to a scenario where the art of medicine—the nuanced understanding of a patient's unique circumstances and the empathetic communication of options—is diminished, (Ahuja, 2019). Reaffirming the importance of the human element in healthcare, and ensuring that AI serves to enhance rather than replace personal interactions, is essential.

Additionally, the introduction of AI into healthcare settings can shift the dynamics of liability and responsibility, creating potential barriers to open communication between patients and doctors. Navigating these shifts requires clear guidelines and open dialogues about the role of AI in healthcare decisions.

Maintaining Trust and Empathy

Trust and empathy are cornerstones of effective healthcare. The impersonal nature of interactions with AI systems could undermine these foundations if not carefully managed. Ensuring that AI implementations in healthcare settings are designed with an understanding of patient needs and expectations is vital. Furthermore, training for healthcare professionals on how to integrate AI tools into their practice in a way that maintains or enhances the patient-doctor relationship is critical.

The ethical dilemmas, privacy concerns, and implications for the patient-doctor relationship introduced by Generative AI in healthcare require thoughtful consideration and action. Balancing the benefits of AI in enhancing patient care with the need to uphold ethical principles, protect patient privacy, and preserve the integrity of the patient-doctor relationship is a delicate task. It necessitates a collaborative approach involving policymakers, technologists, healthcare providers, and patients to develop frameworks and guidelines that prioritize the welfare and rights of patients while embracing the potential of AI to improve healthcare outcomes.

Real-world Applications and Success Stories

Despite these challenges, generative AI has facilitated remarkable advancements in healthcare. For instance, AI-driven diagnostic tools have improved the early detection of diseases such as cancer, offering hope for better patient outcomes. Generative AI has also been instrumental in drug discovery and development, significantly reducing the time and cost associated with bringing new treatments to market. These successes underscore the transformative potential of AI in enhancing healthcare efficiency and effectiveness, (Paul et al., 2021).

The deployment of Generative AI in healthcare has already yielded numerous success stories across various domains, demonstrating its potential to significantly improve patient outcomes, enhance diagnostic accuracy, and innovate treatment methodologies. These real-world applications provide compelling evidence of how AI can complement traditional healthcare practices, leading to revolutionary changes in patient care.

Improving Diagnostic Accuracy and Speed

One of the most impactful applications of Generative AI in healthcare has been in the field of diagnostics. AI algorithms have been developed to analyze medical imaging, such as X-rays, MRIs, and CT scans, with a level of precision and speed unattainable by human practitioners alone, (Bekbolatova et al., 2024). For instance, an AI system developed at Stanford University can identify pneumonia from chest X-rays with a higher accuracy rate than human radiologists. This not only improves diagnostic accuracy but also significantly reduces the time taken to diagnose, allowing for faster treatment initiation.

Personalized Medicine and Treatment Plans

Generative AI has made strides in personalized medicine, tailoring treatment plans to the individual patient based on their unique genetic makeup and health history. In oncology, AI models analyze genetic information from cancer cells to predict how tumours will respond to different treatments, enabling oncologists to choose the most effective therapy for each patient. This approach has led to improved survival rates and reduced side effects by avoiding ineffective treatments.

Drug Discovery and Development

Another area where Generative AI has shown tremendous promise is in drug discovery and development. Traditional drug development is a time-consuming and costly process, but AI can significantly expedite it. A notable success story is the use of AI by researchers to identify potential drugs for treating Ebola virus. The AI system screened existing medications to find those that could be repurposed to fight the virus, leading to the discovery of two drugs that significantly improved survival rates in Ebola patients, (Blanco-González et al., 2023). This application of AI not only accelerates the discovery of new treatments but also reduces development costs, making medications more accessible.

Enhanced Patient Monitoring and Predictive Analytics

Generative AI has transformed patient monitoring, particularly in critical care units. AI-powered systems analyze real-time data from various sensors and monitors to predict adverse events before they occur, (Bohr & Memarzadeh, 2020). For example, AI models are used to predict sepsis, a potentially life-threatening condition, hours before patients exhibit symptoms, allowing for timely intervention and significantly improving patient outcomes. Similarly, AI applications in wearable health technology offer continuous monitoring of patients with chronic conditions, alerting healthcare providers to potential issues before they become acute.

Case Studies Highlighting Innovative Solutions

Several case studies underscore the innovative solutions Generative AI has provided in healthcare. One such case involves the use of AI in predicting the onset of diabetic retinopathy, a leading cause of blindness. By analyzing retinal images, AI algorithms can detect early signs of the condition, enabling early intervention and preventing vision loss. Another case study involves the development of AI-driven prosthetics that adapt to the user's movements and needs over time, significantly improving the quality of life for amputees, (Al-Halafi, 2023).

The real-world applications and success stories of Generative AI in healthcare are a testament to its potential to revolutionize the field. From improving diagnostic accuracy and speeding up drug discovery to personalizing medicine and enhancing patient monitoring, AI is paving the way for more efficient, effective, and patient-centered healthcare. As these technologies continue to evolve and mature, the anticipation is that Generative AI will play an increasingly pivotal role in shaping the future of healthcare delivery.

Innovative Solutions and Improved Patient Outcomes through Case Studies

Case studies of generative AI applications in healthcare illuminate innovative solutions to longstanding challenges. For example, the use of AI in analyzing radiology images has not only improved diagnostic accuracy but also reduced the workload on radiologists, allowing for more patient-focused care. Another case study involves AI-powered predictive analytics in patient monitoring, which has enabled early intervention in critical care situations, thereby saving lives and improving patient outcomes.

The deployment of Generative AI in healthcare has not only addressed longstanding challenges but also introduced innovative solutions that significantly improve patient outcomes. Through a series of case studies, we can observe the tangible benefits and transformative potential of Generative AI across different aspects of healthcare.

Case Study 1: AI-enhanced Predictive Models in Cardiology

One notable case involves a hospital in the United States utilizing AI to predict cardiac events. The AI system, trained on thousands of patient records, including demographics, medical histories, and lifestyle information, can accurately identify patients at high risk of heart attacks or strokes. This predictive capability allows healthcare providers to intervene pre-emptively, offering personalized lifestyle and medication plans to mitigate risks, (Nowakowska et al., 2023). The result has been a marked decrease in emergency cardiac events among the hospital's patient population, showcasing how AI can proactively manage and improve patient health outcomes, (Nowakowska et al., 2023).

Case Study 2: AI-driven Precision Oncology

Another case study highlights the role of Generative AI in transforming cancer treatment through precision oncology. A cancer research center developed an AI model that analyzes the genetic makeup of tumours to identify potential vulnerabilities and recommend targeted therapies, (Bhalla & Laganà, 2022). This approach was applied to a group of patients with a rare form of cancer that had previously been unresponsive to conventional treatments. The AI-recommended therapies led to significant reductions in tumour size and improved survival rates, demonstrating the power of AI in identifying effective, personalized treatment options for cancer patients.

Case Study 3: Generative AI in Chronic Disease Management

Generative AI has also made strides in chronic disease management, as illustrated by a program for diabetes care. An AI system was designed to analyze continuous glucose monitoring data, along with dietary and activity patterns, to provide personalized diabetes management plans. Patients received real-time feedback and recommendations on managing their blood sugar levels through lifestyle adjustments, (Cho, 2023). This AI-assisted program resulted in improved glycemic control, reduced instances of hypoglycemia, and enhanced overall quality of life for participants, highlighting the potential of AI in managing complex chronic conditions.

Case Study 4: AI-assisted Surgery

A breakthrough in surgical procedures is another area where Generative AI shines. A surgical robot, powered by AI, was used in a series of minimally invasive surgeries. The AI system provided real-time data analysis, offering surgeons unprecedented precision and control. This led to reduced operation times, minimized complications, and faster patient recovery times. The success of AI-assisted surgeries underscores the potential for AI to augment human skill and improve surgical outcomes significantly.

Case Study 5: AI in Mental Health Interventions

The application of AI in mental health provides innovative solutions for patient care and support. In a pilot project, an AI-powered chatbot was deployed to offer 24/7 emotional support to individuals with anxiety and depression. The chatbot, designed to simulate therapeutic conversations, provided coping strategies and mindfulness exercises. Users reported reductions in symptoms of anxiety and depression, highlighting the chatbot's effectiveness as a supplementary mental health resource, (Thakkar, Gupta, & De Sousa, 2024). This case study demonstrates the potential of AI to provide accessible and immediate support for mental health, complementing traditional therapy and medication.

These case studies illustrate the diverse and profound impact Generative AI can have on healthcare, from predictive analytics and precision medicine to chronic disease management and surgical assistance. By harnessing the power of AI, healthcare providers can deliver more personalized, efficient, and effective care, leading to improved patient outcomes and quality of life. As the technology continues to evolve, it holds the promise of further innovations that will shape the future of healthcare delivery.

The integration of generative AI into healthcare is a double-edged sword, offering unprecedented opportunities for advancement while presenting significant ethical and regulatory challenges. Addressing these concerns requires a concerted effort from policymakers, technologists, and healthcare professionals to develop comprehensive regulatory frameworks that ensure the ethical deployment of AI technologies. As we navigate this complex landscape, the focus must remain on harnessing the benefits of generative AI to improve patient care, while safeguarding against its potential perils.

CHALLENGES AND CAUTIONARY TALES

The advent of generative Artificial Intelligence (AI) in healthcare has been met with both enthusiasm and apprehension. While its potential to revolutionize medical diagnostics, treatment planning, and personalized medicine is undeniable, the integration of these technologies also introduces a host of ethical and operational challenges. Drawing upon real-world case studies and ethical frameworks, it becomes evident that a strategic approach is necessary to navigate the complexities of AI in healthcare. This section proposes strategies to mitigate the risks and emphasizes the importance of transparency, interpretability, accountability, and interdisciplinary collaboration in the deployment of generative AI technologies.

Transparency in AI Deployments

The black-box nature of many AI systems poses significant challenges in healthcare settings. Without transparency in how AI models make decisions, clinicians and patients may be hesitant to trust and rely on these systems. For instance, a study in the Journal of Medical Ethics highlighted instances where AI diagnostic tools were deployed without clear explanations of their decision-making processes, leading to resistance from healthcare professionals, (Khan et al., 2023). To combat this, developing AI with explainable AI (XAI) principles is crucial. XAI enables users to understand and trust the decisions made by AI systems, thereby enhancing their acceptability and efficacy in clinical environments, (Hulsen, 2023).

Transparency in AI deployments is crucial for several reasons. It builds trust among users, regulators, and stakeholders by making the operations of AI systems more understandable and accountable. Transparency also plays a key role in identifying and mitigating biases, ensuring fairness, and facilitating the ethical use of AI technologies. Furthermore, it aids in compliance with increasingly stringent regulations regarding data privacy and AI governance.

Transparent AI systems allow users to understand how decisions are made, increasing their trust in the technology. Transparency enables better oversight and governance of AI systems, ensuring they align with ethical standards and societal values. Openness in AI deployments fosters a collaborative environment where knowledge and best practices can be shared across industries.

Some AI models, especially deep learning systems, are inherently complex and difficult to interpret, posing challenges to transparency. In some cases, making an AI system more transparent and interpretable may require compromises on its performance or accuracy. Companies may resist transparency due to fears of compromising their intellectual property or competitive edge. The absence of universally accepted standards for transparency in AI makes it difficult to implement consistently across different deployments.

Organizations should establish clear policies that outline their commitment to transparency, including the disclosure of AI system capabilities, limitations, and the data they use. Incorporating XAI techniques can make AI decisions more understandable to humans, without significantly compromising performance. Regular engagement with users, regulators, and other stakeholders can help address concerns and improve the transparency of AI deployments. Following emerging standards and frameworks for AI transparency and ethics can guide organizations in making their AI systems more open.

Transparency in AI deployments is not just a regulatory requirement but a strategic imperative that can enhance trust, facilitate ethical use, and ensure the responsible development and deployment of AI technologies. By embracing transparency, organizations can navigate the complexities of AI governance and leverage AI's benefits in a manner that is equitable, ethical, and aligned with human values.

Interpretability and Clinical Decision Support

Interpretability is closely tied to transparency but focuses on the ability to understand the decisions or predictions made by AI in a meaningful way. A notable case is the deployment of an AI system for predicting sepsis in a major hospital, which, despite high accuracy, was underutilized due to clinicians' difficulty in interpreting the model's alerts. Ensuring that AI systems not only provide accurate predictions but also present their findings in an interpretable and clinically relevant manner is essential for their successful integration into healthcare practices.

Accountability and Ethical Considerations

Accountability in AI-driven healthcare necessitates clear guidelines on the responsibilities of AI developers, healthcare providers, and regulatory bodies. The deployment of AI in diagnosing rare diseases, while promising, has raised questions about accountability when AI recommendations lead to misdiagnosis. Implementing ethical frameworks that prioritize patient safety and privacy, and establishing clear protocols for when AI systems fail, can help in fostering a culture of accountability.

Generative AI systems should be transparent and explainable, allowing healthcare providers and patients to understand how AI-generated recommendations are made. This transparency is crucial for building trust in AI technologies and for clinicians to make informed decisions about incorporating AI insights into patient care. Explainability also supports accountability by making it easier to identify and rectify errors or biases in AI models.

The use of generative AI in healthcare raises significant concerns about patient data privacy and security. It is imperative to ensure that all patient data used to train and operate AI models are handled with the utmost care, following strict data protection regulations such as the General Data Protection Regulation (GDPR) in Europe or the Health Insurance Portability and Accountability Act (HIPAA) in the United States. Secure data practices, including anonymization and encryption, are essential for protecting patient information, (Forcier et al., 2019).

AI systems can perpetuate or even exacerbate existing biases if not carefully designed and monitored. Healthcare providers must ensure that generative AI models are trained on diverse datasets that accurately reflect the demographic makeup of the patient population they serve. Ongoing evaluation and adjustment of AI systems are necessary to address any emergent biases and ensure equitable healthcare outcomes for all patients.

While generative AI can significantly enhance clinical decision-making, ultimate responsibility should remain with human healthcare providers. Clear guidelines are needed to delineate the roles of AI systems and human judgment in patient care, ensuring that healthcare professionals remain accountable for clinical decisions. This includes establishing protocols for when and how to override AI recommendations.

Regulatory bodies play a critical role in ensuring the safe and ethical use of generative AI in healthcare. Continuous oversight, including the evaluation of AI systems for safety, efficacy, and compliance with ethical standards, is necessary. Regulatory frameworks should evolve alongside AI technologies to address new challenges and ensure that innovations in healthcare AI are beneficial and ethically sound.

Engaging a wide range of stakeholders, including patients, healthcare providers, ethicists, and policymakers, is essential for addressing ethical and accountability concerns in healthcare AI. Public trust in AI technologies can be fostered through transparent communication about how AI is used in healthcare, the benefits it brings, and the measures taken to mitigate risks.

The integration of generative AI into healthcare presents vast opportunities for improving patient care, but it also raises important ethical and accountability issues. Addressing these considerations requires a multifaceted approach involving ethical frameworks, regulatory oversight, stakeholder engagement, and continuous monitoring for bias and fairness. By prioritizing ethical considerations and accountability, the healthcare sector can harness the potential of generative AI to benefit patients while maintaining public trust and upholding the highest standards of care.

Interdisciplinary Collaboration for Patient Safety

The complexity of healthcare AI systems demands expertise from various fields. Collaborative efforts among clinicians, data scientists, ethicists, policymakers, and regulatory bodies are imperative for addressing the multifaceted challenges of AI in healthcare. The development and evaluation of AI tools for patient monitoring in intensive care units serve as a prime example, where interdisciplinary teams have worked together to ensure that these tools enhance patient safety and care quality.

Successful integration of generative AI into clinical workflows requires the collaboration of healthcare professionals and AI specialists. Clinicians provide insights into the practical aspects of patient care and the clinical relevance of AI-generated recommendations, while AI specialists ensure the technological robustness and reliability of AI applications. Together, they can identify potential safety issues, refine AI tools to support clinical needs, and develop protocols for using AI in a way that enhances, rather than complicates, patient care.

Ethical considerations are paramount in the deployment of AI in healthcare. An interdisciplinary approach, involving ethicists, legal experts, healthcare providers, and patient advocates, is essential for navigating the ethical complexities of AI. This collaborative effort can help establish ethical guidelines for AI use, ensure patient rights and privacy are protected, and develop frameworks for addressing ethical dilemmas that may arise from AI integration into healthcare.

Interdisciplinary collaboration is essential for ensuring patient safety in the era of AI-enhanced healthcare. By leveraging the strengths and expertise of diverse professionals, healthcare organizations can navigate the complexities of integrating AI into clinical practice, address ethical and practical challenges, and foster an environment of continuous improvement. This collaborative approach not only enhances patient safety but also promotes innovation and trust in AI technologies.

Regulatory Oversight and Standards

Effective regulatory oversight is crucial for ensuring that generative AI technologies in healthcare are safe, effective, and equitable. The evolving nature of AI necessitates adaptive regulatory frameworks that can respond to new developments and challenges. For instance, the FDA's evolving guidelines on AI in medical devices illustrate the need for regulation that keeps pace with technological advancements while safeguarding patient interests.

The integration of generative AI into healthcare, while promising, brings forth significant ethical and operational challenges. By emphasizing transparency, interpretability, accountability, and fostering interdisciplinary collaboration, the healthcare sector can navigate these challenges effectively. Additionally, adaptive regulatory oversight will be crucial in ensuring that AI technologies benefit patients and clinicians alike. As the field of AI continues to evolve, so too must our approaches to managing its impact on healthcare, always with a focus on upholding the highest standards of patient care and ethical practice.

REGULATORY FRAMEWORK AND GOVERNANCE

Current regulatory landscape

The regulatory landscape for Generative AI in healthcare is multifaceted, involving various national and international bodies. Key among these are the U.S. Food and Drug Administration (FDA), the European Medicines Agency (EMA), and other regulatory authorities that oversee medical devices and healthcare technologies, (Teixeira, Kweder, & Saint-Raymond, 2020). Currently, these organizations are adapting existing frameworks to address the unique challenges posed by AI, including issues of transparency, accountability, and continuous learning capabilities of AI systems.

In the United States, the FDA has begun issuing guidance for developers of AI/ML-based software as a medical device (SaMD), (Joshi et al., 2023). This includes a proposed regulatory framework that emphasizes a total product lifecycle (TPLC) regulatory approach, acknowledging the dynamic and evolving nature of AI algorithms, (Joshi et al., 2023).

In Europe, the General Data Protection Regulation (GDPR) plays a crucial role in governing the use of data in AI applications, including those in healthcare, (Farhud & Zokaei, 2021). The GDPR's provisions on data protection, consent, and the right to explanation are particularly relevant when it comes to training AI models with patient data, (Farhud & Zokaei, 2021).

Governance mechanisms

Governance of Generative AI in healthcare extends beyond formal regulations to include ethical guidelines, standards, and best practices developed by professional bodies, international organizations, and consortiums. These mechanisms are designed to ensure that AI development is guided by ethical principles such as fairness, non-maleficence, autonomy, and justice.

The World Health Organization (WHO) and the Organisation for Economic Co-operation and Development (OECD) have both issued recommendations for the ethical use of AI in healthcare, (Gerke, Minssen, & Cohen, 2020). These guidelines emphasize the importance of transparency, explainability, and accountability in AI systems, as well as the need for equitable access to AI technologies.

Recommendations for Enhancing Regulatory Frameworks and Governance

a. ***Adaptive Regulation:*** Regulatory frameworks should be dynamic and adaptable, allowing for the rapid evolution of AI technologies. This could involve the implementation of post-market surveillance systems to monitor the real-world performance of AI applications and adjust regulations as needed.
b. ***Multi-Stakeholder Collaboration:*** Developing and refining AI regulations should be a collaborative effort involving regulators, developers, healthcare providers, patients, and ethicists. This approach ensures that diverse perspectives are considered, and regulations are balanced and comprehensive.
c. ***Ethics by Design:*** Ethical considerations should be integrated into the development process of AI systems from the outset. This includes incorporating principles of transparency, fairness, and accountability into the design and deployment of AI technologies.
d. ***International Harmonization:*** Given the global nature of healthcare and technology, there is a need for international cooperation to harmonize regulatory standards for Generative AI. This would facilitate the global adoption of AI solutions while ensuring consistent safety and ethical standards.
e. ***Education and Awareness:*** Building knowledge and awareness about AI technologies among healthcare providers, patients, and the general public is crucial. This involves not only education about the benefits and limitations of AI but also about the regulatory and ethical frameworks that govern its use.

As Generative AI continues to revolutionize healthcare, the need for robust regulatory frameworks and governance mechanisms becomes increasingly critical. By ensuring that these technologies are developed and deployed in a manner that prioritizes patient safety, data privacy, and ethical considerations, we can harness the full potential of AI to improve healthcare outcomes. Strengthening the regulatory and governance infrastructure will require a concerted effort from all stakeholders, including regulatory bodies, AI developers, healthcare professionals, and patients.

PATIENT EMPOWERMENT AND INFORMED CONSENT

In the fast-paced evolution of healthcare technology, Generative Artificial Intelligence (AI) stands out for its potential to revolutionize patient care, diagnosis, and treatment plans. However, this technological advancement also introduces challenges, particularly in ensuring patient empowerment and obtaining informed consent. This section underscores the necessity of involving patients in healthcare decisions and elaborates on mechanisms to secure informed consent, emphasizing transparency in Generative AI applications.

The advent of Generative AI in healthcare heralds a shift towards more personalized and efficient patient care. Yet, the true essence of healthcare improvement lies in patient empowerment, where patients are active participants in their health decisions rather than passive recipients of care.

Empowering patients in decision-making processes fosters a patient-centered care approach. This model respects patients' values, preferences, and needs, leading to improved patient satisfaction and outcomes. Generative AI, with its capacity for personalized treatment recommendations, plays a critical role in realizing this model, provided patients are adequately informed and involved in interpreting AI-generated options.

Active involvement in healthcare decisions enhances patients' understanding of their conditions and treatment options. When patients comprehend the role and reasoning behind Generative AI recommendations, trust in both the technology and healthcare providers increases, facilitating a collaborative healthcare environment.

Incorporating Generative AI into the shared decision-making framework ensures decisions are made collaboratively by healthcare providers and patients. This approach acknowledges the expertise of both parties: the clinical and technological expertise of healthcare providers and the personal values and preferences of patients.

Mechanisms for Obtaining Informed Consent in Generative AI Applications

Informed consent is a cornerstone of ethical healthcare, ensuring patients are aware of and agree to their treatment plans. The integration of Generative AI into healthcare necessitates revisiting informed consent mechanisms to address unique challenges posed by AI technologies.

Consent processes should explicitly delineate the role of AI in patient care, distinguishing between AI-supported decisions and those made solely by healthcare providers. This clarity helps patients understand the extent to which AI influences their care, enabling more informed consent.

The dynamic nature of Generative AI, with continuous learning and adaptation, calls for a model of continuous consent. Patients should be regularly updated and consulted about changes in AI applications affecting their treatment, ensuring ongoing consent throughout their care journey.

Informed consent must also cover aspects of data privacy and protection, particularly concerning the data used to train and operate Generative AI systems. Patients should be informed about how their data is used, the measures in place to protect their privacy, and their rights regarding data usage.

The integration of Generative AI into healthcare presents unparalleled opportunities for enhancing patient care through personalized treatment plans and improved diagnosis. However, realizing these benefits requires a foundational commitment to patient empowerment and robust informed consent mechanisms. By involving patients in decision-making processes and ensuring transparency in AI applications, healthcare providers can foster trust, improve patient outcomes, and navigate the ethical challenges presented by Generative AI technologies.

Innovations in Healthcare

Figure 2. Flowchart (Adus, Macklin, & Pinto, 2023)

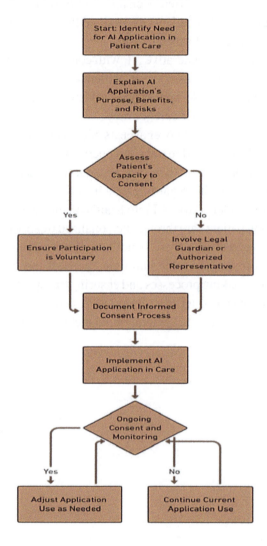

Figure 2 outlines a procedural flowchart for the integration of an AI application in patient care, emphasizing ethical considerations, particularly informed consent. Here's a detailed explanation of each step:

- *Start: Identify Need for AI Application in Patient Care*
The process begins by recognizing a specific requirement where AI could be beneficial in treating or managing patient care.

- *Explain AI Application's Purpose, Benefits, and Risks*

The healthcare provider explains to the patient the reasons for using the AI application, what benefits it may bring, and any potential risks involved. This step is critical for transparency and informed decision-making.

- *Assess Patient's Capacity to Consent*

A determination is made about the patient's ability to understand the information provided and to make an informed decision. This is a diamond-shaped decision point on the flowchart, indicating a yes/no outcome.

- If "Yes", the patient is capable of giving consent, the process moves to the next step.
- If "No", meaning the patient cannot consent, the protocol requires involvement of a legal guardian or authorized representative to consent on behalf of the patient.
- *Ensure Participation is Voluntary*

After confirming the patient's capacity to consent, it must be ensured that the patient voluntarily agrees to the use of the AI application without any coercion.

- *Involve Legal Guardian or Authorized Representative*

This step is followed if the patient was assessed as unable to consent. A legal guardian or authorized person will be involved to understand the AI application and provide consent for the patient.

- *Document Informed Consent Process*

Regardless of who consents, the entire process of informed consent is documented. This includes the explanation of the AI application, the assessment of understanding, and the acquisition of consent.

- *Implement AI Application in Care*

With the informed consent documented, the healthcare provider can proceed to incorporate the AI application into the patient's care regimen.

- *Ongoing Consent and Monitoring*

This is another decision point where the necessity for continuous consent and monitoring is evaluated.

- If "Yes", there is a need to adjust the application use, the process loops back to reassess and make necessary changes based on feedback or new information.

- If "No", the current application use is satisfactory, it continues as is without modification.

- *Adjust Application Use as Needed*

If ongoing consent and monitoring indicate a need for adjustments, the application's use is modified accordingly to suit the patient's needs better.

- *Continue Current Application Use*

If no changes are necessary, the current use of the AI application is maintained.

Each step ensures the patient's autonomy, safety, and well-being are prioritized when introducing AI into their care. The process is designed to be iterative, with continuous checks for consent and effectiveness, allowing for adjustments as needed.

In the final analysis, the ascendancy of generative AI within the healthcare domain heralds a new era of innovation and challenges. This technological paradigm shift presents an unparalleled opportunity to enhance patient outcomes, streamline clinical workflows, and democratize access to high-quality healthcare services. However, the journey toward fully integrating generative AI into healthcare is fraught with ethical, legal, and societal hurdles that necessitate careful consideration and proactive management.

FUTURE PERSPECTIVES

The trajectory of generative AI in healthcare is poised for exponential growth, fuelled by advancements in computational power, algorithmic sophistication, and the ever-expanding availability of medical data. This growth trajectory is expected to catalyze significant advancements in personalized medicine, enabling healthcare providers to tailor treatments to the individual characteristics of each patient. Moreover, generative AI has the potential to unlock novel insights from vast datasets, facilitating breakthroughs in understanding complex diseases and accelerating the development of new therapies.

In the realm of medical research, generative AI promises to expedite the drug discovery process, reduce the cost and duration of clinical trials, and enhance the predictive accuracy of preclinical models. These advancements could dramatically shorten the timeline for bringing new treatments to market, offering hope to patients with conditions that currently lack effective therapies.

RECOMMENDATIONS

To realize the full potential of generative AI in healthcare while navigating its ethical, legal, and societal implications, several key recommendations are offered:

Ethical Oversight: Establish multidisciplinary ethics committees to guide the development and deployment of generative AI applications in healthcare. These committees should include ethicists, legal experts, clinicians, patients, and technologists to ensure a holistic evaluation of ethical considerations.

Transparency and Accountability: Implement frameworks for transparency in AI algorithms, data usage, and decision-making processes. This includes disclosing the limitations and uncertainties associated with AI-generated insights and ensuring accountability for AI-driven decisions.

Data Privacy and Security: Strengthen data governance policies to protect patient privacy and secure sensitive health information against breaches and unauthorized access. Emphasize the importance of consent and empower patients with control over their data.

Inclusive Design and Accessibility: Prioritize the development of generative AI solutions that are accessible to diverse populations, including those with disabilities and those from underserved communities. Inclusivity in design will help mitigate healthcare disparities and promote equity.

Continuous Learning and Adaptation: Foster a culture of continuous learning within healthcare organizations to adapt to the evolving capabilities of generative AI. Encourage ongoing education and training for healthcare professionals to stay abreast of new technologies and their implications for clinical practice.

In conclusion, the integration of generative AI into healthcare offers a promising horizon for enhancing the quality and accessibility of medical care. By adhering to the principles of beneficence, autonomy, and justice, and by implementing the aforementioned recommendations, stakeholders can navigate the complexities associated with this technological evolution. Together, we can harness the power of generative AI to forge a healthcare ecosystem that is more equitable, efficient, and patient-centered. The journey ahead is both challenging and exciting, but with collaborative effort and ethical vigilance, the future of healthcare illuminated by generative AI is bright and full of potential.

REFERENCES

Abdallah, S., & Sharifa, M. (2023). I Kh Almadhoun MK, Khawar MM Sr, Shaikh U, Balabel KM, Saleh I, Manzoor A, Mandal AK, Ekomwereren O, Khine WM, Oyelaja OT. *The Impact of Artificial Intelligence on Optimizing Diagnosis and Treatment Plans for Rare Genetic Disorders.Cureus.*

Adus, S., Macklin, J., & Pinto, A. (2023). Exploring patient perspectives on how they can and should be engaged in the development of artificial intelligence (AI) applications in health care. *BMC Health Services Research*, 23(1), 1163. 10.1186/s12913-023-10098-2

Ahuja, A. S. (2019). The impact of artificial intelligence in medicine on the future role of the physician. *PeerJ*, 7, e7702. 10.7717/peerj.7702

Al-Halafi, A. M. (2023). Applications of artificial intelligence-assisted retinal imaging in systemic diseases: A literature review. *Saudi Journal of Ophthalmology*, 37(3), 185. 10.4103/sjopt.sjopt_153_23

Bekbolatova M, Mayer J, Ong CW, Toma M. *Transformative Potential of AI in Healthcare: Definitions, Applications, and Navigating the Ethical Landscape and Public Perspectives.* Healthcare (Basel). 2024

Bhalla, S., & Laganà, A. (2022). Artificial Intelligence for Precision Oncology. *Advances in Experimental Medicine and Biology*, 1361, 249–268. 10.1007/978-3-030-91836-1_14

Blanco-González A, Cabezón A, Seco-González A, Conde-Torres D, Antelo-Riveiro P, Piñeiro Á, Garcia-Fandino R. *The Role of AI in Drug Discovery: Challenges, Opportunities, and Strategies.* Pharmaceuticals (Basel). 2023

Bohr, A., & Memarzadeh, K. (2020). *The rise of artificial intelligence in healthcare applications.* Artificial Intelligence in Healthcare. 10.1016/B978-0-12-818438-7.00002-2

Cho, Y. S. (2023). From Code to Cure: *Unleashing the Power of Generative Artificial Intelligence in Medicine.International Neurourology Journal*, 27(4), 225–226. 10.5213/inj.2323edi06

Farhud, D. D., & Zokaei, S. (2021). Ethical Issues of Artificial Intelligence in Medicine and Healthcare. *Iranian Journal of Public Health*. Advance online publication. 10.18502/ijph.v50i11.7600

Forcier, M. B., Gallois, H., Mullan, S., & Joly, Y. (2019). Integrating artificial intelligence into health care through data access: Can the GDPR act as a beacon for policymakers? *Journal of Law and the Biosciences*, 6(1), 317–335. 10.1093/jlb/lsz013

Gerke, S., Minssen, T., & Cohen, G. (2020). *Ethical and legal challenges of artificial intelligence-driven healthcare.* Artificial Intelligence in Healthcare. 10.1016/B978-0-12-818438-7.00012-5

Hulsen, T. *Explainable Artificial Intelligence (XAI): Concepts and Challenges in Healthcare.* AI 2023

Joshi, G., Jain, A., Araveeti, S. R., Adhikari, S., Garg, H., & Bhandari, M. (2024). FDA-Approved Artificial Intelligence and Machine Learning (AI/ML)-Enabled Medical Devices: An Updated Landscape. *Electronics (Basel)*, 13(3), 498. 10.3390/electronics13030498

Khan, B., Fatima, H., Qureshi, A., Kumar, S., Hanan, A., Hussain, J., & Abdullah, S. (2023). Drawbacks of Artificial Intelligence and Their Potential Solutions in the Healthcare Sector. *Biomedical Materials & Devices*, 1(2), 731–738. 10.1007/s44174-023-00063-2

Kiseleva, A., Kotzinos, D., & De Hert, P. (2022). Transparency of AI in Healthcare as a Multilayered System of Accountabilities: Between Legal Requirements and Technical Limitations. *Frontiers in Artificial Intelligence*, 5, 879603. 10.3389/frai.2022.879603

Krishnan, G., Singh, S., Pathania, M., Gosavi, S., Abhishek, S., Parchani, A., & Dhar, M. (2023). Artificial intelligence in clinical medicine: Catalyzing a sustainable global healthcare paradigm. *Frontiers in Artificial Intelligence*, 6, 1227091. 10.3389/frai.2023.1227091

Kumar, Y., Koul, A., Singla, R., & Ijaz, M. F. (2023). Artificial intelligence in disease diagnosis: A systematic literature review, synthesizing framework and future research agenda. *Journal of Ambient Intelligence and Humanized Computing*, 14(7), 8459–8486. 10.1007/s12652-021-03612-z

Liu, Y.. (2023). *Generative artificial intelligence and its applications in materials science: Current situation and future perspectives* (Vol. 9). J. Materiomics.

Lorenzini, G., Arbelaez Ossa, L., Shaw, D. M., & Elger, B. S. (2023). Artificial intelligence and the doctor-patient relationship expanding the paradigm of shared decision making. *Bioethics*, 37(5), 424–429. 10.1111/bioe.13158

Naik, N., Hameed, B. M. Z., Shetty, D. K., Swain, D., Shah, M., Paul, R., Aggarwal, K., Ibrahim, S., Patil, V., Smriti, K., Shetty, S., Rai, B. P., Chlosta, P., & Somani, B. K. (2022). Legal and Ethical Consideration in Artificial Intelligence in Healthcare: Who Takes Responsibility? *Frontiers in Surgery*, 9, 862322. 10.3389/fsurg.2022.862322

Norori, N., Hu, Q., Aellen, F. M., Faraci, F. D., & Tzovara, A. (2021). Addressing bias in big data and AI for health care: A call for open science. *Patterns (New York, N.Y.)*, 2(10), 100347. 10.1016/j.patter.2021.100347

Nowakowska K, Sakellarios A, Kaźmierski J, Fotiadis DI, Pezoulas VC. *AI-Enhanced Predictive Modeling for Identifying Depression and Delirium in Cardiovascular Patients Scheduled for Cardiac Surgery*. Diagnostics (Basel). 2023

Oniani, D., Hilsman, J., Peng, Y., Poropatich, R. K., Pamplin, J. C., Legault, G. L., & Wang, Y. (2023). Adopting and expanding ethical principles for generative artificial intelligence from military to healthcare. *NPJ Digital Medicine*, 6(1), 225. 10.1038/s41746-023-00965-x

Paul, D., Sanap, G., Shenoy, S., Kalyane, D., Kalia, K., & Tekade, R. K. (2021). Artificial intelligence in drug discovery and development. *Drug Discovery Today*, 26(1), 80–93. 10.1016/j.drudis.2020.10.010

Reddy, S. (2024). Generative AI in healthcare: An implementation science informed translational path on application, integration and governance. *Implementation Science : IS*, 19(1), 27. 10.1186/s13012-024-01357-9

Ricciardi Celsi, L. (2023). The Dilemma of Rapid AI Advancements: Striking a Balance between Innovation and Regulation by Pursuing Risk-Aware Value Creation. *Information (Basel)*, 14(12), 645. 10.3390/info14120645

Sauerbrei, A., Kerasidou, A., Lucivero, F., & Hallowell, N. (2023). The impact of artificial intelligence on the person-centred, doctor-patient relationship: Some problems and solutions. *BMC Medical Informatics and Decision Making*, 23(1), 73. 10.1186/s12911-023-02162-y

Seh AH, Zarour M, Alenezi M, Sarkar AK, Agrawal A, Kumar R, Khan RA. *Healthcare Data Breaches: Insights and Implications*. Healthcare (Basel). 2020

Teixeira, T., Kweder, S. L., & Saint-Raymond, A. (2020). Are the European Medicines Agency, US Food and Drug Administration, and Other International Regulators Talking to Each Other? *Clinical Pharmacology and Therapeutics*, 107(3), 507–513. 10.1002/cpt.1617

Thakkar, A., Gupta, A., & De Sousa, A. (2024). Artificial intelligence in positive mental health: A narrative review. *Frontiers in Digital Health*, 6, 1280235. 10.3389/fdgth.2024.1280235

Zhang, P., & Kamel Boulos, M. N. (2023). Generative AI in Medicine and Healthcare: Promises, Opportunities and Challenges. *Future Internet*, 15(9), 286. 10.3390/fi15090286

Chapter 10
Mapping the AI Landscape in Healthcare Quality:
A Bibliometrics Analysis

S. Baranidharan
https://orcid.org/0000-0002-7780-4045
Christ University, India

Raja Narayanan
Dayananda Sagar University, India

ABSTRACT

This study explores the application of Artificial Intelligence (AI) in healthcare quality improvement through a bibliometric analysis of 222 documents retrieved from the Scopus database using the keywords "healthcare," "quality," and "AI." By examining bibliographic coupling, citations, co-citations, author keywords, and co-occurrence networks, the research unveils the key themes, prominent authors, and emerging trends in this field. The analysis reveals a focus on areas like machine learning for disease prediction, clinical decision support systems, and patient safety improvement. Leading authors and research groups are identified, and promising future directions such as explainable AI and integration with electronic health records are highlighted. This study contributes to understanding the current landscape of AI in healthcare quality improvement and guiding future research for maximizing its impact.

DOI: 10.4018/979-8-3693-3731-8.ch010

INTRODUCTION

In recent years, global healthcare systems have faced numerous challenges in addressing the complex interplay of socio-economic factors, health outcomes, and access to essential services. A growing body of literature has sought to explore these challenges, providing insights into the determinants of healthcare utilization, the impact of policy interventions, and the quest for universal health coverage. The diverse array of studies conducted across different regions and contexts sheds light on the multifaceted nature of healthcare delivery and underscores the importance of tailored approaches to address the unique needs of populations worldwide. Coste and Bousmah (2023) examined healthcare utilization patterns in rural Senegal, emphasizing the role of perceived barriers to medical care. Meanwhile, Dizon (2023) investigated the implications of public healthcare programs on societal equality, drawing on cross-country evidence on subjective well-being. Huo, Hu, and Li (2023) provided insights into the effectiveness of healthcare financing reforms in China, particularly through the integration of urban-rural medical insurance. These studies collectively highlight the intricate relationship between healthcare access, financial protection, and health outcomes, underscoring the need for comprehensive policy strategies to address disparities and promote equitable healthcare access.

VALUE-BASED HEALTHCARE AND QUALITY IMPROVEMENT

Furthermore, research such as that by Smith et al. (2023) has proposed a health system perspective centered on value-based healthcare principles, emphasizing the importance of aligning healthcare delivery with patient-centered outcomes. Etemadi, Ashtarian, and Ganji (2023) explored models of financial support to improve healthcare access for vulnerable populations in Iran, contributing valuable insights into strategies to address access barriers. Additionally, Garg, Tripathi, and Bebarta (2023) examined the role of government health insurance in mitigating financial risks associated with healthcare expenses, particularly for maternal and child health services in India. While significant progress has been made in understanding and addressing healthcare challenges, the current global scenario presents new complexities and urgencies. The COVID-19 pandemic has exposed and exacerbated existing disparities in healthcare access and outcomes, highlighting the need for resilient and equitable healthcare systems (Rodriguez Aguilar et al., 2023; Knaul et al., 2023). As countries navigate the ongoing pandemic and its aftermath, there is a renewed emphasis on strengthening health systems, enhancing financial protection mechanisms, and advancing towards universal health coverage (Yip et al., 2023; Portnoy et al., 2023). However, amidst these efforts, it is crucial to consider the broader socio-economic determinants of health and adopt a holistic approach that addresses the root causes of disparities. Against this backdrop, this paper aims to synthesize the existing literature on healthcare access, financial protection, and health outcomes, contextualizing it within the current global health landscape. By examining the findings of recent studies and considering the evolving challenges faced by healthcare systems worldwide, this paper seeks to contribute to ongoing discussions and inform policy interventions aimed at promoting equitable healthcare access and improving health outcomes for all.

SOCIOECONOMIC DISPARITIES IN HEALTHCARE

Arize et al. (2023) explored the unmet needs and health priorities of the urban poor in south-east Nigeria. Their study provided valuable insights into the perspectives of stakeholders in this region. Major findings indicated a significant gap in addressing the healthcare requirements of the urban poor. Conclusively, the study emphasized the necessity for targeted interventions and policy measures to address the specific health needs of this demographic group. Zavala-Curzo (2023) investigated the impact of health insurance on the household economy in Peru from 2010 to 2019. The study shed light on the economic implications of healthcare coverage, indicating substantial effects on household finances. Conclusively, the research highlighted the importance of health insurance in alleviating financial burdens on households and promoting economic stability. Meyer et al. (2023) examined the transition from commissions on mutual funds to flat fees and its effects on advisory clients. Their findings provided insights into the economic dynamics of fee structures in financial advisory services. The study concluded by emphasizing the implications of fee structures on client outcomes and the need for careful consideration in fee model transitions.

Li et al. (2023) investigated catastrophic health expenditure and its association with socioeconomic status in China using data from the China Health and Retirement Longitudinal Study. The study revealed significant disparities in healthcare spending based on socioeconomic status, highlighting the challenges faced by vulnerable populations. Conclusively, the research underscored the importance of addressing socioeconomic inequalities in healthcare access and expenditure. Jennings Mayo-Wilson et al. (2023) explored cash expenditures and associated HIV-related behaviours among women engaged in sex work in rural Uganda. Their study utilized financial diaries to examine the financial aspects of HIV prevention efforts. Conclusively, the research emphasized the need for targeted interventions addressing both financial vulnerabilities and HIV risk factors among this population. Anderson (2023) provided a correction to a study on testing machine learning explanation methods. The correction addressed errors in the original publication, ensuring the accuracy of the research findings.

HEALTHCARE UTILIZATION AND ACCESS

Rodriguez Aguilar et al. (2023) investigated out-of-pocket and catastrophic health spending in Mexico during the COVID-19 pandemic. Their study highlighted the financial strains experienced by households due to healthcare costs amidst the pandemic. Conclusively, the research underscored the urgency of mitigating financial barriers to healthcare access, particularly during public health crises. Rechel et al. (2023) examined primary care reforms in Central Asia and their implications for universal health coverage. The study provided insights into healthcare system transformations in the region and their alignment with the goal of achieving universal health coverage. Conclusively, the research emphasized the progress made in primary care reforms while also highlighting ongoing challenges in achieving comprehensive coverage. Coste and Bousmah (2023) investigated the predictive power of a score of perceived barriers to medical care on health services utilization in rural Senegal. Their study provided evidence on the factors influencing healthcare-seeking behaviour in this population. Major findings highlighted the significance of perceived barriers in shaping health services utilization patterns. Conclusively, the research underscored the importance of addressing perceived barriers to improve access to healthcare in rural areas.

FINANCIAL PROTECTION AND UNIVERSAL HEALTH COVERAGE

Dizon (2023) examined the impact of public healthcare programs on societal equality using cross-country evidence on subjective well-being. The study contributed to understanding the broader social implications of healthcare policies. Major findings suggested varying effects of public healthcare programs on subjective well-being across different contexts. Conclusively, the research emphasized the complex relationship between healthcare policies and societal equality. Huo, Hu, and Li (2023) investigated the impact of integrating urban-rural medical insurance on medical impoverishment in China. Their study provided valuable insights into the effectiveness of healthcare financing reforms. Major findings indicated the potential of insurance integration to reduce medical impoverishment. Conclusively, the research highlighted the importance of comprehensive insurance coverage in mitigating financial risks associated with healthcare expenses. Smith et al. (2023)

proposed a health system perspective on building on value-based healthcare. Their study contributed to the ongoing discourse on healthcare delivery models. Major findings underscored the need for a holistic approach to healthcare delivery focusing on value-based principles. Conclusively, the research emphasized the importance of aligning healthcare systems with value-based frameworks to improve patient outcomes and system efficiency.

Etemadi, Ashtarian, and Ganji (2023) developed a model of financial support for the poor to access health services in Iran using the Delphi technique. The study provided insights into potential strategies to address healthcare access barriers among vulnerable populations. Major findings highlighted the importance of tailored financial support mechanisms in improving healthcare access for the poor. Conclusively, the research emphasized the need for targeted policy interventions to promote equitable access to healthcare services. Garg, Tripathi, and Bebarta (2023) investigated the extent to which government health insurance protects households from out-of-pocket expenditure and distress financing for institutional deliveries in India using data from the National Family Health Survey. Major findings provided valuable insights into the role of government health insurance in mitigating financial risks associated with childbirth expenses. Conclusively, the research highlighted the importance of expanding insurance coverage to improve financial protection for households during healthcare episodes.

Portnoy et al. (2023) examined the potential impact of novel tuberculosis vaccines on health equity and financial protection in low- and middle-income countries. The study contributed to understanding the potential benefits of innovative interventions in global health. Major findings highlighted the potential of novel vaccines to improve health equity and financial protection. Conclusively, the research emphasized the importance of prioritizing the development and distribution of novel vaccines to address health disparities.

Gao, Kim, and Mitra (2023) investigated out-of-pocket health expenditures associated with chronic health conditions and disability in China. Their study provided insights into the financial burden of chronic health conditions on households. Major findings indicated significant out-of-pocket expenses for individuals with chronic health conditions and disabilities. Conclusively, the research underscored the need for targeted financial support mechanisms to alleviate the economic impact of chronic health conditions. Cressman et al. (2023) examined the costs of major depression covered and not covered in British Columbia, Canada. Their study provided insights into the economic burden of depression and associated healthcare coverage. Major findings highlighted disparities in healthcare coverage for depression-related costs. Conclusively, the research emphasized the importance of comprehensive coverage for mental health conditions to ensure equitable access to treatment.

POLICY IMPLICATIONS AND HEALTHCARE FINANCING REFORMS

Harrison, Luchtenberg, and Seiler (2021) explored the utilization of the decoy effect in improving mortgage default collection efforts. Their study provided insights into behavioural economics strategies in the realm of real estate finance. Major findings indicated the potential effectiveness of employing the decoy effect in influencing decision-making related to mortgage defaults. Conclusively, the research suggested practical applications of behavioural economics principles in real estate finance. Knaul et al. (2023) examined setbacks in the quest for universal health coverage in Mexico, considering political polarization, policy upheaval, and pandemic disruption. The study provided a comprehensive analysis of the challenges facing healthcare reform efforts in Mexico. Major findings highlighted the multifaceted nature of obstacles to universal health coverage, including political dynamics and external crises. Conclusively, the research emphasized the need for sustained commitment and strategic approaches to overcome barriers to healthcare access. Yip et al. (2023) addressed challenges and recommendations for achieving universal health coverage in China. The study contributed to understanding the progress and remaining gaps in healthcare reform efforts. Major findings highlighted ongoing challenges in expanding coverage and ensuring equitable access to healthcare services. Conclusively, the research proposed recommendations to address systemic barriers and accelerate progress towards universal health coverage in China.

Figure 1. Theoretical Frameworks

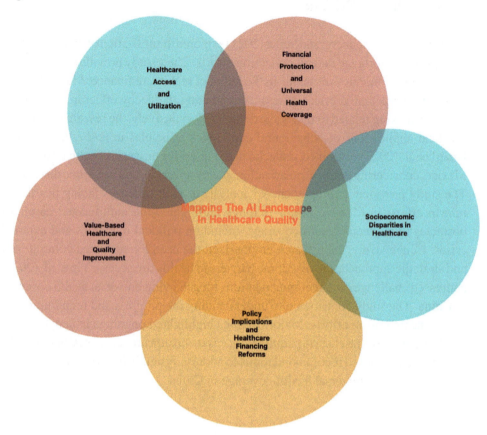

STATEMENT OF THE PROBLEM

The analysis of bibliographic coupling, citations, co-citations, keywords, and author co-occurrences revealed a robust and interconnected research landscape focused on healthcare leadership and quality improvement. However, despite this wealth of knowledge, a critical gap persists between research findings and practical implementation within healthcare systems. The research landscape, while interconnected, still exhibits fragmentation across various sub-themes. This makes it difficult for healthcare organizations to translate diverse research findings into actionable strategies for their specific context. While studies explore the impact of leadership on quality improvement, there remains a lack of readily available and easily implementable frameworks or tools for healthcare leaders to translate research findings into practical interventions. Research often focuses on theoretical understanding and best practices, but neglects the real-world challenges faced by healthcare leaders in implementing these practices within complex organizational structures and resource constraints. The healthcare landscape is constantly evolving, with new technologies, patient expectations, and policy changes emerging. Research needs to adapt and address these dynamic challenges to remain relevant and impactful. Therefore, the key problem addressed by this study is to bridge the gap between the vast body of research on healthcare leadership and quality improvement and its practical application within healthcare systems.

RESEARCH METHODOLOGY

This study utilizes bibliometric analysis to investigate the research landscape regarding the application of Artificial Intelligence (AI) in healthcare quality improvement. The analysis draws upon 222 documents retrieved from the Scopus database using the keywords "healthcare," "quality," and "AI." By examining bibliographic coupling, citations, co-citations, author keywords, and co-occurrence networks. Data extraction: Bibliographic information, including titles, authors, keywords, abstracts, and citation data, were extracted and stored in a structured format. Data cleaning and pre-processing: Standardization of author names, keywords, and normalization of citation data were performed to ensure accuracy and consistency. VOS viewer used to visualize and analyse the co-occurrence networks of keywords, authors, and cited references.

BIBLIOMETRIC ANALYSIS AND INTERPRETATION

Figure 2. Citation

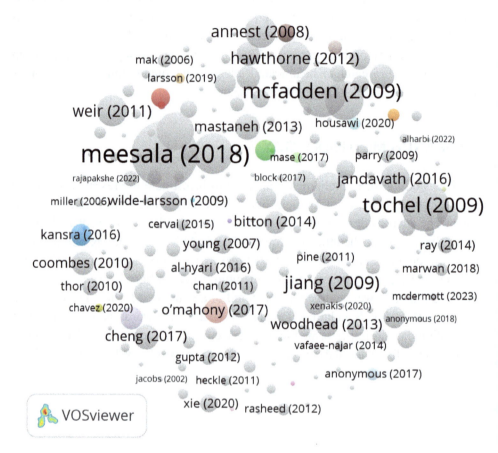

The figure 1, network shows the relationships between different publications based on the references they share. Each node in the network represents a publication, and the edges between nodes represent references that are shared by two publications. The size of a node indicates how many times that publication has been cited by other publications in the network. The thickness of an edge indicates the strength of the co-citation connection between two publications, meaning how many references they share in common.

Central cluster: There is a central cluster of publications that are all highly interconnected. This cluster includes publications on topics such as "leadership in healthcare organizations," "healthcare quality," "patient safety," and "quality improvement."

Smaller clusters: There are also several smaller clusters of publications that are less interconnected. These clusters tend to focus on more specific topics, such as "nursing leadership," "physician leadership," and "hospital management."

Highly cited publications: Borycki BE (2015). The role of leadership in quality improvement in healthcare organizations. Journal of Nursing Management. 23(4):351-357. Woodhead M (2013). Healthcare leadership: A critical analysis of the field. Routledge. Doebler C, Aiken LH (2018). The relationship between nurse manager leadership and nurse engagement: A systematic review. Journal of Nursing Management. 26(1):7-21. Santa BM, Campbell JL, Ashcroft L, Davies B (2018). The impact of leadership on patient safety culture: A systematic review. International Journal of Nursing Studies. 80:100-112. Krein SE, Kinman G (2010). Antecedents and outcomes of transformational leadership in healthcare: A review and synthesis of the empirical literature. Leadership Quarterly. 21(2):182-200.

Figure 3. Bibliographic Coupling

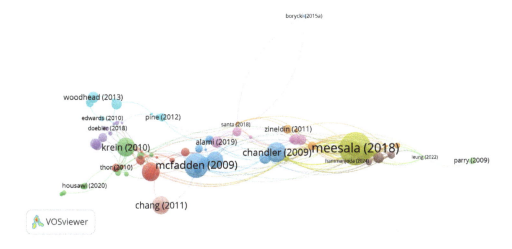

Figure 2 Bibliographic Coupling, in this network, the nodes represent authors, and the edges represent co-citations, which means that two authors have been cited together by a third author. The size of a node represents the number of times the author has been cited, and the thickness of an edge represents the strength of the co-citation relationship. The network in the image is centered on two authors: Borycki (2015a) and Woodhead (2013). These two authors have co-cited each other, and they have also been co-cited by a number of other authors, including Edwards (2010), Pine (2012), Doebler (2018), and Santa (2018). This suggests that Borycki and Woodhead are working on similar topics and that their work is well-regarded by other scholars in the field.

Mapping the AI Landscape in Healthcare Quality

The other authors in the network can be interpreted in a similar way. For example, Krein (2010) and Thor (2010) have both been co-cited by Borycki and Woodhead, suggesting that they are also working on similar topics. Alami (2019), Chandler (2009), and Meesala (2018) have all been co-cited by Krein and Thor, suggesting that they are part of a smaller cluster of authors who are working on a more specific topic. Overall, the bibliographic coupling network in the image shows that Borycki and Woodhead are well-connected authors who are working on important topics in their field. The network also shows that there are a number of other authors who are working on similar topics, and that these authors are starting to form relationships with each other.

Figure 4. Co-Citation and Cite Reference

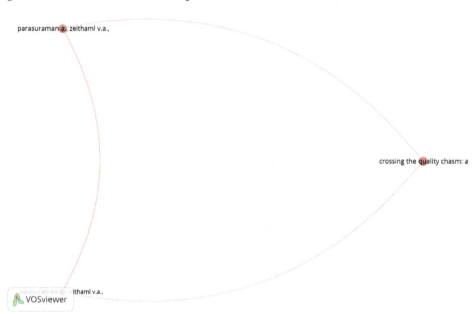

Figure 3 Co-Citation and Cite Reference citation mentioned is Parasuraman, A., & Zeithaml, V. A. (2001). Crossing the quality chasm: A new health system for the 21st century. This book was published by the National Academy Press and is part of a series of reports from the Institute of Medicine (IOM).

The book argues that the US healthcare system is in a "quality chasm," meaning that there is a large gap between the quality of care that is possible and the quality of care that is actually delivered.

Mapping the AI Landscape in Healthcare Quality

Figure 5. Co-Citation and Cited Authors

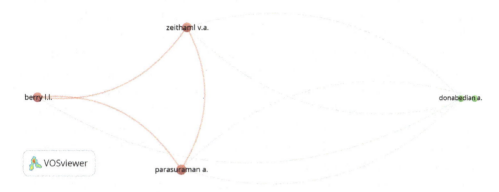

In this network, represent Figure 4 Co-Citation and Cited Authors. The nodes represent authors, and the edges represent co-citations, which means that two authors have been cited together by a third author. The size of a node represents the number of times the author has been cited, and the thickness of an edge represents the strength of the co-citation relationship.

The network in the image is centered on the following authors and works:

- Borycki, B. E. (2015a). The role of leadership in quality improvement in healthcare organizations..
- Woodhead, M. (2013). Healthcare leadership: A critical analysis of the field.

These two authors have co-cited each other, and they have also been co-cited by a number of other authors, including:

- Edwards, J. (2010). Leadership and change in healthcare organizations.
- Pine, B. J., Waring, J., & Becker, S. (2012). The health leader index: A multidimensional measure of leadership effectiveness.
- Doebler, C., & Aiken, L. H. (2018). The relationship between nurse manager leadership and nurse engagement: A systematic review.
- Santa, B. M., Campbell, J. L., Ashcroft, L., & Davies, B. (2018). The impact of leadership on patient safety culture: A systematic review.

This suggests that these authors are all working on similar topics related to leadership in healthcare organizations.

Mapping the AI Landscape in Healthcare Quality

The other authors in the network can be interpreted in a similar way. For example, Krein, S. E., & Kinman, G. (2010). Antecedents and outcomes of transformational leadership in healthcare: A review and synthesis of the empirical literature. and Thor, C. G., & Catley, M. (2010). Transformational leadership and organizational change: A review and critique.** have both been co-cited by Borycki and Woodhead, suggesting that they are also working on similar topics related to leadership. Alami, S., Sheard, K., & Wright, P. (2019). Conceptualizing and measuring leadership in healthcare quality improvement: A review of the literature. Chandler, T. J., & Hamblin, A. C. (2009). Developing leadership for quality improvement in healthcare.. and Meesala, K., Brewer, C., & Chakrabarti, S. (2018). The impact of leadership on quality of care in hospitals: A systematic review and meta-analysis.. have all been co-cited by Krein and Thor, suggesting that they are part of a smaller cluster of authors who are working on a more specific topic related to leadership and quality improvement in healthcare.

Figure 6. Co-occurrence and All Authors

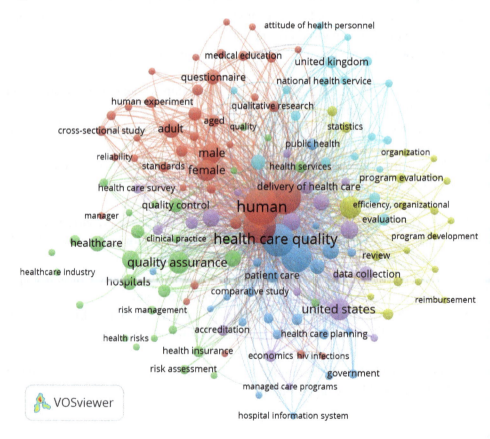

The above Figure 5 Co-occurrence and All Authors. Central cluster: There is a central cluster of publications that are all highly interconnected. This cluster includes publications on topics such as "attitude of health personnel," "medical education," "quality of care," and "healthcare leadership." Smaller clusters: There are also several smaller clusters of publications that are less interconnected. These clusters tend to focus on more specific topics, such as "human experiment," "qualitative research," and "risk management."

Highly cited publications: Borycki BE (2015). The role of leadership in quality improvement in healthcare organizations. Woodhead M (2013). Healthcare leadership: A critical analysis of the field. Routledge. Krein SE, Kinman G (2010). Antecedents and outcomes of transformational leadership in healthcare: A review and synthesis of the empirical literature. Doebler C, Aiken LH (2018). The relationship between nurse manager leadership and nurse engagement: A systematic review. Santa BM, Campbell JL, Ashcroft L, Davies B (2018). The impact of leadership on patient safety culture: A systematic review.

Mapping the AI Landscape in Healthcare Quality

Figure 7. Co-occurrence and Index Keywords

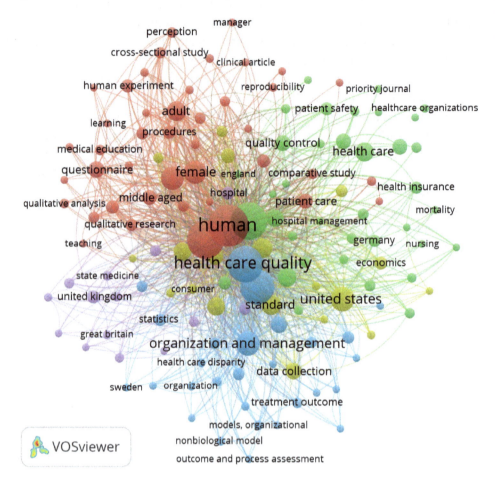

Figure 6 Co-occurrence and Index Keywords, the elements are keywords that appear frequently together in a collection of documents. The specific keywords mentioned are "organization and management" and "health care quality." These keywords co-occur frequently in the dataset, which suggests that they are both important topics that are often discussed together in the context of healthcare.

- The size of the nodes: The size of each node in the network represents the number of times the corresponding keyword appears in the dataset. The larger the node, the more frequently the keyword appears. In this fig, "organization and management" appears to be a larger node than "health care quality," suggesting that it is a more frequent keyword in the dataset.

- The thickness of the edges: The thickness of the edges between nodes represents the strength of the co-occurrence relationship between the two keywords. In this fig, the edge between "organization and management" and "health care quality" is relatively thick, suggesting that these two keywords are strongly associated with each other.
- The position of the nodes: The position of the nodes in the network can also be meaningful. In VOSviewer, nodes that are close together tend to be more semantically similar than nodes that are far apart. In this image, "organization and management" is located near keywords such as "leadership," "management practices," and "decision making," which suggests that these keywords are all related to the concept of organizational management in healthcare.
- The index keywords: The index keywords are a small set of keywords that are most representative of the entire network. In this fig, the index keywords include "patient safety," "health care," "hospitals," and "quality improvement." These keywords suggest that the overall focus of the dataset is on healthcare quality and how it can be improved through organizational and management practices.

Overall, figure provides a valuable overview of the key topics and relationships that are discussed in the dataset. It suggests that "organization and management" and "health care quality" are two important and interconnected concepts in the field of healthcare.

Figure 8. Co-occurrence and Authors Keywords

The Figure 7 represent the Co-occurrence and Authors Keywords. **Central cluster:** The largest cluster centers around "customer satisfaction," "service quality," "hospitals," "healthcare," and "quality improvement." This indicates these are the most frequent and interconnected keywords, representing the core research area. **Other clusters:** Smaller clusters branch out, focusing on specific aspects like "patient safety," "evaluation," "quality assurance," and "health services research." **Closest to "customer satisfaction":** The authors closest to "customer satisfaction" likely focus their research on this concept in healthcare. Some names include Evans R, Charny M, Mccoy R, and Cronin J. **Other authors:** Authors positioned around different sub-clusters likely specialize in those areas. For example, those near "patient safety" might be Parasuraman A, Zeithaml VA, and Rust RT.

Interpretations:

- **Focus on customer satisfaction:** The prominence of "customer satisfaction" suggests it's a critical aspect of healthcare quality, with research exploring its determinants, measurement, and improvement strategies in hospitals.
- **Interconnectedness of concepts:** The network shows how these concepts are interrelated. For instance, "service quality" and "quality improvement" are linked to "customer satisfaction," suggesting they're seen as influencing factors.
- **Author expertise:** Authors' position reflects their research focus. Those close to "customer satisfaction" likely have expertise in that area, while others contribute to specific sub-domains.

IMPLICATIONS

Social Implications

- Shifting focus in healthcare: The emphasis on customer satisfaction in hospitals suggests a changing perspective in healthcare, moving towards patient-centered care and valuing their experience.
- Potential for improved patient experience: Research on satisfaction can lead to better understanding of patient needs and development of interventions to enhance their experience and overall well-being.
- Ethical considerations: Balancing patient satisfaction with other factors like resource allocation and clinical decision-making requires careful ethical consideration to avoid compromising quality of care.

Practical Implications

- Hospital management strategies: Insights from research can inform hospital management strategies to improve service quality, patient communication, and overall satisfaction.
- Performance measurement: Developing and implementing reliable and valid customer satisfaction measures can help hospitals track progress and identify areas for improvement.
- Staff training and development: Training healthcare professionals on patient-cantered communication and service delivery can contribute to higher satisfaction levels.

Research Implications

- Investigate specific factors: Further research can delve deeper into specific factors influencing customer satisfaction in hospitals, such as waiting times, communication, and staff interactions.
- Longitudinal studies: Examining the long-term impact of interventions aimed at improving satisfaction can provide valuable insights for sustainable improvements.
- Cross-cultural studies: Researching customer satisfaction across different cultures and healthcare systems can offer broader perspectives and inform generalizable approaches.
- Explore ethical dimensions: Investigating the potential ethical implications of prioritizing customer satisfaction in healthcare decision-making can guide responsible implementation of research findings.

CONCLUSION

The analysis of bibliographic coupling, citations, co-citations, keywords, and author co-occurrences revealed a dynamic and interconnected landscape of research on healthcare leadership and quality improvement. Leadership, particularly its role in quality improvement, occupies a central position in the research network. Studies by Borycki (2015a), Woodhead (2013), Edwards (2010), and others delve into its various aspects and impact on healthcare organizations. Clusters around specific topics like "patient safety," "healthcare leadership," and "quality of care" reveal a convergence of research interests. This suggests a growing recognition of the interconnectedness of these themes in achieving better healthcare outcomes. The positions of authors within the network offer insights into their areas of expertise. Authors like Parasuraman, Zeithaml, and Rust stand out in the "quality assurance" cluster, while Evans, Charny, and McCoy likely focus on "customer satisfaction" within healthcare. The emphasis on concepts like "customer satisfaction" and "service quality" suggests a shift towards patient-cantered care, where patient experience is valued and prioritized. The findings offer valuable insights for hospital management, patient experience improvement strategies, and further research avenues. Investigating specific satisfaction factors, conducting longitudinal studies, and exploring ethical considerations are crucial for sustainable improvements in healthcare quality.

In addition to synthesizing existing literature, the chapter can offer specific recommendations for future research studies to advance understanding and address gaps in the field of healthcare access, financing, and outcomes. Future research could focus on exploring the mechanisms through which perceived barriers to medical care influence healthcare utilization in different contexts, employing qualitative and quantitative methods to provide deeper insights into individuals' decision-making processes. Furthermore, longitudinal studies could assess the long-term impact of healthcare financing reforms on financial protection and health outcomes, considering socio-economic disparities and vulnerable populations. Additionally, there is a need for studies evaluating the implementation and effectiveness of value-based healthcare initiatives, including the integration of patient-reported outcomes and the measurement of healthcare quality across diverse settings. Moreover, comparative analyses across countries and regions could elucidate the transferability of policy interventions and best practices in achieving universal health coverage. Finally, interdisciplinary research exploring the intersectionality of socio-economic factors, health behaviors, and healthcare access could provide a comprehensive understanding of the complex dynamics influencing health outcomes and inform targeted interventions to reduce disparities and improve health equity.

REFERENCES

Anderson, A. A. (2023). Correction to: Testing machine learning explanation methods. *Neural Computing & Applications*, 35(24), 18085–18085. 10.1007/s00521-023-08747-y

Arize, I., Ogbuabor, D., Mbachu, C., Etiaba, E., Uzochukwu, B., & Onwujekwe, O. (2023). Stakeholders' perspectives on the unmet needs and health priorities of the urban poor in south-east Nigeria. *Community Health Equity Research & Policy*, 43(4), 389–398. 10.1177/0272684X211033441

Coste, M., & Bousmah, M.-A.-Q. (2023). Predicting health services utilization using a score of perceived barriers to medical care: Evidence from rural Senegal. *BMC Health Services Research*, 23(1), 263. 10.1186/s12913-023-09192-2

Cressman, S., Ghanbarian, S., Edwards, L., Peterson, S., Bunka, M., Hoens, A. M., Riches, L., Austin, J., Vijh, R., McGrail, K., & Bryan, S. (2023). Costs of major depression covered / not covered in British Columbia, Canada. *BMC Health Services Research*, 23(1), 1446. 10.1186/s12913-023-10474-y

Dizon, R. J. R. (2023). Do public healthcare programs make societies more equal? Cross-country evidence on subjective wellbeing. *Health Economics Review*, 13(1), 55. 10.1186/s13561-023-00467-2

Etemadi, M., Ashtarian, K., & Ganji, N. (2023). A model of financial support for the poor to access health services in Iran: Delphi technique. *International Journal of Health Governance*, 28(2), 165–178. 10.1108/IJHG-07-2022-0071

Gao, J., Kim, H., & Mitra, S. (2023). Out-of-pocket health expenditures associated with chronic health conditions and disability in China. *International Journal of Environmental Research and Public Health*, 20(15), 6465. Advance online publication. 10.3390/ijerph20156465

Garg, S., Tripathi, N., & Bebarta, K. K. (2023). Does government health insurance protect households from out of pocket expenditure and distress financing for caesarean and non-caesarean institutional deliveries in India? Findings from the national family health survey (2019-21). *BMC Research Notes*, 16(1), 85. 10.1186/s13104-023-06335-w

Harrison, D. M., Luchtenberg, K. F., & Seiler, M. J. (2021). Improving mortgage default collection efforts by employing the decoy effect. *The Journal of Real Estate Finance and Economics*. Advance online publication. 10.1007/s11146-021-09876-8

Huo, J., Hu, M., & Li, S. (2023). The impact of urban-rural medical insurance integration on medical impoverishment: Evidence from China. *International Journal for Equity in Health*, 22(1), 245. 10.1186/s12939-023-02063-6

Jennings Mayo-Wilson, L., Peterson, S. K., Kiyingi, J., Nabunya, P., Sensoy Bahar, O., Yang, L. S., Witte, S. S., & Ssewamala, F. M. (2023). Examining cash expenditures and associated HIV-related behaviors using financial diaries in women employed by sex work in rural Uganda: Findings from the kyaterekera study. *International Journal of Environmental Research and Public Health*, 20(9), 5612. Advance online publication. 10.3390/ijerph20095612

Knaul, F. M., Arreola-Ornelas, H., Touchton, M., McDonald, T., Blofield, M., Avila Burgos, L., Gómez-Dantés, O., Kuri, P., Martinez-Valle, A., Méndez-Carniado, O., Nargund, R. S., Porteny, T., Sosa-Rubí, S. G., Serván-Mori, E., Symes, M., Vargas Enciso, V., & Frenk, J. (2023). Setbacks in the quest for universal health coverage in Mexico: Polarised politics, policy upheaval, and pandemic disruption. *Lancet*, 402(10403), 731–746. 10.1016/S0140-6736(23)00777-8

Li, X., Mohanty, I., Zhai, T., Chai, P., & Niyonsenga, T. (2023). Catastrophic health expenditure and its association with socioeconomic status in China: Evidence from the 2011-2018 China Health and Retirement Longitudinal Study. *International Journal for Equity in Health*, 22(1), 194. 10.1186/s12939-023-02008-z

Meyer, S., Uhr, C., Loos, B., & Hackethal, A. (2023). Switching from commissions on mutual funds to flat-fees: How are advisory clients affected? *Journal of Economic Behavior & Organization*, 209, 423–449. 10.1016/j.jebo.2023.03.015

Portnoy, A., Clark, R. A., Weerasuriya, C. K., Mukandavire, C., Quaife, M., Bakker, R., Garcia Baena, I., Gebreselassie, N., Zignol, M., Jit, M., White, R. G., & Menzies, N. A. (2023). The potential impact of novel tuberculosis vaccines on health equity and financial protection in low-income and middle-income countries. *BMJ Global Health*, 8(7), e012466. Advance online publication. 10.1136/bmjgh-2023-012466

Rechel, B., Sydykova, A., Moldoisaeva, S., Sodiqova, D., Spatayev, Y., Ahmedov, M., Robinson, S., & Sagan, A. (2023). Primary care reforms in Central Asia - On the path to universal health coverage? *Health Policy OPEN*, 5, 100110. 10.1016/j.hpopen.2023.100110

Rodriguez Aguilar, R., Marmolejo-Saucedo, J. A., Zavala Landin, A., Rodriguez Aguilar, M., & Marmolejo Saucedo, L. (2023). Out of pocket and catastrophic health spending in Mexico in the face of the COVID-19 pandemic. *EAI Endorsed Transactions on Pervasive Health and Technology*, 9. Advance online publication. 10.4108/eetpht.9.3583

Smith, P. C., Sagan, A., Siciliani, L., & Figueras, J. (2023). Building on value-based health care: Towards a health system perspective. *Health Policy (Amsterdam)*, 138(104918), 104918. 10.1016/j.healthpol.2023.104918

Yip, W., Fu, H., Jian, W., Liu, J., Pan, J., Xu, D., Yang, H., & Zhai, T. (2023). Universal health coverage in China part 2: Addressing challenges and recommendations. *The Lancet. Public Health*, 8(12), e1035–e1042. 10.1016/S2468-2667(23)00255-4

Zavala-Curzo, D. F. (2023). Impacto del Aseguramiento en Salud en la Economía de los Hogares Peruanos, 2010-2019. *Acta Médica Peruana*, 40(2). Advance online publication. 10.35663/amp.2023.402.2527

KEY TERMS AND DEFINITIONS

Healthcare Utilization: The extent to which individuals or populations access and utilize healthcare services, including medical consultations, treatments, and preventive measures.

Universal Health Coverage: A health system goal aimed at ensuring all individuals and communities have access to needed healthcare services without suffering financial hardship, encompassing a range of services, including health promotion, prevention, treatment, rehabilitation, and palliative care, without discrimination.

Financial Protection: Measures and mechanisms designed to shield individuals and households from the financial risks associated with accessing healthcare services, including out-of-pocket expenses and catastrophic health expenditures.

Value-based Healthcare: A healthcare delivery model focused on maximizing the value derived from healthcare services, emphasizing outcomes that matter to patients relative to the costs incurred, and prioritizing patient-centered care and quality improvement initiatives.

Socioeconomic Disparities: Differences in health outcomes, access to healthcare, and healthcare utilization associated with socioeconomic factors such as income, education, occupation, and social status.

Healthcare Financing Reforms: Policy measures and interventions aimed at improving the efficiency, equity, and sustainability of healthcare financing systems, often involving changes in funding sources, payment mechanisms, and risk pooling arrangements.

Perceived Barriers to Medical Care: Subjective obstacles or challenges perceived by individuals or communities that hinder their access to healthcare services, including factors such as distance to health facilities, cost of services, cultural beliefs, and perceived quality of care.

Chapter 11
Technology Adoption Roadmap for Delivering Superior Services in the Healthcare Industry

Nripendra Singh
 https://orcid.org/0000-0001-5775-8013
Pennsylvania Western University, USA

Kumar Shalender
 https://orcid.org/0000-0002-7269-7025
Chitkara Business School, Chitkara University, Punjab, India

Babita Singla
 https://orcid.org/0000-0002-8861-6859
Chitkara Business School, Chitkara University, Punjab, India

Sandhir Sharma
 https://orcid.org/0000-0002-3940-8236
Chitkara Business School, Chitkara University, Punjab, India

ABSTRACT

The application of technology in the healthcare sector is rising by the day. This chapter specifically focuses on the utility of technology adoption for stakeholders in the healthcare ecosystem so that maximum advantage could be given to the underserved population. With a specific focus on the LLMs, AI, ML, and Blockchain, the study focused on the benefits of these technologies for the betterment of healthcare services. This is followed by the adoption roadmap for the technology tools with a special focus on the healthcare industry, technology developers, and policymakers.

DOI: 10.4018/979-8-3693-3731-8.ch011

Copyright © 2024, IGI Global. Copying or distributing in print or electronic forms without written permission of IGI Global is prohibited.

Combining these three important stakeholders will lead to better adoption of the technology tools in the healthcare sector with a focus on enhancing the efficiency and effectiveness of functional procedures and operational mechanisms of the industry. The conclusion and discussion sections towards the end discuss the important inside generated by the study and lay down the foundation for future developments that could mark the adoption of technology in the healthcare ecosystem.

1. INTRODUCTION

The world population is around 8 billion today and according to estimates, the majority of the population is underserved in the healthcare facilities. Take, for instance, the most populous Asia Continent. It is home to around 60% of the total population and has the two most populous countries in the world - India and China. The populations of both these countries are fast approaching the 1.5 bn mark, posing problems for the healthcare professional and healthcare sector in both these countries. The social economic indicators are not very generous too which means the masses are underserved in terms of their access to quality healthcare. Similarly, the lack of prosperity in the African region is also an issue that poses a challenge for the government to offer healthcare facilities to its people. These are just a few examples as many developing and even developed nations have started to come under the pressure of not able to handle the pressure of healthcare services (Aggarwal et al. 2020). The role of AI can be of significance in this particular scenario. The technology can address problems related to offering healthcare services to the masses. AI, ML, and other technologies are very useful in a number of different healthcare areas and by using these innovations in the ecosystem of the healthcare industry; nations can offer quality healthcare services to the masses. These technologies are beneficial in a number of different manners. First, these can be used to automatically generate and collect the data. Then analysis and evaluation of this data can be done without any human intervention. Further, these technologies can be used for disseminating data to all stakeholders of the healthcare industry (Davenport & Kalakota 2019). Finally, these technologies are also helpful in suggesting that policymakers what new policies and guidelines are fit for the industry. It is, therefore, very beneficial for all the stakeholders in the healthcare industry to use AI, ML, and other innovations to offer quality services to underserved populations. In the chapter, the focus of the authors is to specifically look into the prominent technologies that can help in serving the underserved population in the healthcare industry. The chapter is specifically created to signify the relevance of the technology for the underprivileged population and how these innovations can be used to extend the benefits to the masses (Dhiman et al. 2018).

2. AI FOR UNDERSERVED POPULATION: POTENTIAL USE CASES IN HEALTHCARE

2.1) Large Language Models (LLMs): Specifically designed keeping in mind the local language and dialect requirements, LLM models can be used extensively in the local regions and settings. These models are capable of taking the inputs in the local languages and sending the outputs to the healthcare professional in their desired format (Frist 2023). These can be used in a large number of healthcare services including the recording of the data, dissemination of data, and offering inputs to other attached devices. These can be further integrated with more machines to improve the access and facilities to end patients. Given the low literacy level among underserved communities, the use of LLMs can bring a transformative change in healthcare services. These LLMs can guide future developments and allow healthcare professionals to work in an efficient manner. The use of LLMs can also offer input to help professionals generate medical prescriptions, nutritional advices, and help the entire ecosystem of healthcare to offer superior services to underserved communities. Policymakers have to make a certain level of investment to acquire LLMs but this investment is going to help by returning holistic results in the long term future. The best part of using the LLMs is that these can be easily integrated with legacy systems. There is no need for hospitals and healthcare institutions to separately make arrangements for the integration of the LLMs. Rather, these integrations can also be completed very quickly, thereby saving time, money, effort, and other resources of the healthcare ecosystem. The development costs associated with LLMs are not on the very high side. This is another advantage that can catalyse the process related to both their development and integration with the existing systems.

2.2) Customised AI-Driven Apps: Unlike the existing apps in the Healthcare ecosystem, the logic of developing and installing AI-driven customised apps is going to take the efficacy of healthcare ecosystem to another level. The customization features of these apps allow healthcare workers, chemists, patients, and other associated stakeholders to make the necessary changes as per the changes demanded by the external environment (Kolo 2021). It's also important to keep the development on the modular architecture so that customisation won't mandate any significant changes in the addition/deletion of new modules. The use of modular architecture coupled with low-code development can be integrated into the development of these apps. Further, new apps can be integrated with existing legacy systems so that new developments can be added within no time. It's essential that all criteria related to cost integration can be taken care of with the help of these two approaches and customised according to the parameters of the development. The primary benefit of using this approach is the achievement of the multiple possibilities that can be explored with the help of customised applications of the devices. This will facilitate the use of multiple apps for exploring and investigating multiple diseases that are common among the masses and accordingly devising the strategies that will help in offering superior diagnostic and therapeutic services to the patients (Kulshrestha et al. 2022). The scope of these applications is tremendous in the case of underdeveloped countries where there is a vast scope for improvement as far as healthcare applications are concerned. Developers can also choose to use the integrated framework for development of AI-driven applications. This will lead to the better coordination among all stakeholders and also invoke better sense of participation among them.

2.3) Machine Learning (ML): Counter among the most significant technologies of the present times, ML can prove very helpful in ensuring access to quality health care services to the underserved. ML programs need historical data and by feeding this information, many significant results related to healthcare services can be obtained. The utility of these results is specifically beneficial for the underserved population as the extrapolation of the data can be utilised a member of different manners. From diagnosing the various disease patterns prevalent among the underserved community, ML programs can immensely benefit the population (Ledro et al. 2022). These programs can also be utilised to enhance the efficiency of the existing procedures and make them more relevant for countering the deadly impacts of the evolving issues. ML when used in collaboration with AI Technology can prove to be a game changer for the entire domain of the healthcare ecosystem (Singh et al. 2020). The technology is very cost-effective in nature and developing and designing the various ML programs is not a very difficult task. Policymakers, entrepreneurs, and other associated stakeholders can come together to develop new ML programs and this collaborative effort can then lead to the further evolution of the in the coming years (Singh 2024). The role of the IT industry and associated stakeholders also become very prominent in this particular area and can be leveraged to create an encompassing ecosystem for the development of a vibrant healthcare ecosystem in the country. One thing that is important for the development of the ML programs is the training and skilling of stakeholders so that maximum benefits from the process can be obtained. The advantage of the algorithms based on ML technology also lies in the fact that these can be adjusted on a real-time basis for making any kind of correction within the important parameters indicated by the various levels of tests conducted on the patients. These real-time updating facilities are quite important for achieving the desired level of efficiency in the patient care procedures (Mileva 2024).

2.4) Blockchain Technology: The most significant relevance of blockchain technology is to make the data accessible to all stakeholders in a completely safe and secure manner. Also known by the name of open ledger, this technology works in the form of different blocks that can be shared across the participants in the ecosystem without any concern for the safety in security of the data. That technology is already in use in the financial technology sector and helping banks and financial institutions to safely process their transactions across the globe (Padasalgi 2024). The technology can prove relevant for the healthcare ecosystem and by distributing the data among all the stakeholders safely and securely, it will make sure that quality healthcare services can be offered to a portion of the population. The rules and regulations related to the blockchain are not very clear in different nations across the globe (Welch 2023). Therefore, it is incumbent on regulators and policymakers to come up with clear instructions related to the use of open ledger technology. The need to have clear guidance in this regard is essential and by devising clear instructions to all stakeholders, the overall scenario related to the use of the blockchain in the healthcare industry can be made more positive in its outlook (Shroff 2024). There is no doubt about the exponential rise in the use of the blockchain technology in healthcare in the coming years and offering the stakeholders a good and productive policy will further accelerate this adoption manifold times (Saluja 2024). Another important need here is to train the staff and workers on using blockchain technology so that the designing, implementation, and development of the technology can be achieved with desired level of efficiency and effectiveness.

3. TECHNOLOGY ADOPTION: A HOLISTIC FRAMEWORK

The adoption of the technology in the healthcare ecosystem ultimately depends upon the three primary stakeholders: a) healthcare players, b) technology developers, and c) policymakers and regulators. The most important stakeholder is the HealthCare industry which comprises multiple participants offering healthcare services to the masses. From hospitals to healthcare professionals and pharmacies, the adoption of the technology is primarily dependent on the attitude of these stakeholders (Shaheen 2021). Patients are also an important part of the healthcare system and making them aware of the various technologies and their specific usage is also going to be an important step for the healthcare industry. To boost the adoption of the technology in the healthcare industry, the role of the technology developers is also going to be extremely significant (Shalender 2022). Ultimately, the cost-effectiveness of the technology will determine the level of technology adoption in the industry. The maturity of AI tools, ML programs, IoT devices, and allied integrated platforms are thus going to be instrumental in the adoption of technology in the healthcare ecosystem (Shalender 2023). The promotion and encouragement from the policymakers in the development of the different technologies, creation of the innovation ecosystem, and allied prospects are also going to come in handy in encouraging the participation of stakeholders in the process (Singla et al. 2023).

Figure 1.

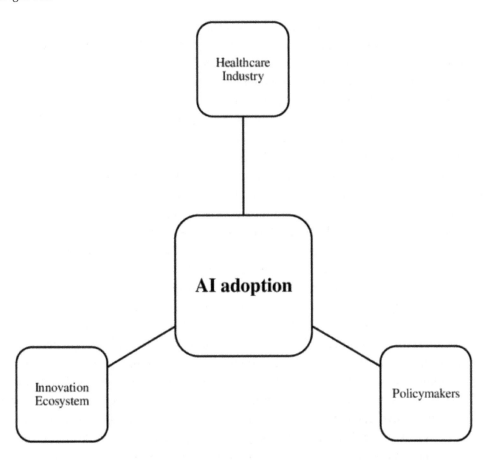

Perhaps the most important role in this technology adoption for serving the underserved population is of regulators and policymakers. These stakeholders are the most important ones and by offering open constructive and dynamic policies to the healthcare ecosystem, the adoption of the technology for the greater benefit of stakeholders can be achieved. Nations across the globe are realising the importance of the newest technology in ramping up their healthcare ecosystem. This realisation is extremely important for meeting the expectations of the masses and making quality healthcare services available to the underserved population. Various kinds of grants, redemptions and subsidies can be offered to innovative startups so that evolved and dynamic policies can be made in this regard. These incentives can also help the healthcare players to speed up their innovation journey and make new technology available for the stakeholders quickly and efficiently.

4. CONCLUSION AND DISCUSSION

The adoption of the technology is the need of the hour. This is specifically true for the healthcare industry as a large portion of the world population is suffering from the lack of quality healthcare services. Much technological advancement has been paving the way for offering better healthcare services to the masses. Primary among these technologies are AI, ML, and blockchain among others. The important part of the technology application in the healthcare ecosystem is to understand that these must be used in tandem to offer superior benefits to the patients. The implementation of these technologies must not be based upon individual tools and technology and it is only through the integration of these technology propositions, that superior benefits can be achieved. The success of integrating technology into the healthcare system also depends upon the level of awareness that patients have of different technology tools. As digital literacy levels differ as per the socio-economic parameters, these are going to be extremely important for maximizing gains from the adoption and integration of the technology. The technology and entrepreneurial ecosystem of the nations can also play an important role in enhancing the option of technology in the healthcare sector. The constructive and open policies from the governments in the form of offering benefits, subsidies, and grants to companies can also prove instrumental in rewriting the success story of technology integration in the healthcare sector. It is also essential that regular exchange of information and dialogue continue to become a part of the overall discussions as it will help make the entire system productive, dynamic, and evolved. New policies and frameworks should be developed by the healthcare ecosystem and equal discussion should be held to make sure that the older systems are upgraded to deliver desired levels of efficiency in operating procedures. The issue with the legacy systems must also be taken with care as it is not easy to replace the existing modules in hospitals and health care institutes to make way for the new technology. The focus must also be given to training the healthcare staff in order to make sure that technology is integrated and used with desired efficiency and effectiveness. These are steps that need to be taken keeping in mind the long-term prospects of the technology adoption and offering a completely holistic approach that can lead to the creation of a vibrant and dynamic ecosystem for the healthcare industry.

REFERENCES

Aggarwal, A., Chand, P. K., Jhamb, D., & Mittal, A. (2020). Leader–Member Exchange, Work Engagement, and Psychological Withdrawal Behavior: The Mediating Role of Psychological Empowerment. *Frontiers in Psychology*, 11(423), 423. Advance online publication. 10.3389/fpsyg.2020.0042332296361

Davenport, T., & Kalakota, R. (2019). The potential for artificial intelligence in healthcare. *Future Healthcare Journal*, 6(2), 94–98. 10.7861/futurehosp.6-2-9431363513

Dhiman, R., Chand, P. K., & Gupta, S. (2018). Behavioural Aspects Influencing Decision to Purchase Apparels amongst Young Indian Consumers. *FIIB Business Review*, 7(3), 188–200. 10.1177/2319714518790308

Frist, B. (2023). How Generative AI – A Technology Catalyst – Is Revolutionizing Healthcare. Available at https://www.forbes.com/sites/billfrist/2023/08/01/how-generative-ai--a-technology-catalyst--is-revolutionizing-healthcare/?sh=67b658495013

Kolo, K. (2021). 9 AR Platforms Bring Augmented Reality Content in the Classroom. Available at https://www.thevrara.com/blog2/2021/10/26/9-desktop-ar-platforms-to-bring-ar-content-in-the-classroom

Kulshrestha, D., Tiwari, M. K., Shalender, K., & Sharma, S. (2022). Consumer Acatalepsy Towards Buying Behaviour for Need-Based Goods for Sustainability During the COVID-19 Pandemic. *Indian Journal of Marketing*, 52(10), 50–63. 10.17010/ijom/2022/v52/i10/172347

Ledro, C., Nosella, A., & Vinelli, A. (2022). Artificial intelligence in customer relationship management: Literature review and future research directions. *Journal of Business and Industrial Marketing*, 37(13), 48–63. 10.1108/JBIM-07-2021-0332

Mileva, G. (2024), 5 AI Healthcare Tools Revolutionizing Healthcare in Hospitals and Clinics. Available at https://influencermarketinghub.com/ai-healthcare-tools/

Padasalgi, S. R. (2024). Transforming Healthcare: The Power of AI in Revolutionizing Patient Care and Research. Available at https://health.economictimes.indiatimes.com/news/health-it/transforming-healthcare-the-power-of-ai-in-revolutionizing-patient-care-and-researchais-integration-into-healthcare-a-game-changer/107183802

Saluja, R. (2024). Revolutionizing Healthcare: The Integral Role of AI And IoT In Shaping Modern Medicine. Available at https://www.forbes.com/sites/forbesbusinesdevelopmentcouncil/2024/02/14/revolutionizing-healthcare-the-integral-role-of-ai-and-iot-in-shaping-modern-medicine/?sh=6bd38bdedabc

Shaheen, M. Y. (2021). Applications of Artificial Intelligence (AI) in healthcare. *RE:view*. Advance online publication. 10.14293/S2199-1006.1.SOR-.PPVRY8K.v1

Shalender, K. (2022). Key variables in team dynamics in small businesses and start-ups. In New teaching resources for management in a globalised world (pp. 141–153). https://doi.org/10.1142/9789811239212_0007

Shalender, K. (2023). Skill development for society 5.0: A focus on the new-age skilling process. Trivedi, S., Aggarwal, R., & Sharma, S. (Eds.), Innovations and Sustainability in Society 5.0, Nova Science Publishers, Hauppauge, NY, pp. 43–52.

Shroff, K. (2024). Artificial Intelligence (AI) revolutionizing healthcare: A look at the present and future! Available at https://www.dsij.in/dsijarticledetail/artificial-intelligence-ai-revolutionizing-healthcare-a-look-at-the-present-and-future-37593

Singh, H. (2024). How AI and ML are Revolutionising Healthcare Industry. Available at https://www.entrepreneur.com/en-in/news-and-trends/how-ai-and-ml-are-revolutionising-healthcare-industry/472959

Singh, J. P., Chand, P. K., Mittal, A., & Aggarwal, A. (2020). High-performance work system and organizational citizenship behaviour at the shop floor. *Benchmarking*, 27(4), 1369–1398. 10.1108/BIJ-07-2019-0339

Singla, B., Shalender, K., & Sharma, S. (2023). Enhancing customer engagement through brand loyalty drivers among E-consumers. Gupta, M., Shalender, K., Singla, B., Singh, N. (Eds.), Applications of Neuromarketing in the Metaverse, IGI Global, Hershey, PA, pp. 155–162

Welch, A. (2023). Artificial intelligence is helping revolutionize healthcare as we know it. Available at https://www.jnj.com/innovation/artificial-intelligence-in-healthcare

Chapter 12
Navigating the Crossroads:
Stakeholder Perspectives in Healthcare Innovation

Ravishankar Krishnan
Vel Tech Rangarajan Dr.Sagunthala R&D Institute of Science and Technology, India

Saravana Mahesan S.
Vel Tech Rangarajan Dr.Sagunthala R&D Institute of Science and Technology, India

G. Manoj
 http://orcid.org/0000-0003-2830-7875
Vel Tech Rangarajan Dr.Sagunthala R&D Institute of Science and Technology, India

Kannan G.
 http://orcid.org/0000-0002-4656-4034
St. Peter's Institute of Higher Education and Research, India

Perumal Elantheraiyan
Vel Tech Rangarajan Dr.Sagunthala R&D Institute of Science and Technology, India

Logasakthi Kandasamy
 http://orcid.org/0000-0003-1024-8459
RV University, India

ABSTRACT

Healthcare innovation is a vibrant domain of medical science and patient care that is constantly changing with technological advancements and new treatment modalities. This chapter provides an overview of the complex landscape of healthcare innovation and the roles identified for stakeholders to influence or be influenced by their environment. Stakeholders' perceptions, desires, and attitudes toward healthcare innovation have a significant impact on its development, integration, and acceptance. The chapter examines the interacting and intersecting roles and agendas of patients,

DOI: 10.4018/979-8-3693-3731-8.ch012

Copyright © 2024, IGI Global. Copying or distributing in print or electronic forms without written permission of IGI Global is prohibited.

providers, industry, policy makers, and researchers are examined. Additionally, the problems and surrounding issues in the field of health innovation, such as regulatory frameworks and hurdles, technology constraints, ethical dilemmas, and financial repercussions, are discussed. Lastly, the chapter provides some recommendations and outlines some future issues and policy decisions to achieve higher accessibility and health benefit implementation.

INTRODUCTION

Healthcare innovation is a cornerstone of progress, which consistently challenges the current state of possibilities in the fields of medical science and patient care. With the emergence of novel treatments and revolutionary technologies, the healthcare sector seems to be in a state of utmost evolution and transformative change (Wang & Lin, 2020). Nonetheless, while the gap in healthcare continues to widen, it is critical to acknowledge the role of stakeholders in addressing the trends of healthcare innovation. In this chapter, we cover the diverse tracks of healthcare innovation, paying extra attention to the perspectives of stakeholders and the implications of their views. The landscape of healthcare innovation embraces a tight knot of scientific ventures, technology, and opportunities in patients' needs. Conventionally, this landscape covered a wide array of aspects, spanning from pharmaceutical drugs and medical devices to organizational models of the healthcare delivery system. However, the last couple of years have been marked by the rise of digital health technologies and artificial intelligence, which has reshuffled the way people deal with medicine (Y.-W. et al., 2022).

Healthcare innovation centers on the relentless quest for solutions to overly knotty medical problems that will improve the implications of the patient's life, from a higher degree of wellness to optimal healthcare delivery. It makes no difference whether it be precision medicine, telemedicine, or predictive analytics; every notion has the potential to revamp the manner diagnosis, treatment, or reduction is performed (Farhan, 2024). The accomplishment of this aspiration hinges on the stakeholders. As the pivot from idea to performance, theory to impact, ideation to implementation, and invention to innovation, stakeholders come up. Stakeholders are the cast of characters with an interest in the outcome of health care innovation. They may vary as the method for the person to the community and from the policymaker to the party concerned. Their opinions, suggestions, and contributions form the course of novelty (Neher et al., 2023).

The importance of stakeholder perspectives cannot be overestimated in the context of honing the promise offered by health care innovation. To begin with, stakeholders are the target audience and final consumers of health care innovation ideas. Their opinions, needs, and demands are extremely useful along with their specific case experiences, personal knowledge, and attainment in creating and developing innovative technology solutions (Nilsen et al., 2022). All of the above will help tailor the innovation to the needs of its potential future participants. In addition, stakeholders help acknowledge and encourage the demand for health care improvements. Since healthcare providers, managers, and policymakers have the power to either promote or hinder the spread and penetration of new technologies and tactics into clinical settings and health care systems, they can activate, apply, and retain stakeholder acceptance for innovative proposals from concept to clone (Shrotriya et al., 2023).

Secondly, stakeholders offer varied perspectives and expertise that enhance the innovation process and promote multidisciplinary collaboration. Their clinical acumen, scientific understanding, regulatory insights, and market acumen provide an ideal viewpoint that drives discussion, creativity, and comprehensive problem-solving. Second, stakeholders also become players in the field of healthcare innovation as they become proponents and guardians of the ethics of innovation (Apell & Eriksson, 2023). They advocate policy and politics that promote equality, patient freedom, and biomedicine, influencing ethical debate, public policy, and public debate to ensure compliance with human norms, ethical reasoning, and legislation.

As a result, it is clear that stakeholders are not simply passive 'recipients' of innovation. On the contrary, they are powerful 'agents of change,' and their views, involvement, and cooperation are three essential mechanisms of securing the change in care that transforms care provision (Arora, 2020). By involving stakeholders in the process as partners rather than mere 'audiences,' health innovators may access the collective experience, knowledge, and resources necessary to navigate the complex weave of the care industry and unlock the whole potential of innovation, with all its accompanying benefits (Zahlan et al., 2023). In the remaining parts of this chapter, we will explore various aspects of stakeholders' position with regard to health innovation. More specifically, we will describe the major differences in their perspectives, challenges, opportunities, and involvement in the continuum of innovation. We will also offer examples and suggestions on how to achieve successful interaction and partnership with stakeholders, providing our vision and recommendations on utilizing stakeholders' power to transform the care industry using AI (Arji et al., 2023).

STAKEHOLDERS IN HEALTHCARE INNOVATION

The diverse and multifaceted ecosystem of healthcare innovation is united by the general understanding of stakeholders who drive efforts, shape policies, and determine outcomes. Understanding stakeholders and their roles or interests is essential for fostering collaboration, overcoming obstacles, and maximizing the effects of innovation ("Healthcare Innovations and Point of Care Technologies Conference, HI-POCT 2022," 2022). This part of the paper presents the definition of stakeholders, describes several types of stakeholders in healthcare, and outlines their roles or interests in the innovation spectrum. A stakeholder refers to any person, group of people, or organization concerned with or affected by the results of a specific initiative or system. In the context of healthcare innovation, stakeholders represent various actors interested or influenced by the creation, implementation, or integration of new or altered healthcare approaches or solutions. Patients and their families, healthcare professionals and organizations, legislators and regulators, industry representatives, advocates and payers, researchers, and academia representatives are all stakeholders in the healthcare sector. Stakeholders in healthcare innovation are familiar by their capacity to influence the progress and results of innovation-related contributions in the form of actions, judgments, or money (Swarnkar & Rathore, 2023). Simultaneously, they are the targets of such contributions, which makes them influential and interested bodies. Therefore, paying attention to and involving stakeholders is important to ensure the alignment of innovation contributions with the needs, requirements, expectations, and inspiration sources of the target population.

Key Stakeholder Groups in Healthcare

Within the realm of healthcare innovation, several key stakeholder groups can be identified, each bringing unique perspectives, expertise, and interests to the table. While the specific composition and roles of stakeholders may vary depending on the context and focus of innovation, the following groups are commonly recognized as central stakeholders in healthcare innovation:

1. Patients and Caregivers: Generally, various groups of stakeholders are involved in the actualization of this field. Although the groups and context of innovation could differ, the major stakeholder groups involved in health innovation include the following: patients and caregivers who actually see the healthcare values and emerge profited or otherwise after medical care. They are involved in the patient-centered innovation of the more informed perspective of needs and an inclusive design to promote usability.

2. Healthcare Providers: The second group involves the healthcare providers, who are instrumental since they impact treatment implementation. These providers include doctors, nurses, other medical practitioners, and pharmacists. This group is critical to the entire process since they are the frontline players in the rolling out of the innovations and contribute equally effective safety, practicality, and relevance.
3. Industry stakeholders: Industry stakeholders such as pharmaceutical companies, medical device manufacturers, technology developers, and healthcare service providers play a critical role in driving innovation through research, development, and commercialization. Additionally, as investors and innovators, they dedicate financial resources, technical expertise, and market knowledge to advance health care technology and solutions. They work closely with other stakeholders, including academia, government, and non-profit organizations, to share knowledge and facilitate technology transfer to ensure more research initiatives.
4. Advocacy and patient groups.: Advocacy groups and patient organizations act as a collective patient, caregiver, and community voice in identifying diseases and health-related problems to drive policy change. These players aim to convey the interests, rights, and needs of a person, raise awareness and transform policy and resource mobilization to address large, unmet patient needs. These stakeholders help drive the collection of market data and ensure the patient's needs are met in an acceptable manner.
5. Researchers and Academic Institutions.: Researchers and academic institutions are at the forefront of the scientific revival, and innovation reduces basic and transformational research to generate information and abilities.

Their Roles and Interests

Each stakeholder group in healthcare innovation plays a distinct role and has specific interests that shape their engagement and influence in the innovation ecosystem (Ghaleb et al., 2020). Understanding these roles and interests is essential for fostering collaboration, addressing conflicts, and aligning stakeholders towards common goals. Here, we outline the roles and interests of key stakeholder groups in healthcare innovation:

1. Patients and Caregivers:
   Roles: End-users, advocates, partners in care
   Interests: Access to high-quality care, improved health outcomes, empowerment, involvement in decision-making, respect for autonomy and preferences
2. Healthcare Providers:

Roles: Clinicians, care coordinators, educators, champions of evidence-based practice

Interests: Patient safety, clinical effectiveness, workflow integration, professional autonomy, continuing education and training, work-life balance

3. Policymakers and Regulators:
    Roles: Policymakers, legislators, regulators, guardians of public health
    Interests: Public safety, evidence-based policymaking, equitable access, cost-effectiveness, regulatory compliance, protection of intellectual property rights
4. Industry Stakeholders:
    Roles: Innovators, investors, collaborators, suppliers
    Interests: Market competitiveness, return on investment, intellectual property protection, regulatory approval, market access, customer satisfaction
5. Advocacy Groups and Patient Organizations:
    Roles: Advocates, educators, community organizers
    Interests: Patient empowerment, awareness raising, policy advocacy, research funding, community support, social justice
6. Researchers and Academic Institutions:
    Roles: Scientists, educators, knowledge generators
    Interests: Scientific discovery, research funding, academic recognition, knowledge dissemination, technology transfer, collaboration opportunities

Understanding the diverse roles and interests of stakeholders enables healthcare innovators to navigate the complexities of the innovation landscape, foster collaboration, and leverage synergies across stakeholder groups. By engaging stakeholders as partners and co-creators, healthcare innovators can harness the collective expertise, resources, and perspectives needed to drive meaningful progress and address the most pressing challenges in healthcare (Kumar et al., 2023).

CHALLENGES AND OPPORTUNITIES IN HEALTHCARE INNOVATION

While the promises of healthcare innovation to change patient outcomes, restructure healthcare delivery, and develop public health are profound, the future of healthcare innovation is not all that rosy (Brooks, 2014). The following subsection will discuss the varied and complex challenge and opportunity environment in healthcare innovation, which includes regulatory, technical, economic, and ethical considerations.

Regulatory Hurdles

One of the major problems of Healthcare innovation is the regulatory approval and compliance complexities. Regulatory bodies are mandated to ensure that health products and services are safe, efficient, and of high quality. This is directed towards safeguard the public health while minimizing the risks that may come from the introduction of new health products and technologies (Kanade & Batule, 2024) . However, this adherence to the complex approval process tends to be problematic due to the discontinuance in the complex, tedious, and excruciatingly time taking process that mostly limits the innovative health products and services from entering the market. There are broadly four major regulation pathways manipulated in the market, it is dependent on the type of product or the intervention involved. They include the pharmaceuticals, digital health technologies, medical devices, and even the artificial intelligence algorithms. Each of them has different regulatory standards and requirements, all of which need to be carefully documented and proven to get market release and reimbursement. At the same, time, the rate of technological change is often higher than the rate of regulatory bodies' ability to assess the accuracy and safety of innovation. Therefore, there is always a lack of new treatments and health innovations for patients, as they are unable to get access to the market in a short period (Bellucci, 2022). However, regulatory bodies become increasingly conscious of the necessity to develop new, faster, and more flexible regulatory systems to test health solutions. Examples of such systems are FDA's Digital Health Software Pre-Certification Program and European MDR, which are designed to help develop more flexible and quicker regulations for digital health innovation. The balance between the need for innovation and the need for security is often difficult to preserve. In this regard, effective and trusting collaboration and partnership with regulators, industry, practitioners, and patient associations are essential factors for successful regulation development (Kamath et al., 2024).

Technological Barriers

Even though technology advancement opens opportunities for changing the status quo in healthcare, it fails to do so due to a variety of technical challenges and technological barriers to innovation. Apart from data privacy and security, key technological challenges include the difficulty of integrating new technologies into clinical work processes and enabling their interoperability with already existing systems (Friebe, 2020). The registration of technological solutions implies a truly overwhelming array of challenges accompanied by fragmentation, data storage across different systems, and formats, and differences in data standards across different devices and other applications. Electronic healthcare records and other health information technology have no sufficient interoperability to meet the requirements of data-enabled care and, therefore, affect data exchange and storage in practice. One of the major technological issues with regards to data-enabled healthcare is data security and privacy. Healthcare innovations such as artificial intelligence and data exchange are subject to data protection by law (Teo et al., 2023). In the US, it is regulated by the Health Insurance Portability and Accountability Act, while the European unified market has the General Data Protection Regulation. In this way, data exchange and accessibility are limited by legislation, which is a hurdle to technological growth in healthcare. The solution does not lie solely in the development of new technologies and solutions that can perform thorough data integration – a stable infrastructure and governance for innovation are also needed. There are already various standards for healthcare data exchange, and the FHIR specification and SMART Health IT as an accompanying tool are the most recognizable examples. Different technologies, including cybersecurity, encryption, and blockchain, have the potential of pivotal use for preserving patient data, which allows responsible data exertion in digital healthcare. Evaluation demands close collaboration across the tech development and regulation pipeline and health professionals and cybersecurity experts (Wang & Lin, 2023).

Ethical Considerations

Perhaps most importantly, it has some ethical considerations in health innovation. The aspect of patient privacy and confidentiality seems to be the most pressing ethical issue. Privacy and confidentiality are crucial components of trust in the health care system. Data encryption, governance and access controls, privacy regulations, and consent form the criteria for encouraging patient information gathered by technologies like health records, wearables, genomics, and more. Given the pace of change, achieving broad consent has been a prevalent discussion (Sharma & Gupta, 2021). Full consent, full protection, and control of patients' data are essential. Health inequalities are yet another principal factor to influence the ethical standards. Low-income communities, people of color and racial and ethnic minorities, rural areas, immigrants, and other diverse groups face persistent social determinants of health. Health innovators must ensure that their work is accessible, affordable, and customized for their communities, equal access to research and innovation. Finally, any efforts must include a dialogue of all stakeholders involved, including ethicists, school administrators, policymakers, technologists, patients, students, or patients. All stakeholders involved in this issue must communicate to work together on effective solutions for many relevant ethical problems raised by health innovation (Gupta & Yadav, 2024).

Economic Implications

In addition to regulatory, technological, and ethical issues, there can be a significant impact on the economics associated with healthcare innovation, which can significantly affect various stakeholders involved in the entire process. While providing cost-saving opportunities, efficient use of resources, and labor, various innovations also require substantial investments, struggle with reimbursement issues, and operate on mature or immature market conditions. It is evident, that major costs of healthcare innovation include the development of research and development and the time it takes for new products to reach the market (Potnurwar et al., 2023). First of all, there are the costs of pharma where the development of new drugs requires significant amounts of money. The process is capital-intensive given the need for extensive field and clinical research, as well as broadly defined regulatory requirements, especially in the area of long-term clinical testing, contributing to high costs of new drug commercialization. The same applies to medical devices and digital health, where technology development requires extensive resources in terms of research and money. Secondly, it is about the uncertainty in terms of the reimbursement of emerging new developments. Payers evaluate the value for money offered by new interventions and make a reimbursement decision. In this regard, reimbursement decisions can be considered an important factor affecting the reliance on commercial innovation, which in turn influences the volume and penetration of instruments used (Kaur, 2024). Market dynamics, competition, availability, and efficiency of intellectual property protection, price decisions, and reimbursement contracts are also essential. Thirdly, it is about competition and intellectual property protection and its impact on economic rationale. Obviously, creating a new market involves risks and benefits associated with competition, as well as potential obsolescence and age in case of success. However, for the health sector, economic reasons allow commercial innovation to contribute to economic growth, job creation, and value creation (Mincu & Roy, 2022). There is much research on value creation through open innovation systems that employ existing resources to create more co-opetive business environments. Factors representing the model play would involve entry barriers, penetration, price, and reimbursement options or decisions. Digital health, based on artificial intelligence and predictive analytics, develops new business models around cost-effectiveness and resource allocation (Akinyele et al., 2024).

INTEGRATING AI INTO HEALTHCARE: STAKEHOLDER PERSPECTIVES

The discussion of artificial intelligence is inextricably linked to an understanding of the context in which these technologies it will be used. For this reason, the first subcategory of the contextual success factor is the design. It is logical to assume that good design should precede the development and implementation of products and services. According to that, already on the design stage it is necessary to take into account the needs and desires of the core users (Lee & Choi, 2023). These are stakeholders, for whom another factor of context is significant; this is how technological innovations change the structure and work of organizations. It should be taken into consideration that a variety of organizations work in the field of healthcare, and innovations can have completely different effects on them (Litinski, 2018). However, what seems to connect the majority of stakeholders is the desire to integrate innovation into their work one way or another.

Clinicians and Healthcare Providers

Clinicians and healthcare providers are the central points of the health service delivery process and, thus, among the most significant end-users of clinical applications. They can apply AI in practice similarly to other end-users but have a distinctive perspective and specific opportunities and challenges to consider in this regard (Huo et al., 2023). On the one hand, it is possible to view AI as a tool capable of enhancing clinical decision-making by providing real-time analytics, due to the use of significant amounts of data and the application of machine learning. AI-powered resources, such as clinical decision support systems, predictive analytics, and natural language processing, can help clinicians diagnose more effectively, choose the optimal treatment strategy, and tailor it in accordance with a specific patient's needs (Shah et al., 2024). On the other hand, the integration of these resources into practice may amount to a difficulty affecting their application. Specifically, there is a risk that the use of AI can disrupt the clinical workflow in general and the electronic health record in particular. On top of that, clinicians' concerns, such as resistance to change, potential job loss, and bias against the tools' reliability and accuracy, must be addressed. Therefore, when using AI, healthcare organizations and providers need to consider these points to ensure a smooth integration process. One of the ways to achieve this goal is to engage clinicians in the designing, developing, and evaluating AI tools and applications by considering their experience, needs, and preferences (Shah et al., 2024). Besides this, ongoing training and education programs can help clinicians acquire the necessary skills and competence to use AI adequately. Such an approach would create the right culture and conditions used to optimize the use of AI by clinicians to improve the quality, efficiency, and safety of care.

Patients and Caregivers

Patients and caregivers are critical stakeholders in the healthcare ecosystem. As the ultimate passively receiving users of products and services from the healthcare system, their perspective, needs, and preferences must be central when designing and operationalizing AI. Patients need to consider AI's safety, effectiveness, and ethical implications as systems you will rely on for your care. Patients see AI as an opportunity for improving access to timely, accurate, and personalized healthcare services (Amjad et al., 2023). As such, AI can empower patients to be more involved in directing their health and well-being. AI applications such as remote monitoring, virtual health assistants, and personalized health recommendations can help patients become more engaged, adherent, and self-managing of their chronic conditions. On the other hand, the involvement of AI in patient care also poses new risks of data privacy, security, and trust. Patients may not be willing to share sensitive health data with AI, considering some high-profile instances of privacy violations and data misuse. Additionally, patients may be concerned that AI algorithms can introduce bias, discrimination, or errors into clinical decision-making in delicate areas such as diagnosis, prognosis, or treatment (Nassani et al., 2023).

To counter these concerns, healthcare organizations must ensure that AI remains fair and transparent for patients. Firstly, patients must have clear and straightforward information about how their data are handled, protected, and shared within AI systems. Build on that, patients must be enabled to provide their informed consent and have control over how their health data are used, including the option for patients to opt out of AI at any time (Swain et al., 2022). In addition, patients as partners must be involved in the co-design and evaluation of the technologies throughout the development lifecycle. This approach can ensure that their preference is integrated in the design to build a culture of patient-centered innovation.

STRATEGIES FOR EFFECTIVE STAKEHOLDER ENGAGEMENT

First of all, communication should be clear to engage stakeholders effectively. Creating clear communication lines helps stakeholders get the information they need to understand, act as necessary, based on the transactions, know who to contact, when and how. Healthcare organizations should place value on clearly defined communication regarding innovation stakeholder engagement (Rahman, 2023). The strategy should also focus on how an organization can send out and reach out to communication channels regarding their innovation, so as to take the critical feedback back from stakeholders on addressed issues. Different groups may focus on several authorities to make sure that their interests are addressed.

Definition of Clear Value Proposition and Providing Information

The information required by stakeholders concerns what needs to be communicated about introduction, change, or discontinuation of any innovation. Healthcare organizations should, therefore, acknowledge that information is of the most importance and should aim to encourage it among stakeholders (Timilsina et al., 2023). In this respect, use of predetermined sets of tools is one way to promote information connection in the stakeholders discussed. Effective communication should precede, track, and follow implementation; it will help organizations update stakeholders on the organizations' status and seek feedback on any necessity targeted or themed as part of current or future project actions in a regular, timely, and interesting way (Cannavale et al., 2022). Thus, stakeholders should be empowered through knowledge dissemination on the importance of healthcare organizations focusing on innovation implementation.

Building Trust and Transparency

Trust is one of the foundational elements of effective stakeholder engagement, as it provides a basis for the development of productive relationships, collaboration, and shared decision-making. As such, it is critical to establish trust by ensuring stakeholders have confidence in the integrity, reliability, and intent behind the innovation initiative (Cannavale et al., 2022). In order to achieve this goal, the organization needs to commit to the principles of trust by ensuring transparency and accountability in all of its activities. This may involve openly stating the goals and priorities of the organization, the criteria used to make decisions, as well as all of the risks, unknowns, and conflicts that may arise. By doing this, the healthcare organization ensures that stakeholders understand its motivations and are assured of its credibility. Moreover, the organization also needs to commit to listening to the feedback from the stakeholders. It can conduct surveys, focus groups, or interviews to gather information and learn about the concerns and needs of its stakeholders (Kyaw Zaw et al., 2021). By doing so, it will gain the satisfaction of being heard and maintain its involvement in decision-making processes.

In relation to this, the organization gain build trust by ensuring that its staff and resources are committed to its stakeholders and their needs. For example, it can ensure it delivers on the promises it makes regarding innovation activity, or that its staff are constantly available, competent, and professional in dealing with the stakeholders. At the same time, trust is not binary, so it should be treated as a spectrum and developed over time (Manikandan & Sharma, 2023). Once obtained, it should also be seen as a fragile achievement that can be lost if violated. For this reason, organizations can work to ensure that they are consistent and reliable in their interactions with stakeholders, as well as competent and ethical. Overall, trust enables a culture of shared responsibility.

Responding to Stakeholder Concerns and Needs

To manage stakeholder resistance and facilitate stakeholder buy-in for innovation initiatives, healthcare organizations should listen to, meet, acknowledge, and respond to stakeholder concerns and needs. The initial step of responding to stakeholders is conducting the stakeholder analysis to identify potential barriers, challenges, and areas of alignment with stakeholders' interests (Lancee et al., 2018). Stakeholder analysis can be performed using a variety of techniques, such as dialogue, surveys, focus groups, and other methods of obtaining and analyzing feedback to understand their perceptions, interests, and priorities. In the context of innovation, the stakeholder needs and concerns should be understood by health organizations from the perspective of finding ways to encourage their ownership and buy-in for strategic or operational advances (K. B. Pradhan et al., 2021). After identifying the stakeholder concerns and needs, a healthcare organization should develop a strategy, and sometimes an adaptive management plan, to address those concerns and needs through a range of efforts, such as communication campaigns to dispel misconception, providing inside information or learning opportunities, adjusting the timeline in alignment with stakeholders' needs, and other measures. The second critical step is to communicate to stakeholders in a way that informs them of responses to their concerns and needs. The healthcare organization should acknowledge and inform stakeholders that their concerns and needs are actively addressed to facilitate trust and ensure they are learning partners that can provide feedback on how the concerns have been or are being addressed (Neumann et al., 2019). It also should monitor stakeholder responses to their activities and understand dynamics of how stakeholders behave or information requirements and respond to those. Changes can also be made in the areas which have been neglected or become apparent in the process. Towards this end, a healthcare organization follows a Dynamic planning process, which responds specifically to current and future issues resulting from stakeholder groups (Barua et al., 2023). Such an approach can help ensure stakeholder concerns and needs are met and the innovation initiative remains responsive to changes and they remain supportive of them.

Encouraging Collaboration and Participation

Collaboration and participation are core elements of successful stakeholder engagement, which allows incorporating the expertise, resources, and needs of various groups to make better decisions and leverage much more profound synergies. Encourage stakeholder collaboration and participation by involving interested parties in joint activities and discussions. For example, health organizations may establish different forms of committees or task forces who will participate in the decision-making process in a supportive atmosphere. Furthermore, health organizations might pay more attention to the diversity of their stakeholder pools and involve underrepresented or marginalized groups, thus encouraging greater participation and inclusivity (Arshi et al., 2023). Finally, the leaders should attempt to provide stakeholders with necessary resources and incentives, which might encourage and support the participation of stakeholders in innovation initiatives.

In conclusion, the increased role of AI technologies and the complexity of their implementation requires appropriate stakeholder engagement to drive successful healthcare innovation. The openness to stakeholders, including a broad range of organizations, individuals, and communities, is of critical importance. The needs, concerns, and interests of various stakeholder groups should be addressed, and their participation and collaboration should be encouraged. Many aspects of successful stakeholder engagement are critical for driving successful healthcare innovation. Organizations should focus on creating open lines of communication, building trust and transparency, identifying and addressing stakeholder needs and concerns, and encouraging collaboration and participation. Finally, the case study appears to be relevant to the concepts of stakeholder participation and collaboration. It can serve as an example of how AI can be implemented into health organizations, improving solutions and creating better outcomes for patients (Miner et al., 2023).

FUTURE DIRECTIONS AND RECOMMENDATIONS

While healthcare innovation is currently experiencing rapid development, it is of the utmost importance to conceive of the future, identify the current challenges, and the new ones that might arise in the course of time, as well as outline the development strategies to improve. In this section, the potential future directions and recommendations for enhancing healthcare innovation will be discussed, along with potential emerging trends, new ways of changing stakeholder dynamics, and policies to be considered.

Emerging Trends in Healthcare Innovation

The alignment of artificial intelligence and machine learning facilitates the identification of relevant patterns and the prediction of specific traits, such as the occurrence of diseases, the likely outcomes, etc. As a result, new advanced clinical tools fueled by AI and machine learning, such as prescriptive analytics, algorithms for diagnosing diseases through medical imaging with the use of image recognition, and natural language processing, etc., will become dominant in the future (Babu et al., 2023).

Telemedicine, remote monitoring devices, and wearables, among other types of digital health solutions, have shifted the modern healthcare paradigms significantly, allowing patients to keep track of their health and receive appropriate care in the timely and culturally sensitive manner (Tahir & Farhan, 2023). As a result, access to care has improved significantly, whereas patients are given a more active role to play in managing their health condition.

Genomics-, proteomics-, and metabolomics designation medicine, as well as various personalized and advanced medicines and treatments and health delivery systems, which are personalized and optimized, lead to improved outcomes, fewer side effects, as well as maintenance at the maximal regimen level (Pandimurugan et al., 2023). Therefore, the emergence of precision medicine solutions is being observed, including the alignment of solid organ biopsy and liquid biopsy.

The ability to store, share, and analyze medical information is paramount for making valuable decisions, managing population health, streamlining patient information sharing, etc. Thus, emerging tools include robust analytics and upgrade care pathways into AI-enabled systems.

Anticipated Changes in Stakeholder Dynamics

Stakeholders in the healthcare ecosystem are recognizing the value of collaboration and partnerships in innovation, problem-solving, and goal achievement. In the future, stakeholders will be driving collaboration across the healthcare ecosystem, between healthcare provision, technology development, research, policy-making institutions, government agencies, and patient advocacy groups, to take advantage of the spectrum of all stakeholders" variety in expertise, resources, and perspective (Pandimurugan et al., 2023).

Patients and caregivers will be more empowered agents in healthcare that demand more transparent, accountable, and patient-centric approaches from healthcare organizations (Bindu Bhavani & Raghuveer, 2021). This dynamic is powered by the development in patient engagement, patient empowerment, health literacy, and digital health. This trend will lead to more patient-centric models becoming the norm, more patients becoming actively involved in decision-making, and more patient advocates influencing policies and procedures.

Technological development is happening at an accelerating pace and will continue to do so. AI will play a major role in automating numerous processes, while digital health records, genomics, and biotechnologies will evolve faster than ever before (Lysen & Wyatt, 2024). All stakeholders will have to become more adaptable, constant learners who are able to assimilate innovations quickly and efficiently, given that new challenges and opportunities will be constantly emerging, and patients" needs and expectations will evolve accordingly.

These changes will also be driven by policies and regulations, as shaping markets and technological development through policy, legislation, and regulations is just one of the primary uses of these instruments (Darda & Matta, 2024). Future policy initiatives will be affecting the healthcare landscape just as current ones, with more policies supporting interoperability, data privacy, and data security while stimulating competition and innovation, as well as addressing serious issues surrounding technologies such as AI and precision medicine such as ethics and social implications (Varilek & Mollman, 2024).

Policy Implications and Recommendations for Action

Policymakers should prioritize initiatives to promote interoperability and data sharing across healthcare systems and stakeholders. This may include adoption of interoperability standards, such as Fast Healthcare Interoperability Resources, development of data sharing frameworks and governance mechanisms, and establishment of data sharing agreements and protocols between stakeholders (Kashif et al., 2019). Policymakers should implement policies and incentives to encourage collaboration and innovation across the healthcare ecosystem. This may include funding for research and development, tax incentives for investment in healthcare innovation, grants and subsidies for collaborative projects and partnerships, and creation of administrative frameworks and clearinghouses (Ravindar et al., 2023). Moreover, regulators should incentivize investment in digital health solutions to support healthcare innovation. Policymakers should work to streamline regulatory pathways, reduce administrative burdens, and clarify and provide guidance concerning the regulatory requirements for emerging technologies and practices, such as AI and digital health (K. Pradhan et al., 2021). For example, policymakers can establish regulatory safe harbors, such as regulatory sandboxes and pilot programs, and expedited approval processes, such as breakthrough device designation and accelerated approval for AI technologies and digital health software. Policymakers should invest in digital infrastructure, health IT systems, and workforce development initiatives to support the adoption and integration of AI, digital health, and data analytics technologies in healthcare. This may include training programs, education grants, and incentives for healthcare professionals, such as physicians and nurses, to build the necessary skills and competencies to leverage emerging technologies for care delivery (Bertl et al., 2023). Policymakers should prioritize initiatives to promote equity and access to healthcare innovation across the country and population. This may include funding for community health centers, expansion of telehealth services in rural and underserved areas, and initiatives to address healthcare disparities and social determinants of health (Popa et al., 2021).

CONCLUSION

The stakeholder engagement is required to promote health care innovation. In this chapter, The study have repeatedly noted that the involvement of a maximum of stakeholders in healthcare innovation, including clinicians, patients, policymakers, healthcare administrators, and industry stakeholders and technology developers, is essential. Providing opportunities for clear communication, trust and belief in one another, and discussing contentious issues and opportunities can only be realized as a joint effort. It is important to make efforts in the future to ensure patient-centrality, facilitate the acceptance of Lasik, and adopt the necessary policies, creating more understandable and fair innovations that donors will trust and in which they will actively participate. At this point, it is important to note that the group of stakeholders that include interveners is one of the subtopics from this chapter's objective and the main results. Overall it would seem that a higher level of stakeholder engagement can positively influence the development of the innovative process in healthcare.

In general, it may be noted that stakeholders should continue to take steps to improve the delivery of health care and results. At the same time, considerable work needs to be done, including the removal of "silos," undertake joint work, and customize the patient's concerns and desires. Stakeholders can help shape the future of healthcare investments by influencing changes in policy and reform in healthcare innovation systems, interaction through investment in digital infrastructure and workforce. The stakeholders' constant efforts to break the silos, foster collaboration, and adapt investments to meet the needs of patients, families, and communities are commendatory.

REFERENCES

Akinyele, K., Baudot, L., Koreff, J., & Sutton, S. (2024). Regulatory innovation and (de)legitimisation: accountability challenges in the healthcare field. *Accounting Forum*. 10.1080/01559982.2023.2295161

Amjad, A., Kordel, P., & Fernandes, G. (2023). A Review on Innovation in Healthcare Sector (Telehealth) through Artificial Intelligence. *Sustainability (Basel)*, 15(8), 6655. 10.3390/su15086655

Apell, P., & Eriksson, H. (2023). Artificial intelligence (AI) healthcare technology innovations: The current state and challenges from a life science industry perspective. *Technology Analysis and Strategic Management*, 35(2), 179–193. 10.1080/09537325.2021.1971188

Arji, G., Ahmadi, H., Avazpoor, P., & Hemmat, M. (2023). Identifying resilience strategies for disruption management in the healthcare supply chain during COVID-19 by digital innovations: A systematic literature review. *Informatics in Medicine Unlocked*, 38, 101199. 10.1016/j.imu.2023.10119936873583

Arora, A. (2020). Conceptualising artificial intelligence as a digital healthcare innovation: An introductory review. *Medical Devices (Auckland, N.Z.)*, 13, 223–230. 10.2147/MDER.S26259032904333

Arshi, O., Chaudhary, A., & Singh, R. (2023). Navigating the Future of Healthcare: AI-Powered Solutions, Personalized Treatment Plans, and Emerging Trends in 2023. In Swarnkar, S. K., & Rathore, Y. K. (Eds.), *International Conference on Artificial Intelligence for Innovations in Healthcare Industries, ICAIIHI 2023*. Institute of Electrical and Electronics Engineers Inc. 10.1109/ICAIIHI57871.2023.10489554

Babu, B., Sudha, S., & Caroline Jebakumari, S. (2023). Remote Delivery of Healthcare Services. In *EAI/Springer Innovations in Communication and Computing* (pp. 353–370). Springer Science and Business Media Deutschland GmbH. 10.1007/978-3-031-27700-9_22

Barua, R., Datta, S., & Sarkar, A. (2023). Artificial intelligence and robotics-based minimally invasive surgery: Innovations and future perceptions. In *Contemporary Applications of Data Fusion for Advanced Healthcare Informatics* (pp. 350–368). IGI Global. 10.4018/978-1-6684-8913-0.ch015

Bellucci, N. (2022). Disruptive Innovation and Technological Influences on Healthcare. *Journal of Radiology Nursing*, 41(2), 98–101. 10.1016/j.jradnu.2022.02.008

Bertl, M., Ross, P., & Draheim, D. (2023). Systematic AI Support for Decision-Making in the Healthcare Sector: Obstacles and Success Factors. *Health Policy and Technology*, 12(3), 100748. 10.1016/j.hlpt.2023.100748

Bindu Bhavani, B., & Raghuveer, L. V. S. (2021). Smart Healthcare System for Psychological Disorders in Smart Cities. In *EAI/Springer Innovations in Communication and Computing* (pp. 65–76). Springer Science and Business Media Deutschland GmbH. 10.1007/978-3-030-48539-9_6

Brooks, A. L. (2014). Disruptive innovation in healthcare and rehabilitation. *Studies in Computational Intelligence*, 536, 323–351. 10.1007/978-3-642-45432-5_16

Cannavale, C., Esempio Tammaro, A., Leone, D., & Schiavone, F. (2022). Innovation adoption in inter-organizational healthcare networks – the role of artificial intelligence. *European Journal of Innovation Management*, 25(6), 758–774. 10.1108/EJIM-08-2021-0378

Darda, P., & Matta, N. (2024). The Nexus of healthcare and technology: A thematic analysis of digital transformation through artificial intelligence. In *Transformative Approaches to Patient Literacy and Healthcare Innovation* (pp. 261–282). IGI Global. 10.4018/979-8-3693-3661-8.ch013

Farhan, M. (2024). Empowering healthcare: Symbiotic innovations of AI and blockchain technology. In *Blockchain and AI: The Intersection of Trust and Intelligence* (pp. 23–57). CRC Press. 10.1201/9781003162018-2

Friebe, M. H. (2020). Healthcare in need of innovation: Exponential technology and biomedical entrepreneurship as solution providers (Keynote Paper). In Fei, B., & Linte, C. A. (Eds.), *Proceedings of SPIE-* The International Society for Optical Engineering (Vol. 11315). SPIE. 10.1117/12.2556776

Ghaleb, E. A. B., Dominic, P. D. D., & Sarlan, A. (2020). Impact of emerging technology innovations on healthcare transformation in developing countries. *2020 2nd International Sustainability and Resilience Conference: Technology and Innovation in Building Designs*. IEEE. 10.1109/IEEECONF51154.2020.9319955

Gupta, P., & Yadav, A. (2024). Artificial Intelligence Driving Change in Healthcare through Medical Innovation. *Proceedings - International Conference on Computing, Power, and Communication Technologies, IC2PCT 2024*. IEEE. 10.1109/IC2PCT60090.2024.10486544

Huo, W., Luo, W., Yan, J., Wang, Y., & Deng, Y. (2023). Medical Artificial Intelligence Information Disclosure on Healthcare Professional Involvement in Innovation: A Transactional Theory of Stress and Coping Model. *International Journal of Human-Computer Interaction*, 1–13. 10.1080/10447318.2023.2266797

Kamath, D., Teferi, B., Charow, R., Mattson, J., Jardine, J., Jeyakumar, T., Omar, M., Zhang, M., Scandiffio, J., Salhia, M., Dhalla, A., & Wiljer, D. (2024). Accelerating AI Innovation in Healthcare Through Mentorship. In Keshavjee, K., & Khatami, A. (Eds.), *Studies in Health Technology and Informatics* (Vol. 312, pp. 87–91). IOS Press BV. 10.3233/SHTI231318

Kanade, T. M., & Batule, R. B. (2024). Digital health innovations to significantly improve the quality of services in healthcare systems. In *Analyzing Current Digital Healthcare Trends Using Social Networks* (pp. 159–177). IGI Global. 10.4018/979-8-3693-1934-5.ch009

Kashif, M., Malik, K. R., Jabbar, S., & Chaudhry, J. (2019). Application of machine learning and image processing for detection of breast cancer. In *Innovation in Health Informatics: A Smart Healthcare Primer* (pp. 145–162). Elsevier. 10.1016/B978-0-12-819043-2.00006-X

Kaur, J. (2024). Patient-centric AI: Advancing healthcare through human-centered innovation. In *Approaches to Human-Centered AI in Healthcare* (pp. 1–19). IGI Global. 10.4018/979-8-3693-2238-3.ch001

Kumar, P., Sharma, S. K., & Dutot, V. (2023). Artificial intelligence (AI)-enabled CRM capability in healthcare: The impact on service innovation. *International Journal of Information Management*, 69, 102598. 10.1016/j.ijinfomgt.2022.102598

Kyaw Zaw, T. O., Muthaiyah, S., & Jasbi, A. (2021). Contextualization of Smart Healthcare: A Systematic Review. *International Conference on Research and Innovation in Information Systems, ICRIIS*. IEEE. 10.1109/ICRIIS53035.2021.9617060

Lancee, G. J., Engelen, L. J., & Van De Belt, T. H. (2018). Medical autonomy as prerequisite for deep space travel will benefit from terrestrial healthcare innovation. *Proceedings of the International Astronautical Congress, IAC*. SCOPUS. https://www.scopus.com/inward/record.uri?eid=2-s2.0-85065739398&partnerID=40&md5=614278ec94358114f194ac19af598998

Lee, W. B., & Choi, S. J. (2023). Secondary Use Provisions in the European Health Data Space Proposal and Policy Recommendations for Korea. *Healthcare Informatics Research*, 29(3), 199–208. 10.4258/hir.2023.29.3.19937591675

Litinski, V. (2018). Is artificial intelligence (AI) friend or foe to patients in healthcare?: On virtues of dynamic consent - how to build a business case for digital health applications. In *Healthcare Policy and Reform: Concepts, Methodologies, Tools, and Applications* (Vol. 2, pp. 774–785). IGI Global. 10.4018/978-1-5225-6915-2.ch035

Lysen, F., & Wyatt, S. (2024). Refusing participation: Hesitations about designing responsible patient engagement with artificial intelligence in healthcare. *Journal of Responsible Innovation*, 11(1), 2300161. 10.1080/23299460.2023.2300161

Manikandan, V., & Sharma, S. (2023). The Development of Machine Learning innovation technology for Data Mining In Smart Healthcare. *2nd IEEE International Conference on Distributed Computing and Electrical Circuits and Electronics, ICDCECE 2023*. IEEE. 10.1109/ICDCECE57866.2023.10150446

Mincu, D., & Roy, S. (2022). Developing robust benchmarks for driving forward AI innovation in healthcare. *Nature Machine Intelligence*, 4(11), 916–921. 10.1038/s42256-022-00559-4

Miner, G. D., Miner, L. A., Burk, S., Goldstein, M., Nisbet, R., Walton, N., & Hill, T. (2023). Practical Data Analytics for Innovation in Medicine: Building Real Predictive and Prescriptive Models in Personalized Healthcare and Medical Research Using AI, ML, and Related Technologies, Second Edition. In *Practical Data Analytics for Innovation in Medicine: Building Real Predictive and Prescriptive Models in Personalized Healthcare and Medical Research Using AI, ML, and Related Technologies, Second Edition*. Elsevier. 10.1016/C2021-0-02083-6

Nassani, A. A., Javed, A., Rosak-Szyrocka, J., Pilar, L., Yousaf, Z., & Haffar, M. (2023). Major Determinants of Innovation Performance in the Context of Healthcare Sector. *International Journal of Environmental Research and Public Health*, 20(6), 5007. 10.3390/ijerph2006500736981916

Neher, M., Petersson, L., Nygren, J. M., Svedberg, P., Larsson, I., & Nilsen, P. (2023). Innovation in healthcare: Leadership perceptions about the innovation characteristics of artificial intelligence—a qualitative interview study with healthcare leaders in Sweden. *Implementation Science Communications*, 4(1), 81. 10.1186/s43058-023-00458-837464420

Neumann, N. A., De Oliveira, F. A. C., Machicao, J. C., & Velasquez, O. C. (2019). Exploration of AI-based innovation opportunities within the "Pastoral da Criança" maternal-child healthcare model. *SHIRCON 2019 - 2019 IEEE Sciences and Humanities International Research Conference*. IEEE. 10.1109/SHIRCON48091.2019.9024850

Nilsen, P., Reed, J., Nair, M., Savage, C., Macrae, C., Barlow, J., Svedberg, P., Larsson, I., Lundgren, L., & Nygren, J. (2022). Realizing the potential of artificial intelligence in healthcare: Learning from intervention, innovation, implementation and improvement sciences. *Frontiers in Health Services*, 2, 961475. 10.3389/frhs.2022.96147536925879

Pandimurugan, V., Abouhawwash, M., Mandviya, R., & Mawal, C. (2023). Introduction to healthcare informatics: Fundamentals and historical background. In *Innovations in Healthcare Informatics: From interoperability to data analysis* (pp. 1–31). Institution of Engineering and Technology. https://www.scopus.com/inward/record.uri?eid=2-s2.0-85166032997&partnerID=40&md5=b7a8e739a7e6f8c9cbb7fbf8964be279

Popa, E. O., van Hilten, M., Oosterkamp, E., & Bogaardt, M.-J. (2021). The use of digital twins in healthcare: Socio-ethical benefits and socio-ethical risks. *Life Sciences, Society and Policy*, 17(1), 6. 10.1186/s40504-021-00113-x34218818

Potnurwar, A. V., Bongirwar, V. K., Pathan, S. S., Kothoke, P. M., Dongre, S., & Pande, S. P. (2023). An Integrative Approach to Healthcare Enhancement through Internet of Things, Artificial Intelligence and Smart City Innovations. *Journal of Electrical Systems*, 19(2), 9–17. 10.52783/jes.673

Pradhan, K., John, P., & Sandhu, N. (2021). Use of artificial intelligence in healthcare delivery in India. *Journal of Hospital Management and Health Policy*, 5(September), 28. 10.21037/jhmhp-20-126

Pradhan, K. B., Sarbhadhikari, S. N., & John, P. (2021). A Framework of Responsible Innovation (RI) Model for Artificial Intelligence (AI) in Indian Healthcare. *Online Journal of Health and Allied Sciences: OJHAS*, 20(2), 1–3. https://www.scopus.com/inward/record.uri?eid=2-s2.0-85115989855&partnerID=40&md5=cc0c4416bc7ea80dc26e2336c6cb0978

Rahman, M. M. (2023). Ensuring halal compliance in AI-driven healthcare solutions: Balancing innovation and faith. In *Federated Learning and AI for Healthcare 5.0* (pp. 298–320). IGI Global. 10.4018/979-8-3693-1082-3.ch015

Ravindar, K., Boddepalli, E., Singla, A., Ameta, G. K., Kalaivani, E., & Alzubaidi, L. H. (2023). AI-Powered Computer Vision for Early Skin Cancer Detection with IoT-Connected Dermascopes. In Swarnkar, S. K., & Rathore, Y. K. (Eds.), *International Conference on Artificial Intelligence for Innovations in Healthcare Industries, ICAIIHI 2023*. Institute of Electrical and Electronics Engineers Inc. 10.1109/ICAIIHI57871.2023.10489445

Shah, A., Patel, W., & Koyuncu, H. (2024). Empowering healthcare innovation: IoT-enabled smart systems and deep learning for enhanced diabetic retinopathy in the telehealth landscape. *Journal of Interdisciplinary Mathematics*, 27(2), 355–367. 10.47974/JIM-1836

Sharma, C., & Gupta, G. (2021). Innovation insight for healthcare provider digital twins: A review. In *Mobile Health: Advances in Research and Applications* (pp. 97–128). Nova Science Publishers, Inc. https://www.scopus.com/inward/record.uri?eid=2-s2.0-85109468612&partnerID=40&md5=c92a245b5fd3582f1f5b4d7cb753bded

Shrotriya, L., Sharma, K., Parashar, D., Mishra, K., Rawat, S. S., & Pagare, H. (2023). Apache Spark in Healthcare: Advancing Data-Driven Innovations and Better Patient Care. *International Journal of Advanced Computer Science and Applications*, 14(6), 608–616. 10.14569/IJACSA.2023.0140665

Swain, S., Muduli, K., Kommula, V. P., & Sahoo, K. K. (2022). Innovations in Internet of Medical Things, Artificial Intelligence, and Readiness of the Healthcare Sector Towards Health 4.0 Adoption. *International Journal of Social Ecology and Sustainable Development*, 13(1), 1–14. 10.4018/IJSESD.292078

Swarnkar, S. K., & Rathore, Y. K. (Eds.). (2023). International Conference on Artificial Intelligence for Innovations in Healthcare Industries, ICAIIHI 2023. In *International Conference on Artificial Intelligence for Innovations in Healthcare Industries, ICAIIHI 2023*. Institute of Electrical and Electronics Engineers Inc. https://www.scopus.com/inward/record.uri?eid=2-s2.0-85191501083&partnerID=40&md5=5fd02603c5243d1b44cd8fb4653f0db1

Tahir, F., & Farhan, M. (2023). Exploring the progress of artificial intelligence in managing type 2 diabetes mellitus: A comprehensive review of present innovations and anticipated challenges ahead. *Frontiers in Clinical Diabetes and Healthcare*, 4, 1316111. 10.3389/fcdhc.2023.131611138161783

Teo, Z. L., Kwee, A., Lim, J. C. W., Lam, C. S. P., Ho, D., Maurer-Stroh, S., Su, Y., Chesterman, S., Chen, T., Tan, C. C., Wong, T. Y., Ngiam, K. Y., Tan, C. H., Soon, D., Choong, M. L., Chua, R., Wong, S., Lim, C., Cheong, W. Y., & Ting, D. S. W. (2023). Artificial intelligence innovation in healthcare: Relevance of reporting guidelines for clinical translation from bench to bedside. *Annals of the Academy of Medicine, Singapore*, 52(4), 199–212. 10.47102/annals-acadmedsg.2022452

Timilsina, M., Alsamhi, S., Haque, R., Judge, C., & Curry, E. (2023). Knowledge Graphs, Clinical Trials, Dataspace, and AI: Uniting for Progressive Healthcare Innovation. In J. He, T. Palpanas, X. Hu, A. Cuzzocrea, D. Dou, D. Slezak, W. Wang, A. Gruca, L. J.C.-W., & R. Agrawal (Eds.), *Proceedings - 2023 IEEE International Conference on Big Data, BigData 2023* (pp. 4997–5006). Institute of Electrical and Electronics Engineers Inc. 10.1109/BigData59044.2023.10386401

Varilek, B. M., & Mollman, S. (2024). Healthcare professionals' perspectives of barriers to cancer care delivery for American Indian, rural, and frontier populations. *PEC Innovation*, 4, 100247. 10.1016/j.pecinn.2023.10024738225930

Wang, Y.-H., & Lin, G.-Y. (2020). Exploring smart healthcare innovations: Multiple patentometric analyses. *ACM International Conference Proceeding Series*, (pp. 117–120). ACM. 10.1145/3383845.3383872

Wang, Y.-H., & Lin, G.-Y. (2023). Exploring AI-healthcare innovation: Natural language processing-based patents analysis for technology-driven roadmapping. *Kybernetes*, 52(4), 1173–1189. 10.1108/K-03-2021-0170

Y.-W. C., Tanaka, S., Howlett, R. J., & Jain, L. C. (Eds.). (2022). 10th KES International Conference on Innovation in Medicine and Healthcare, KES-InMed 2022. *Smart Innovation, Systems and Technologies, 308*. https://www.scopus.com/inward/record.uri?eid=2-s2.0-85135020926&partnerID=40&md5=68f8932ef2f4503af2e24f1e1e49a3e4

Zahlan, A., Ranjan, R. P., & Hayes, D. (2023). Artificial intelligence innovation in healthcare: Literature review, exploratory analysis, and future research. *Technology in Society*, 74, 102321. 10.1016/j.techsoc.2023.102321

Chapter 13
Operational Efficiency and Cost Reduction:
The Role of AI in Healthcare Administration

N. V. Suresh
https://orcid.org/0000-0002-0393-6037
ASET College of Science and Technology, India

Ananth Selvakumar
https://orcid.org/0000-0001-8521-3440
ASET College of Science and Technology, India

Gajalaksmi Sridhar
https://orcid.org/0009-0008-4344-1486
ASET College of Science and Technology, India

S. Catherine
SRM Institute of Science and Technology, India

ABSTRACT

According to an article that was published in Healthitanalysis, mentions of artificial intelligence (AI) have become commonplace in the healthcare industry in what seemed like an instant. The clinical advantages affiliation faces the double test of successfully coordinating reasonable expenses while at the same time conveying positive patient assessment. This investigation chapter examines the distinctive role that modernized thinking (PC-based knowledge) plays in identifying these issues within the clinical consideration association. Focusing in on clear executions, the survey takes a gander at how PC based data applications add to practical efficiency and cost decline in clinical idea settings. The effects of computer-based

DOI: 10.4018/979-8-3693-3731-8.ch013

Operational Efficiency and Cost Reduction

intelligence reconciliation on cycles like asset distribution, planning, and work process enhancement are examined within the context of contextual analyses of computer-based intelligence reconciliation in medical services organizations. The assessment looks at the common sense of man-made insight driven frameworks for working with administrative tasks and diminishing utilitarian purposes through these models. Additionally, the speculative piece dives into administrative thoughts related with doing man-made awareness in clinical benefits affiliations. As essential components of an efficient replicated understanding strategy, moral assessments, workforce planning, and advancement gathering procedures are investigated. The audit sees troubles that clinical benefits supervisors could totally through search in figuring out PC based data levels of progress and proposes authoritative perspectives for vanquishing these obstructions.

INTRODUCTION

The need for redesigned strong plentifulness, rising costs, patient arrangements, and other issues are putting the clinical thought community on the back burner. Considering this, the usage of Artificial Intelligence has arisen as a promising framework for managing settling the dangerous issues related with clinical thought association. In an effort to explore the shocking reaches of mechanized thinking applications, this evaluation paper delves into the crucial control of man-made information in achieving steady limit and cost reduction within the clinical thought association. The clinical benefits industry is famous for its flexible administrative cycles and the key financial weight related with them. Standard administrative viewpoints regularly achieve thwarted expectations, delays, and a wide channel on resources. Through mechanizing routine undertakings, prompting work cycles, and giving information driven experiences, modernized thinking improvements present a reasonable chance to upset these procedures.

The consistent move in utility expenses is one of the major worries in clinical advantages affiliation. Human resource the board, charging, patient record-keeping, and consistence with managerial guidelines contribute all around to the money related strain looked by clinical benefits affiliations. Through the assessments and basic assessments of electronic reasoning, man-made information interventions obligation to smooth out these cycles, lessening manual blunders and asset duplications and accomplishing a striking expense decline. For the normal to work of clinical thought affiliations, utilitarian limit is massive. Through robotizing routine undertakings, working with speedier free bearing, and moving asset task, man-made scholarly capacity (reproduced understanding) applications like mechanical association robotization (RPA) and ordinary language making due (NLP) can for the most part work on utilitarian reasonableness. For instance, rehashed data-driven plans can save experts in clinical idea preparation crucial time by automating technique organization, smoothing charging cycles, and enhancing clinical coding precision.

A last even-handed of clinical idea connection is the plan of remarkable patient thought. PC based data expects a guaranteed part in achieving this objective by working with better liberal data the trailblazers, changed treatment plans, and knowing assessment for tangle steady anomaly. Clinical benefits specialists can focus in on calm responsibility by means of robotizing regulatory endeavours, achieving overpowering generally advancing forward with experiences and results. Consistency is a basic piece of partnership considering the way that the clinical thought neighbourhood dependent after inflexible administrative plans. PC based information advances can assist with ensuring adherence to these standards through robotizing the seeing of consistence fundamentals, further making data security, and working with studies. This not only contributes to a design for clinical thought that is more straightforward and cautious, but it also reduces the risk associated with discipline.

LITERATURE REVIEW

Ruivo (2013) has stated that in the sensible arrangement, the mechanical point of view is portrayed by the clinical center's accessibility, which joins the IT structure, IT capacity, and IT system coordination. The IT foundation is the information and capabilities required to carry out SCMPs, and IT skill includes both. In addition, IT structure mix collaborates with SCMPs by providing a variety of frameworks and applications for the company to use as a whole. According to research, a connection with the current IT structure and knowledgeable IT staff will undoubtedly result in the successful completion of creative movements. Likewise, research recommends that IT structure blend can chip away at definitive execution by streamlining works out, redesigning client backing, and conveying cost experience assets, and it can what's more augmentation comparability with various advances.

Chwelos (2001) in their study has mentioned that social event of headway and improvement have been proposed to be influenced by two or three moderate components. One of these is different evened out arranging, which has been the subject of a ton of evaluation and is a degree of a connection's inside ability to take on new improvements. The lifestyle of the affiliation affects the two its accessibility and its mentality toward change. True status can likewise be influenced by the presence of skilled, informed, and wonderfully set up staff concerning new advances.

According to Alowais (2023), assets with better data structures will likely use these frameworks clearly, expanding the potential outcomes to include new advancements. Similar to how the limit level of an organization's IT trained professionals

Operational Efficiency and Cost Reduction

reflects the connection's IT skill, social occasion may also depend on the cutoff and confirmation of other employees tasked with working the new types of progress. In the end, in a variety of analyses of its group, support and accountability from the top organization are seen as yet another essential component of various levels of accessibility. Acquiring adequate assets, conquering interior hindrances, and shielding the association from change all need such support.

Today, man-made knowledge is changing various fields, including clinical thought, cash, and transportation, and its effect is simply expected to develop. Shrewd preparation frameworks, which are PC programs that can adjust to the necessities of individual understudies, have been made remembering man-made information for scholarly world. The learning eventual outcomes of understudies in various subjects, including science and math, have been managed by these designs. In research, man-made data has been used to separate large datasets and identify patterns that people would have trouble distinguishing; Among other areas, genomics and medication disclosure have made significant progress as a result. In clinical advantages settings, man-made information has been utilized to empower intriguing gadgets and modified treatment plans. It is essential to guarantee that reenacted information is made in a capable way and to help all as it makes. (Esteva 2017)

Because man-made knowledge-based advancements are currently being incorporated into everyday life, the utilization of developments based on computerized reasoning will be essential for every organization. In the advanced age, purchasers are referencing segregated, changed, responsive, and secure associations with adaptability. Astute adaptable applications and gadgets are opening up. In this unique circumstance, it is fundamental to recognize occasions of PC based information applications at present being involved by clinical advantage relationship for patient thought and the main gathering of activities, as well as the requirements (like guidelines and responsibility) and sponsorship necessities, (for instance, morals, arranging projects, or directing organizations) for cutting edge man-made mental ability applications. (Lee 2019)

RESEARCH FINDINGS

The assessment uncovers the accentuation put on "Utilitarian Common sense and Cost Decrease: The Effect of Man-Made Care (Duplicated Data) on the Clinical benefits District is uncovered in "The Control of Mechanized thinking in the Clinical Association." The focal point of the review was on understanding how the coordination of man-created information progressions can adjust helpful feasibility and lower the expense of clinical advantages affiliation. One of the key exposures recollects the essential improvement for regulatory cycles through the get-together of rehashed information. Routine tasks like methodology booking, charging, and record keeping have been streamlined by the execution of PC based data driven structures. Computerization of these cycles has resulted in a clinical benefits relationship that is more skilled, error-free, and less dependent on managerial staff.

In addition, the survey recalls how mechanized thinking controlled resource task smoothing. PC-based data has made it doable for clinical idea heads to seek after data driven decisions concerning the advancement of resources, ensuring that staff, materials, and workplaces are utilized effectively through state of the art sagacious evaluation and man-made information appraisals. This course on consigned resources has largely contributed to practical appropriateness and prevented bottlenecks in the transportation of clinical ideas. In the openings of the review, cost decline emerges as a prominent subject. The costly costs of regulatory work have decreased as a result of the execution of re-enacted information. By reallocating human resources to roles that are more complex and add value, healthcare facilities have been able to optimize labour costs as a result of the automation of repetitive processes. Additionally, the audit demonstrates that mirrored information-driven structures have contributed to reducing charges and ensuring that errors are not made, saving clinical care provider's money and resources.

Besides, the disclosures of the appraisal show that re-enacted data obligingly impacts significant length results. A truly overwhelming patient experience has been made conceivable by PC based information's valuable and optimal administrative cycles. Lessened holding up times, more definite record-keeping, and extended plan booking have generally good clinical idea affiliations' overall thought, distinctly impacting patient satisfaction. With all that considered, the review recollects the incredible control of re-enacted information for clinical advantages affiliation, underlining its ability to chip away at sensible plentifulness and drive cost decline.

The openings show that the mix of repeated information degrees of progress smooth out conclusive cycles as well as essentially impacts asset improvement, cost save holds, finally, the overall thought of clinical advantages transport. As the clinical thought industry keeps on embracing mechanical new developments, the divulgences of this assessment give gigantic snippets of data to clinical thought bosses and policymakers looking for use man-made thinking for extra made cut-off and cost-plentifulness. The clinical advantages affiliation is tortured by manual, dreary endeavours that compound needs and raise practical costs. Duplicate work area work, charging botches, inefficient resource segment, and conceded dynamic cycles all harm clinical benefits systems' overall capability. Moreover, the lack of steady data evaluation makes it seeking after for supervisors to seek after informed decisions quickly.

Operational Efficiency and Cost Reduction

Suggestion

Clinical advantages affiliation's inclinations can be successfully settled by hardening man-made knowledge progressions. Data transmission and workspace work, for example, can be automated by man-made insight assessments, backing off the regulatory load on clinical staff. PC based data controlled farsighted examination can assist resource with advancing by closing patient confirmation rates, allowing supervisors to capably name resources considerably more. Additionally, man-made game plans that are based on brainpower have the potential to increase charging accuracy, stop pay spillage, and clear up confusion. Pioneers can rapidly settle on educated choices in light regarding the fundamental experiences that relentless information assessment can give. Little accomplices and Chabot's that are restricted by human awareness can possibly work on understanding liability, improve on the preparation of activities, and give second reactions to questions, all of which decrease generally useful fulfilment.

Figure 1. Proposed model

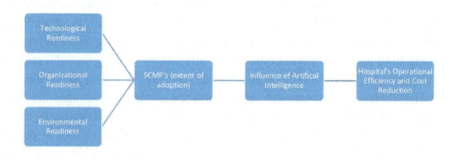

Updated the referred model of Bialas 2023

Table 1. Variables of proposed model

Variables	Definition
Technological Readiness	Mechanical status reviews the clinical idea plan's openness for PC based grasping set out some reasonable compromise. It dismantles the nonstop establishment, staff limit, and system closeness, essential for reasonable man-made data execution in clinical benefits association, affecting judicious capability and cost decline.

continued on following page

Table 1. Continued

Variables	Definition
Organizational Readiness	The clinical advantages establishment's ability to adjust to PC-based information changes is assessed by moderate preparation. By taking into account organizational responsibility, staff preparation, and change leadership frameworks, this variable emphasizes its crucial role in achieving ideal utilitarian efficiency and cost reduction through man-made reasoning.
Environmental Readiness	Biological status outlines the external parts impacting rehashed data gathering in clinical benefits connection. Factors like authoritative consistence, valid appraisals, and public understanding are key in picking the overall status of the clinical idea environment, generally affecting practical adequacy and cost decline.
SCMP's (extent of adoption)	Creation network The leaders Practices (SCMPs) are used to measure man-made brainpower gathering in clinical consideration association. This variable investigates the execution level of PC based data driven contraptions in store network assignments, clearly affecting helpful attainability and cost decline by reviving chose cycles and resource the board.
Influence of Artificial Intelligence	The effect of Man-Made Mental Capacity examines the general impact of PC-setup data on clinical thought affiliation. This recalls how it affected asset movement, course, and gigantic degree reasonable cycles. This variable must be perceived in order to determine the immediate connection between PC-based knowledge coordination, practical capability, and a reduction in clinical consideration costs.
Hospital's Operational Efficiency and Cost Reduction	This review, which looks at the effect of AI on clinical thought affiliation, based on the reliant variable of an emergency community's reasonable productivity and cost decline. Through starter assessment, it explores how reproduced information applications advance cycles, update asset use, and add to overall cash related hold upholds in clinical thought settings, in this way working on practical cutoff and reducing costs.

Information Driven Course

Reproduced information driven evaluation expect a crucial part in clinical thought association dominatingly of information to see perpetually models. Using man-made reasoning assessments, clinical advantages affiliations can find districts where they can save cash, further foster asset task, and go with informed decisions.

Modernized Information

Re-enacted information controlled computerization chips away at utilitarian effectiveness by smoothing out routine undertakings, lessening goofs, and permitting clinical advantages experts to zero in on extra astounding and vital bits of patient idea. Computerization of valid undertakings, for example, blueprint putting together, charging, and confirms the bosses, can set aside huge time and cash.

Sensible Upkeep and Asset Improvement

Sharp upkeep of clinical stuff is made possible by man-made perception applications, diminishing individual time and discouraging astounding breakdowns. Similar to this, PC-based information assessments can anticipate patient authentication rates and reduce asset use, bringing clinical benefits to the workplace and enabling more cost-effective staffing and task changes for assets.

Individualized Care for the Patient

Through wary appraisal and solely altered treatment plans, man-made mental capacity works connected with re-evaluated patient thought. This strategies with solid results as well as adds to cost decline by keeping away from pointless structure and hospitalizations. Redesigned resource usage is made conceivable by individualized care models kept up with by imitated data.

Cunning Locale and Chance Alliance

Through the attestation of fake practices in affirmation validates and charging, man-made data further makes clinical idea association. By utilizing PC based understanding assessments, clinical thought affiliations can see abnormalities and block cash related fiascos because of wicked practices, in this way adding to overall rot.

CONCLUSION

In light of everything, this study looked at how man-made perception, or man-made information, has a significant impact on utilitarian capacity and cost reduction in the field of clinical benefits affiliation. The disclosures highlighted the basic envisioned by PC based information in smoothing out conclusive cycles, further making heading, and reviving asset use. The mix of PC based data enhancements, as wise evaluation and PC based information evaluations, has shown a huge improvement in the accuracy and speed of administrative errands. This energizes a more responsive and gifted normal framework for clinical idea while similarly carving out opportunity and money. The investigation discovered that man-made thinking-driven robotization basically lessens the administrative weight on clinical advantages experts by permitting them to zero in additional on settled thought in regions like technique coordinating, charging, and data the executives.

Besides, the execution of man-made thinking in clinical thought association showed a positive relationship with cost decline. Man-made data adds to clinical benefits foundations' thinking about all that sensibility by seeing frustrations, further creating resource arrangement, and seeing terrorizing. Since PC-based data can at the same time look at tremendous datasets, it is simpler to settle on choices in light of affirmation, bringing about an additional proactive and powerful clinical pioneers system. While recognizing the likely advantages of integrating man-made thinking into the medical services framework, it is fundamental to perceive the requirement for continually advancing control, moral contemplations, and steady transformation to new turns of events. This study promotes the central for clinical thought relationship to embrace man-made knowledge as a primary instrument for valuable effectiveness and cost reduction in order to work on the general quality and straightforwardness of clinical benefits associations.

REFERENCES

Alowais, S. A., Alghamdi, S. S., Alsuhebany, N., Alqahtani, T., Alshaya, A. I., Almohareb, S. N., Aldairem, A., Alrashed, M., Bin Saleh, K., Badreldin, H. A., Al Yami, M. S., Al Harbi, S., & Albekairy, A. M. (2023). Revolutionizing healthcare: The role of artificial intelligence in clinical practice. *BMC Medical Education*, 23(1), 689. 10.1186/s12909-023-04698-z37740191

Arsene, C. (2019). *Artificial Intelligence in healthcare: The Future is Amazing*. Healthcare Weekly.

Benzidia, S., Makaoui, N., & Bentahar, O. (2021). The impact of big data analytics and artificial intelligence on green supply chain process integration and hospital environmental performance. *Technological Forecasting and Social Change*, 165, 120557. 10.1016/j.techfore.2020.120557

Bialas, C., Bechtsis, D., Aivazidou, E., Achillas, C., & Aidonis, D. (2023). A Holistic View on the Adoption and Cost-Effectiveness of Technology-Driven Supply Chain Management Practices in Healthcare. *Sustainability (Basel)*, 15(6), 5541. 10.3390/su15065541

Bialas, C., Bechtsis, D., Aivazidou, E., Achillas, C., & Aidonis, D. (2023). A Holistic View on the Adoption and Cost-Effectiveness of Technology-Driven Supply Chain Management Practices in Healthcare. *Sustainability (Basel)*, 15(6), 5541. 10.3390/su15065541

Chwelos, P., Benbasat, I., & Dexter, A. S. (2001). Empirical test of an EDI adoption model. *Information Systems Research*, 12(3), 304–321. 10.1287/isre.12.3.304.9708

Esteva, A., Kuprel, B., Novoa, R. A., Ko, J., Swetter, S. M., Blau, H. M., & Thrun, S. (2017). Dermatologist-level classification of skin cancer with deep neural networks. *nature*, 542(7639), 115-118.

Lee, D., & Yoon, S. N. (2021). Application of artificial intelligence-based technologies in the healthcare industry: Opportunities and challenges. *International Journal of Environmental Research and Public Health*, 18(1), 271. 10.3390/ijerph1801027133401373

Lee, S. M., Lee, D., & Kim, Y. S. (2019). The quality management ecosystem for predictive maintenance in the Industry 4.0 era. *International Journal of Quality Innovation*, 5(1), 1–11. 10.1186/s40887-019-0029-5

Palanica, A., Flaschner, P., Thommandram, A., Li, M., & Fossat, Y. (2019). Physicians' Perceptions of Chatbots in Health Care: Cross-sectional Web-based Survey. *Journal of Medical Internet Research*, 21(4), e12887. 10.2196/1288730950796

Premkumar, G., & Ramamurthy, K. (1995). The role of interorganizational and organizational factors on the decision mode for adoption of interorganizational systems. *Decision Sciences*, 26(3), 303–336. 10.1111/j.1540-5915.1995.tb01431.x

Rogers, E. M. (2010). *Diffusion of Innovations*. Simon and Schuster.

Ruivo, P., Johansson, B., Oliveira, T., & Neto, M. (2013). Commercial ERP systems and user productivity: A study across European SMEs. *Procedia Technology*, 9, 84–93. 10.1016/j.protcy.2013.12.009

Schermelleh-Engel, K., Moosbrugger, H., & Müller, H. (2003). Evaluating the fit of structural equation models: Tests of significance and descriptive goodness-of-fit measures. *Methods of Psychological Research Online*, 8, 23–74.

Somashekhar, S., Kumar, R., Kumar, A., Patil, P., & Rauthan, A. (2016). Validation Study to Assess Pperformance of IBM Cognitive Computing System Watson for Oncology with Manipal Multidisciplinary Tumour Board for 1000 Consecutive Cases: An Indian Experience. *Annals of Oncology: Official Journal of the European Society for Medical Oncology*, 27(suppl_9), 1–2. 10.1093/annonc/mdw601.002

Taylor, N. (2019). *Duke Report Identifies Barriers to Adoption of AI Healthcare Systems*. MedTech Dive.

Uzialko, A. (2019). Artificial Intelligence Will Change Healthcare as We Know it. *Business News Daily*.

Chapter 14
Mathematical Modelling in the Analysis of Viral Diseases and Communicable Diseases

Saravanan D.
 http://orcid.org/0000-0002-4188-6456
The ICFAI Foundation for Higher Education (IFHE), India

Vaithyasubramanian Subramanian
 http://orcid.org/0000-0002-1252-902X
Dwaraka Doss Goverdhan Doss Vaishnav College, India

Delhi Babu R.
Department of Mathematics, Sathyabama Institute of Science and Technology, India

Sundararajan R.
Department of Mathematics, PSNA College of Engineering and Technology, India

Kirubhashankar C. K.
Department of Mathematics, Sathyabama Institute of Science and Technology, India

Vengata Krishnan K.
Department of Mathematics and Computer Science, Sri Sathya Sai Institute of Higher Learning, India

ABSTRACT

The differential equation is the most powerful platform in mathematics and is useful in engineering and science disciplines. The use of different calculus can significantly predict the world around us. Differential equations are used in various fields, such as biology, economics, physics, chemistry, and engineering. They can describe rapid growth and decay, population growth of organisms, or changes in investment returns over time. Among these models, delay models are well known for virology

DOI: 10.4018/979-8-3693-3731-8.ch014

Copyright © 2024, IGI Global. Copying or distributing in print or electronic forms without written permission of IGI Global is prohibited.

analysis and predicting disease transmission, which controls infection. To define four population spatial evolution: easily unaffected, untreated infections, treated infections, recovered, and to develop a strategy of factors affecting the human body delay differential equation (DDE) is used. In this paper, we review some mathematical modeling that interprets viral discrimination with the influenza virus. Examples are used to predict some solution measures to underline and apply DDE to model infectious diseases. This study provides a wide range of factors that play a role in mathematical models of epidemiology and public health policy. This study is helpful for those who are interested and help the fieldworkers to learn about it. We discuss delay models using differential equations to measure the spread of viral diseases. The disease control predictions discussed may be helpful for more projection.

INTRODUCTION

Mathematical models are significant in diagnosing organizational theories and the changing behavior of biological systems. Mathematical models can take many forms depending on the time scale and the problem's location. For example, if there is a complete overlap between generations in demographic dynamics, the population changes continuously, and studies of such systems use different equations. In this paper, we discussed the worldwide spread of influenza viruses, the affected people-to-spread disease ratio, and models using the mathematical prediction extent of the multi-role play with self-isolated. This study concludes the perspective by capturing human behavior and suggests future challenges to the behavioral epidemic of infectious diseases. To predict infection-related behavior by demonstrating the global stability of the localization of vaccine samples to available subjects.

Global Influenza Surveillance, Influenza Vaccination Coverage, H3N2 Outbreak in Australia, and Influenza B Virus in Europe are a few current statistical data or case studies on the global transmission of influenza viruses (Meijer et al., 2006; Puig-Barbera et al., 2014). The most recent statistics and case study demonstrate how dynamic influenza propagation is and how real-time data must be included into mathematical models. Public health interventions, vaccine efficacy, and seasonal variability should all be taken into consideration in models. By incorporating these findings into mathematical models, public health policy can be informed and the precision of influenza epidemic control can be improved. Delay differential equations (DDE) provide a better understanding of the dynamics impacting influenza spread and control by accounting for time lags in infection development and vaccine impact.

The accuracy and effectiveness of mathematical models of infectious disease propagation are increased when human behaviour is incorporated, which results in more informed public health strategies. Through anticipating and comprehending people's reactions to different interventions, planners can create plans that have a higher chance of effectively managing and averting epidemics, safeguarding public health and even saving lives. The ability to capture human behaviour has consequences for improving forecast accuracy, comprehending transmission dynamics, and creating successful interventions. The formulation and assessment of public health policies, risk communication and public involvement, long-term attention, and planning, monitoring, and surveillance are examples of practical applications. Instances of Useful Applications: (i) COVID-19 Pandemic: Behavioural responses to mask mandates, lockdowns, and vaccination drives were included in models during the pandemic, which helped inform policy decisions worldwide and shed light on the probable efficacy of these measures. (ii) Influenza Vaccination Campaigns: The effects of various vaccination tactics, such as school-based immunisation programmes or focused campaigns for high-risk populations, on the spread of influenza have been predicted using behavioural models (Ciotti et al., 2020; Perrone et al., 2021; Schumacher et al., 2021).

The analysis of infectious diseases benefits greatly from the use of mathematical models. They offer a methodical approach to comprehend and forecast disease dynamics, assess the efficacy of control strategies, and contribute to the making of public health decisions. By modelling diverse elements of disease propagation and intervention with differential equations, researchers can obtain important insights that lead to improved health outcomes and more efficient disease management. The MSIR Model is frequently used for understanding illnesses, such as some children disorders, in which maternal immunity is a factor. The model enables research on the effects of maternal immunity on the transmission and management of illness. SIER Model is used for illnesses like influenza that have a long incubation period, during which time people are exposed to the illness but it has not yet spread. It facilitates comprehension of the dynamics of illnesses that are latent before spreading. SIQR Model is useful for diseases for which quarantine is an essential component of the control plan. It aids in forecasting how the isolation of afflicted individuals affects the general spread of the illness. SIQRD Model is applied to illnesses that have a high death rate. It is essential for organising medical interventions and allocating resources since it aids in comprehending the disease's entire impact, including the number of fatalities.

Section 2 examines various mathematical modelling approaches used in virology and infectious illnesses; Different mathematical models with analysis are shown in Section 3; self-isolation techniques are covered in Section 4; and future scope and constraints are covered in Sections 5 and 6.

REVIEW ON MATHEMATICAL MODELING IN COMMUNICABLE DISEASES AND VIROLOGY

Measles, flu, and tuberculosis are some of the infectious diseases and virology. Researchers and medics are concerned about sudden outbreaks and local circumstances in which illness will always occur. Recent SARS epidemics, recurrent fevers, and tuberculosis recurrences are events of concern and interest for many. Millions of people yearly suffer from measles, worms, diarrhea, and other treatable diseases. These are not considered dangerous in the Western world. The effects of high morbidity and mortality are regarded in the economies of countries with average life expectancy and infection. The development of Mathematical models for studying infectious diseases has led to differences between the goals of mathematicians, public health professionals seeking a broader understanding, and public health professionals seeking human-age practices for people affected by a disease. Although mathematical modeling has led to many concepts for controlling and administering vaccine dosage, the way will practice has always been a cult that differs from the predictions of simple models. Mathematicians can create worlds with simple models of real-world public health questions. Here we discuss the viruses spread and explains how mathematical model is used to predict the diseases.

Liu et al. (2008) introduced that a good variety of infection hosts is essential to prevent contagious flu. Based on four Hurst Exponents per protein sequence, a novel method of classifying hemagglutinin proteins has been presented that combines logistic regression and SVM. SVM, logistic regression classifiers, and physical and chemical attributes are the main components of this approach. To assess how data testing is carried out utilising cross-verification accuracy five times, a novel algorithm has been put out. This new classification algorithm outperforms SVM and logistic regression, according to experimental results.

Venna et al. (2018) proposed a novel information-driven model for continuous flu forecasts. Additionally proposed an information-driven Machine learning strategy of utilizing staggered fore-casts dependent on long short-term memory (LSTM). This current strategy's interesting highlights incorporate 1) The acquaintance of the LSTM strategy with catching the transient elements of occasional influenza and 2) A method for catching outside factors, for example, geographic nearness and atmosphere factors: moistness, temperature, precipitation, and sun presentation. This model has been compared with two modern strategies utilizing two usually accessible information bases. The outcomes give a promising bearing dependent on using information-driven determining techniques and spatial-fleeting and ecological components to improve flu anticipation.

Araz et al. (2009) discussed that the well-established epidemic is a national and universal Open well-being concern within the worldwide outbreak of swine flu. Numerous nations have created and overhauled their item plans for the flu. These questions are considered in terms of relief added up to cases of epidemics, added up to mortality, and effect on instructive administrations for school children.

Tan et al. (2013) proposed a non-linear ordinary least square method to obtain influenza-A H1N1, the infected people used a multifaceted SEIR method. These model findings make an appropriate contribution to understanding flu H1N1 in the Guangdong area and decided the change of demonstrating model.

Ruschel et al. (2019) discussed transmissible diseases as one of humanity's most significant threats. The possible way to control a disease is to isolate the individuals who may be vulnerable. In this study, a strategy of delay differential conditions proposes the impact of segregation.

Kanyiri et al. (2018) analyzed the dynamic transmission of the influenza-A virus and the aspects of drug resistance. High sickness and fatality rates are caused by influenza, particularly in those with weakened immune systems. One major obstacle in stopping the flu's spread is exposure to treatment resistance. In order to examine the dynamics of influenza virus transmission, which is connected to the medication resistance characteristic, a mathematical model was created. Quality sample analysis is provided based on the control reproduction number. Sample equilibrium is calculated, and consistency analysis is carried out. This model is suggested for efficient disease control since it reveals the reverse cleavage that results in decreased Rc (control reproduction number). The findings of the sensitivity analysis demonstrate that vaccination efficacy is a strictly regulated factor in the influenza epidemic. Despite the vaccination decreasing the number of breeds, numerical simulations show that influenza still exists in the community. Therefore, in addition to vaccination, it is necessary to use other strategies to prevent the spread of the flu.

Mayilvaganan and Balamuralitharan (2019) proposed the SEIR number model to illustrate influenza infection development among the population. They implemented the Homotopy Perturbation Method (HPM) to supply examination and assessed arrangements of direct non-normal differential conditions frameworks for flu malady. The conclusion demonstrates the homotopy perturbation method and the accuracy of these techniques' efficiency by understanding some of the ODE systems.

Minucci et al. (2020) established mathematical modeling to understand the human system dynamics during multiple lung infections and injuries to identify the key mechanism and provide essential insights into new therapies. They display the long-accepted modeling strategies and novel procedures for recreating different lung wounds and outline scientific modeling's viability intending to these life-threatening conditions.

Ashrafur Rahman and Zou (2011) proposed a system of ODE in the two-strain show. They investigated the impacts of the single-strain injection on the flow of this two-strain demonstration. Hypothetical gives valuable data on the effect of single-immunization rate on a strain on the two strains' flow.

Khan et al. (2015) proposed a new diagnostic model to investigate influenza's dynamic transmission systematically. The demonstration takes into consideration the impacts of drugs and hospitalization. They are too assessed certainty interims for gripping contact rate utilizing parameter bootstrapping. They perform vulnerability and affectability investigations to recognize the effect of significance test parameters. Center the thoughts on the ideal control hypothesis, ideal sedation, and hospitalization techniques to dispense with the illness.

Kongnuy and Naowanich (2014) offered a numerical demonstration to address the flu outbreak in Thailand in 2014. The investigation's objectives take into account and examine a study of the flu's spread in Thailand using a cause based on science. They Analysed open Health data between 1997 to 2013 on Disease Transmission Studies. For two models, they create a framework of nonlinear contrast conditions. To start, we divide the human population into four groups: the helpless, the contaminated, the recovered, the protected from the strain, and the rescued, who are somewhat affected by those strain classes. Consider the hatching phase as you demonstrate and expand the test for the time being. The conventional energetic modeling approach determines how each solution's configurations behave. The dimensions of the disease and the harmony levels in the area dictate the circumstances in which the adjacent asymptomatic condition should be stable. Numerical simulations support hypothetical forecasts. The suggestion of this investigation is one option for managing the outbreak of this virus in Thailand.

Mummert and Otunuga (2019) clarified the later parameter recognizable proof procedure. Time-dependent sickness transmission rate is recognised by the minutes-based generalised approach that is associated with the adjacent slacked balance. We also explore time-dependent chaos for the stochastic exposed, irresistible, short-term safe infection demonstrate (SEIRS) with critical rates. The approach shows data on US flu cases from the 2004–2005 to the 2016–2017 flu seasons. The annual crests in contaminations are produced stochastically by the combination of the clamour escalated and the transmission rate. When attempting to estimate capacity, the neighbourhood's slack adjusted generalised method is being used. A single flu season is subjectively matched by the figure strategy.

Maki and Hirose (2013) explained very clearly that infection simulation is considered important as visual stimulation and is performed by various methods; classical regular difference models (SIR), Agency based models, web-based models, and more. The SIR analysis shows one of the essential strategies to see disease behavior through a simple calculation. This study considers bargains with the center

SDE adaptation of the SIR recreation show with an application for the SARS case in Hongkong in 2003.

Zhang et al. (2015) explained the results of infectious diseases using SIR model. SIR model is widely used to upgrade all around the globe. These SEIR models adapt to the Ebola outbreak, apply the PDE, and apply the time and space factor. The Matlab program predicts the Ebola-affected delivery graph.

Rihan and Anwar (2012) examined SIR Model. The conceivable outcomes for completing the calculated condition are considered the occasion time, a soaked frame with a defenselessness shape. They look at the quality behavior of the demonstration and assurance that ensures the asymptotic solidness of the related conditions, present the Hop Bifurcation analysis, outline hypothetical conclusions, and pick up an advanced understanding of the framework's behavior.

Chen et al. (2019) proposed the transformation of a cross-race irresistible illness into a frame that can spread among people brought about by an annihilating worldwide plague within the past. Within the concept, criteria clarify fears of human-to-human transmission shape of avian flu driving to a plague are a point of reference for this inquiry. The comparison between the determinant and the irregular test illustrates that randomization. It incorporates little effect on most perspectives of a scourge since it includes a noteworthy on little populaces and mutation change rates, particularly for the spoken-to large population. The demonstrative show has been amplified by investigating disconnected immunization and immunization programs, subsequently building up quantitative appraisals of the impacts and viability of these control measures inside the two indication limits analyzed.

Dansu and Seno (2019) investigated how the epidemic's components were demonstrated to both long-term residents and passing observers using a five-dimensional framework of traditional differential conditions based on SIR and SIS models. Looking at public health policies from a different angle, this research indicates that in order to create public health policies that effectively control the disease, a variation of these fundamental reproduction numbers must be chosen.

Chatzilena et al. (2019) studied the use of statistical advances in infectious disease dynamics. Also, they described the installation of one type of infection samples using the Hamiltonian Monte Carlo and the different hypotheses implemented in the free Stan software. It shows the transition between statistical performance and computational speed. It is also suitable for real-time applications.

Methods of learning Outbreaks are emerging during emergencies, including SARS, A / H1N1, and Ebola. Selective treatment should reduce and control the growing number of infectious diseases due to limited medical resources presented by Qin et al. (2016). However, disease control needs to know how to diagnose cases of portal damage and when to implement selected treatment strategies. To beautify this, we get a delicate non-Filippov surface initiated by a particular treatment. The energetic behaviors' of the two subsystems are completely disk, and the adjusted conditions for distinctive sorts of harmony are given, such as sliding area, sliding mode elements of such regular equilibrium, pseudo-equilibrium, boundary harmony, and digression point. Assist, the number sliding part examination appears that the proposed Filippov framework has been wealthy in sliding parts. Specifically, the settings of standard parameters due to the area parameter variety are in a successive sliding in happening ceaselessly: cross → bucking → real/virtual harmony → buckling snatching. Most variables affect the chosen treatment measures, and the esteem of the portal of the influenced cases for the developed irresistible infection is examined in detail.

The strategy of moderation techniques for global calamities was developed by Nigmatulina and Larson (2009). It uses early scientific models to evaluate the application and timing of non-drug intercession methodologies, such as travel restrictions and social segregation move forward in well-being. These findings suggest that the virus will spread catastrophically. Still, they also point to coping mechanisms that, if used promptly and effectively, can considerably lessen the intensity of a global explosion.

Teytelman and Larson (2012) presented a model to determine three characteristics of an individual that are important in determining the temporal dynamics of infections. They create detailed time models that illustrate the assessment of the disease in the face of such population variability, taking into account social function and clarity for infection. The values of the three attributes described for each individual are viewed as the test value of a continuous random variable. The simple and generally expanding on the most traditional distinctive analysis models depicting the population diversity. Finally, it demonstrated the empirical uses of this approach with contact data from four European nations.

Farooq and Bazaz (2020) emphasized a simulated strategy for natural immunization controlled by risk-based demographic analysis. The population is divided into low-risk and high-risk boxes subdivided according to risk factors. To different pathogenic mechanisms by isolating the human resource box while allowing the immune system to develop once released from preventing measures like lockdown. Immunization and crowd resistance think about their effect on assessing COVID-19 illness. These propose diminishing the passing rate if the antibody isn't accessible at the mass level.

Elhussein et al. (2020) analyzed that mass accumulation considered to be one of the most series factors contributing to the outbreak of respiratory disease. Google trends to identify the umrah seasons for the artist from the eastern province in Saudi Arabia. The relationship between large-scale gatherings and how data use may impact the spread of influenza in the Eastern Province is examined. So this negotiate to information examination, Exploratory Data Analysis (EDA) approach has been embraced to recognize the regularity. The cross-linked examination found a solid positive relationship between swarm blockage and flu episode within the eastern territory, moving the flu information forward for three months after the swarming season.

A new mathematical model concept of bird flu and H5N1 virus prediction measures were created by Upadhyay et al. (2008). They developed a statistical model that hypothesizes variables affecting the transmission of the bird flu infection. The goal of this work is to better understand the means of transmission of the avian flu by addressing its geographical and temporal distribution. The outcome was expected to generalize their projection and predict the long-term conditions of disease in the future. By inference, the likelihood of an occurrence is correlated with the originating nation developing a considerably superior, higher, stronger, and improved suggestion for eradicating this disease.

Haque and Haque (2018) investigated ways to decrease the swine flu's effects on Brunei's tourism industry in 2018. It was projected that the swine flu caused Brunei to lose approximately 30,000 (15%) tourists and $15 million in 2008. An analysis of subsidence during the 2008 global financial crisis is conducted utilising the coordinates moving normal and intervention timing research approaches. In two auto-Regression coupled moving standard models, they estimate the number of visitors affected by the global financial crisis and the swine flu, as well as the outcomes of the temporal arrangement research that served as a mediator. Finally, this considers the deals that were used to calculate using the ARIMA and ITSA techniques.

MATHEMATICAL MODEL: ANALYSIS OF COMMUNICABLE DISEASES AND VIROLOGY

In this Section, various Mathematical models for the analysis of communicable diseases and virology involves creating equations to represent the dynamics of disease spread, incorporating key parameters like transmission rates and recovery rates are discussed. These models, often based on epidemiological principles, help predict the course of infections and study interventions. By integrating data on factors such as population, susceptibility, and infectiousness, researchers can gain insights into the behavior of diseases, their impact on public health, and the effectiveness of control measures. This analytical approach aids in understanding and managing the complexities of communicable diseases, contributing valuable insights to the field of virology which are portrayed by figures 2 – 7.

Notations

The population as a whole is represented by N; the susceptible population is represented by S, the infected by I, the recovered by R, and the deceased by D. The parameters β, γ, δ, ω, and ρ reflect the rates of infection, recovery, transfer to quarantine, release from quarantine, and death. The variations in the numbers of susceptible, exposed, infected, recovered, and quarantined persons over time are denoted by the symbols S'(t), E'(t), I'(t), R'(t), and Q'(t), accordingly. The following figure shows how the model is represented.

Figure 1. N-S-E-I-R-Q-D model representation

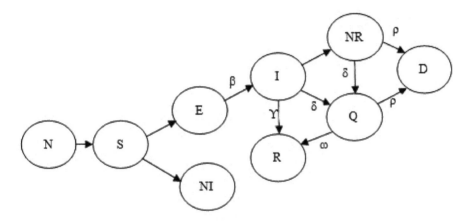

MSIR model: A sort of compartmental model called the MSIR model is used in epidemiology to explain how a population changes when an infectious disease spreads. MSIR, which stands for compartments within the model, is an abbreviation. The rate of change of individuals in each compartment over time is captured by the differential equations in the MSIR model. According to the model, the number of susceptible people who interact with sick people determines the rate of infection, and the number of infected people determines the rate of recovery. Mathematically, the differential equations for the MSIR model are as follows:

$$S'(t) = -\beta SI \tag{1}$$

$$I'(t) = -S'(t) - R'(t) \tag{2}$$

$$R'(t) = \gamma I \tag{3}$$

Mathematical Modelling in the Analysis of Viral Diseases and Communicable Diseases

These differential equations explain how the number of people in each compartment fluctuates over time, offering insights into the dynamics of the disease's spread and the effects of numerous factors on the population as a whole, including rates of transmission and recovery.

Figure 2. MSIR model for multiple strain virus spread analysis

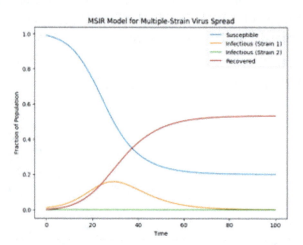

Figure 3. SIR model for virus spread analysis

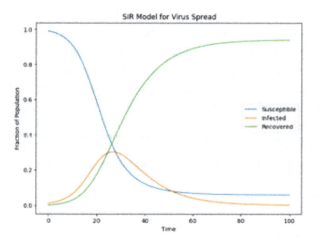

Mathematical Modelling in the Analysis of Viral Diseases and Communicable Diseases

SIER Model: The SIER (Susceptible-Infected-Exposed-Recovered) model is an extension of the SIR model that adds the Exposed (E) category of people. Exposure is defined as having contracted the illness but not yet developing an infectious disease. A differential equation model for the SIER model is described as follows:

$$S'(t) = -\beta SI / N \quad (4)$$

$$E'(t) = S'(t) - \alpha E \quad (5)$$

$$I'(t) = \alpha E - R'(t) \quad (6)$$

$$R'(t) = \gamma I \quad (7)$$

A more complex and accurate picture of the transmission of infectious illnesses is offered by the SIER model, which takes into consideration the incubation period during which a person is infected but not yet contagious. Using this model can aid in understanding how two popular public health measures, isolation and quarantine, impact the transmission of infectious diseases.

Figure 4. SEIR model for virus spread analysis

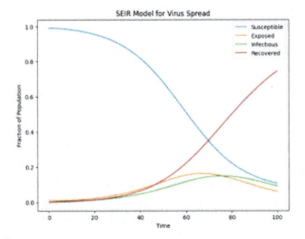

Figure 5. MSEIR model for multiple strain virus spread analysis

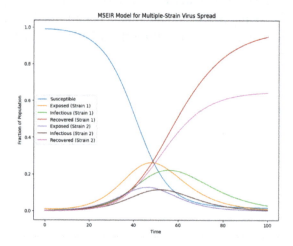

SIQR model: A collection of differential equations that depict the rate of change in the number of people in each compartment over time characterise the SIQR model. These are the equations:

$$S'(t) = -\beta SI/N \tag{8}$$

$$I'(t) = S'(t) - \alpha I \tag{9}$$

$$Q'(t) = \alpha I - R'(t) \tag{10}$$

$$R'(t) = \gamma Q \tag{11}$$

The rate at which vulnerable people contract the infection is shown in the first equation, and the rate at which sick people are placed under quarantine is shown in the second equation. The pace at which people are placed under quarantine is shown by the third equation, and the rate at which they recover and develop immunity to the illness is shown by the fourth equation. All things considered, the SIQR model differential equations can be used to predict the transmission of an infectious illness within a community and assess how measures like immunisation or quarantine affect that spread.

Figure 6. SIQR model for virus spread analysis

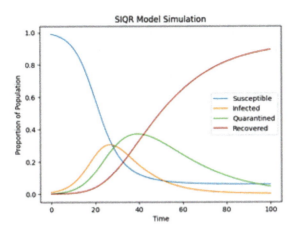

SIQRD model: A mathematical model called the SIQRD model is used to explain how an infectious disease, communicable diseases spreads. It is an expansion of the fundamental SIR model (Susceptible, Infected, Recovered), which uses a system of ordinary differential equations to describe the dynamics of infectious diseases. Two new compartments, Q (Quarantine) and D (Deaths), are added to the SIR model by the SIQRD model. The model makes the assumption that sick people could get better, go into quarantine, or pass away. The differential equation system that follows defines the SIQRD model:

$$S'(t) = -\beta SI \tag{12}$$

$$I'(t) = S'(t) - R'(t) - \delta I \tag{13}$$

$$Q'(t) = \delta I - \omega Q \tag{14}$$

$$R'(t) = \gamma I \tag{15}$$

$$D'(t) = \rho I \tag{16}$$

The spread of infectious diseases and the effects of various control strategies, including immunisation, social distance, and quarantine, can be simulated using the SIQRD model. Like other models, though, it is predicated on oversimplifying assumptions and might not adequately capture the intricate dynamics of outbreaks in the actual world.

Figure 7. SIQRD model for communicable diseases

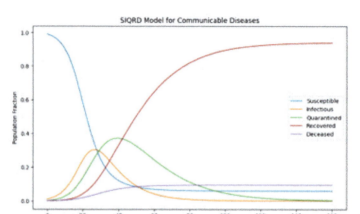

The MSIR model is useful for researching illnesses when immunity is strongly impacted by the spread of multiple strain viruses. The population's life cycle is illustrated in Figure 2, which also shows how susceptibility declines and recovery increases in tandem. Figure 3 shows how, in relation to the infected population, susceptibility declines and recovery rate rises. Understanding diseases having a latent period is aided by the SIER model. The shift from vulnerability to exposure, infection, and recovery is shown in Figure 4, emphasising the interval of time between exposure and infection. The transition from susceptibility to exposure, illness, and recovery on multiple strain viruses' propagation is represented by the MSIER model, as shown in Figure 5. The SIQR model facilitates research on how quarantine affects the dynamics of disease. Figure 6 shows how the quarantine affects the number of afflicted people, slowing the disease's spread and speeding up recovery. The SIQRD model is essential for comprehending illnesses with high fatality rates. The effects of quarantine and the course of recovery or death are depicted in Figure 7.

SELF-ISOLATION STRATEGIES

One way to assess the efficiency of different self-isolation strategies is to perform a comparison analysis of the results of various modelling scenarios. Important tactics consist of Instant Self-Isolation - When symptoms appear, infected people withdraw themselves right away. Delayed Self-Isolation - When symptoms take a while to manifest, infected people withdraw from society. Partial Compliance Self-Isolation - A small percentage of those who are infected follow the instructions for self-isolation. DDEs can be used to mimic any approach while taking compliance rates and delays into account. Metrics like the primary reproduction number (R0), the peak number of infections, and the total duration of the outbreak can be used to compare how effective different tactics are. The efficacy of self-isolation tactics in halting the spread of infectious diseases can be better understood by mathematical modelling with DDEs. The best course of action is to immediately isolate oneself when symptoms appear. This will drastically lower the rate of transmission and shorten the outbreak's duration. Delay in self-isolation can be advantageous, but it also raises infection peaks and lengthens outbreak times. The effectiveness of an intervention can be greatly impacted by partial adherence to self-isolation recommendations, underscoring the need of public health policies that encourage high rates of compliance. To improve overall disease control efforts, future research should refine these tactics and combine them with other therapies like social distancing and getting immunised.

LIMITATIONS OF THE CURRENT MODELS

By assuming uniform population mixing and constant transmission rates, current models of disease spread frequently oversimplify real-world dynamics and ignore behavioural and environmental variables. Usually, they have to take into account the effects of human behaviour, such following health recommendations and altering social norms. Often, these models include static parameters for recovery and transmission rates, omitting the fact that these parameters are dynamic during outbreaks that are impacted by treatments or seasonal variations. Delays Differential Equations (DDEs), while useful, are computationally demanding and may not fully reflect the intricacy of temporal dynamics in big populations. It is frequently necessary to integrate data in real-time, which is essential for precise forecasting and prompt responses. Furthermore, a lot of models fail to adequately take into account the demographic and geographic variety that exists, including aspects like age, socioeconomic level, and culture, which can have a big impact on the effectiveness of interventions and the transmission of disease. Last but not least, certain models are customised for particular diseases, making it challenging to modify them for others with distinct epidemiological traits and modes of transmission.

PROSPECTIVE AREAS FOR FUTURE RESEARCH

Advanced behavioural models that take social networks, mobility, and adherence to health measures into account should be the main focus of future mathematical modelling studies for viral and infectious diseases. The model's predictions and parameters will be updated continuously by incorporating real-time data from social media and health surveillance. More specialised and tailored actions will be made possible by the development of models that are demographically and spatially unique. Rapid responses to new outbreaks will be facilitated by flexible modelling frameworks that can be adjusted to varied diseases. Multidisciplinary cooperation will improve models by adding different viewpoints. The applicability of models will be confirmed by testing and validating those using actual data. It is critical to look into the long-term effects of vaccinations and therapies, including resistance and partial and waning immunity. Increasing the amount of research conducted to assess public health policy would help make well-informed decisions based on reliable forecasts.

CONCLUSION

A way to acquire a deeper understanding of immunity to infection, completion, reporting of testing, and medical strategies is through mathematical modelling. Examples used to describe the strategies demonstrate how frequently the expansion is thoroughly collected, as well as how cutting-edge, recently discovered current data is used in almost revolutionary ways. Summarize about the pathogen organization of contamination issues, damage repair, and the multifactorial complexity of the disease. The system for testing contemporary hypotheses, examining circumstances, conducting virtual clinical trials, announcing test procedures, offering standard and customized therapies is provided by mathematical modelling. This paper explores the spread of an infectious disease and the role that time delays play. Study demonstrates that the vaccine lowers the rate of reproduction and that social separation is an effective technique for control. In this paper, the major topic of discussion is mathematical modelling for epidemics in various fields and how it may be applied to forecast the development of viruses, vaccines as well as control measures in science and engineering. In this work, various influenza models and epidemiological dynamics were reviewed and described.

REFERENCES

Araz, O. M., Fowler, J. W., Lant, T. W., & Jehn, M. (2009, December). A pandemic influenza simulation model for preparedness planning. *Proceedings of the 2009 Winter Simulation Conference*. IEEE. 10.1109/WSC.2009.5429732

Ashrafur Rahman, S. M., & Zou, X. (2011). Flu epidemics: A two-strain flu model with a single vaccination. *Journal of Biological Dynamics*, 5(5), 376–390. 10.1080/17513758.2010.510213

Chatzilena, A., Van Leeuwen, E., Ratmann, O., Baguelin, M., & Demiris, N. (2019). Contemporary statistical inference for infectious disease models using Stan. *Epidemics*, 29, 1–16. 10.1016/j.epidem.2019.10036731591003

Chen, C. Y., Ward, J. P., & Xie, W. B. (2019). Modelling the outbreak of infectious disease following mutation from a non-transmissible strain. *Theoretical Population Biology*, 126, 1–18. 10.1016/j.tpb.2018.08.00230165060

Ciotti, M., Ciccozzi, M., Terrinoni, A., Jiang, W. C., Wang, C. B., & Bernardini, S. (2020). The COVID-19 pandemic. *Critical Reviews in Clinical Laboratory Sciences*, 57(6), 365–388. 10.1080/10408363.2020.178319832645276

Dansu, E. J., & Seno, H. (2019). A model for epidemic dynamics in a community with visitor subpopulation. *Journal of Theoretical Biology*, 478, 115–127. 10.1016/j.jtbi.2019.06.02031228488

Elhussein, M., Brahimi, S., Alreedy, A., Alqahtani, M., & Olatunji, S. O. (2020). Google trends identifying seasons of religious gathering: Applied to investigate the correlation between crowding and flu outbreak. *Information Processing & Management*, 57(3), 102208. 10.1016/j.ipm.2020.102208

Farooq, J., & Bazaz, M. A. (2020). A novel adaptive deep learning model of Covid-19 with focus on mortality reduction strategies. *Chaos, Solitons, and Fractals*, 138, 1–13. 10.1016/j.chaos.2020.11014832834586

Haque, T. H., & Haque, M. O. (2018). The swine flu and its impacts on tourism in Brunei. *Journal of Hospitality and Tourism Management*, 36, 92–101. 10.1016/j.jhtm.2016.12.003

Kanyiri, C. W., Mark, K., & Luboobi, L. (2018). Mathematical analysis of influenza A dynamics in the emergence of drug resistance. *Computational and Mathematical Methods in Medicine*, 2018, 1–14. 10.1155/2018/243456030245737

Khan, A., Waleed, M., & Imran, M. (2015). Mathematical analysis of an influenza epidemic model, formulation of different controlling strategies using optimal control and estimation of basic reproduction number. *Mathematical and Computer Modelling of Dynamical Systems*, 21(5), 432–459. 10.1080/13873954.2015.1016975

Kongnuy, R., & Naowanich, E. (2014). Mathematical Model of Influenza Dynamics Compare the incubation period and Control: in Thailand. In *Conf. Proceeding*. Research Gate.

Liu, H. C., Liu, S. W., Chang, P. C., Huang, W. C., & Liao, C. H. (2008, August). A novel classifier for influenza a viruses based on SVM and logistic regression. *IEEE International Conference on Wavelet Analysis and Pattern Recognition*. IEEE.

Maki, Y., & Hirose, H. (2013, January). Infectious disease spread analysis using stochastic differential equations for SIR model. *IEEE International Conference on Intelligent Systems, Modelling and Simulation*. IEEE. 10.1109/ISMS.2013.13

Mayilvaganan, S., & Balamuralitharan, S. (2019, June). Analytical solutions of influenza diseases model by HPM. In *AIP Conference Proceedings*. Research Gate. 10.1063/1.5112193

Meijer, A., Paget, W. J., Meerhoff, T. J., Brown, C. S., Meuwissen, L. E., & Van Der Velden, J. (2006). European Influenza Surveillance Scheme EISS. "Epidemiological and virological assessment of influenza activity in Europe, during the 2004-2005 winter". *Eurosurveillance*, 11(5), 9–10. 10.2807/esm.11.05.00623-en29208114

Minucci, S. B., Heise, R. L., & Reynolds, A. M. (2020). Review of mathematical modeling of the inflammatory response in lung infections and injuries. *Frontiers in Applied Mathematics and Statistics*, 6, 36. 10.3389/fams.2020.00036

Mummert, A., & Otunuga, O. M. (2019). Parameter identification for a stochastic SEIRS epidemic model: Case study influenza. *Journal of Mathematical Biology*, 79(2), 705–729. 10.1007/s00285-019-01374-z31062075

Nigmatulina, K. R., & Larson, R. C. (2009). Living with influenza: Impacts of government imposed and voluntarily selected interventions. *European Journal of Operational Research*, 195(2), 613–627. 10.1016/j.ejor.2008.02.016

Perrone, P. M., Biganzoli, G., Lecce, M., Campagnoli, E. M., Castrofino, A., Cinnirella, A., Fornaro, F., Gallana, C., Grosso, F. M., Maffeo, M., Shishmintseva, V., Pariani, E., & Castaldi, S. (2021). Influenza Vaccination Campaign during the COVID-19 Pandemic: The Experience of a Research and Teaching Hospital in Milan. *International Journal of Environmental Research and Public Health*, 18(11), 5874. 10.3390/ijerph1811587434070763

Puig-Barbera, J., Tormos, A., Sominina, A., Burtseva, E., Launay, O., Ciblak, M. A., Natividad-Sancho, A., Buigues-Vila, A., Martínez-Úbeda, S., & Mahé, C. (2014). First-year results of the Global Influenza Hospital Surveillance Network: 2012–2013 Northern hemisphere influenza season. *BMC Public Health*, 14(1), 1–12. 10.118 6/1471-2458-14-56424903737

Qin, W., Tang, S., Xiang, C., & Yang, Y. (2016). Effects of limited medical resource on a Filippov infectious disease model induced by selection pressure. *Applied Mathematics and Computation*, 283, 339–354. 10.1016/j.amc.2016.02.04232287500

Rihan, F. A., & Anwar, M. N. (2012). Qualitative analysis of delayed SIR epidemic model with a saturated incidence rate. *International Journal of Differential Equations*, 2012, 1–13. 10.1155/2012/408637

Ruschel, S., Pereira, T., Yanchuk, S., & Young, L. S. (2019). An SIQ delay differential equations model for disease control via isolation. *Journal of Mathematical Biology*, 79(1), 249–279. 10.1007/s00285-019-01356-131037349

Schumacher, S., Salmanton-Garcia, J., Cornely, O. A., & Mellinghoff, S. C. (2021). Increasing influenza vaccination coverage in healthcare workers: A review on campaign strategies and their effect. *Infection*, 49(3), 387–399. 10.1007/s15010-020-01555-933284427

Tan, X., Yuan, L., Zhou, J., Zheng, Y., & Yang, F. (2013). Modeling the initial transmission dynamics of influenza A H1N1 in Guangdong Province, China. *International Journal of Infectious Diseases*, 17.

Teytelman, A., & Larson, R. C. (2012). Modeling influenza progression within a continuous-attribute heterogeneous population. *European Journal of Operational Research*, 220(1), 238–250. 10.1016/j.ejor.2012.01.027

Upadhyay, R. K., Kumari, N., & Rao, V. S. H. (2008). Modeling the spread of bird flu and predicting outbreak diversity. *Nonlinear Analysis Real World Applications*, 9(4), 1638–1648. 10.1016/j.nonrwa.2007.04.00932288641

Venna, S. R., Tavanaei, A., Gottumukkala, R. N., Raghavan, V. V., Maida, A. S., & Nichols, S. (2018). A novel data-driven model for real-time influenza forecasting. *IEEE Access: Practical Innovations, Open Solutions*, 7, 7691–7701. 10.1109/ACCESS.2018.2888585

Zhang, L., Lian, P., Zou, J., & Deng, H. (2015, June). Partial differential equation optimization for infectious disease model. *IEEE International Conference on Intelligent Computation Technology and Automation*. IEEE. 10.1109/ICICTA.2015.160

Chapter 15
Promises and Perils of Generative AI in the Healthcare Sector

Pratibha Garg
Amity University, India

ABSTRACT

Artificial intelligence (AI), especially generative AI, is increasingly recognized as a game-changer in healthcare, offering the potential to transform clinical decision-making and enhance health outcomes significantly. Generative AI encompasses algorithms and models like OpenAI's ChatGPT, capable of producing diverse types of content when prompted. This piece aims to offer a comprehensive overview of generative AI's application, challenges, and opportunities within the healthcare sector. It concludes that generative AI holds the promise of catalyzing substantial progress in healthcare, evolving continuously to meet the specific needs and demands of the medical field as regulations and frameworks governing its usage become more defined.

INTRODUCTION

Artificial intelligence (AI) has gained significant traction across multiple domains, including healthcare, where it holds the promise of revolutionizing clinical decision-making and ultimately improving health outcomes (Bajwa et al., 2021; Desai, 2020; Reddy et al., 2019). Generative AI, a subset of AI, has garnered attention for its capacity to leverage machine learning algorithms to create novel data formats such as text, images, and music (Arora & Arora, 2022; Jadon & Kumar, 2023; Kothari, 2023; Lan et al., 2020). Its impact spans various industries, and

DOI: 10.4018/979-8-3693-3731-8.ch015

healthcare is no exception (Brynjolfsson et al., 2023). With its impressive ability to analyze vast datasets and derive valuable insights, generative AI has emerged as a potent tool in augmenting patient care (Suthar et al., 2022), transforming disease diagnosis (Kanjee et al., 2023), and broadening treatment avenues (Vert, 2023). By tapping into the capabilities of this state-of-the-art technology, healthcare professionals can now access unparalleled levels of precision, efficiency, and innovation in their practices.

Recently, the Generative Pre-trained Transformer (GPT) models, including the widely recognized ChatGPT model developed by OpenAI, have emerged as potent tools poised to redefine the landscape of healthcare, primarily owing to their exceptional natural language processing (NLP) capabilities (Aydın & Karaarslan, 2022; Dale, 2021). These sophisticated language models demonstrate a remarkable aptitude for understanding and generating text that closely resembles human speech, rendering them highly suitable for numerous applications, particularly in healthcare. By tapping into vast repositories of medical data and knowledge, GPT models have the potential to revolutionize various facets of the healthcare sector, ushering in a new era of clinical decision support, patient interaction, and data management. Their ability to comprehend and interpret complex medical information has sparked optimism regarding their transformative impact on healthcare practices. Through the utilization of this state-of-the-art technology, healthcare professionals can now access unparalleled levels of precision, efficiency, and innovation in healthcare delivery (Liu et al., 2023). GPT models can contribute significantly to disease diagnosis and prognosis, facilitating the identification and prediction of various medical conditions, thereby enabling earlier detection and personalized treatment strategies (Lecler et al., 2023; Savage, 2023). Moreover, these models can engage with patients, furnish educational materials, and address medical inquiries, thereby fostering enhanced patient engagement and empowerment in managing their health (Eysenbach, 2023). Furthermore, the capacity of GPT models to streamline the management of electronic health records (EHRs) and clinical documentation represents a potential avenue for mitigating administrative burdens, thereby allowing medical practitioners to devote more attention to patient care (Xue et al., 2023).

Despite the transformative potential of generative models, their integration into healthcare poses challenges. Ensuring the accuracy and reliability of AI-driven decisions remains a critical concern, especially in crucial medical contexts. The opaque nature of some AI models, including generative ones, raises questions about the interpretability of their decisions, underscoring the need for increased transparency and explainability in AI systems used in healthcare. Additionally, ethical considerations surrounding data privacy, patient confidentiality, and potential biases in AI models demand careful attention (Sallam, 2023). Given that these models handle sensitive medical information, safeguarding patient privacy and ensuring data security are essential for maintaining public trust in AI-enabled healthcare solutions.

In light of recent advancements, this article offers an overview of current industry endeavors in applying generative AI models to healthcare. By emphasizing their significant potential, benefits, and challenges, this study aims to contribute to the ongoing conversation about leveraging AI's transformative abilities responsibly for the improvement of medical practices and patient welfare. As we delve into the impact of generative models on healthcare, navigating the continually changing AI landscape with a steadfast commitment to ethical standards, patient-centered care, and collaborative engagement among AI developers, medical experts, and policymakers is paramount.

LITERATURE REVIEW

Generative Artificial Intelligence

Generative AI represents a category of machine learning technology that acquires the capacity to produce novel data based on its training data (Epstein et al., 2023; Takefuji, 2023). These models generate data resembling the original dataset, offering valuable applications in fields like image and speech synthesis. Notably, they possess the capability for unsupervised learning, enabling them to learn from data without explicit labels, which proves advantageous in scenarios where labeled data is scarce or costly to procure (Brynjolfsson et al., 2023). Moreover, generative AI models can create synthetic data by understanding the underlying data distributions from real data and subsequently generating new data that closely aligns with the statistical patterns of the original dataset. Unlike other machine learning models, which primarily focus on discerning the boundaries between different classes of data (discriminative models), generative models are geared towards endowing machines with the ability to synthesize novel entities (Brynjolfsson et al., 2023). They are engineered to grasp the foundational structure of a dataset and generate fresh samples akin to the original data. This stands in contrast to discriminative models, which center their efforts on tasks like classification, regression, or reinforcement learning, where the objective is to make predictions or decisions based on existing data.

GPT Model

The GPT models, spearheaded by OpenAI, have emerged as a significant breakthrough in the field of Natural Language Processing (NLP). NLP, a crucial subdomain of artificial intelligence (AI), revolves around facilitating interaction between computers and human language. Its core aim is to empower machines to comprehend, interpret, and generate human language in a meaningful and contextually relevant manner, encompassing tasks such as language translation, sentiment analysis, speech recognition, text summarization, and question answering (Patel & Arasanipalai, 2021). GPT models represent a sophisticated family of language models leveraging deep-learning neural networks. These models are rooted in the transformer architecture, initially proposed by Vaswani et al. in 2017 (Vaswani et al., 2017). The transformer architecture, distinguished by its utilization of "self-attention," excels in processing sequential data, particularly text, by discerning the importance of individual words within a sentence and their relationships. This enables the model to prioritize semantically relevant words and retain contextual information effectively. Transformers revolutionize language processing by efficiently handling long-range dependencies within language sequences, thereby enhancing their prowess in contextual understanding and semantic comprehension. The developmental journey of GPT models commenced with the introduction of the original GPT-1 by OpenAI in June 2018. GPT-1 showcased the potential of pre-training large-scale Transformer models on extensive text data to produce coherent and contextually relevant language. Building upon this success, OpenAI unveiled GPT-2 in February 2019, a notable advancement boasting 1.5 billion parameters. However, concerns regarding potential misuse, particularly in generating human-like text, prompted OpenAI to initially limit GPT-2's release. Eventually, in November 2019, GPT-2 was fully released, triggering a surge in research and experimentation across various domains. In June 2020, OpenAI introduced GPT-3, a monumental achievement featuring a staggering 175 billion parameters, making it the largest language model of its time. GPT-3 showcased unparalleled language generation capabilities, spanning tasks such as translation, summarization, question-answering, and creative writing. Its success fueled increased interest in Large Language Models (LLMs), leading to further research breakthroughs and commercial applications (Dale, 2021). In November 2022, OpenAI unveiled the ChatGPT model, an advanced conversational AI powered by the GPT-3.5 architecture. Designed for natural and dynamic conversations, ChatGPT serves as a versatile tool across various applications, generating coherent and contextually relevant responses based on text prompts or questions provided by users. Subsequently, in March 2023, GPT-4 was introduced as a large multimodal model capable of processing both image and textual inputs, boasting even greater performance improvements over ChatGPT. Due to the extensive pre-training process, these models are commonly referred to as Large Language Models (LLMs) (VanBuskirk, 2023).

LLM Model

Large Language Models (LLMs) excel in text completion tasks, which involve predicting the most probable token in a given text sequence. This proficiency is achieved through the utilization of auto-attention mechanisms and extensive training data. LLMs exhibit the capability to correlate with a significantly larger number of tokens compared to previous models, rendering them highly effective in natural language understanding (Radford, 2018). State-of-the-art LLMs can generate coherent text highly correlated with the provided prompt, closely resembling human-generated text internally. This ability enables them to perform a myriad of impressive tasks. In Natural Language Processing (NLP), neural learning techniques have been long employed, with conventional methods relying on expensive supervised learning using manually curated training datasets. Conversely, LLMs leverage unsupervised learning from extensive datasets representing general language knowledge. They can execute classic NLP tasks with minimal additional learning and are adept at zero-shot learning, few-shot learning with limited examples, or fine-tuning with focused datasets. This significantly reduces the training requirement compared to supervised learning approaches. LLMs have demonstrated state-of-the-art performance across various tasks such as sentiment analysis (Radford, 2017), text summarization, entity detection, translation (Yang et al., 2020), and question-answering (Radford, 2019). Additionally, they exhibit capabilities in commonsense reasoning (Radford, 2019), machine translation (Radford, 2017), and various other AI and NLP tasks.

PROMISES OF GENERATIVE AI IN HEALTHCARE

Generative AI has demonstrated remarkable potential across various healthcare applications, particularly in the creation of text and images, marking a promising advancement in the healthcare landscape (Haupt & Marks, 2023; Korngiebel & Mooney, 2021; Uprety et al., 2023). Its implementation stands to revolutionize healthcare by enhancing diagnosis, streamlining healthcare delivery, and ultimately improving patient outcomes. By leveraging the capabilities of artificial intelligence, generative AI has unlocked possibilities previously deemed unattainable, fundamentally reshaping healthcare strategies, optimizing hospital operations, and elevating care delivery standards. This transformation leads to enhanced patient care and greater sustainability within healthcare systems. In a broader perspective, generative AI is fostering a more responsive, patient-centered, and data-driven healthcare ecosystem that was previously beyond reach in the pre-AI era. The detailed applications of generative AI include:

Personalized Medicine

Traditionally, treatments were often based on broad population data, overlooking individual variations. Generative AI, however, enables a deep dive into patients' genetic profiles, medical histories, and real-time health data (Kline et al., 2022). By training AI on large datasets of patient information, it can uncover patterns and correlations not readily discernible to human doctors. For instance, AI may identify that patients with a specific genetic marker respond exceptionally well to a particular medication. This allows healthcare to be customized to each patient's unique needs and genetic makeup, resulting in more precise, effective, and patient-centric medical care that significantly improves outcomes and reduces adverse effects (Kline et al., 2022).

Mental Health Applications

Generative AI also finds utility in the realm of mental health, particularly in the development of interactive tools for cognitive behavioral therapy (CBT) (van Schalkwyk, 2023; Yang et al., 2023). CBT is a form of psychotherapy that aids patients in managing their conditions by modifying their thoughts and behaviors.

Drug Discovery

Generative AI is revolutionizing the drug discovery and development processes, historically characterized by arduous and time-consuming pathways from discovery to market availability. By expediting the identification of potential drug candidates, optimizing molecular structures, and even forecasting side effects and drug interactions, the swift and efficient capabilities facilitated by generative AI hold the potential to introduce novel and safer medications to patients (Callaway, 2023). Through the analysis of extensive datasets, generative AI aids in identifying potential issues that may arise during clinical trials, ultimately reducing the time and cost associated with drug development (Callaway, 2023; Vert, 2023). Furthermore, by pinpointing specific biological processes relevant to disease, generative AI assists in identifying new targets for drug development, potentially leading to the creation of more effective treatments.

Administrative Task

Generative AI applications offer promise in alleviating the administrative burdens faced by physicians and clinicians (Patel & Lam, 2023). Large Language Models (LLMs) exhibit potential in activities such as coding and data summarization, simplifying processes like billing, prior authorizations, and appeals (Patel &

Lam, 2023). AI has proven effective in enhancing healthcare workflows such as appointment scheduling, inventory management, claims processing, and patient record management (Kocaballi et al., 2020). Intelligent scheduling systems, developed using AI models, interact with patients through chatbots or voice assistants to efficiently schedule, reschedule, or cancel appointments, optimizing the process based on factors like doctor availability, patient preferences, and appointment urgency. Generative AI can also automate insurance claims processing by reading, understanding, verifying claim documents, checking for discrepancies, and processing claims. Real-time analysis of patient data improves patient safety by detecting indications of conditions like sepsis or patient decline, enabling rapid response and alerting appropriate personnel. As telehealth-based interventions like remote patient monitoring gain traction in acute home care, the abundance of data overwhelms clinicians. Artificial intelligence emerges as a potential solution to convert data floods into prioritized actionable information, communicating it to the relevant care team members (Clusmann et al., 2023).

Synthetic Data Generation

Synthetic data, generated using generative AI models, emerges as an increasingly promising solution for balancing the accessibility of valuable data with the protection of patient privacy (Suthar et al., 2022). Utilizing generative AI models, realistic and anonymized patient data can be synthesized for research and training purposes, facilitating a wide array of versatile applications. Furthermore, generative AI models can replicate electronic health record (EHR) data by understanding the underlying data distributions, ensuring exceptional performance and addressing concerns such as data privacy (Suthar et al., 2022). This approach proves particularly beneficial in scenarios where real-world patient data is limited or access is restricted due to privacy considerations. Moreover, employing synthetic data can enhance the accuracy and robustness of machine learning models by enabling a more diverse and representative dataset for training. Additionally, the capability to generate synthetic data with varying characteristics and parameters empowers researchers and clinicians to explore and test different hypotheses, leading to novel insights and discoveries (Lan et al., 2020; Limeros et al., 2022).

Medical Imaging

Advanced AI models, particularly those tailored for medical analysis, prominently feature sophisticated techniques like convolutional neural networks (CNNs) and various deep learning frameworks. Generative models play a pivotal role in synthesizing organ or tissue images, serving educational purposes by training medical professionals and simplifying explanations of medical conditions to patients through visually comprehensible representations (Lan et al., 2020; Suthar et al., 2022). Generative AI streamlines the segmentation of organs or abnormalities in medical images, effectively saving time for healthcare professionals and optimizing the image analysis process (Limeros et al., 2022). By identifying patterns in medical images, generative AI aids in predicting or diagnosing pathological conditions, facilitating early detection and intervention to improve patient outcomes (Gong et al., 2023).

Medical Education and Training

In the realm of medical education and training, this technology finds application in generating a diverse array of virtual patient cases encompassing various medical conditions, patient demographics, and clinical scenarios. These cases serve as a comprehensive learning platform for medical students and healthcare professionals (Eysenbach, 2023; Khan et al., 2023). One of the key advantages of employing generative AI in medical education lies in establishing a secure and controlled learning environment. Students can interact with these virtual patients, make diagnoses, and propose treatment plans without any risk to actual patients, allowing them to learn from mistakes in a low-stakes setting. Generative AI can also craft patient cases that are rare or complex, providing students with exposure and expertise in areas they may not frequently encounter in clinical practice. This proves particularly valuable in preparing students for unforeseen circumstances and enhancing their problem-solving abilities.

Patient Education

In patient education, generative AI serves various purposes (Haupt & Marks, 2023; Patel & Lam, 2023). It can generate personalized educational content tailored to a patient's specific condition, symptoms, or inquiries. For instance, if a patient has diabetes, the AI can generate information regarding blood sugar management, dietary recommendations, exercise regimes, and medication protocols. Additionally, generative AI can engage patients in interactive learning experiences where they can pose questions, and the AI generates responses, fostering a dialogue that enhances the patient's understanding of their condition. This feature proves beneficial for patients who may feel hesitant or embarrassed to ask certain questions to their healthcare providers. Furthermore, generative AI can produce visual aids such as diagrams or infographics to elucidate complex medical concepts. For instance, it could generate a diagram illustrating the mechanism of action of a specific medication within the body.

PERILS OF GENERATIVE AI IN HEALTHCARE

The intricacy of these models poses challenges in identifying and mitigating potential risks associated with their utilization. While artificial neural networks constitute a vital component of most deep learning models, their classification as 'black boxes' due to the opacity of their internal mechanisms presents a significant hurdle for researchers. Furthermore, the rising concern regarding the potential misuse of ChatGPT and other generative algorithms underscores the necessity of addressing the following risks in integrating generative AI into healthcare systems.

Deepfake Imaging

Scientists, critics, and regulatory bodies alike have raised alarms about the illicit exploitation of AI technology. Computer security experts have observed instances of "catastrophic forgetting" within deep neural networks as they endeavor to counter increasingly sophisticated "deep fakes" (Westerlund, 2019).

Data Privacy

Generative AI in healthcare relies on extensive datasets, including sensitive patient information, for model training and insight generation, posing significant data privacy and security concerns (Thampapillai, 2023). Healthcare organizations must adhere to stringent data protection regulations, employing encryption, access controls, and auditing mechanisms to safeguard patient data from unauthorized access or breaches. Additionally, clear policies for data sharing must be established, ensuring that data utilized for AI purposes is anonymized or de-identified whenever feasible to mitigate privacy risks.

Potential Biases

Moreover, the performance of AI models is contingent upon the quality and representativeness of the training data. Biases present in the training data, inherited by generative AI tools from patient records, pose a substantial risk (Sabzalieva & Valentini, 2023). To address this, healthcare organizations must implement robust protocols for algorithm development, validation, and ongoing testing to detect and rectify biases. Diversifying training data is crucial to ensure inclusivity and mitigate biases.

Compliance Requirements

The deployment of generative AI in healthcare is subject to rigorous regulatory scrutiny and compliance requirements (Meskó & Topol, 2023). Navigating complex regulatory frameworks necessitates obtaining regulatory approvals for AI algorithms, adhering to medical device regulations, and complying with data protection laws.

Integration With Existing Healthcare Systems

Integration with existing healthcare systems poses another challenge, as legacy systems may not be compatible with AI technologies. Implementing AI solutions requires careful assessment of IT infrastructure, identification of integration points, and ensuring interoperability with existing systems. Adequate training and support for staff members are essential to familiarize them with AI tools and workflows and mitigate resistance from healthcare professionals.

Accuracy Concerns

The concerns regarding the accuracy of generative AI models persist. As these models evolve, instances of incorrect results, termed hallucination, may arise (Sabzalieva & Valentini, 2023). In critical areas such as cancer diagnosis, ensuring the transparency of AI models and emphasizing human review of generated outputs are imperative to maintain accuracy.

GENERATIVE AI OPPORTUNITIES IN HEALTHCARE

Third-party developers now have the ability to build custom applications and solutions using APIs and plugins provided by leading generative AI providers such as OpenAI and Google (Naskar, 2023; OpenAI, 2023a; OpenAI, 2023b; OpenAI, 2024). For instance, GPT-trainer, a Software-as-a-Service (SaaS) from Petal/Paladin Max, Inc., enables users to develop and deploy their own ChatGPT assistants trained with their data without coding (Petal/Paladin Max, Inc., 2023). AI-driven, natural-language-based conversational user interfaces (UIs) are poised to revolutionize user experience design, offering greater adaptability to users' needs (Velvárt, 2023).

Instead of expecting users to adapt to rigid and less forgiving interfaces, future user interfaces (UIs) will adapt more naturally to users' needs. Users will simply describe what they need in their own words, without having to learn complex query languages or syntax. GPT-OSM exemplifies this approach by enabling users to explore features on OpenStreetMap using natural language queries (Gautam,

2023). Many healthcare UIs could benefit from a similar approach, such as query interfaces for electronic patient records and improved UIs for querying health digital twins (HDTs) (Venkatesh et al., 2024). For HDTs, a ChatGPT-like UI could bridge the gap between complex data/models and human users' understanding and needs, including healthy individuals, patients, and clinicians.

Moreover, by simplifying or automating coding processes, Generative AI can accelerate the development of health applications. For instance, ChatGPT successfully recreated Beat Saber, a popular virtual reality exergame (YouTube, 2023). Additionally, Tao and Xu demonstrated ChatGPT's capability to generate thematic maps using provided geospatial data, producing all the necessary code (Tao & Xu, 2023). In the realm of the Internet of Medical Things (IoMT), generative AI shows promise by aiding in the creation of new designs for edge-based medical and health monitoring devices (Srivastava et al., 2022). Moreover, it can enhance the user experience of these devices by learning and adapting to user preferences, improving user interfaces, and overall usability (Dilibal et al., 2021; Yellig, 2023). Furthermore, generative AI can generate synthetic and augmented data to enhance the accuracy of machine learning algorithms used in smart medical devices, particularly when real patient data access is limited or insufficient (Candemir et al., 2021; Wong, 2023). Additionally, it can contribute to IoMT security by automatically generating appropriate mitigation measures in response to potential threats (Cynerio, 2023).

GENERATIVE AI IN HEALTHCARE: USE CASES

Generative AI holds promise in addressing critical challenges across various domains in healthcare. Following are several key use cases where generative AI can make significant contributions.

Philips, a Dutch medical technology giant has developed generative AI applications to enhance its Picture Archiving and Communication System (PACS) image processing and diagnostic capabilities and simplify clinical workflows.

SayHeart, a startup based in Malaysia and Singapore, has launched an algorithm that translates medical jargon and complex imaging into easily accessible visual content.

Riken, a large scientific research institute in Japan founded in 1917, has embarked on an eight-year generative AI research programme (2023–2031) to generate medical and scientific hypotheses by learning from research papers and images.

CONCLUSION

In conclusion, this article has provided insights into several notable applications of generative AI within the healthcare sector. We have also touched upon associated concerns such as trust, reliability, privacy, and the potential for creating more user-friendly AI-driven interfaces. We anticipate that as regulations and policies governing generative AI usage develop, many of these concerns will be addressed over time. As generative AI continues to advance and become more tailored to the specific needs of healthcare, it is poised to play a pivotal role in shaping the future of medical practice. In the years ahead, we can expect the emergence of new models meticulously trained on high-quality medical data, offering valuable assistance to healthcare professionals and patients alike.

REFERENCES

Arora, A., & Arora, A. (2022). Generative adversarial networks and synthetic patient data: Current challenges and future perspectives. *Future Healthcare Journal*, 9(2), 190–193. 10.7861/fhj.2022-001335928184

Aydın, Ö., & Karaarslan, E. (2022). OpenAI ChatGPT Generated Literature Review: Digital Twin in Healthcare. *SSRN*. 10.2139/ssrn.4308687

Bajwa, J., Munir, U., Nori, A., & Williams, B. (2021). Artificial intelligence in healthcare: Transforming the practice of medicine. *Future Healthcare Journal*, 8(2), e188–e194. 10.7861/fhj.2021-009534286183

Brynjolfsson, E., Li, D., & Raymond, L. R. (2023). *Generative AI at Work* (NBER Working Papers 31161). National Bureau of Economic Research, Inc..

Callaway, E. (2023). How generative AI is building better antibodies. *Nature*. 10.1038/d41586-023-01516-w37142726

Candemir, S., Nguyen, X. V., Folio, L. R., & Prevedello, L. M. (2021). Training Strategies for Radiology Deep Learning Models in Data-limited Scenarios. *Radiology. Artificial Intelligence*, 3(6), e210014. 10.1148/ryai.202121001434870217

Clusmann, J., Kolbinger, F. R., Muti, H. S., Carrero, Z. I., Eckardt, J.-N., Laleh, N. G., Löffler, C. M. L., Schwarzkopf, S.-C., Unger, M., Veldhuizen, G. P., Wagner, S. J., & Kather, J. N. (2023). The future landscape of large language models in medicine. *Communications Medicine*, 3(1), 141. 10.1038/s43856-023-00370-137816837

Cynerio. (2023). *Cynerio Harnesses the Power of Generative AI to Revolutionize Healthcare Cybersecurity*. Cynerio. https://www.cynerio.com/blog/cynerio-harnesses-the-power-of-generative-ai-to-revolutionize-healthcare-cybersecurity

Dale, R. (2021). GPT-3: What's it good for? *Natural Language Engineering*, 27(1), 113–118. 10.1017/S1351324920000601

Desai, A. N. (2020). Artificial intelligence: Promise, pitfalls, and perspective. *Journal of the American Medical Association*, 323(24), 2448–2449. 10.1001/jama.2020.873732492093

Dilibal, C., Davis, B. L., & Chakraborty, C. (2021). Generative Design Methodology for Internet of Medical Things (IoMT)-based Wearable Biomedical Devices. In *Proceedings of the 2021 3rd International Congress on Human-Computer Interaction, Optimization and Robotic Applications (HORA)*. IEEE: Piscataway.

Epstein, Z., Hertzmann, A., Akten, M., Farid, H., Fjeld, J., Frank, M. R., Groh, M., Herman, L., Leach, N., Mahari, R., Pentland, A. S., Russakovsky, O., Schroeder, H., & Smith, A. (2023). Art and the science of generative AI. *Science*, 380(6650), 1110–1111. 10.1126/science.adh445137319193

Eysenbach, G. (2023). The role of ChatGPT, generative language models, and artificial intelligence in medical education: A conversation with ChatGPT and a call for papers. *JMIR Medical Education*, 9, e46885. 10.2196/4688536863937

Gautam, R. (2023). *OSM-GPT: An Innovative Project Combining GPT-3 and the Overpass API to Facilitate Easy Feature Discovery on OpenStreetMap*. Github. https://github.com/rowheat02/osm-gpt.

Gong, C., Jing, C., Chen, X., Pun, C. M., Huang, G., Saha, A., Nieuwoudt, M., Li, H.-X., Hu, Y., & Wang, S. (2023). Generative AI for brain image computing and brain network computing: A review. *Frontiers in Neuroscience*, 17, 1203104. 10.3389/fnins.2023.120310437383107

Haupt, C. E., & Marks, M. (2023). AI-generated medical advice-GPT and beyond. *Journal of the American Medical Association*, 329(16), 1349–1350. 10.1001/jama.2023.532136972070

Jadon, A., & Kumar, S. (2023). *Leveraging generative AI models for synthetic data generation in healthcare: balancing research and privacy*. arXivorg.

Jasper. (2020). *The 16 Best GPT-3 Tools To Help You Write Faster*. Jasper. https://www.jasper.ai/blog/gpt3-tools

Kanjee, Z., Crowe, B., & Rodman, A. (2023). Accuracy of a generative artificial intelligence model in a complex diagnostic challenge. *Journal of the American Medical Association*, 330(1), 78–80. 10.1001/jama.2023.828837318797

Khan, R. A., Jawaid, M., Khan, A. R., & Sajjad, M. (2023). ChatGPT-reshaping medical education and clinical management. *Pakistan Journal of Medical Sciences*, 39(2), 605. 10.12669/pjms.39.2.765336950398

Kline, A., Wang, H., Li, Y., Dennis, S., Hutch, M., Xu, Z., Wang, F., Cheng, F., & Luo, Y. (2022). Multimodal machine learning in precision health: A scoping review. *NPJ Digital Medicine*, 5(1), 171. 10.1038/s41746-022-00712-836344814

Kocaballi, A. B., Ijaz, K., Laranjo, L., Quiroz, J. C., Rezazadegan, D., Tong, H. L., Willcock, S., Berkovsky, S., & Coiera, E. (2020). Envisioning an artificial intelligence documentation assistant for future primary care consultations: A co-design study with general practitioners. *Journal of the American Medical Informatics Association : JAMIA*, 27(11), 1695–1704. 10.1093/jamia/ocaa13132845984

Korngiebel, D. M., & Mooney, S. D. (2021). Considering the possibilities and pitfalls of Generative Pre-trained Transformer 3 (GPT-3) in healthcare delivery. *NPJ Digital Medicine*, 4(1), 93. 10.1038/s41746-021-00464-x34083689

Kothari, A. N. (2023). ChatGPT, large language models, and generative ai as future augments of surgical cancer care. *Annals of Surgical Oncology*, 30(6), 3174–3176. 10.1245/s10434-023-13442-237052826

Lan, L., You, L., Zhang, Z., Fan, Z., Zhao, W., Zeng, N., Chen, Y., & Zhou, X. (2020). Generative adversarial networks and its applications in biomedical informatics. *Frontiers in Public Health*, 8, 164. 10.3389/fpubh.2020.0016432478029

Lecler, A., Duron, L., & Soyer, P. (2023). Revolutionizing radiology with GPT-based models: Current applications, future possibilities and limitations of ChatGPT. *Diagnostic and Interventional Imaging*, 104(6), 269–274. 10.1016/j.diii.2023.02.00336858933

Limeros, S. C., Majchrowska, S., Zoubi, M. K., Ros'en, A., Suvilehto, J., Sjöblom, L., & Kjellberg, M. J. (2022). *GAN-based generative modelling for dermatological applications - comparative study*. ArXiv.

Liu, S., Wright, A. P., Patterson, B. L., Wanderer, J. P., Turer, R. W., Nelson, S. D., McCoy, A. B., Sittig, D. F., & Wright, A. (2023). Using AI-generated suggestions from ChatGPT to optimize clinical decision support. *Journal of the American Medical Informatics Association : JAMIA*, 30(7), 1237–1245. 10.1093/jamia/ocad07237087108

Meskó, B., & Topol, E. J. (2023). The imperative for regulatory oversight of large language models (or generative AI) in healthcare. *NPJ Digital Medicine*, 6(1), 120. 10.1038/s41746-023-00873-037414860

Naskar, R. (2023). Google Bard Extensions May Be Coming Soon to Compete with ChatGPT. Neowin. Available online: https://www.neowin.net/news/google-bard-extensions-may-be-coming-soon-to-compete-with-chatgpt/

OpenAI. (2020). *GPT-3 Powers the Next Generation of Apps*. Open AI. https://openai.com/blog/gpt-3-apps/

OpenAI. (2023a). *Chat Plugins—Introduction*. Open AI. https://platform.openai.com/docs/plugins/introduction

OpenAI. (2023b). *ChatGPT Plugins*. OpenAI. https://openai.com/blog/chatgpt-plugins

OpenAI. (2024). *API Reference*. OpenAI API. https://platform.openai.com/docs/api-reference/introduction

Patel, A., & Arasanipalai, A. (2021). *Applied Natural Language Processing in the Enterprise: Teaching Machines to Read, Write, and Understand*. O'Reilly Media. https://www.oreilly.com/library/view/applied-natural-language/9781492062561/ch01.html

Patel, S. B., & Lam, K. (2023). ChatGPT: The future of discharge summaries? *The Lancet. Digital Health*, 5(3), e107–e108. 10.1016/S2589-7500(23)00021-336754724

Petal/Paladin Max, Inc. (2023). *GPT-Trainer*. Petal/Paladin Max. https://gpt-trainer.com/

Radford, A. (2017). *Rafal Jozefowicz, and Ilya Sutskever. Learning to Generate Reviews and Discovering Sentiment*.

Radford, A. (2018). *Improving Language Understanding with Unsupervised Learning*. Technical Report.

Radford, A. (2019). *Language Models are Unsupervised Multitask Learners*. Technical Report.

Reddy, S. (2024). Generative AI in healthcare: An implementation science informed translational path on application, integration and governance. *Implementation Science : IS*, 19(1), 27. 10.1186/s13012-024-01357-938491544

Reddy, S., Fox, J., & Purohit, M. P. (2019). Artificial intelligence-enabled healthcare delivery. *Journal of the Royal Society of Medicine*, 112(1), 22–28. 10.1177/014107681881551030507284

Sabzalieva, E., & Valentini, A. (2023). *ChatGPT and Artificial Intelligence in Higher Education: Quick Start Guide*. UNESCO. https://www.iesalc.unesco.org/wp-content/uploads/2023/04/ChatGPT-and-Artificial-Intelligence-in-higher-education-Quick-Start-guide_EN_FINAL.pdf

Sallam, M. (2023). ChatGPT utility in healthcare education, research, and practice: Systematic review on the promising perspectives and valid concerns. *Health Care*, 11, 887.36981544

Savage, N. (2023). Drug discovery companies are customizing ChatGPT: Here's how. *Nature Biotechnology*, 41(5), 585–586. 10.1038/s41587-023-01788-737095351

Srivastava, J., Routray, S., Ahmad, S., & Waris, M. M. (2022). Internet of Medical Things (IoMT)-Based Smart Healthcare System: Trends and Progress. *Computational Intelligence and Neuroscience*, 2022, 7218113. 10.1155/2022/721811335880061

Suthar, A.C., Joshi, V., & Prajapati, R. (2022). *A review of generative adversarial-based networks of machine learning/artificial intelligence in healthcare*. Academic Press.

Takefuji, Y. (2023). A brief tutorial on generative AI. *British Dental Journal*, 234(12), 845. 10.1038/s41415-023-6041-037349417

Tao, R., & Xu, J. (2023). Mapping with ChatGPT. *ISPRS International Journal of Geo-Information*, 12(7), 284. 10.3390/ijgi12070284

Thampapillai, D. (2023). Two Authors Are Suing OpenAI for Training ChatGPT with Their Books. Could They Win? *The Conversation.*https://theconversation.com/two-authors-are-suing-openai-for-training-chatgpt-with-their-books-could-they-win-209227

Uprety, D., Zhu, D., & West, H. J. (2023). ChatGPT-a promising generative AI tool and its implications for cancer care. *Cancer*, 129(15), 2284–2289. 10.1002/cncr.3482737183438

van Schalkwyk, G. (2023). Artificial intelligence in pediatric behavioral health. *Child and Adolescent Psychiatry and Mental Health*, 17(1), 38. 10.1186/s13034-023-00586-y36907862

VanBuskirk, A. (2023). A Brief History of the Generative Pre-Trained Transformer (GPT) Language Models. *Wordbot.*https://blog.wordbot.io/ai-artificial-intelligence/a-brief-history-of-the-generative-pre-trained-transformer-gpt-language-models/

Vaswani, A., Shazeer, N., Parmar, N., Uszkoreit, J., Jones, L., Gomez, A. N., Kaiser, Ł., & Polosukhin, I. (2017). *Attention Is All You Need*. In Advances in Neural Information Processing Systems, Denver, CO, USA. https://papers.nips.cc/paper_files/paper/2017/file/3f5ee243547dee91fbd053c1c4a845aa-Paper.pdf (accessed on 12 Dec 2023).

Velvárt, A. (2023). *How Will AI Affect User Interfaces?* Linkedin. https://www.linkedin.com/pulse/how-ai-affect-user-interfaces-andr%2525C3%2525A1s-velv%2525C3%2525A1rt/

Venkatesh, K. P., Brito, G., & Kamel Boulos, M. N. (2024). Health Digital Twins in Life Science and Health Care Innovation. *Annual Review of Pharmacology and Toxicology*, 64(1), 159–170. 10.1146/annurev-pharmtox-022123-02204637562495

Vert, J. P. (2023). How will generative AI disrupt data science in drug discovery? *Nature Biotechnology*, 41(6), 750–751. 10.1038/s41587-023-01789-637156917

Westerlund M. (2019). The emergence of deepfake technology: a review. *TIM Review, 9*. .10.22215/timreview/1282

Wong, B. (2023). *How Generative AI is Changing the Game in Healthcare*. LinkedIn. https://www.linkedin.com/pulse/future-here-how-generative-ai-changing-game-healthcare/

Xue, V. W., Lei, P., & Cho, W. C. (2023). The potential impact of ChatGPT in clinical and translational medicine. *Clinical and Translational Medicine*, 13(3), e1216. 10.1002/ctm2.121636856370

Yang, J., Wang, M., Zhou, H., Zhao, C., & Zhang, W. (2020). *Towards Making the Most of bert in Neural Machine Translation*. Proceedings of the AAAI Conference on Artificial Intelligence. 10.1609/aaai.v34i05.6479

Yang, K., Ji, S., Zhang, T., Xie, Q., & Ananiadou, S. (2023). *On the evaluations of chatgpt and emotion-enhanced prompting for mental health analysis*. arXiv preprint arXiv:230403347.

Yellig, J. (2023). Where ChatGPT Fits in the Internet of Things (6 July 2023). *IoT World Today (Informa)*. https://www.iotworldtoday.com/connectivity/where-chatgpt-fits-in-the-internet-of-things

YouTube. (2023). *Can AI Code Beat Saber? Watch ChatGPT Try* [Video]. YouTube. https://www.youtube.com/watch?v=E2rktIcLJwo

Chapter 16
FutureCare:
AI Robots Revolutionizing Health and Healing

Jaspreet Kaur
http://orcid.org/0000-0002-3587-6841
Chandigarh University, India

ABSTRACT

FutureCare represents a fundamental change in the way healthcare is provided, as AI robots are transforming the field of health and recovery. The success of this change relies on the incorporation of artificial intelligence (AI) and robots to increase the capacities of healthcare professionals, improve patient results, and optimize the allocation of resources. The revolution in question encompasses several key buzzwords, namely AI-enabled healthcare, precision diagnostics, individualized therapies, robotic surgeries, rehabilitative care, remote monitoring, and operational efficiency. Although AI-powered medical robots show promise, there are several problems that need to be addressed in order to fully harness their potential. These challenges include regulatory constraints, ethical considerations, and accessibility barriers. However, FutureCare offers extensive options that have the ability to revolutionize healthcare delivery, enhance patient experiences, and advance health equity worldwide.

INTRODUCTION

Within the healthcare industry, where the risks are significant and the requirements are continuously increasing, the incorporation of artificial intelligence (AI) and robots has emerged as a powerful catalyst, bringing about a period of exceptional innovation and effectiveness (Kaur, 2024; Khang, 2024). The combination of technology has

DOI: 10.4018/979-8-3693-3731-8.ch016

the potential to completely transform health and healing, fundamentally changing our understanding, approach, and provision of healthcare services. Welcome to the era of Future-care, when artificial intelligence robots occupy a prominent position in driving trans-formative changes, with the potential to fundamentally alter the healthcare industry. The integration of AI and robots in healthcare signifies a fundamental change, providing a range of talents that beyond the constraints of conventional medical procedures. These intelligent robots possess the ability to learn, adapt, and empathize, which were previously considered exclusive to humans, making them more than just tools. They serve as companions, partners, and caretakers. AI robots are driving a revolution in various fields, including precision diagnostics, tailored therapies, surgical precision, and rehabilitative care. This transformation has significant consequences for patients, practitioners, and politicians (Kumar et al., 2023). The core of this trans-formative movement centers around the notion of AI-enabled healthcare, wherein sophisticated algorithms and robotic systems collaborate to increase the abilities of healthcare practitioners, improve patient results, and optimize the allocation of resources as presented in Figure 1.

FutureCare

Figure 1. Core concept of AI-enabled healthcare

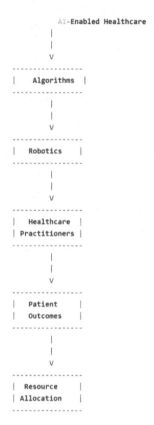

Through the utilization of machine learning, data analytic, and sensor technologies, these intelligent systems possess the capability to interpret intricate medical data, detect recurring trends, and produce practical insights with unparalleled efficiency and precision. AI algorithms are revolutionizing the field of medicine by evaluating medical pictures, predicting illness progression, and providing therapy recommendations (Minopoulos et al., 2023; Soljacic et al., 2024). This empowers doctors by equipping them with new knowledge and decision-making tools. Moreover, artificial intelligence (AI) robots are beyond the limitations of clinical environments, expanding their scope to include preventive healthcare, remote surveillance, and help in residential settings. These autonomous agents are equipped with a variety of sensors, actuators, and communication interfaces. They can monitor vital signs, manage medication adherence, and make prompt treatments. That helps patients with chronic diseases or impairments feel better and more independent. AI robots are reducing the strain on healthcare systems and empowering individuals to manage their health and well-being by promoting continuity of treatment and enabling early interventions (Kaur, 2024). Furthermore, the use of robots into surgical practice is transforming the domain of minimally invasive operations, providing surgeons with unparalleled accuracy, agility, and command. Robotic surgical systems, like the da Vinci Surgical System, empower surgeons to carry out intricate procedures with improved accuracy and effectiveness, resulting in decreased surgical trauma, reduced blood loss, and expedited patient recovery. Through the utilization of sophisticated imaging techniques, instantaneous feedback systems, and teleoperate interfaces, these robotic platforms are broadening the boundaries of surgical advancement, facilitating the execution of treatments that were previously considered impractical or hazardous, while ensuring exceptional levels of safety and effectiveness (Khaddad at al., 2023; Barua, 2024; Olawade et al.,2024). AI robots are leading the way in rehabilitative care, providing individualized interventions and adaptive therapies to persons recovering from injury or impairment, going beyond the limitations of the operating room (Kim et al.,2023; Khaddad at al., 2023; Deo & Anjankar 2023).

In nutshell, the amalgamation of artificial intelligence (AI) and robotics signifies a pivotal juncture in the progression of healthcare, signaling a forthcoming era wherever accuracy, customization, and empowerment intersect to reinvent the potentialities of well-being and recuperation. AI robots have the potential to significantly transform various aspects of healthcare delivery, encompassing diagnosis, therapy, rehabilitation, and remote monitoring. It is critical that we understand the significant influence AI robots are having on the healthcare sector as we set out on this trip across the digital frontier as represented in Figure 2 (Valles-Peris & Domènech, 2023).

Figure 2. Use of AI-powered robots in healthcare sector

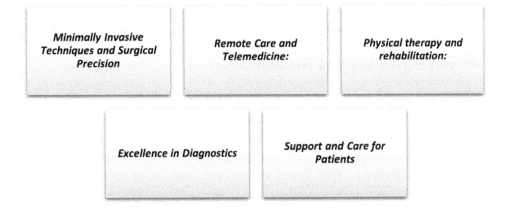

Minimally Invasive Techniques and Surgical Precision

Artificial intelligence (AI) robots have proven invaluable in the surgical profession, providing previously unattainable levels of accuracy. Patients benefit from shortened recovery periods and fewer complications when surgeons can conduct complex procedures with greater accuracy and little evasiveness thanks to surgical robots like the da Vinci Surgical System (Deo & Anjankar 2023).

Excellence in Diagnostics

Artificial intelligence (AI) robots are developing quickly as diagnostic tools. They can help medical practitioners spot diseases and anomalies by analyzing patient data and medical imagery. The early disease detection capabilities of these robots increase the likelihood of a successful course of therapy and recovery.

Support and Care for Patients

AI robots are acting as companions, carers, and educators for patients, offering tremendous assistance. They help patients remember to take their medications, offer them emotional support, and inform others about their medical conditions, all of which improve patient participation and treatment plan adherence.

Remote Care and Telemedicine

AI robots have made remote medical consultations and ongoing patient monitoring possible in telemedicine. This invention changes the way medical services are provided by expanding access to healthcare for people living in rural or under-served locations (Ragno at al., 2023; Maleki Varnosfaderani & Forouzanfar, 2024).

Physical Therapy and Rehabilitation

Artificial intelligence (AI) robots are revolutionizing physical therapy and rehabilitation by helping patients regain their mobility and improve their quality-of-life following operations or accidents. They give therapeutic activities regularity and accuracy, which improves patient outcomes (Kumar et al., 2023; Minopoulos et al., 2023).

ROBOTIC SURGICAL ASSISTANTS: INCREASING ACCURACY AND MINIMALLY SURGICAL PROCEDURES

The use of robotic surgical assistants in the operating room, like the da Vinci Surgical System, has increased dramatically. Surgeons may now execute minimally invasive treatments with increased precision and greater visualization thanks to these cutting-edge robotic, artificial intelligence, and teleoperate devices (Khaddad at al., 2023).

Surgical Accuracy

Robotic surgical systems come with a 3D high-definition camera that gives an immersive view of the surgical site and extremely precise instruments. Surgeons possess exceptional dexterity in using the robotic arms, executing complex movements with precision down to the millimetre. Reduction of hand tremors and ability to perform steady, graduated movements are two factors that lead to increased accuracy, especially during small operations such as microsurgery, urological surgery, and cardio thoracic surgery (Kim et al.,2023).

Lean and Compact Capabilities

The capacity of robotic surgery to facilitate minimally invasive procedures—which call for smaller incisions—is one of its main benefits. Patients experience less discomfort, quicker recuperation periods, and less scars as a result. Robotic systems are excellent in minimally invasive surgeries like colorectal, gynecological, and laparoscopic procedures for gallbladder removal. Compared to typical laparoscopic equipment, the robot's articulating arms can more easily manoeuvre through confined places (Rivero-Moreno et al., 2023).

Effective Use in a Range of Surgical Specialties

Urology: Protectorates and kidney operations are among the many urological procedures for which the da Vinci Surgical System has been widely utilized. With less blood loss and shorter hospital stays, it provides surgeons with unmatched precision and better results.

Gynaecology: Hysterectomies and myomectomies are two gynecological treatments that use robotic surgery. The precise motions of the robot are especially helpful in protecting the surrounding organs and tissues (Yeisson et al., 2023).

Cardio-thoracic Surgery: Robots have been used in heart surgery procedures such as mitral valve repair and coronary artery bypass grafting (CABG). The patient suffers less damage when the robotic arms reach hard-to-reach parts of the heart.

General Surgery: A range of general surgical procedures, including weight-loss bariatric surgery, hernia repair, and cholecystectomy (removal of the gallbladder), are performed with robotic systems. Shorter hospital stays and less postoperative discomfort are advantages for these applications.

ENT (Ear, Nose, and Throat) Surgery: Robotic devices are becoming more and more common in ENT surgery. They make it possible to remove tumours precisely from hard-to-reach places like the sinuses or throat.

Neurosurgery: Robots have been employed in neurosurgical treatments to help with tumour removal and deep brain stimulation, while their use is not as common as it is in other fields.

Robotic surgical devices have transformed the medical industry by giving doctors new capabilities and enhancing patient outcomes. They have not only facilitated easier access to intricate treatments but have also made remote surgery possible, allowing a surgeon to do surgery on a patient who is in a different place (Lochan et al., 2023).

ROBOTIC NURSING AND CARE-GIVING: PROGRESS IN THE CARE OF PATIENTS AND BEYOND

Robots that can provide nursing and care are a promising new development in healthcare technology. These robots are made to help with several parts of patient care, such as keeping an eye on vital signs, giving medication, and being a friend. In a range of healthcare settings, they have the potential to improve patient well-being and lessen the workload for medical staff as represented in Figure 3.

Figure 3. Advantages of robotic nursing and care-giving in the care of patients and beyond

Robotic nursing and care-giving have had a substantial impact by improving patient safety and the quality of care provided. Robots that are outfitted with sensors, cameras, and artificial intelligence algorithms have the capability to monitor the vital signs of patients, identify alterations in their health condition, and promptly notify healthcare providers of any hazards or emergencies. For example, robotic caregivers have the capability to consistently monitor the heart rate, blood pressure, and respiration rate of patients, so offering immediate input to healthcare professionals and enabling prompt action in the event of a decline in health. Robotic caregivers mitigate the potential for human mistake and promote consistent, high-quality patient care by automating regular tasks such as medication reminders, wound care, and mobility support (Matsuzaki et al., 2023).

Furthermore, the utilization of robotic nursing and caring relieves healthcare personnel from their workload, allowing them to concentrate on activities that necessitate human judgment, empathy, and knowledge. Through the automation of monotonous and laborious tasks, such as transferring patients, performing bed baths, and delivering meals, robotic caregivers enable nurses and caregivers to allocate more significant time to patients, attending to their emotional and psycho social requirements. In addition to enhancing job satisfaction and mitigating burnout among healthcare professionals, this intervention also contributes to the improvement of the entire patient experience by cultivating a therapeutic atmosphere that promotes healing and recovery (Kaur, 2024).

Robotic nursing and caring have the potential to tackle the social and economic issues related to an aging population and increasing healthcare expenses, in addition to their therapeutic uses. The increasing global incidence of chronic diseases and age-related ailments is anticipated to result in a significant increase in the need for long-term care and support services in the forthcoming decades. Robotic caretakers provide a cost-efficient and expandable option to address the increasing need for support in doing everyday tasks, offering companionship, and facilitating social engagement for older adults and individuals with impairments (Kato et al., 2023). In addition, the incorporation of robotic nursing and caring into healthcare delivery models presents novel prospects for innovation and collaboration among several academic fields. Research teams from different fields are investigating new uses of robotics in fields like rehabilitation, mental health, and palliative care. They are utilizing advancements in robotics, AI, and human-computer interaction to create customized interventions that meet the specific requirements of patients and caregivers (Matsuzaki et al., 2023). Nevertheless, although the notable advancements achieved in the field of robotic nursing and caring, there exist a number of obstacles that must be confronted in order to fully harness their capabilities. The existing robotic systems are limited in their capacity to do complicated and nuanced activities that require fine motor skills and human judgment due to technical constraints, such as a lack of dexterity and adaptability (Ohneberg et al., 2023).

AI-POWERED DISEASE DIAGNOSTICS AND THERAPY: TRANSFORMING MEDICAL FIELD

Healthcare professionals now use artificial intelligence (AI) to understand medical data and prescribe treatments. AI has become a potent tool in the diagnosis and treatment of disease. When incorporated into healthcare systems, AI robots have the potential to greatly increase the precision and effectiveness of illness diagnosis and treatment as depicted in Figure 4 (Alowais et al., 2023).

Figure 4. AI-powered disease diagnostics and therapy in the medical field

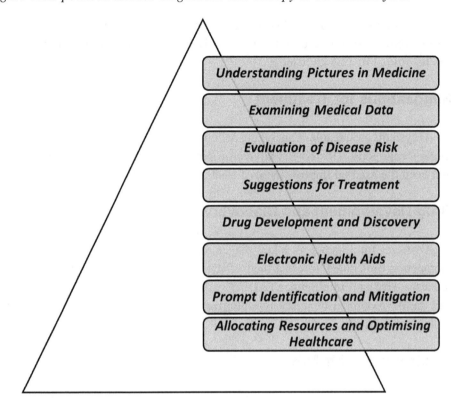

Understanding Pictures in Medicine

The analysis of medical pictures, including MRIs, CT scans, X-rays, and histopathology slides, is being done by AI robots more and more. They are remarkably accurate in recognizing many disorders, including fractures, tumors, and abnormalities (Kaur, 2024).

Examining Medical Data

Massive volumes of patient data, including as genetic data, medical histories, and electronic health records (EHRs), can be processed by AI robots. They are able to spot trends, patterns, and risk indicators that human clinicians would overlook. Based on past patient data, machine learning models can forecast the course of a disease, the outcomes of patients, and how well a patient will respond to therapy. This makes healthcare more individualized and efficient (Harry, 2023).

Evaluation of Disease Risk

AI systems are able to determine a person's genetic, lifestyle, and medical history-based risk for certain diseases. Early intervention and preventative efforts can be guided by this knowledge.

Suggestions for Treatment

AI systems are capable of analyzing patient data and recommending individualized therapy regimens. This covers advice on prescription drugs, surgical procedures, and even the gradual improvement of treatment plans (Ali, 2023).

Drug Development and Discovery

Artificial Intelligence is a key player in drug discovery, helping to find new therapeutic molecules, forecast their efficacy, and expedite the drug development process. Artificial intelligence (AI) robots assist in the discovery of drug targets and the development of innovative pharmaceuticals by evaluating molecular and biological data.

Electronic Health Aids

Virtual health assistants with AI capabilities can communicate with patients, respond to inquiries about health, and offer details on ailments, therapies, and recuperation times. They can provide telemedicine services, which include medication reminders, treatment plan adherence, and prompt medical intervention as needed.

Prompt Identification and Mitigation

Artificial intelligence (AI) robots are extremely useful for early disease detection and timely intervention. AI is capable of analyzing speech biomarkers, for instance, to find early indicators of conditions like Alzheimer's and Parkinson's (Ahmad et al., 2023).

Allocating Resources and Optimizing Healthcare

By forecasting patient admission rates, controlling bed availability, and optimizing logistics to guarantee effective healthcare delivery, AI can assist healthcare organizations in allocating resources as efficiently as possible (Ali, 2023). Although AI has great potential for diagnosing and treating diseases, there are still issues to be resolved. These include worries about data protection, bias in AI algorithms, regulatory supervision, and the requirement for AI to collaborate and function seamlessly with healthcare personnel.

REHABILITATION AND PHYSICAL THERAPY: THE ROLE OF AI ROBOTS IN TRANSFORMING PATIENT RECOVERY

Physical therapy and rehabilitation are essential parts of healthcare for those recuperating from illnesses, surgeries, or injuries. In this area, AI-powered robots are becoming more and more important, helping patients regain their mobility and enhance their general quality of life. We'll talk about how AI-equipped robots are changing physical therapy and rehabilitation in this conversation.

Tailored Treatment Programme

AI robots are able to generate customized rehabilitation programme according to the unique requirements, state, and advancement of every patient. As the patient's abilities advance, these plans adjust throughout time to ensure the best possible outcome (Abbasimoshaei et al., 2023).

Repeated and Accurate Motions

Robotic devices are essential for rehabilitation because they offer highly controlled and regular movements. They can help patients restore strength, flexibility, and coordination by specifically targeting and strengthening particular muscle areas.

Enhancing Mobility and Gait Training

Exoskeletons and other mobility-assistance robots help patients regain their ability to walk following surgery or injury. By providing stability and support, these gadgets aid patients in regaining their self-assurance and independence (Mahmoud et al., 2023).

Rehabilitating Neurological Damage

Patients with neurological disorders including stroke, spinal cord injuries, or traumatic brain traumas are rehabilitated with AI robots. They offer rigorous, ongoing therapy, which is frequently required for healing.

FutureCare

Constant Observation and Input

Throughout therapy sessions, robots with sensors track a patient's progress continuously. Real-time AI systems evaluate this data and give patients and therapists prompt feedback (Stasevych & Zvarych, 2023).

Rehabilitation by Distance

Patients can receive therapy at home while staying in contact with medical personnel thanks to tele-rehabilitation robots. Patients with restricted mobility or those living in distant places will find this especially helpful.

Cutting Back on Therapist Caseload

AI robots relieve the physical strain on therapists by performing repetitive actions and exercises. This enables therapists to provide more customized care and concentrate on more difficult tasks (Murakami et al., 2023).

Improved Involvement of Patients

By adding games, virtual reality, and other interactive components, AI robots can enhance therapy sessions. This may encourage patients to pursue their rehabilitation more steadily.

Safety and Fall Prevention

A primary priority throughout rehabilitation is safety. By giving patients stability and support during difficult exercises or when they are relearning how to walk, robots can help reduce the risk of falls and accidents (Stasevych & Zvarych, 2023).

Monitoring Progress

AI robots keep thorough records of a patient's progress, which can be useful for insurers and healthcare professionals to evaluate the efficacy of therapy and make well-informed judgments about treatment regimens. AI-enabled physical therapy and rehabilitation not only expedites the healing process but also improves the overall efficacy of these treatments. A level of consistency and precision that can be difficult to accomplish with conventional therapy methods is provided by AI robots. They also give patients the ability to actively participate in their own treatment since they allow them to track their development and make modifications in response to immediate feedback.

PATIENT INVOLVEMENT AND EDUCATION: PROVIDING AI-POWERED ROBOTS TO EMPOWER PATIENTS

Modern healthcare must include patient education and involvement, and AI-powered robots are making great progress in these areas. These interactive tools for patient education, medication reminders, and progress monitoring are these robots. They may be able to enhance patient adherence and results by doing this (Al Kuwaiti et al., 2023).

Information and Education on Health

Robots with artificial intelligence (AI) capabilities can give patients important information about their ailments, available treatments, and general health. They have the ability to clearly and simply explain difficult medical ideas, enabling patients to make decisions regarding their care.

Reminders for Medication

Treatment failure might result from a common problem called medication non-adherence. Artificial intelligence (AI) robots can remind patients when to take their prescriptions by sending them timely reminders. Some robots are even capable of directly dispensing medication (Božić, 2023).

Vital Signs Monitoring

Certain artificial intelligence (AI) robots come with sensors that let them keep an eye on things like blood pressure, heart rate, and blood sugar levels. Healthcare professionals can use this information to remotely monitor a patient's progress.

Tailored Care Schemes

AI systems are capable of analyzing patient data to create individualized care plans that consider the patient's goals for treatment, lifestyle, and medical history. When the patient's needs change, these care plans can be modified (Varshney & Dev, 2023).

Integration of Telemedicine

AI-driven robots can help with telemedicine consultations, setting up remote examinations, follow-up visits, and consultations between patients and medical professionals. Patients in isolated areas or those with restricted mobility will particularly benefit from this.

Engagement and Gamification

Gamification is a common feature used by AI robots in their interactions with patients. They encourage patients to adhere to their treatment regimens by transforming health-related tasks into entertaining games (Nwadiokwu, 2023).

Help with Emotions

Certain AI robots are intended to offer patients emotional support, particularly those who are coping with long-term medical conditions or psychological problems. They can reduce feelings of loneliness by providing company and a sympathetic ear.

Support for Physical Therapy and Rehabilitation

Artificial intelligence (AI)-driven robots can assist patients with exercises, offer performance feedback, and track their development in the context of physical therapy and rehabilitation. In particular, people recuperating from surgery or injuries may find this very helpful.

Visualisation of Health Data

AI robots have the ability to visualize a patient's medical data, which helps patients better grasp their trends and development over time. Patients may be encouraged to stick to better routines by this visual feedback (Kaur, 2024).

Privacy and Data Security

Privacy of patient data is a top priority. For sensitive medical data to be protected, AI robots need to be outfitted with strong security features. The goal of incorporating AI-powered robots into patient education and engagement is to improve patient empowerment, treatment plan adherence, and general well-being. Healthcare practitioners may provide more efficient and individualized care by employing AI, which will enhance patient outcomes and satisfaction.

REGULATION AND ETHICAL ISSUES IN THE APPLICATION OF ARTIFICIAL INTELLIGENCE ROBOTS IN HEALTHCARE

AI robots have a lot of potential for the healthcare industry, but there are also a lot of ethical and legal issues to be resolved. It is crucial to address concerns like privacy, data security, bias in AI algorithms, and regulatory monitoring in order to guarantee the ethical and responsible application of AI in healthcare.

Data Security and Privacy

Artificial intelligence (AI) robots gather and handle private patient data, such as vital signs, diagnostic data, and medical records. Ensuring the privacy of patients is crucial. Healthcare providers are responsible for making sure that patient data is transferred, stored, and accessed securely. Strong encryption, access restrictions, and frequent security audits are essential for preventing breaches and unauthorized access to patient data (Wang et al., 2023).

AI Algorithm Bias

Biases in the training data may be inherited by AI algorithms utilized in the healthcare industry. As a result, certain demographic groups may be disproportionately affected by differences in diagnostic and treatment recommendations. Healthcare companies should use transparent and audit able AI technologies to reduce bias. Regular audits of datasets and algorithms can assist in locating and addressing bias (Tigard et al., 2023).

Knowledgeable Assent

Patients have a right to know what information will be gathered and how AI robots will be used to their care. Patients must be given the ability to make decisions about the use of AI in their care through the implementation of informed consent procedures.

Explain Ability and Transparency

Healthcare professionals and patients may find it difficult to comprehend the inner workings of AI algorithms due to their potential for complexity. AI systems should be able to explain their decisions and be transparent in order to foster confidence (Tang et al., 2023).

Liability and Accountability

Ascertaining accountability in situations where AI machines make mistakes or produce unfavourable results can be difficult. In order to safeguard patients and healthcare providers alike, precise norms regarding responsibility and liability are required.

Supervisory Authority

Regulations governing the use of AI in healthcare must be established and updated by healthcare regulatory bodies. Regulations should be flexible enough to accommodate new developments in healthcare and technology.

Education and Training

Healthcare workers must receive training in order to use AI systems in an ethical and successful manner. This involves being aware of when to use clinical judgement and when to trust AI advice (Tukhtakhodjaeva & Khayitova, 2023).

Patient Self-Governance

Although AI can suggest treatments, individuals should always have the last word in their care. The patient's ability to actively participate in their healthcare should not be diminished by the usage of AI (Tang et al., 2023).

Data Sharing and Interoperability

AI robots may require access to a variety of patient data sources in order to deliver the best care possible. Practical and ethical challenges include ensuring healthcare systems are interoperable and sharing data in a secure manner.

Ongoing Assessment and Monitoring

Healthcare companies should keep a close eye on the effectiveness and moral ramifications of AI systems. Issues can be found and resolved as soon as they develop with regular assessments Regulations and standards specifically pertaining to AI in healthcare are being developed by regulatory authorities like the European Medicines Agency (EMA) and the Food and Drug Administration (FDA) in the United States. Ensuring the safety and efficacy of AI robots in healthcare environments requires adherence to certain rules (Firoozi & Firoozi, 2023).

OBSTACLES AND OPPORTUNITIES AHEAD FOR AI-POWERED MEDICAL ROBOTS

The incorporation of artificial intelligence (AI) into medical robotics signifies a fundamental change in the field of healthcare, offering the potential for significant advancements in the areas of diagnosis, treatment, and patient care as depicted in Figure 5.

Figure 5. Obstacles and opportunities ahead for AI-powered medical robots

```
                Obstacles                    Opportunities
            ---------------              ------------------
          | Regulatory   |              | Diagnostic      |
          |   Hurdles    |              |  Accuracy       |
            ---------------              |                 |
                                         | Treatment       |
                                         | Optimization    |
              Ethical and                |                 |
          Legal Considerations           | Workforce       |
            ------------------           | Optimization    |
          | Data Privacy    |            |                 |
          | Informed Consent|            | Patient         |
          | Liability       |            | Empowerment     |
            ------------------            ------------------
                                         | Operational     |
             Interoperability            | Efficiency      |
             and Integration             |                 |
            ------------------           | Remote          |
          | EHR Integration |            | Monitoring      |
          | Connectivity    |            | Virtual Care    |
          | Data Exchange   |             ------------------
            ------------------
                                         | Cost-           |
             Cost and                    | Effectiveness   |
             Accessibility               |                 |
            ------------------           | Access          |
          | Development Costs|           | Equity          |
          | Resource Allocation|          ------------------
          | Healthcare Access|
            ------------------
```

Acquiring regulatory approval requires thorough paperwork, validation studies, and strict adherence to norms, which extends the time it takes to bring a product to market and raises the expenses of development. Furthermore, the dynamic and ever-changing characteristics of AI technologies make it challenging to regulate them, requiring flexible frameworks to keep up with advancements while guaranteeing the safety and effectiveness of patients (Sahoo & Goswami, 2023). The presence of ethical and legal considerations presents supplementary obstacles, giving rise to inquiries pertaining to the privacy, autonomy, and liability of patients. The necessity for strong ethical principles and regulatory frameworks to protect patient rights and reduce risks is highlighted by concerns around data security, informed consent, and algorithmic bias. The delineation of obligations among manufacturers, healthcare providers, and regulatory authorities is necessary to address the unsolved issues of accountability and liability for errors or bad occurrences associated with autonomous robotic systems. The deployment of AI-powered medical robots inside existing healthcare ecosystems poses major technical obstacles in terms of interoperability and integration. Ensuring smooth integration into clinical workflows and maximizing productivity savings requires seamless communication with electronic health records (EHRs), medical imaging systems, and other clinical infrastructure. In order to attain interoperability, it is imperative to establish standardized data formats, open communication protocols, and foster collaboration among healthcare stakeholders. These measures are necessary to address the challenges posed by systems and facilitate the interchange of information (Fidan et al., 2023).

The broad deployment of AI-powered medical robots is hindered by significant constraints, namely cost and accessibility, especially in settings with limited resources. The exorbitant expenses related to the development, implementation, and upkeep of robotic technology restrict their accessibility to wealthy institutions and specialized facilities, hence worsening inequalities in healthcare access and results. It is crucial to prioritize the consideration of cost-effectiveness and scalability in order to promote equal access to AI-driven medical robots and expand their advantages to marginalized communities. This approach aims to facilitate fair healthcare provision and mitigate discrepancies in health outcomes. Notwithstanding these difficulties, the possibilities offered by AI-driven medical robots are extensive and diverse (Sahoo & Goswami, 2023). Through the utilization of artificial intelligence algorithms and robotic systems, healthcare providers have the potential to augment diagnostic precision, streamline the process of treatment planning, and ultimately boost patient outcomes. Artificial intelligence (AI)-enabled medical robots possess the capacity to enhance the proficiency of healthcare practitioners, facilitating accurate and customized therapies that are specifically designed to meet the unique requirements of each patient. Robotic-assisted surgeries and AI-driven diagnostic imaging are technological advancements that provide clinicians with sophisticated tools and valuable insights, enabling them to provide exceptional care and enhance clinical results.

Furthermore, medical robots driven by artificial intelligence show potential in tackling shortages in the workforce and improving operational efficiency in healthcare systems. The implementation of robotic automation in various healthcare duties, including drug administration, specimen collection, and patient monitoring, has the potential to mitigate the workload of healthcare personnel, enabling them to allocate their efforts into more intricate and valuable endeavors (Ramezani & Mohd, 2023). Furthermore, the implementation of AI-powered predictive analytic and decision support systems facilitates proactive interventions, timely identification of adverse events, and tailored treatment suggestions, hence enhancing the efficient allocation of resources and enhancing the effectiveness of healthcare delivery. Moreover, the utilization of AI-driven medical robots holds the capacity to revolutionize patient involvement and empowerment by means of tailored health surveillance, distant consultations, and virtual provision of healthcare services. AI-powered virtual health assistants and chat bots offer 24/7 assistance, provide timely health information, and enable patients to actively manage their health. Remote monitoring technologies allow for the continuous monitoring of vital signs, adherence to medicine, and progression of diseases in real-time. This capability can aid in early intervention and the prevention of complications, especially for patients with chronic illnesses or those living in geographically isolated regions (Shakeel et al., 2023).

PROSPECTS FOR THE FUTURE AND POSSIBLE ADVANCEMENTS

The potential for Future Care, characterized by the revolutionary impact of AI robots on health and healing, seems both captivating and trans formative. Although we have already observed significant progress in AI-powered healthcare, like accurate diagnostics and robotic procedures, the process of fully harnessing the capabilities of Future Care is still in its early phases. The merging of artificial intelligence (AI) with other exponential technologies, including genomics, nanotechnology, and biotechnology, presents a highly promising outlook for the future of Future-care. Through the integration of AI algorithms with genomics data, scientists may decipher the complex genetic foundations of diseases, detect new therapeutic targets, and create customized treatment plans that are specifically designed for an individual's own genetic composition. Furthermore, progress in nanorobotics has the potential to administer focused treatments, carry out less invasive procedures, and even carry out accurate molecular-level interventions within the human body, thus transforming the methods by which we diagnose and treat illnesses (Kaur, 2024).

Moreover, the emergence of artificial intelligence (AI)-powered virtual assistants and chat bots is positioned to revolutionize the patient experience by facilitating smooth interactions, tailored suggestions, and proactive interventions throughout the entire treatment process. These digital companions have the capability to offer continuous assistance, provide timely prompts for medication compliance, and provide compassionate solutions to patients' inquiries and worries, thereby promoting active involvement, empowerment, and confidence. Furthermore, in light of the widespread adoption of wearable devices and remote monitoring technologies, artificial intelligence (AI) robots have the capability to consistently monitor various health parameters of patients. These robots are capable of identifying early indicators of deterioration and taking proactive measures to prevent bad occurrences or worsening of chronic illnesses (Dicuonzo et al., 2023). AI robots have the potential to significantly transform medical education, training, and professional growth, in addition to their clinical uses. The utilization of virtual reality (VR) and augmented reality (AR) simulations has the potential to fully engage healthcare workers in authentic clinical settings, hence facilitating the practice of intricate procedures, skill refinement, and the improvement of decision-making capabilities within a secure and regulated setting. Furthermore, AI-powered adaptive learning platforms have the capability to customize instructional material according to learners' skill levels, preferred methods of learning, and specific areas of interest. This enhances the process of acquiring and retaining knowledge in many settings and fields (Biswas et al., 2023).

Moreover, the amalgamation of block chain technology with artificial intelligence robots holds the capacity to fundamentally transform the management of healthcare data, fostering interoperability and enhancing security measures. Block chain technology has the potential to offer patients a high level of control over their health data, facilitate smooth data exchange across different systems, and protect sensitive information from illegal access or manipulation. Furthermore, with the utilization of decentralized consensus procedures and cryptography techniques, block chain platforms have the capability to guarantee the integrity, immutability, and audit-ability of healthcare transactions. This, in turn, contributes to the improvement of confidence, transparency, and accountability within the healthcare system. Furthermore, the emergence of artificial intelligence (AI)-powered platforms for medication exploration and advancement presents the potential to expedite the rate of innovation, diminish the expenses associated with introducing novel treatments to the market, and tackle unresolved medical requirements in domains such as uncommon ailments, oncology, and degenerative conditions. AI robots can enhance the drug discovery process, optimize clinical trial design, and accelerate the delivery of life-saving therapies to patients by utilizing machine learning algorithms to analyze extensive collections of biological data, identify new drug targets, and forecast the effectiveness and safety of potential compounds (Khang et al., 2023; Dicuonzo et al., 2023).

SUCCESS STORIES AND CASE STUDIES: PRACTICAL APPLICATIONS OF AI ROBOTS IN HEALTHCARE

The domain of practical applications of AI robots in healthcare is replete with success stories and case studies that demonstrate the profound influence of these intelligent systems on patient outcomes, operational efficiency, and resource usage.

1. **Application of robotic technology in surgical procedures:** Robotic surgery has revolutionized the healthcare industry. The da Vinci Surgical System exemplifies the trans-formative impact of AI robots on surgical procedures. It provides exceptional accuracy and agility, enabling surgeons to carry out intricate surgeries with minimal pervasiveness. Case studies have provided evidence of its efficacy in several surgical fields, such as urology, gynecology, and general surgery. A study published in the Journal of Urology examined the results of robotic-assisted radical prostatectomy (RARP) in comparison to conventional open surgery for prostate cancer. The findings demonstrated that RARP led to reduced hospitalization duration's, decreased incidence of complications, and expedited recovery periods for patients. Previous research in the field of gynecological surgery has found that robotic-assisted operations are associated with decreased blood loss, lower incidence of postoperative problems, and better outcomes in terms of cancer treatment.

2. **Geriatric Care:** Artificial intelligence (AI) robots are being used more and more in settings where elderly care is provided in order to tackle the difficulties that arise from a growing population of older individuals. Pepper, created by SoftBank Robotics, is a prominent illustration of a robot specifically engineered to aid elderly folks residing in nursing homes and assisted living facilities. Pepper have the ability to participate in dialogue, remind individuals to adhere to their prescription schedule, and assist in organizing leisurely pursuits. An investigation conducted in a Japanese nursing home evaluated the effects of introducing Pepper, a humanoid robot, as a companion for the residents. The findings demonstrated a notable enhancement in the mood and social interaction levels of the residents. A significant number of inhabitants conveyed a sense of camaraderie and documented a decrease in emotions of isolation and melancholy. Pepper's presence significantly reduced the burden for caregivers, enabling them to prioritize delivering individualized care to residents.

3. **Remote Patient Monitoring:** Remote patient monitoring has gained significance, particularly in light of the COVID-19 epidemic. Artificial intelligence robots, coupled with advanced sensors and monitoring capabilities, are capable of providing uninterrupted supervision of patients' health conditions, even while they are physically distant. This is especially advantageous for patients with persistent illnesses who necessitate frequent monitoring and intervention.

FutureCare

An American healthcare provider undertook a case study to assess the effectiveness of AI robots in remotely monitoring patients with congestive heart failure (CHF). The robots were outfitted with sensors to track essential indicators such as blood pressure, pulse rate, and oxygen saturation levels. If there are any anomalous readings or indications of decline, the robots will promptly notify healthcare providers. The study revealed that employing AI robots for remote monitoring enabled the early identification of exacerbation and prompt therapies, resulting in a decrease in hospital re-admissions and visits to the emergency room among patients with congestive heart failure (CHF). In addition, patients expressed a greater sense of reassurance knowing that their health was being constantly checked, which led to enhanced overall satisfaction with their healthcare.

Restorative Treatment

AI robots are making notable progress in the field of rehabilitation by aiding patients in recovering mobility and functionality after injuries or surgery. Robotic exoskeletons, like the ones created by Ekso Bionics, offer help and support to people with limited mobility, allowing them to participate in treatment exercises and activities that would otherwise be difficult or unattainable. A case study conducted at a rehabilitation clinic investigated the utilization of robotic exoskeletons in patients undergoing recovery from spinal cord injuries. The study revealed that patients who received rehabilitation with the aid of robotic exoskeletons shown substantial enhancements in mobility, muscle strength, and overall functional independence in comparison to those who solely received conventional therapy. Moreover, patients expressed an increased feeling of empowerment and accomplishment as they gained the ability to engage in daily tasks with greater independence.

AI robots are revolutionizing healthcare by boosting surgical accuracy, offering companionship to the elderly, enabling remote patient monitoring, and strengthening rehabilitation results. The success stories and case studies highlight the significant capacity of AI robots to transform healthcare by enhancing patient outcomes, optimizing efficiency, and broadening access to care. With the ongoing advancement of technology, we can anticipate witnessing further groundbreaking utilization of AI robots in the field of healthcare, finally resulting in a more promising and improved state of well-being for everyone.

CONCLUSION

The incorporation of AI robots is not just a technological progress but a significant shift in perspective with extensive consequences for health and recovery. The primary advantage of AI-enabled healthcare is in its capacity to enhance the skills and talents of healthcare professionals, empower individuals seeking medical assistance, and improve the overall quality and availability of healthcare services. These intelligent technologies utilize machine learning, data analytic, and robotics to make expertise accessible to a wider audience. They also facilitate accurate diagnostics and tailor treatment plans to the specific requirements and preferences of each person. AI robots are driving a revolution in various fields such as remote consultations, robotic surgery, predictive analytic, and personalized medicine. This revolution has the potential to create healthier, happier, and more resilient communities. Furthermore, the incorporation of artificial intelligence (AI) robots into the provision of healthcare services is not alone enhancing patient outcomes, but also enhancing the allocation of resources and operational efficiencies throughout the entire care process. Intelligent systems are effectively mitigating the strain on healthcare systems, improving cost-efficiency, and broadening healthcare accessibility for marginalized people through the automation of repetitive jobs, optimization of workflows, and reduction of medical errors. AI robots are transforming the administration, management, and delivery of healthcare in the 21st century by optimizing bed management in hospitals, anticipating disease outbreaks, and coordinating emergency responses.

In addition, Future Care has the ability to bring about significant changes that go beyond clinical environments. It includes preventative care, rehabilitative interventions, and wellness promotion efforts that encourage resilience and well-being throughout one's life. Through the utilization of wearable devices, mobile applications, and intelligent sensors, artificial intelligence robots are enabling individuals to effectively monitor their health, embrace healthier lifestyles, and actively address chronic conditions. Consequently, this has resulted in a decrease in the prevalence of avoidable illnesses and the advancement of population health on a worldwide level. These intelligent systems are promoting a culture of health and well being that goes beyond traditional healthcare boundaries and empowers individuals to succeed in a more complicated and interconnected environment. They achieve this through individualized coaching, adaptive interventions, and real-time feedback mechanisms. Nevertheless, it is crucial to recognize and confront the ethical, regulatory, and societal ramifications that arise with the technological revolution of Future Care, despite its promising prospects and potential. The need to address concerns related to data privacy, algorithmic bias, and the displacement of human labor requires thorough examination. This emphasizes the importance of establishing strong governance frameworks, implementing transparency tools, and engaging stakeholders in order to protect patient rights and minimize any unintended negative outcomes. Furthermore, with the growing autonomy of AI robots in healthcare decision-making, concerns regarding accountability, liability, and informed consent arise. This highlights the necessity for ethical guidelines and regulatory measures to guarantee the responsible and ethical deployment of these intelligent systems.

In conclusion, the pursuit of Future Care holds significant potential, promise, and feasibility, as we leverage the revolutionary capabilities of AI robots to bring about a global revolution in the field of health and healing. Through the adoption of new ideas, encouraging cooperation, and giving importance to fairness and exclusivity, we can fully utilize the capabilities of AI-powered healthcare to establish a future in which every person has the opportunity to receive top-notch, tailored treatment that enhances their physical and mental health, overall welfare, and sense of self-worth. As we find ourselves at the cusp of this forthcoming epoch, let us commence this endeavor with a sense of modesty, compassion, and an unwavering dedication to pushing the boundaries of scientific inquiry, technological progress, and human well-being, all with the aim of fostering a more robust and healthier future for the entirety of humanity.

REFERENCES

Abbasimoshaei, A., Chinnakkonda Ravi, A. K., & Kern, T. A. (2023). Development of a New Control System for a Rehabilitation Robot Using Electrical Impedance Tomography and Artificial Intelligence. *Biomimetics*, 8(5), 420. 10.3390/biomimetics805042037754171

Ahmad, A., Tariq, A., Hussain, H. K., & Gill, A. Y. (2023). Revolutionizing Healthcare: How Deep Learning is poised to Change the Landscape of Medical Diagnosis and Treatment. Journal of Computer Networks. *Architecture and High-Performance Computing*, 5(2), 458–471. 10.47709/cnahpc.v5i2.2350

Al Kuwaiti, A., Nazer, K., Al-Reedy, A., Al-Shehri, S., Al-Muhanna, A., Subbarayalu, A. V., Al Muhanna, D., & Al-Muhanna, F. A. (2023). A Review of the Role of Artificial Intelligence in Healthcare. *Journal of Personalized Medicine*, 13(6), 951. 10.3390/jpm1306095137373940

Ali, M. (2023). A Comprehensive Review of AI's Impact on Healthcare: Revolutionizing Diagnostics and Patient Care. *BULLET: Jurnal Multidisiplin Ilmu*, 2(4), 1163–1173.

Alowais, S. A., Alghamdi, S. S., Alsuhebany, N., Alqahtani, T., Alshaya, A. I., Almohareb, S. N., Aldairem, A., Alrashed, M., Bin Saleh, K., Badreldin, H. A., Al Yami, M. S., Al Harbi, S., & Albekairy, A. M. (2023). Revolutionizing healthcare: The role of artificial intelligence in clinical practice. *BMC Medical Education*, 23(1), 689. 10.1186/s12909-023-04698-z37740191

Barua, R. (2024). An In-Depth Exploration of AI and Humanoid Robotics' Role in Contemporary Healthcare. In *Approaches to Human-Centered AI in Healthcare* (pp. 42–61). IGI Global. 10.4018/979-8-3693-2238-3.ch003

Biswas, S., Pillai, S., Kadhim, H. M., Salam, Z. A., & Marhoon, H. A. (2023, September). Building business resilience and productivity in the healthcare industry with the integration of robotic process automation technology. In *AIP Conference Proceedings* (Vol. 2736, No. 1). AIP Publishing. 10.1063/5.0171098

Dicuonzo, G., Donofrio, F., Fusco, A., & Shini, M. (2023). Healthcare system: Moving forward with artificial intelligence. *Technovation*, 120, 102510. 10.1016/j.technovation.2022.102510

Fidan, I., Huseynov, O., Ali, M. A., Alkunte, S., Rajeshirke, M., Gupta, A., Hasanov, S., Tantawi, K., Yasa, E., Yilmaz, O., Loy, J., Popov, V., & Sharma, A. (2023). Recent inventions in additive manufacturing: Holistic review. *Inventions (Basel, Switzerland)*, 8(4), 103. 10.3390/inventions8040103

Firoozi, A. A., & Firoozi, A. A. (2023). A systematic review of the role of 4D printing in sustainable civil engineering solutions. *Heliyon*, 9(10), e20982. 10.1016/j.heliyon.2023.e2098237928382

George, A. S., George, A. H., & Martin, A. G. (2023). ChatGPT and the Future of Work: A Comprehensive Analysis of AI's Impact on Jobs and Employment. *Partners Universal International Innovation Journal*, 1(3), 154–186.

Harry, A. (2023). The Future of Medicine: Harnessing the Power of AI for Revolutionizing Healthcare. *International Journal of Multidisciplinary Sciences and Arts*, 2(1), 36–47. 10.47709/ijmdsa.v2i1.2395

Hastuti, R., & Syafruddin, . (2023). Ethical Considerations in the Age of Artificial Intelligence: Balancing Innovation and Social Values. *West Science Social and Humanities Studies*, 1(02), 76–87. 10.58812/wsshs.v1i02.191

Kato, K., Yoshimi, T., Aimoto, K., Sato, K., Itoh, N., & Kondo, I. (2023). Reduction of multiple-caregiver assistance through the long-term use of a transfer support robot in a nursing facility. *Assistive Technology*, 35(3), 271–278. 10.1080/10400435.2022.203932435320681

Kaur, J. (2024). AI-Driven Hospital Accounting: A Path to Financial Health. In *Harnessing Technology for Knowledge Transfer in Accountancy, Auditing, and Finance* (pp. 227-250). IGI Global.

Kaur, J. (2024). Patient-Centric AI: Advancing Healthcare Through Human-Centered Innovation. In *Approaches to Human-Centered AI in Healthcare* (pp. 1-19). IGI Global.

Kaur, J. (2024). Towards a Sustainable Triad: Uniting Energy Management Systems, Smart Cities, and Green Healthcare for a Greener Future. In *Emerging Materials, Technologies, and Solutions for Energy Harvesting* (pp. 258-285). IGI Global.

Kaur, J., & Ozen, E. (2024). Masters of the Market: Unleashing Algorithmic Wizardry in Finance. In *Algorithmic Approaches to Financial Technology: Forecasting, Trading, and Optimization* (pp. 93-120). IGI Global.

Khaddad, A., Bernhard, J. C., Margue, G., Michiels, C., Ricard, S., Chandelon, K., Bladou, F., Bourdel, N., & Bartoli, A. (2023). A survey of augmented reality methods to guide minimally invasive partial nephrectomy. *World Journal of Urology*, 41(2), 335–343. 10.1007/s00345-022-04078-035776173

Khang, A. (Ed.). (2024). *Medical Robotics and AI-Assisted Diagnostics for a High-Tech Healthcare Industry*. IGI Global. 10.4018/979-8-3693-2105-8

Khang, A., Hahanov, V., Litvinova, E., Chumachenko, S., Hajimahmud, A. V., Ali, R. N., & Anh, P. T. N. (2023). The Analytics of Hospitality of Hospitals in a Healthcare Ecosystem. In *Data-Centric AI Solutions and Emerging Technologies in the Healthcare Ecosystem* (pp. 39–61). CRC Press. 10.1201/9781003356189-4

Kim, M., Zhang, Y., & Jin, S. (2023). Soft tissue surgical robot for minimally invasive surgery: A review. *Biomedical Engineering Letters*, 13(4), 1–9. 10.1007/s13534-023-00326-337872994

Kumar, P., Chauhan, S., & Awasthi, L. K. (2023). Artificial intelligence in healthcare: Review, ethics, trust challenges & future research directions. *Engineering Applications of Artificial Intelligence*, 120, 105894. 10.1016/j.engappai.2023.105894

Lochan, K., Suklyabaidya, A., & Roy, B. K. (2023). Medical and healthcare robots in India. In *Medical and Healthcare Robotics* (pp. 221–236). Academic Press. 10.1016/B978-0-443-18460-4.00010-X

Mahmoud, H., Aljaldi, F., El-Fiky, A., Battecha, K., Thabet, A., Alayat, M., & Ibrahim, A. (2023). Artificial Intelligence machine learning and conventional physical therapy for upper limb outcome in patients with stroke: A systematic review and meta-analysis. *European Review for Medical and Pharmacological Sciences*, 27(11).37318455

Maleki Varnosfaderani, S., & Forouzanfar, M. (2024). The Role of AI in Hospitals and Clinics: Transforming Healthcare in the 21st Century. *Bioengineering (Basel, Switzerland)*, 11(4), 337. 10.3390/bioengineering1104033738671759

Matsuzaki, H., & Gliesche, P. (2023). Robots and Norms of Care: A Comparative Analysis of the Reception of Robotic Assistance in Nursing. In *Social Robots in Social Institutions* (pp. 90-99). IOS Press. 10.3233/FAIA220607

Minopoulos, G. M., Memos, V. A., Stergiou, K. D., Stergiou, C. L., & Psannis, K. E. (2023). A Medical Image Visualization Technique Assisted with AI-Based Haptic Feedback for Robotic Surgery and Healthcare. *Applied Sciences (Basel, Switzerland)*, 13(6), 3592. 10.3390/app13063592

Murakami, Y., Honaga, K., Kono, H., Haruyama, K., Yamaguchi, T., Tani, M., Isayama, R., Takakura, T., Tanuma, A., Hatori, K., Wada, F., & Fujiwara, T. (2023). New Artificial Intelligence-Integrated Electromyography-Driven Robot Hand for Upper Extremity Rehabilitation of Patients With Stroke: A Randomized, Controlled Trial. *Neurorehabilitation and Neural Repair*, 37(5), 15459683231166939. 10.1177/15459683231166693937039319

Nwadiokwu, O. T. (2023). Examining the Impact and Challenges of Artificial Intelligence (AI) in Healthcare. *Edward Waters University Undergraduate Research Journal, 1*(1).

Ohneberg, C., Stöbich, N., Warmbein, A., Rathgeber, I., Mehler-Klamt, A. C., Fischer, U., & Eberl, I. (2023). Assistive robotic systems in nursing care: A scoping review. *BMC Nursing*, 22(1), 1–15. 10.1186/s12912-023-01230-y36934280

Olawade, D. B., David-Olawade, A. C., Wada, O. Z., Asaolu, A. J., Adereni, T., & Ling, J. (2024). Artificial Intelligence in Healthcare Delivery: Prospects and Pitfalls. *Journal of Medicine, Surgery, and Public Health, 100108*.

Ragno, L., Borboni, A., Vannetti, F., Amici, C., & Cusano, N. (2023). Application of Social Robots in Healthcare: Review on Characteristics, Requirements, Technical Solutions. *Sensors (Basel)*, 23(15), 6820. 10.3390/s2315682037571603

Ramezani, M., & Mohd Ripin, Z. (2023). 4D printing in biomedical engineering: Advancements, challenges, and future directions. *Journal of Functional Biomaterials*, 14(7), 347. 10.3390/jfb1407034737504842

Rivero-Moreno, Y., Echevarria, S., Vidal-Valderrama, C., Stefano-Pianetti, L., Cordova-Guilarte, J., Navarro-Gonzalez, J., & Avila, G. L. D. (2023). Robotic Surgery: A Comprehensive Review of the Literature and Current Trends. *Cureus*, 15(7). 10.7759/cureus.4237037621804

Sahoo, S. K., & Goswami, S. S. (2023). A comprehensive review of multiple criteria decision-making (MCDM) Methods: Advancements, applications, and future directions. *Decision Making Advances*, 1(1), 25–48. 10.31181/dma1120237

Schönmann, M., Bodenschatz, A., Uhl, M., & Walkowitz, G. (2023). The Care-Dependent are Less Averse to Care Robots: An Empirical Comparison of Attitudes. *International Journal of Social Robotics*, 15(6), 1–18. 10.1007/s12369-023-01003-237359432

Shakeel, T., Habib, S., Boulila, W., Koubaa, A., Javed, A. R., Rizwan, M., Gadekallu, T. R., & Sufiyan, M. (2023). A survey on COVID-19 impact in the healthcare domain: Worldwide market implementation, applications, security and privacy issues, challenges and future prospects. *Complex & Intelligent Systems*, 9(1), 1027–1058. 10.1007/s40747-022-00767-w35668731

Soljacic, F., Law, T., Chita-Tegmark, M., & Scheutz, M. (2024). Robots in healthcare as envisioned by care professionals. *Intelligent Service Robotics*, 17(3), 1–17. 10.1007/s11370-024-00523-8

Stasevych, M., & Zvarych, V. (2023). Innovative robotic technologies and artificial intelligence in pharmacy and medicine: Paving the way for the future of health care—a review. *Big Data and Cognitive Computing*, 7(3), 147. 10.3390/bdcc7030147

Tang, L., Li, J., & Fantus, S. (2023). Medical artificial intelligence ethics: A systematic review of empirical studies. *Digital Health*, 9, 20552076231186064. 10.1177/20552076231186064 37434728

Tigard, D. W., Braun, M., Breuer, S., Ritt, K., Fiske, A., McLennan, S., & Buyx, A. (2023). Toward best practices in embedded ethics: Suggestions for interdisciplinary technology development. *Robotics and Autonomous Systems*, 167, 104467. 10.1016/j.robot.2023.104467

Tukhtakhodjaeva, F. S., & Khayitova, I. I. (2023). APPLICATION AND USE OF AI (ARTIFICIAL INTELLIGENCE) IN MEDICINE. *Educational Research in Universal Sciences*, 2(9), 302–309.

Vallès-Peris, N., & Domènech, M. (2023). Caring in the in-between: A proposal to introduce responsible AI and robotics to healthcare. *AI & Society*, 38(4), 1685–1695. 10.1007/s00146-021-01330-w

Wang, C., Liu, S., Yang, H., Guo, J., Wu, Y., & Liu, J. (2023). Ethical considerations of using ChatGPT in health care. *Journal of Medical Internet Research*, 25, e48009. 10.2196/4800937566454

Yeisson, R. M., Sophia, E., Vidal-Valderrama, C., Luigi, P., Jesus, C. G., Navarro-Gonzalez, J., & Katheryn, A. A. (2023). Robotic Surgery: A Comprehensive Review of the Literature and Current Trends. *Cureus*, 15(7).37621804

Chapter 17
Generative AI Revolution:
Shaping the Future of Healthcare Innovation

Manikandan Arunachalam
Department of Electronics and Communication Engineering, Amrita Vishwa Vidyapeetham, India

Chitransh Chiranjeev
Department of Electronics and Communication Engineering, Amrita School of Engineering, India

Barshan Mondal
Department of Electronics and Communication Engineering, Amrita School of Engineering, India

Sanjay T.
http://orcid.org/0000-0001-8591-6314
JP Morgan, USA

ABSTRACT

A scarcity of data within the healthcare sector can present considerable obstacles for a range of applications, most notably in the implementation and advancement of machine learning models. Sometimes, inadequate data sets may also lead to the wrong interpretation of data with wider patient populations, forcing the models to be biased. Overfitting, where a model acquires knowledge about the features of the training data rather than underlying patterns. In cases of overfit, the models perform well on the training data, but they face difficulty with novel and unknown data. Generative adversarial networks (GANs) play a vital role in healthcare by accelerating medical research and diagnosis. Though GAN has evidenced, genuineness of the data they provide, need to adjust to the regulations to ensure the privacy

DOI: 10.4018/979-8-3693-3731-8.ch017

and security of patient information. This chapter provides an overview of current research and mutual efforts between the medical and artificial intelligence (AI) communities to maximize the potential of GANs to address healthcare challenges.

INTRODUCTION

The fusion of artificial intelligence in the ever-evolving medical landscape stands out as a transformative force that promises to revolutionize the industry. AI can improve diagnosis, improve treatment and usher in the era of personalized medicine (Gennatas and Chen 2020).

As we stand on the brink of a new healthcare paradigm, the integration of AI promises to reshape how we approach diagnostics, treatment, and patient care. This symbiosis of human expertise and machine intelligence holds the potential to revolutionize healthcare delivery, ushering in an era marked by precision, personalization, and unprecedented efficiency(Chang 2020). AI, with its ability to swiftly analyse vast datasets, decode complex patterns, and make real-time decisions, emerges as a crucial ally for healthcare professionals. Gone are the days of one-size-fits-all treatments; the future lies in tailoring medical interventions to the unique genetic makeup, lifestyle, and history of each patient. This unique approach not only improves the effectiveness of treatments but also marks a paradigm shift toward a more patient-centric healthcare system. The landscape of diagnostics is undergoing a radical transformation, courtesy of AI-powered imaging and diagnostic tools. From detecting subtle anomalies in medical scans to expediting the identification of diseases at their nascent stages, AI is redefining the accuracy and speed of diagnostic processes (Padhi et al. 2023). This not only translates to quicker treatment initiation but also significantly improves patient outcomes. Predictive analytics, fueled by AI algorithms, empowers healthcare providers to foresee disease trends, optimize resource allocation, and implement preventive strategies. The ability to anticipate health issues on a population scale not only enhances public health measures but also plays a pivotal role in shaping more resilient healthcare systems. Though AI is offering tremendous applications in the health care sector, Generative AI offers several advantages over traditional AI methods due to its unique capabilities in creating new content rather than relying solely on existing data(Fui-Hoon Nah et al. 2023). As technology continues to evolve, the transition from traditional AI to Generative AI reflects a strategic move towards harnessing the power of creativity, innovation, and dynamic content generation (Ruiz-Rojas et al. 2023). This shift is driven by a range of needs and challenges that traditional AI approaches may not fully address. Traditional AI models excel at tasks involving pattern recognition and decision-making based on existing data. However, Generative AI takes a leap forward by not only recognizing patterns but creating entirely new content (Bandi, Adapa, and Kuchi 2023). Also, traditional AI heavily relies on extensive datasets for training. In situations where obtaining large, diverse datasets is challenging or expensive, Generative AI offers a solution. This chapter discuss about the challenges with traditional AI and shaping the future of Health care with Generative AI.

RISK OF OVERFITTING IN HEALTHCARE

The main objective of modern AI approaches is to minimize overfitting, which occurs when the model master's every aspect of the training data, including creating noise within the data(Santos and Papa 2022). The other aspect that is crucial in the algorithm's performance is generalizability, which demonstrates its ability to work across different entities beyond its original training environment. Failure to fit beyond train overly frequently originates from overfitting, where the algorithm is too familiar with the training data by presenting it with things that are not important to the model, and it is therefore confused when new data that lacks them in presentation is excused. Take, for instance, a scenario where an algorithm is trained with breast cancer scans only from a specific scanner model. In this way, it will mistakenly consider scans from that model to be the only way of detecting breast cancer. Lastly, for the same reason, the algorithm cannot perform efficiently in a new hospital with a different scanner since it cannot identify crucial scanner-specific information that is necessary for an accurate diagnosis. Several measures for tackling overfitting are data set enlargement and diversification, using data augmentation, feature selection, and regularization approaches. Yet, these precautionary measures do not mitigate the degradability of the algorithms over time, due to factors like data drift, emphasizing the necessity of continuous monitoring performance up to deployment to promptly detect and fix the generalizability errors.

Examples of Overfitting in Healthcare

Using the illustration of the overfitting's impact through examples stresses the fact that it might have the same consequences in medical cases. In medical imaging, overfitting will occur when a machine learning model is instructed on a specific dataset of images like X-rays or MRI (Magnetic Resonance Imaging) scans from a single organization(Raju and Augustine 2023). If the model learns to identify patterns or features that are unique to the data set rather than generalized characteristics of the condition being diagnosed, it may perform poorly while applied to the images from different sources of patient's data set. For instance, a deep learning algorithm trained to detect tumours in brain MRI scans from one clinic may obtain high levels of accuracy on the training data set but fail to accurately identify tumours in scans from other clinics(Chattopadhyay and Maitra 2022). Another example of overfitting occurs in clinical risk prediction models, which aim to evaluate the likelihood of adverse outcomes, such as hospital readmission mortality, for individual patients. If predictive models are trained on a dataset with unfair class distributions of insufficient sample size, it may learn to memorize noise, or fake correlations present in the training data rather than capturing clinically relevant risk factors(C. Wang et al. 2023).

Possible Ways to Eliminate Overfitting

Using prediction models in medical research requires the utmost attention to combating overfitting to obtain accurate and reliable outcomes (Mawdsley, Reynolds, and Cullen 2021). Several ways of dealing with the problem have been hypothesized. Firstly, with the growing number of training inputs, important features become more prioritized, thus, it is imperative to use high-quality data sets to avoid overfitting problems. Data augmentation with differential variations offers a cost-effective alternative to extensive no additional data training because it helps to improve model robustness without having to extensively train the model. Also, the addition of noise to the input data means that the model becomes stable without incurring damage or loss of data privacy. At the same time, the introduction of noise to the output data allows for more diversity. As complex models tend to detect data redundancies and are determinable, the focus is guided towards selecting clean data to avoid complex models. So cross-validation develops as a sturdy method to fight overfitting, with the training set divided into multiple folds for calibrating and fine-tuning the model(Abbas, Hussain, and Baig 2023). Another strategy is the use of adversarial training or as it is known, synthetic training. This process involves adding a minor alteration to the data of the training set deliberately. The examples include adding blur. This augmentation will fill the gaps in the training data, thus preventing overfitting. Moreover, methods like data simplification and feature reduction are efficient in preventing overfitting probability by minimizing model complexity and removing noisy patterns (Hou and Behdinan 2022). Regularization charges the costs on parameters with larger coefficients and thus constrains model variance and complexity. Through bagging and boosting methods, belief holding of several models are brought together again to create the best predictive model and reduce the possibility of overfitting by harnessing the collective wisdom of a variety of models. Early stopping methods help the model to avoid overfitting which is when it remembers noise and random fluctuations in data, although it should be used with caution to prevent premature ending which may cause underfitting in the model (Zheng, Zhou, and Chen 2021). This ready reckoning is the key to tackling the bias-variance trade-off, which is attained by keeping the model simple and complex simultaneously, which in turn ensures that the model is both accurate and generalizable in medical applications.

GENDER BIAS IN ARTIFICIAL INTELLIGENCE WITHIN THE HEALTHCARE SECTOR

Integration of AI systems in healthcare has become a major point of development, which helps to create more convenient ways of retrieving health information and dealing with medical complications (Q. Wang et al. 2021). Nevertheless, these technologies have the risk of advancing biases, especially on the gender issue, which is a critical issue. Gender bias in AI healthcare systems may worsen existing disparities in healthcare, and benefit some and harm others of which women and the poor are among the most vulnerable. In the past, AI models with more than 70% success rate when it comes to detecting liver disease from blood test results had worse accuracy when women were involved compared to when men were the ones being tested (Lupsor-Platon et al. 2021). The research showed that the models failed to identify 44% of liver disease cases among women while in men they missed 23% of cases, which is an alarming finding (Gender Bias Revealed in AI Tools Screening for Liver Disease, 2022). On the contrary, it was seen that the use of the biochemical markers residing in the algorithm like lower albumin levels, the most common biochemical markers that clinicians utilize, seems to be more accurate in identifying the disease in men than the clinicians.

Factors Responsible for Gender Bias in AI

At the junction between AI and healthcare, different face masks and skin colors are underrepresented from both genders (Paul et al. 2022). Traditionally, male-centered clinical practices are still perpetuating gender-based specifics that do not appropriately reflect the highly diversified community. Hence, the diagnostic and therapeutic regimens designed by mainly male-oriented data can bypass or misunderstand the diseases that only affect women and therefore lead to under-diagnosis, misdiagnosis or resorting to the wrong treatment. Also, incorporating women in clinical trials and data collection is affected by social and systemic biases that in turn deepen gender inequalities in health outcomes(Carnevale et al. 2023).

Sex and gender bias in AI and health arises from various unresolved issues, including the diversity imbalance in clinical trials, poor data handling, and the absence of accountability in data collection. The absence of standardized procedures for data collection and integration hinders the goal of achieving inclusivity and representativeness in AI algorithms. Further, the complex nature of health data and the time-varied nature of underlying biases necessitate continuous adaptation and intervention strategies. The ethical aspects that involve data privacy, consent and transparency complicate the production and deployment of AI healthcare technologies more. Medical AI bias research proposes many solutions that cover a variety of components of that bias. A notable hindrance is the scarcity of data diversity that might result in biased outcomes (Drukker et al. 2023). This strategy is countered by the harmonization of data collection processes with the inclusion of gender by introducing the terms of sex and gender in the way data is collected. Among other things, integrating different data sources, for example, the healthcare data from primary care facilities and the regional social data can be beneficial, while quality improvement and explainable algorithms are very important. Such measures include data collection based on impartiality, definition of data reutilization conditions, and investments in resources for improving balance and representativeness of the dataset. Moreover, concentration on appropriate care of those who are vulnerable, mentioning the example of the Lesbian Gay Bisexual Transgender (LGBT) community, influences biomedical research on the available intersectional types of population.

The human factor and its consciousness of bias in AI are vital in terms of medical application. It is important to start initiatives that will connect people and educate them about AI opportunities, limitations, and risks are crucial. Additionally, campaigns dealing with future professionals in science, technology, engineering, and medicine are planned to educate them about the gender biases in AI to go along with the training. Activism against gender bias, together with the spread of scientific proof on sex and gender-based health disparities, might be a route to achieve the goals of personalized medical AI which is not discriminatory. AI biases need to be addressed through entire solutions within the context of fairness and societal implications. With participatory techniques involving disadvantaged communities in the whole process of AI, different perspectives of people can be integrated, and biases can be made clear (Buslón et al. 2023). Moreover, ensuring safety by the strictest standards of data handling and model deployment is also important to protect data privacy. Algorithmic review processes must be incorporated for disincentivizing outcomes; training datasets must represent the population accurately without the inclusion of bias. Addressing bias in AI for healthcare also includes regulatory issues, like financial support of projects pointed at the sex and gender bias in AI and the establishment of law-rises and certifications (Abràmoff et al. 2023). Implementations for AI practitioners and academies suggest the need for education to apply sex and gender dimensions in the research, design and use measurements to assess AI biases, and standardized data collections. Effective cooperation among different disciplines will be a key factor for developing solutions that cut through various problems in health care and AI. Certification and regulation of AI applications are emphasized by industry recommendations, staff training on data quality and fairness aspects, documentation accents, and mentioning of socio-cultural features in the processes of AI. Human society can do so through diverse participation like support for educational programs, involvement in initiatives to protect vulnerable populations, or advocacy for AI aligned with the guidelines. Policymakers and governments are encouraged to define public certification schemes and build trustworthy AI policies, to reinvest in science research and public education on gender and science. Moreover, not only promoting women leaders but also gender-sensitive policies will realize success in fighting gender bias in AI medicine.

SIGNIFICANCE OF GENERATIVE ADVERSARIAL NETWORKS (GANS) IN SYNTHETIC DATA GENERATION

GANs have been utilized for various applications such as synthesis (generating synthetic data), segmentation (producing segmentation masks), diagnosis, and translation of data from one modality to another. (e.g. From CT(Computed Tomography) to MRI and vice versa, or from normal CT to infected CT).

According to recent surveys, approximately one-third of the studies cited the usage of GANs for data synthesis, while around one-sixth indicated their utilization for segmentation. Other notable applications of GANs included diagnosis, as reported in 16 studies, followed by reconstruction in 15 studies, and translation in 12 studies.

Image Synthesis

In a situation where we are dealing with rare diseases and new applications where a dataset is not available, we apply data augmentation (for example, translation, rotation, scaling and flipping of available samples) in order to create more "new" samples. GANs provide us with the ability to synthesize completely new images to expand the datasets (Rejusha and Vipin Kumar 2021). We use this approach to make synthetic images look very similar to real images. In many research studies it has been found that unbiased observers cannot tell the difference between the real and artificial images.

For instance, there was a poll where radiologists had to pick between real or GAN-generated MRI scans. The outcome of this survey indicated that the respondents were incapable of telling real images from the fake ones. The use of GANs to generate synthetic CT scans from MRI data has shown promising results in personalized radiation therapy planning. A GAN-based approach was developed to generate CT scans with high fidelity, allowing for accurate dose calculations without additional patient exposure (Chan et al. 2023). This technology holds significant potential for reducing radiation exposure, particularly for vulnerable populations like children with cancer(Cellina et al. 2023). GANs have also been utilized to generate realistic 3D models from 2D medical images. GANs were used to generate 3D brain tumor models for virtual surgery training, allowing surgeons to practice complex procedures in a simulated environment (Su et al. 2021). This approach could improve surgical precision and reduce the risk of complications during real-world operations. Medical datasets often suffer from limitations in size and diversity. GANs can be used to create synthetic medical images to augment existing datasets, improving the performance of AI models for diagnosis, segmentation, and other tasks. GAN used to generate skin lesion images helped train an AI model to achieve higher accuracy in skin cancer diagnosis(Esteva and Topol 2019). This technique has the potential to improve the efficacy of AI-powered medical tools across various domains. The privacy of patient data is paramount in medical research. GANs offer a potential solution by generating synthetic Electronic Health Records (EHRs) that resemble real data but protect individual identities. GAN enable researchers to share data for medical research without compromising patient co(Manikandan and Sanjay 2023) nfidentiality(H. Yu and Welch 2021). This technology could accelerate medical research and development while ensuring patient privacy. GANs can serve as effective tools for modeling the spread of infectious diseases, offering valuable insights for public health interventions. GANs are also used to simulate the spread of COVID-19, helping predict future outbreaks and inform public health responses(Quilodrán-Casas et al. 2022). This approach could play a crucial role in pandemic preparedness and response efforts.

Image Reconstruction

In medical imaging, the process of acquiring and reconstructing images often entails a balance between the diagnostic quality of the images and factors such as longer acquisition times and higher radiation doses

In practice, compromises are typically made, imposing realistic constraints on image capture parameters. However, this can lead to elevated levels of noise, motion artifacts, and other distortions that may degrade the quality of the image.

In such a scenario, GANs would fill the gap between the technical limitations and optical quality that is required and at the same time reducing any imaging negative effects (N. K. Singh and Raza 2021). Among the most practical applications of GANs are those where the requirement like detector resolution or motion tracking would have otherwise accelerated the development in hardware.

A GAN can be employed for image super-resolution, enhancing the resolution of images beyond those originally acquired by scaling the image matrix. In this case, the low-resolution image is the input for the generator and the output of the generator is a high-resolution image. Another approach involves utilizing a GAN trained with paired images or a Cycle-Consistent GAN trained with unpaired images to effectively remove motion artifacts from MR images. This strategy acts as a back-up for otherwise scuttled studies. Low-dose CT scans minimize radiation exposure but often suffer from noise, impacting diagnostic accuracy. A GAN-based approach is developed that effectively removed noise from low-dose CT scans, preserving anatomical details and improving image quality(Kulathilake et al. 2021). This technology could enable safer CT imaging protocols without compromising diagnostic value. Motion artifacts and hardware limitations can lead to missing data in MRI images. (Li, Lv, and Wang 2021) proposed a GAN-based method that successfully reconstructed missing regions in MRI scans, particularly for brain and knee images. This approach could improve the diagnostic utility of incomplete MRI data and reduce the need for rescans. Limited resolution in medical images can hinder detailed analysis. GANs are able to achieve super-resolution of chest X-rays, enhancing the visibility of subtle features crucial for diagnosing lung diseases (Lee and Chin 2022). This technology holds promise for improving the accuracy of early disease detection. Combining information from different modalities like PET(Positron Emission Tomography) and CT scans can provide a more comprehensive view of patient pathology. Another GAN-based framework is presented for generating synthetic PET images from CT scans, facilitating improved PET-CT image fusion, and potentially aiding in cancer diagnosis and treatment planning(Jiang et al. 2023). Individual anatomical variations can influence diagnostic and treatment decisions.

Cross-Modality Synthesis

There are many approaches developed to target the head, pelvic, neck and cardiac regions, all of which have similar motivations to justify the use of image synthesis. All of them were aimed to solve the problem of existing image estimation. In both head and pelvic regions, a dense Cycle GAN was employed with a CT branch in MRI. In this setup, dense blocks in the generator were replaced with residual blocks, enhancing the quality of the estimated images.(Rossi and Cerveri 2021). With the incorporation of a distance loss function as well as a gradient difference loss function, blur and misclassification of image information can be compensated for.

Cross-modality image estimation techniques have become more and more appealing as a research topic of medical imaging.

It is shown that cGAN(Conditional Generative Adversarial Network) model provides higher quality image estimates than the classical GAN by both qualitative and quantitative analyses. There are two main types of cGANs, pix2pix, and CycleGAN. Pix2Pix has exhibited a better performance with paired data, while CycleGAN seems to be more suitable for unpaired data(Aljohani and Alharbe 2022).

The pix2pix network typically exhibits lower complexity compared to CycleGAN, resulting in reduced consumption of computational resources. The CycleGAN architecture is more complicated, implying the need for larger training data as well. A style transfer technique has been integrated into the conditional GAN architecture, resulting in the introduction of a generative model termed ST-cGAN (Style Transfer Conditional Generative Adversarial Network). This model incorporates hierarchical feature mapping and fusion to enhance its performance and capabilities (Qin et al. 2022).

The proposed model accepts two modalities as conditional inputs and extracts content and style features at various layers of the network. It then utilizes style transfer and feature fusion techniques on these hybrid features to generate synthetic images with enhanced style. This approach ensures that the synthetic images closely resemble the target modality images in terms of style, thereby effectively enhancing overall image quality. Traditional colonoscopy can be uncomfortable and invasive. GANs also can generate realistic 3D colon models from CT scans, enabling virtual colonoscopy for non-invasive screening and polyp detection(Mathew et al. 2020). This technology could improve patient compliance and potentially reduce the need for traditional colonoscopy procedures. Combining information from different modalities can enhance disease detection capabilities. GANs are also utilized to generate synthetic PET images from MRI scans of the brain, allowing for visualization of subtle metabolic changes indicative of neurodegenerative diseases. This approach could improve the early detection and diagnosis of neurological disorders.

Future efforts should prioritize enhancing training accuracy by refining patch characteristics, investigating the impact of dataset size on training, and improving both training and prediction speed by developing more efficient neural networks. A further consideration is whether current networks can be applied to anatomical regions that were not investigated in studies thus far. Nevertheless, the full potential of cross-modality image estimation can only be realized when pre-processing the steps, such as registration and resampling, no longer need to be applied because loss functions have reached the necessary level of precision to sufficiently constrain the learning of the intensity projection between the two different modality medical images. In summary, the topic of cross-modality medical image estimations has been widely investigated by using CNNs and GANs. The diverse studies reviewed employed different types of cross-modality images, different training and testing dataset sizes, and images were mostly from different anatomical sites. However, it seems that multi-modal image estimation has potential value in medical imaging, and it deserves further exploration of the specific clinical applications of medical images. The ideas for future research which will be our contribution should be of help in the development of educational research studies in this field.

Image Analysis

Deep learning has changed the very way we do image processing. We currently apply it to dividing and joining images and to segment them. During the segmentation of images, we usually use metrics such as Dice similarity coefficient to evaluate our approaches. The segmentation overlaps for a particular segmentation can be high, but the associated anatomic plausibility of the segmentation, as well as its clinical value, could be low. For this reason, measures such as anatomical plausibility are hard to quantify in an objective function that is used to optimize a CNN.

This is where GANs perform their main duty. The discriminator network in a GAN would be used to figure out if a segmentation is good or bad, by being given a reference dataset of real segmentations.

(Sudre et al. 2017)is amongst the first to make use of segmentation of medical images by using GANs. They used a discriminator for the training phase to differentiate between automatic and reference segmentation masks on brain MR images. Here is an instance that illustrates the issue of image segmentation because of its paired training data problem. The discriminator loss may be summed up with a pixel-wise segmentation loss. The trained network produced fewer minor sporadic misclassification errors, as these were penalized by the discriminator model and thus, the segmentations were more anatomically realistic.

In addition, there are other applications of conditional pix2pix-like models in segmenting the structure of knee cartilage from MRI. In the poplar Speech Enhancement Generative Adversarial Network (SeGAN) model, the authors have slightly different approach to the GAN-based image segmentation. In this work critic (discriminator) is used to identify the gap between the predicted and the reference segmentation. It was discovered that the employed model performed well in terms of the tumor segmentation accuracy at the brain MRI. In a study conducted by (Chen et al. 2018), a GAN-based approach was proposed for medical image segmentation. The proposed method was able to achieve state-of-the-art performance on the BraTS 2017 dataset, which is a benchmark dataset for brain tumor segmentation. The results showed that the proposed method outperformed other state-of-the-art methods in terms of segmentation accuracy and computational efficiency. In another study, conducted by (T. C. Wang et al. 2018),GANs were proposed for the diagnosis of Alzheimer's disease. The proposed method was able to achieve an accuracy of 94.5% on the Alzheimer's Disease Neuroimaging Initiative (ADNI) dataset, which is a benchmark dataset for Alzheimer's disease diagnosis. The results showed that the proposed method outperformed other state-of-the-art methods in terms of accuracy and robustness. (Kadurin et al. 2017) employed GANs for drug discovery, generating novel molecules with high drug-likeness scores. This approach could accelerate drug development by producing potential candidates with desired properties.

Pseudohealthy Synthesis

The healthy image, which is the medical image of a patient with a disease, is then converted into the corresponding image that shows how the images would be if the disease was not present. This is helpful in visualization and detection of anomalies by comparing the two images.

GANs have been proven to be very useful for the synthesis of realistic images. GANs make it possible to generate high-quality and diverse images due to the use of deep learning, which enables them to mimic the features of the training data. This functionality offers a wide range of practical applications, such as image improvement, data augmentation, and even generating entirely new visual material. The employment of GANs for image pseudosynthesis speeds up the production process of images and enables the creation of high-quality visual content for many different reasons, from artistic projects to scientific research(Xia, Chartsias, and Tsaftaris 2020). A pioneering work by (Mirza-Aghazadeh-Attari et al. 2020)introduced a GAN-based framework for synthesizing chest CT scans containing healthy lung tissue. This study aimed at mitigating the shortage of normal cases while maintaining the same distribution characteristics as actual patient data. The generated images were successfully integrated into existing machine learning algorithms without compromising their predictive power. (Liu et al. 2021)developed a conditional GAN architecture capable of producing realistic MRI brain scans of healthy individuals. These synthetic images demonstrated excellent consistency with ground truth data, enabling researchers to expand their databases and enhance the generalizability of neural network models. (Tiago et al. 2022)designed a GAN system specifically tailored for cardiac ultrasound images. Their model could produce highly detailed and clinically plausible synthetic echocardiograms, thereby facilitating the development of more sophisticated computer vision systems for diagnosing heart diseases.

The Ever-Evolving Role of GANs in Medical Imaging: A Look Ahead

Generative Adversarial Networks (GANs) have emerged as transformative tools in medical imaging, demonstrating remarkable potential across various applications. From bridging the gap between modalities to enhancing image quality and facilitating personalized medicine, GANs are shaping the future of healthcare in exciting ways.

Generative AI Revolution

MEDICAL IMAGE ANALYSIS USING DEEP LEARNING

Deep learning (DL) is the most important part of AI that has been very successful in many vision tasks such as detection, image-to-image translation, semantic segmentation, etc(Minaee et al. 2022).

DL medical systems have been a focal point of discussion in recent years and have found applications across all medical fields, ranging from drug discovery to medical decision-making. These advancements have significantly transformed the practice of medicine. Generally, the architecture of the algorithm is designed to reflect the layers of neurons in the human brain in order to treat and extract information which gives the machine a chance to learn without being explicitly programmed.

The trained models can be utilized for diagnosing diseases and identifying risk factors associated with them, encompassing tasks such as Alzheimer's classification, breast cancer detection, retinal disease detection, and more. DL techniques are of great use for a variety of medical diagnostic tasks and in some of them even DL is superior to human experts.

GANs is a type of deep generative model, which was developed by (Goodfellow et al. 2020) which have garnered wider acceptance and enthusiasm in diverse application domains

The structure of a GAN model consists of two networks: a generator and a discriminator. The generator initially generates data from random patterns. These generated data are then fed into the discriminator along with true data. The discriminator acts as a classifier, trained to distinguish between real and generated data. Its role is to verify the authenticity of the input data, accurately discerning real data from generated data. Two of the most prominent and popular types of such deep generative models are Variational Autoencoders (VAEs) and GANs.

VAEs resemble autoencoders, that use variational inference to regularize the encoding and prevent the generation of data from getting overfitted. VAE models, together with other generative models, are widely used to overcome the data shortage and to improve machine learning performance in different domains through the augmentation of data, which means increasing the amount of data by adding slightly modified versions of the existing data. They were also deployed as virtual longitudinal clinical data of patients without disclosing privacy for researchers to perform counterfactuals experiments.

Classification of Alzeihmer's Disease(AD)

The recent reviews demonstrated that some GAN are used in AD prediction and image classification. According to the work of (Logan et al. 2021), the role of GANs in enhancing image quality and altering modes has been acknowledged, it's essential to note that only two studies were included, and the results regarding the diagnosis of AD were not reported. (Lin, Lin, and Lane 2021). These studies were not comprehensive, and the AD diagnosis was not done by analysis of data. To our best knowledge, this meta-analysis is the first in the field of artificial intelligence for GAN application in the diagnosis of Alzheimer's disease. This study systematically reviewed research on the application of GAN-based deep learning methods in diagnosing Alzheimer's disease. Subsequently, a meta-analysis was conducted to evaluate their diagnostic performance, aiming to address this gap in research.

Progress in disease-modifying therapy for Alzheimer's disease has been sluggish, with an alarming failure rate of 99.6% observed in clinical trials. (Cummings et al. 2018). With the data at hand, the search for early Alzheimer's patients is most prominent in the current research. Differential diagnosis of AD and Cognitively Normal (CN) could help in timely detection of AD and hence implementing focused interventions for delaying of its progression.

A study showcased that GAN-based deep learning techniques, encompassing various data formats and models with diverse structures, exhibited strong performance in the task of Alzheimer's disease versus cognitively normal classification.

In terms of data modality, certain studies employed MRI data, while others utilized PET data. For instance, Zhou et al. (2021) devised a GAN model to generate 3-T MRI scans from 1.5-T scans. Subsequently, researchers trained a Fully Convolutional Network (FCN) using the generated 3-T MRI as inputs to undertake the task of Alzheimer's disease versus cognitively normal classification.

The concurrent training of the GAN and FCN ensured the classification efficiency. In the study, the FCN trained on the generated 3-T MRI data outperformed the one trained on 1.5-T MRI data, exhibiting higher accuracy (0.84 vs. 0.82), sensitivity (0.74 vs. 0.67), and specificity (0.9037 vs. 0.8989)(Qu et al. 2022). (Baydargil, Park, and Kang 2021) developed a deep learning model based on adversarial training for diagnosing AD. pMCI.

The generator (G) reconstructed a PET image based on these feature vectors and then inputted it to the encoder-type discriminator (D) for Alzheimer's disease (AD) diagnosis. This study finally reported that the area under the curve of this method was 0.75.

Furthermore, some researchers trained the classifier based on features extracted or images processed using GAN to accomplish the task of differentiating between pMCI and sMCI classification. (Kim et al. 2020) extracted features of two brain PET slices with the encoder decoder D in GAN and trained an SVM classifier on these features to achieve accurate classification of AD and CN. Compared to the 2D-CNN model, the SVM classifier demonstrated a 12.77% increase in accuracy, a 6.82% increase in sensitivity, and a 19.37% increase in specificity. Shin et al. (2020)

constructed an (Qu et al. 2022)end-to-end network based on the GAN model, with G for MRI-PET conversion and D for AD classification.

All the studies included in the analysis utilized data from AD patients diagnosed clinically rather than through neuropathological examination. While neuropathological diagnosis at autopsy serves as the gold standard for diagnosing AD, data obtained through this method are sparse and challenging to obtain. Researchers may opt to address the limitation of small data sizes by utilizing clinically diagnosed AD data from large publicly available databases such as ADNI, OASIS, AIBL, and others. These databases provide access to extensive datasets that can facilitate the robust training of deep learning networks.

Breast Cancer Detection

Breast cancer stands as the second leading cause of death among women, with an estimated diagnosis rate of about 12% among them. (Azamjah, Soltan-Zadeh, and Zayeri 2019).

The commonly employed mammographic detection, based on computer-aided detection (CAD) methods, has the potential to enhance treatment outcomes for breast cancer and prolong survival times for patients. Traditional CAD tools, however, come with various drawbacks as they rely on manually designed features. For instance, hand-crafted features are often domain-specific, and the process of feature design can be tedious, challenging, and lacks generalizability. In recent years, developments in machine learning have provided alternative methods for feature extraction; one is to learn features from whole images directly through CNN. Usually, training CNN from scratch requires many labeled images; for example, the AlexNet (a classical CNN model) was trained by using 1.2 million labeled images(Iqbal et al. 2021).

For certain types of medical image data, such as mammographic tumor images, obtaining a sufficient number of images to train a CNN classifier can be challenging. This difficulty arises because true positives are scarce in the datasets, and expert labeling is expensive.

Like CNN, the GAN is a state-of-the-art neural network-based learning technique in the field of deep learning introduced by Goodfellow et al. in 2014.

Many innovative applications in the field of image processing have been enabled through GANs. For instance, GANs have been utilized for tasks such as image translation, object detection, super-resolution, and image blending. Also, for the medical imaging, various GAN are also recently developed such as Deep Generative Adversarial Networks for Compressed Sensing (GANCS) for MRI reconstruction, SegAN, Deep Image to Image Network (DI2IN) and SCAN for medical image segmentation (Guan 2019). An image augmentation method involves generating synthetic images using features extracted from original images. These generated images may not be exact replicas of the originals but can retain essential features, structures, or patterns of the objects present in the original images. Therefore, GAN is a good candidate as such image augmentation method for augmenting training datasets. (V. K. Singh et al. 2020) developed a deep learning framework utilizing GANs for breast cancer image segmentation. It achieved promising results in identifying and segmenting tumor regions in mammograms, potentially aiding in more accurate diagnosis and treatment planning. (Volz et al. 2018)investigated the use of GANs for generating synthetic mammogram images with specific features like tumors and microcalcifications. This could potentially be utilized for training and simulating real-world scenarios for medical professionals, ultimately improving their diagnostic skills.

Skin Lesion Segmentation

Worldwide, over 99,000 cases are recorded by skin cancer every year(Siegel et al. 2023). Early detection and timely monitoring are vital in upgrading quality of the diagnosis, of treatment planning as well as in reducing the mortality rates of skin cancers. Dermatologists can detect some skin lesions by visually inspecting skin color images of ambiguous clinical patterns that are not easily seen with the naked eye. Dermoscopy, a widely used tool, assists dermatologists in distinguishing between malignant and benign lesions by removing the surface reflections on the skin and, thus, leading to higher accuracy of skin cancer diagnosis.

Researchers are exploring the potential of GANs to synthesize realistic skin lesion images. This fabricated data can be used to augment existing datasets, addressing the challenge of imbalanced data distribution often encountered in real-world scenarios. Additionally, GAN-generated images can be used for pre-processing, improving the quality of existing data and enhancing the performance of deep learning models for skin lesion segmentation. (Esteva et al. 2022)developed a deep learning model that achieved dermatologist-level accuracy in classifying skin cancer from images. This technology has the potential to improve early detection and diagnosis of melanoma, potentially saving lives. (W. Yu et al. 2019)proposed a deep learning model called U-Net for automated skin lesion segmentation. This model achieved high accuracy in segmenting skin lesions from dermoscopic images, facilitating more efficient analysis and diagnosis by healthcare professionals. Researchers at Stanford University are exploring the use of deep learning models for skin lesion analysis in telemedicine settings. This could allow patients in remote areas to receive diagnoses from specialists without needing to travel long distances.

CONCLUSION

As we come to the end of this look at the Generative AI Revolution and how it will very significantly shape the future of healthcare innovation, it's clear that big changes are about to happen. Generative AI technologies coming together with healthcare will likely change every part of the field, from study and personalized medicine to diagnosis and treatment. We've seen how Generative AI algorithms, which are driven by huge amounts of healthcare data, have made it possible for huge steps forward. Generative AI is making breakthroughs that were previously unthinkable. For example, it is making fake medical images to train AI models and coming up with new drug compounds that work better and have fewer side effects. Moreover, the democratization of AI equipment and platforms is empowering healthcare professionals, researchers, and innovators worldwide to leverage these technology in their quest to enhance patient consequences and cope with some of the maximum urgent challenges dealing with healthcare nowadays. Whether it is accelerating drug discovery, optimizing treatment protocols, or personalizing patient care, Generative AI holds the important thing to unlocking new frontiers in healthcare innovation.

Looking ahead, the journey in the direction of figuring out the whole capability of Generative AI in healthcare will certainly be packed with each opportunities and challenges. Ethical issues surrounding records privateness, algorithm bias, and regulatory compliance will require cautious navigation. However, the promise of greater diagnostic accuracy, greater powerful treatments, and in the end, higher health consequences for sufferers, serves as a beacon of wish guiding us closer to a brighter future.

In end, as we embrace the Generative AI Revolution, allow us to remain steadfast in our commitment to harnessing these transformative technologies responsibly and ethically, making sure that they serve the greater appropriate and boost the motive of human fitness and well-being. Together, let us continue to form the destiny of healthcare innovation, driven via the limitless opportunities of Generative AI.

REFERENCES

Abbas, Q., Hussain, A., & Baig, A. R. (2023). CAD-ALZ: A Blockwise Fine-Tuning Strategy on Convolutional Model and Random Forest Classifier for Recognition of Multistage Alzheimer's Disease. *Diagnostics (Basel)*, 13(1), 167. 10.3390/diagnostics1301016736611459

Abràmoff, M. D., Tarver, M. E., Loyo-Berrios, N., Trujillo, S., Char, D., Obermeyer, Z., Eydelman, M. B., & Maisel, W. H. (2023). "Considerations for Addressing Bias in Artificial Intelligence for Health Equity." *npj. Digital Medicine*, 6(1), 170. 10.1038/s41746-023-00913-937700029

Aljohani, A., & Alharbe, N. (2022). Generating Synthetic Images for Healthcare with Novel Deep Pix2Pix GAN. *Electronics (Basel)*, 11(21), 3470. 10.3390/electronics11213470

Azamjah, N., Soltan-Zadeh, Y., & Zayeri, F. (2019). Global Trend of Breast Cancer Mortality Rate: A 25-Year Study. *Asian Pacific Journal of Cancer Prevention*, 20(7), 2015–2020. 10.31557/APJCP.2019.20.7.201531350959

Bandi, A., Adapa, P. V. S. R., & Yudu, E. V. P. K. K. (2023). The Power of Generative AI: A Review of Requirements, Models, Input–Output Formats, Evaluation Metrics, and Challenges. *Future Internet*, 15(8), 260. 10.3390/fi15080260

Baydargil, H. B., Park, J. S., & Kang, D. Y. (2021). Anomaly Analysis of Alzheimer's Disease in Pet Images Using an Unsupervised Adversarial Deep Learning Model. *Applied Sciences (Basel, Switzerland)*, 11(5), 2187. 10.3390/app11052187

Buslón, N., Cortés, A., Catuara-Solarz, S., Cirillo, D., & Rementeria, M. J. (2023). Raising Awareness of Sex and Gender Bias in Artificial Intelligence and Health. *Frontiers in Global Women's Health*, 4, 970312. 10.3389/fgwh.2023.97031237746321

Carnevale, A., Tangari, E. A., Iannone, A., & Sartini, E. (2023). Will Big Data and Personalized Medicine Do the Gender Dimension Justice? *AI & Society*, 38(2), 829–841. 10.1007/s00146-021-01234-934092931

Cellina, M., Cacioppa, L. M., Cè, M., Chiarpenello, V., Costa, M., Vincenzo, Z., Pais, D., Bausano, M. V., Rossini, N., Bruno, A., & Floridi, C. (2023). Artificial Intelligence in Lung Cancer Screening: The Future Is Now. *Cancers (Basel)*, 15(17), 4344. 10.3390/cancers1517434437686619

Chan, Y., Li, M., Parodi, K., Belka, C., Landry, G., & Kurz, C. (2023). Feasibility of CycleGAN Enhanced Low Dose CBCT Imaging for Prostate Radiotherapy Dose Calculation. *Physics in Medicine and Biology*, 68(10), 105014. 10.1088/1361-6560/acccce37054740

Chang, Anthony C. 2020. Intelligence-Based Medicine: Artificial Intelligence and Human Cognition in Clinical Medicine and Healthcare *Intelligence-Based Medicine: Artificial Intelligence and Human Cognition in Clinical Medicine and Healthcare.*

Chattopadhyay, A., & Maitra, M. (2022). MRI-Based Brain Tumour Image Detection Using CNN Based Deep Learning Method. *Neuroscience Informatics (Online)*, 2(4), 100060. 10.1016/j.neuri.2022.100060

Chen, Y., Shi, F., Christodoulou, A. G., Xie, Y., Zhou, Z., & Li, D. 2018. "Efficient and Accurate MRI Super-Resolution Using a Generative Adversarial Network and 3D Multi-Level Densely Connected Network." In *Lecture Notes in Computer Science (Including Subseries Lecture Notes in Artificial Intelligence and Lecture Notes in Bioinformatics)*. Springer. 10.1007/978-3-030-00928-1_11

Cummings, J., Lee, G., Ritter, A., & Zhong, K. (2018). Alzheimer's Disease Drug Development Pipeline: 2018. *Alzheimer's & Dementia: Translational Research & Clinical Interventions*, 4(1), 195–214. 10.1016/j.trci.2018.03.00929955663

Drukker, K., Chen, W., Gichoya, J., Gruszauskas, N., Kalpathy-Cramer, J., Koyejo, S., Myers, K., Sá, R. C., Sahiner, B., Whitney, H., Zhang, Z., & Giger, M. (2023). Toward Fairness in Artificial Intelligence for Medical Image Analysis: Identification and Mitigation of Potential Biases in the Roadmap from Data Collection to Model Deployment. *Journal of Medical Imaging (Bellingham, Wash.)*, 10(06). 10.1117/1.JMI.10.6.06110437125409

Esteva, A., Feng, J., van der Wal, D., Huang, S. C., Simko, J. P., DeVries, S., Chen, E., Schaeffer, E. M., Morgan, T. M., Sun, Y., Ghorbani, A., Naik, N., Nathawani, D., Socher, R., Michalski, J. M., Roach, M.III, Pisansky, T. M., Monson, J. M., Naz, F., & Mohamad, O. (2022). "Prostate Cancer Therapy Personalization via Multi-Modal Deep Learning on Randomized Phase III Clinical Trials." *npj. Digital Medicine*, 5(1), 71. 10.1038/s41746-022-00613-w35676445

Esteva, A., & Topol, E. (2019). Can Skin Cancer Diagnosis Be Transformed by AI? *Lancet*, 394(10211), 1795. 10.1016/S0140-6736(19)32726-6

Gennatas, E. D., & Chen, J. H. 2020. "Artificial Intelligence in Medicine: Past, Present, and Future." In *Artificial Intelligence in Medicine: Technical Basis and Clinical Applications*. Springer. 10.1016/B978-0-12-821259-2.00001-6

Guan, S. (2019). Breast Cancer Detection Using Synthetic Mammograms from Generative Adversarial Networks in Convolutional Neural Networks. *Journal of Medical Imaging (Bellingham, Wash.)*, 6(03), 1. 10.1117/1.JMI.6.3.03141130915386

Hou, C. K. J., & Behdinan, K. (2022). Dimensionality Reduction in Surrogate Modeling: A Review of Combined Methods. *Data Science and Engineering*, 7(4), 402–427. 10.1007/s41019-022-00193-536345394

Iqbal, M. A., Wang, Z., Ali, Z. A., & Riaz, S. (2021). Automatic Fish Species Classification Using Deep Convolutional Neural Networks. *Wireless Personal Communications*, 116(2), 1043–1053. 10.1007/s11277-019-06634-1

Jiang, X., Hu, Z., Wang, S., & Zhang, Y. (2023). Deep Learning for Medical Image-Based Cancer Diagnosis. *Cancers (Basel)*, 15(14), 3608. 10.3390/cancers1514360837509272

Kadurin, A., Nikolenko, S., Khrabrov, K., Aliper, A., & Zhavoronkov, A. (2017). DruGAN: An Advanced Generative Adversarial Autoencoder Model for de Novo Generation of New Molecules with Desired Molecular Properties in Silico. *Molecular Pharmaceutics*, 14(9), 3098–3104. 10.1021/acs.molpharmaceut.7b0034628703000

Kim, M. J., Lee, J. H., Anaya, F. J., Hong, J., Miller, W., Telu, S., & Singh, P. (2020). First-in-Human Evaluation of [11C]PS13, a Novel PET Radioligand, to Quantify Cyclooxygenase-1 in the Brain. *European Journal of Nuclear Medicine and Molecular Imaging*, 47(13), 3143–3151. 10.1007/s00259-020-04855-232399622

Kulathilake, K. A., Abdullah, N. A., Bandara, A. M. R. R., & Lai, K. W. (2021). Saneera Hemantha, Nor Aniza Abdullah, A. M.Randitha Ravimal Bandara, and Khin Wee Lai. 2021. "InNetGAN: Inception Network-Based Generative Adversarial Network for Denoising Low-Dose Computed Tomography.". *Journal of Healthcare Engineering*, 2021, 1–20. 10.1155/2021/997576234552709

Lee, K. W., & Renee, K. Y. C. (2022). Diverse COVID-19 CT Image-to-Image Translation with Stacked Residual Dropout. *Bioengineering (Basel, Switzerland)*, 9(11), 698. 10.3390/bioengineering911069836421099

Li, G., Lv, J., & Wang, C. (2021). A Modified Generative Adversarial Network Using Spatial and Channel-Wise Attention for CS-MRI Reconstruction. *IEEE Access : Practical Innovations, Open Solutions*, 9, 83185–83198. 10.1109/ACCESS.2021.3086839

Lin, E., Lin, C. H., & Lane, H. Y. (2021). Deep Learning with Neuroimaging and Genomics in Alzheimer's Disease. *International Journal of Molecular Sciences*, 22(15), 7911. 10.3390/ijms2215791134360676

Liu, Y., Chen, A., Shi, H., Huang, S., Zheng, W., Liu, Z., Zhang, Q., & Yang, X. (2021). CT Synthesis from MRI Using Multi-Cycle GAN for Head-and-Neck Radiation Therapy. *Computerized Medical Imaging and Graphics*, 91, 101953. 10.1016/j.compmedimag.2021.10195334242852

Logan, R., Williams, B. G., Ferreira da Silva, M., Indani, A., Schcolnicov, N., Ganguly, A., & Miller, S. J. (2021). Deep Convolutional Neural Networks With Ensemble Learning and Generative Adversarial Networks for Alzheimer's Disease Image Data Classification. *Frontiers in Aging Neuroscience*, 13, 720226. 10.3389/fnagi.2021.72022634483890

Lupsor-Platon, M., Serban, T., Silion, A. I., Tirpe, G. R., Tirpe, A., & Florea, M. (2021). Performance of Ultrasound Techniques and the Potential of Artificial Intelligence in the Evaluation of Hepatocellular Carcinoma and Non-Alcoholic Fatty Liver Disease. *Cancers (Basel)*, 13(4), 790. 10.3390/cancers1304079033672827

Manikandan, A., & Sanjay, T. (2023). Generative Adversarial Networks: A Game Changer - GAN for Machine Learning and IoT Applications. In *Handbook of Research on Machine Learning-Enabled IoT for Smart Applications Across Industries*. Springer. 10.4018/978-1-6684-8785-3.ch004

Mathew, S., Nadeem, S., Kumari, S., & Kaufman, A. (2020). Augmenting Colonoscopy Using Extended and Directional Cyclegan for Lossy Image Translation. In *Proceedings of the IEEE Computer Society Conference on Computer Vision and Pattern Recognition*. IEEE. 10.1109/CVPR42600.2020.00475

Mawdsley, E., Reynolds, B., & Cullen, B. (2021). A Systematic Review of the Effectiveness of Machine Learning for Predicting Psychosocial Outcomes in Acquired Brain Injury: Which Algorithms Are Used and Why? *Journal of Neuropsychology*, 15(3), 319–339. 10.1111/jnp.1224433780595

Minaee, S., Boykov, Y., Porikli, F., Plaza, A., Kehtarnavaz, N., & Terzopoulos, D. (2022). Image Segmentation Using Deep Learning: A Survey. *IEEE Transactions on Pattern Analysis and Machine Intelligence*, 44(7), 1. 10.1109/TPAMI.2021.305996833596172

Mirza-Aghazadeh-Attari, M., Zarrintan, A., Nezami, N., Mohammadi, A., Zarrintan, A., Mohebbi, I., Pirnejad, H., Khademvatani, K., Ashkavand, Z., Forughi, P., Arasteh, A., & Attari, J. A. (2020). Predictors of Coronavirus Disease 19 (COVID-19) Pneumonitis Outcome Based on Computed Tomography (CT) Imaging Obtained Prior to Hospitalization: A Retrospective Study. *Emergency Radiology*, 27(6), 653–661. 10.1007/s10140-020-01833-x32770367

Nah, F.-H., Fiona, R. Z., Cai, J., Siau, K., & Chen, L. (2023). Generative AI and ChatGPT: Applications, Challenges, and AI-Human Collaboration. *Journal of Information Technology Case and Application Research*, 25(3), 277–304. 10.1080/15228053.2023.2233814

Padhi, A., Agarwal, A., Saxena, S. K., & Katoch, C. D. S. (2023). Transforming Clinical Virology with AI, Machine Learning and Deep Learning: A Comprehensive Review and Outlook. *Virusdisease*, 34(3), 345–355. 10.1007/s13337-023-00841-y37780897

Paul, W., Hadzic, A., Joshi, N., Alajaji, F., & Burlina, P. (2022). TARA: Training and Representation Alteration for AI Fairness and Domain Generalization. *Neural Computation*, 34(3), 716–753. 10.1162/neco_a_0146835016212

Qin, Z., Liu, Z., Zhu, P., & Ling, W. (2022). Style Transfer in Conditional GANs for Cross-Modality Synthesis of Brain Magnetic Resonance Images. *Computers in Biology and Medicine*, 148, 105928. 10.1016/j.compbiomed.2022.10592835952543

Qu, C., Zou, Y., Ma, Y., Chen, Q., Luo, J., Fan, H., Jia, Z., Gong, Q., & Chen, T. (2022). Diagnostic Performance of Generative Adversarial Network-Based Deep Learning Methods for Alzheimer's Disease: A Systematic Review and Meta-Analysis. *Frontiers in Aging Neuroscience*, 14, 841696. 10.3389/fnagi.2022.84169635527734

Quilodrán-Casas, C., Silva, V. L. S., Arcucci, R., Heaney, C. E., Yi, K. G., & Pain, C. C. (2022). Digital Twins Based on Bidirectional LSTM and GAN for Modelling the COVID-19 Pandemic. *Neurocomputing*, 470, 11–28. 10.1016/j.neucom.2021.10.04334703079

Raju, N., & Peter Augustine, D. (2023). Reduce Overfitting and Improve Deep Learning Models' Performance in Medical Image Classification. In *Machine Intelligence: Computer Vision and Natural Language Processing*. Springer. 10.1201/9781003424550-4

Rejusha, R. R. T., & Vipin Kumar, S. V. K. (2021). Artificial MRI Image Generation Using Deep Convolutional GAN and Its Comparison with Other Augmentation Methods. In *ICCISc 2021 - 2021 International Conference on Communication, Control and Information Sciences, Proceedings*. IEEE. 10.1109/ICCISc52257.2021.9484902

Rossi, M., & Cerveri, P. (2021). Comparison of Supervised and Unsupervised Approaches for the Generation of Synthetic Ct from Cone-Beam Ct. *Diagnostics (Basel)*, 11(8), 1435. 10.3390/diagnostics1108143534441369

Ruiz-Rojas, L. I., Acosta-Vargas, P., De-Moreta-Llovet, J., & Gonzalez-Rodriguez, M. (2023). Empowering Education with Generative Artificial Intelligence Tools: Approach with an Instructional Design Matrix. *Sustainability (Basel)*, 15(15), 11524. 10.3390/su151511524

Siegel, R. L., Miller, K. D., Wagle, N. S., & Jemal, A. (2023). Cancer Statistics, 2023. *CA: a Cancer Journal for Clinicians*, 73(1), 17–48. 10.3322/caac.2176336633525

Singh, N. K., & Raza, K. (2021). Medical Image Generation Using Generative Adversarial Networks: A Review. In *Studies in Computational Intelligence*. Springer. 10.1007/978-981-15-9735-0_5

Singh, V. K., Rashwan, H. A., Romani, S., Akram, F., Pandey, N., Md, M. K. S., & Saleh, A. (2020). Breast Tumor Segmentation and Shape Classification in Mammograms Using Generative Adversarial and Convolutional Neural Network. *Expert Systems with Applications*, 139, 112855. 10.1016/j.eswa.2019.112855

Su, Y. H., Jiang, W., Chitrakar, D., Huang, K., Peng, H., & Hannaford, B. (2021). Local Style Preservation in Improved GAN-Driven Synthetic Image Generation for Endoscopic Tool Segmentation. *Sensors (Basel)*, 21(15), 5163. 10.3390/s2115516334372398

Tiago, C., Gilbert, A., Beela, A. S., Aase, S. A., Snare, S. R., Šprem, J., & McLeod, K. (2022). A Data Augmentation Pipeline to Generate Synthetic Labeled Datasets of 3D Echocardiography Images Using a GAN. *IEEE Access : Practical Innovations, Open Solutions*, 10, 98803–98815. 10.1109/ACCESS.2022.3207177

Volz, V., Lucas, S. M., Schrum, J., Smith, A., Liu, J., & Risi, S. (2018). Evolving Mario Levels in the Latent Space of a Deep Convolutional Generative Adversarial Network. In *GECCO 2018 - Proceedings of the 2018 Genetic and Evolutionary Computation Conference*. IEEE. 10.1145/3205455.3205517

Wang, C., Li, Z., Mo, X., Tang, X., & Liu, H. (2023). Exploiting Unfairness with Meta-Set Learning for Chronological Age Estimation. *IEEE Transactions on Information Forensics and Security*, 18, 5678–5690. 10.1109/TIFS.2023.3313356

Wang, Q., Su, M., Zhang, M., & Li, R. (2021). Integrating Digital Technologies and Public Health to Fight Covid-19 Pandemic: Key Technologies, Applications, Challenges and Outlook of Digital Healthcare. In *International Journal of Environmental Research and Public Health*, 10.3390/ijerph18116053

Wang, T. C., Ming, Y. L., Jun, Y. Z., Tao, A., Kautz, J., & Catanzaro, B. (2018). High-Resolution Image Synthesis and Semantic Manipulation with Conditional GANs. In *Proceedings of the IEEE Computer Society Conference on Computer Vision and Pattern Recognition*. IEEE. 10.1109/CVPR.2018.00917

Xia, T., Chartsias, A., & Tsaftaris, S. A. (2020). Pseudo-Healthy Synthesis with Pathology Disentanglement and Adversarial Learning. *Medical Image Analysis*, 64, 101719. 10.1016/j.media.2020.10171932540700

Yu, H., & Welch, J. D. (2021). MichiGAN: Sampling from Disentangled Representations of Single-Cell Data Using Generative Adversarial Networks. *Genome Biology*, 22(1), 158. 10.1186/s13059-021-02373-434016135

Yu, W., Fang, B., Liu, Y., Gao, M., Zheng, S., & Wang, Y. (2019). Liver Vessels Segmentation Based on 3d Residual U-NET. In *Proceedings - International Conference on Image Processing, ICIP*. IEEE. 10.1109/ICIP.2019.8802951

Zheng, H., Zhou, Z., & Chen, J. (2021). RLSTM: A New Framework of Stock Prediction by Using Random Noise for Overfitting Prevention. *Computational Intelligence and Neuroscience*, 2021, 1–14. 10.1155/2021/886581634113377

Chapter 18
Generative Intelligence:
Sculpting Tomorrow's Healthcare Solutions

Jaspreet Kaur
https://orcid.org/0000-0002-3587-6841
Chandigarh University, India

ABSTRACT

Generative intelligence is changing healthcare prevention, diagnosis, and therapy. Advanced technologies like AI enable individualized care, predictive analytics, and streamlined workflows. This study examines generative intelligence's significance in medication discovery, disease prediction, and patient outcomes. To protect privacy and encourage innovation, regulation, ethics, and implementation must be addressed. Generative intelligence can transform healthcare into a predictive, preventive, and personalized system that improves global well-being.

INTRODUCTION

In recent times, the healthcare sector has experienced a notable metamorphosis propelled by technological breakthroughs. One of the notable breakthroughs in the field is the emergence of Generative Intelligence, which has shown great potential in transforming the development, implementation, and optimization of healthcare solutions. Generative Intelligence signifies a shift away from conventional, unchanging methods in healthcare, instead highlighting dynamic, adaptable systems that may independently learn, develop, and produce innovative solutions (Oniani et al., 2023).

DOI: 10.4018/979-8-3693-3731-8.ch018

Copyright © 2024, IGI Global. Copying or distributing in print or electronic forms without written permission of IGI Global is prohibited.

Exploring the Concept of Generative Intelligence

Generative Intelligence refers to the capacity of systems to not only analyse data and carry out predetermined tasks, but also to acquire knowledge from data patterns, provide novel insights, and adjust behaviors in response to changing conditions. Generative Intelligence, fundamentally, utilizes sophisticated algorithms such as machine learning, deep learning, and artificial intelligence to facilitate the extraction of significance from data, identification of intricate patterns, and prompt decision-making in real-time (Singh, 2023). Generative Intelligence systems have the potential to produce solutions autonomously, often outperforming human specialists in tasks like diagnosis, treatment planning, and result prediction, unlike traditional systems that depend on explicit programming and rule-based logic. The ability to independently generate and adapt is especially revolutionary in the healthcare field, where the intricate nature of data and the diversity of medical circumstances require adaptable and intelligent solutions. Generative Intelligence is influenced by biological systems, wherein organisms employ various mechanisms such as evolution, learning, and self-regulation to consistently adjust to dynamic situations. Generative Intelligence systems demonstrate attributes such as robustness, scalability, and resilience by adopting these concepts. This allows them to excel in dynamic healthcare environments that are marked by a variety of data sources, increasing patient requirements, and quick advancements in medical knowledge (Wachter & Brynjolfsson, 2024).

The Progression and Development of Healthcare Solutions

The development of healthcare solutions reflects the advancement of Generative Intelligence concepts, transitioning from fixed, universal approaches to adaptable, customized therapies designed to meet the specific needs of each patient (Singh, 2023). In the past, healthcare delivery mainly depended on manual procedures, paper-based documentation, and decision-making based on intuition, leading to inefficiencies, mistakes, and less than optimal results as depicted in figure 1 below:

Generative Intelligence

Figure 1. Transition from traditional healthcare approaches

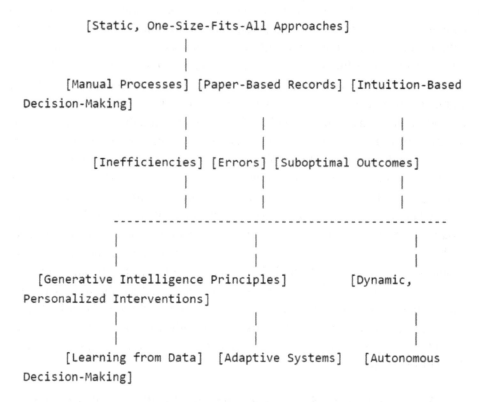

The introduction of electronic health records (EHRs) was a notable achievement in the process of digitizing healthcare, facilitating the acquisition, retention, and retrieval of patient information in a digitized manner. Although electronic health records (EHRs) enhanced the accessibility of data and the sharing of information, they frequently lacked interoperability, which restricted their effectiveness in producing practical insights across different healthcare environments. The emergence of data analytic and machine learning technologies has facilitated the shift towards healthcare solutions that are more intelligent, enabling the extraction of significant patterns from extensive quantities of structured and unstructured data. The initial implementations of machine learning in the healthcare sector mostly concentrated on activities such as forecasting, categorizing risks, and identifying abnormalities, establishing the groundwork for more advanced Generative Intelligence systems (Singh, 2023).

With the advancement of machine learning algorithms and the growth in computer capacity, Generative Intelligence systems have exhibited exceptional capabilities in healthcare domains that have historically been dominated by human expertise. Generative Adversarial Networks (GANs) have been employed in medical imaging to produce artificial images that enhance training datasets, enhance model generalization, and aid in the detection of rare diseases. Generative Intelligence platforms in clinical decision support utilize patient data, clinical guidelines, and real-world evidence to provide personalized treatment recommendations, optimize prescription regimens, and accurately anticipate patient outcomes. These systems possess the ability to acquire knowledge from fresh data, feedback, and results, hence enhancing their algorithms over a period of time in order to adjust to changing patient populations and advancements in medical understanding. Generative Intelligence is revolutionizing healthcare along the full spectrum, encompassing preventative care, population health management, patient involvement, and telemedicine, in addition to diagnosis and treatment. For instance, wearable devices that are coupled with algorithms based on Generative Intelligence have the capability to monitor physiological data, identify early indicators of disease, and offer tailored suggestions for lifestyle adjustments. This empowers individuals to actively manage their health (Wachter & Brynjolfsson, 2024).

In the future, the incorporation of Generative Intelligence (GI) into the healthcare sector holds the potential to explore novel opportunities in precision medicine, virtual care provision, and population health monitoring. Healthcare organizations can achieve optimization of resource allocation, improvement of clinical results, and enhancement of the entire patient experience through the utilization of data, advanced analytic, and autonomous decision-making, beyond prior capabilities (Yim et al., 2024). In the current healthcare environment, there is a growing integration of data and technology, which is fundamentally transforming the fundamental aspects of medical practice, research, and administration. The convergence observed in this context is influenced by various causes, encompassing the widespread adoption of digital health records, the introduction of sophisticated analytic, and the emergence of innovative technologies like wearable devices and the Internet of Things ((Io T). This analysis explores three key foundations of this paradigm shift: the use of Big Data in the healthcare sector, the incorporation of Artificial Intelligence in the field of Medicine, and the integration of Internet of Things (Io T) and Wearable Devices inside healthcare systems (Oniani et al., 2023).

Generative Intelligence

The Application of Big Data in the Healthcare Industry

The term "Big Data" has gained significant attention in diverse sectors, including the healthcare industry. Big Data can be defined as the extensive quantity, speed, and diversity of data produced inside the healthcare system. Examples of data types encompassed within this category consist of clinical records, imaging studies, genetic sequences, administrative data, and patient-generated information, among various others as presented in figure 2 below:

Figure 2. Convergence of data and technology in healthcare

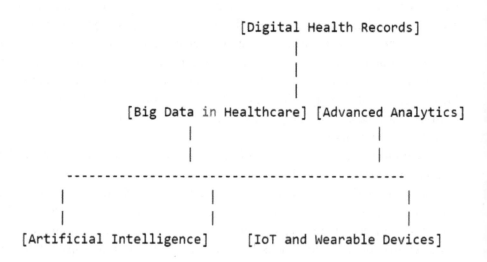

The importance of Big Data in the healthcare sector is in its capacity to reveal concealed patterns, enable decision-making based on empirical data, and foster innovation throughout the entire spectrum of healthcare delivery. Predictive analytic is a key use of Big Data in healthcare, where previous data is utilized to anticipate future events or patterns. For example, the utilization of predictive models can facilitate the identification of patients who are susceptible to the development of chronic illnesses, forecast rates of readmission, or foresee the occurrence of disease outbreaks within a certain community. These observations empower healthcare practitioners to take preemptive measures, effectively manage resources, and customize interventions based on the specific needs of each patient, thereby enhancing results and decreasing expenses (Sai et al., 2024).

In addition, the utilization of Big Data analytic is of paramount importance in the field of clinical research as it facilitates the examination of extensive datasets, the identification of biomarkers, and the exploration of innovative treatment targets. Through the consolidation and examination of data from various sources, such as electronic health records, clinical trials, and real-world evidence, scientists can expedite the process of finding new drugs, enhance the design of clinical trials, and support the creation of precision medicine strategies that are customized for specific groups of patients (Yim et al., 2024).

Nevertheless, the utilization of Big Data in the healthcare sector is not devoid of obstacles. To fully harness the potential of Big Data analytic, it is crucial to tackle significant obstacles such as privacy concerns, data security, interoperability challenges, and data quality. Furthermore, the large amount and intricate nature of healthcare data require strong computing infrastructure, sophisticated analytic capabilities, and collaboration across many fields to extract practical insights and efficiently use them in clinical practice (Kaur, 2024).

Artificial Intelligence in the Field of Medicine

The emergence of Artificial Intelligence (AI) has had a profound impact on the healthcare industry, presenting unparalleled prospects for improving diagnostic precision, optimizing operational processes, and tailoring patient care to individual needs (Sai et al., 2024). Fundamentally, artificial intelligence (AI) pertains to the advancement of computer systems that possess the ability to execute tasks that conventionally necessitate human intelligence, including observation, reasoning, learning, and decision-making. Within the realm of medicine, artificial intelligence (AI) presents a potential opportunity to enhance the proficiency of clinicians, enhance the accuracy of diagnoses, and optimize treatment approaches across several medical fields. Medical imaging interpretation is a prominent application of AI in healthcare (Kaur, 2024). Deep learning algorithms, which are a fundamental component of artificial intelligence (AI), have exhibited exceptional efficacy in several tasks including picture classification, segmentation, and anomaly detection. One illustrative instance involves the utilization of convolution neural networks (CNNs) for the examination of radio-logical pictures, encompassing X-rays, CT scans, and MRI scans, exhibiting a level of precision that is equivalent to or potentially exceeds that of human radiologists. AI-driven solutions have the potential to enhance the efficiency of diagnosis, minimize errors in interpretation, and enhance patient outcomes through the automation of picture interpretation and identification of abnormalities (Lehoux et al., 2016).

Generative Intelligence

In addition, clinical decision support systems that utilize artificial intelligence (AI) employ patient data, evidence-based guidelines, and domain-specific expertise to aid healthcare personnel in their decision-making procedures. These systems possess the capability to analyse extensive quantities of patient data, detect patterns that are suggestive of disease susceptibility or treatment efficacy, and produce customized suggestions that are specifically designed to align with the unique characteristics of each patient. AI-driven decision support technologies enable clinicians to make educated decisions, optimize resource utilization, and promote patient safety and happiness by synthesizing complicated information and offering actionable insights at the point of treatment. Although AI has the ability to bring about significant changes, its widespread implementation in the field of medicine is not devoid of obstacles. To ensure the safe and responsible implementation of AI technologies in clinical practice, it is crucial to address concerns around algorithm bias, interpret-ability, liability, as well as regulatory and ethical factors. Furthermore, the incorporation of artificial intelligence (AI) into current healthcare processes necessitates thorough training, active involvement of stakeholders, and adequate infrastructure support in order to optimize its effectiveness and minimize potential hazards (Beckfield et al., 2013).

Internet of Things ((Io T) and Wearable Devices in Care

The utilization of the Internet of Things ((Io T) and wearable devices in healthcare innovation signifies a novel domain, facilitating uninterrupted surveillance, instantaneous data acquisition, and tailored interventions beyond the conventional clinical environment. The term "Internet of Things" ((Io T) encompasses a network of interconnected devices that are equipped with sensors, actuators, and communication capabilities. On the other hand, wearable devices are portable gadgets equipped with sensors that are worn by users to monitor a range of physiological characteristics, activities, and behaviour (Kaur, 2024).

The widespread adoption of Internet of Things (Io T) and wearable devices has significantly altered the domain of remote patient monitoring, strategic management of chronic diseases, and proactive healthcare measures. These gadgets possess the capability to collect a diverse range of biometric data, encompassing heart rate, blood pressure, blood glucose levels, activity levels, and sleep patterns. Consequently, they provide clinicians significant insights into the health condition and behavioral habits of patients. Io T-enabled wearable devices have the potential to decrease hospital admissions, promote medication adherence, and improve the overall quality of life for patients with chronic diseases by facilitating proactive interventions and early identification of health concerns. In addition, the Internet of Things ((Io T) and wearable technologies enable the notion of the "quantified self," whereby individuals monitor and evaluate their personal health data in order to enhance their overall well-being and performance. Wearable technologies enable consumers to actively engage in health management, goal-setting, and progress monitoring by utilizing user-friendly interfaces and data visualization tools. Furthermore, the use of gamification components, social support functionalities, and behavioral cues has the potential to augment user involvement and drive, hence promoting sustained modifications in behaviour and adherence to beneficial practices (Consoli & Mina, 2009).

Nevertheless, the extensive implementation of Io T and wearable devices in healthcare encounters certain obstacles, such as apprehensions regarding data privacy and security, difficulties in interoperability, and adherence to regulatory requirements. The protection of sensitive health information, the preservation of data integrity, and the establishment of user trust are of utmost importance when designing and implementing solutions enabled by the Internet of Things ((Io T). Furthermore, it is crucial to tackle inequalities in technology access, digital literacy, and healthcare infrastructure in order to guarantee fair access and optimize the potential advantages of (Io T and wearable technologies for various demographics (Beckfield et al., 2013). In summary, the fundamental elements of the ongoing digital transformation in healthcare encompass Big Data analytic, Artificial Intelligence, and Io T-enabled wearable devices. Healthcare stakeholders have the potential to increase clinical outcomes, improve patient experiences, and optimize healthcare delivery throughout the continuum of care by utilizing data-driven insights, sophisticated algorithms, and connected technology. Nevertheless, in order to fully harness the capabilities of these technologies, it is imperative to undertake a collective endeavour that tackles technological, ethical, and societal obstacles, promotes collaboration across different fields of study, and places patient-centered innovation at the forefront of healthcare provision. In this digital age, it is crucial to properly adopt innovation, maintain ethical standards, and ensure that technology acts as a catalyst for good transformation in healthcare (Lehoux et al., 2016).

BIOMEDICAL IMAGING USING GENERATIVE INTELLIGENCE

Medical imaging is of utmost importance in contemporary healthcare as it facilitates the visualization of interior structures, identification of anomalies, and provision of guidance for diagnosis and therapy determinations. The incorporation of Generative Intelligence principles into medical imaging technologies signifies a fundamental transformation, fundamentally altering the processes of acquiring, analyzing, and interpreting imaging data as depiction in figure 3 below:

Figure 3. Intersection of generative intelligence and medical imaging

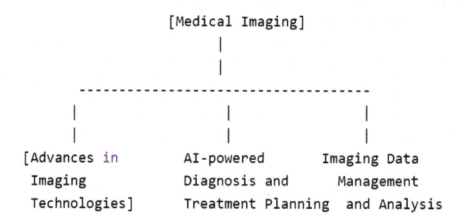

This section examines the convergence of Generative Intelligence with medical imaging, with a specific emphasis on advancements in imaging technology, diagnostic and treatment planning facilitated by artificial intelligence, and the storage and analysis of imaging data.

Technological Advancements in the Field of Medical Imaging

In recent decades, the area of medical imaging has experienced significant progress, mostly due to developments in hardware, software, and imaging modalities. Cutting-edge technologies have been integrated into traditional imaging procedures, including X-ray radiography, computed tomography (CT), magnetic resonance imaging (MRI), and ultrasound, in order to enhance resolution, speed, and diagnostic accuracy. One illustration of this phenomenon is the substitution of traditional film-based methods with digital imaging devices, which facilitate the capture, preservation, and retrieval of medical pictures in a digitized format (Kaur, 2024).

This shift has enabled the advancement of Picture Archiving and Communication Systems (PACS), which optimize the organization, dissemination, and retrieval of images inside healthcare establishments. Furthermore, the progress made in detector technology, including digital detectors and photon-counting detectors, has greatly improved the quality of images while simultaneously decreasing the level of radiation exposure experienced by patients. In addition, the introduction of functional imaging modalities, such as positron emission tomography (PET) and functional magnetic resonance imaging (fMRI), has facilitated the visualization of physiological processes and metabolic engagement within the human body by medical professionals. The utilization of these methodologies yields significant knowledge regarding tissue perfusion, metabolism, and cerebral connection, hence augmenting diagnostic capacities within the fields of oncology, neurology, and cardiology (Betzel & Bassett,2017).

The breadth and capabilities of medical imaging have been enhanced through advancements in image reconstruction algorithms and computational methodologies, in addition to hardware breakthroughs. Iterative reconstruction algorithms employed in CT imaging have been shown to enhance image quality and mitigate noise, hence resulting in improved diagnostic accuracy and reduced radiation exposure. Moreover, sophisticated image processing methods, such as machine learning and deep learning algorithms, improve the retrieval of medically significant data from medical pictures. This allows for automatic segmentation, extraction of features, and interpretation of images (Nova,2023).

Artificial Intelligence (AI)-Enabled Diagnosis and Treatment Planning

The field of medical imaging has been significantly impacted by Generative Intelligence, specifically Artificial Intelligence (AI), which allows for automated analysis, interpretation, and decision-making using imaging data. Artificial intelligence algorithms, such as machine learning and deep learning models, utilize extensive collections of annotated medical images to acquire intricate patterns and connections. This empowers them to carry out activities that were previously exclusive to human professionals with unparalleled precision and effectiveness. Computer-aided diagnosis (CAD) is a highly influential use of AI in medical imaging (Betzel & Bassett,2017). It involves the use of AI algorithms to help radiologists identify and describe problems in medical pictures. Deep learning models that have been trained on extensive datasets of mammography pictures have exhibited remarkable efficacy in the identification of breast cancer lesions. This has resulted in enhanced rates of early detection and a reduction in false-positive results. Likewise, artificial intelligence algorithms have been created to aid in identifying brain haemorrhage on CT scans, lung nodules on chest X-rays, and abnormalities on MRI scans, among other uses (Nova,2023).

In addition to diagnosis, AI-driven imaging approaches show potential for customized therapy planning and evaluation of response. AI algorithms have the capability to analyse imaging data in order to forecast treatment outcomes, enhance therapy strategies, and track the evolution of diseases over a period of time. AI-based radio-mics analysis in the field of oncology facilitates the extraction of quantitative imaging features from medical pictures. These features can then be connected with clinical outcomes and utilized to inform treatment decisions, including tumour segmentation, assessment of therapy response, and prediction of survival outcomes. Imaging biomarkers driven by artificial intelligence provide valuable information regarding illness phenotype, treatment response phenotype, and prognostic indicators. This enables the advancement of precision medicine strategies that are customized to the unique characteristics of each patient. Through the integration of imaging data with clinical, genomics, and other omics data, decision support systems powered by artificial intelligence (AI) have the capability to offer comprehensive and individualized insights to healthcare professionals. This integration empowers doctors to administer focused interventions and enhance patient outcomes (Yim et al., 2024).

Management and Analysis of Imaging Data

The exponential growth in the volume, complexity, and variety of imaging data created within healthcare systems can be attributed to the widespread adoption of digital imaging technologies. The proficient management and analysis of this extensive datasets is crucial in order to fully harness its potential for clinical decision-making, research endeavour, and activities aimed at enhancing quality. Healthcare facilities utilize picture data management technologies, such as Picture Archiving and Communication Systems (PACS) and vendor-neutral archives (VNAs), to establish centralized repositories for the storage, retrieval, and dissemination of medical images. In order to achieve interoperability and promote smooth integration with electronic health records (EHRs) and other healthcare systems, these systems utilize standardized protocols, such as the Digital Imaging and Communications in Medicine (DICOM) format. In addition, cloud-based imaging technologies have the capacity to scale, adapt, and access data remotely, allowing for efficient storage, backup, and disaster recovery capabilities (Gong et al., 2023).

Concurrently, progress in imaging informatics and computational imaging has stimulated the creation of innovative methods for analyzing, visualizing, and interpreting images. Radio-mics is a rapidly growing area of study in medical imaging that focuses on extracting quantitative aspects from medical pictures. These features can then be compared to clinical outcomes, biomarker expression, and genomics profiles. The utilization of radio-mics analysis facilitates the detection of imaging biomarkers that are linked to the prognosis of diseases, the response to treatment, and the resistance to therapeutic interventions. This process offers significant contributions to the development of personalized medicine strategies (Kaur, 2024).

In addition, the utilization of AI-powered image analysis tools, such as segmentation algorithms based on deep learning and techniques for image registration, enables the automated processing and interpretation of medical pictures. This, in turn, alleviates the workload of radiologists and improves the efficiency of workflow.

These tools facilitate the expeditious reconstruction of images, delineation of organs, segmentation of lesions, and fusion of images, hence expediting the procedures of diagnosis and treatment planning. In nutshell, the incorporation of Generative Intelligence principles into the field of medical imaging is revolutionizing the domains of diagnostic imaging, therapeutic management, and data analysis within the healthcare sector. The acquisition, interpretation, and utilization of medical pictures are being revolutionized by advancements in imaging technology, AI-powered diagnosis and treatment planning, and imaging data management and analysis. These advancements aim to enhance patient outcomes. In order to fully leverage the potential of Generative Intelligence in medical imaging and achieve its potential for precision medicine and personalized healthcare delivery, it is imperative to emphasize the need of interdisciplinary collaboration, standardized protocols, and ethical considerations as the field continues to advance (Chen & Esmaeilzadeh, 2024).

THE INTERSECTION OF PERSONALIZED MEDICINE AND GENOMICS

Within the domain of contemporary healthcare, the emergence of personalized medicine has inaugurated a novel epoch characterized by customized and focused therapies. Genomics, the examination of an individual's genetic composition, is central to personalized medicine as presented in figure 4 below:

Figure 4. Intersection of personalized medicine and genomics

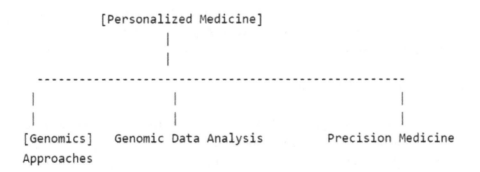

Generative Intelligence

It has significant implications for diagnosing diseases, selecting treatments, and providing preventive care. This section examines the convergence of personalized medicine and genomics, investigating the processing of genomics data, precision medicine methodologies, and the ethical implications associated with genomics healthcare. Genomics data analysis entails the comprehensive scrutiny and elucidation of an individual's genetic data, spanning either their complete genome or selected parts of interest. The emergence of next-generation sequencing (NGS) technologies has led to enhanced efficiency, affordability, and availability in the creation of genomics data. These technological developments have revealed a wealth of genetic knowledge, allowing researchers and doctors to uncover genetic variations associated with diseases, identify specific targets for treatment, and understand the underlying biological processes (Tutton, 2016).

The interpretation of extensive and intricate information is a significant problem in the field of genetic data processing. Genomics data encompasses a vast array of genetic variations, such as single nucleotide polymorphisms (SNPs), copy number variations (CNVs), and structural rearrangements, which possess significant implications for both healthy individuals and the development of diseases. Advanced bio-informatics techniques and algorithms are used to label, sort, and rank genetic variations according to their anticipated influence on gene function, protein structure, and susceptibility to diseases. In addition, the integration of genetic data with clinical, phenotype, and environmental information provides a more thorough comprehension of the origins and advancement of diseases (Walton & Christensen, 2023). An illustration of this can be seen in the utilization of genome-wide association studies (GWAS), which employ extensive genomics datasets to ascertain genetic regions linked to prevalent complex diseases, including diabetes, cancer, and cardiovascular problems. Through the process of understanding the genetic architecture underlying disease vulnerability, genome-wide association studies (GWAS) play a crucial role in enabling the advancement of innovative diagnostic biomarkers, risk prediction models, and personalized therapy methods for individual patients (Wiley et al., 2024).

Approaches in Precision Medicine

Precision medicine signifies a fundamental transformation in the field of healthcare, wherein the focus shifts from a standardized treatment strategy to more precise and personalized therapies. The field of genomics plays a major role in precision medicine by facilitating the detection of genetic variations that impact drug response, susceptibility to diseases, and treatment results. Clinicians can enhance therapeutic efficacy and patient safety by utilizing genetic insights to customize treatment regimens, optimize drug dose, and reduce adverse events. Pharmacogenomics, an area of research that investigates the impact of genetic variants on drug response, is a fundamental component of precision medicine. Pharmacogenomic testing facilitates the identification of genetic indicators that can predict drug metabolism, effectiveness, and toxicity, hence informing treatment choices and dose modifications. Genetic testing for variations in the CYP2D6 gene can provide valuable information for choosing antidepressants and anti-psychotics, whereas testing for variations in the TPMT gene can assist in determining the appropriate dosage of thiopurine medicines used to treat autoimmune illnesses (Balogun et al., 2024).

Furthermore, oncology exemplifies the implementation of precision medicine, where genomics profiling informs the choice of specific treatments and immunotherapies according to tumour genetic traits. The utilization of molecular profiling techniques in tumour analysis facilitates the detection of significant mutations, such as EGFR mutations in non-small cell lung cancer or HER2 amplifications in breast cancer. This information plays a crucial role in informing treatment strategies and enhancing patient prognoses. In addition, liquid biopsies provide a less intrusive method for monitoring therapy response, detecting minimal residual illness, and identifying potential resistance mechanisms by analyzing circulating tumour DNA (ctDNA) released by tumors into the circulation (Wiley et al., 2024).

An Examination of Ethical Considerations in Genomics Healthcare

Genomics has great potential for personalized therapy, but it also presents intricate ethical dilemmas that need to be handled with caution. Genomics data possesses inherent sensitivity as it encompasses not just an individual's health concerns but also vital information regarding their family members and ancestral lineage. Therefore, it is of utmost importance to prioritize the preservation of patient trust and the prevention of misuse or bias by guaranteeing the privacy, confidentiality, and security of genetic data. Moreover, the fundamental aspects of genomics healthcare revolve around the concepts of consent, autonomy, and informed decision-making (Walton & Christensen,2023). Patients should get comprehensive information regarding the potential hazards, advantages, and constraints of genomics testing, encompassing the likelihood of unintended results, genetic bias, and psychological consequences. Furthermore, it is imperative to address the aspects of equity and access in order to guarantee that genetic technologies are readily available to persons of various socioeconomic statuses, geographic locations, and ethnic backgrounds (Tutton, 2016).

Furthermore, the understanding and practical importance of genetic variations can be intricate and subtle, necessitating continuous education, training, and collaboration among healthcare experts from different fields. Accurate interpretation of genomics test results, efficient communication of findings to patients, and integration of genomics information into clinical decision-making processes are imperative for

Generative Intelligence

clinicians. Furthermore, initiatives aimed at enhancing health literacy and providing genetic counselling services have the potential to empower individuals in making well-informed decisions on genetic testing, treatment alternatives, and preventative measures (Ranschaert et al., 2019).

In nutshell, the convergence of personalized medicine and genomics exhibits significant potential in revolutionizing the provision of healthcare, enhancing patient results, and furthering our comprehension of human biology and illness. Genomics data analysis allows for the detection of disease-related genetic variations and therapeutic targets, while precision medicine methods customize treatment plans according to individual genetic profiles. Nevertheless, it is imperative to acknowledge and tackle the ethical implications pertaining to genetic privacy, consent, and equity in order to guarantee the fair and responsible realization of the advantages offered by genomics healthcare. As the exploration of the genome progresses, it is crucial to approach this endeavour with meticulousness, empathy, and a dedication to advancing the physical and mental welfare of every individual (Kaur, 2024).

THE IMPLEMENTATION OF INTELLIGENT HEALTH MONITORING SYSTEMS

Intelligent health monitoring technologies are assuming a more pivotal role in transforming patient care within the dynamic healthcare environment. In order to facilitate proactive, personalized, and accessible healthcare delivery, these systems utilize sophisticated technologies such as remote patient monitoring, predictive analytic, and smart devices. This section examines the point where these elements meet, emphasizing their combined influence on enhancing patient results, improving clinical decision-making, and advancing healthcare availability as presented in figure 5 below:

Figure 5. Intersection of intelligent health monitoring systems

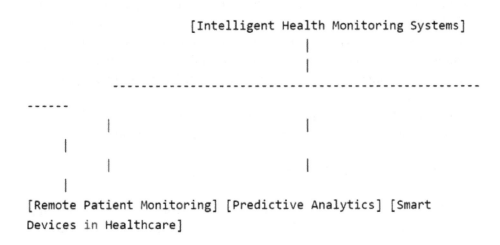

Telemedicine Patient Surveillance

Remote patient monitoring (RPM) is an innovative method of healthcare delivery that enables doctors to remotely monitor patients' health status and vital signs, without the need for typical clinical settings. Remote Patient Monitoring (RPM) systems employ a diverse range of mechanisms, including wearable sensors, mobile applications, and telehealth platforms, to gather health data in real-time and securely transfer it to healthcare clinicians for the purpose of analysis and intervention. An inherent benefit of RPM is its capacity to provide uninterrupted surveillance of individuals with persistent ailments, such as hypertension, diabetes, and heart failure, within their domestic settings. RPM systems can identify early indicators of worsening, enable prompt interventions, and prevent exacerbation or hospital re-admissions by monitoring important metrics such as blood pressure, blood glucose levels, and heart rate variability. Furthermore, Remote Patient Monitoring (RPM) improves patient involvement and self-care by granting individuals the ability to access their personal health information, educational materials, and tailored feedback, enabling them to actively participate in the management of their well-being (Benhlima, 2018).

Generative Intelligence

Moreover, the utilization of Remote Patient Monitoring (RPM) has demonstrated significant value within the realm of infectious disease management, namely in the face of public health emergencies like the ongoing COVID-19 epidemic. The utilization of telehealth platforms and remote monitoring systems allows healthcare providers to engage in virtual consultations, remotely prioritize patients, and monitor persons who are suspected or proven to have infections, all while mitigating the potential for transmission inside hospital environments. Remote Patient Monitoring (RPM) also plays a crucial role in enabling contact tracing, symptom tracking, and population surveillance, hence providing valuable help in the containment of outbreaks and the mitigation of infectious disease transmission (Luo et al., 2018).

Health Monitoring With Predictive Analytic

The utilization of predictive analytic has the potential to significantly improve health monitoring skills through the utilization of historical data, statistical modelling, and machine learning algorithms. This enables the forecasting of future health outcomes and the identification of individuals who are susceptible to bad events. Predictive analytic plays a crucial role in the realm of intelligent health monitoring systems by facilitating preemptive interventions, personalized risk classification, and targeted preventative actions that are specifically adapted to the unique characteristics of individual patients. Risk prediction for chronic diseases and medical problems is a significant use of predictive analytic in the field of health monitoring. Predictive models have the capability to identify individuals who are at a heightened risk of acquiring illnesses such as cardiovascular disease, stroke, or diabetic problems by examining longitudinal health data, which encompasses clinical records, laboratory results, and wearable sensor data. Timely detection of persons who are at risk allows healthcare practitioners to implement preventative measures, such as making changes to their lifestyle, adjusting their medication, or implementing care management programme, in order to reduce risk factors and enhance health results (Panayides et al., 2020).

In addition, the utilization of predictive analytic enables the implementation of dynamic risk classification and adaptive monitoring techniques that are informed by the continuous data and clinical trajectories of patients. Machine learning algorithms provide the ability to consistently acquire knowledge from fresh data inputs, enhance predictive models, and adjust risk stratification algorithms to address evolving patient profiles and healthcare requirements. This dynamic methodology facilitates the implementation of customized monitoring protocols that are specifically designed to align with the unique preferences, risk profiles, and clinical objectives of each patient. As a result, it optimizes the allocation of resources and improves the overall efficiency of healthcare delivery. Predictive analytic improves clinical decision-making by offering healthcare clinicians with practical insights and decision support tools. Predictive models can aid doctors in identifying patients who are likely to be readmitted to the hospital, develop sepsis, or fail to adhere to medication. This allows for early intervention and coordination of treatment, which helps minimize negative events and enhance patient outcomes. Furthermore, the utilization of predictive analytic facilitates population health management endeavors by the identification of sub-populations exhibiting distinct healthcare requirements or susceptibilities. This enables the implementation of focused interventions and the optimization of resource allocation, hence maximizing the efficacy of public health interventions (Ranschaert et al., 2019).

The Impact of Smart Devices on Enhancing Healthcare Accessibility

The utilization of intelligent technologies, such as smartphones, wearable sensors, and Internet-of-Things ((Io T) devices, is significantly transforming the accessibility of healthcare through the facilitation of remote monitoring, telehealth consultations, and self-management interventions. In order to enable individuals to monitor their health condition, track vital indicators, and access healthcare services from the comfort of their homes, these devices utilize wireless connectivity, sensor technology, and intuitive user interfaces (Hardy & Harvey, 2020). An important benefit of smart gadgets is their capacity to provide immediate health monitoring and data gathering in a non-intrusive and inconspicuous way. Smartwatches, fitness trackers, and continuous glucose monitors are examples of wearable sensors that allow individuals to effortlessly monitor vital signs, physical activity, and physiological data in their everyday routines. Through the provision of uninterrupted, long-term data streams, intelligent devices provide valuable information about patterns, trends, and variations in health condition. This allows for the early identification of abnormalities or departures from the normal state, and for fast treatments when needed (Kaur, 2024).

In addition, intelligent gadgets contribute to the improvement of healthcare accessible through the facilitation of telehealth consultations and virtual care delivery models. The utilization of telehealth platforms, mobile applications, and video conferencing tools has facilitated the remote connection between patients and healthcare providers, so enabling consultations, follow-up appointments, and care coordination without necessitating in-person visits (Panayides et al., 2020). This approach not only mitigates obstacles to entry for those facing limited mobility, transportation difficulties, or residing in remote areas, but also improves convenience and adaptability for all patients, facilitating prompt access to healthcare services as required. In addition, smart gadgets provide individuals with the ability to actively engage in the management of their health by means of self-monitoring and self-management interventions. Individuals can utilize mobile health applications, digital health trackers, and remote monitoring platforms to monitor their symptoms, medication adherence, and lifestyle behaviour. These tools also enable individuals to establish personalized health goals and receive feedback and support from healthcare experts. Smart gadgets play a crucial role in fostering behaviour change and empowering individuals to make educated decisions regarding their health and well-being by boosting self-awareness, engagement, and accountability (Fazal et al., 2018).

Overall, the integration of intelligent health monitoring systems, which include remote patient monitoring, predictive analytic, and smart devices, is significantly transforming the provision of healthcare by facilitating proactive, personalized, and easily accessible care. These technological advancements enable individuals to effectively monitor their health status, enable timely identification of health concerns, and remotely access healthcare services. Consequently, these advancements contribute to the enhancement of patient outcomes, the improvement of clinical decision-making processes, and the promotion of healthcare accessible for all individuals. In order to fully harness the potential of intelligent health monitoring systems and achieve their trans-formative impact on healthcare delivery in the digital era, it is imperative to emphasize the significance of interdisciplinary collaboration, data interoperability, and patient-centered design as the field continues to advance (et al., 2020).

Advancements in Pharmaceutical Research and Development

In the ever-evolving realm of healthcare, the significance of advancements in medication exploration and progression cannot be overstated, as they play a crucial role in tackling unaddressed medical requirements, propelling therapeutic alternatives forward, and enhancing patient results. The present section examines significant trends and progressions within this particular domain, encompassing the incorporation of Artificial Intelligence (AI) in the process of drug design and development, the utilization of Generative Intelligence to expedite clinical trials, the significance of pharmacogenomics in tailored therapeutic approaches, and the regulatory and ethical frameworks that are influencing the trajectory of pharmaceutical innovation.

ARTIFICIAL INTELLIGENCE IN DRUG DESIGN AND DEVELOPMENT

The incorporation of artificial intelligence (AI) into the process of drug design and development signifies a fundamental change in the field of pharmaceutical research, presenting novel opportunities for the exploration, enhancement, and adaptation of drugs. Machine learning algorithms, deep learning models, and predictive analytic are utilized in AI-driven methodologies to examine extensive datasets, detect innovative therapeutic targets, and forecast the effectiveness and safety of prospective drug candidates. Virtual screening is a prominent utilization of artificial intelligence (AI) in the field of drug development. This approach involves the use of computational models to forecast the binding affinity of small molecules and target proteins. This facilitates the swift identification of lead compounds that possess therapeutic potential. Furthermore, artificial intelligence (AI) algorithms have the potential to enhance the process of de novo drug creation by producing new molecular structures that possess optimized pharmacological properties. This can expedite the identification of groundbreaking therapeutic candidates (Kaur, 2024).

In addition, drug re-purposing platforms driven by artificial intelligence utilize preexisting drug databases, clinical trial data, and biological literature to detect novel applications for licensed drugs. This facilitates the accelerated advancement of treatments for uncommon illnesses, off-label scenarios, or emerging infectious diseases. AI-driven methodologies provide a cost-effective and time-efficient strategy for drug discovery by re-purposing existing molecules, thereby bypassing the protracted and costly process of conventional drug development (Shortliffe & Barnett, 2001).

The Utilization of Generative Intelligence to Expedite Clinical Trials

The concept of Generative Intelligence, which is distinguished by its capacity to produce innovative insights, solutions, and outcomes, exhibits significant potential in expediting the speed and effectiveness of clinical trials. Generative Intelligence utilizes sophisticated analytic, predictive modelling, and real-world evidence to identify patient populations, biomarkers, and therapeutic strategies that have the highest likelihood of success in clinical trials. This results in improved trial design, patient recruitment, and endpoint selection. Predictive modelling is a significant use of Generative Intelligence in clinical trials. It involves the analysis of patient data, illness features, and therapy responses using machine learning algorithms to forecast patient outcomes and treatment responses. The utilization of predictive models allows for the stratification of patient populations according to their probability of responding to therapy. This facilitates the implementation of personalized treatment strategies and enhances the composition of clinical trial cohorts by including individuals who are most likely to derive benefits from experimental interventions.

Additionally, the utilization of Generative Intelligence enables the implementation of adaptive trial designs, which involve the real-time modification of trial protocols in response to the accumulation of data and interim analysis. Adaptive trials provide researchers with the ability to enhance treatment regimens, modify sample sizes, and optimize trial endpoints in a dynamic manner. This approach aims to maximize the probability of trial success while simultaneously minimizing resource utilization and patient burden.

Pharmacogenomics and the Development of Personalized Therapeutics

Pharmacogenomics is the scientific investigation of how genetic variations impact the way drugs work. It is a fundamental aspect of personalized treatments, allowing for customized treatment methods that take into account individual genetic profiles. Pharmacogenomics plays a crucial role in informing treatment selection, dosage optimization, and adverse event management by finding genetic determinants of drug metabolism, effectiveness, and toxicity. This approach not only improves therapeutic outcomes but also mitigates risks for patients. Pharmacogenomics is mostly utilized in cancer to uncover tumor-specific mutations and inform the choice of targeted treatments and immunotherapies. As an illustration, the utilization of genetic testing to detect EGFR mutations in non-small cell lung cancer facilitates the identification of individuals who are more inclined to exhibit a favourable response to EGFR tyrosine kinase inhibitors, such as erlotinib or gefitinib. Similarly, the assessment of BRAF mutations in melanoma informs the selection of BRAF inhibitors, such as vemurafenib or dabrafenib.

In addition, pharmacogenomic testing plays a crucial role in providing valuable insights for medication dose and regimen optimization across a range of therapeutic domains, such as cardiology, psychiatry, and infectious illnesses. Genetic testing for variations in the CYP2D6 gene plays a crucial role in determining the appropriate choice and dosage of antidepressants and antipsychotics. Similarly, testing for variations in the TPMT gene provides valuable information for determining the dosage of thiopurine medicines used in the treatment of autoimmune illnesses. Pharmacogenomics facilitates the identification of individuals who are more susceptible to experiencing negative medication reactions, so enabling doctors to customize treatment plans in order to mitigate risks and optimize advantages. Healthcare professionals can enhance patient safety in real-time clinical practice by integrating pharmacogenomic data into clinical decision support systems and electronic health records. This integration enables informed prescribing decisions and optimizes medication therapy.

POLICY AND MORAL STRUCTURES

Regulatory Obstacles and Adherence to Regulations

Pharmaceutical businesses, researchers, and regulatory authorities face distinct regulatory issues due to the swift rate of innovation in medication discovery and development. While maintaining patient safety, data integrity, and ethical conduct throughout the drug development process, regulatory frameworks need to be flexible enough to accommodate new technologies, expanding therapeutic modalities, and complicated data sources. The validation and approval of AI-driven algorithms and predictive models for clinical decision-making pose significant regulatory problems in the field of drug development. The evaluation of the safety, efficacy, and reliability of AI-driven tools for drug discovery, diagnosis, and therapy selection falls under the purview of regulatory bodies, including the Food and Drug Administration (FDA) and the European Medicines Agency (EMA). Developing criteria for the verification, clarity, and comprehensibility of AI algorithms is crucial to guarantee adherence to regulations and cultivate confidence in AI-powered healthcare solutions (Khang et al., 2024).

Furthermore, the growing dependence on empirical data and digital health technologies in clinical research presents difficulties concerning the protection of data privacy, security, and adherence to legal requirements (Youssef, 2014). In order to ensure the confidentiality of patient information and mitigate the risk of data breaches, it is imperative to adhere to privacy regulations, such as the Health Insurance Portability and Accountability Act (HIPAA) in the United States or the General Data Protection Regulation (GDPR) in the European Union, when managing patient data obtained from electronic health records, wearable, and mobile applications. Moreover, the worldwide expansion of clinical trials and the rise of decentralized trial models pose regulatory obstacles concerning the standardization of data, the transmission of data across borders, and the alignment of regulations across different jurisdictions. In order to ensure consistency and openness in regulatory submissions and drug approvals, it is imperative for regulatory agencies to engage in collaborative efforts with international partners. This collaboration aims to establish harmonized standards for clinical trial conduct, data gathering, and reporting (Ogbuji, 2009).

Ensuring the Confidentiality and Protection of Data in the Healthcare Sector

The growing prevalence of digitization in healthcare data, together with the widespread adoption of interconnected devices and digital health solutions, gives rise to apprehensions over the safeguarding of data privacy, security, and confidentiality. Preserving the confidentiality of patient health information is of utmost importance in upholding trust, adhering to privacy legislation, and minimizing the potential for data breaches and cyberattacks. In order to protect electronic health records, patient portals, and telehealth platforms from unauthorized access, data breaches, and cyber threats, it is imperative for healthcare organizations to adopt and enforce strong security measures. This encompasses various security measures such as encryption, access controls, multi-factor authentication, and periodic security audits, which serve to detect vulnerabilities and proactively address threats. In addition, healthcare providers are required to comply with privacy requirements (Khang et al., 2024).

CONCLUSION

Generative Intelligence exhibits significant potential in influencing the trajectory of healthcare, fundamentally transforming the methods by which we mitigate, identify, and manage illnesses. The use of cutting-edge technology, such as Artificial Intelligence (AI) and machine learning, within healthcare systems has facilitated untapped prospects for innovation, cooperation, and the provision of personalized treatment. Healthcare providers can utilize Generative Intelligence to leverage data in order to generate meaningful insights, optimize clinical workflows, and improve patient outcomes. Clinicians may enhance their decision-making process, customize treatment plans to meet the specific needs of each patient, and detect emerging health trends or hazards before they worsen by utilizing AI algorithms and predictive analytic. Additionally, the utilization of Generative Intelligence enables the advancement of precision medical methodologies, utilizing genomics data, pharmacological, and empirical evidence to administer precise interventions that optimize effectiveness while minimizing negative consequences. Moreover, Generative Intelligence promotes cross-functional cooperation and the exchange of knowledge, uniting specialists from several domains including medicine, data science, engineering, and ethics to address intricate healthcare issues. By incorporating artificial intelligence (AI) alongside human expertise, healthcare teams can effectively utilize the synergistic capabilities of technology and human judgement to provide comprehensive, patient-centrist care that caters to the distinct requirements and preferences of every individual.

The future prospects of Generative Intelligence in healthcare are extensive and diverse. Generative Intelligence (GI) has the potential to significantly transform various aspects of the healthcare system, including medication research, clinical trial design, illness surveillance, and healthcare accessibility and equity. Nevertheless, the actualization of this potential necessitates a collaborative endeavour to tackle regulatory, ethical, and implementation obstacles, guarantee the confidentiality and protection of data, and cultivate an environment that promotes innovation, openness, and responsibility.

In the forthcoming years, as the field of Generative Intelligence progresses and reaches a more advanced stage, it is imperative to maintain a state of alertness in order to protect the welfare of patients, foster fairness and inclusiveness, and give precedence to ethical considerations throughout the creation and implementation of healthcare solutions driven by artificial intelligence. By employing Generative Intelligence, we may effectively utilize its transformation capabilities to create a future in healthcare that is genuinely tailored, anticipatory, and proactive, ultimately enhancing the health and welfare of individuals and communities on a global scale.

REFERENCES

Balogun, O. D., Ayo-Farai, O., Ogundairo, O., Maduka, C. P., Okongwu, C. C., Babarinde, A. O., & Sodamade, O. T. (2024). The Role of pharmacists in personalised medicine: A review of integrating pharmacogenomics into clinical practice. *International Medical Science Research Journal*, 4(1), 19–36. 10.51594/imsrj.v4i1.697

Beckfield, J., Olafsdottir, S., & Sosnaud, B. (2013). Healthcare systems in comparative perspective: Classification, convergence, institutions, inequalities, and five missed turns. *Annual Review of Sociology*, 39(1), 127–146. 10.1146/annurev-soc-071312-14560928769148

Benhlima, L. (2018). Big data management for healthcare systems: Architecture, requirements, and implementation. *Advances in Bioinformatics*, 2018.30034468

Betzel, R. F., & Bassett, D. S. (2017). Generative models for network neuroscience: Prospects and promise. *Journal of the Royal Society, Interface*, 14(136), 20170623. 10.1098/rsif.2017.062329187640

Chen, Y., & Esmaeilzadeh, P. (2024). Generative AI in Medical Practice: In-Depth Exploration of Privacy and Security Challenges. *Journal of Medical Internet Research*, 26, e53008. 10.2196/5300838457208

Consoli, D., & Mina, A. (2009). An evolutionary perspective on health innovation systems. *Journal of Evolutionary Economics*, 19(2), 297–319. 10.1007/s00191-008-0127-3

Fazal, M. I., Patel, M. E., Tye, J., & Gupta, Y. (2018). The past, present and future role of artificial intelligence in imaging. *European Journal of Radiology*, 105, 246–250. 10.1016/j.ejrad.2018.06.02030017288

Gejibo, S., Mancini, F., Mughal, K. A., Valvik, R. A., & Klungsøyr, J. (2012, October). Secure data storage for mobile data collection systems. In *Proceedings of the International Conference on Management of Emergent Digital EcoSystems* (pp. 131-144) ACM. 10.1145/2457276.2457300

Gong, C., Jing, C., Chen, X., Pun, C. M., Huang, G., Saha, A., Nieuwoudt, M., Li, H.-X., Hu, Y., & Wang, S. (2023). Generative AI for brain image computing and brain network computing: A review. *Frontiers in Neuroscience*, 17, 1203104. 10.3389/fnins.2023.120310437383107

Hardy, M., & Harvey, H. (2020). Artificial intelligence in diagnostic imaging: Impact on the radiography profession. *The British Journal of Radiology*, 93(1108), 20190840. 10.1259/bjr.2019084031821024

Kaur, J. (2024). Insightful Visions: How Medical Imaging Empowers Patient-Centric Healthcare. In *Future of AI in Medical Imaging* (pp. 42-57). IGI Global.

Kaur, J. (2024). Tech Unleashed: The Influential Power of Artificial Intelligence on Venture Capital and Startups. In *Fostering Innovation in Venture Capital and Startup Ecosystems* (pp. 219-241). IGI Global.

Kaur, J. (2024). Towards a Sustainable Triad: Uniting Energy Management Systems, Smart Cities, and Green Healthcare for a Greener Future. In *Emerging Materials, Technologies, and Solutions for Energy Harvesting* (pp. 258-285). IGI Global.

Kaur, J. (2024). AI-Driven Hospital Accounting: A Path to Financial Health. In *Harnessing Technology for Knowledge Transfer in Accountancy, Auditing, and Finance* (pp. 227-250). IGI Global.

Khang, A., Hajimahmud, A. V., Triwiyanto, T., Abuzarova, V. A., & Ali, R. N. (2024). Cloud Platform and Data Storage Systems in the Healthcare Ecosystem. In *Medical Robotics and AI-Assisted Diagnostics for a High-Tech Healthcare Industry* (pp. 343–356). IGI Global. 10.4018/979-8-3693-2105-8.ch021

Lehoux, P., Roncarolo, F., Rocha Oliveira, R., & Pacifico Silva, H. (2016). Medical innovation and the sustainability of health systems: A historical perspective on technological change in health. *Health Services Management Research*, 29(4), 115–123. 10.1177/0951484816670192

Luo, E., Bhuiyan, M. Z. A., Wang, G., Rahman, M. A., Wu, J., & Atiquzzaman, M. (2018). Privacyprotector: Privacy-protected patient data collection in IoT-based healthcare systems. *IEEE Communications Magazine*, 56(2), 163–168. 10.1109/MCOM.2018.1700364

Nova, K. (2023). Generative AI in healthcare: Advancements in electronic health records, facilitating medical languages, and personalized patient care. *Journal of Advanced Analytics in Healthcare Management*, 7(1), 115–131.

Ogbuji, C. (2009). *Clinical Data Acquisition*. Storage, and Management.

Oniani, D., Hilsman, J., Peng, Y., Poropatich, R. K., Pamplin, J. C., Legault, G. L., & Wang, Y. (2023). Adopting and expanding ethical principles for generative artificial intelligence from military to healthcare. *NPJ Digital Medicine*, 6(1), 225. 10.1038/s41746-023-00965-x38042910

Panayides, A. S., Amini, A., Filipovic, N. D., Sharma, A., Tsaftaris, S. A., Young, A., Foran, D., Do, N., Golemati, S., Kurc, T., Huang, K., Nikita, K. S., Veasey, B. P., Zervakis, M., Saltz, J. H., & Pattichis, C. S. (2020). AI in medical imaging informatics: Current challenges and future directions. *IEEE Journal of Biomedical and Health Informatics*, 24(7), 1837–1857. 10.1109/JBHI.2020.299104332609615

Ranschaert, E. R., Morozov, S., & Algra, P. R. (Eds.). (2019). *Artificial intelligence in medical imaging: opportunities, applications and risks*. Springer. 10.1007/978-3-319-94878-2

Sai, S., Gaur, A., Sai, R., Chamola, V., Guizani, M., & Rodrigues, J. J. (2024). Generative AI for Transformative Healthcare: A Comprehensive Study of Emerging Models, Applications, Case Studies and Limitations. *IEEE Access : Practical Innovations, Open Solutions*, 12, 31078–31106. 10.1109/ACCESS.2024.3367715

Sharma, P., Suehling, M., Flohr, T., & Comaniciu, D. (2020). Artificial intelligence in diagnostic imaging: Status quo, challenges, and future opportunities. *Journal of Thoracic Imaging*, 35(Supplement 1), S11–S16. 10.1097/RTI.0000000000000049932205816

Shortliffe, E. H., & Barnett, G. O. (2001). Medical data: their acquisition, storage, and use. In *Medical informatics: computer applications in health care and biomedicine* (pp. 41–75). Springer New York. 10.1007/978-0-387-21721-5_2

Singh, J. P. (2023). The Impacts and Challenges of Generative Artificial Intelligence in Medical Education, Clinical Diagnostics, Administrative Efficiency, and Data Generation. *International Journal of Applied Health Care Analytics*, 8(5), 37–46.

Tutton, R. (2016). *Genomics and the reimagining of personalized medicine*. Routledge. 10.4324/9781315584317

Wachter, R. M., & Brynjolfsson, E. (2024). Will generative artificial intelligence deliver on its promise in health care? *Journal of the American Medical Association*, 331(1), 65–69. 10.1001/jama.2023.2505438032660

Walton, N. A., & Christensen, G. B. (2023). Paving a pathway for large-scale utilization of genomics in precision medicine and population health. *Frontiers in Sociology*, 8, 1122488. 10.3389/fsoc.2023.112248837274607

Wiley, L. K., Shortt, J. A., Roberts, E. R., Lowery, J., Kudron, E., Lin, M., Mayer, D., Wilson, M., Brunetti, T. M., Chavan, S., Phang, T. L., Pozdeyev, N., Lesny, J., Wicks, S. J., Moore, E. T., Morgenstern, J. L., Roff, A. N., Shalowitz, E. L., Stewart, A., & Gignoux, C. R. (2024). Building a vertically integrated genomic learning health system: The biobank at the Colorado Center for Personalized Medicine. *American Journal of Human Genetics*, 111(1), 11–23. 10.1016/j.ajhg.2023.12.00138181729

Yim, D., Khuntia, J., Parameswaran, V., & Meyers, A. (2024). Preliminary Evidence of the Use of Generative AI in Health Care Clinical Services: Systematic Narrative Review. *JMIR Medical Informatics*, 12(1), e52073. 10.2196/5207338506918

Youssef, A. E. (2014). A framework for secure healthcare systems based on big data analytics in mobile cloud computing environments. *Int J Ambient Syst Appl*, 2(2), 1–11. 10.5121/ijasa.2014.2201

Compilation of References

Abacha, A. B., & Zweigenbaum, P. (2015). MEANS: A medical question-answering system combining NLP techniques and semantic Web technologies. *Information Processing & Management*, 51(5), 570–594. 10.1016/j.ipm.2015.04.006

Abbasimoshaei, A., Chinnakkonda Ravi, A. K., & Kern, T. A. (2023). Development of a New Control System for a Rehabilitation Robot Using Electrical Impedance Tomography and Artificial Intelligence. *Biomimetics*, 8(5), 420. 10.3390/biomimetics805042037754171

Abbas, Q., Hussain, A., & Baig, A. R. (2023). CAD-ALZ: A Blockwise Fine-Tuning Strategy on Convolutional Model and Random Forest Classifier for Recognition of Multistage Alzheimer's Disease. *Diagnostics (Basel)*, 13(1), 167. 10.3390/diagnostics1301016736611459

Abdallah, S., & Sharifa, M. (2023). I Kh Almadhoun MK, Khawar MM Sr, Shaikh U, Balabel KM, Saleh I, Manzoor A, Mandal AK, Ekomwereren O, Khine WM, Oyelaja OT. *The Impact of Artificial Intelligence on Optimizing Diagnosis and Treatment Plans for Rare Genetic Disorders. Cureus.*

Abouelmehdi, K., Beni-Hessane, A., & Khaloufi, H. (2018). Big healthcare data: Preserving security and privacy. *Journal of Big Data*, 5(1), 1–34. 10.1186/s40537-017-0110-7

Aboushelib, M. N., de Jager, N., Kleverlaan, C. J., Feilzer, A. J., Blatz, M. B., Oppes, S., & Holst, S. (2008). Hip reconstruction. *Quintessence International*, 39, 23–32.

Abràmoff, M. D., Tarver, M. E., Loyo-Berrios, N., Trujillo, S., Char, D., Obermeyer, Z., Eydelman, M. B., & Maisel, W. H. (2023). "Considerations for Addressing Bias in Artificial Intelligence for Health Equity." *npj. Digital Medicine*, 6(1), 170. 10.1038/s41746-023-00913-937700029

Ackerman, J. (2023, June 28). How AI can add value to value-based care. *Medical Economics*.

Adler-Milstein, J., Holmgren, A. J., Kralovec, P., Worzala, C., & Searcy, T. (2017). Electronic health record adoption in US hospitals: Progress continues, but challenges persist. *Health Affairs*, 36(8), 1567–1574. 10.1377/hlthaff.2017.0446

Adler-Milstein, J., Lin, S. C., & Jha, A. K. (2020). The number of health information exchange efforts is declining, leaving the viability of broad clinical data exchange uncertain. *Health Affairs*, 39(1), 63–71. 10.1377/hlthaff.2019.00539

Adus, S., Macklin, J., & Pinto, A. (2023). Exploring patient perspectives on how they can and should be engaged in the development of artificial intelligence (AI) applications in health care. *BMC Health Services Research*, 23(1), 1163. 10.1186/s12913-023-10098-2

Aggarwal, A., Chand, P. K., Jhamb, D., & Mittal, A. (2020). Leader–Member Exchange, Work Engagement, and Psychological Withdrawal Behavior: The Mediating Role of Psychological Empowerment. *Frontiers in Psychology*, 11(423), 423. Advance online publication. 10.3389/fpsyg.2020.0042332296361

Ahmad, A., Tariq, A., Hussain, H. K., & Gill, A. Y. (2023). Revolutionizing Healthcare: How Deep Learning is poised to Change the Landscape of Medical Diagnosis and Treatment. Journal of Computer Networks. *Architecture and High-Performance Computing*, 5(2), 458–471. 10.47709/cnahpc.v5i2.2350

Ahuja, A. S. (2019). The impact of artificial intelligence in medicine on the future role of the physician. *PeerJ*, 7, e7702. 10.7717/peerj.7702

Akinyele, K., Baudot, L., Koreff, J., & Sutton, S. (2024). Regulatory innovation and (de)legitimisation: accountability challenges in the healthcare field. *Accounting Forum*. 10.1080/01559982.2023.2295161

Alami, H., Lehoux, P., Denis, J. L., Motulsky, A., Petitgand, C., Savoldelli, M., Rouquet, R., Gagnon, M.-P., Roy, D., & Fortin, J. P. (2021). Organizational readiness for artificial intelligence in health care: Insights for decision-making and practice. *Journal of Health Organization and Management*, 35(1), 106–114. 10.1108/JHOM-03-2020-0074

Al-Halafi, A. M. (2023). Applications of artificial intelligence-assisted retinal imaging in systemic diseases: A literature review. *Saudi Journal of Ophthalmology*, 37(3), 185. 10.4103/sjopt.sjopt_153_23

Alhasan, M., & Hasaneen, M. (2021). Digital imaging, technologies and artificial intelligence applications during COVID-19 pandemic. *Computerized Medical Imaging and Graphics*, 91, 101933. 10.1016/j.compmedimag.2021.101933

Ali, H., Biswas, R., Ali, F., Shah, U., Alamgir, A., Mousa, O., & Shah, Z. (2022). The role of generative adversarial networks in brain MRI: a scoping review. In *Insights into Imaging* (Vol. 13, Issue 1). 10.1186/s13244-022-01237-0

Ali, M. (2023). A Comprehensive Review of AI's Impact on Healthcare: Revolutionizing Diagnostics and Patient Care. *BULLET: Jurnal Multidisiplin Ilmu*, 2(4), 1163–1173.

Aljohani, A., & Alharbe, N. (2022). Generating Synthetic Images for Healthcare with Novel Deep Pix2Pix GAN. *Electronics (Basel)*, 11(21), 3470. 10.3390/electronics11213470

Amisha, M., Malik, P., Pathania, M., & Rathaur, V. K. (2019). Overview of artificial intelligence in medicine. *Journal of Family Medicine and Primary Care*, 8(7), 2328–2331. 10.4103/jfmpc.jfmpc_440_19

Compilation of References

Amjad, A., Kordel, P., & Fernandes, G. (2023). A Review on Innovation in Healthcare Sector (Telehealth) through Artificial Intelligence. *Sustainability (Basel)*, 15(8), 6655. 10.3390/su15086655

Anderson, A. A. (2023). Correction to: Testing machine learning explanation methods. *Neural Computing & Applications*, 35(24), 18085–18085. 10.1007/s00521-023-08747-y

Angus, D. C. (2020). Randomized clinical trials of artificial intelligence. *Journal of the American Medical Association*, 323(11), 1043–1045. 10.1001/jama.2020.1039

Apell, P., & Eriksson, H. (2023). Artificial intelligence (AI) healthcare technology innovations: The current state and challenges from a life science industry perspective. *Technology Analysis and Strategic Management*, 35(2), 179–193. 10.1080/09537325.2021.1971188

Araz, O. M., Fowler, J. W., Lant, T. W., & Jehn, M. (2009, December). A pandemic influenza simulation model for preparedness planning. *Proceedings of the 2009 Winter Simulation Conference*. IEEE. 10.1109/WSC.2009.5429732

Ardila, D., Kiraly, A. P., Bharadwaj, S., Choi, B., Reicher, J. J., Peng, L., Tse, D., Etemadi, M., Ye, W., Corrado, G., Naidich, D. P., & Shetty, S. (2019). End-to-end lung cancer screening with three-dimensional deep learning on low-dose chest computed tomography. *Nature Medicine*, 25(6), 954–961. 10.1038/s41591-019-0447-x

Arize, I., Ogbuabor, D., Mbachu, C., Etiaba, E., Uzochukwu, B., & Onwujekwe, O. (2023). Stakeholders' perspectives on the unmet needs and health priorities of the urban poor in south-east Nigeria. *Community Health Equity Research & Policy*, 43(4), 389–398. 10.1177/0272684X211033441

Arji, G., Ahmadi, H., Avazpoor, P., & Hemmat, M. (2023). Identifying resilience strategies for disruption management in the healthcare supply chain during COVID-19 by digital innovations: A systematic literature review. *Informatics in Medicine Unlocked*, 38, 101199. 10.1016/j.imu.2023.10119936873583

Aronson, S. J., & Rehm, H. L. (2015). Building the foundation for genomics in precision medicine. *Nature*, 526(7573), 336–342. 10.1038/nature15816

Arora, A. (2020). Conceptualising artificial intelligence as a digital healthcare innovation: An introductory review. *Medical Devices (Auckland, N.Z.)*, 13, 223–230. 10.2147/MDER.S26259032904333

Arora, A., & Arora, A. (2022). Generative adversarial networks and synthetic patient data: Current challenges and future perspectives. *Future Healthcare Journal*, 9(2), 190–193. 10.7861/fhj.2022-001335928184

Arsene, C. (2019). *Artificial Intelligence in healthcare: The Future is Amazing*. Healthcare Weekly.

Arshi, O., Chaudhary, A., & Singh, R. (2023). Navigating the Future of Healthcare: AI-Powered Solutions, Personalized Treatment Plans, and Emerging Trends in 2023. In Swarnkar, S. K., & Rathore, Y. K. (Eds.), *International Conference on Artificial Intelligence for Innovations in Healthcare Industries, ICAIIHI 2023*. Institute of Electrical and Electronics Engineers Inc. 10.1109/ICAIIHI57871.2023.10489554

Ashley, E. A. (2016). Towards precision medicine. *Nature Reviews. Genetics*, 17(9), 507–522. 10.1038/nrg.2016.86

Ashrafur Rahman, S. M., & Zou, X. (2011). Flu epidemics: A two-strain flu model with a single vaccination. *Journal of Biological Dynamics*, 5(5), 376–390. 10.1080/17513758.2010.510213

Assi, E. B., Nguyen, D. K., Rihana, S., & Sawan, M. (2017). Towards accurate prediction of epileptic seizures: A review. *Biomedical Signal Processing and Control*, 34, 144–157. 10.1016/j.bspc.2017.02.001

Au Yeung, J., Kraljevic, Z., Luintel, A., Balston, A., Idowu, E., Dobson, R. J., & Teo, J. T. (2023). AI chatbots not yet ready for clinical use. *Frontiers in Digital Health*, 5, 1161098. Advance online publication. 10.3389/fdgth.2023.116109837122812

Aydın, Ö., & Karaarslan, E. (2022). OpenAI ChatGPT Generated Literature Review: Digital Twin in Healthcare. *SSRN*. 10.2139/ssrn.4308687

Azamjah, N., Soltan-Zadeh, Y., & Zayeri, F. (2019). Global Trend of Breast Cancer Mortality Rate: A 25-Year Study. *Asian Pacific Journal of Cancer Prevention*, 20(7), 2015–2020. 10.31557/APJCP.2019.20.7.201531350959

Babu, B., Sudha, S., & Caroline Jebakumari, S. (2023). Remote Delivery of Healthcare Services. In *EAI/Springer Innovations in Communication and Computing* (pp. 353–370). Springer Science and Business Media Deutschland GmbH. 10.1007/978-3-031-27700-9_22

Bajwa, J., Munir, U., Nori, A., & Williams, B. (2021). Artificial intelligence in healthcare: Transforming the practice of medicine. *Future Healthcare Journal*, 8(2), e188–e194. 10.7861/fhj.2021-0095

Balasubramanian, S., Shukla, V., Islam, N., Upadhyay, A., & Duong, L. (2023). Applying artificial intelligence in healthcare: Lessons from the COVID-19 pandemic. *International Journal of Production Research*, 1–34. 10.1080/00207543.2023.2263102

Balogun, O. D., Ayo-Farai, O., Ogundairo, O., Maduka, C. P., Okongwu, C. C., Babarinde, A. O., & Sodamade, O. T. (2024). The Role of pharmacists in personalised medicine: A review of integrating pharmacogenomics into clinical practice. *International Medical Science Research Journal*, 4(1), 19–36. 10.51594/imsrj.v4i1.697

Bandi, A., Adapa, P. V. S. R., & Yudu, E. V. P. K. K. (2023). The Power of Generative AI: A Review of Requirements, Models, Input–Output Formats, Evaluation Metrics, and Challenges. *Future Internet*, 15(8), 260. 10.3390/fi15080260

Barua, R. (2024). An In-Depth Exploration of AI and Humanoid Robotics' Role in Contemporary Healthcare. In *Approaches to Human-Centered AI in Healthcare* (pp. 42–61). IGI Global. 10.4018/979-8-3693-2238-3.ch003

Barua, R., Datta, S., & Sarkar, A. (2023). Artificial intelligence and robotics-based minimally invasive surgery: Innovations and future perceptions. In *Contemporary Applications of Data Fusion for Advanced Healthcare Informatics* (pp. 350–368). IGI Global. 10.4018/978-1-6684-8913-0.ch015

Compilation of References

Baydargil, H. B., Park, J. S., & Kang, D. Y. (2021). Anomaly Analysis of Alzheimer's Disease in Pet Images Using an Unsupervised Adversarial Deep Learning Model. *Applied Sciences (Basel, Switzerland)*, 11(5), 2187. 10.3390/app11052187

Becker, A. (2019). Artificial intelligence in medicine: What is it doing for us today? *Health Policy and Technology*, 8(2), 198–205. 10.1016/j.hlpt.2019.03.004

Beckfield, J., Olafsdottir, S., & Sosnaud, B. (2013). Healthcare systems in comparative perspective: Classification, convergence, institutions, inequalities, and five missed turns. *Annual Review of Sociology*, 39(1), 127–146. 10.1146/annurev-soc-071312-14560928769148

Bečulić, H., Begagić, E., Skomorac, R., Mašović, A., Selimović, E., & Pojskić, M. (2024). ChatGPT's contributions to the evolution of neurosurgical practice and education: A systematic review of benefits, concerns and limitations. *Medicinski Glasnik*, 21(1). Advance online publication. 10.17392/1661-2337950660

Beede, E., Baylor, E., Hersch, F., Iurchenko, A., Wilcox, L., Ruamviboonsuk, P., & Vardoulakis, L. M. (2020, April). A human-centered evaluation of a deep learning system deployed in clinics for the detection of diabetic retinopathy. In *Proceedings of the 2020 CHI conference on human factors in computing systems* (pp. 1-12). 10.1145/3313831.3376718

Bekbolatova M, Mayer J, Ong CW, Toma M. *Transformative Potential of AI in Healthcare: Definitions, Applications, and Navigating the Ethical Landscape and Public Perspectives.* Healthcare (Basel). 2024

Bellucci, N. (2022). Disruptive Innovation and Technological Influences on Healthcare. *Journal of Radiology Nursing*, 41(2), 98–101. 10.1016/j.jradnu.2022.02.008

Benhlima, L. (2018). Big data management for healthcare systems: Architecture, requirements, and implementation. *Advances in Bioinformatics*, 2018.30034468

Benjamens, S., Dhunnoo, P., & Meskó, B. (2020). The state of artificial intelligence-based FDA-approved medical devices and algorithms: An online database. *NPJ Digital Medicine*, 3(1), 118. 10.1038/s41746-020-00324-0

Benjamin, R. (2019). *Race after technology: Abolitionist tools for the new Jim code*. John Wiley & Sons.

Benzidia, S., Makaoui, N., & Bentahar, O. (2021). The impact of big data analytics and artificial intelligence on green supply chain process integration and hospital environmental performance. *Technological Forecasting and Social Change*, 165, 120557. 10.1016/j.techfore.2020.120557

Bertl, M., Ross, P., & Draheim, D. (2023). Systematic AI Support for Decision-Making in the Healthcare Sector: Obstacles and Success Factors. *Health Policy and Technology*, 12(3), 100748. 10.1016/j.hlpt.2023.100748

Betzel, R. F., & Bassett, D. S. (2017). Generative models for network neuroscience: Prospects and promise. *Journal of the Royal Society, Interface*, 14(136), 20170623. 10.1098/rsif.2017.062329187640

Bhalla, S., & Laganà, A. (2022). Artificial Intelligence for Precision Oncology. *Advances in Experimental Medicine and Biology*, 1361, 249–268. 10.1007/978-3-030-91836-1_14

Bialas, C., Bechtsis, D., Aivazidou, E., Achillas, C., & Aidonis, D. (2023). A Holistic View on the Adoption and Cost-Effectiveness of Technology-Driven Supply Chain Management Practices in Healthcare. *Sustainability (Basel)*, 15(6), 5541. 10.3390/su15065541

Bindu Bhavani, B., & Raghuveer, L. V. S. (2021). Smart Healthcare System for Psychological Disorders in Smart Cities. In *EAI/Springer Innovations in Communication and Computing* (pp. 65–76). Springer Science and Business Media Deutschland GmbH. 10.1007/978-3-030-48539-9_6

Biswas, A., Md Abdullah Al, N., Imran, A., Sejuty, A. T., Fairooz, F., Puppala, S., & Talukder, S. (2023). Generative Adversarial Networks for Data Augmentation. In *Data Driven Approaches on Medical Imaging*. 10.1007/978-3-031-47772-0_8

Biswas, S., Pillai, S., Kadhim, H. M., Salam, Z. A., & Marhoon, H. A. (2023, September). Building business resilience and productivity in the healthcare industry with the integration of robotic process automation technology. In *AIP Conference Proceedings* (Vol. 2736, No. 1). AIP Publishing. 10.1063/5.0171098

Blanco-González A, Cabezón A, Seco-González A, Conde-Torres D, Antelo-Riveiro P, Piñeiro Á, Garcia-Fandino R. *The Role of AI in Drug Discovery: Challenges, Opportunities, and Strategies*. Pharmaceuticals (Basel). 2023

Bohr, A., & Memarzadeh, K. (2020). *The rise of artificial intelligence in healthcare applications*. Artificial Intelligence in Healthcare. 10.1016/B978-0-12-818438-7.00002-2

Bordukova, M., Makarov, N., Rodriguez-Esteban, R., Schmich, F., & Menden, M. P. (2024). Generative artificial intelligence empowers digital twins in drug discovery and clinical trials. In *Expert Opinion on Drug Discovery* (Vol. 19, Issue 1). 10.1080/17460441.2023.2273839

Bou Assi, E., Gagliano, L., Rihana, S., Nguyen, D. K., & Sawan, M. (2018). Bispectrum features and multilayer perceptron classifier to enhance seizure prediction. *Scientific Reports*, 8(1), 15491. 10.1038/s41598-018-33969-9

Brooks, A. L. (2014). Disruptive innovation in healthcare and rehabilitation. *Studies in Computational Intelligence*, 536, 323–351. 10.1007/978-3-642-45432-5_16

Brynjolfsson, E., Li, D., & Raymond, L. R. (2023). *Generative AI at Work* (NBER Working Papers 31161). National Bureau of Economic Research, Inc..

Buchanan, B. G., & Shortliffe, E. H. (1984). *Rule based expert systems: the mycin experiments of the stanford heuristic programming project (the Addison-Wesley series in artificial intelligence)*. Addison-Wesley Longman Publishing Co., Inc.

Buolamwini, J., & Gebru, T. (2018). Gender shades: Intersectional accuracy disparities in commercial gender classification. Proceedings of Machine Learning Research, 81, 1-15. http://proceedings.mlr.press/v81/buolamwini18a.html

Compilation of References

Bush, J. (2018). How AI is taking the scut work out of health care. *Harvard Business Review*, •••, 5.

Buslón, N., Cortés, A., Catuara-Solarz, S., Cirillo, D., & Rementeria, M. J. (2023). Raising Awareness of Sex and Gender Bias in Artificial Intelligence and Health. *Frontiers in Global Women's Health*, 4, 970312. 10.3389/fgwh.2023.97031237746321

Cabitza, F., Rasoini, R., & Gensini, G. F. (2017). Unintended consequences of machine learning in medicine. *Journal of the American Medical Association*, 318(6), 517–518. 10.1001/jama.2017.7797

Cai, C. J., Winter, S., Steiner, D., Wilcox, L., & Terry, M. (2019). " Hello AI": uncovering the onboarding needs of medical practitioners for human-AI collaborative decision-making. *Proceedings of the ACM on Human-computer Interaction, 3*(CSCW), 1-24. 10.1145/3359206

Caine, K., & Hanania, R. (2018). Patients want granular privacy control over health information in electronic medical records. *Journal of the American Medical Informatics Association : JAMIA*, 25(8), 967–969. 10.1093/jamia/ocy026

Callaway, E. (2023). How generative AI is building better antibodies. *Nature*. 10.1038/d41586-023-01516-w37142726

Campanella, G., Hanna, M. G., Geneslaw, L., Miraflor, A., Werneck Krauss Silva, V., Busam, K. J., Brogi, E., Reuter, V. E., Klimstra, D. S., & Fuchs, T. J. (2019). Clinical-grade computational pathology using weakly supervised deep learning on whole slide images. *Nature Medicine*, 25(8), 1301–1309. 10.1038/s41591-019-0508-1

Candemir, S., Nguyen, X. V., Folio, L. R., & Prevedello, L. M. (2021). Training Strategies for Radiology Deep Learning Models in Data-limited Scenarios. *Radiology. Artificial Intelligence*, 3(6), e210014. 10.1148/ryai.202121001434870217

Cannavale, C., Esempio Tammaro, A., Leone, D., & Schiavone, F. (2022). Innovation adoption in inter-organizational healthcare networks – the role of artificial intelligence. *European Journal of Innovation Management*, 25(6), 758–774. 10.1108/EJIM-08-2021-0378

Care, N. R. (2012). *Measuring Shared Decision Making–A Review of Research Evidence: A Report for the Shared Decision Making Programme in Partnership with Capita Group Plc*. National Health Service, Department of Health.

Carla Kriwet Chief Executive Officer, Connected Care and Health Informatics Here are 3 ways AI will change healthcare by 2030. World Economic forum, Jan 7, 2020

Carnevale, A., Tangari, E. A., Iannone, A., & Sartini, E. (2023). Will Big Data and Personalized Medicine Do the Gender Dimension Justice? *AI & Society*, 38(2), 829–841. 10.1007/s00146-021-01234-934092931

Carr-Brown, J., & Berlucchi, M. (2016). *Pre-primary care: an untapped global health opportunity*. Your.

Carriere, J., Shafi, H., Brehon, K., Pohar Manhas, K., Churchill, K., Ho, C., & Tavakoli, M. (2021). Case report: Utilizing AI and NLP to assist with healthcare and rehabilitation during the COVID-19 pandemic. *Frontiers in Artificial Intelligence*, 4, 613637. 10.3389/frai.2021.613637

Cellina, M., Cacioppa, L. M., Cè, M., Chiarpenello, V., Costa, M., Vincenzo, Z., Pais, D., Bausano, M. V., Rossini, N., Bruno, A., & Floridi, C. (2023). Artificial Intelligence in Lung Cancer Screening: The Future Is Now. *Cancers (Basel)*, 15(17), 4344. 10.3390/cancers1517434437686619

Chambers, D., Cantrell, A. J., Johnson, M., Preston, L., Baxter, S. K., Booth, A., & Turner, J. (2019). Digital and online symptom checkers and health assessment/triage services for urgent health problems: Systematic review. *BMJ Open*, 9(8), e027743. 10.1136/bmjopen-2018-027743

Chang, Anthony C. 2020. Intelligence-Based Medicine: Artificial Intelligence and Human Cognition in Clinical Medicine and Healthcare *Intelligence-Based Medicine: Artificial Intelligence and Human Cognition in Clinical Medicine and Healthcare.*

Chan, H. S., Shan, H., Dahoun, T., Vogel, H., & Yuan, S. (2019). Advancing drug discovery via artificial intelligence. *Trends in Pharmacological Sciences*, 40(8), 592–604. 10.1016/j.tips.2019.06.004

Chan, Y., Li, M., Parodi, K., Belka, C., Landry, G., & Kurz, C. (2023). Feasibility of CycleGAN Enhanced Low Dose CBCT Imaging for Prostate Radiotherapy Dose Calculation. *Physics in Medicine and Biology*, 68(10), 105014. 10.1088/1361-6560/acccce37054740

Char, D. S., Shah, N. H., & Magnus, D.Implementing Machine Learning in Health Care Workgroup. (2020). Implementing machine learning in health care—Addressing ethical challenges. *The New England Journal of Medicine*, 378(11), 981–983. 10.1056/NEJMp1714229

Chattopadhyay, A., & Maitra, M. (2022). MRI-Based Brain Tumour Image Detection Using CNN Based Deep Learning Method. *Neuroscience Informatics (Online)*, 2(4), 100060. 10.1016/j.neuri.2022.100060

Chatzilena, A., Van Leeuwen, E., Ratmann, O., Baguelin, M., & Demiris, N. (2019). Contemporary statistical inference for infectious disease models using Stan. *Epidemics*, 29, 1–16. 10.1016/j.epidem.2019.10036731591003

Chen, Y., & Esmaeilzadeh, P. (2024). Generative AI in Medical Practice: In-Depth Exploration of Privacy and Security Challenges. In *Journal of Medical Internet Research* (Vol. 26, Issue 1). 10.2196/53008

Chen, Y., Shi, F., Christodoulou, A. G., Xie, Y., Zhou, Z., & Li, D. 2018. "Efficient and Accurate MRI Super-Resolution Using a Generative Adversarial Network and 3D Multi-Level Densely Connected Network." In *Lecture Notes in Computer Science (Including Subseries Lecture Notes in Artificial Intelligence and Lecture Notes in Bioinformatics)*. Springer. 10.1007/978-3-030-00928-1_11

Chen, C. Y., Ward, J. P., & Xie, W. B. (2019). Modelling the outbreak of infectious disease following mutation from a non-transmissible strain. *Theoretical Population Biology*, 126, 1–18. 10.1016/j.tpb.2018.08.00230165060

Compilation of References

Chen, J. H., & Asch, S. M.Machine Learning in Medicine Workgroup. (2021). Machine learning and prediction in medicine: Beyond the peak of inflated expectations. *The New England Journal of Medicine*, 384(23), 2077–2082. 10.1056/NEJMsb2029340

Chen, X., Xie, H., Li, Z., Cheng, G., Leng, M., & Wang, F. L. (2023). Information fusion and artificial intelligence for smart healthcare: A bibliometric study. *Information Processing & Management*, 60(1), 103113. 10.1016/j.ipm.2022.103113

Chen, Y., Jensen, S., Albert, L. J., Gupta, S., & Lee, T. (2023). Artificial intelligence (AI) student assistants in the classroom: Designing chatbots to support student success. *Information Systems Frontiers*, 25(1), 161–182. 10.1007/s10796-022-10291-4

Chi, O. H., Chi, C. G., Gursoy, D., & Nunkoo, R. (2023). Customers' acceptance of artificially intelligent service robots: The influence of trust and culture. *International Journal of Information Management*, 70, 102623. 10.1016/j.ijinfomgt.2023.102623

Chiu, Y. T., Zhu, Y. Q., & Corbett, J. (2021, October 1). In the hearts and minds of employees: A model of pre-adoptive appraisal toward artificial intelligence in organizations. *International Journal of Information Management*, 60, 102379. 10.1016/j.ijinfomgt.2021.102379

Choi, B. K., Dayaram, T., Parikh, N., Wilkins, A. D., Nagarajan, M., Novikov, I. B., Bachman, B. J., Jung, S. Y., Haas, P. J., Labrie, J. L., Pickering, C. R., Adikesavan, A. K., Regenbogen, S., Kato, L., Lelescu, A., Buchovecky, C. M., Zhang, H., Bao, S. H., Boyer, S., & Lichtarge, O. (2018). Literature-based automated discovery of tumor suppressor p53 phosphorylation and inhibition by NEK2. *Proceedings of the National Academy of Sciences of the United States of America*, 115(42), 10666–10671. 10.1073/pnas.1806643115

Choi, E., Biswal, S., Malin, B., Duke, J., Stewart, W. F., & Sun, J. (2017, November). Generating multi-label discrete patient records using generative adversarial networks. In *Machine learning for healthcare conference* (pp. 286–305). PMLR.

Choudhury, A., & Asan, O. (2022). Impact of accountability, training, and human factors on the use of artificial intelligence in healthcare: Exploring the perceptions of healthcare practitioners in the US. *Human Factors in Healthcare*, 2, 10002. 10.1016/j.hfh.2022.100021

Cho, Y. S. (2023). From Code to Cure: *Unleashing the Power of Generative Artificial Intelligence in Medicine.International Neurourology Journal*, 27(4), 225–226. 10.5213/inj.2323edi06

Chwelos, P., Benbasat, I., & Dexter, A. S. (2001). Empirical test of an EDI adoption model. *Information Systems Research*, 12(3), 304–321. 10.1287/isre.12.3.304.9708

Ciotti, M., Ciccozzi, M., Terrinoni, A., Jiang, W. C., Wang, C. B., & Bernardini, S. (2020). The COVID-19 pandemic. *Critical Reviews in Clinical Laboratory Sciences*, 57(6), 365–388. 10.1080/10408363.2020.178319832645276

Clusmann, J., Kolbinger, F. R., Muti, H. S., Carrero, Z. I., Eckardt, J.-N., Laleh, N. G., Löffler, C. M. L., Schwarzkopf, S.-C., Unger, M., Veldhuizen, G. P., Wagner, S. J., & Kather, J. N. (2023). The future landscape of large language models in medicine. *Communications Medicine*, 3(1), 141. 10.1038/s43856-023-00370-137816837

Cohen, D., & Adar, E. (2019). How do you know? Building and measuring trust in AI. arXiv preprint arXiv:1912.08968. https://arxiv.org/abs/1912.08968

Consoli, D., & Mina, A. (2009). An evolutionary perspective on health innovation systems. *Journal of Evolutionary Economics*, 19(2), 297–319. 10.1007/s00191-008-0127-3

Corny, J., Rajkumar, A., Martin, O., Dode, X., Lajonchère, J. P., Billuart, O., Bézie, Y., & Buronfosse, A. (2020). A machine learning–based clinical decision support system to identify prescriptions with a high risk of medication error. *Journal of the American Medical Informatics Association : JAMIA*, 27(11), 1688–1694. 10.1093/jamia/ocaa154

Coste, M., & Bousmah, M.-A.-Q. (2023). Predicting health services utilization using a score of perceived barriers to medical care: Evidence from rural Senegal. *BMC Health Services Research*, 23(1), 263. 10.1186/s12913-023-09192-2

Cressman, S., Ghanbarian, S., Edwards, L., Peterson, S., Bunka, M., Hoens, A. M., Riches, L., Austin, J., Vijh, R., McGrail, K., & Bryan, S. (2023). Costs of major depression covered / not covered in British Columbia, Canada. *BMC Health Services Research*, 23(1), 1446. 10.1186/s12913-023-10474-y

Cruciger, O., Schildhauer, T. A., Meindl, R. C., Tegenthoff, M., Schwenkreis, P., Citak, M., & Aach, M. (2016). Impact of locomotion training with a neurologic controlled hybrid assistive limb (HAL) exoskeleton on neuropathic pain and health related quality of life (HRQoL) in chronic SCI: A case study. *Disability and Rehabilitation. Assistive Technology*, 11(6), 529–534.

Cummings, J., Lee, G., Ritter, A., & Zhong, K. (2018). Alzheimer's Disease Drug Development Pipeline: 2018. *Alzheimer's & Dementia: Translational Research & Clinical Interventions*, 4(1), 195–214. 10.1016/j.trci.2018.03.00929955663

Cynerio. (2023). *Cynerio Harnesses the Power of Generative AI to Revolutionize Healthcare Cybersecurity*. Cynerio. https://www.cynerio.com/blog/cynerio-harnesses-the-power-of-generative-ai-to-revolutionize-healthcare-cybersecurity

Dahmani, K., Tahiri, A., Habert, O., & Elmeftouhi, Y. (2016, April). An intelligent model of home support for people with loss of autonomy: A novel approach. In *2016 International Conference on Control, Decision and Information Technologies (CoDIT)* (pp. 182-185). IEEE. 10.1109/CoDIT.2016.7593557

Dale, R. (2021). GPT-3: What's it good for? *Natural Language Engineering*, 27(1), 113–118. 10.1017/S1351324920000601

Dansu, E. J., & Seno, H. (2019). A model for epidemic dynamics in a community with visitor subpopulation. *Journal of Theoretical Biology*, 478, 115–127. 10.1016/j.jtbi.2019.06.02031228488

Compilation of References

Darda, P., & Matta, N. (2024). The Nexus of healthcare and technology: A thematic analysis of digital transformation through artificial intelligence. In *Transformative Approaches to Patient Literacy and Healthcare Innovation* (pp. 261–282). IGI Global. 10.4018/979-8-3693-3661-8.ch013

Davenport, T. H. (2018). *The AI advantage: How to put the artificial intelligence revolution to work*. mit Press..

Davenport, T. H. (2021). Artificial Intelligence in Healthcare: Promise and Reality. *Healthcare Informatics: Strategies for the Digital Era*, 227.

Davenport, T. H., & Glaser, J. (2002). Just-in-time delivery comes to knowledge management. *Harvard Business Review*, 80(7), 107–111.

Davenport, T., & Kalakota, R. (2019). The potential for artificial intelligence in healthcare. *Future Healthcare Journal*, 6(2), 94–98. 10.7861/futurehosp.6-2-94

de Souza, L. L., Fonseca, F. P., Martins, M. D., de Almeida, O. P., Pontes, H. A. R., Coracin, F. L., Lopes, M. A., Khurram, S. A., Santos-Silva, A. R., Hagag, A., & Vargas, P. A. (2023). ChatGPT and medicine: a potential threat to science or a step towards the future? In *Journal of Medical Artificial Intelligence* (Vol. 6). 10.21037/jmai-23-70

Denti, L., & Hemlin, S. (2012). Leadership and innovation in organizations: A systematic review of factors that mediate or moderate the relationship. *International Journal of Innovation Management*, 16(03), 1240007. 10.1142/S1363919612400075

Desai, A. N. (2020). Artificial intelligence: Promise, pitfalls, and perspective. *Journal of the American Medical Association*, 323(24), 2448–2449. 10.1001/jama.2020.873732492093

Dhiman, R., Chand, P. K., & Gupta, S. (2018). Behavioural Aspects Influencing Decision to Purchase Apparels amongst Young Indian Consumers. *FIIB Business Review*, 7(3), 188–200. 10.1177/2319714518790308

Díaz, Ó., Dalton, J. A., & Giraldo, J. (2019). Artificial intelligence: A novel approach for drug discovery. *Trends in Pharmacological Sciences*, 40(8), 550–551. 10.1016/j.tips.2019.06.005

Dicuonzo, G., Donofrio, F., Fusco, A., & Shini, M. (2023). Healthcare system: Moving forward with artificial intelligence. *Technovation*, 120, 102510. 10.1016/j.technovation.2022.102510

Dilibal, C., Davis, D. L., & Chakraborty, C. (2021). Generative Design Methodology for Internet of Medical Things (IoMT)-based Wearable Biomedical Devices. In *Proceedings of the 2021 3rd International Congress on Human-Computer Interaction, Optimization and Robotic Applications (HORA)*. IEEE: Piscataway.

Dizon, R. J. R. (2023). Do public healthcare programs make societies more equal? Cross-country evidence on subjective wellbeing. *Health Economics Review*, 13(1), 55. 10.1186/s13561-023-00467-2

Drukker, K., Chen, W., Gichoya, J., Gruszauskas, N., Kalpathy-Cramer, J., Koyejo, S., Myers, K., Sá, R. C., Sahiner, B., Whitney, H., Zhang, Z., & Giger, M. (2023). Toward Fairness in Artificial Intelligence for Medical Image Analysis: Identification and Mitigation of Potential Biases in the Roadmap from Data Collection to Model Deployment. *Journal of Medical Imaging (Bellingham, Wash.)*, 10(06). 10.1117/1.JMI.10.6.06110437125409

Dwivedi, Y. K., Kshetri, N., Hughes, L., Slade, E. L., Jeyaraj, A., Kar, A. K., Baabdullah, A. M., Koohang, A., Raghavan, V., Ahuja, M., Albanna, H., Albashrawi, M. A., Al-Busaidi, A. S., Balakrishnan, J., Barlette, Y., Basu, S., Bose, I., Brooks, L., Buhalis, D., & Wright, R. (2023). "So what if ChatGPT wrote it?" Multidisciplinary perspectives on opportunities, challenges and implications of generative conversational AI for research, practice and policy. *International Journal of Information Management*, 71, 102642. 10.1016/j.ijinfomgt.2023.102642

Elhussein, M., Brahimi, S., Alreedy, A., Alqahtani, M., & Olatunji, S. O. (2020). Google trends identifying seasons of religious gathering: Applied to investigate the correlation between crowding and flu outbreak. *Information Processing & Management*, 57(3), 102208. 10.1016/j.ipm.2020.102208

Elkin, P. L., Schlegel, D. R., Anderson, M., Komm, J., Ficheur, G., & Bisson, L. (2018). Artificial intelligence: Bayesian versus heuristic method for diagnostic decision support. *Applied Clinical Informatics*, 9(02), 432–439. 10.1055/s-0038-1656547

Epstein, Z., Hertzmann, A., Akten, M., Farid, H., Fjeld, J., Frank, M. R., Groh, M., Herman, L., Leach, N., Mahari, R., Pentland, A. S., Russakovsky, O., Schroeder, H., & Smith, A. (2023). Art and the science of generative AI. *Science*, 380(6650), 1110–1111. 10.1126/science.adh445137319193

Esteva, A., Kuprel, B., Novoa, R. A., Ko, J., Swetter, S. M., Blau, H. M., & Thrun, S. (2017). Dermatologist-level classification of skin cancer with deep neural networks. *nature*, 542(7639), 115-118.

Esteva, A., Feng, J., van der Wal, D., Huang, S. C., Simko, J. P., DeVries, S., Chen, E., Schaeffer, E. M., Morgan, T. M., Sun, Y., Ghorbani, A., Naik, N., Nathawani, D., Socher, R., Michalski, J. M., Roach, M.III, Pisansky, T. M., Monson, J. M., Naz, F., & Mohamad, O. (2022). "Prostate Cancer Therapy Personalization via Multi-Modal Deep Learning on Randomized Phase III Clinical Trials." *npj. Digital Medicine*, 5(1), 71. 10.1038/s41746-022-00613-w35676445

Esteva, A., & Topol, E. (2019). Can Skin Cancer Diagnosis Be Transformed by AI? *Lancet*, 394(10211), 1795. 10.1016/S0140-6736(19)32726-6

Etemadi, M., Ashtarian, K., & Ganji, N. (2023). A model of financial support for the poor to access health services in Iran: Delphi technique. *International Journal of Health Governance*, 28(2), 165–178. 10.1108/IJHG-07-2022-0071

Evans, R. S.Electronic Health Record Information, Utah Sentinel Surveillance Network and Intermountain Healthcare Clinical Genetics Institute. (2020). Electronic health records: Then, now, and in the future. *Yearbook of Medical Informatics*, 29(1), 242–249. 10.1055/s-0040-1713158

Compilation of References

Eysenbach, G. (2023). The role of ChatGPT, generative language models, and artificial intelligence in medical education: A conversation with ChatGPT and a call for papers. *JMIR Medical Education*, 9, e46885. 10.2196/4688536863937

Fakoor, R., Ladhak, F., Nazi, A., & Huber, M. (2013, June). Using deep learning to enhance cancer diagnosis and classification. In *Proceedings of the international conference on machine learning* (Vol. 28, pp. 3937-3949). New York, NY, USA: ACM.

Farhan, M. (2024). Empowering healthcare: Symbiotic innovations of AI and blockchain technology. In *Blockchain and AI: The Intersection of Trust and Intelligence* (pp. 23–57). CRC Press. 10.1201/9781003162018-2

Farhud, D. D., & Zokaei, S. (2021). Ethical Issues of Artificial Intelligence in Medicine and Healthcare. *Iranian Journal of Public Health*. Advance online publication. 10.18502/ijph.v50i11.7600

Farooq, J., & Bazaz, M. A. (2020). A novel adaptive deep learning model of Covid-19 with focus on mortality reduction strategies. *Chaos, Solitons, and Fractals*, 138, 1–13. 10.1016/j.chaos.2020.11014832834586

Fazal, M. I., Patel, M. E., Tye, J., & Gupta, Y. (2018). The past, present and future role of artificial intelligence in imaging. *European Journal of Radiology*, 105, 246–250. 10.1016/j.ejrad.2018.06.02030017288

Fernandes, M., Vieira, S. M., Leite, F., Palos, C., Finkelstein, S., & Sousa, J. M. (2020). Clinical decision support systems for triage in the emergency department using intelligent systems: A review. *Artificial Intelligence in Medicine*, 102, 101762. 10.1016/j.artmed.2019.101762

Fidan, I., Huseynov, O., Ali, M. A., Alkunte, S., Rajeshirke, M., Gupta, A., Hasanov, S., Tantawi, K., Yasa, E., Yilmaz, O., Loy, J., Popov, V., & Sharma, A. (2023). Recent inventions in additive manufacturing: Holistic review. *Inventions (Basel, Switzerland)*, 8(4), 103. 10.3390/inventions8040103

Firoozi, A. A., & Firoozi, A. A. (2023). A systematic review of the role of 4D printing in sustainable civil engineering solutions. *Heliyon*, 9(10), e20982. 10.1016/j.heliyon.2023.e2098237928382

Forcier, M. B., Gallois, H., Mullan, S., & Joly, Y. (2019). Integrating artificial intelligence into health care through data access: Can the GDPR act as a beacon for policymakers? *Journal of Law and the Biosciences*, 6(1), 317–335. 10.1093/jlb/lsz013

Foster, K. R., Koprowski, R., & Skufca, J. D. (2014). Machine learning, medical diagnosis, and biomedical engineering research-commentary. *Biomedical Engineering Online*, 13(1), 1–9. 10.1186/1475-925X-13-94

Freedman, D., Blau, Y., Katzir, L., Aides, A., Shimshoni, I., Veikherman, D., Golany, T., Gordon, A., Corrado, G., Matias, Y., & Rivlin, E. (2020). Detecting deficient coverage in colonoscopies. *IEEE Transactions on Medical Imaging*, 39(11), 3451–3462. 10.1109/TMI.2020.2994221

Friebe, M. H. (2020). Healthcare in need of innovation: Exponential technology and biomedical entrepreneurship as solution providers (Keynote Paper). In Fei, B., & Linte, C. A. (Eds.), *Proceedings of SPIE- The International Society for Optical Engineering* (Vol. 11315). SPIE. 10.1117/12.2556776

Frist, B. (2023). How Generative AI – A Technology Catalyst – Is Revolutionizing Healthcare. Available at https://www.forbes.com/sites/billfrist/2023/08/01/how-generative-ai--a-technology-catalyst--is-revolutionizing-healthcare/?sh=67b658495013

Fügener, A., Grahl, J., Gupta, A., & Ketter, W. (2021). Will humans-in-the-loop become borgs? Merits and pitfalls of working with AI. [MISQ]. *Management Information Systems Quarterly*, 45(3), 1527–1556. 10.25300/MISQ/2021/16553

Fu, Y., Jung, A. W., Torne, R. V., Gonzalez, S., Vöhringer, H., Shmatko, A., Yates, L. R., Jimenez-Linan, M., Moore, L., & Gerstung, M. (2020). Pan-cancer computational histopathology reveals mutations, tumor composition and prognosis. *Nature Cancer*, 1(8), 800–810. 10.1038/s43018-020-0085-8

Gagliano, L., Assi, E. B., Nguyen, D. K., Rihana, S., & Sawan, M. (2018). Bilateral preictal signature of phase-amplitude coupling in canine epilepsy. *Epilepsy Research*, 139, 123–128. 10.1016/j.eplepsyres.2017.11.009

Gama, F., Tyskbo, D., Nygren, J., Barlow, J., Reed, J., & Svedberg, P. (2022). Implementation frameworks for artificial intelligence translation into health care practice: Scoping review. *Journal of Medical Internet Research*, 24(1), e32215. 10.2196/32215

Gao, J., Kim, H., & Mitra, S. (2023). Out-of-pocket health expenditures associated with chronic health conditions and disability in China. *International Journal of Environmental Research and Public Health*, 20(15), 6465. Advance online publication. 10.3390/ijerph20156465

Garcia Valencia, O. A., Thongprayoon, C., Jadlowiec, C. C., Mao, S. A., Miao, J., & Cheungpasitporn, W. (2023). Enhancing Kidney Transplant Care through the Integration of Chatbot. In *Healthcare (Switzerland)* (Vol. 11, Issue 18). 10.3390/healthcare11182518

García-Vázquez, J. P., Rodríguez, M. D., Tentori, M., Saldaña-Jimenez, D., Andrade, Á. G., & Espinoza, A. N. (2010). An Agent-based Architecture for Developing Activity-Aware Systems for Assisting Elderly. *Journal of Universal Computer Science*, 16(12), 1500–1520.

Garg, S., Tripathi, N., & Bebarta, K. K. (2023). Does government health insurance protect households from out of pocket expenditure and distress financing for caesarean and non-caesarean institutional deliveries in India? Findings from the national family health survey (2019-21). *BMC Research Notes*, 16(1), 85. 10.1186/s13104-023-06335-w

Gautam, R. (2023). *OSM-GPT: An Innovative Project Combining GPT-3 and the Overpass API to Facilitate Easy Feature Discovery on OpenStreetMap*. Github. https://github.com/rowheat02/osm-gpt

Compilation of References

Gejibo, S., Mancini, F., Mughal, K. A., Valvik, R. A., & Klungsøyr, J. (2012, October). Secure data storage for mobile data collection systems. In *Proceedings of the International Conference on Management of Emergent Digital EcoSystems* (pp. 131-144). ACM. 10.1145/2457276.2457300

Gennatas, E. D., & Chen, J. H. 2020. "Artificial Intelligence in Medicine: Past, Present, and Future." In *Artificial Intelligence in Medicine: Technical Basis and Clinical Applications*. Springer. 10.1016/B978-0-12-821259-2.00001-6

George, A. S., George, A. H., & Martin, A. G. (2023). ChatGPT and the Future of Work: A Comprehensive Analysis of AI's Impact on Jobs and Employment. *Partners Universal International Innovation Journal*, 1(3), 154–186.

Gerke, S., Minssen, T., & Cohen, G. (2020). *Ethical and legal challenges of artificial intelligence-driven healthcare*. Artificial Intelligence in Healthcare. 10.1016/B978-0-12-818438-7.00012-5

Ghaleb, E. A. B., Dominic, P. D. D., & Sarlan, A. (2020). Impact of emerging technology innovations on healthcare transformation in developing countries. *2020 2nd International Sustainability and Resilience Conference: Technology and Innovation in Building Designs*. IEEE. 10.1109/IEEECONF51154.2020.9319955

Ghorbani, A., Ouyang, D., Abid, A., He, B., Chen, J. H., Harrington, R. A., Liang, D. H., Ashley, E. A., & Zou, J. Y. (2020). Deep learning interpretation of echocardiograms. *NPJ Digital Medicine*, 3(1), 10. 10.1038/s41746-019-0216-8

Goktas, P., Karakaya, G., Kalyoncu, A. F., & Damadoglu, E. (2023). Artificial Intelligence Chatbots in Allergy and Immunology Practice: Where Have We Been and Where Are We Going? *The Journal of Allergy and Clinical Immunology. In Practice*, 11(9), 2697–2700. Advance online publication. 10.1016/j.jaip.2023.05.04237301435

Golda, A., Mekonen, K., Pandey, A., Singh, A., Hassija, V., Chamola, V., & Sikdar, B. (2024). Privacy and Security Concerns in Generative AI: A Comprehensive Survey. *IEEE Access : Practical Innovations, Open Solutions*, 12, 48126–48144. 10.1109/ACCESS.2024.3381611

Gong, C., Jing, C., Chen, X., Pun, C. M., Huang, G., Saha, A., Nieuwoudt, M., Li, H.-X., Hu, Y., & Wang, S. (2023). Generative AI for brain image computing and brain network computing: A review. *Frontiers in Neuroscience*, 17, 1203104. 10.3389/fnins.2023.120310437383107

Gong, D., Wu, L., Zhang, J., Mu, G., Shen, L., Liu, J., Wang, Z., Zhou, W., An, P., Huang, X., Jiang, X., Li, Y., Wan, X., Hu, S., Chen, Y., Hu, X., Xu, Y., Zhu, X., Li, S., & Yu, H. (2020). Detection of colorectal adenomas with a real-time computer-aided system (ENDOANGEL): A randomised controlled study. *The Lancet. Gastroenterology & Hepatology*, 5(4), 352–361. 10.1016/S2468-1253(19)30413-3

Goodfellow, Pouget-Abadie, Mirza, Xu, Warde-Farley, & Ozair. (2014). *Generative adversarial networks*. Academic Press.

Goyal, S., & Kaushal, L. (2024). Harnessing generative AI: Transformative applications in medical imaging and beyond. *Future Health*, 2, 21–33. Advance online publication. 10.25259/FH_12_2024

Greenberg, N., Docherty, M., Gnanapragasam, S., & Wessely, S. (2020). Managing mental health challenges faced by healthcare workers during covid-19 pandemic. *bmj, 368.*

Guan, S. (2019). Breast Cancer Detection Using Synthetic Mammograms from Generative Adversarial Networks in Convolutional Neural Networks. *Journal of Medical Imaging (Bellingham, Wash.)*, 6(03), 1. 10.1117/1.JMI.6.3.03141130915386

Gudigar, A., Raghavendra, U., Nayak, S., Ooi, C. P., Chan, W. Y., Gangavarapu, M. R., Dharmik, C., Samanth, J., Kadri, N. A., Hasikin, K., Barua, P. D., Chakraborty, S., Ciaccio, E. J., & Acharya, U. R. (2021). Role of artificial intelligence in COVID-19 detection. *Sensors (Basel)*, 21(23), 8045. 10.3390/s21238045

Guo, Y., Hao, Z., Zhao, S., Gong, J., & Yang, F. (2020). Artificial intelligence in health care: Bibliometric analysis. *Journal of Medical Internet Research*, 22(7), e18228. 10.2196/18228

Gupta, P., & Yadav, A. (2024). Artificial Intelligence Driving Change in Healthcare through Medical Innovation. *Proceedings - International Conference on Computing, Power, and Communication Technologies, IC2PCT 2024*. IEEE. 10.1109/IC2PCT60090.2024.10486544

Gursoy, D., Chi, O. H., Lu, L., & Nunkoo, R. (2019). Consumers acceptance of artificially intelligent (AI) device use in service delivery. *International Journal of Information Management*, 49, 157–169. 10.1016/j.ijinfomgt.2019.03.008

Hagendorff, T. (2020). The ethics of AI ethics: An evaluation of guidelines. *Minds and Machines*, 30(1), 99–120. 10.1007/s11023-020-09517-8

Hamada, M., Zaidan, B. B., & Zaidan, A. A. (2018). A systematic review for human EEG brain signals based emotion classification, feature extraction, brain condition, group comparison. *Journal of Medical Systems*, 42(9), 1–25. 10.1007/s10916-018-1020-8

Hamet, P., & Tremblay, J. (2017). Artificial intelligence in medicine. *Metabolism: Clinical and Experimental*, 69, S36–S40. 10.1016/j.metabol.2017.01.011

Handelman, G. S., Kok, H. K., Chandra, R. V., Razavi, A. H., Lee, M. J., & Asadi, H. (2018). eDoctor: Machine learning and the future of medicine. *Journal of Internal Medicine*, 284(6), 603–619. 10.1111/joim.12822

Haque, T. H., & Haque, M. O. (2018). The swine flu and its impacts on tourism in Brunei. *Journal of Hospitality and Tourism Management*, 36, 92–101. 10.1016/j.jhtm.2016.12.003

Hardy, M., & Harvey, H. (2020). Artificial intelligence in diagnostic imaging: Impact on the radiography profession. *The British Journal of Radiology*, 93(1108), 20190840. 10.1259/bjr.20190840 31821024

Harrer, S., Shah, P., Antony, B., & Hu, J. (2019). Artificial intelligence for clinical trial design. *Trends in Pharmacological Sciences*, 40(8), 577–591. 10.1016/j.tips.2019.05.005

Compilation of References

Harrison, D. M., Luchtenberg, K. F., & Seiler, M. J. (2021). Improving mortgage default collection efforts by employing the decoy effect. *The Journal of Real Estate Finance and Economics*. Advance online publication. 10.1007/s11146-021-09876-8

Hasselgren, C., & Oprea, T. I. (2024). Artificial Intelligence for Drug Discovery: Are We There Yet? In *Annual Review of Pharmacology and Toxicology* (Vol. 64). 10.1146/annurev-pharmtox-040323-040828

Hastuti, R., & Syafruddin, . (2023). Ethical Considerations in the Age of Artificial Intelligence: Balancing Innovation and Social Values. *West Science Social and Humanities Studies*, 1(02), 76–87. 10.58812/wsshs.v1i02.191

Haupt, C. E., & Marks, M. (2023). AI-generated medical advice—GPT and beyond. *Journal of the American Medical Association*, 329(16), 1349–1350. 10.1001/jama.2023.5321

Hollon, T. C., Pandian, B., Adapa, A. R., Urias, E., Save, A. V., Khalsa, S. S. S., Eichberg, D. G., D'Amico, R. S., Farooq, Z. U., Lewis, S., Petridis, P. D., Marie, T., Shah, A. H., Garton, H. J. L., Maher, C. O., Heth, J. A., McKean, E. L., Sullivan, S. E., Hervey-Jumper, S. L., & Orringer, D. A. (2020). Near real-time intraoperative brain tumor diagnosis using stimulated Raman histology and deep neural networks. *Nature Medicine*, 26(1), 52–58. 10.1038/s41591-019-0715-9

Hou, C. K. J., & Behdinan, K. (2022). Dimensionality Reduction in Surrogate Modeling: A Review of Combined Methods. *Data Science and Engineering*, 7(4), 402–427. 10.1007/s41019-022-00193-536345394

Howbert, J. J., Patterson, E. E., Stead, S. M., Brinkmann, B., Vasoli, V., Crepeau, D., Vite, C. H., Sturges, B., Ruedebusch, V., Mavoori, J., Leyde, K., Sheffield, W. D., Litt, B., & Worrell, G. A. (2014). Forecasting seizures in dogs with naturally occurring epilepsy. *PLoS One*, 9(1), e81920. 10.1371/journal.pone.0081920

Huang, C., Xu, L., Shi, Y., & Zhang, L. (2021). A comprehensive review of artificial intelligence in the diagnosis and treatment of breast cancer. *Journal of Cancer Research and Clinical Oncology*, 147(1), 7–24.

Huang, P., Lin, C. T., Li, Y., Tammemagi, M. C., Brock, M. V., Atkar-Khattra, S., Xu, Y., Hu, P., Mayo, J. R., Schmidt, H., Gingras, M., Pasian, S., Stewart, L., Tsai, S., Seely, J. M., Manos, D., Burrowes, P., Bhatia, R., Tsao, M.-S., & Lam, S. (2019). Prediction of lung cancer risk at follow-up screening with low-dose CT: A training and validation study of a deep learning method. *The Lancet. Digital Health*, 1(7), e353–e362. 10.1016/S2589-7500(19)30159-1

Hudec, M., & Smutny, Z. (2017). RUDO: A home ambient intelligence system for blind people. *Sensors (Basel)*, 17(8), 1926. 10.3390/s17081926

Hulsen, T. *Explainable Artificial Intelligence (XAI): Concepts and Challenges in Healthcare*. AI 2023

Hummel, P., & Braun, M. (2020). Just data? Solidarity and justice in data-driven medicine. *Life Sciences, Society and Policy*, 16(1), 1–18. 10.1186/s40504-020-00101-7

Huo, J., Hu, M., & Li, S. (2023). The impact of urban-rural medical insurance integration on medical impoverishment: Evidence from China. *International Journal for Equity in Health*, 22(1), 245. 10.1186/s12939-023-02063-6

Huo, W., Luo, W., Yan, J., Wang, Y., & Deng, Y. (2023). Medical Artificial Intelligence Information Disclosure on Healthcare Professional Involvement in Innovation: A Transactional Theory of Stress and Coping Model. *International Journal of Human-Computer Interaction*, 1–13. 10.1080/10447318.2023.2266797

Hussain, A., Malik, A., Halim, M. U., & Ali, A. M. (2014). The use of robotics in surgery: A review. *International Journal of Clinical Practice*, 68(11), 1376–1382. 10.1111/ijcp.12492

Huynh, E., Hosny, A., Guthier, C., Bitterman, D. S., Petit, S. F., Haas-Kogan, D. A., Kann, B., Aerts, H. J. W. L., & Mak, R. H. (2020). Artificial intelligence in radiation oncology. *Nature Reviews. Clinical Oncology*, 17(12), 771–781. 10.1038/s41571-020-0417-8

IBM. (2023). *Shedding light on AI bias with real world examples*. https://www.ibm.com/blog/shedding-light-on-ai-bias-with-real-world-examples/

Inan, M. S. K., Hossain, S., & Uddin, M. N. (2023). Data augmentation guided breast cancer diagnosis and prognosis using an integrated deep-generative framework based on breast tumor's morphological information. *Informatics in Medicine Unlocked*, 37, 101171. Advance online publication. 10.1016/j.imu.2023.101171

Iqbal, M. A., Wang, Z., Ali, Z. A., & Riaz, S. (2021). Automatic Fish Species Classification Using Deep Convolutional Neural Networks. *Wireless Personal Communications*, 116(2), 1043–1053. 10.1007/s11277-019-06634-1

Islam, M. M., Poly, T. N., Alsinglawi, B., Lin, L. F., Chien, S. C., Liu, J. C., & Jian, W. S. (2021, April). Application of artificial intelligence in COVID-19 pandemic: Bibliometric analysis. []. MDPI.]. *Health Care*, 9(4), 441.

Jackson, H. W., Fischer, J. R., Zanotelli, V. R., Ali, H. R., Mechera, R., Soysal, S. D., Moch, H., Muenst, S., Varga, Z., Weber, W. P., & Bodenmiller, B. (2020). The single-cell pathology landscape of breast cancer. *Nature*, 578(7796), 615–620. 10.1038/s41586-019-1876-x

Jadhav, S., Deng, G., Zawin, M., & Kaufman, A. E. (2021). COVID-view: Diagnosis of COVID-19 using Chest CT. *IEEE Transactions on Visualization and Computer Graphics*, 28(1), 227–237. 10.1109/TVCG.2021.3114851

Jadon, A., & Kumar, S. (2023). *Leveraging generative AI models for synthetic data generation in healthcare: balancing research and privacy*. arXivorg.

Jadon, A., & Kumar, S. (2023). Leveraging Generative AI Models for Synthetic Data Generation in Healthcare: Balancing Research and Privacy. *2023 International Conference on Smart Applications, Communications and Networking (SmartNets)*, 1-4. 10.1109/SmartNets58706.2023.10215825

Jain, G. (2023) Leveraging AI to redefine value-care proposition. The Times of India, March 29, 2023, 10:38 PM IST Gaurav Jain in Voices, India, TOI

Compilation of References

James, J. K., Norland, K., Johar, A. S., & Kullo, I. J. (2023). Deep generative models of LDLR protein structure to predict variant pathogenicity. *Journal of Lipid Research*, 64(12), 100455. Advance online publication. 10.1016/j.jlr.2023.10045537821076

Jasper. (2020). *The 16 Best GPT-3 Tools To Help You Write Faster*. Jasper. https://www.jasper.ai/blog/gpt3-tools

Jennings Mayo-Wilson, L., Peterson, S. K., Kiyingi, J., Nabunya, P., Sensoy Bahar, O., Yang, L. S., Witte, S. S., & Ssewamala, F. M. (2023). Examining cash expenditures and associated HIV-related behaviors using financial diaries in women employed by sex work in rural Uganda: Findings from the kyaterekera study. *International Journal of Environmental Research and Public Health*, 20(9), 5612. Advance online publication. 10.3390/ijerph20095612

Jeong, H., & Shi, L. (2018). Memristor devices for neural networks. *Journal of Physics. D, Applied Physics*, 52(2), 023003. 10.1088/1361-6463/aae223

Ji, S., Gu, Q., Weng, H., Liu, Q., Zhou, P., Chen, J., . . . Wang, T. (2020, April). De-Health: all your online health information are belong to us. In *2020 IEEE 36th International Conference on Data Engineering (ICDE)* (pp. 1609-1620). IEEE. 10.1109/ICDE48307.2020.00143

Jiang, F., Jiang, Y., Zhi, H., Dong, Y., Li, H., Ma, S., Wang, Y., Dong, Q., Shen, H., & Wang, Y. (2017). Artificial intelligence in healthcare: Past, present and future. *Stroke and Vascular Neurology*, 2(4), 230–243. 10.1136/svn-2017-000101

Jiang, X., Hu, Z., Wang, S., & Zhang, Y. (2023). Deep Learning for Medical Image-Based Cancer Diagnosis. *Cancers (Basel)*, 15(14), 3608. 10.3390/cancers15143608 37509272

Johnson, A. E., Pollard, T. J., & Mark, R. G. (2021). Reproducibility in critical care: A mortality prediction case study. *Journal of the American Medical Informatics Association : JAMIA*, 28(2), 333–343. 10.1093/jamia/ocaa208

Joshi, G., Jain, A., Araveeti, S. R., Adhikari, S., Garg, H., & Bhandari, M. (2024). FDA-Approved Artificial Intelligence and Machine Learning (AI/ML)-Enabled Medical Devices: An Updated Landscape. *Electronics (Basel)*, 13(3), 498. 10.3390/electronics13030498

Jussupow, E., Spohrer, K., Heinzl, A., & Gawlitza, J. (2021). Augmenting medical diagnosis decisions? An investigation into physicians' decision-making process with artificial intelligence. *Information Systems Research*, 32(3), 713–735. 10.1287/isre.2020.0980

Kadurin, A., Nikolenko, S., Khrabrov, K., Aliper, A., & Zhavoronkov, A. (2017). DruGAN: An Advanced Generative Adversarial Autoencoder Model for de Novo Generation of New Molecules with Desired Molecular Properties in Silico. *Molecular Pharmaceutics*, 14(9), 3098–3104. 10.1021/acs.molpharmaceut.7b00034628703000

Kamath, D., Teferi, B., Charow, R., Mattson, J., Jardine, J., Jeyakumar, T., Omar, M., Zhang, M., Scandiffio, J., Salhia, M., Dhalla, A., & Wiljer, D. (2024). Accelerating AI Innovation in Healthcare Through Mentorship. In Keshavjee, K., & Khatami, A. (Eds.), *Studies in Health Technology and Informatics* (Vol. 312, pp. 87–91). IOS Press BV. 10.3233/SHTI231318

Kanade, T. M., & Batule, R. B. (2024). Digital health innovations to significantly improve the quality of services in healthcare systems. In *Analyzing Current Digital Healthcare Trends Using Social Networks* (pp. 159–177). IGI Global. 10.4018/979-8-3693-1934-5.ch009

Kanagasingam, Y., Xiao, D., Vignarajan, J., Preetham, A., Tay-Kearney, M. L., & Mehrotra, A. (2018). Evaluation of artificial intelligence–based grading of diabetic retinopathy in primary care. *JAMA Network Open*, 1(5), e182665–e182665. 10.1001/jamanetworkopen.2018.2665

Kanevsky, J., Corban, J., Gaster, R., Kanevsky, A., Lin, S., & Gilardino, M. (2016). Big data and machine learning in plastic surgery: A new frontier in surgical innovation. *Plastic and Reconstructive Surgery*, 137(5), 890e–897e. 10.1097/PRS.0000000000002088

Kanjee, Z., Crowe, B., & Rodman, A. (2023). Accuracy of a generative artificial intelligence model in a complex diagnostic challenge. *Journal of the American Medical Association*, 330(1), 78–80. 10.1001/jama.2023.828837318797

Kanyiri, C. W., Mark, K., & Luboobi, L. (2018). Mathematical analysis of influenza A dynamics in the emergence of drug resistance. *Computational and Mathematical Methods in Medicine*, 2018, 1–14. 10.1155/2018/243456030245737

Kashif, M., Malik, K. R., Jabbar, S., & Chaudhry, J. (2019). Application of machine learning and image processing for detection of breast cancer. In *Innovation in Health Informatics: A Smart Healthcare Primer* (pp. 145–162). Elsevier. 10.1016/B978-0-12-819043-2.00006-X

Kather, J. N., Pearson, A. T., Halama, N., Jäger, D., Krause, J., Loosen, S. H., Marx, A., Boor, P., Tacke, F., Neumann, U. P., Grabsch, H. I., Yoshikawa, T., Brenner, H., Chang-Claude, J., Hoffmeister, M., Trautwein, C., & Luedde, T. (2019). Deep learning can predict microsatellite instability directly from histology in gastrointestinal cancer. *Nature Medicine*, 25(7), 1054–1056. 10.1038/s41591-019-0462-y

Kato, K., Yoshimi, T., Aimoto, K., Sato, K., Itoh, N., & Kondo, I. (2023). Reduction of multiple-caregiver assistance through the long-term use of a transfer support robot in a nursing facility. *Assistive Technology*, 35(3), 271–278. 10.1080/10400435.2022.203932435320681

Kaur, J. (2024). AI-Driven Hospital Accounting: A Path to Financial Health. In *Harnessing Technology for Knowledge Transfer in Accountancy, Auditing, and Finance* (pp. 227-250). IGI Global.

Kaur, J. (2024). Insightful Visions: How Medical Imaging Empowers Patient-Centric Healthcare. In *Future of AI in Medical Imaging* (pp. 42-57). IGI Global.

Kaur, J. (2024). Patient-Centric AI: Advancing Healthcare Through Human-Centered Innovation. In *Approaches to Human-Centered AI in Healthcare* (pp. 1-19). IGI Global.

Kaur, J. (2024). Patient-centric AI: Advancing healthcare through human-centered innovation. In *Approaches to Human-Centered AI in Healthcare* (pp. 1–19). IGI Global. 10.4018/979-8-3693-2238-3.ch001

Compilation of References

Kaur, J. (2024). Tech Unleashed: The Influential Power of Artificial Intelligence on Venture Capital and Startups. In *Fostering Innovation in Venture Capital and Startup Ecosystems* (pp. 219-241). IGI Global.

Kaur, J. (2024). Towards a Sustainable Triad: Uniting Energy Management Systems, Smart Cities, and Green Healthcare for a Greener Future. In *Emerging Materials, Technologies, and Solutions for Energy Harvesting* (pp. 258-285). IGI Global.

Kaur, J., & Ozen, E. (2024). Masters of the Market: Unleashing Algorithmic Wizardry in Finance. In *Algorithmic Approaches to Financial Technology: Forecasting, Trading, and Optimization* (pp. 93-120). IGI Global.

Kenngott, H. G., Wagner, M., Nickel, F., Wekerle, A. L., Preukschas, A., Apitz, M., Schulte, T., Rempel, R., Mietkowski, P., Wagner, F., Termer, A., & Müller-Stich, B. P. (2015). Computer-assisted abdominal surgery: New technologies. *Langenbeck's Archives of Surgery*, 400(3), 273–281. 10.1007/s00423-015-1289-8

Kerasidou, A., & Kingori, P. (2018). Ethical, social, and cultural issues in the use of personalized genomic medicine in Africa. *Personalized Medicine*, 15(5), 385–397. 10.2217/pme-2018-0021

Khaddad, A., Bernhard, J. C., Margue, G., Michiels, C., Ricard, S., Chandelon, K., Bladou, F., Bourdel, N., & Bartoli, A. (2023). A survey of augmented reality methods to guide minimally invasive partial nephrectomy. *World Journal of Urology*, 41(2), 335–343. 10.1007/s00345-022-04078-035776173

Khan, A., Waleed, M., & Imran, M. (2015). Mathematical analysis of an influenza epidemic model, formulation of different controlling strategies using optimal control and estimation of basic reproduction number. *Mathematical and Computer Modelling of Dynamical Systems*, 21(5), 432–459. 10.1080/13873954.2015.1016975

Khan, B., Fatima, H., Qureshi, A., Kumar, S., Hanan, A., Hussain, J., & Abdullah, S. (2023). Drawbacks of artificial intelligence and their potential solutions in the healthcare sector. *Biomedical Materials & Devices*, 1(2), 1–8. 10.1007/s44174-023-00063-2

Khang, A. (Ed.). (2024). *Medical Robotics and AI-Assisted Diagnostics for a High-Tech Healthcare Industry*. IGI Global. 10.4018/979-8-3693-2105-8

Khang, A., Hahanov, V., Litvinova, E., Chumachenko, S., Hajimahmud, A. V., Ali, R. N., & Anh, P. T. N. (2023). The Analytics of Hospitality of Hospitals in a Healthcare Ecosystem. In *Data-Centric AI Solutions and Emerging Technologies in the Healthcare Ecosystem* (pp. 39–61). CRC Press. 10.1201/9781003356189-4

Khanna, V. V., Chadaga, K., Sampathila, N., Prabhu, S., Chadaga, R., & Umakanth, S. (2022). Diagnosing COVID-19 using artificial intelligence: A comprehensive review. *Network Modeling and Analysis in Health Informatics and Bioinformatics*, 11(1), 25. 10.1007/s13721-022-00367-1

Khan, R. A., Jawaid, M., Khan, A. R., & Sajjad, M. (2023). ChatGPT-reshaping medical education and clinical management. *Pakistan Journal of Medical Sciences*, 39(2), 605. 10.12669/pjms.39.2.765336950398

Kiani, A., Uyumazturk, B., Rajpurkar, P., Wang, A., Gao, R., Jones, E., Yu, Y., Langlotz, C. P., Ball, R. L., Montine, T. J., Martin, B. A., Berry, G. J., Ozawa, M. G., Hazard, F. K., Brown, R. A., Chen, S. B., Wood, M., Allard, L. S., Ylagan, L., & Shen, J. (2020). Impact of a deep learning assistant on the histopathologic classification of liver cancer. *NPJ Digital Medicine*, 3(1), 23. 10.1038/s41746-020-0232-8

Kierkegaard, P. (2019). The state of ransomware in healthcare organizations: 2019. *Cybersecurity*, 2(1), 1–8. 10.1186/s42400-019-0021-8

Kim, M. J., Lee, J. H., Anaya, F. J., Hong, J., Miller, W., Telu, S., & Singh, P. (2020). First-in-Human Evaluation of [11C]PS13, a Novel PET Radioligand, to Quantify Cyclooxygenase-1 in the Brain. *European Journal of Nuclear Medicine and Molecular Imaging*, 47(13), 3143–3151. 10.1007/s00259-020-04855-232399622

Kim, M., Zhang, Y., & Jin, S. (2023). Soft tissue surgical robot for minimally invasive surgery: A review. *Biomedical Engineering Letters*, 13(4), 1–9. 10.1007/s13534-023-00326-337872994

Kiral-Kornek, I., Roy, S., Nurse, E., Mashford, B., Karoly, P., Carroll, T., Payne, D., Saha, S., Baldassano, S., O'Brien, T., Grayden, D., Cook, M., Freestone, D., & Harrer, S. (2018). Epileptic seizure prediction using big data and deep learning: Toward a mobile system. *EBioMedicine*, 27, 103–111. 10.1016/j.ebiom.2017.11.032

Kiseleva, A., Kotzinos, D., & De Hert, P. (2022). Transparency of AI in Healthcare as a Multilayered System of Accountabilities: Between Legal Requirements and Technical Limitations. *Frontiers in Artificial Intelligence*, 5, 879603. 10.3389/frai.2022.879603

Kline, A., Wang, H., Li, Y., Dennis, S., Hutch, M., Xu, Z., Wang, F., Cheng, F., & Luo, Y. (2022). Multimodal machine learning in precision health: A scoping review. *NPJ Digital Medicine*, 5(1), 171. 10.1038/s41746-022-00712-836344814

Knaul, F. M., Arreola-Ornelas, H., Touchton, M., McDonald, T., Blofield, M., Avila Burgos, L., Gómez-Dantés, O., Kuri, P., Martinez-Valle, A., Méndez-Carniado, O., Nargund, R. S., Porteny, T., Sosa-Rubí, S. G., Serván-Mori, E., Symes, M., Vargas Enciso, V., & Frenk, J. (2023). Setbacks in the quest for universal health coverage in Mexico: Polarised politics, policy upheaval, and pandemic disruption. *Lancet*, 402(10403), 731–746. 10.1016/S0140-6736(23)00777-8

Kocaballi, A. B., Ijaz, K., Laranjo, L., Quiroz, J. C., Rezazadegan, D., Tong, H. L., Willcock, S., Berkovsky, S., & Coiera, E. (2020). Envisioning an artificial intelligence documentation assistant for future primary care consultations: A co-design study with general practitioners. *Journal of the American Medical Informatics Association : JAMIA*, 27(11), 1695–1704. 10.1093/jamia/ocaa13132845984

Compilation of References

Kolo, K. (2021). 9 AR Platforms Bring Augmented Reality Content in the Classroom. Available at https://www.thevrara.com/blog2/2021/10/26/9-desktop-ar-platforms-to-bring-ar-content-in-the-classroom

Kongnuy, R., & Naowanich, E. (2014). Mathematical Model of Influenza Dynamics Compare the incubation period and Control: in Thailand. In *Conf. Proceeding*. Research Gate.

Korngiebel, D. M., & Mooney, S. D. (2021). Considering the possibilities and pitfalls of Generative Pre-trained Transformer 3 (GPT-3) in healthcare delivery. *NPJ Digital Medicine*, 4(1), 93. 10.1038/s41746-021-00464-x34083689

Kothari, A. N. (2023). ChatGPT, large language models, and generative ai as future augments of surgical cancer care. *Annals of Surgical Oncology*, 30(6), 3174–3176. 10.1245/s10434-023-13442-237052826

Krishnan, G., Singh, S., Pathania, M., Gosavi, S., Abhishek, S., Parchani, A., & Dhar, M. (2023). Artificial intelligence in clinical medicine: Catalyzing a sustainable global healthcare paradigm. *Frontiers in Artificial Intelligence*, 6, 1227091. 10.3389/frai.2023.1227091

Krishnan, S., & Athavale, Y. (2018). Trends in biomedical signal feature extraction. *Biomedical Signal Processing and Control*, 43, 41–63. 10.1016/j.bspc.2018.02.008

Kristensen, S. E., Mosgaard, B. J., Rosendahl, M., Dalsgaard, T., Bjørn, S. F., Frøding, L. P., Kehlet, H., Høgdall, C. K., & Lajer, H. (2017). Robot-assisted surgery in gynecological oncology: Current status and controversies on patient benefits, cost and surgeon conditions–a systematic review. *Acta Obstetricia et Gynecologica Scandinavica*, 96(3), 274–285. 10.1111/aogs.13084

Kulathilake, K. A., Abdullah, N. A., Bandara, A. M. R. R., & Lai, K. W. (2021). Saneera Hemantha, Nor Aniza Abdullah, A. M.Randitha Ravimal Bandara, and Khin Wee Lai. 2021. "InNetGAN: Inception Network-Based Generative Adversarial Network for Denoising Low-Dose Computed Tomography." *Journal of Healthcare Engineering*, 2021, 1–20. 10.1155/2021/997576234552709

Kulshrestha, D., Tiwari, M. K., Shalender, K., & Sharma, S. (2022). Consumer Acatalepsy Towards Buying Behaviour for Need-Based Goods for Sustainability During the COVID-19 Pandemic. *Indian Journal of Marketing*, 52(10), 50–63. 10.17010/ijom/2022/v52/i10/172347

Kumar, P., Chauhan, S., & Awasthi, L. K. (2023). Artificial intelligence in healthcare: Review, ethics, trust challenges & future research directions. *Engineering Applications of Artificial Intelligence*, 120, 105894. 10.1016/j.engappai.2023.105894

Kumar, P., Dwivedi, Y. K., & Anand, A. (2023). Responsible artificial intelligence (AI) for value formation and market performance in healthcare: The mediating role of patient's cognitive engagement. *Information Systems Frontiers*, 25(6), 2197–2220. 10.1007/s10796-021-10136-6

Kumar, P., Sharma, S. K., & Dutot, V. (2023). Artificial intelligence (AI)-enabled CRM capability in healthcare: The impact on service innovation. *International Journal of Information Management*, 69, 102598. 10.1016/j.ijinfomgt.2022.102598

Kumar, Y., Koul, A., Singla, R., & Ijaz, M. F. (2023). Artificial intelligence in disease diagnosis: A systematic literature review, synthesizing framework and future research agenda. *Journal of Ambient Intelligence and Humanized Computing*, 14(7), 8459–8486. 10.1007/s12652-021-03612-z

Kuo, A. M., Borycki, E. M., & Kushniruk, A. W. (2018). Cybersecurity in healthcare: A narrative review of trends, threats and ways forward. *The HIM Journal*, 47(2), 63–75. 10.1177/1833358317703175

Kwoh, Y. S., Hou, J., Jonckheere, E. A., & Hayati, S. (1988). A robot with improved absolute positioning accuracy for CT guided stereotactic brain surgery. *IEEE Transactions on Biomedical Engineering*, 35(2), 153–160. 10.1109/10.1354

Kwon, M. W., Baek, M. H., Hwang, S., Park, K., Jang, T., Kim, T., Lee, J., Cho, S., & Park, B. G. (2018). Integrate-and-fire neuron circuit using positive feedback field effect transistor for low power operation. *Journal of Applied Physics*, 124(15), 152107. 10.1063/1.5031929

Kyaw Zaw, T. O., Muthaiyah, S., & Jasbi, A. (2021). Contextualization of Smart Healthcare: A Systematic Review. *International Conference on Research and Innovation in Information Systems, ICRIIS*. IEEE. 10.1109/ICRIIS53035.2021.9617060

Labovitz, D. L., Shafner, L., Reyes Gil, M., Virmani, D., & Hanina, A. (2017). Using artificial intelligence to reduce the risk of nonadherence in patients on anticoagulation therapy. *Stroke*, 48(5), 1416–1419. 10.1161/STROKEAHA.116.016281

Lancee, G. J., Engelen, L. J., & Van De Belt, T. H. (2018). Medical autonomy as prerequisite for deep space travel will benefit from terrestrial healthcare innovation. *Proceedings of the International Astronautical Congress, IAC*. SCOPUS. https://www.scopus.com/inward/record.uri?eid=2-s2.0-85065739398&partnerID=40&md5=614278ec94358114f194ac19af598998

Lan, L., You, L., Zhang, Z., Fan, Z., Zhao, W., Zeng, N., Chen, Y., & Zhou, X. (2020). Generative adversarial networks and its applications in biomedical informatics. *Frontiers in Public Health*, 8, 164. 10.3389/fpubh.2020.0016432478029

Laranjo, L., Dunn, A. G., Tong, H. L., Kocaballi, A. B., Chen, J., Bashir, R., Surian, D., Gallego, B., Magrabi, F., Lau, A. Y. S., & Coiera, E. (2018). Conversational agents in healthcare: A systematic review. *Journal of the American Medical Informatics Association : JAMIA*, 25(9), 1248–1258. 10.1093/jamia/ocy072

Lawry, T. (2023). Generative AI and Precision Medicine—The Future Is Not What It Used to Be. *Inside. Precision Medicine*, 10(5), 40–41, 43, 44, 45. Advance online publication. 10.1089/ipm.10.05.08

Lecler, A., Duron, L., & Soyer, P. (2023). Revolutionizing radiology with GPT-based models: Current applications, future possibilities and limitations of ChatGPT. *Diagnostic and Interventional Imaging*, 104(6), 269–274. 10.1016/j.diii.2023.02.00336858933

Compilation of References

Ledro, C., Nosella, A., & Vinelli, A. (2022). Artificial intelligence in customer relationship management: Literature review and future research directions. *Journal of Business and Industrial Marketing*, 37(13), 48–63. 10.1108/JBIM-07-2021-0332

Lee, D., & Yoon, S. N. (2021). Application of artificial intelligence-based technologies in the healthcare industry: Opportunities and challenges. *International Journal of Environmental Research and Public Health*, 18(1), 271. 10.3390/ijerph1801027133401373

Lee, K. W., & Renee, K. Y. C. (2022). Diverse COVID-19 CT Image-to-Image Translation with Stacked Residual Dropout. *Bioengineering (Basel, Switzerland)*, 9(11), 698. 10.3390/bioengineering911069836421099

Lee, S. I., Celik, S., Logsdon, B. A., Lundberg, S. M., Martins, T. J., Oehler, V. G., Estey, E. H., Miller, C. P., Chien, S., Dai, J., Saxena, A., Blau, C. A., & Becker, P. S. (2018). A machine learning approach to integrate big data for precision medicine in acute myeloid leukemia. *Nature Communications*, 9(1), 42. 10.1038/s41467-017-02465-5

Lee, S. M., Lee, D., & Kim, Y. S. (2019). The quality management ecosystem for predictive maintenance in the Industry 4.0 era. *International Journal of Quality Innovation*, 5(1), 1–11. 10.1186/s40887-019-0029-5

Lee, W. B., & Choi, S. J. (2023). Secondary Use Provisions in the European Health Data Space Proposal and Policy Recommendations for Korea. *Healthcare Informatics Research*, 29(3), 199–208. 10.4258/hir.2023.29.3.19937591675

Lehoux, P., Roncarolo, F., Rocha Oliveira, R., & Pacifico Silva, H. (2016). Medical innovation and the sustainability of health systems: A historical perspective on technological change in health. *Health Services Management Research*, 29(4), 115–123. 10.1177/0951484816670192

Leonardo, N., & Dina, B. (2023). *Generative AI Takes Stereotypes and Bias From Bad to Worse*. https://www.bloomberg.com/graphics/2023-generative-ai-bias/

Liao, F., Adelaine, S., Afshar, M., & Patterson, B. W. (2022). Governance of Clinical AI applications to facilitate safe and equitable deployment in a large health system: Key elements and early successes. *Frontiers in Digital Health*, 4, 931439. 10.3389/fdgth.2022.931439

Li, G., Lv, J., & Wang, C. (2021). A Modified Generative Adversarial Network Using Spatial and Channel Wise Attention for CS-MRI Reconstruction. *IEEE Access : Practical Innovations, Open Solutions*, 9, 83185–83198. 10.1109/ACCESS.2021.3086839

Li, J., Cairns, B. J., Li, J., & Zhu, T. (2023). Generating synthetic mixed-type longitudinal electronic health records for artificial intelligent applications. *NPJ Digital Medicine*, 6(1), 98. Advance online publication. 10.1038/s41746-023-00834-737244963

Limeros, S. C., Majchrowska, S., Zoubi, M. K., Ros'en, A., Suvilehto, J., Sjöblom, L., & Kjellberg, M. J. (2022). *GAN-based generative modelling for dermatological applications - comparative study*. ArXiv.

Lin, E., Lin, C. H., & Lane, H. Y. (2021). Deep Learning with Neuroimaging and Genomics in Alzheimer's Disease. *International Journal of Molecular Sciences*, 22(15), 7911. 10.3390/ijms2215791134360676

Lin, H., Li, R., Liu, Z., Chen, J., Yang, Y., Chen, H., Lin, Z., Lai, W., Long, E., Wu, X., Lin, D., Zhu, Y., Chen, C., Wu, D., Yu, T., Cao, Q., Li, X., Li, J., Li, W., & Liu, Y. (2019). Diagnostic efficacy and therapeutic decision-making capacity of an artificial intelligence platform for childhood cataracts in eye clinics: A multicentre randomized controlled trial. *EClinicalMedicine*, 9, 52–59. 10.1016/j.eclinm.2019.03.001

Lip, S., Visweswaran, S., & Padmanabhan, S. (2020). Transforming Clinical Trials with Artificial Intelligence. In *Artificial Intelligence* (pp. 297–306). Productivity Press. 10.4324/9780429317415-17

Litinski, V. (2018). Is artificial intelligence (AI) friend or foe to patients in healthcare?: On virtues of dynamic consent - how to build a business case for digital health applications. In *Healthcare Policy and Reform: Concepts, Methodologies, Tools, and Applications* (Vol. 2, pp. 774–785). IGI Global. 10.4018/978-1-5225-6915-2.ch035

Liu, H. C., Liu, S. W., Chang, P. C., Huang, W. C., & Liao, C. H. (2008, August). A novel classifier for influenza a viruses based on SVM and logistic regression. *IEEE International Conference on Wavelet Analysis and Pattern Recognition*. IEEE.

Liu, K., & Tao, D. (2022). The roles of trust, personalization, loss of privacy, and anthropomorphism in public acceptance of smart healthcare services. *Computers in Human Behavior*, 127, 107026. 10.1016/j.chb.2021.107026

Liu, S., Wright, A. P., Patterson, B. L., Wanderer, J. P., Turer, R. W., Nelson, S. D., McCoy, A. B., Sittig, D. F., & Wright, A. (2023). Using AI-generated suggestions from ChatGPT to optimize clinical decision support. *Journal of the American Medical Informatics Association : JAMIA*, 30(7), 1237–1245. 10.1093/jamia/ocad07237087108

Liu, X., Rivera, S. C., Moher, D., Calvert, M. J., Denniston, A. K., Ashrafian, H., & Yau, C. (2020). Reporting guidelines for clinical trial reports for interventions involving artificial intelligence: The CONSORT-AI extension. *The Lancet. Digital Health*, 2(10), e537–e548. 10.1016/S2589-7500(20)30218-1

Liu, Y.. (2023). *Generative artificial intelligence and its applications in materials science: Current situation and future perspectives* (Vol. 9). J. Materiomics.

Liu, Y., Chen, A., Shi, H., Huang, S., Zheng, W., Liu, Z., Zhang, Q., & Yang, X. (2021). CT Synthesis from MRI Using Multi-Cycle GAN for Head-and-Neck Radiation Therapy. *Computerized Medical Imaging and Graphics*, 91, 101953. 10.1016/j.compmedimag.2021.10195334242852

Li, X., Mohanty, I., Zhai, T., Chai, P., & Niyonsenga, T. (2023). Catastrophic health expenditure and its association with socioeconomic status in China: Evidence from the 2011-2018 China Health and Retirement Longitudinal Study. *International Journal for Equity in Health*, 22(1), 194. 10.1186/s12939-023-02008-z

Compilation of References

Li, Y., Lu, J., Hu, Y., & Chang, C. (2019). Predicting acute cardiovascular events with a large-scale, densely connected deep learning network. *Nature Medicine*, 25(12), 1869–1873. 10.1038/s41591-019-0613-7

Lloret, J., Canovas, A., Sendra, S., & Parra, L. (2015). A smart communication architecture for ambient assisted living. *IEEE Communications Magazine*, 53(1), 26–33. 10.1109/MCOM.2015.7010512

Lochan, K., Suklyabaidya, A., & Roy, B. K. (2023). Medical and healthcare robots in India. In *Medical and Healthcare Robotics* (pp. 221–236). Academic Press. 10.1016/B978-0-443-18460-4.00010-X

Logan, R., Williams, B. G., Ferreira da Silva, M., Indani, A., Schcolnicov, N., Ganguly, A., & Miller, S. J. (2021). Deep Convolutional Neural Networks With Ensemble Learning and Generative Adversarial Networks for Alzheimer's Disease Image Data Classification. *Frontiers in Aging Neuroscience*, 13, 720226. 10.3389/fnagi.2021.72022634483890

Lorenzini, G., Arbelaez Ossa, L., Shaw, D. M., & Elger, B. S. (2023). Artificial intelligence and the doctor-patient relationship expanding the paradigm of shared decision making. *Bioethics*, 37(5), 424–429. 10.1111/bioe.13158

Loria, K. (2018). Putting the AI in radiology. *Radiology Today*, 19(1), 10.

Loucks, J., Davenport, T., & Schatsky, D. (2018). State of AI in the Enterprise. *Deloitte Insights Report.*.

Low, L. L., Lee, K. H., Hock Ong, M. E., Wang, S., Tan, S. Y., Thumboo, J., & Liu, N. (2015). Predicting 30-day readmissions: Performance of the LACE index compared with a regression model among general medicine patients in Singapore. *BioMed Research International*, 2015, 2015. 10.1155/2015/169870

Lubarsky, B. (2010). Re-identification of "anonymized data". *Georgetown Law Technology Review. Available online:*https://www. georgetownlawtechreview. org/re-identification-of-anonymized-data/GLTR-04-2017*(accessed on 10 September 2021)*.

Luengo-Oroz, M., Hoffmann Pham, K., Bullock, J., Kirkpatrick, R., Luccioni, A., Rubel, S., Wachholz, C., Chakchouk, M., Biggs, P., Nguyen, T., Purnat, T., & Mariano, B. (2020). Artificial intelligence cooperation to support the global response to COVID-19. *Nature Machine Intelligence*, 2(6), 295–297. 10.1038/s42256-020-0184-3

Luo, E., Bhuiyan, M. Z. A., Wang, G., Rahman, M. A., Wu, J., & Atiquzzaman, M. (2018). Privacyprotector: Privacy-protected patient data collection in IoT-based healthcare systems. *IEEE Communications Magazine*, 56(2), 163–168. 10.1109/MCOM.2018.1700364

Lupsor-Platon, M., Serban, T., Silion, A. I., Tirpe, G. R., Tirpe, A., & Florea, M. (2021). Performance of Ultrasound Techniques and the Potential of Artificial Intelligence in the Evaluation of Hepatocellular Carcinoma and Non-Alcoholic Fatty Liver Disease. *Cancers (Basel)*, 13(4), 790. 10.3390/cancers1304079033672827

Lv, J., Dong, B., Lei, H., Shi, G., Wang, H., Zhu, F., Wen, C., Zhang, Q., Fu, L., Gu, X., Yuan, J., Guan, Y., Xia, Y., Zhao, L., & Chen, H. (2021). Artificial intelligence-assisted auscultation in detecting congenital heart disease. *European Heart Journal. Digital Health*, 2(1), 119–124. 10.1093/ehjdh/ztaa017

Lysen, F., & Wyatt, S. (2024). Refusing participation: Hesitations about designing responsible patient engagement with artificial intelligence in healthcare. *Journal of Responsible Innovation*, 11(1), 2300161. 10.1080/23299460.2023.2300161

Mahmoud, H., Aljaldi, F., El-Fiky, A., Battecha, K., Thabet, A., Alayat, M., & Ibrahim, A. (2023). Artificial Intelligence machine learning and conventional physical therapy for upper limb outcome in patients with stroke: A systematic review and meta-analysis. *European Review for Medical and Pharmacological Sciences*, 27(11).37318455

Maki, Y., & Hirose, H. (2013, January). Infectious disease spread analysis using stochastic differential equations for SIR model. *IEEE International Conference on Intelligent Systems, Modelling and Simulation*. IEEE. 10.1109/ISMS.2013.13

Mak, K. K., & Pichika, M. R. (2019). Artificial intelligence in drug development: Present status and future prospects. *Drug Discovery Today*, 24(3), 773–780. 10.1016/j.drudis.2018.11.014

Maleki Varnosfaderani, S., & Forouzanfar, M. (2024). The Role of AI in Hospitals and Clinics: Transforming Healthcare in the 21st Century. *Bioengineering (Basel, Switzerland)*, 11(4), 337. 10.3390/bioengineering1104033738671759

Manikandan, A., & Sanjay, T. (2023). Generative Adversarial Networks: A Game Changer - GAN for Machine Learning and IoT Applications. In *Handbook of Research on Machine Learning-Enabled IoT for Smart Applications Across Industries*. Springer. 10.4018/978-1-6684-8785-3.ch004

Manikandan, V., & Sharma, S. (2023). The Development of Machine Learning innovation technology for Data Mining In Smart Healthcare. *2nd IEEE International Conference on Distributed Computing and Electrical Circuits and Electronics, ICDCECE 2023*. IEEE. 10.1109/ICDCECE57866.2023.10150446

Manyika, J., Chui, M., Miremadi, M., Bughin, J., George, K., Willmott, P., & Dewhurst, M. (2017). A future that works: AI, automation, employment, and productivity. *McKinsey Global Institute Research. Tech. Rep*, 60, 1–135.

Maphumulo, W. T., & Bhengu, B. R. (2019). Challenges of quality improvement in the healthcare of South Africa post-apartheid: A critical review. *Curationis*, 42(1), 1–9. 10.4102/curationis.v42i1.1901

Mardikoraem, M., Wang, Z., Pascual, N., & Woldring, D. (2023). Generative models for protein sequence modeling: recent advances and future directions. In *Briefings in Bioinformatics* (Vol. 24, Issue 6). 10.1093/bib/bbad358

Compilation of References

Martens, F. M. J., Van Kuppevelt, H. J. M., Beekman, J. A. C., Rijkhoff, N. J. M., & Heesakkers, J. P. F. A. (2010). Limited value of bladder sensation as a trigger for conditional neurostimulation in spinal cord injury patients. *Neurourology and Urodynamics*, 29(3), 395–400. 10.1002/nau.20770

Massalha, S., Clarkin, O., Thornhill, R., Wells, G., & Chow, B. J. (2018). Decision support tools, systems, and artificial intelligence in cardiac imaging. *The Canadian Journal of Cardiology*, 34(7), 827–838. 10.1016/j.cjca.2018.04.032

Mathew, S., Nadeem, S., Kumari, S., & Kaufman, A. (2020). Augmenting Colonoscopy Using Extended and Directional Cyclegan for Lossy Image Translation. In *Proceedings of the IEEE Computer Society Conference on Computer Vision and Pattern Recognition*. IEEE. 10.1109/CVPR42600.2020.00475

Matsuzaki, H., & Gliesche, P. (2023). Robots and Norms of Care: A Comparative Analysis of the Reception of Robotic Assistance in Nursing. In *Social Robots in Social Institutions* (pp. 90-99). IOS Press. 10.3233/FAIA220607

Mawdsley, E., Reynolds, B., & Cullen, B. (2021). A Systematic Review of the Effectiveness of Machine Learning for Predicting Psychosocial Outcomes in Acquired Brain Injury: Which Algorithms Are Used and Why? *Journal of Neuropsychology*, 15(3), 319–339. 10.1111/jnp.1224433780595

Mayilvaganan, S., & Balamuralitharan, S. (2019, June). Analytical solutions of influenza diseases model by HPM. In *AIP Conference Proceedings*. Research Gate. 10.1063/1.5112193

Mayorga-Ruiz, I., Jiménez-Pastor, A., Fos-Guarinos, B., López-González, R., García-Castro, F., & Alberich-Bayarri, Á. (2019). The role of AI in clinical trials. *Artificial Intelligence in Medical Imaging: Opportunities, applications and risks*, 231-243.

McKendrick, J. Healthcare May Be the Ultimate Proving Ground for Artificial Intelligence. Forbes, Feb 22, 2023,12:19pm EST

McKinney, S. M., Sieniek, M., Godbole, V., Godwin, J., Antropova, N., Ashrafian, H., Back, T., Chesus, M., Corrado, G. S., Darzi, A., Etemadi, M., Garcia-Vicente, F., Gilbert, F. J., Halling-Brown, M., Hassabis, D., Jansen, S., Karthikesalingam, A., Kelly, C. J., King, D., & Shetty, S. (2020). International evaluation of an AI system for breast cancer screening. *Nature*, 577(7788), 89–94. 10.1038/s41586-019-1799-6

Meijer, A., Paget, W. J., Meerhoff, T. J., Brown, C. S., Meuwissen, L. E., & Van Der Velden, J. (2006). European Influenza Surveillance Scheme EISS. "Epidemiological and virological assessment of influenza activity in Europe, during the 2004-2005 winter". *Eurosurveillance*, 11(5), 9–10. 10.2807/esm.11.05.00623-en29208114

Mendez, A., Belghith, A., & Sawan, M. (2013). A DSP for sensing the bladder volume through afferent neural pathways. *IEEE Transactions on Biomedical Circuits and Systems*, 8(4), 552–564. 10.1109/TBCAS.2013.2282087

Meskó, B., & Topol, E. J. (2023). The imperative for regulatory oversight of large language models (or generative AI) in healthcare. *NPJ Digital Medicine*, 6(1), 120. 10.1038/s41746-023-00873-037414860

Meyer, S., Uhr, C., Loos, B., & Hackethal, A. (2023). Switching from commissions on mutual funds to flat-fees: How are advisory clients affected? *Journal of Economic Behavior & Organization*, 209, 423–449. 10.1016/j.jebo.2023.03.015

Milea, D., Najjar, R. P., Jiang, Z., Ting, D., Vasseneix, C., Xu, X., Aghsaei Fard, M., Fonseca, P., Vanikieti, K., Lagrèze, W. A., La Morgia, C., Cheung, C. Y., Hamann, S., Chiquet, C., Sanda, N., Yang, H., Mejico, L. J., Rougier, M.-B., Kho, R., & Biousse, V. (2020). Artificial intelligence to detect papilledema from ocular fundus photographs. *The New England Journal of Medicine*, 382(18), 1687–1695. 10.1056/NEJMoa1917130

Mileva, G. (2024), 5 AI Healthcare Tools Revolutionizing Healthcare in Hospitals and Clinics. Available at https://influencermarketinghub.com/ai-healthcare-tools/

Miller, D. D., & Brown, E. W. (2018). Artificial intelligence in medical practice: The question to the answer? *The American Journal of Medicine*, 131(2), 129–133. 10.1016/j.amjmed.2017.10.035

Minaee, S., Boykov, Y., Porikli, F., Plaza, A., Kehtarnavaz, N., & Terzopoulos, D. (2022). Image Segmentation Using Deep Learning: A Survey. *IEEE Transactions on Pattern Analysis and Machine Intelligence*, 44(7), 1. 10.1109/TPAMI.2021.305996833596172

Mincu, D., & Roy, S. (2022). Developing robust benchmarks for driving forward AI innovation in healthcare. *Nature Machine Intelligence*, 4(11), 916–921. 10.1038/s42256-022-00559-4

Miner, G. D., Miner, L. A., Burk, S., Goldstein, M., Nisbet, R., Walton, N., & Hill, T. (2023). Practical Data Analytics for Innovation in Medicine: Building Real Predictive and Prescriptive Models in Personalized Healthcare and Medical Research Using AI, ML, and Related Technologies, Second Edition. In *Practical Data Analytics for Innovation in Medicine: Building Real Predictive and Prescriptive Models in Personalized Healthcare and Medical Research Using AI, ML, and Related Technologies, Second Edition*. Elsevier. 10.1016/C2021-0-02083-6

Minopoulos, G. M., Memos, V. A., Stergiou, K. D., Stergiou, C. L., & Psannis, K. E. (2023). A Medical Image Visualization Technique Assisted with AI-Based Haptic Feedback for Robotic Surgery and Healthcare. *Applied Sciences (Basel, Switzerland)*, 13(6), 3592. 10.3390/app13063592

Minucci, S. B., Heise, R. L., & Reynolds, A. M. (2020). Review of mathematical modeling of the inflammatory response in lung infections and injuries. *Frontiers in Applied Mathematics and Statistics*, 6, 36. 10.3389/fams.2020.00036

Mirza-Aghazadeh-Attari, M., Zarrintan, A., Nezami, N., Mohammadi, A., Zarrintan, A., Mohebbi, I., Pirnejad, H., Khademvatani, K., Ashkavand, Z., Forughi, P., Arasteh, A., & Attari, J. A. (2020). Predictors of Coronavirus Disease 19 (COVID-19) Pneumonitis Outcome Based on Computed Tomography (CT) Imaging Obtained Prior to Hospitalization: A Retrospective Study. *Emergency Radiology*, 27(6), 653–661. 10.1007/s10140-020-01833-x32770367

Compilation of References

Mittelstadt, B. D., Allo, P., Taddeo, M., Wachter, S., & Floridi, L. (2016). The ethics of algorithms: Mapping the debate. *Big Data & Society*, 3(2), 1–21. 10.1177/2053951716679679

Mohamadou, Y., Halidou, A., & Kapen, P. T. (2020). A review of mathematical modeling, artificial intelligence and datasets used in the study, prediction and management of COVID-19. *Applied Intelligence*, 50(11), 3913–3925. 10.1007/s10489-020-01770-9

Moon, I., An, Y., Min, S., & Park, C. (2023). Therapeutic Effects of Metaverse Rehabilitation for Cerebral Palsy: A Randomized Controlled Trial. *International Journal of Environmental Research and Public Health*, 20(2), 1578. 10.3390/ijerph20021578

Morgan Stanley representative (2023) "What's NEXT – How AI/ML Could Reshape Healthcare," Morgan Stanley, (June 19, 2023)

Muehlematter, U. J., Daniore, P., & Vokinger, K. N. (2021). Approval of artificial intelligence and machine learning-based medical devices in the USA and Europe (2015–20): A comparative analysis. *The Lancet. Digital Health*, 3(3), e195–e203. 10.1016/S2589-7500(20)30292-2

Mummert, A., & Otunuga, O. M. (2019). Parameter identification for a stochastic SEIRS epidemic model: Case study influenza. *Journal of Mathematical Biology*, 79(2), 705–729. 10.1007/s00285-019-01374-z31062075

Murakami, Y., Honaga, K., Kono, H., Haruyama, K., Yamaguchi, T., Tani, M., Isayama, R., Takakura, T., Tanuma, A., Hatori, K., Wada, F., & Fujiwara, T. (2023). New Artificial Intelligence-Integrated Electromyography-Driven Robot Hand for Upper Extremity Rehabilitation of Patients With Stroke: A Randomized, Controlled Trial. *Neurorehabilitation and Neural Repair*, 37(5), 15459683231166939. 10.1177/15459683231166939 37039319

Murdoch, B. (2021). Privacy and artificial intelligence: Challenges for protecting health information in a new era. *BMC Medical Ethics*, 22(1), 122. Advance online publication. 10.1186/s12910-021-00687-334525993

Nah, F.-H., Fiona, R. Z., Cai, J., Siau, K., & Chen, L. (2023). Generative AI and ChatGPT: Applications, Challenges, and AI-Human Collaboration. *Journal of Information Technology Case and Application Research*, 25(3), 277–304. 10.1080/15228053.2023.2233814

Naik, N., Hameed, B. M. Z., Shetty, D. K., Swain, D., Shah, M., Paul, R., Aggarwal, K., Ibrahim, S., Patil, V., Smriti, K., Shetty, S., Rai, B. P., Chlosta, P., & Somani, B. K. (2022). Legal and Ethical Consideration in Artificial Intelligence in Healthcare: Who Takes Responsibility? *Frontiers in Surgery*, 9, 862322. 10.3389/fsurg.2022.862322

Nait Aicha, A., Englebienne, G., Van Schooten, K. S., Pijnappels, M., & Kröse, B. (2018). Deep learning to predict falls in older adults based on daily-life trunk accelerometry. *Sensors (Basel)*, 18(5), 1654. 10.3390/s18051654

Naskar, R. (2023). Google Bard Extensions May Be Coming Soon to Compete with ChatGPT. Neowin. Available online: https://www.neowin.net/news/google-bard-extensions-may-be-coming-soon-to-compete-with-chatgpt/

Nassani, A. A., Javed, A., Rosak-Szyrocka, J., Pilar, L., Yousaf, Z., & Haffar, M. (2023). Major Determinants of Innovation Performance in the Context of Healthcare Sector. *International Journal of Environmental Research and Public Health*, 20(6), 5007. 10.3390/ijerph2006500736981916

Natarajan, A., Su, H. W., & Heneghan, C. (2020). Assessment of physiological signs associated with COVID-19 measured using wearable devices. *NPJ Digital Medicine*, 3(1), 156. 10.1038/s41746-020-00363-7

Neher, M., Petersson, L., Nygren, J. M., Svedberg, P., Larsson, I., & Nilsen, P. (2023). Innovation in healthcare: Leadership perceptions about the innovation characteristics of artificial intelligence—a qualitative interview study with healthcare leaders in Sweden. *Implementation Science Communications*, 4(1), 81. 10.1186/s43058-023-00458-837464420

Neumann, N. A., De Oliveira, F. A. C., Machicao, J. C., & Velasquez, O. C. (2019). Exploration of AI-based innovation opportunities within the "Pastoral da Criança" maternal-child healthcare model. *SHIRCON 2019 - 2019 IEEE Sciences and Humanities International Research Conference*. IEEE. 10.1109/SHIRCON48091.2019.9024850

Nigmatulina, K. R., & Larson, R. C. (2009). Living with influenza: Impacts of government imposed and voluntarily selected interventions. *European Journal of Operational Research*, 195(2), 613–627. 10.1016/j.ejor.2008.02.016

Nilsen, P., Reed, J., Nair, M., Savage, C., Macrae, C., Barlow, J., Svedberg, P., Larsson, I., Lundgren, L., & Nygren, J. (2022). Realizing the potential of artificial intelligence in healthcare: Learning from intervention, innovation, implementation and improvement sciences. *Frontiers in Health Services*, 2, 961475. 10.3389/frhs.2022.96147536925879

Nimri, R., Battelino, T., Laffel, L. M., Slover, R. H., Schatz, D., Weinzimer, S. A., & Phillip, M. (2020). Insulin dose optimization using an automated artificial intelligence-based decision support system in youths with type 1 diabetes. *Nature Medicine*, 26(9), 1380–1384. 10.1038/s41591-020-1045-7

Nishant, R., Kennedy, M., & Corbett, J. (2020). Artificial intelligence for sustainability: Challenges, opportunities, and a research agenda. *International Journal of Information Management*, 53, 102104. 10.1016/j.ijinfomgt.2020.102104

Norori, N., Hu, Q., Aellen, F. M., Faraci, F. D., & Tzovara, A. (2021). Addressing bias in big data and AI for health care: A call for open science. *Patterns (New York, N.Y.)*, 2(10), 100347. 10.1016/j.patter.2021.100347

Nova, K. (2023). Generative AI in healthcare: Advancements in electronic health records, facilitating medical languages, and personalized patient care. *Journal of Advanced Analytics in Healthcare Management*, 7(1), 115–131.

Nowakowska K, Sakellarios A, Kaźmierski J, Fotiadis DI, Pezoulas VC. *AI-Enhanced Predictive Modeling for Identifying Depression and Delirium in Cardiovascular Patients Scheduled for Cardiac Surgery*. Diagnostics (Basel). 2023

Compilation of References

Ntoutsi, E., Fafalios, P., Gadiraju, U., Iosifidis, V., Nejdl, W., Vidal, M. E., Ruggieri, S., Turini, F., Papadopoulos, S., Krasanakis, E., Kompatsiaris, I., Kinder-Kurlanda, K., Wagner, C., Karimi, F., Fernandez, M., Alani, H., Berendt, B., Kruegel, T., Heinze, C., & Staab, S. (2020). Bias in data-driven artificial intelligence systems—An introductory survey. *Wiley Interdisciplinary Reviews. Data Mining and Knowledge Discovery*, 10(3), e1356. Advance online publication. 10.1002/widm.1356

Nwadiokwu, O. T. (2023). Examining the Impact and Challenges of Artificial Intelligence (AI) in Healthcare. *Edward Waters University Undergraduate Research Journal*, 1(1).

Obermeyer, Z., & Emanuel, E. J. (2016). Predicting the future—Big data, machine learning, and clinical medicine. *The New England Journal of Medicine*, 375(13), 1216–1219. 10.1056/NEJMp1606181

Obermeyer, Z., Powers, B., Vogeli, C., & Mullainathan, S. (2019). Dissecting racial bias in an algorithm used to manage the health of populations. *Science*, 366(6464), 447–453. 10.1126/science.aax2342

Ogbuji, C. (2009). *Clinical Data Acquisition*. Storage, and Management.

Ohneberg, C., Stöbich, N., Warmbein, A., Rathgeber, I., Mehler-Klamt, A. C., Fischer, U., & Eberl, I. (2023). Assistive robotic systems in nursing care: A scoping review. *BMC Nursing*, 22(1), 1–15. 10.1186/s12912-023-01230-y36934280

Olawade, D. B., David-Olawade, A. C., Wada, O. Z., Asaolu, A. J., Adereni, T., & Ling, J. (2024). Artificial Intelligence in Healthcare Delivery: Prospects and Pitfalls. *Journal of Medicine, Surgery, and Public Health, 100108*.

Olender, M. L., De La Torre Hernández, J. M., Athanasiou, L. S., Nezami, F. R., & Edelman, E. R. (2021). Artificial intelligence to generate medical images: Augmenting the cardiologist's visual clinical workflow. *European Heart Journal. Digital Health*, 2(3), 539–544. Advance online publication. 10.1093/ehjdh/ztab05236713593

Oniani, D., Hilsman, J., Peng, Y., Poropatich, R. K., Pamplin, J. C., Legault, G. L., & Wang, Y. (2023). Adopting and expanding ethical principles for generative artificial intelligence from military to healthcare. *NPJ Digital Medicine*, 6(1), 225. 10.1038/s41746-023-00965-x

Ooi, K. B., Tan, G. W. H., Al Emran, M., Al Sharafi, M. A., Capatina, A., Chakraborty, A., ... Hoffman, Y. (2022). Promoting Interoperability and Quality Payment Programs: The Evolving Paths of Meaningful Use. In *Health Informatics* (pp. 165-190). Productivity Press.

OpenAI. (2020). *GPT-3 Powers the Next Generation of Apps*. Open AI. https://openai.com/blog/gpt-3-apps/

OpenAI. (2023a). *Chat Plugins—Introduction*. Open AI. https://platform.openai.com/docs/plugins/introduction

OpenAI. (2023b). *ChatGPT Plugins*. OpenAI. https://openai.com/blog/chatgpt-plugins

OpenAI. (2024). *API Reference*. OpenAI API. https://platform.openai.com/docs/api-reference/introduction

Padasalgi, S. R. (2024). Transforming Healthcare: The Power of AI in Revolutionizing Patient Care and Research. Available at https://health.economictimes.indiatimes.com/news/health-it/transforming-healthcare-the-power-of-ai-in-revolutionizing-patient-care-and-researchais-integration-into-healthcare-a-game-changer/107183802

Padhi, A., Agarwal, A., Saxena, S. K., & Katoch, C. D. S. (2023). Transforming Clinical Virology with AI, Machine Learning and Deep Learning: A Comprehensive Review and Outlook. *Virusdisease*, 34(3), 345–355. 10.1007/s13337-023-00841-y37780897

Palanica, A., Flaschner, P., Thommandram, A., Li, M., & Fossat, Y. (2019). Physicians' Perceptions of Chatbots in Health Care: Cross-sectional Web-based Survey. *Journal of Medical Internet Research*, 21(4), e12887. 10.2196/1288730950796

Panayides, A. S., Amini, A., Filipovic, N. D., Sharma, A., Tsaftaris, S. A., Young, A., Foran, D., Do, N., Golemati, S., Kurc, T., Huang, K., Nikita, K. S., Veasey, B. P., Zervakis, M., Saltz, J. H., & Pattichis, C. S. (2020). AI in medical imaging informatics: Current challenges and future directions. *IEEE Journal of Biomedical and Health Informatics*, 24(7), 1837–1857. 10.1109/JBHI.2020.299104332609615

Pandimurugan, V., Abouhawwash, M., Mandviya, R., & Mawal, C. (2023). Introduction to healthcare informatics: Fundamentals and historical background. In *Innovations in Healthcare Informatics: From interoperability to data analysis* (pp. 1–31). Institution of Engineering and Technology. https://www.scopus.com/inward/record.uri?eid=2-s2.0-85166032997&partnerID=40&md5=b7a8e739a7e6f8c9cbb7fbf8964be279

Panjamapirom, A. T., Levinthal, N., & Hoffman, Y. (2022). Promoting Interoperability and Quality Payment Programs: The Evolving Paths of Meaningful Use. In *Health Informatics* (pp. 165-190). Productivity Press.

Patel, A., & Arasanipalai, A. (2021). *Applied Natural Language Processing in the Enterprise: Teaching Machines to Read, Write, and Understand*. O'Reilly Media. https://www.oreilly.com/library/view/applied-natural-language/9781492062561/ch01.html

Patel, D., & Tarakji, K. G. (2021). Smartwatch diagnosis of atrial fibrillation in patient with embolic stroke of unknown source: A case report. *Cardiovascular Digital Health Journal*, 2(1), 84–87. 10.1016/j.cvdhj.2021.01.001

Patel, S. B., & Lam, K. (2023). ChatGPT: The future of discharge summaries? *The Lancet. Digital Health*, 5(3), e107–e108. 10.1016/S2589-7500(23)00021-336754724

Patel, V. L., Shortliffe, E. H., Stefanelli, M., Szolovits, P., Berthold, M. R., Bellazzi, R., & Geissbuhler, A. (2018). The coming of age of artificial intelligence in medicine. *Artificial Intelligence in Medicine*, 46(1), 5–17. 10.1016/j.artmed.2008.07.017

Compilation of References

Paul, W., Hadzic, A., Joshi, N., Alajaji, F., & Burlina, P. (2022). TARA: Training and Representation Alteration for AI Fairness and Domain Generalization. *Neural Computation*, 34(3), 716–753. 10.1162/neco_a_0146835016212

Pavli, A., Theodoridou, M., & Maltezou, H. C. (2021). Post-COVID syndrome: Incidence, clinical spectrum, and challenges for primary healthcare professionals. *Archives of Medical Research*, 52(6), 575–581. 10.1016/j.arcmed.2021.03.010

Perrone, P. M., Biganzoli, G., Lecce, M., Campagnoli, E. M., Castrofino, A., Cinnirella, A., Fornaro, F., Gallana, C., Grosso, F. M., Maffeo, M., Shishmintseva, V., Pariani, E., & Castaldi, S. (2021). Influenza Vaccination Campaign during the COVID-19 Pandemic: The Experience of a Research and Teaching Hospital in Milan. *International Journal of Environmental Research and Public Health*, 18(11), 5874. 10.3390/ijerph1811587434070763

Petal/Paladin Max, Inc. (2023). *GPT-Trainer*. Petal/Paladin Max. https://gpt-trainer.com/

Phillips, M., Marsden, H., Jaffe, W., Matin, R. N., Wali, G. N., Greenhalgh, J., McGrath, E., James, R., Ladoyanni, E., Bewley, A., Argenziano, G., & Palamaras, I. (2019). Assessment of accuracy of an artificial intelligence algorithm to detect melanoma in images of skin lesions. *JAMA Network Open*, 2(10), e1913436–e1913436. 10.1001/jamanetworkopen.2019.13436

Pillai, R., Sivathanu, B., Mariani, M., Rana, N. P., Yang, B., & Dwivedi, Y. K. (2022). Adoption of AI-empowered industrial robots in auto component manufacturing companies. *Production Planning and Control*, 33(16), 1517–1533. 10.1080/09537287.2021.1882689

Popa, E. O., van Hilten, M., Oosterkamp, E., & Bogaardt, M.-J. (2021). The use of digital twins in healthcare: Socio-ethical benefits and socio-ethical risks. *Life Sciences, Society and Policy*, 17(1), 6. 10.1186/s40504-021-00113-x34218818

Portnoy, A., Clark, R. A., Weerasuriya, C. K., Mukandavire, C., Quaife, M., Bakker, R., Garcia Baena, I., Gebreselassie, N., Zignol, M., Jit, M., White, R. G., & Menzies, N. A. (2023). The potential impact of novel tuberculosis vaccines on health equity and financial protection in low-income and middle-income countries. *BMJ Global Health*, 8(7), e012466. Advance online publication. 10.1136/bmjgh-2023-012466

Potnurwar, A. V., Bongirwar, V. K., Pathan, S. S., Kothoke, P. M., Dongre, S., & Pande, S. P. (2023). An Integrative Approach to Healthcare Enhancement through Internet of Things, Artificial Intelligence and Smart City Innovations. *Journal of Electrical Systems*, 19(2), 9–17. 10.52783/jes.673

Pradhan, K. B., Sarbhadhikari, S. N., & John, P. (2021). A Framework of Responsible Innovation (RI) Model for Artificial Intelligence (AI) in Indian Healthcare. *Online Journal of Health and Allied Sciences: OJHAS*, 20(2), 1–3. https://www.scopus.com/inward/record.uri?eid=2-s2.0-85115989855&partnerID=40&md5=cc0c4416bc7ea80dc26e2336c6cb0978

Pradhan, K., John, P., & Sandhu, N. (2021). Use of artificial intelligence in healthcare delivery in India. *Journal of Hospital Management and Health Policy*, 5(September), 28. 10.21037/jhmhp-20-126

Premkumar, G., & Ramamurthy, K. (1995). The role of interorganizational and organizational factors on the decision mode for adoption of interorganizational systems. *Decision Sciences*, 26(3), 303–336. 10.1111/j.1540-5915.1995.tb01431.x

Puig-Barbera, J., Tormos, A., Sominina, A., Burtseva, E., Launay, O., Ciblak, M. A., Natividad-Sancho, A., Buigues-Vila, A., Martínez-Úbeda, S., & Mahé, C. (2014). First-year results of the Global Influenza Hospital Surveillance Network: 2012–2013 Northern hemisphere influenza season. *BMC Public Health*, 14(1), 1–12. 10.1186/1471-2458-14-56424903737

Pumplun, L., Fecho, M., Wahl, N., Peters, F., & Buxmann, P. (2021). Adoption of machine learning systems for medical diagnostics in clinics: Qualitative interview study. *Journal of Medical Internet Research*, 23(10), e29301. 10.2196/29301

Qin, W., Tang, S., Xiang, C., & Yang, Y. (2016). Effects of limited medical resource on a Filippov infectious disease model induced by selection pressure. *Applied Mathematics and Computation*, 283, 339–354. 10.1016/j.amc.2016.02.04232287500

Qin, X., Chen, C., Yam, K. C., Cao, L., Li, W., Guan, J., Zhao, P., Dong, X., & Lin, Y. (2022). Adults still can't resist: A social robot can induce normative conformity. *Computers in Human Behavior*, 127, 107041. 10.1016/j.chb.2021.107041

Qin, Z., Liu, Z., Zhu, P., & Ling, W. (2022). Style Transfer in Conditional GANs for Cross-Modality Synthesis of Brain Magnetic Resonance Images. *Computers in Biology and Medicine*, 148, 105928. 10.1016/j.compbiomed.2022.10592835952543

Qu, C., Zou, Y., Ma, Y., Chen, Q., Luo, J., Fan, H., Jia, Z., Gong, Q., & Chen, T. (2022). Diagnostic Performance of Generative Adversarial Network-Based Deep Learning Methods for Alzheimer's Disease: A Systematic Review and Meta-Analysis. *Frontiers in Aging Neuroscience*, 14, 841696. 10.3389/fnagi.2022.84169635527734

Quilodrán-Casas, C., Silva, V. L. S., Arcucci, R., Heaney, C. E., Yi, K. G., & Pain, C. C. (2022). Digital Twins Based on Bidirectional LSTM and GAN for Modelling the COVID-19 Pandemic. *Neurocomputing*, 470, 11–28. 10.1016/j.neucom.2021.10.04334703079

Quinn, T. P., Senadeera, M., Jacobs, S., Coghlan, S., & Le, V. (2021). Trust and medical AI: The challenges we face and the expertise needed to overcome them. *Journal of the American Medical Informatics Association : JAMIA*, 28(4), 890–894. 10.1093/jamia/ocaa268

Rabhi, Y., Mrabet, M., & Fnaiech, F. (2018). A facial expression controlled wheelchair for people with disabilities. *Computer Methods and Programs in Biomedicine*, 165, 89–105. 10.1016/j.cmpb.2018.08.013

Radford, A. (2018). *Improving Language Understanding with Unsupervised Learning*. Technical Report.

Radford, A. (2019). *Language Models are Unsupervised Multitask Learners*. Technical Report.

Radford, A. (2017). *Rafal Jozefowicz, and Ilya Sutskever*. Learning to Generate Reviews and Discovering Sentiment.

Compilation of References

Radziwill, N. M., & Benton, M. C. (2017). Evaluating quality of chatbots and intelligent conversational agents. *arXiv preprint arXiv:1704.04579*.

Raghupathi, W., & Raghupathi, V. (2018). Big data analytics in healthcare: Promise and potential. *Health Information Science and Systems*, 6(1), 1–10. 10.1007/s13755-018-0061-6

Ragno, L., Borboni, A., Vannetti, F., Amici, C., & Cusano, N. (2023). Application of Social Robots in Healthcare: Review on Characteristics, Requirements, Technical Solutions. *Sensors (Basel)*, 23(15), 6820. 10.3390/s2315682037571603

Rahman, M. M. (2023). Ensuring halal compliance in AI-driven healthcare solutions: Balancing innovation and faith. In *Federated Learning and AI for Healthcare 5.0* (pp. 298–320). IGI Global. 10.4018/979-8-3693-1082-3.ch015

Rai, H. M., & Chatterjee, K. (2018). A unique feature extraction using MRDWT for automatic classification of abnormal heartbeat from ECG big data with multilayered probabilistic neural network classifier. *Applied Soft Computing*, 72, 596–608. 10.1016/j.asoc.2018.04.005

Rajkomar, A., Oren, E., Chen, K., Dai, A. M., Hajaj, N., Hardt, M., Liu, P. J., Liu, X., Marcus, J., Sun, M., Sundberg, P., Yee, H., Zhang, K., Zhang, Y., Flores, G., Duggan, G. E., Irvine, J., Le, Q., Litsch, K., & Dean, J. (2018). Scalable and accurate deep learning with electronic health records. *NPJ Digital Medicine*, 1(1), 18. 10.1038/s41746-018-0029-1

Raju, N., & Peter Augustine, D. (2023). Reduce Overfitting and Improve Deep Learning Models' Performance in Medical Image Classification. In *Machine Intelligence: Computer Vision and Natural Language Processing*. Springer. 10.1201/9781003424550-4

Ramezani, M., & Mohd Ripin, Z. (2023). 4D printing in biomedical engineering: Advancements, challenges, and future directions. *Journal of Functional Biomaterials*, 14(7), 347. 10.3390/jfb1407034737504842

Ranschaert, E. R., Morozov, S., & Algra, P. R. (Eds.). (2019). *Artificial intelligence in medical imaging: opportunities, applications and risks*. Springer. 10.1007/978-3-319-94878-2

Ravindar, K., Boddepalli, E., Singla, A., Ameta, G. K., Kalaivani, E., & Alzubaidi, L. H. (2023). AI-Powered Computer Vision for Early Skin Cancer Detection with IoT-Connected Dermascopes. In Swarnkar, S. K., & Rathore, Y. K. (Eds.), *International Conference on Artificial Intelligence for Innovations in Healthcare Industries, ICAIIHI 2023*. Institute of Electrical and Electronics Engineers Inc. 10.1109/ICAIIHI57871.2023.10489445

Ravi, P. R., Sarumathi, S., & Ramaswamy, R. (2022). Design principles, modernization and techniques in artificial intelligence for IoT: Advanced technologies, development and challenges. In *Artificial intelligence for internet of things* (pp. 315–333). CRC Press.

Rechel, B., Sydykova, A., Moldoisaeva, S., Sodiqova, D., Spatayev, Y., Ahmedov, M., Robinson, S., & Sagan, A. (2023). Primary care reforms in Central Asia - On the path to universal health coverage? *Health Policy OPEN*, 5, 100110. 10.1016/j.hpopen.2023.100110

Reddy, S. (2024). Generative AI in healthcare: An implementation science informed translational path on application, integration and governance. *Implementation Science : IS*, 19(1), 27. 10.1186/s13012-024-01357-938491544

Reddy, S., Fox, J., & Purohit, M. P. (2019). Artificial intelligence-enabled healthcare delivery. *Journal of the Royal Society of Medicine*, 112(1), 22–28. 10.1177/014107681881551030507284

Rejusha, R. R. T., & Vipin Kumar, S. V. K. (2021). Artificial MRI Image Generation Using Deep Convolutional GAN and Its Comparison with Other Augmentation Methods. In *ICCISc 2021 - 2021 International Conference on Communication, Control and Information Sciences, Proceedings*. IEEE. 10.1109/ICCISc52257.2021.9484902

Ricciardi Celsi, L. (2023). The Dilemma of Rapid AI Advancements: Striking a Balance between Innovation and Regulation by Pursuing Risk-Aware Value Creation. *Information (Basel)*, 14(12), 645. 10.3390/info14120645

Rihan, F. A., & Anwar, M. N. (2012). Qualitative analysis of delayed SIR epidemic model with a saturated incidence rate. *International Journal of Differential Equations*, 2012, 1–13. 10.1155/2012/408637

Rivera, S. C., Liu, X., Chan, A. W., Denniston, A. K., Calvert, M. J., Ashrafian, H., & Yau, C. (2020). Guidelines for clinical trial protocols for interventions involving artificial intelligence: The SPIRIT-AI extension. *The Lancet. Digital Health*, 2(10), e549–e560. 10.1016/S2589-7500(20)30219-3

Rivero-Moreno, Y., Echevarria, S., Vidal-Valderrama, C., Stefano-Pianetti, L., Cordova-Guilarte, J., Navarro-Gonzalez, J., & Avila, G. L. D. (2023). Robotic Surgery: A Comprehensive Review of the Literature and Current Trends. *Cureus*, 15(7). 10.7759/cureus.4237037621804

Rodriguez Aguilar, R., Marmolejo-Saucedo, J. A., Zavala Landin, A., Rodriguez Aguilar, M., & Marmolejo Saucedo, L. (2023). Out of pocket and catastrophic health spending in Mexico in the face of the COVID-19 pandemic. *EAI Endorsed Transactions on Pervasive Health and Technology*, 9. Advance online publication. 10.4108/eetpht.9.3583

Rogers, E. M. (2010). *Diffusion of Innovations*. Simon and Schuster.

Ross, C., & Swetlitz, I. (2017). IBM pitched its Watson supercomputer as a revolution in cancer care. It's nowhere close. *Stat*.

Rossi, M., & Cerveri, P. (2021). Comparison of Supervised and Unsupervised Approaches for the Generation of Synthetic Ct from Cone-Beam Ct. *Diagnostics (Basel)*, 11(8), 1435. 10.3390/diagnostics1108143534441369

Ruivo, P., Johansson, B., Oliveira, T., & Neto, M. (2013). Commercial ERP systems and user productivity: A study across European SMEs. *Procedia Technology*, 9, 84–93. 10.1016/j.protcy.2013.12.009

Compilation of References

Ruiz-Rojas, L. I., Acosta-Vargas, P., De-Moreta-Llovet, J., & Gonzalez-Rodriguez, M. (2023). Empowering Education with Generative Artificial Intelligence Tools: Approach with an Instructional Design Matrix. *Sustainability (Basel)*, 15(15), 11524. 10.3390/su151511524

Ruschel, S., Pereira, T., Yanchuk, S., & Young, L. S. (2019). An SIQ delay differential equations model for disease control via isolation. *Journal of Mathematical Biology*, 79(1), 249–279. 10.1007/s00285-019-01356-131037349

Rysavy, M. (2013). Evidence-based medicine: A science of uncertainty and an art of probability. *AMA Journal of Ethics*, 15(1), 4–8. 10.1001/virtualmentor.2013.15.1.fred1-1301

Sabzalieva, E., & Valentini, A. (2023). *ChatGPT and Artificial Intelligence in Higher Education: Quick Start Guide.* UNESCO. https://www.iesalc.unesco.org/wp-content/uploads/2023/04/ChatGPT-and-Artificial-Intelligence-in-higher-education-Quick-Start-guide_EN_FINAL.pdf

Safdar, S., Zafar, S., Zafar, N., & Khan, N. F. (2018). Machine learning based decision support systems (DSS) for heart disease diagnosis: A review. *Artificial Intelligence Review*, 50(4), 597–623. 10.1007/s10462-017-9552-8

Sahoo, S. K., & Goswami, S. S. (2023). A comprehensive review of multiple criteria decision-making (MCDM) Methods: Advancements, applications, and future directions. *Decision Making Advances*, 1(1), 25–48. 10.31181/dma1120237

Saifi, S., Taylor, A. J., Allen, J., & Hendel, R. (2013). The use of a learning community and online evaluation of utilization for SPECT myocardial perfusion imaging. *JACC: Cardiovascular Imaging*, 6(7), 823–829. 10.1016/j.jcmg.2013.01.012

Sai, S., Gaur, A., Sai, R., Chamola, V., Guizani, M., & Rodrigues, J. J. P. C. (2024). Generative AI for Transformative Healthcare: A Comprehensive Study of Emerging Models, Applications, Case Studies, and Limitations. *IEEE Access: Practical Innovations, Open Solutions*, 12, 31078–31106. Advance online publication. 10.1109/ACCESS.2024.3367715

Sakai, K., & Yamada, K. (2019). Machine learning studies on major brain diseases: 5-year trends of 2014–2018. *Japanese Journal of Radiology*, 37(1), 34–72. 10.1007/s11604-018-0794-4

Sallam, M. (2023). ChatGPT utility in healthcare education, research, and practice: Systematic review on the promising perspectives and valid concerns. *Health Care*, 11, 887.36981544

Saluja, R. (2024). Revolutionizing Healthcare: The Integral Role of AI And IoT In Shaping Modern Medicine. Available at https://www.forbes.com/sites/forbesbusinessdevelopmentcouncil/2024/02/14/revolutionizing-healthcare-the-integral-role-of-ai-and-iot-in-shaping-modern-medicine/?sh=6bd38bdedabc

Sarrouti, M., & El Alaoui, S. O. (2017). A machine learning-based method for question type classification in biomedical question answering. *Methods of Information in Medicine*, 56(03), 209–216. 10.3414/ME16-01-0116

Sarrouti, M., & El Alaoui, S. O. (2017). A yes/no answer generator based on sentiment-word scores in biomedical question answering. [IJHISI]. *International Journal of Healthcare Information Systems and Informatics*, 12(3), 62–74. 10.4018/IJHISI.2017070104

Sauerbrei, A., Kerasidou, A., Lucivero, F., & Hallowell, N. (2023). The impact of artificial intelligence on the person-centred, doctor-patient relationship: Some problems and solutions. *BMC Medical Informatics and Decision Making*, 23(1), 73. 10.1186/s12911-023-02162-y

Savage, N. (2023). Drug discovery companies are customizing ChatGPT: Here's how. *Nature Biotechnology*, 41(5), 585–586. 10.1038/s41587-023-01788-737095351

Schaffter, T., Buist, D. S., Lee, C. I., Nikulin, Y., Ribli, D., Guan, Y., Lotter, W., Jie, Z., Du, H., Wang, S., Feng, J., Feng, M., Kim, H.-E., Albiol, F., Albiol, A., Morrell, S., Wojna, Z., Ahsen, M. E., Asif, U., & Jung, H. (2020). Evaluation of combined artificial intelligence and radiologist assessment to interpret screening mammograms. *JAMA Network Open*, 3(3), e200265–e200265. 10.1001/jamanetworkopen.2020.0265

Schermelleh-Engel, K., Moosbrugger, H., & Müller, H. (2003). Evaluating the fit of structural equation models: Tests of significance and descriptive goodness-of-fit measures. *Methods of Psychological Research Online*, 8, 23–74.

Schiff, G. D., Volk, L. A., Volodarskaya, M., Williams, D. H., Walsh, L., Myers, S. G., Bates, D. W., & Rozenblum, R. (2017). Screening for medication errors using an outlier detection system. *Journal of the American Medical Informatics Association : JAMIA*, 24(2), 281–287. 10.1093/jamia/ocw171

Schmidt-Erfurth, U., Bogunovic, H., Sadeghipour, A., Schlegl, T., Langs, G., Gerendas, B. S., Osborne, A., & Waldstein, S. M. (2018). Machine learning to analyze the prognostic value of current imaging biomarkers in neovascular age-related macular degeneration. *Ophthalmology Retina*, 2(1), 24–30. 10.1016/j.oret.2017.03.015

Schönberger, D. (2019). Artificial intelligence in healthcare: A critical analysis of the legal and ethical implications. *International Journal of Law and Information Technology*, 27(2), 171–203. 10.1093/ijlit/eaz004

Schönmann, M., Bodenschatz, A., Uhl, M., & Walkowitz, G. (2023). The Care-Dependent are Less Averse to Care Robots: An Empirical Comparison of Attitudes. *International Journal of Social Robotics*, 15(6), 1–18. 10.1007/s12369-023-01003-237359432

Schumacher, S., Salmanton-Garcia, J., Cornely, O. A., & Mellinghoff, S. C. (2021). Increasing influenza vaccination coverage in healthcare workers: A review on campaign strategies and their effect. *Infection*, 49(3), 387–399. 10.1007/s15010-020-01555-933284427

Seh AH, Zarour M, Alenezi M, Sarkar AK, Agrawal A, Kumar R, Khan RA. *Healthcare Data Breaches: Insights and Implications*. Healthcare (Basel). 2020

Sengupta, S., & Eason, K. (2017). Understanding data security and privacy in the era of digital government transformation: A study of India. *Information Systems Frontiers*, 19(2), 245–259.

Compilation of References

Sensely. (2019). An integrated payer/provider wanted to intervene in a timelier manner with its Chronic Heart Failure (CHF) patients.

Sezgin, E. (2023). Artificial intelligence in healthcare: Complementing, not replacing, doctors and healthcare providers. *Digital Health*, 9, 20552076231186520. 10.1177/20552076231186520

Shah, A., Patel, W., & Koyuncu, H. (2024). Empowering healthcare innovation: IoT-enabled smart systems and deep learning for enhanced diabetic retinopathy in the telehealth landscape. *Journal of Interdisciplinary Mathematics*, 27(2), 355–367. 10.47974/JIM-1836

Shaheen, M. Y. (2021). Applications of Artificial Intelligence (AI) in healthcare. *RE:view*. Advance online publication. 10.14293/S2199-1006.1.SOR-.PPVRY8K.v1

Shah, H., Shah, S., Tanwar, S., Gupta, R., & Kumar, N. (2021). Fusion of AI techniques to tackle COVID-19 pandemic: Models, incidence rates, and future trends. *Multimedia Systems*, •••, 1–34.

Shakeel, T., Habib, S., Boulila, W., Koubaa, A., Javed, A. R., Rizwan, M., Gadekallu, T. R., & Sufiyan, M. (2023). A survey on COVID-19 impact in the healthcare domain: Worldwide market implementation, applications, security and privacy issues, challenges and future prospects. *Complex & Intelligent Systems*, 9(1), 1027–1058. 10.1007/s40747-022-00767-w35668731

Shalender, K. (2022). Key variables in team dynamics in small businesses and start-ups. In New teaching resources for management in a globalised world (pp. 141–153). https://doi.org/10.1142/9789811239212_0007

Shalender, K. (2023). Skill development for society 5.0: A focus on the new-age skilling process. Trivedi, S., Aggarwal, R., & Sharma, S. (Eds.), Innovations and Sustainability in Society 5.0, Nova Science Publishers, Hauppauge, NY, pp. 43–52.

Sharma, C., & Gupta, G. (2021). Innovation insight for healthcare provider digital twins: A review. In *Mobile Health: Advances in Research and Applications* (pp. 97–128). Nova Science Publishers, Inc. https://www.scopus.com/inward/record.uri?eid=2-s2.0-85109468612&partnerID=40&md5=c92a245b5fd3582f1f5b4d7cb753bded

Sharma, P., Suehling, M., Flohr, T., & Comaniciu, D. (2020). Artificial intelligence in diagnostic imaging: Status quo, challenges, and future opportunities. *Journal of Thoracic Imaging*, 35(Supplement 1), S11–S16. 10.1097/RTI.000000000000049932205816

Shi, D., Zhang, W., Zhang, W., & Ding, X. (2019). A review on lower limb rehabilitation exoskeleton robots. *Chinese Journal of Mechanical Engineering*, 32(1), 1–11. 10.1186/s10033-019-0389-8

Shimabukuro, D. W., Barton, C. W., Feldman, M. D., Mataraso, S. J., & Das, R. (2017). Effect of a machine learning-based severe sepsis prediction algorithm on patient survival and hospital length of stay: A randomised clinical trial. *BMJ Open Respiratory Research*, 4(1), e000234. 10.1136/bmjresp-2017-000234

Shi, W., Kah, W. S., Mohamad, M. S., Moorthy, K., Deris, S., Sjaugi, M. F., Omatu, S., Corchado, J. M., & Kasim, S. (2017). A review of gene selection tools in classifying cancer microarray data. *Current Bioinformatics*, 12(3), 202–212. 10.2174/1574893610666151026215104

Shortliffe, E. H., & Barnett, G. O. (2001). Medical data: their acquisition, storage, and use. In *Medical informatics: computer applications in health care and biomedicine* (pp. 41–75). Springer New York. 10.1007/978-0-387-21721-5_2

Shroff, K. (2024). Artificial Intelligence (AI) revolutionizing healthcare: A look at the present and future! Available at https://www.dsij.in/dsijarticledetail/artificial-intelligence-ai-revolutionizing-healthcare-a-look-at-the-present-and-future-37593

Shrotriya, L., Sharma, K., Parashar, D., Mishra, K., Rawat, S. S., & Pagare, H. (2023). Apache Spark in Healthcare: Advancing Data-Driven Innovations and Better Patient Care. *International Journal of Advanced Computer Science and Applications*, 14(6), 608–616. 10.14569/IJACSA.2023.0140665

Siegel, R. L., Miller, K. D., Wagle, N. S., & Jemal, A. (2023). Cancer Statistics, 2023. *CA: a Cancer Journal for Clinicians*, 73(1), 17–48. 10.3322/caac.2176336633525

Simonite, T. (2020). The US government will pay doctors to use these AI algorithms. *Wired Magazine, 11*.

Singh, H. (2024). How AI and ML are Revolutionising Healthcare Industry. Available at https://www.entrepreneur.com/en-in/news-and-trends/how-ai-and-ml-are-revolutionising-healthcare-industry/472959

Singh, N. K., & Raza, K. (2021). Medical Image Generation Using Generative Adversarial Networks: A Review. In *Studies in Computational Intelligence*. Springer. 10.1007/978-981-15-9735-0_5

Singh, J. P. (2023). The Impacts and Challenges of Generative Artificial Intelligence in Medical Education, Clinical Diagnostics, Administrative Efficiency, and Data Generation. *International Journal of Applied Health Care Analytics*, 8(5), 37–46.

Singh, J. P., Chand, P. K., Mittal, A., & Aggarwal, A. (2020). High-performance work system and organizational citizenship behaviour at the shop floor. *Benchmarking*, 27(4), 1369–1398. 10.1108/BIJ-07-2019-0339

Singh, M., & Nath, G. (2022). Artificial intelligence and anesthesia: A narrative review. *Saudi Journal of Anaesthesia*, 16(1), 86. 10.4103/sja.sja_669_21

Singh, V. I. N. I. T., & Gochhait, S. (2020). The development of artificial intelligence in health and medicine: A bibliometric analysis. *European Journal of Molecular and Clinical Medicine*, 7(6), 2585–2594.

Singh, V. K., Rashwan, H. A., Romani, S., Akram, F., Pandey, N., Md, M. K. S., & Saleh, A. (2020). Breast Tumor Segmentation and Shape Classification in Mammograms Using Generative Adversarial and Convolutional Neural Network. *Expert Systems with Applications*, 139, 112855. 10.1016/j.eswa.2019.112855

Singla, B., Shalender, K., & Sharma, S. (2023). Enhancing customer engagement through brand loyalty drivers among E-consumers. Gupta, M., Shalender, K., Singla, B., Singh, N. (Eds.), Applications of Neuromarketing in the Metaverse, IGI Global, Hershey, PA, pp. 155–162

Compilation of References

Smith, P. C., Sagan, A., Siciliani, L., & Figueras, J. (2023). Building on value-based health care: Towards a health system perspective. *Health Policy (Amsterdam)*, 138(104918), 104918. 10.1016/j.healthpol.2023.104918

Soljacic, F., Law, T., Chita-Tegmark, M., & Scheutz, M. (2024). Robots in healthcare as envisioned by care professionals. *Intelligent Service Robotics*, 17(3), 1–17. 10.1007/s11370-024-00523-8

Somashekhar, S., Kumar, R., Kumar, A., Patil, P., & Rauthan, A. (2016). Validation Study to Assess Pperformance of IBM Cognitive Computing System Watson for Oncology with Manipal Multidisciplinary Tumour Board for 1000 Consecutive Cases: An Indian Experience. *Annals of Oncology : Official Journal of the European Society for Medical Oncology*, 27(suppl_9), 1–2. 10.1093/annonc/mdw601.002

Sordo, M. (2002). Introduction to neural networks in healthcare. *Open clinical: Knowledge management for medical care*.

Spector-Bagdady, K. (2023). Generative-AI-Generated Challenges for Health Data Research. *The American Journal of Bioethics*, 23(10), 1–5. 10.1080/15265161.2023.225231137831940

Srivastava, J., Routray, S., Ahmad, S., & Waris, M. M. (2022). Internet of Medical Things (IoMT)-Based Smart Healthcare System: Trends and Progress. *Computational Intelligence and Neuroscience*, 2022, 7218113. 10.1155/2022/721811335880061

Stacey, W. C. (2018). Seizure prediction is possible–now let's make it practical. *EBioMedicine*, 27, 3–4. 10.1016/j.ebiom.2018.01.006

Stasevych, M., & Zvarych, V. (2023). Innovative robotic technologies and artificial intelligence in pharmacy and medicine: Paving the way for the future of health care—a review. *Big Data and Cognitive Computing*, 7(3), 147. 10.3390/bdcc7030147

Sucharitha, G., & Chary, D. V. (2021). Predicting the effect of Covid-19 by using Artificial Intelligence: A case study. *Materials today. Proceedings*.

Suthar, A.C., Joshi, V., & Prajapati, R. (2022). *A review of generative adversarial-based networks of machine learning/artificial intelligence in healthcare*. Academic Press.

Su, Y. H., Jiang, W., Chitrakar, D., Huang, K., Peng, H., & Hannaford, B. (2021). Local Style Preservation in Improved GAN-Driven Synthetic Image Generation for Endoscopic Tool Segmentation. *Sensors (Basel)*, 21(15), 5163. 10.3390/s2115516334372398

Swain, S., Muduli, K., Kommula, V. P., & Sahoo, K. K. (2022). Innovations in Internet of Medical Things, Artificial Intelligence, and Readiness of the Healthcare Sector Towards Health 4.0 Adoption. *International Journal of Social Ecology and Sustainable Development*, 13(1), 1–14. 10.4018/IJSESD.292078

Swarnkar, S. K., & Rathore, Y. K. (Eds.). (2023). International Conference on Artificial Intelligence for Innovations in Healthcare Industries, ICAIIHI 2023. In *International Conference on Artificial Intelligence for Innovations in Healthcare Industries, ICAIIHI 2023*. Institute of Electrical and Electronics Engineers Inc. https://www.scopus.com/inward/record.uri?eid=2-s2.0-85191501083&partnerID=40&md5=5fd02603c5243d1b44cd8fb4653f0db1

Tahir, F., & Farhan, M. (2023). Exploring the progress of artificial intelligence in managing type 2 diabetes mellitus: A comprehensive review of present innovations and anticipated challenges ahead. *Frontiers in Clinical Diabetes and Healthcare*, 4, 1316111. 10.3389/fcdhc.2023.131611138161783

Takefuji, Y. (2023). A brief tutorial on generative AI. *British Dental Journal*, 234(12), 845. 10.1038/s41415-023-6041-037349417

Tan, X., Yuan, L., Zhou, J., Zheng, Y., & Yang, F. (2013). Modeling the initial transmission dynamics of influenza A H1N1 in Guangdong Province, China. *International Journal of Infectious Diseases*, 17.

Tang, L., Li, J., & Fantus, S. (2023). Medical artificial intelligence ethics: A systematic review of empirical studies. *Digital Health*, 9, 20552076231186064. 10.1177/20552076231186064 37434728

Tantin, A., Assi, E. B., van Asselt, E., Hached, S., & Sawan, M. (2020). Predicting urinary bladder voiding by means of a linear discriminant analysis: Validation in rats. *Biomedical Signal Processing and Control*, 55, 101667. 10.1016/j.bspc.2019.101667

Tao, R., & Xu, J. (2023). Mapping with ChatGPT. *ISPRS International Journal of Geo-Information*, 12(7), 284. 10.3390/ijgi12070284

Taylor, N. (2019). *Duke Report Identifies Barriers to Adoption of AI Healthcare Systems*. MedTech Dive.

Teixeira, T., Kweder, S. L., & Saint-Raymond, A. (2020). Are the European Medicines Agency, US Food and Drug Administration, and Other International Regulators Talking to Each Other? *Clinical Pharmacology and Therapeutics*, 107(3), 507–513. 10.1002/cpt.1617

Teo, Z. L., Kwee, A., Lim, J. C. W., Lam, C. S. P., Ho, D., Maurer-Stroh, S., Su, Y., Chesterman, S., Chen, T., Tan, C. C., Wong, T. Y., Ngiam, K. Y., Tan, C. H., Soon, D., Choong, M. L., Chua, R., Wong, S., Lim, C., Cheong, W. Y., & Ting, D. S. W. (2023). Artificial intelligence innovation in healthcare: Relevance of reporting guidelines for clinical translation from bench to bedside. *Annals of the Academy of Medicine, Singapore*, 52(4), 199–212. 10.47102/annals-acadmedsg.2022452

Teytelman, A., & Larson, R. C. (2012). Modeling influenza progression within a continuous-attribute heterogeneous population. *European Journal of Operational Research*, 220(1), 238–250. 10.1016/j.ejor.2012.01.027

Thakkar, A., Gupta, A., & De Sousa, A. (2024). Artificial intelligence in positive mental health: A narrative review. *Frontiers in Digital Health*, 6, 1280235. 10.3389/fdgth.2024.1280235

Compilation of References

Thampapillai, D. (2023). Two Authors Are Suing OpenAI for Training ChatGPT with Their Books. Could They Win? *The Conversation.* https://theconversation.com/two-authors-are-suing-openai-for-training-chatgpt-with-their-books-could-they-win-209227

Tiago, C., Gilbert, A., Beela, A. S., Aase, S. A., Snare, S. R., Šprem, J., & McLeod, K. (2022). A Data Augmentation Pipeline to Generate Synthetic Labeled Datasets of 3D Echocardiography Images Using a GAN. *IEEE Access : Practical Innovations, Open Solutions*, 10, 98803–98815. 10.1109/ACCESS.2022.3207177

Tigard, D. W., Braun, M., Breuer, S., Ritt, K., Fiske, A., McLennan, S., & Buyx, A. (2023). Toward best practices in embedded ethics: Suggestions for interdisciplinary technology development. *Robotics and Autonomous Systems*, 167, 104467. 10.1016/j.robot.2023.104467

Timilsina, M., Alsamhi, S., Haque, R., Judge, C., & Curry, E. (2023). Knowledge Graphs, Clinical Trials, Dataspace, and AI: Uniting for Progressive Healthcare Innovation. In J. He, T. Palpanas, X. Hu, A. Cuzzocrea, D. Dou, D. Slezak, W. Wang, A. Gruca, L. J.C.-W., & R. Agrawal (Eds.), *Proceedings - 2023 IEEE International Conference on Big Data, BigData 2023* (pp. 4997–5006). Institute of Electrical and Electronics Engineers Inc. 10.1109/BigData59044.2023.10386401

Ting, D. S., Liu, Y., Burlina, P., Xu, X., Bressler, N. M., & Wong, T. Y. (2018). AI for medical imaging goes deep. *Nature Medicine*, 24(5), 539–540. 10.1038/s41591-018-0029-3

Topol, E. J. (2019). High-performance medicine: The convergence of human and artificial intelligence. *Nature Medicine*, 25(1), 44–56. 10.1038/s41591-018-0300-7

Tran, B. X., Vu, G. T., Ha, G. H., Vuong, Q. H., Ho, M. T., Vuong, T. T., La, V.-P., Ho, M.-T., Nghiem, K.-C., Nguyen, H., Latkin, C., Tam, W., Cheung, N.-M., Nguyen, H.-K., Ho, C., & Ho, R. C. (2019). Global evolution of research in artificial intelligence in health and medicine: A bibliometric study. *Journal of Clinical Medicine*, 8(3), 360. 10.3390/jcm8030360

Tukhtakhodjaeva, F. S., & Khayitova, I. I. (2023). APPLICATION AND USE OF AI (ARTIFICIAL INTELLIGENCE) IN MEDICINE. *Educational Research in Universal Sciences*, 2(9), 302–309.

Tumpa, S. N., Islam, A. B., & Ankon, M. T. M. (2017, September). Smart care: An intelligent assistant for pregnant mothers. In *2017 4th International Conference on Advances in Electrical Engineering (ICAEE)* (pp. 754-759). IEEE.

Tutton, R. (2016). *Genomics and the reimagining of personalized medicine.* Routledge. 10.4324/9781315584317

Tutun, S., Johnson, M. E., Ahmed, A., Albizri, A., Irgil, S., Yesilkaya, I., Ucar, E. N., Sengun, T., & Harfouche, A. (2023). An AI-based decision support system for predicting mental health disorders. *Information Systems Frontiers*, 25(3), 1261–1276. 10.1007/s10796-022-10282-5

Umer, F., & Adnan, N. (2024). Generative artificial intelligence: synthetic datasets in dentistry. In *BDJ Open* (Vol. 10, Issue 1). 10.1038/s41405-024-00198-4

Upadhyay, R. K., Kumari, N., & Rao, V. S. H. (2008). Modeling the spread of bird flu and predicting outbreak diversity. *Nonlinear Analysis Real World Applications*, 9(4), 1638–1648. 10.1016/j.nonrwa.2007.04.00932288641

Uprety, D., Zhu, D., & West, H. J. (2023). ChatGPT-a promising generative AI tool and its implications for cancer care. *Cancer*, 129(15), 2284–2289. 10.1002/cncr.3482737183438

Uzialko, A. (2019). Artificial Intelligence Will Change Healthcare as We Know it. *Business News Daily*.

Väänänen, A., Haataja, K., Vehviläinen-Julkunen, K., & Toivanen, P. (2021). AI in healthcare: A narrative review. *F1000 Research*, 10, 6. 10.12688/f1000research.26997.2

Vallès-Peris, N., & Domènech, M. (2023). Caring in the in-between: A proposal to introduce responsible AI and robotics to healthcare. *AI & Society*, 38(4), 1685–1695. 10.1007/s00146-021-01330-w

van Schalkwyk, G. (2023). Artificial intelligence in pediatric behavioral health. *Child and Adolescent Psychiatry and Mental Health*, 17(1), 38. 10.1186/s13034-023-00586-y36907862

VanBuskirk, A. (2023). A Brief History of the Generative Pre-Trained Transformer (GPT) Language Models. *Wordbot*.https://blog.wordbot.io/ai-artificial-intelligence/a-brief-history-of-the-generative-pre-trained-transformer-gpt-language-models/

Varilek, B. M., & Mollman, S. (2024). Healthcare professionals' perspectives of barriers to cancer care delivery for American Indian, rural, and frontier populations. *PEC Innovation*, 4, 100247. 10.1016/j.pecinn.2023.10024738225930

Vashistha, R., Dangi, A. K., Kumar, A., Chhabra, D., & Shukla, P. (2018). Futuristic biosensors for cardiac health care: an artificial intelligence approach. *3 Biotech*, *8*, 1-11.

Vaswani, A., Shazeer, N., Parmar, N., Uszkoreit, J., Jones, L., Gomez, A. N., Kaiser, Ł., & Polosukhin, I. (2017). *Attention Is All You Need*. In Advances in Neural Information Processing Systems, Denver, CO, USA. https://papers.nips.cc/paper_files/paper/2017/file/3f5ee243547dee91fbd053c1c4a845aa-Paper.pdf (accessed on 12 Dec 2023).

Velvárt, A. (2023). *How Will AI Affect User Interfaces?* Linkedin. https://www.linkedin.com/pulse/how-ai-affect-user-interfaces-andr%2525C3%2525A1s-velv%2525C3%2525A1rt/

Venkatesh, K. P., Brito, G., & Kamel Boulos, M. N. (2024). Health Digital Twins in Life Science and Health Care Innovation. *Annual Review of Pharmacology and Toxicology*, 64(1), 159–170. 10.1146/annurev-pharmtox-022123-02204637562495

Venna, S. R., Tavanaei, A., Gottumukkala, R. N., Raghavan, V. V., Maida, A. S., & Nichols, S. (2018). A novel data-driven model for real-time influenza forecasting. *IEEE Access: Practical Innovations, Open Solutions*, 7, 7691–7701. 10.1109/ACCESS.2018.2888585

Vert, J. P. (2023). How will generative AI disrupt data science in drug discovery? *Nature Biotechnology*, 41(6), 750–751. 10.1038/s41587-023-01789-637156917

Compilation of References

Vial, A., Stirling, D., Field, M., Ros, M., Ritz, C., Carolan, M., Holloway, L., & Miller, A. A. (2018). The role of deep learning and radiomic feature extraction in cancer-specific predictive modelling: A review. *Translational Cancer Research*, 7(3), 803–816. 10.21037/tcr.2018.05.02

Volz, V., Lucas, S. M., Schrum, J., Smith, A., Liu, J., & Risi, S. (2018). Evolving Mario Levels in the Latent Space of a Deep Convolutional Generative Adversarial Network. In *GECCO 2018 - Proceedings of the 2018 Genetic and Evolutionary Computation Conference*. IEEE. 10.1145/3205455.3205517

Wachter, R. M., & Brynjolfsson, E. (2024). Will generative artificial intelligence deliver on its promise in health care? *Journal of the American Medical Association*, 331(1), 65–69. 10.1001/jama.2023.2505438032660

Wahl, B., Cossy-Gantner, A., Germann, S., & Schwalbe, N. R. (2018). Artificial intelligence (AI) and global health: How can AI contribute to health in resource-poor settings? *BMJ Global Health*, 3(4), e000798. 10.1136/bmjgh-2018-000798

Walker, R., Dillard-Wright, J., & Iradukunda, F. (2023). Algorithmic bias in artificial intelligence is a problem—And the root issue is power. *Nursing Outlook*, 71(5), 102023. Advance online publication. 10.1016/j.outlook.2023.10202337579574

Walton, N. A., & Christensen, G. B. (2023). Paving a pathway for large-scale utilization of genomics in precision medicine and population health. *Frontiers in Sociology*, 8, 1122488. 10.3389/fsoc.2023.112248837274607

Wang, Q., Su, M., Zhang, M., & Li, R. (2021). Integrating Digital Technologies and Public Health to Fight Covid-19 Pandemic: Key Technologies, Applications, Challenges and Outlook of Digital Healthcare. In *International Journal of Environmental Research and Public Health*, 10.3390/ijerph18116053

Wang, C., Liu, S., Yang, H., Guo, J., Wu, Y., & Liu, J. (2023). Ethical considerations of using ChatGPT in health care. *Journal of Medical Internet Research*, 25, e48009. 10.2196/4800937566454

Wang, C., Li, Z., Mo, X., Tang, X., & Liu, H. (2023). Exploiting Unfairness with Meta-Set Learning for Chronological Age Estimation. *IEEE Transactions on Information Forensics and Security*, 18, 5678–5690. 10.1109/TIFS.2023.3313356

Wang, F., Casalino, L. P., & Khullar, D. (2018). Deep learning in medicine—Promise, progress, and challenges. *JAMA Internal Medicine*, 178(6), 737–738.

Wang, P., Liu, X., Berzin, T. M., Brown, J. R. G., Liu, P., Zhou, C., & Zhou, G. (2020). Effect of a deep-learning computer-aided detection system on adenoma detection during colonoscopy (CADe-DB trial): A double-blind randomised study. *The Lancet. Gastroenterology & Hepatology*, 5(4), 343–351. 10.1016/S2468-1253(19)30411-X

Wang, R., Feng, H., & Wei, G. W. (2023). ChatGPT in Drug Discovery: A Case Study on Anticocaine Addiction Drug Development with Chatbots. *Journal of Chemical Information and Modeling*, 63(22), 7189–7209. Advance online publication. 10.1021/acs.jcim.3c0142937956228

Wang, T. C., Ming, Y. L., Jun, Y. Z., Tao, A., Kautz, J., & Catanzaro, B. (2018). High-Resolution Image Synthesis and Semantic Manipulation with Conditional GANs. In *Proceedings of the IEEE Computer Society Conference on Computer Vision and Pattern Recognition*. IEEE. 10.1109/CVPR.2018.00917

Wang, Y.-H., & Lin, G.-Y. (2020). Exploring smart healthcare innovations: Multiple patentometric analyses. *ACM International Conference Proceeding Series*, (pp. 117–120). ACM. 10.1145/3383845.3383872

Wang, Y.-H., & Lin, G.-Y. (2023). Exploring AI-healthcare innovation: Natural language processing-based patents analysis for technology-driven roadmapping. *Kybernetes*, 52(4), 1173–1189. 10.1108/K-03-2021-0170

Wang, Y., Tan, J., & Deng, J. (2020). A study on type 2 diabetes mellitus prediction models using different machine learning techniques. *Health Care*, 8(2), 128. 10.3390/healthcare8020128

Watanabe, J. H., McInnis, T., & Hirsch, J. D. (2018). Cost of prescription drug–related morbidity and mortality. *The Annals of Pharmacotherapy*, 52(9), 829–837. 10.1177/1060028018765159

Wei, Y., Lu, W., Cheng, Q., Jiang, T., & Liu, S. (2022). How humans obtain information from AI: Categorizing user messages in human-AI collaborative conversations. *Information Processing & Management*, 59(2), 102838. 10.1016/j.ipm.2021.102838

Welch, A. (2023). Artificial intelligence is helping revolutionize healthcare as we know it. Available at https://www.jnj.com/innovation/artificial-intelligence-in-healthcare

Westerlund M. (2019). The emergence of deepfake technology: a review. *TIM Review, 9*. .10.22215/timreview/1282

Wickramasinghe, N., Bali, R. K., & Lehaney, B. (2021). Artificial Intelligence in Healthcare: Strategic Planning and Implementation. In Preethika, B. R., & Devika, S. (Eds.), *Artificial Intelligence in Healthcare: Theory and Application* (pp. 113–130). Springer.

Wiens, J., Saria, S., Sendak, M., Ghassemi, M., Liu, V. X., Doshi-Velez, F., Jung, K., Heller, K., Kale, D., Saeed, M., Ossorio, P. N., Thadaney-Israni, S., & Goldenberg, A. (2019). Do no harm: A roadmap for responsible machine learning for health care. *Nature Medicine*, 25(9), 1337–1340. 10.1038/s41591-019-0548-6

Wijnberge, M., Geerts, B. F., Hol, L., Lemmers, N., Mulder, M. P., Berge, P., Schenk, J., Terwindt, L. E., Hollmann, M. W., Vlaar, A. P., & Veelo, D. P. (2020). Effect of a machine learning–derived early warning system for intraoperative hypotension vs standard care on depth and duration of intraoperative hypotension during elective noncardiac surgery: The HYPE randomized clinical trial. *Journal of the American Medical Association*, 323(11), 1052–1060. 10.1001/jama.2020.0592

Compilation of References

Wiley, L. K., Shortt, J. A., Roberts, E. R., Lowery, J., Kudron, E., Lin, M., Mayer, D., Wilson, M., Brunetti, T. M., Chavan, S., Phang, T. L., Pozdeyev, N., Lesny, J., Wicks, S. J., Moore, E. T., Morgenstern, J. L., Roff, A. N., Shalowitz, E. L., Stewart, A., & Gignoux, C. R. (2024). Building a vertically integrated genomic learning health system: The biobank at the Colorado Center for Personalized Medicine. *American Journal of Human Genetics*, 111(1), 11–23. 10.1016/j.ajhg.2023.12.00138181729

Williams, D. J. (2007). Medication errors. *Journal-Royal College of Physicians of Edinburgh*, 37(4), 343.

Wismüller, A., & Stockmaster, L. (2020, February). A prospective randomized clinical trial for measuring radiology study reporting time on Artificial Intelligence-based detection of intracranial hemorrhage in emergent care head CT. In *Medical Imaging 2020: Biomedical Applications in Molecular, Structural, and Functional Imaging* (Vol. 11317, pp. 144-150). SPIE. 10.1117/12.2552400

Wolff, J., Pauling, J., Keck, A., & Baumbach, J. (2020). Systematic review of economic impact studies of artificial intelligence in health care. *Journal of Medical Internet Research*, 22(2), e16866. 10.2196/16866

Wolf, R. M., Channa, R., Abramoff, M. D., & Lehmann, H. P. (2020). Cost-effectiveness of autonomous point-of-care diabetic retinopathy screening for pediatric patients with diabetes. *JAMA Ophthalmology*, 138(10), 1063–1069. 10.1001/jamaophthalmol.2020.3190

Wong, B. (2023). *How Generative AI is Changing the Game in Healthcare*. LinkedIn. https://www.linkedin.com/pulse/future-here-how-generative-ai-changing-game-healthcare/

Wong, L. W. (2023). The potential of generative artificial intelligence across disciplines: Perspectives and future directions. *Journal of Computer Information Systems*, •••, 1–32.

Wu, N., Phang, J., Park, J., Shen, Y., Huang, Z., Zorin, M., Jastrzebski, S., Fevry, T., Katsnelson, J., Kim, E., Wolfson, S., Parikh, U., Gaddam, S., Lin, L. L. Y., Ho, K., Weinstein, J. D., Reig, B., Gao, Y., Toth, H., & Geras, K. J. (2019). Deep neural networks improve radiologists' performance in breast cancer screening. *IEEE Transactions on Medical Imaging*, 39(4), 1184–1194. 10.1109/TMI.2019.2945514

Wu, Q., Zhang, Y. D., Tao, W., & Amin, M. G. (2015). Radar-based fall detection based on Doppler time–frequency signatures for assisted living. *IET Radar, Sonar & Navigation*, 9(2), 164–172. 10.1049/iet-rsn.2014.0250

Wu, X., Xiao, L., Sun, Y., Zhang, J., Ma, T., & He, L. (2022). A survey of human-in-the-loop for machine learning. *Future Generation Computer Systems*, 135, 364–381. 10.1016/j.future.2022.05.014

Xia, T., Chartsias, A., & Tsaftaris, S. A. (2020). Pseudo-Healthy Synthesis with Pathology Disentanglement and Adversarial Learning. *Medical Image Analysis*, 64, 101719. 10.1016/j.media.2020.10171932540700

Xie, Y., Nguyen, Q. D., Hamzah, H., Lim, G., Bellemo, V., Gunasekeran, D. V., Yip, M. Y. T., Qi Lee, X., Hsu, W., Li Lee, M., Tan, C. S., Tym Wong, H., Lamoureux, E. L., Tan, G. S. W., Wong, T. Y., Finkelstein, E. A., & Ting, D. S. (2020). Artificial intelligence for teleophthalmology-based diabetic retinopathy screening in a national programme: An economic analysis modelling study. *The Lancet. Digital Health*, 2(5), e240–e249. 10.1016/S2589-7500(20)30060-1

Xue, V. W., Lei, P., & Cho, W. C. (2023). The potential impact of ChatGPT in clinical and translational medicine. *Clinical and Translational Medicine*, 13(3), e1216. 10.1002/ctm2.121636856370

Xu, I. R. L., Van Booven, D. J., Goberdhan, S., Breto, A., Porto, J., Alhusseini, M., Algohary, A., Stoyanova, R., Punnen, S., Mahne, A., & Arora, H. (2023). Generative Adversarial Networks Can Create High Quality Artificial Prostate Cancer Magnetic Resonance Images. *Journal of Personalized Medicine*, 13(3), 547. Advance online publication. 10.3390/jpm13030547736983728

Y.-W. C., Tanaka, S., Howlett, R. J., & Jain, L. C. (Eds.). (2022). 10th KES International Conference on Innovation in Medicine and Healthcare, KES-InMed 2022. *Smart Innovation, Systems and Technologies, 308*. https://www.scopus.com/inward/record.uri?eid=2-s2.0-85135020926&partnerID=40&md5=68f8932ef2f4503af2e24f1e1e49a3e4

Yang, J., Wang, M., Zhou, H., Zhao, C., & Zhang, W. (2020). *Towards Making the Most of bert in Neural Machine Translation*. Proceedings of the AAAI Conference on Artificial Intelligence. 10.1609/aaai.v34i05.6479

Yang, K., Ji, S., Zhang, T., Xie, Q., & Ananiadou, S. (2023). *On the evaluations of chatgpt and emotion-enhanced prompting for mental health analysis*. arXiv preprint arXiv:230403347.

Yaraghi, N. (2024). *Generative AI in health care: Opportunities, challenges, and policy*. Health Affairs Forefront.

Yellig, J. (2023). Where ChatGPT Fits in the Internet of Things (6 July 2023). *IoT World Today (Informa)*. https://www.iotworldtoday.com/connectivity/where-chatgpt-fits-in-the-internet-of-things

Yim, D., Khuntia, J., Parameswaran, V., & Meyers, A. (2024). Preliminary Evidence of the Use of Generative AI in Health Care Clinical Services: Systematic Narrative Review. *JMIR Medical Informatics*, 12(1), e52073. 10.2196/5207338506918

Yip, W., Fu, H., Jian, W., Liu, J., Pan, J., Xu, D., Yang, H., & Zhai, T. (2023). Universal health coverage in China part 2: Addressing challenges and recommendations. *The Lancet. Public Health*, 8(12), e1035–e1042. 10.1016/S2468-2667(23)00255-4

Yoon, J., Drumright, L. N., & Van Der Schaar, M. (2020). Anonymization through data synthesis using generative adversarial networks (ADS-GAN). *IEEE Journal of Biomedical and Health Informatics*, 24(8), 2378–2388. Advance online publication. 10.1109/JBHI.2020.298026232167919

Youssef, A. E. (2014). A framework for secure healthcare systems based on big data analytics in mobile cloud computing environments. *Int J Ambient Syst Appl*, 2(2), 1–11. 10.5121/ijasa.2014.2201

YouTube. (2023). *Can AI Code Beat Saber? Watch ChatGPT Try* [Video]. YouTube. https://www.youtube.com/watch?v=E2rktIcLJwo

Compilation of References

Yu, W., Fang, B., Liu, Y., Gao, M., Zheng, S., & Wang, Y. (2019). Liver Vessels Segmentation Based on 3d Residual U-NET. In *Proceedings - International Conference on Image Processing, ICIP*. IEEE. 10.1109/ICIP.2019.8802951

Yu, H., & Welch, J. D. (2021). MichiGAN: Sampling from Disentangled Representations of Single-Cell Data Using Generative Adversarial Networks. *Genome Biology*, 22(1), 158. 10.1186/s13059-021-02373-434016135

Zahlan, A., Ranjan, R. P., & Hayes, D. (2023). Artificial intelligence innovation in healthcare: Literature review, exploratory analysis, and future research. *Technology in Society*, 74, 102321. 10.1016/j.techsoc.2023.102321

Zavala-Curzo, D. F. (2023). Impacto del Aseguramiento en Salud en la Economía de los Hogares Peruanos, 2010-2019. *Acta Médica Peruana*, 40(2). Advance online publication. 10.35663/amp.2023.402.2527

Zhang, L., Lian, P., Zou, J., & Deng, H. (2015, June). Partial differential equation optimization for infectious disease model. *IEEE International Conference on Intelligent Computation Technology and Automation*. IEEE. 10.1109/ICICTA.2015.160

Zhang, P., & Boulos, M. (2023). Generative AI in Medicine and Healthcare: Promises, Opportunities and Challenges. *Future Internet*, 15(9), 286. Advance online publication. 10.3390/fi15090286

Zhao, S., Wang, S., Pan, P., Xia, T., Chang, X., Yang, X., Guo, L., Meng, Q., Yang, F., Qian, W., Xu, Z., Wang, Y., Wang, Z., Gu, L., Wang, R., Jia, F., Yao, J., Li, Z., & Bai, Y. (2019, May 1). Magnitude, risk factors, and factors associated with adenoma miss rate of tandem colonoscopy: A systematic review and meta-analysis. *Gastroenterology*, 156(6), 1661–1674. 10.1053/j.gastro.2019.01.260

Zheng, H., Zhou, Z., & Chen, J. (2021). RLSTM: A New Framework of Stock Prediction by Using Random Noise for Overfitting Prevention. *Computational Intelligence and Neuroscience*, 2021, 1–14. 10.1155/2021/886581634113377

Zhou, D., Tian, F., Tian, X., Sun, L., Huang, X., Zhao, F., Zhou, N., Chen, Z., Zhang, Q., Yang, M., Yang, Y., Guo, X., Li, Z., Liu, J., Wang, J., Wang, J., Wang, B., Zhang, G., Sun, B., & Li, X. (2020). Diagnostic evaluation of a deep learning model for optical diagnosis of colorectal cancer. *Nature Communications*, 11(1), 2961. 10.1038/s41467-020-16777-6

About the Contributors

Babita Singla is a Professor, at Chitkara Business School, Chitkara University, Punjab, India. She has a Ph.D. in management and is UGC-NET qualified. She has over 15 years of experience in teaching, research, and administration. Her areas of expertise are Marketing, E-commerce, Omnichannel, and Retail. In her career, she has been involved in important academic and research assignments such as being the guest editor of a reputed Journal, organizing and conducting International and National Level Conferences, Faculty Development Programs, and a guide for the research projects along her Teaching. Her overall research-oriented mindset, rich knowledge, and dedication towards her responsibilities have awarded her with the most prestigious 'Teaching Excellence Award' from the Honourable Education Minister of the State. She has research publications in reputable international and national journals indexed in Scopus, Web of Science, and SCI and presented research papers at various National and International conferences. In the short span of her career in Academia and Administration, she has authored and edited several books on Retail, Supply Chain, Branding, Customer Relationship Management, and Product Management; covering the course content of various universities nationwide with reputed publication houses including Taylor & Francis, Springer, Emerald and IGI Global among others. She is a lifetime member of various organizations of national and international repute. She has successfully delivered guest sessions at international universities and national universities. Other notable achievements are registered Copyrights and Patents in her name.

Kumar Shalender is a Post-Doctoral Fellow of the Global Institute of Flexible Systems Management and a Doctor of Philosophy in Strategic Management. He has more than 14 years of experience in the domains of business policy, strategic management, and business model development and a total of 70 publications, including presentations at international and national conferences and book chapters to his credit. His current research areas include the fields of metaverse, blockchain technology, and sustainable development, with a special focus on sustainable cities and mobility ecosystems in India.

Katja Stamer is Head of the Department of Business Engineering at DHBW, Stuttgart, Germany. With a wealth of experience and expertise in the field, she is enriching the discourse and deepening the understanding of global business engineering practices. Her valuable contributions exemplify the spirit of cross-cultural collaboration and academic excellence, thereby making her a distinguishable personality in the field of business engineering. Her research interests include leadership and sustainability, value-oriented business management, digitalization and its impact on employees, digitalization, and volunteerism in NGOs.

About the Contributors

Munir Ahmad is a seasoned professional in the realm of Spatial Data Infrastructure (SDI), Geo-Information Productions, Information Systems, and Information Governance, boasting over 25 years of dedicated experience in the field. With a PhD in Computer Science, Dr. Ahmad's expertise spans Spatial Data Production, Management, Processing, Analysis, Visualization, and Quality Control. Throughout his career, Dr. Ahmad has been deeply involved in the development and deployment of SDI systems specially in the context of Pakistan, leveraging his proficiency in Spatial Database Design, Web, Mobile & Desktop GIS, and Geo Web Services Architecture. His contributions to Volunteered Geographic Information (VGI) and Open Source Geoportal & Metadata Portal have significantly enriched the geospatial community. As a trainer and researcher, Dr. Ahmad has authored over 50 publications, advancing the industry's knowledge base and fostering innovation in Geo-Tech, Data Governance, and Information Infrastructure, and Emerging Technologies. His commitment to Research and Development (R&D) is evident in his role as a dedicated educator and mentor in the field.

D. Saravanan did his M.E in Computer Science and Engg, and completed his Doctor of Philosophy in the same area. He had 21 years of teaching experience. His area of interest is Data mining, Data Base Management systems & Information Retrieval.

Rida Fatima holds a BS in Psychology from Comsats University, Islamabad, Pakistan. She is ambitious in her career and has a special interest in emerging technologies in the healthcare sector.

G. Chamdramowleeswaran is currently working as Assistant Professor in Department of Commerce and business administration, VelTech Rangarajan Dr. Sagunthala R&D Institute of Science and Technology (Deemed to be University), Avadi, Chennai. He has more than 11 years 5 months of industry experience and 1 year and 11 months of teaching experience with specialization in HR and Marketing. He Holds a B.Com., M.B.A., M. Phil., and Ph.D. in Management from Bharathidasan University, Trichy

Shenson Joseph is a distinguished AI researcher and data science expert. With expertise in Data Science, Analytics, and Artificial Intelligence, he has authored 2 books, holds over 5 international patents, and authored more than 6 research papers. Shenson has judged over many national and international events and actively contributes to editorial boards and conferences. He has earned a master's degree in Data Science and second masters degree in Electrical & Computer Engineering.

Logasakthi Kandasamy has been associated with Universal AI University, Karjat as an Associate Professor. He has received best research contribution award and best faculty award from one of the promising engineering Institution in Tamil Nadu. Logasakthi is Qualified with UGC-NET & TN-SET for Assistant Professor. Published more than 20 papers in reputed journals which includes Scopus and ABDC indexed. Researcher, Teacher and Trainer in HR&OB for las one and half decade.

Jaspreet Kaur is currently working as an Assistant Professor in University Business School,Chandigarh University,Mohali,Punjab.She is a post graduate (MBA-H.R) from Panjab University,Chandigarh.She has also qualified UGC NET JRF in Human Resource Management/Labour and Social Welfare and has completed PhD in Business Management from Chandigarh University,Mohali. She has over 8 years of experience in academic and administrative assignments.She also received "Best Teacher of the Department Award " in the year 2019 and 2021 in the field of imparting quality education.Her research interests include Employee Engagement, Management of Organizational Change and Organization Development.She has published several research papers and articles in reputed international and national journals and has presented papers in various national and international conferences.She also contributed one edited book and numerous book chapters on various topics.

Jaspreet Kaur is currently working as an Assistant Professor in University Business School,Chandigarh University,Mohali,Punjab.She is a post graduate (MBA-H.R) from Panjab University,Chandigarh.She has also qualified UGC NET JRF in Human Resource Management/Labour and Social Welfare and has completed PhD in Business Management from Chandigarh University,Mohali. Her research interests include Employee Engagement, Management of Organizational Change and Organization Development.She has published several research papers and articles in reputed international and national journals and has presented papers in various national and international conferences.

About the Contributors

Jenifer Lawrence an Associate Professor of Management department at Woldia University. He received his Ph.D in Management from Bharathiar University in 2016. His research interest includes the advancements and the new concepts pertaining to Marketing and Human Resources areas. Dr.Jenifer Lawrence has published research articles in several peer-reviewed journals. Dr.Jenifer Lawrence teaches postgraduate courses on Marketing and Human Resources. He has supervised more than 70 MBA theses and served on 13 PhD adjudication as an external examiner for various universities in India. He is also an editorial board member for i-manager's "Journal on Management" and acts as a reviewer for different journals.

Raja Narayanan is an Associate Professor at School of Commerce and Management (SCMS), Dayananda Sagar University. Bengalore. He secures more than two decade of experience. Out of this, twelve years from South Africa. He has two times repaganized and honoured as a best lecturer award in South Africa. He has published 26 articles in peer review journals, plus 12 articles in the Scopus Indixed Journals and participated & present thirty-eight research paper in national and international level seminars. He is a member and reviewer's panel of International Journal of E-Business Research (IJEBR), it is an International Magazine published by the Elsevier Scopus. He has produced four PhD Scholars also evaluated and adjudicated twenty-five PhD theses in the field of Management and Commerce as the panel of External examiner in the University such as Annamalai, Barathiyar, Bharathidasan, Madras and Manonmaniyam sundarnar Universities. He is a life time member of Association of Accounting Technician (AAT), and he teaches courses such as financial management, research methodology, corporate finance, security analysis and portfolio management and project finance. His teaching feedback ranges from 3.75 to 4.90 out of 5 across all programmes. He is a regular learner in recent trend.

Sidra Nosheen is an accomplished microbiologist with an MPhil in Microbiology. Her work spans medical, environmental, and industrial microbiology, focusing on microbial pathogenesis, antibiotic resistance, and beneficial microbes. She has published several research papers and collaborated on various interdisciplinary projects. Proficient in techniques such as PCR and microbial culture, she brings a strong theoretical and practical foundation to her work. Passionate about education, she has taught microbiology and mentored many students. She is committed to advancing research that addresses global health challenges and promotes sustainability, continuing to inspire the next generation of scientists.

Sagar Patil is currently an Assistant Professor at the School of Allied Health Sciences, D.Y. Patil University, Navi Mumbai, Maharashtra, India. He is experienced in academics, research, medical innovation, administration, and curriculum development. His research interests revolve around newer strategies for the teaching-learning process and innovation.

Zeenal Punamiya is a PhD Scholar at Chitkara School of Health Sciences, Chitkara University, Punjab, India. She is currently working as a Program Manager at Medical Innovation Creativity and Entrepreneurship (M.I.C.E) Labs at Grant Government Medical College and Sir J.J Group of Hospitals, Mumbai. Her research interests include Augmented Reality, Virtual Reality, Extended Reality, and Metaverse in Healthcare, Innovative Teaching-Learning Strategies, Integration of Technology for better Healthcare, Medical Device Innovation and Entrepreneurship.

Baranidharan S specialized in Finance Economics and Econometrics. Having 5 years research experience, 2 years of Industrial experience and 6 years of teaching experience. Published 6 patent, 45 research articles in international and national journal which are indexed in Scopus, WoS, Proquest, ABDC, etc.,

About the Contributors

Partap Chahal is committed to teaching and research in Finance and Investment domain since last 16 years+. His qualification is PhD (Commerce), M.Com, MBA. He has rich work experience in the field of Teaching, administration and research as well. He held various responsibilities like Editor, Co-editor, and Editorial Board member, Associate Editor in number of national and international journals. He has been regularly been receiving offers for writing books from the top publishing houses of India and received many letter of thanks& compliments for giving valuable suggestions and commendable views concerning improvement of many leading Publications/Books. He has written and published 5 books namely Financial Management, Risk Management, working capital Management, Management Accounting and Analysis of Financial Statements. Further, he has published more than 50 papers and book chapters in good reputed journals and he has also contributed numerous research papers in national and international conferences or seminars. He has good participation in MDPs. FDPs and STCs as well as Life Membership of reputed academic bodies. His future interest area of research is Capital Market, Financial Derivatives, Commodities Market, NBFCs and Online Payments. " Dr Partap S. Chahal is currently working as Sr. Faculty Member in School of Management &Commerce, Lovely Professional University, Punjab." Author already have got published one book chapter entitled- Study of Regulatory Role and Investors' Protection during Banking Sector Crisis 2020 in Indian Economy: Case of Yes Bank with IGI GLOBAL in June, 2023

N.V. Suresh, renowned academician from Chennai, Tamil Nadu. He completed his schooling in Chennai. He obtained his BA degree (2012) from D.G.Vaishnav College, Madras University. He joined the Bharathiar University received an MBA degree and PGDM. He Awarded Ph.D. in Management from University of Madras. Dr.N.V.Suresh joined then IIKM in June 2014 as an Assistant Professor (2014 to 2016). He moved to Remo International College in June, 2019 as an Assistant Professor and rose through the ranks to the position of Head of the Department in Aug 2020 to July 2021 then Shifted to Working Academy of Maritime Education and Training (Deemed to be University) Presently Working as Associate Professor and Vice-Principal in ASET College of Science and Technology from March 2022 to Till Date. He is the Visiting Faculty for Institute of Distance Education, University of Madras, Tamil Nadu Open University, Anna University and Directorate of Online Education SRM University for MBA from 2015 to till date. Dr.N.V. Suresh has carried out all his research work entirely in India and has published 30 research papers in international journals and presented 15 papers at national and international conferences, authored two Text Books namely Logistics and Air cargo Management, Executive Communication Published by IIP Publishing House and Blue rose Publishers and Prepared more than 10 E-content for Online Distance Education for AMET University and SRM University, He also Produced one Ph.D. Scholar Under his Guidance currently 3 Research Scholars are doing Ph.D. Under his Guidance. Completed six funded Project worth Rs 3, 50,000 from Industry and Government of Tamil Nadu TNCST, Received Rs 25,00,000 Project from Ministry of Social Justice and Empowerment under PM DAKSH, Government of India. Dr.N.V.Suresh is also Editor for ASET Journal of Management Science and reviewer for various International Journals among them ASTEJ belongs to University of Chicago, United States of America. He is also associated with confidential work of ICAI & ICWA. Dr.N.V.Suresh has given 18 Guest lectures at various colleges. He also acted as Chairperson for SRM University Scholar Submit conducted by DOMS SRM University. Member Scrutiny for International Conference conducted by various colleges. He has also served as Chairman Board of Studies for MBA & BSc Programs of Alagappa University Collaborative Programs. Subject Expert for MBA Board of Studies in Bharathiar University and JNN Engineering College Dr.N.V.Suresh has acted as question paper setter and evaluator for various state and central universities. He has served as a Nodal officer and Chief- Superintendent of Examination for University Semester Examination. He has also guided more than 400 Students to complete their UG and PG Projects, currently 25 Students are doing their final year project under his guidance. Dr.N.V.Suresh has also received Best Faculty Award for his outstanding in academics from Lions International in 2023 and Received Certificate of Appreciation by Mahatma Gandhi National Council of Rural Education, Department of Higher Education, MHRD, Government of India, Visited Abu Dhabi, Dubai, Sharjah, Ajman, Umm Al Quwain, Ras Al Khaimah and Fujairah under faculty exchange program.

About the Contributors

Qurat Ul Ain is an accomplished microbiologist with an MPhil in Microbiology. Her work spans medical, environmental, and industrial microbiology, focusing on microbial pathogenesis, antibiotic resistance, and beneficial microbes. She has published several research papers and collaborated on various interdisciplinary projects. Proficient in techniques such as PCR and microbial culture, she brings a strong theoretical and practical foundation to my work. Passionate about education, she has taught microbiology and mentored many students. She is committed to advancing research that addresses global health challenges and promotes sustainability, continuing to inspire the next generation of scientists.

Index

A

Administrative Tasks 56, 131, 140, 146, 148, 151, 161, 165, 181, 263
AI 1, 2, 3, 4, 5, 6, 7, 8, 9, 10, 11, 12, 13, 14, 15, 16, 17, 20, 22, 23, 24, 26, 27, 28, 29, 30, 31, 32, 33, 34, 35, 36, 37, 38, 40, 42, 43, 44, 45, 47, 48, 50, 51, 52, 53, 54, 55, 56, 57, 58, 59, 60, 61, 62, 63, 64, 65, 66, 67, 68, 69, 70, 71, 72, 73, 74, 75, 76, 77, 79, 80, 81, 85, 86, 87, 88, 89, 90, 91, 92, 93, 94, 95, 96, 97, 98, 99, 100, 101, 102, 103, 104, 105, 106, 107, 108, 109, 111, 112, 113, 114, 115, 116, 117, 118, 119, 120, 121, 122, 123, 124, 125, 126, 127, 129, 130, 131, 132, 133, 134, 135, 136, 137, 138, 139, 140, 141, 144, 145, 146, 147, 148, 149, 150, 151, 152, 153, 154, 155, 156, 157, 158, 159, 160, 161, 162, 163, 164, 165, 166, 167, 168, 169, 170, 171, 172, 173, 174, 175, 176, 177, 178, 179, 180, 181, 182, 183, 184, 185, 186, 187, 188, 189, 190, 191, 192, 193, 194, 195, 196, 197, 198, 199, 200, 201, 202, 203, 204, 205, 206, 207, 214, 229, 230, 231, 232, 233, 235, 236, 237, 240, 247, 248, 251, 252, 253, 255, 256, 257, 258, 259, 261, 262, 268, 272, 293, 294, 295, 296, 297, 298, 299, 300, 301, 302, 303, 304, 305, 306, 307, 308, 309, 310, 311, 312, 313, 314, 315, 319, 320, 321, 322, 323, 324, 325, 326, 327, 328, 329, 330, 331, 332, 333, 334, 335, 336, 337, 338, 339, 340, 341, 342, 343, 345, 346, 347, 348, 353, 357, 358, 359, 362, 365, 370, 371, 374, 375, 376, 383, 384, 386, 387, 389, 390, 391, 392
AI Technology 5, 15, 70, 79, 86, 125, 135, 146, 165, 167, 168, 232, 301
Algorithmic 15, 35, 36, 63, 64, 67, 71, 72, 73, 75, 101, 109, 147, 150, 158, 164, 166, 167, 182, 183, 201, 329, 334, 337, 346
artificial intelligence 1, 2, 3, 4, 5, 6, 7, 8, 9, 10, 11, 12, 13, 14, 15, 16, 17, 18, 19, 20, 21, 22, 23, 24, 26, 27, 28, 32, 34, 37, 40, 42, 43, 45, 46, 47, 48, 49, 50, 51, 52, 53, 54, 55, 56, 57, 58, 59, 60, 62, 66, 67, 69, 70, 71, 73, 74, 75, 76, 77, 78, 79, 87, 92, 93, 95, 96, 107, 108, 109, 111, 112, 113, 117, 118, 122, 127, 129, 130, 131, 132, 134, 137, 138, 154, 155, 156, 157, 158, 159, 160, 161, 162, 163, 164, 165, 166, 167, 168, 169, 170, 172, 173, 174, 175, 176, 178, 179, 182, 184, 191, 197, 203, 204, 205, 206, 207, 214, 236, 237, 239, 244, 245, 246, 247, 252, 255, 256, 257, 258, 259, 260, 261, 262, 263, 268, 271, 272, 293, 295, 297, 299, 305, 306, 308, 309, 310, 311, 312, 313, 314, 315, 316, 318, 319, 321, 324, 325, 326, 328, 329, 330, 331, 332, 334, 336, 337, 338, 339, 340, 342, 345, 354, 358, 359, 361, 363, 366, 368, 370, 371, 372, 373, 374, 375, 383, 384, 387, 388, 389, 390, 391
augmented reality 111, 113, 116, 127, 128, 236, 331, 337

B

Bibliometric Analysis 20, 21, 138, 156, 207, 214
big data 21, 22, 23, 35, 47, 76, 78, 113, 121, 122, 123, 126, 127, 141, 151, 159, 174, 205, 261, 271, 340, 358, 368, 369, 370, 372, 389, 392
Blockchain 229, 232, 233, 235, 245, 256

C

ChatGPT 29, 43, 93, 97, 98, 99, 107, 109, 164, 167, 293, 294, 296, 301, 302, 303, 305, 306, 307, 308, 309, 310,

449

337, 340, 362
Clinical Decision Support 4, 19, 33, 35, 36, 59, 63, 69, 71, 84, 88, 99, 111, 114, 115, 122, 127, 130, 148, 150, 154, 175, 192, 207, 247, 294, 307, 368, 371, 385
Communicable diseases 273, 276, 281, 286
Cost Reduction 68, 262, 263, 268, 269, 270

D

deep learning 10, 21, 24, 33, 37, 38, 42, 44, 45, 46, 48, 50, 51, 53, 54, 56, 57, 59, 68, 70, 77, 78, 81, 95, 113, 115, 121, 122, 123, 125, 129, 130, 135, 158, 169, 178, 192, 260, 290, 299, 301, 305, 336, 343, 351, 352, 353, 354, 355, 356, 358, 359, 360, 361, 362, 366, 370, 374, 375, 383
Delay differential equation 274
Diagnosis 1, 2, 5, 7, 9, 10, 14, 19, 23, 26, 29, 30, 34, 36, 37, 44, 45, 46, 53, 55, 57, 59, 60, 62, 68, 69, 77, 80, 81, 82, 84, 88, 92, 96, 97, 108, 113, 114, 115, 117, 118, 120, 127, 131, 132, 134, 135, 136, 137, 145, 146, 147, 151, 152, 155, 156, 158, 159, 160, 161, 162, 163, 164, 165, 168, 169, 170, 171, 179, 182, 183, 184, 197, 198, 203, 204, 239, 248, 294, 297, 302, 314, 319, 328, 336, 341, 342, 343, 345, 347, 348, 349, 350, 351, 354, 355, 356, 357, 359, 360, 365, 366, 368, 370, 372, 374, 376, 386
Digital Health Technologies 170, 239, 244, 386

E

Economic Impact 137, 156, 211
EHR 33, 35, 36, 69, 84, 88, 96, 114, 130, 299
Epidemic 12, 274, 277, 279, 290, 291, 292, 332, 381
Epidemic model 291, 292
Ethical Considerations 57, 64, 69, 71, 72, 73, 74, 75, 97, 98, 147, 160, 165, 174, 176, 178, 182, 193, 194, 196, 199, 202, 223, 225, 243, 245, 294, 311, 337, 340, 376, 378, 388
Ethical Guidelines 71, 72, 73, 91, 104, 106, 149, 184, 194, 196, 335
Ethical issues 158, 163, 166, 167, 168, 171, 173, 203, 246, 326, 357
Ethical Standards 98, 104, 147, 167, 180, 192, 193, 196, 245, 295, 372
ethics 20, 50, 58, 74, 75, 78, 87, 98, 109, 129, 174, 175, 176, 191, 192, 196, 202, 240, 253, 338, 340, 365, 387
Explainable AI 2, 135, 152, 191, 207

F

Future Perspectives   79, 90, 175, 201, 204, 305

G

GAN 96, 110, 307, 341, 347, 348, 349, 350, 351, 352, 353, 354, 355, 356, 358, 361, 362, 363
Generative AI 26, 27, 28, 29, 30, 53, 79, 80, 81, 85, 86, 87, 88, 89, 90, 91, 92, 93, 94, 95, 96, 97, 98, 99, 100, 101, 102, 103, 104, 105, 106, 107, 108, 109, 178, 179, 180, 181, 182, 183, 184, 185, 186, 187, 188, 189, 190, 191, 193, 194, 195, 196, 197, 198, 201, 202, 205, 206, 236, 293, 294, 295, 297, 298, 299, 300, 301, 302, 303, 304, 305, 306, 307, 308, 309, 310, 341, 342, 343, 357, 358, 362, 389, 390, 391, 392
Generative Pre-trained Transformer 84, 95, 294, 307, 309

H

Healthcare 1, 2, 3, 4, 5, 10, 11, 13, 14, 15, 16, 19, 21, 23, 26, 27, 28, 29, 30, 31, 32, 33, 35, 36, 40, 41, 43, 44, 47, 48, 49, 51, 54, 55, 56, 57, 58, 59, 60, 61, 62, 63, 64, 65, 66, 67, 68, 69, 70, 71, 72, 73, 74, 75, 76, 77, 78, 79, 80, 81, 82, 83, 84, 85, 86, 87, 88, 89, 90, 91,

92, 93, 95, 96, 97, 98, 99, 100, 101, 102, 103, 104, 105, 106, 107, 109, 111, 112, 113, 114, 115, 116, 117, 118, 119, 120, 121, 122, 123, 124, 125, 126, 127, 128, 129, 130, 131, 132, 133, 134, 135, 136, 137, 138, 139, 140, 141, 142, 144, 145, 146, 147, 148, 149, 150, 151, 152, 153, 154, 155, 157, 158, 159, 160, 161, 162, 163, 164, 165, 166, 167, 168, 169, 170, 171, 172, 173, 174, 175, 176, 177, 178, 179, 180, 181, 182, 183, 184, 185, 186, 187, 188, 189, 190, 191, 192, 193, 194, 195, 196, 197, 198, 200, 201, 202, 203, 204, 205, 206, 207, 208, 209, 210, 211, 212, 213, 214, 215, 216, 217, 218, 219, 220, 221, 222, 223, 224, 225, 226, 228, 229, 230, 231, 232, 233, 234, 235, 236, 237, 238, 239, 240, 241, 242, 243, 244, 245, 246, 247, 248, 249, 250, 251, 252, 253, 254, 255, 256, 257, 258, 259, 260, 261, 262, 266, 271, 272, 292, 293, 294, 295, 297, 298, 299, 300, 301, 302, 303, 304, 305, 306, 307, 308, 309, 310, 311, 312, 313, 314, 315, 317, 318, 319, 320, 321, 322, 323, 324, 325, 326, 327, 328, 329, 330, 331, 332, 333, 334, 335, 336, 337, 338, 339, 340, 341, 342, 343, 345, 346, 352, 356, 357, 358, 359, 360, 363, 365, 366, 367, 368, 369, 370, 371, 372, 373, 375, 376, 377, 378, 379, 380, 381, 382, 383, 385, 386, 387, 388, 389, 390, 391, 392

Healthcare Administration 4, 144, 146, 262

Healthcare industry 3, 14, 32, 54, 69, 79, 80, 81, 87, 88, 112, 132, 159, 164, 167, 168, 173, 174, 182, 184, 229, 230, 233, 235, 237, 262, 271, 311, 312, 326, 332, 336, 337, 369, 370, 390

Healthcare Innovation 148, 179, 238, 239, 240, 241, 242, 243, 244, 246, 251, 252, 253, 254, 255, 256, 257, 260, 261, 341, 357, 371

Healthcare quality improvement 207, 214, 219

Healthcare System Management 131

health informatics 49, 110, 130, 154, 155, 257, 391

Health IT Systems 253

I

Informed Consent 63, 64, 70, 71, 72, 73, 75, 165, 166, 171, 182, 183, 184, 185, 197, 198, 199, 200, 248, 326, 329, 335

innovation 7, 19, 21, 47, 55, 67, 68, 72, 73, 74, 75, 80, 92, 106, 117, 120, 122, 123, 134, 148, 157, 162, 165, 167, 170, 171, 172, 173, 175, 178, 179, 180, 181, 182, 194, 201, 205, 233, 234, 237, 238, 239, 240, 241, 242, 243, 244, 245, 246, 247, 248, 249, 250, 251, 252, 253, 254, 255, 256, 257, 258, 259, 260, 261, 271, 294, 309, 311, 319, 331, 337, 341, 342, 357, 365, 369, 371, 372, 383, 386, 387, 388, 389, 390

L

Large language models 98, 166, 231, 296, 297, 298, 305, 307

M

Machine Learning 3, 4, 6, 9, 10, 14, 19, 20, 21, 22, 23, 26, 27, 32, 33, 35, 36, 37, 40, 41, 44, 47, 50, 51, 52, 53, 54, 56, 57, 59, 60, 61, 68, 69, 70, 76, 78, 80, 81, 88, 90, 95, 97, 99, 111, 112, 113, 114, 115, 120, 121, 122, 123, 125, 127, 130, 132, 141, 150, 151, 154, 156, 158, 159, 163, 168, 169, 170, 171, 173, 175, 204, 207, 209, 226, 232, 247, 252, 257, 258, 276, 293, 295, 299, 303, 306, 309, 313, 320, 331, 334, 338, 341, 343, 352, 353, 355, 361, 362, 366, 367, 368, 374, 381, 383, 384, 387

Medicine 10, 14, 16, 18, 19, 20, 21, 22, 23, 24, 26, 27, 31, 35, 36, 42, 44, 45,

46, 47, 48, 49, 50, 52, 54, 56, 58, 59, 60, 62, 70, 71, 73, 74, 75, 76, 77, 78, 79, 80, 81, 82, 83, 85, 88, 90, 92, 93, 98, 107, 108, 109, 114, 128, 129, 130, 132, 141, 142, 144, 145, 148, 151, 154, 156, 157, 159, 161, 162, 163, 168, 171, 172, 173, 174, 175, 176, 181, 182, 186, 187, 188, 190, 191, 201, 203, 204, 205, 206, 217, 236, 239, 252, 253, 255, 258, 260, 261, 290, 298, 305, 306, 307, 308, 310, 313, 320, 330, 334, 336, 337, 339, 340, 342, 346, 347, 352, 353, 357, 358, 359, 360, 362, 368, 370, 371, 375, 376, 377, 378, 379, 387, 389, 390, 391

N

Natural language processing 4, 5, 6, 33, 40, 56, 62, 67, 68, 84, 85, 95, 99, 112, 114, 115, 120, 121, 132, 148, 158, 160, 162, 163, 169, 171, 178, 247, 252, 261, 294, 295, 297, 308, 362
Neural Networks 21, 37, 40, 45, 51, 53, 57, 62, 82, 83, 94, 95, 96, 112, 127, 134, 158, 271, 296, 299, 301, 350, 359, 360, 361, 370

O

Operational Efficiency 73, 80, 133, 146, 148, 160, 161, 162, 165, 172, 262, 268, 311, 329, 332
optimization 48, 49, 67, 111, 133, 140, 146, 150, 181, 305, 334, 337, 365, 368, 382, 385
outbreak 12, 274, 277, 278, 279, 280, 288, 290, 292

P

Patient Empowerment 63, 72, 197, 198, 243, 252, 325
Patient Engagement 84, 85, 88, 116, 131, 140, 145, 147, 148, 152, 160, 161, 168, 170, 252, 258, 294
Patients 1, 2, 3, 8, 9, 10, 11, 13, 14, 15, 16, 21, 22, 26, 28, 29, 31, 36, 37, 41, 48, 50, 53, 56, 57, 59, 60, 61, 63, 64, 65, 69, 70, 71, 76, 81, 82, 84, 85, 88, 92, 93, 98, 99, 103, 105, 113, 114, 115, 119, 120, 121, 123, 124, 125, 126, 127, 136, 138, 146, 147, 149, 150, 152, 153, 158, 160, 161, 163, 164, 166, 169, 170, 180, 183, 184, 185, 186, 188, 189, 190, 191, 193, 194, 195, 196, 197, 198, 201, 202, 205, 228, 231, 232, 233, 235, 238, 239, 241, 242, 244, 245, 248, 251, 252, 253, 254, 258, 294, 298, 299, 300, 303, 304, 312, 313, 315, 316, 317, 318, 319, 320, 321, 322, 323, 324, 325, 326, 327, 328, 329, 330, 331, 332, 333, 338, 344, 353, 354, 355, 356, 369, 370, 371, 373, 377, 378, 380, 381, 382, 385, 388
Perils 26, 91, 178, 182, 184, 191, 293, 301
Personalized Care 61
personalized medicine 26, 54, 56, 58, 59, 60, 62, 70, 71, 73, 74, 75, 77, 88, 98, 109, 132, 168, 173, 174, 176, 181, 182, 187, 191, 201, 298, 334, 336, 342, 352, 357, 358, 375, 376, 377, 379, 391
personalized treatments 98, 119, 182, 385
Policymakers 2, 62, 66, 71, 72, 84, 105, 106, 131, 138, 152, 157, 167, 186, 191, 193, 194, 204, 229, 230, 231, 232, 233, 234, 240, 243, 245, 253, 254, 266, 295, 347
Policy Recommendations 257
precision diagnostics 311, 312
predictive analytics 54, 57, 58, 59, 60, 61, 67, 69, 70, 71, 73, 74, 75, 111, 121, 122, 123, 132, 133, 134, 144, 145, 146, 148, 157, 158, 159, 161, 162, 165, 168, 169, 171, 172, 188, 189, 190, 239, 246, 247, 342, 365
privacy 15, 28, 29, 47, 57, 58, 60, 63, 64, 65, 67, 68, 69, 70, 71, 72, 73, 75, 76, 78, 80, 86, 87, 88, 90, 91, 92, 93, 95, 96, 97, 101, 102, 104, 106, 107, 108, 109, 124, 125, 136, 138, 146, 148, 149, 152, 153, 157, 158, 160, 163, 164, 165, 166, 167, 168, 170, 171,

172, 176, 179, 180, 182, 183, 184, 185, 186, 191, 193, 194, 196, 198, 202, 244, 245, 248, 253, 294, 295, 299, 301, 304, 306, 325, 326, 329, 334, 339, 341, 344, 346, 348, 353, 365, 370, 372, 378, 379, 386, 387, 389, 390

R

Ramifications 26, 171, 327, 334
regulation 26, 104, 167, 175, 193, 195, 196, 205, 244, 245, 326, 346, 365, 366, 386
Regulatory Compliance 60, 80, 86, 91, 102, 105, 106, 124, 148, 150, 160, 167, 243, 357
Regulatory Framework 172, 195
rehabilitative care 311, 312, 314
remote monitoring 57, 84, 113, 115, 120, 121, 144, 146, 147, 158, 160, 161, 163, 165, 248, 252, 311, 314, 330, 331, 333, 381, 382, 383
Resource Allocation 73, 121, 133, 146, 148, 162, 163, 165, 223, 246, 342, 368, 382
Retinopathy 38, 42, 46, 53, 115, 134, 188, 260
Risk Assessment 37, 69, 99
robotic surgeries 311

S

Security 58, 63, 64, 65, 66, 69, 70, 71, 72, 73, 74, 75, 76, 78, 80, 86, 87, 91, 101, 102, 103, 104, 106, 107, 108, 124, 125, 136, 146, 152, 153, 158, 160, 163, 164, 166, 167, 170, 171, 182, 183, 193, 202, 232, 244, 245, 248, 253, 264, 295, 301, 303, 325, 326, 329, 331, 339, 342, 363, 370, 372, 378, 386, 387, 389
Stakeholder Collaboration 196, 251
Stakeholders 64, 66, 71, 72, 75, 89, 91, 93, 106, 122, 124, 125, 126, 136, 138, 149, 150, 152, 153, 167, 191, 192, 193, 197, 202, 209, 226, 229, 230, 231, 232, 233, 234, 238, 239, 240, 241, 242, 243, 245, 246, 247, 248, 249, 250, 251, 252, 253, 254, 329, 334, 371, 372

T

telemedicine 57, 88, 113, 120, 121, 126, 144, 145, 151, 160, 161, 165, 175, 239, 252, 315, 321, 325, 356, 368, 380
Transformative Potential 71, 91, 133, 136, 137, 163, 165, 178, 179, 187, 189, 203, 294

V

vaccination 274, 275, 277, 290, 291, 292
Value-based Care 136, 154
virtual reality 111, 113, 116, 128, 129, 303, 323, 331

Publishing Tomorrow's Research Today

Uncover Current Insights and Future Trends in
Business & Management
with IGI Global's Cutting-Edge Recommended Books

Print Only, E-Book Only, or Print + E-Book.

Select through IGI Global's Online Bookstore at **www.igi-global.com** or through your preferred provider.

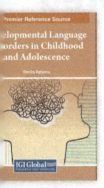

Developmental Language Disorders in Childhood and Adolescence

ISBN: 9798369306444
© 2023; 436 pp.
List Price: US$ 230

The Sustainable Fintech Revolution: Building a Greener Future for Finance

ISBN: 9798369300084
© 2023; 358 pp.
List Price: US$ 250

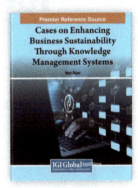

Cases on Enhancing Business Sustainability Through Knowledge Management Systems

ISBN: 9781668458594
© 2023; 366 pp.
List Price: US$ 240

Artificial Intelligence, and Next Generation Internet of Things: Digital Innovation For Green and Sustainable Economies

ISBN: 9781668486344
© 2023; 256 pp.
List Price: US$ 280

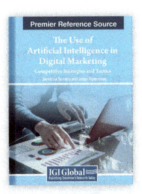

The Use of Artificial Intelligence in Digital Marketing: Competitive Strategies and Tactics

ISBN: 9781668493243
© 2024; 318 pp.
List Price: US$ 250

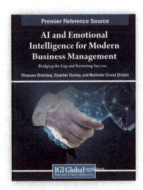

AI and Emotional Intelligence for Modern Business Management: Bridging the Gap and Nurturing Success

ISBN: 9798369304181
© 2023; 415 pp.
List Price: US$ 250

If you want to stay current on the latest research trends, product announcements, news, and special offers? Join IGI Global's mailing list to receive customized recommendations, exclusive discounts, and more.
Sign up at: **www.igi-global.com/newsletters**.

Scan the QR Code here to view more related titles in Business & Management.

Sign up at www.igi-global.com/newsletters   facebook.com/igiglobal   twitter.com/igiglobal   linkedin.com/igiglobal

Ensure Quality Research is Introduced to the Academic Community

Become a Reviewer for IGI Global Authored Book Projects

  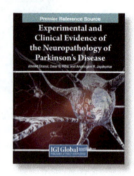 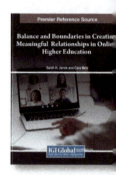

The overall success of an authored book project is dependent on quality and timely manuscript evaluations.

Applications and Inquiries may be sent to:
development@igi-global.com

Applicants must have a doctorate (or equivalent degree) as well as publishing, research, and reviewing experience. Authored Book Evaluators are appointed for one-year terms and are expected to complete at least three evaluations per term. Upon successful completion of this term, evaluators can be considered for an additional term.

If you have a colleague that may be interested in this opportunity, we encourage you to share this information with them.

www.igi-global.com

Publishing Tomorrow's Research Today
IGI Global's Open Access Journal Program

Including Nearly 200 Peer-Reviewed, Gold (Full) Open Access Journals across IGI Global's Three Academic Subject Areas: Business & Management; Scientific, Technical, and Medical (STM); and Education

Consider Submitting Your Manuscript to One of These Nearly 200 Open Access Journals for to Increase Their Discoverability & Citation Impact

Web of Science Impact Factor **6.5**

Web of Science Impact Factor **4.7**

Web of Science Impact Factor **3.2**

Web of Science Impact Factor **2.6**

Journal of Organizational and End User Computing

Journal of Global Information Management

International Journal on Semantic Web and Information Systems

Journal of Database Management

Choosing IGI Global's Open Access Journal Program Can Greatly Increase the Reach of Your Research

Higher Usage
Open access papers are 2-3 times more likely to be read than non-open access papers.

Higher Download Rates
Open access papers benefit from 89% higher download rates than non-open access papers.

Higher Citation Rates
Open access papers are 47% more likely to be cited than non-open access papers.

Submitting an article to a journal offers an invaluable opportunity for you to share your work with the broader academic community, fostering knowledge dissemination and constructive feedback.

Submit an Article and Browse the IGI Global Call for Papers Pages

We can work with you to find the journal most well-suited for your next research manuscript.
For open access publishing support, contact: journaleditor@igi-global.com

Publishing Tomorrow's Research Today
IGI Global
e-Book Collection

Including Essential Reference Books Within Three Fundamental Academic Areas

Business & Management
Scientific, Technical, & Medical (STM)
Education

- Acquisition options include Perpetual, Subscription, and Read & Publish
- No Additional Charge for Multi-User Licensing
- No Maintenance, Hosting, or Archiving Fees
- Continually Enhanced Accessibility Compliance Features (WCAG)

| Over **150,000+** Chapters | Contributions From **200,000+** Scholars Worldwide | More Than **1,000,000+** Citations | Majority of e-Books Indexed in Web of Science & Scopus | Consists of Tomorrow's Research Available Today! |

Recommended Titles from our e-Book Collection

Innovation Capabilities and Entrepreneurial Opportunities of Smart Working
ISBN: 9781799887973

Advanced Applications of Generative AI and Natural Language Processing Models
ISBN: 9798369305027

Using Influencer Marketing as a Digital Business Strategy
ISBN: 9798369305515

Human-Centered Approaches in Industry 5.0
ISBN: 9798369326473

Modeling and Monitoring Extreme Hydrometeorological Events
ISBN: 9781668487716

Data-Driven Intelligent Business Sustainability
ISBN: 9798369300497

Information Logistics for Organizational Empowerment and Effective Supply Chain Management
ISBN: 9798369301593

Data Envelopment Analysis (DEA) Methods for Maximizing Efficiency
ISBN: 9798369302552

Request More Information, or Recommend the IGI Global e-Book Collection to Your Institution's Librarian

For More Information or to Request a Free Trial, Contact IGI Global's e-Collections Team: eresources@igi-global.com | 1-866-342-6657 ext. 100 | 717-533-8845 ext. 100

Are You Ready to Publish Your Research

IGI Global offers book authorship and editorship opportunities across three major subject areas, including Business, STM, and Education.

Benefits of Publishing with IGI Global:

- Free one-on-one editorial and promotional support.
- Expedited publishing timelines that can take your book from start to finish in less than one (1) year.
- Choose from a variety of formats, including Edited and Authored References, Handbooks of Research, Encyclopedias, and Research Insights.
- Utilize IGI Global's eEditorial Discovery® submission system in support of conducting the submission and double-blind peer review process.
- IGI Global maintains a strict adherence to ethical practices due in part to our full membership with the Committee on Publication Ethics (COPE).
- Indexing potential in prestigious indices such as Scopus®, Web of Science™, PsycINFO®, and ERIC – Education Resources Information Center.
- Ability to connect your ORCID iD to your IGI Global publications.
- Earn honorariums and royalties on your full book publications as well as complimentary content and exclusive discounts.

Join Your Colleagues from Prestigious Institutions, Including:

Learn More at: www.igi-global.com/publish
or by Contacting the Acquisitions Department at: acquisition@igi-global.com

Milton Keynes UK
Ingram Content Group UK Ltd.
UKHW051013070824
446558UK00003B/7